The Heritage of WORLD Civilizations

SECOND EDITION

Albert M. Craig *Harvard University*

William A. Graham *Harvard University*

Donald Kagan *Yale University*

Steven Ozment *Harvard University*

Frank M. Turner *Yale University*

VOLUME **I**

To 1600

Macmillan Publishing Company

New York

A portion of this book previously appeared in *The Western
Heritage* by Donald Kagan, Steven Ozment, and Frank M.
Turner.

Earlier edition copyright © 1986 by Macmillan Publishing
Company

Macmillan Publishing Company
866 Third Avenue, New York, New York 10022

Collier Macmillan Canada, Inc.

Library of Congress Cataloging in Publication Data

The Heritage of world civilizations / Albert M. Craig . . . [et al.].—
    2nd ed.
        p.   cm.
    Includes bibliographical references.
    Contents: v. 1. To 1600.
    ISBN 0-02-325492-0 (v. 1)
    1. Civilization—History.   I. Craig, Albert M.
    CB69.H45   1990   89-12994
    909—dc20   CIP

Printing: 1 2 3 4 5 6 7 8   Year: 0 1 2 3 4 5 6 7 8 9

Acquisitions Editor: Eben Ludlow
Developmental Editor: Johnna Barto
Production Supervisor: J. Edward Neve
Production Manager: Richard C. Fischer
Text Designer: Andrew P. Zutis
Cover Designer: Eileen Burke
Photo Researchers: Barbara and John Schultz

This book was set in Orion typeface by York Graphic Services,
Inc., printed and bound by Rand McNally and Company.
The cover was printed by: Lehigh Press.

Preface

Today, more than during any previous era of history, we live in a time of interaction and interdependence of nations around the entire globe. More people with differing cultural heritages and religious outlooks live more closely together than in any other period. Economic, political, and military developments in one part of the world quickly affect millions of people in other parts. The common problems of environmental pollution, overpopulation, and urban sprawl affect every continent. The vast expansion of markets for products as diverse as oil, electronics, and fast food have changed the standard of living virtually everywhere. Furthermore, never before in human history have fervent adherents of so many of the major religious traditions lived in such close proximity throughout the world. No people or nation today can live without an awareness of its place in what has rapidly become a global village.

The current situation is itself the result of a major historical development—the close of the European era of world history. Between approximately 1500 and the middle of the twentieth century Europeans and their colonists in North America and elsewhere dominated the world scene through the strength of their political organization, economic productivity, and military might. That era came to an end during the third quarter of this century as the nations of Asia, the Near East, and Africa achieved new positions on the world scene. Their new political independence, their control over strategic natural resources (especially oil), the expansion of their economies (particularly those of the nations on the Pacific rim of Asia), and their control over nuclear weapons have changed the shape of world affairs in virtually every respect. Because of these developments Europe and the United States now play a lesser role in world affairs than they did a half century ago or even a quarter century ago.

As citizens of the world, we confront political and economic relationships virtually unimagined even half a century ago. These conditions demand that we learn and teach history from a global perspective. It is the goal of this volume to provide just that perspective. It is our hope that students—and teachers for that matter—who now live in the global village may, through the study of the various world civilizations, better understand and appreciate other citizens of that village.

On this transformed world stage the students who read this book will spend their lives. It is our hope that through the exploration of the diverse world civilizations they may enter that world better informed and more culturally sensitive. We have aimed not merely to describe the several civilizations, but also to convey an inner sense of what each civilization meant to those who have lived in it. For that reason we have paid very special attention to the emergence of the major religious traditions of world civilizations. These represent on the one hand the most ancient roots of those civilizations and on the other the most relevant factors in contemporary human interaction.

We are also quite aware of the vast array of new tools and concepts that historians have brought to bear on the treatment of history. Our coverage has attempted to introduce students to the various aspects of social and intellectual history as well as to the more traditional political and diplomatic coverage. We firmly believe that only through an appreciation of all pathways to understanding of the past can the real heritage of world civilizations be achieved.

Changes in Second Edition

In undertaking this second edition we have attempted to make a number of major revisions to aid both teachers and students.

- Much more extensive coverage of topics in social history with special emphasis on women and the family.
- Extensively revised and expanded sections on African history in Chapters 7, 11, 15, 22, 31, and 37.
- A new statement regarding Neo-Confucian philosophy in Chapter 9 and a new section on women in warrior society Japan in Chapter 10.
- A new section on Meso-American civilization in Chapter 21.
- An extensively revised chapter (Chapter 23) that integrates the seventeenth-century European scientific revolution with the eighteenth-century Enlightenment.
- A completely new chapter (Chapter 27) on the history of North America during the nineteenth century.
- New sections incorporating the twentieth-century history of the United States in Chapters 34 and 36.
- Extensively revised treatment of the world since 1945 in Chapters 36 and 37.

Pedagogical Elements

We have concentrated our efforts on improving the pedagogy to make the text more accessible to all students.

- *Part Essays* open each of the seven major sections of the book. These serve to preview the coverage in the subsequent chapters while highlighting major trends and movements.
- *Part Timelines* show the major events that occurred in five different civilizations during the same period. These provide quick reference for events occurring concurrently in the Middle East, Africa, East Asia, Europe, and the Americas.
- *Chapter Outlines* display major headings and subheadings on the opening page of each chapter. A quick glance helps to organize material before reading the chapter and provides a quick review after completing the chapter.
- *Primary Source Documents* include selections from sacred books, poems, philosophy, political manifestos, and travel accounts. They will aid both teachers and students to experience the general character of the major civilizations. Along with the photographs, they convey the experiences and voices of even ancient societies with immediacy and concreteness.
- *In World Perspective Sections* serve as chapter conclusions and place the materials of each chapter into an integrated worldview.
- *Color Portfolios* include photographs accompanied by interpretive essays that are organized around

the major world religions: Judaism, Christianity, Islam, Buddhism, Hinduism, and contemporary religious revival.

We should note that most scholarship on China uses the Wade-Giles system of romanizaton for Chinese names and terms. In order that students may be able to move easily from the present text to advanced works of scholarship in Chinese history, we have used the Wade-Giles system throughout. China today, however, uses another system known as pinyin. Virtually all Western newspapers have adopted it. Therefore, for Chinese history since 1949 (See Chapter 37) we have included the pinyin spellings in parentheses after the Wade-Giles.

Also, we have followed the most accurate currently accepted English transliteration of Arabic words. For example, today *Koran* is being replaced by the more accurate *Qur'an*; similarly *Muhammad* is preferable to *Mohammed* and *Muslim* to *Moslem*. We have not tried to distinguish the letters *'ayn* and *hamza*: both are rendered by a simple apostrophe ('), as in *shi'ite*.

With regard to Sanskritic transliteration, we have not distinguished linguals and dentals, and both palatal and lingual "s" are rendered "sh," as in *Shiva* and *Upanishad*.

Teaching Supplements

To help ease the burden of teaching such a comprehensive course as world civilization, we have made available several very useful supplements.

- INSTRUCTOR'S MANUAL. Prepared by Perry Rogers, Ph. D., Ohio State University, this item includes summary and multiple choice questions for each part essay; chapter summaries, outline of key points and concepts, identification questions, multiple choice and essay questions to be used for tests, and a suggested list of relevant films and videos.
- COMPUTERIZED TEST BANK. The test items are also available on computer disk which allows the instructor to choose different configurations of questions as well as add original questions. The result is greater flexibility in the administration of tests.
- MAP TRANSPARENCIES. A number of maps from the text have been computer colorized and are available as full-color acetates. These transparencies provide strong visual support during lectures.
- COMPUTERIZED STUDY GUIDE. Students may review their comprehension of the text presentation by answering questions included on a computer disk.

Acknowledgments

In developing this second edition of *The Heritage of World Civilizations*, we are grateful to the many scholars and teachers who responded to our surveys and who read the manuscript and offered valuable insights. We wish to acknowledge the following academic reviewers:

Sarah J. Adams, *University of Charleston*
David Bard, *Concord College*
Gerald W. Berkley, *University of Hawaii at Manoa*
Richard M. Berthold, *University of New Mexico*
Charmarie J. Blaisdell, *Northeastern University*
C. Dewey Caldwell, *U. of Hawaii, Honolulu Community College*
Richard J. Carey, *Chaminade University of Honolulu*
Daniel Crecelius, *California State University, Los Angeles*
Allen Cronenburg, *Auburn University*
Elton L. Daniel, *University of Hawaii, Honolulu*
Lawrence E. Daxton, *University of Southern Colorado*
Wayne A. DeJohn, *St. Ambrose University*
Samuel E. Dicks, *Emporia State University*
Joel Epstein, *Olivet College*
John D. Fair, *Auburn University at Montgomery*
Harvey M. Feinberg, *Southern Connecticut State University*
Peter J. Frederick, *Wabash College*
Richard Geiger, *St. Ambrose University*
Stephen S. Gosch, *University of Wisconsin, Eau Claire*

C. Wilfred Griggs, *Brigham Young University*
Roland L. Guyotte, *University of Minnesota, Morris*
Edward S. Haynes, *Winthrop College*
John M. Hirschfield, *St. Mary's College of Maryland*
Sarah Hughes, *Hampton University*
Gregory C. Kozlowski, *DePaul University*
Dennis E. Lawther, *West Liberty State College*
Donald L. Layton, *Indiana State University, Terre Haute*
Robert L. Lembright, *James Madison University*
Richard D. Lewis, *St. Cloud State University*
William G. Morris, *Midland College*
John P. Mueller, *Aims Community College*
William O. Oldson, *Florida State University, Tallahassee*
Richard V. Pierard, *Indiana State University, Terre Haute*
Philip F. Riley, *James Madison University*
Anthony W. Snyder, *Brookdale Community College*
David B. Stenzel, *California State University, Stanislaus*
Janet D. Stone, *Armstrong State College*
Teddy J. Uldricks, *University of North Carolina at Asheville*
James Weland, *Bentley College*
Allan M. Winkler, *Miami University (of Ohio)*

We are especially grateful to Theodore M. Ludwig of Valparaiso University who offered many helpful suggestions on the essays that accompany the color sections.

About the Authors

ALBERT M. CRAIG is the Harvard-Yenching Professor of History at Harvard University where he has taught since 1959. A graduate of Northwestern University, he took his Ph.D. at Harvard University. He has studied at Strasbourg University, and at Kyoto and Tokyo universities in Japan. He is the author of *Chóshú in the Meiji Restoration* (1961), and, with others, of *East Asia, Tradition and Transformation* (1978). He is the editor of *Japan, A Comparative View* (1973) and co-editor of *Personality in Japanese History* (1970). At present he is engaged in research on the thought of Fukuzawa Yukichi. For eleven years (1976–1987) he was the director of the Harvard-Yenching Institute. In 1988 he was awarded the Order of the Rising Sun by the Japanese government.

WILLIAM A. GRAHAM is Professor of the History of Religion and Islamic Studies at Harvard University. He has taught there for sixteen years in the Department of Near Eastern Languages and Civilizations and currently chairs the Committee on the Study of Religion. He is the author of *Divine Word and Prophetic Word in Early Islam* (1977), which was awarded the American Council of Learned Societies prize for the "Best First Book in the History of Religions" in 1977–1978. His most recent book is *Beyond the Written Word: Oral Aspects of Scripture in the History of Religion* (1987). He studied for his B.A. in comparative literature (Classics, German, French) as a Morehead Scholar at the University of North Carolina in Chapel Hill, and for the A.M. and Ph.D. degrees in the comparative study of religion as a Woodrow Wilson and Danforth Graduate Fellow at Harvard University. He is the recipient of John Simon Guggenheim (1981) and Alexander von Humboldt (1982) research fellowships.

DONALD KAGAN received the A.B. degree in history from Brooklyn College, the M.A. in classics from Brown University, and the Ph.D. in history from Ohio State University. During 1958–1959 he studied at the American School of Classical Studies as a Fulbright Scholar. Richard M. Colgate Professor at Yale University, where he has taught since 1969, he has received three awards for undergraduate teaching at Cornell and Yale. He is the author of *The Great Dialogue* (1965), a history of Greek political thought, a four volume history of the Peloponnesian War: *The Origins of the Peloponnesian War* (1969), *The Archidamian War* (1974), *The Peace of Nicias and the Sicilian Expedition* (1981), *The Fall of the Athenian Empire* (1987), and he has just completed a biography of Pericles. With Brian Tierney and L. Pearce Williams he is the editor of *Great Issues in Western Civilization*, a collection of readings in the same subject. He is currently Dean of Yale College.

STEVEN OZMENT is Professor of History at Harvard University. He is the author of *The Reformation in the Cities: The Appeal of Protestantism in Sixteenth Century Germany and Switzerland* (1975); *The Age of Reform, 1250–1550: An Intellectual and Religious History of Late Medieval and Reformation Europe* (1980), winner of the Schaff Prize and nominated for the 1981 American Book Award; *When Fathers Ruled: Family Life in Reformation Europe* (1983); *Magdalena and Balthasar: An Intimate Portrait of Life in Sixteenth Century Europe* (1986). Mr. Ozment's new book, *Three Behaim Boys: Growing Up in Early Modern Germany*, will appear in 1990.

FRANK M. TURNER is Professor of History at Yale University. He also serves as University Provost. He received his B.A. degree at the College of William and Mary and his Ph.D. from Yale. He has received the Yale College Award for Distinguished Undergraduate Teaching. He has directed a National Endowment for the Humanities Summer Institute. His scholarly research has received the support of fellowships from the National Endowment for the Humanities and the Guggenheim Foundation. He is the author of *Between Science and Religion: The Reaction to Scientific Naturalism in Late Victorian England* (1974) and *The Greek Heritage in Victorian Britain* (1981). The latter study received the British Council Prize of the Conference on British Studies and the Yale Press Governors Award. He has also contributed numerous articles to journals and has served in the editorial advisory boards of *The Journal of Modern History*, *Isis*, and *Victorian Studies*.

Brief Contents

Detailed Contents

The Coming of Civilization

Empires and Cultures of the Ancient World

Consolidation and Interaction of World Civilizations: 500–1500

11 Africa, Iran, and India Before Islam

12 The Formation of Islamic Civilization (622–945)

13 The Early Middle Ages in the West to 1000: The Birth of Europe

The World in Transition: 1500–1800

Enlightenment and Revolution in the West

Toward the Modern World

31 India, the Islamic Heartlands, and Africa: The Encounter with Western Modernity (1800–1945)

32 Modern East Asia

33 Imperialism, Alliances, and War

Global Conflict and Detente

Documents

Maps

Color Plates

The Coming of Civilization

THE way of life of prehistoric cavepeople differed immensely from that of today's civilized world. Yet the few millennia in which we have been civilized are but a tiny fraction of the long span of human existence. Especially during the recent millennia, changes in our culture have far outpaced changes in our bodies. We live a highly organized and often sedentary life but still retain the emotional make-up and motor reflexes of primitive men and women.

Homo sapiens—modern man—first appeared about 100,000 years ago. Since then, the pace of human control over the environment has constantly accelerated. It took tens of thousands of years to learn to use fire and to make stone tools, to domesticate the dog, and to master the rudiments of agriculture. It took another seven to nine thousand years to develop cities, systems of writing, and then, bronze and iron. Several hundred years later occurred the great religious and philosophical revolutions of the ancient world, followed by the empires of China, India, Iran, and Rome that straddled the B.C.–A.D. divide.

Now, two thousand years later, humans have unlocked the power of the atom, walked on the moon, and broken the genetic code. The pace of new discoveries continues to quicken. If we compare the invention of writing late in the fourth millennium B.C. with the breaking of the genetic code, the latter was far more complex, but the former may have been more difficult.

The timetable for the development of river valley civilizations varied. The Near Eastern cultures began earlier, followed by India and China. But the parallelism in stages of development is remarkable. First came agriculture and pottery, then cities, writing, and bronze, and, finally, iron and empire. Does the logic of nature dictate that once agriculture develops, cities will arise in alluvial river valleys favorable to intensive cultivation? Was it inevitable that the firing of clay to produce pots would reduce metallic oxides and lead to the discovery of smelting? Did the formation of the aristocratic and priestly classes, who controlled the resources of cities, automatically lead to record keeping and writing?

That is to say, did agriculture set in motion a train of similar events in widely separated river valleys? Or, is diffusion a more likely cause? Is it not conceivable that contacts between the early civilizations were more numerous than we now imagine? The earliest written languages—the Sumerian cuneiform, the Egyptian hieroglyphs, and the Chinese ideographs—probably had independent origins. They are too dissimilar to be the result of diffusion. But what of seeds, bronze, and iron? Might not migrating peoples or wandering merchants have carried these over long distances? Both hypotheses — diffusion and independent origins — are plausible. However, in the absence of evidence, a definitive answer cannot be given. Little remains even of the material culture of the men and women of these earliest civilizations. Understanding their lives is like reconstructing a dinosaur from a broken tooth and a fragment of jawbone.

In or near the same river valleys that saw the birth of civilization occurred the religious and philosophical revolutions that permanently marked the world thereafter: monotheistic Judaism, from which would later develop the world religions of Christianity and Islam; Hinduism and Buddhism in South Asia; and the philosophies of China and Greece. The simultaneity of their appearance was striking. The Hebrew prophets, Buddha, Confucius, and Socrates, if not all contemporaries, were grouped within a few hundred years of each other in the first millennium B.C. Most founders of the great religions based their teachings on intensely personal religious experiences, on experiences that cannot be analyzed in historical terms. Yet, we can examine their historical contexts and can note certain similarities.

The coming of the bronze and iron ages — and we speak of bronze and iron partly as a shorthand for many complex developments — led to a series of political and spiritual crises across the world of the early civilizations. The founders of the great religions and philosophies responded to these crises with new visions of man's place in the universe, and with new and more universal ethics. It is their greater universalism that distinguishes the world religions from those centered more narrowly on a particular tribe or people. Of course, all religions spring from a common human impulse, and treat the questions of how to live and what life means in the face of death. But Buddhism, Christianity, and Islam differed from the Shinto of Japan, the religions of the Egyptians or Mayas, or even the Zoroastrianism of ancient Iran, in contending that their answers were true for all peoples and times. It was this universalism that made them missionary religions.

Similarly, the philosophies of China and Greece were more universal than previous systems of thought. Confucianism eventually spread to Korea, Japan, and Vietnam, countries whose customs were quite different from those of China. It became the basis for laws in these countries because its ethics transcended particular Chinese institutions.

Greek ideas played an equivalent role in the West. They joined Judaic concepts to form Christianity. The gospel according to Saint John starts: "In the beginning was the Word (*logos*), and the Word was with God, and the Word was God." In Greek, *logos* means something like "Universal Principle" or "Reason." Universal Greek conceptions also lay at the base of the Roman law code (*ius gentium*) used to govern provinces with different peoples and widely varying customs. This last example also says something about the transition from the older civilizations to the empires of the ancient world. These empires, to be sure, were built by armies, not philosophies. But for their leaders to govern, for their bureaucracies to function, they had to have philosophies and laws. ❏

A Sumerian wall plaque carved in relief. It shows Ur-Nanshe, ruler of Lagash (2494–2465 B.C.). The upper portion shows him carrying a basket of bricks for building a temple; in the lower he sits among his children. The plaque is covered with inscriptions in a very old form of Sumerian writing.

1 The Birth of Civilization

"Prehistory": Early Human Beings and Their Culture

Scientists estimate that the earth may be as many as six billion years old, that creatures very much like humans may have appeared three to five million years ago, and that our own species of human beings goes back at least one hundred thousand years. Humans are different from other animals in that they are capable of producing and passing on a culture. *Culture* may be defined as the ways of living built up by a group and passed on from one generation to another. It may include behavior, material things, ideas, institutions, and religious faith. The source of human creativity is our large and convoluted brain. We create ideas and institutions. We formulate our thoughts in speech, allowing us to transmit our culture to future generations. We also can bring together our fingers and thumb, enabling us to make and hold tools. The combination of speech and material invention was necessary for the development of human culture.

The anthropologist designates early human cultures by their tools. The earliest period is the Paleolithic (from Greek, "old stone") Age. In this immensely long period (from perhaps 600,000 to 10,000 B.C.), people were hunters, fishers, and gatherers, but not producers, of food. They learned to make and use tools of stone and of perishable materials like wood, to make and control fire, and to pass on what they learned in language. In the regions where civilization ultimately was born, people depended on nature for their food and were very vulnerable to attacks from wild beasts and to natural disasters. Because their lives were often "solitary, poor, nasty, brutish, and short," as Thomas Hobbes put it, their responses to troubles may have been rooted in fear of the unknown. Their fear concerned the uncertainties of human life or the overpowering forces of nature. Such fear is often one element in

3

Paleolithic cave painting from Dordogne in France. Deep in caves in southern France and northern Spain are wall paintings of hundreds of animals—bison, deer, horses, and oxen. They are shown in remarkable realism. Often they are shown as hunted by men, sometimes with a spear sticking in them. [Bettmann Archive.]

human recourse to magic as an effort to coerce—or to religion to propitiate—superhuman forces often thought to animate or direct the natural world.

But preliterate human beings are, and were, also much closer to nature than more civilized peoples. This closeness to nature seems to be another primary reason for the evidence of religious faith and practice, as well as magic, that goes as far back as archaeology can take us. Fear or awe, exultation, gratitude, and empathy with the natural world must all have figured in the cave art and in the ritual practices, such as burial, that we find evidenced at Paleolithic sites around the globe. Human life itself is a kind of miracle. The concern in all known societies with life's major transitions—birth, puberty, marriage, and death—was probably a source of "rites of passage" among the earliest human beings as well. For example, the many figurines of pregnant women (or goddesses?) that have been found at prehistoric sites might have been used in rites aimed at ensuring fertility or successful childbirth. However, given the sparse evidence, all we can say is that the sense that there is more to the world than meets the eye— in other words, the religious response to the world—seems to be as old as humankind.

The style of life and the level of technology of the Paleolithic period could support only a sparsely settled society. If the hunters were too numerous, the available game would not suffice. In Paleolithic times, people were subject to the same natural and ecological constraints that today maintain a balance between wolves and deer in Alaska.

Human life in the Paleolithic Age easily lent itself to division of labor by sex. The men engaged in hunting, fishing, making tools and weapons, and fighting against other families, clans, and tribes. The women, less mobile because of frequent childbearing, smaller in stature, and less strong and swift than the men, gathered nuts, berries, and wild grains; wove baskets; and made clothing. Women gathering food probably discovered how to plant and care for seeds. This knowledge eventually made possible the Age of Agriculture—the Neolithic revolution.

Of the early Paleolithic societies, only a few developed into Neolithic or New Stone Age agricultural societies, and anthropologists and archaeologists disagree on why that revolutionary development occurred. In many areas, right into our own time, some isolated portions of humankind have been content to continue to live in the "Stone Age" unless compelled by more advanced cultures to change. The reasons for the shift to agriculture by late Paleolithic groups are unclear. In the past, some scientists thought that climatic change—a drop in temperature and rainfall—forced people to be inventive and to seek new ways of acquiring food. But newer evidence suggests that there was little climatic variation in Neolithic times. Other theories focus on the human element: a possible growth in population, an increased sense of territoriality, and a resulting interference with the pursuit of herds for hunting.

However it happened, some ten thousand years ago parts of what we now call the Near East began to shift from a hunter–gatherer culture to a settled agricultural one. People began to use precisely carved stone tools, so we call this period the Neolithic (from Greek, "new stone") Age. Animals as well as food crops were domesticated. The important invention of pottery made it possible to store surplus liquids, just as the invention of baskets had earlier made it possible to store dry foods. Cloth came to be made from flax and wool. Crops required constant care from planting to harvest, so the Neolithic people built permanent buildings, usually in clusters near the best fields.

The agricultural revolution may not, however, have produced an immediate population explosion. Anthropologists suggest that village living produced a much greater incidence of disease, there being no provision for the disposal of human and animal waste. The Neolithic villages also provided attractive targets for raiders.

Still, agriculture provided a steadier source of food and a greater production of food in a given area. It thus provided the basis for a denser population over time. It was a major step in the human control of nature, and it was a vital precondition for the emergence of civilization. The earliest Neolithic societies appeared in the Near East about 8000 B.C., in China about 4000 B.C., and in India by at least 3600 B.C.. The Neolithic revolution in the Near East and India was based on wheat, in China on millet and rice; in Meso-America, several millennia later, it would be based on corn.

Neolithic villages and their culture, gradually having grown from and having replaced Paleolithic culture, could be located on almost any kind of terrain. But beginning about four thousand years before the Christian era, people began to settle in substantive numbers in the river-watered lowlands of Mesopotamia, Egypt, northern China, and northwestern India. Here a new style of life evolved: an urban society and civilization. The shift was accompanied by the gradual introduction of new technologies and by the invention of writing.

Again, we do not know why people first chose to live in cities, with their inherent disadvantages: overcrowding, epidemics, wide separation from sources of

MAP 1-1   THE FOUR GREAT RIVER VALLEY CIVILIZATIONS TO CA. 1000 B.C.
By CA. 2000 B.C. *urban life was established along the Tigris-Euphrates in Mesopotamia, the Nile in Egypt, the Indus and Ganges in India, and the Yellow River in China.*

food and raw materials, and the concentration of wealth that permitted organized warfare. Perhaps cities were created because, to quote the Greek philosopher Aristotle, "Man is by nature a political animal." Perhaps they arose merely because they offered more possibilities for amusement, occupational choice, and enrichment than had the Neolithic villages. In any event, by about 3000 B.C., when the invention of writing gave birth to history, urban life was established in the valleys of the Tigris and Euphrates rivers in Mesopotamia (modern Iraq) and of the Nile in Egypt. Somewhat later, urban life arose in the Indus valley of India and the Yellow River basin of China. The development of urban centers by no means meant the disappearance of numerous outlying peasant agricultural villages. Nevertheless, with the coming of cities, writing, and metals, humankind had attained civilization.

Early Civilizations in the Near East

Civilization, then, is a form of human culture in which many people live in urban centers, have mastered the art of smelting metals, and have developed a method of writing. The rich alluvial plains where civilization began made possible the production of unprecedented surpluses of food—but only if there was an intelligent management of the water supply. Proper flood control and irrigation called for the control of the river by some strong authority capable of managing the distribution of water. This control and management required careful observation and record keeping. The first use of writing may have been to record the behavior of the river and the astronomical events that gave clues about it. It was also used by the powerful individuals (the kings) who dominated the life of the river valleys to record their possessions, by priests to record omens and religious texts, by merchants and artisans to record business transactions, and by others to record acts of government, laws, and different kinds of literature.

This widely varied use of writing reflects the complex culture of the urban centers in the river valleys. Commerce was important enough to support a merchant class. Someone discovered how to smelt tin and copper to make a stronger and more useful material—bronze—which replaced stone in the making of tools and weapons: The importance of this technological development is reflected in the term *Bronze Age*. The great need for record keeping created a class of scribes, because the picture writing and complicated scripts of these cultures took many years to learn and could not be mastered by many. To deal with the gods, temples were built, and many priests attended and administered them. The collection of all these people

into cities gave the settlements an entirely new character. Unlike Neolithic villages, they were communities established for purposes other than agriculture. The city was an administrative, religious, manufacturing, entertainment, and commercial center.

The logic of nature pointed in the direction of the unification of an entire river valley. As a result, these civilizations in time produced unified kingdoms under powerful monarchs who often came to be identified with divinity. The typical king in a river-valley civilization was regarded either as a god or as the delegate of a god. Around him developed a rigid class structure. Beneath the monarch was a class of hereditary military aristocrats and a powerful priesthood. Below them were freemen, mostly peasants, and at the bottom were serfs or slaves. Most of the land was owned or controlled by the king, the nobility, and the priests. These were conservative cultures of numerous peasant villages and a few urban centers. Such cultural patterns took form early and changed only slowly and grudgingly.

The Fertile Crescent: Mesopotamian Civilization

The first civilization appears to have arisen in the valley of the Tigris and Euphrates rivers: Mesopotamia (the term means land "between the rivers" in Greek). Its founders seem to have been a people called Sumerians, who controlled the southern part of the valley (Sumer) close to the head of the Persian Gulf by the dawn of history, around 3000 B.C. (see Map 1.2). At first, city-states about one hundred square miles in size dotted the landscape. Ur, Erech, Lagash, and Eridu are examples of such cities that archaeologists have revealed to us. Quarrels over water rights and frontiers led to incessant fighting, and in time, stronger towns conquered weaker ones and expanded to form larger units, usually kingdoms.

While the Sumerians were fighting with their neighbors and among themselves for supremacy in the south, a people, called Semites, from the Arabian Desert on the west had been moving into Mesopotamia north of Sumer. Their language and society were different from those of the Sumerians, but they soon absorbed Sumerian culture and established their own kingdom, with its capital at Akkad, near a later city known to us as Babylon. The most famous Akkadian king was Sargon, who conquered Sumer and extended his empire in every direction. Legends grew up around his name, and he is said to have conquered the "cedar forests" of Lebanon, far to the west near the coast of the Mediterranean Sea. He ruled about 2340 B.C. and established a family, or dynasty, of Semitic kings that ruled Sumer and Akkad for two centuries.

External attack and internal weakness destroyed

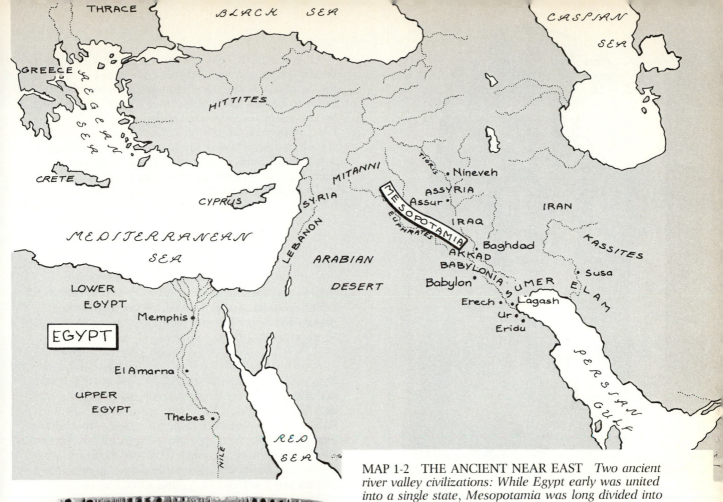

In Mesopotamia inscriptions on stone like this one are much less common than those on clay. This stele records the deeds of Enkhegal, king of Lagash, one of the earliest Sumerian city states. Before the rise of Akkad, Lagash dominated much of Mesopotamia. [Copyrighted by University Museum, University of Pennsylvania.]

MAP 1-2   THE ANCIENT NEAR EAST *Two ancient river valley civilizations: While Egypt early was united into a single state, Mesopotamia was long divided into a number of city states.*

Akkad. About 2125 B.C., the city of Ur in Sumer revolted and became the dominant power, and this Third Dynasty of Ur established a large empire of its own. About 2000 B.C., however, it was swept aside by another Semitic invasion, which ended Sumerian rule forever. Thereafter, Semites ruled Mesopotamia, but the foundations of their culture were Sumerian. The Semites changed much of what they inherited; but in law, government, religion, art, science, and all other areas of culture, their debt to the Sumerians was enormous.

The fall of the Third Dynasty of Ur (CA. 2100–2000 B.C.) put an end to the Sumerians as an identifiable group. The Sumerian language survived only in writing, as a kind of sacred language known only to priests and scribes, preserving the cultural heritage of Sumer. For about a century after the fall of Ur, dynastic chaos reigned, but about 1900 B.C., a Semitic people called the Amorites gained control of the region, establishing their capital at Babylon. The high point of this Amorite, or Old Babylonian, dynasty came more than a hundred years later under its most famous king, Hammurabi (CA. 1792–1750 B.C.)

Hammurabi is best known for the law code connected with his name. Codes of law existed as early as the Sumerian period, and Hammurabi's plainly owed much to earlier models, but it is the fullest and best preserved legal code we have from ancient Mesopotamia, or indeed, from anywhere. The code reveals a society strictly divided in class: There were nobles, commoners, and slaves, and the law did not treat them equally. In general, punishments were harsh, literally applying the principle "an eye for an eye, a tooth for a tooth." The prologue to the code makes it clear that law and justice came from the gods through the king.

About 1600 B.C., the Babylonian kingdom fell apart under the impact of invasions from the north and east by the Hittites and the Kassites. The Hittites were a raiding party who plundered what they could and then withdrew to their home in Asia Minor. The Kassites, a people from the Iranian plateau, stayed and ruled Mesopotamia for five centuries.

GOVERNMENT. From the earliest historical records, it is clear that the Sumerians were ruled by monarchs in some form. Some scholars have thought that they could detect a "primitive democracy" in early Sumer, but the evidence, which is poetic and hard to interpret, shows no more than a limited check on royal power even in early times. The first historical city-states had kings or priest-kings who led the army, administered the economy, and served as judges and as intermediaries between their people and the gods. At first, the kings were thought of as favorites and representatives of the gods; later, on some occasions and for relatively short periods, they instituted cults that worshiped them as divine. This union of church and state (to use modern terminology) in the person of the king reflected the centralization of power typical of Mesopotamian life. The economy was managed from the center by priests and kings and was planned very carefully. Each year, the land was surveyed, fields were assigned to specific farmers, and the amount of seed to be used was designated. The government estimated the size of the crop and planned its distribution even before it was planted.

This process required a large and competent staff, the ability to observe and record natural phenomena, a good knowledge of mathematics, and , for all of this,

The code of Hammurabi. This is a cast of the stele on which is inscribed in cuneiform characters the law code issued by the Babylonian king Hammurabi (CA. 1792–1750 B.C.). In the relief at the top the king stands before the sun god and receives the law from him. The original stele is in the Louvre in Paris. [Courtesy of the Oriental Institute, University of Chicago.]

Hammurabi Creates a Code of Law in Mesopotamia

Hammurabi's Babylonian empire stretched from the Persian Gulf to the Mediterranean Sea. Building on earlier laws, Hammurabi compiled one of the great ancient codes. It was discovered about seventy-five years ago in what is now Iran. Hammurabi, like other rulers before and after, represented himself and his laws as under the protection and sponsorship of all the right gods. Property was at least as sacred as persons, and the eye-for-an-eye approach characterizes the code. Here are a few examples from it.

LAWS

If a son has struck his father, they shall cut off his hand.

If a seignior has destroyed the eye of a member of the aristocracy, they shall destroy his eye.

If he has broken another seignior's bone, they shall break his bone.

If he has destroyed the eye of a commoner or broken the bone of a commoner, he shall pay one mina of silver.

If he has destroyed the eye of a seignior's slave or broken the bone of a seignior's slave, he shall pay one-half his value.

If a seignior has knocked out a tooth of a seignior of his own rank, they shall knock out his tooth.

If he has knocked out a commoner's tooth, he shall pay one-third mina of silver. . . .

EPILOGUE

I, Hammurabi, the perfect king,
was not careless (or) neglectful of the black-headed
  (people),
whom Enlil had presented to me,
(and) whose shepherding Marduk had committed to
  me;
I sought out peaceful regions for them;
I overcame grievous difficulties; . . .
With the mighty weapon which Zababa and Inanna
  entrusted to me,
with the insight that Enki allotted to me,
with the ability that Marduk gave me,
I rooted out the enemy above and below;
I made an end of war;
I promoted the welfare of the land;
I made the peoples rest in friendly habitations; . . .
The great gods called me,
so I became the beneficent shepherd whose scepter is
  righteous. . . . ❑

James B. Pritchard, *Ancient Near Eastern Texts*, 3rd ed. (Princeton: Princeton University Press, 1969), pp. 164–180.

---

a system of writing. The Sumerians invented the writing system known as *cuneiform* (from the Latin *cuneus*, "wedge"). The name comes from the wedge-shaped stylus with which they wrote on clay tablets; the writing also came to be used in beautifully cut characters in stone. Sumerians also began the development of a sophisticated system of mathematics. The calendar they invented had twelve lunar months. To make it agree with the solar year and to make possible accurate designation of the seasons, they introduced a thirteenth month about every three years.

RELIGION. The Sumerians and their Semitic successors believed in gods in the shape of humans who were usually identified with some natural phenomenon. They were pictured as frivolous, quarrelsome, selfish, and often childish, differing from humans only in their greater power and their immortality. They each appear to have begun as a local deity. The people of Mesopotamia had a negative and gloomy picture of

the afterworld as a "land of no return." Their religion dealt with problems of this world, and they employed prayer, sacrifice, and magic to achieve their ends. Expert knowledge was required to reach the perfection in wisdom and ritual needed to influence the gods, so the priesthood flourished. A high percentage of the cuneiform writing that we now have is devoted to religious texts: prayers, incantations, curses, and omens.

It was important to discover the will and intentions of the gods, and the Sumerians sought hints in several places. The movements of the heavenly bodies were an obvious evidence of divine action, so astrology was born. They also sought to discover the divine will by examining the entrails of sacrificial animals for symbolic signs in their particular features. All of this religious activity required numerous scribes to keep records, as well as learned priests to interpret them.

Religious thought, in the form of myth, played a large part in the literature and art of Mesopotamia. A *myth* (from the Greek, "story" or "plot") is a narrative that deals with truths about relationships between the human and the transcendent. In the poetic language of myth, the Sumerians and their successors told tales of the creation of the world, of a great flood that almost destroyed human life, of an island paradise from which the god Enki was expelled for eating forbidden plants, of a hero named Gilgamesh who tried to gain immortality, and many more.

Religion was also the inspiration for the most interesting architectural achievement in Mesopotamia: the ziggurat. The ziggurat was an artificial stepped mound surmounted by a temple. It may have been a symbolic representation of the cosmic mountain that many cultures have thought lies at the center of the world. Neighbors and successors of the Sumerians adopted the style, and the eroded remains of many of these monumental structures, some partly restored, still dot the Iraqi landscape.

SOCIETY. We have a very full and detailed picture of the way people in ancient Mesopotamia conducted their lives and of the social conditions in which they lived during the reign of Hammurabi. More than fifty royal letters, many business contracts, and especially the Code of Hammurabi are the sources of our knowledge. We find that society was legally divided into three classes: nobles, commoners, and slaves. Punishment for crimes committed against freemen was harsher than for those against slaves, and crimes committed against nobles were considered more serious than those against commoners.

Slaves were chiefly captives from wars, although some native Babylonians were enslaved for committing certain crimes, such as kicking one's mother or striking an elder brother. Parents could sell their children into slavery or pledge themselves and their entire family as surety for a debt. In case of default, they

Sumerian statuettes from Tell Asmar. The tallest figure in this collection of gods, priests, and worshipers is the god Abu, the "lord of vegetation." The group was found buried beside the altar of a temple at a site near modern Baghdad dating from 3000–2500 B.C. [Courtesy of the Oriental Institute, University of Chicago.]

Reconstruction of the temple oval at Khafaje. The remains of this temple complex (not far from Baghdad in modern Iraq) have made a probable reconstruction possible. It reveals an elaborate religious establishment of the early third millenium B.C. that was even earlier than the ziggurat at Ur and the major pyramids of Egypt. [H. D. Darby. Courtesy of the Oriental Institute, University of Chicago.]

would all become slaves of the creditor for a stated period of time. Some slaves worked for the king and the state, others for the temple and the priests, and still others for private citizens. Their tasks varied accordingly. Most of the temple slaves appear to have been women, who were probably used to spin and weave and grind flour. The royal slaves did the heavy work of building palaces, canals, and fortifications. Private owners used their slaves chiefly as domestic servants. Some female slaves were used as concubines.

Laws against fugitive slaves or slaves who denied their masters were harsh, but in some respects, Mesopotamian slavery appears enlightened compared to other slave systems in history. Slaves could engage in business and, with certain restrictions, hold property. They could marry free men or women, and the result-

KEY EVENTS AND PEOPLE IN MESOPOTAMIAN HISTORY

CA. 3500 B.C.	Sumerians arrive
CA. 2800–2340 B.C.	Sumerian city-states: early dynastic period
CA. 2340 B.C.	Sargon establishes Semitic dynasty at Akkad
CA. 2125–2027 B.C.	Third Dynasty of Ur
CA. 1900 B.C.	Amorites at Babylon
1792–1750 B.C.	Reign of Hammurabi
CA. 1600 B.C.	Invasion by Hittites and Kassites

ing children would be free. A slave who acquired the necessary wealth could buy his or her own freedom. Children of a slave by the master might be allowed to share in his property after his death.

The Nile Valley: Egyptian Civilization

While a great civilization arose in the valley of the Tigris and Euphrates, another, no less important, emerged in Egypt. The center of Egyptian civilization was the Nile River. From its source in central Africa, the Nile runs north some four thousand miles to the Mediterranean, with long navigable stretches broken by several cataracts. Ancient Egypt included the 750 miles of the valley from the First Cataract northward to the sea and was shaped like a long-necked funnel with two distinct parts. Upper (southern) Egypt was the stem, consisting of the narrow valley of the Nile. The broad, triangular delta, which branches out about 150 miles from the sea, formed the mouth of the funnel, or Lower Egypt (see Map 1.1). The Nile alone made life possible in the almost rainless desert that surrounded it. Each year, the river flooded and covered the land, and when it receded, it left a fertile mud that could produce two crops a year. The construction and maintenance of irrigation ditches to preserve the river's water, with careful planning and organization of planting and harvesting, produced an agricultural prosperity unmatched in the ancient world.

The Nile also served as a highway connecting the long, narrow country and encouraging its unification. Upper and Lower Egypt were, in fact, already united into a single kingdom at the beginning of our historical record, about 3100 B.C. Nature helped protect and isolate the ancient Egyptians from outsiders. The cataracts, the sea, and the desert made it difficult for foreigners to reach Egypt for friendly or hostile purposes. Egypt knew far more peace and security than Mesopotamia. This security, along with the sunny, predictable climate, gave Egyptian civilization a more optimistic outlook than the civilizations of the Tigris–Euphrates, which were always in fear of assault from storm, flood, earthquake, and hostile neighbors.

The more than three-thousand-year span of ancient Egyptian history is traditionally divided into thirty-one royal dynasties. They range from the first, founded by Menes, the unifier of Upper and Lower Egypt, to the last, established by Alexander the Great, who conquered Egypt in 322 B.C. The dynasties are conventionally arranged into periods (see table on page 16). The unification of Egypt was vital, for even more than in Mesopotamia, the entire river valley required the central control of irrigation. By the time of the Third Dynasty, the king had achieved full supremacy and had imposed internal peace and order; his kingdom enjoyed great prosperity. The capital was at Memphis in Lower Egypt, just above the delta. The king was no mere representative of the gods but a god himself. The land was his own personal possession, and the people were his servants.

Nothing better illustrates the extent of royal power than the three great pyramids built as tombs by the kings of the Fourth Dynasty. The largest, that of Khufu, was originally 481 feet high and 756 feet long on each side; it was made up of 2,300,000 stone blocks

Pharaoh Menkaure and his queen. This Fourth Dynasty monarch built the third and smallest of the great pyramids at Giza. The frontality of the two figures and the extension of the left foot of each in this slate sculpture from Giza are typical of Egyptian statues. (About 2550 B.C.) [Courtesy of the Museum of Fine Arts, Boston; MFA Expedition Fund.]

averaging 2.5 tons each. It was said by the much later Greek historian Herodotus to have taken 100,000 men twenty years to build. The pyramids are remarkable not only for the technical skill that was needed to build them but even more for what they tell us of the royal power. They give evidence that the Egyptian kings had enormous wealth, the power to concentrate so much effort on a personal project, and the confidence to undertake one of such a long duration. There were earlier pyramids and many were built later, but those of the Fourth Dynasty were never surpassed.

THE OLD KINGDOM. In the Old Kingdom, royal power was absolute. The pharaoh, as he was later called (the term originally meant "great house" or "palace"), governed his kingdom through his family and appointed officials removable at his pleasure. The peasants were carefully regulated, their movement was limited, and they were taxed heavily, perhaps as much as one fifth of what they produced. Luxury accompanied the king in life and death, and he was raised to a remote and exalted level by his people. Such power and eminence could not be sustained long by force alone. The Egyptians worked for the king and obeyed him because he was a living god on whom their life, safety, and prosperity depended. He was the direct source of law and justice, so no law codes were needed.

In such a world, government was merely one aspect of religion, and religion dominated Egyptian life. The gods of Egypt had many forms: animals, humans, and natural forces. In time, Re, the sun god, came to have a special dominant place, but for centuries, there seems to have been little clarity or order in the Egyptian pantheon. Unlike the Mesopotamians, the Egyptians had a rather precise idea of an afterlife. They took great care to bury their dead according to their custom and supplied the grave with things that the departed would need for a pleasant life after death. The king and some nobles had their bodies preserved as mummies. Their tombs were beautifully decorated with paintings and religious texts useful in the next life; food and furnishings were provided at burial and even after. Some royal tombs were equipped with full-sized ships for the voyage to heaven. At first only kings were thought to achieve eternal life; then nobles were included; finally, all Egyptians could hope for immortality. The dead had to be properly embalmed, and the proper spells had to be written and spoken.

The Egyptians developed a system of writing not much later than the Sumerians. Though the idea may have come from Mesopotamia, the form of their script was independent. It began as picture writing and later combined pictographs with sound signs to produce a difficult and complicated script that the Greeks called *hieroglyphics* ("sacred carvings"). Though much of

The Sphinx. The great Sphinx is located at Giza, near modern Cairo. It seems to have been associated with the pyramid of Khafre, a king who ruled Egypt some time after 2600 B.C. The origin of the colossal lion with the head of a man is unknown, but the face is thought to be a likeness of the pharaoh himself. [Hirmer Fotoarchiv München.]

what we have is preserved on wall paintings and carvings, most of Egyptian writings was done with pen and ink on a fine paper made from the papyrus reed found in the delta. Egyptian literature was more limited in depth and imagination than the Mesopotamian writings. Hymns, myths, magical formulas, tales of travel, and "wisdom literature," or bits of advice to help one get on well in the world, have been preserved. But nothing as serious and probing as the story of Gilgamesh was produced in the more optimistic world of Egypt.

THE MIDDLE KINGDOM. The power of the kings of the Old Kingdom waned as priests and nobles gained more independence and influence. The governors of the regions of Egypt, called *nomes*, gained hereditary claim to their offices, and their families acquired large estates. About 2200 B.C., the Old Kingdom collapsed and gave way to the decentralization and disorder of the First Intermediate Period (CA. 2200–2052 B.C.). Finally, the nomarchs (governors) of Thebes in Upper Egypt gained control of the country and established the Middle Kingdom in about 2052 B.C.

The rulers of the Twelfth Dynasty restored the pharaoh's power over the whole of Egypt, though they could not completely control the nobles who ruled the nomes. Still, they brought order, peace, and prosperity to a troubled land. They encouraged trade and extended Egyptian power and influence northward toward Palestine and southward toward Ethiopia. Though they moved the capital back to the more defensible site at Memphis, they gave great prominence to Amon, a god especially connected with Thebes. He became identified with Re, emerging as Amon-Re, the main god of Egypt.

The kings of this period seem to have emphasized their role in doing justice. In their statues, they are often shown as burdened with care, presumably concern for their people. Tales of the period place great emphasis on the king as interested in right and in the welfare of his people. Much later, in the New Kingdom, ethical concerns appeared, as they had in the law codes of Mesopotamia, but the divine status of the kings gave them a strong religious tinge.

THE NEW KINGDOM (THE EMPIRE). The Middle Kingdom disintegrated in the Thirteenth Dynasty with the resurgence of the power of the local nobility. About 1700 B.C., Egypt suffered an invasion. Tradition speaks of a people called the Hyksos who came from the east and conquered the Nile Delta. They seem to

Akhnaton Intones New Hymns to Aton, the One God

These hymns were composed in the reign of Amenhotep IV (1367–1350 B.C.), or Akhnaton, as he called himself after instituting a religious revolution in Egypt.

Thou makest the Nile in the Nether World,
Thou bringest it as thou desirest,
To preserve alive the people of Egypt
For thou hast made them for thyself,
Thou lord of them all, who weariest thyself for them;
Thou lord of every land, who risest for them.
Thou Sun of day, great in glory,
All the distant highland countries,
Thou makest also their life,
Thou didst set a Nile in the sky.
When it falleth for them,
It maketh waves upon the mountains,
Like the great green sea,
Watering their fields in their towns.

How benevolent are thy designs, O lord of eternity!
There is a Nile in the sky for the strangers
And for the antelopes of all the highlands that go about
  upon their feet.
But the Nile, it cometh from the Nether World for
  Egypt.

Thou didst make the distant sky in order to rise
  therein,
In order to behold all that thou hast made,
While thou wast yet alone
Shining in thy form as living Aton,
Dawning, glittering, going afar and returning.
Thou makest millions of forms
Through thyself alone;
Cities, villages, and fields, highways and rivers,
All eyes see thee before them,
For thou art Aton of the day over the earth,
When thou hast gone away,
And all men, whose faces thou hast fashioned
In order that thou mightest no longer see thyself
  alone;

[Have fallen asleep, so that not] one [seeth] that which
  thou hast made,
Yet art thou still in my heart.

REVELATION TO THE KING
There is no other that knoweth thee
Save thy son Akhnaton.
Thou hast made him wise
In thy designs and in thy might.

UNIVERSAL MAINTENANCE
The world subsists in thy hand,
Even as thou hast made them
When thou hast risen they live,
When thou settest they die;
For thou art length of life of thyself,
Men live through thee.

The eyes of men see beauty
Until thou settest.
All labour is put away
When thou settest in the west.
When thou risest again
[Thou] makest [every hand] to flourish for the king
And [prosperity] is in every foot,
Since thou didst establish the world,
And raise them up for thy son,
Who came forth from thy flesh,
The king of Upper and Lower Egypt,
Living in Truth, Lord of the Two Lands,
Nefer-khepru-Re, Wan-Re [Akhnaton],
Son of Re, living in Truth, lord of diadems,
Akhnaton, whose life is long;
[And for] the chief royal wife, his beloved,
Mistress of the Two Lands, Nefer-nefru-Aton,
  Nofretete,
Living and flourishing for ever and ever. ❑

James H. Breasted, *The Dawn of Conscience* (New York: Charles Scribners' Sons, 1933, 1961), p. 137.

---

have been a collection of Semitic peoples from the area of Palestine and Syria at the eastern end of the Mediterranean. Egyptian nationalism reasserted itself in about 1575 B.C., when a dynasty from Thebes drove out the Hyksos and reunited the kingdom. In reaction to the humiliation of the Second Intermediate Period, the pharaohs of the Eighteenth Dynasty, the most prominent of whom was Thutmose III (1490–1436 B.C.), created an absolute government based on a powerful army and an Egyptian empire extending far beyond the Nile valley.

From the Hyksos, the Egyptians learned new military techniques and obtained new weapons. To these they added determination, a fighting spirit, and an increasingly military society. They pushed the southern frontier back a long way and extended Egyptian power farther into Palestine and Syria and beyond to the upper Euphrates River. They were not checked until they came into conflict with the powerful Hittite empire of Asia Minor. Both powers were weakened by the struggle, and though Egypt survived, it again became the victim of foreign invasion and rule, as one

Akhnaton worshiping Aton. The scene curved into this stone stele shows Eighteenth-Dynasty Pharaoh Akhnaton (1367–1350 B.C.) paying homage to the newly enthroned god, Aton, the disk of the sun. [Library of the Egyptian Museum, Cairo.]

was the growth in power of the priests of Amon and the threat it posed to the position of the king. When young Amenhotep IV (1367–1350 B.C.) came to the throne before the middle of the fourteenth century B.C., he was apparently determined to resist the priesthood of Amon. He was supported by his family and advisers and ultimately made a clean break with the worship of Amon-Re. He moved his capital from Thebes, the center of Amon worship, and built an entirely new city about three hundred miles to the north at a place now called El Amarna. Its god was Aton the physical disk of the sun, and the new city was called Akhtaton. The king changed his own name to Akhnaton, "It pleases Aton." The new god was different from any that had come before him, for he was believed to be universal, not merely Egyptian. Unlike the other gods, he had no cult statue but was represented in painting and relief sculpture by the symbol of the sun disk.

The universal claims for Aton led to religious intolerance of the worshipers of the other gods. Their temples were shut down, and the name of Amon-Re was chiseled from the monuments on which it was carved. The old priests, of course, were deprived of their posts and privileges, and the people who served the pharaoh and his god were new, sometimes even foreign. The new religion, moreover, was more remote than the old. Only the pharaoh and his family worshiped Aton directly, and the people worshiped the pharaoh. Akhnaton's interest in religious reform apparently led him to ignore foreign affairs, which proved disastrous. The Asian possessions of Egypt fell away. This imperial decline and its economic consequences presumably caused further hostility to the new religion. When the king died, a strong counterrevolution swept away the work of his lifetime.

His chosen successor was soon put aside and replaced by Tutankhamon (1347–1339 B.C.), the young husband of one of the daughters of Akhnaton, the beautiful Nefertiti. The new pharaoh restored the old religion and wiped out as much as he could of the memory of the worship of Aton. He restored Amon to the center of the Egyptian pantheon, abandoned El Amarna, and returned the capital to Thebes. There, he and his successors built his magnificent tomb, which remained remarkably intact until its discovery in 1922. The end of the El Amarna age restored power to the priests of Amon and to the military officers. A general named Horemhab became king (1335–1308? B.C.), restored order, and recovered much of the lost empire. He referred to Akhnaton as "the criminal of Akhtaton" and erased his name from the records. Akhnaton's city and memory disappeared for over three thousand years, to be rediscovered only by chance about a century ago.

For the rest of its independent history, Egypt returned to its traditional culture, but its mood was more

foreign empire after another took possession of the ancient kingdom.

The Eighteenth Dynasty, however, witnessed an interesting religious change. One of the results of the successful imperial ventures of the Egyptian pharaohs pessimistic. The Book of the Dead, a product of this late period, was a collection of spells whereby the dead could get safely to the next world without being destroyed by a hideous monster. Egypt itself would soon be devoured by powerful empires, and the Pharaonic civilization would pass from history forever.

Ancient Near Eastern Empires

In the time of the Eighteenth Dynasty in Egypt, new groups of peoples had established themselves in the Near East: the Kassites in Babylonia, the Hittites in Asia Minor, and the Mitannians in northern Mesopotamia. They all spoke languages in the Indo-European group, which includes Greek, Latin, Sanskrit, Persian, Celtic, and the Germanic languages and is thought to have originated in the Ukraine (now the southwestern Soviet Union) or to the east of it. The Kassites and the Mitannians were warrior peoples who ruled as a minority over more civilized folk and absorbed their culture without changing it.

THE HITTITES. The Hittites arrived in Asia Minor about 2000 B.C., and by about 1500 B.C., they had established a strong, centralized government with a capital at Hattusas (near Ankara, the capital of modern Turkey). Between 1400 and 1200 B.C., the Hittites contested Egypt's control of Palestine and Syria. They were strong enough to achieve a dynastic marriage with the daughter of the powerful Nineteenth Dynasty pharaoh Ramses II, in about 1265 B.C. By 1200 B.C., the Hittite kingdom was gone, swept away by the arrival of new, mysterious Indo-Europeans. However, Neo-Hittite centers flourished in Asia Minor and Mesopotamia for a few centuries longer.

In most respects, the Hittites reflected the influence of the dominant Mesopotamian culture of the region, but their government resembled more closely what we know of other Indo-European cultures. Their kings did not claim to be divine or even to be the chosen representatives of the gods. In the early period, the king's power was checked by a council of nobles, and the assembled army had to ratify his succession to the throne. The Hittites appear to have been responsible for a great technological advance, the smelting of iron. They also played an important role in transmitting the ancient cultures of Mesopotamia and Egypt to the Greeks, who lived on their frontiers.

THE ASSYRIANS. The fall of the Hittites was followed shortly by the formation of empires that dominated the Near East's ancient civilizations and even extended them to new areas. The first of these empires was established by the Assyrians, whose homeland was in the valleys and hills of northern Mesopotamia along, and to the east of, the Tigris River. They had a series of capitals, of which the great city of Nineveh is perhaps best known (modern Mosul, Iraq). They spoke a Semitic language and, from early times, were a part of the culture of Mesopotamia. Akkadians, Sumerians, Amorites, and Mitannians had dominated Assyria in turn.

The Hittites' defeat of Mitanni liberated the Assyrians and prepared the way for their greatness from earlier than 1000 B.C. By 665 B.C., they had come to control everything from the southern frontier of Egypt, through Palestine, Syria, and much of Asia Minor, down to the Persian Gulf in the southeast. They succeeded in part because they made use of iron weapons. Because iron was more common than copper and tin, it was possible for them to arm more men cheaply. The Assyrians were also fierce, well disciplined, and cruel. Their cruelty was calculated, at least in part, to terrorize real and potential enemies, for the Assyrians boasted of their brutality.

Unlike earlier empires, the Assyrian Empire systematically and profitably exploited the area it held. The Assyrians employed different methods of control, ranging from the mere collection of tribute, to the sta-

A late Hittite war chariot. The Hittites were probably the earliest major users of iron implements and of the horse. This relief, now in the Ankara museum, shows a pair of horse-drawn Hittite fighters oblivious to the defeated enemy below. It is from the eighth century B.C., by which time the formerly unified empire had been succeeded by several scattered Hittite groups. [AHM.]

tioning of garrisons in conquered territory, to removing entire populations from their homelands and scattering them elsewhere, as they did to the people of the kingdom of Israel. Because of their military and administrative skills, they were able to hold vast areas even as they absorbed the teachings of the older cultures under their sway.

In addition to maintaining their own empire, the Assyrians had to serve as a buffer of the civilized Middle East against the barbarians on its frontiers. In the seventh century B.C., the task of fighting off the barbarians so drained the overextended Assyrians that the empire fell because of internal revolution. A new dy-

An Assyrian palace. This is a reconstruction drawing of the palace complex of King Sargon II (722–705 B.C.) at Khorsabad (in modern Iraq). [Charles Altman. Courtesy of the Oriental Institute, University of Chicago.]

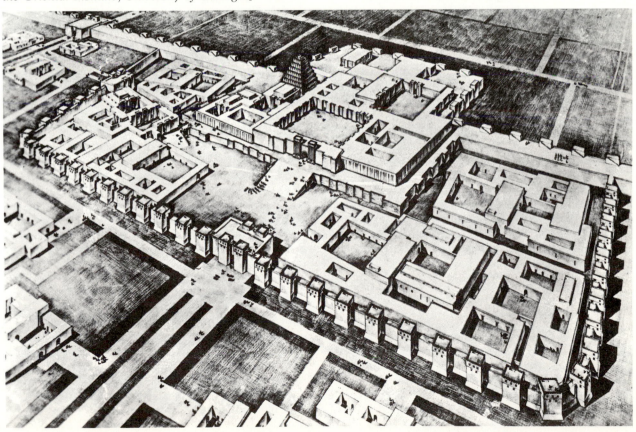

nasty in Babylon joined with the rising kingdom of Media to the east (in modern Iran) to defeat the Assyrians and destroy Nineveh in 612 B.C. The successor kingdoms, the Chaldean or Neo-Babylonian and the Median, did not last long; they were swallowed, by 539 B.C., by yet another great eastern empire, that of the Persians.

Early Indian Civilization

To the east of Mesopotamia, beyond the Iranian plateau and the mountains of Baluchistan, the Asian continent bends sharply southward into the southern oceans. This great triangular projection of Asia south of the massive mountain barrier of the Himalaya is known today as the *Indian subcontinent*. From sites well north in modern Pakistan and Afghanistan to the southern tip of India and Sri Lanka (Ceylon), archaeologists have unearthed evidence of diverse Paleolithic cultures. The latest of these probably existed side by side with the many Neolithic and Bronze Age sites also found on the subcontinent.

The earliest Neolithic pottery and agricultural hunting tools, together with evidence of settled life, have been dated as early as about 5500 B.C. These are in present-day Pakistan in the foothills of Sind and Baluchistan. The Neolithic revolution thus came to the subcontinent somewhat later than in the Near East. Some used to believe that it was imported from the west, but today scholars think that it was of independent origin in much, if not all, of the subcontinent.

The beginning of identifiable civilization in India was unusual, in that the initial breakthrough to literate, urban culture in the Indus valley lasted only a few hundred years. The Aryan culture that replaced the Indus civilization was foreign and bore little relation or resemblance to it. It centered on a different part of northern India, first the extreme northwest (Gandhara, the Punjab), then the plains west of the upper Ganges, and then along the Ganges itself. Although this Aryan culture provided the base for all later Indian civilization, it existed for nearly a millennium without taking up writing or building large cities. Because of the different character of these two cultures, we shall look at each separately.

The Harappan Civilization on the Indus River

The first breakthrough to civilization in the subcontinent came in the region of modern Pakistan. Here, there emerged a culture boasting Bronze age tools, developed cities, a writing system, and diversified social and economic organization. As one might expect, this civilization flourished on the fertile floodplains of one of the two largest river systems of the subcontinent, the Indus and its tributaries. Several sizable rivers flow west and south out of the Himalaya in Kashmir and the Punjab (*Panjab*, "five rivers") to merge into the single stream of the Indus as it crosses Sind to empty into the Indian Ocean. (The second great river system of the subcontinent, the Ganges and its tributaries, also rises in the Himalaya but flows south and east to the Bay of Bengal on the opposite side of the subcontinent.) The Indus culture is sometimes also called *Harappan*, from the name of the site, Harappa, where archaeologists first discovered it. Until the excavations began in the 1920s, no one knew of its existence. Today, two cities, Harappa and Mohenjo-Daro, and numerous lesser towns of this culture have been unearthed and studied.

Of the four great river-valley civilizations that mark the beginnings of literate, urban culture, the Indus is the one about which we know the least. Our relative ignorance is due to two factors.

First, this civilization disappeared as a living cultural tradition sometime before the middle of the second millennium B.C. It was once commonly assumed that this culture was destroyed by invading steppe peoples from the northwest, the Indo-European-speaking tribes who migrated in the second millennium B.C. from the Eurasian steppelands west, south, and eastward into new territories. (The groups that entered India and, at about the same time, Iran, are known as Aryans.) Now scholars recognize that there is no firm evidence to support this hypothesis, and without new evidence, the true cause of the passing of Indus civilization must remain one of history's unsolved mysteries.

Second, although we have many Indus inscriptions (mostly small stamp seals cut into soapstone), no one has been able to decipher them. Many scholars think that the Indus language was a Dravidian tongue, which would place it in the same family as some languages still spoken in the subcontinent, the most important of which is Tamil in southern India. Until it can be read, we have no self-testimony of the Indus peoples to guide us. Without the patient, still-unfolding work of modern archaeologists, this once great and widely dispersed civilization would have remained a wholly "vanished" culture. Now, however, we know that it flourished for at least five hundred years, and perhaps longer, before it passed from history's stage forever. Although material remains do not give us access to the history of the rise and fall of the Indus society, or to its precise institutions, they do yield indisputable evidence of a high culture. We can make some educated guesses about the Indus civilization, based on archaeological data and inferences from later Indian life and culture.

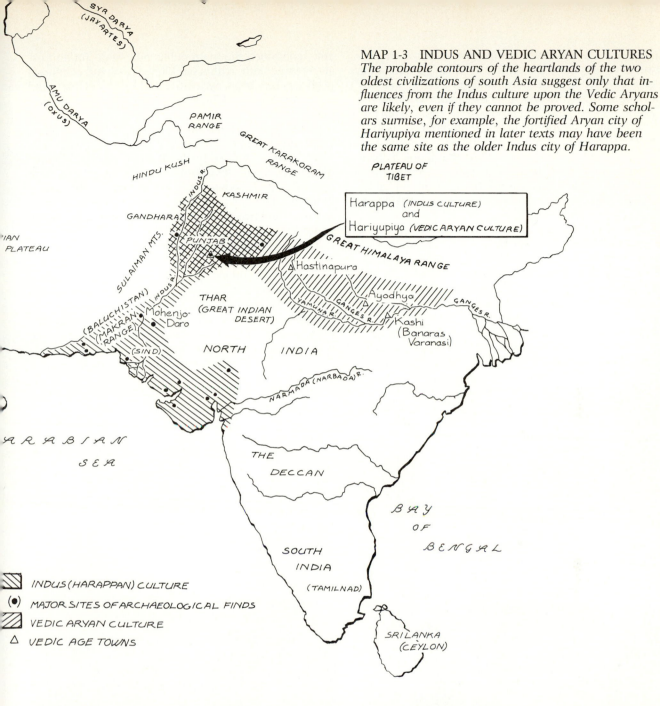

MAP 1-3 INDUS AND VEDIC ARYAN CULTURES
The probable contours of the heartlands of the two oldest civilizations of south Asia suggest only that influences from the Indus culture upon the Vedic Aryans are likely, even if they cannot be proved. Some scholars surmise, for example, that the fortified Aryan city of Hariyupiya mentioned in later texts may have been the same site as the older Indus city of Harappa.

Harappa (INDUS CULTURE)
and
Hariyupiya (VEDIC ARYAN CULTURE)

INDUS (HARAPPAN) CULTURE
MAJOR SITES OF ARCHAEOLOGICAL FINDS
VEDIC ARYAN CULTURE
VEDIC AGE TOWNS

GENERAL CHARACTER. The Indus or Harappan civilization covered an area many times larger than either of its contemporaries, Middle Kingdom Egypt and Third Dynasty Ur. Yet this vast territory was united in a culture of remarkable homogeneity, as the archaeological finds tell us. The similarities in city layouts, building construction, weights and measures, seal inscriptions, artifacts, and even the size of the burnt brick used in all the Indus towns for buildings and floodwalls point to the unusual uniformity of this civilization. Such uniformity suggests a strong, perhaps centralized, government, an integrated economic system, and good internal communications.

The Indus culture is thought to have remained strikingly unchanged over the centuries that it endured (probably from about 2250 to 1750 B.C., although some scholars argue for as long as 2500–1500 B.C.). Change does not seem to have been prized. Because the main cities and towns lay in river lowlands subject to periodic flooding, they had to be rebuilt numerous times in

Indus history. The excavations show that each new level of construction closely followed the pattern of the previous one. Similarly, we find no evidence of any development in the Indus pictographic script in the more than two thousand stamp seals thus far uncovered. Stability, regularity, and traditionalism seem to have been hallmarks of this society. Such unusual continuity has led scholars to speculate that Indus civilization may have flourished under a single conservative, theocratic, priestly state rather than a more unstable, secular state or states dominated by a royal court.

THE CITIES. The major sites at Harappa and Mohenjo-Daro appear to have been two centers of Indus culture. Each probably had a population of at least thirty-five thousand and was meticulously laid out on a similar plan. On the western side of the city stood a large, walled citadel on a raised rectangular platform about 800 by 1400 feet in size; east of this platform lay the town proper, which was laid out on a careful north-south–east-west grid of main avenues, some of which were 30 feet wide. The citadel appar-ently contained the main public buildings. An impressively large bath, with a brick-lined pool and columned porticos, has been excavated at Mohenjo-Daro, and both sites have buildings tentatively identified as temples.

Each city boasted a large granary for food storage. Cemeteries were laid out on the periphery of each. The town "blocks" formed by the main avenues were crisscrossed by small, less rigidly planned lanes, off which opened private houses of various sizes, sometimes more than one story. The typical house was built around a central courtyard and presented only blank walls to the outside lanes. This arrangement is recalled by houses in many Near Eastern and Indian cities today.

Perhaps the most striking feature of these cities, however, was a complex system of covered drains and sewers. Private houses were serviced by wells, bathrooms, and latrines, and the great bath at Mohenjo-Daro was filled from its own large well. The drainage system that served these facilities in the Indus towns was an engineering feat unrivaled in the ancient world

Ancient Mohenjo-Daro, like most cities of the Indus Valley civilization, was built principally of mud brick. The structures are laid on straight lines; streets cross each other at right angles. The impression is one of order, prosperity, and civic discipline.

Stone torso from Mohenjo-Dara. [Borromeo/Art Resource.]

until the time of the Romans, nearly two thousand years later.

ECONOMIC LIFE. The Indus state had an economy based on a thriving agriculture. Wheat and barley were the main crops; peas, lentils, sesame, and cotton were also important. Whether artificial irrigation or only flood control was used is not known, but indications are that the whole Indus region was more densely vegetated and productive than it is today. Cattle, dogs, goats, sheep, and fowl were raised, and elephants and water buffalo were known and possibly tamed for work as well. Cotton weaving, metalworking, and wheel-driven pottery making were practiced. Trade contacts abroad are indicated by Indus stamp seals found in Mesopotamia; the "Melukka" region mentioned in ancient Akkadian texts as a source of ivory, precious stones, and other wares may have been the Indus basin.

Excavations in the Persian Gulf indicate that the island of Bahrain may have been a staging point for Indus-Mesopotamian sea trade. Metals and semiprecious stones were apparently imported from present-day Iran and Afghanistan, as well as from central Asia, modern Rajasthan, and Mysore in peninsular India, and perhaps from Arabia. There are also indications from shared drawing motifs that these trade contacts resulted in cultural borrowings.

MATERIAL CULTURE. Without literary remains, we must look to pottery, tools, sculpture, ornaments, and other objects unearthed at Indus sites to glean some idea of arts, crafts, and technology. The chief evidence of creative art is found in the fine bronze and stone statues that have been recovered. We find also an accomplished mastery of design and production techniques in various artifacts: copper and bronze tools and vessels, impressive black-on-red painted pottery, dressed stonework, stone and terra-cotta figurines and toys, silver vessels and ornaments, gold jewelry, and dyed woven fabric. The numerous flat stamp seals of stone are our major source, along with some pottery painting and small copper-tablet engravings, for both the Indus script and portrayals of animals, humans, and what are thought to be divine or semidivine beings.

Such handiwork shows the Indus capabilities at their best. Unfortunately, no monumental or wall art, beyond some decorative brickwork, has been found in the excavations. There are no friezes, mosaics, or large-scale sculpture. In general, the range of art and artifacts seems limited by comparison with that of ancient Egypt or Mesopotamia.

RELIGION. The Indus remains give us somewhat more to speculate about in the religious realm. The elaborate bath facilities suggest practices like the ritual bathing and water purification rites that are so important in Indian life even in the present day. Later Hindu (and possibly even elements of Indo-Aryan) polytheism and image worship may also have historical links with Indus ideas and practices. This possibility is suggested by the stone images from the so-called "temples" of Mohenjo-Daro and the far more common terra-cotta figurines found at many sites. Later symbols important to Hindus, such as the pipal tree or the swastika sign, are also found on Indus artifacts.

Among the most common images, the large number of male animals—above all, the humped bull—might be symbols of power and fertility or may conceivably indicate some kind of animal worship. Other animals depicted are the tiger, the snake, and a unicornlike animal. The recurring figure of a male with a leafy headdress and horns, often seated in a posture associated later in India with yogic mediation, has been likened to the Aryan "Lord of All Creatures." This figure merges with the major god Shiva in Hindu piety. Such a comparison is strengthened by some pictures in which the seated figure has three faces and an erect phallus, both common elements of Shiva iconography.

The many terra-cotta figurines of females, often pregnant or carrying a child, could be a prefiguration of the goddess (Devi, Durga, and so on) who, as the consort of Shiva, is widely worshiped in India today. Similar female images have been found in other prehistoric cultures, but their actual significance is purely conjectural. If goddess worship did exist in the Indus culture, this may be one of the elements of pre-Aryan religion that survived in folk tradition; it reemerged

This terra-cotta suggests links with later Hindu image worship. [Borromeo/Art Resource.]

us that the Indus peoples, like all others, had their own ways of coming to terms with the mysteries of birth, life, and death, even if we can only guess at what these were.

THE PASSING OF INDUS CIVILIZATION. This distant culture has thus far kept more secrets than it has revealed. Its ruins tell us that sometime in the early second millennium B.C., it went into decline. Some think that it was destroyed by abnormal flooding or changes in the course of the Indus even before the first Aryan invaders arrived. These warlike peoples probably first appeared in the upper Indus area about 1800 B.C. They later swept with their horse-drawn chariots in successive waves across the northern plains of the subcontinent as far as the Ganges valley. As we have indicated, the culture that they established across much of northern India exhibits little trace of clear Indus survivals. The sacred texts of this culture, the Vedas, refer only occasionally either to enemies whose strongholds were destroyed with the help of the gods, or to "dark," "snub-nosed," small and ugly "slaves" brought under subjection by the conquerors.

The Indus civilization remains too much in the shadows of prehistory for its full influence to be seen. Even the common theory that India's Dravidian-speaking people are descendants of the Indus peoples remains to be proved. Still, these forgotten predecessors of the Aryans probably made significant contributions to later life in the subcontinent in ways yet to be discovered.

The Vedic Aryan Civilization of North India

By comparison with the Indus civilization, we know much more about the Aryan culture that effectively "refounded" Indian civilization. Unlike the Indus culture, that of the Indo-Aryans was not an urban civilization. It left behind neither city ruins nor substantial

over a millennium later, after 500 B.C., as a prominent feature of Hindu culture. Other aspects of Indus religion—the burial customs, for example—do not seem to have later Hindu analogies. However, they remind

Indus stone stamp seals. Note the familiar humped bull of India. [Borromeo/EPA.]

artifacts beyond tools, weapons, and pottery. But the Vedas did survive, and we give the name *Vedic* to the early Aryan culture of northern India because the Vedic texts are virtually the exclusive source of our knowledge of it. Although the latest portions of the Vedas date from perhaps 500 B.C., the oldest may go back to 1700 B.C. Because these texts are not historical, but ritual, priestly, and speculative works, they tell us little about specific events. But the Vedas do offer evidence for some general inferences about religion, society, values, and thought in early Aryan India.

Veda, which means "knowledge," is the collective term for the texts still recognized today by most Indians as the holiest sources of their tradition. In Hindu perspective, Veda is the eternal wisdom realized by the most ancient seers and preserved over thousands of years by generations of professional reciters in unbroken oral transmission. We speak of "the Vedas" in the plural to refer to the four major compilations of Vedic ritual texts and the explanatory and speculative texts associated with each. The most significant of the four main collections for the history of the early Aryans is the collection of 1,028 religious hymns known as the Rig Veda, which contains the oldest materials. The latest Rigvedic hymns date from CA. 1000 B.C., the oldest from perhaps 1700–1200 B.C., when the Aryans spread across the northern Indian plains as far as the upper reaches of the Ganges.

Aryan is a different kind of term. The second-millennium invaders of northern India called themselves *Aryas* to distinguish themselves from the peoples that they conquered. Vedic Sanskrit, the language of the invaders, gave this word to later Sanskrit as a term for "noble," or "free-born" *(arya)*. The word is found also in old Iranian texts *(Iran* is itself a name derived from the Old Persian equivalent of *Arya)*. It seems to have been originally the name of peoples who migrated out of the steppeland between eastern Europe and central Asia into Europe, Greece, Anatolia, the Iranian plateau, and India in the second and first millennia B.C. Those who moved into India can thus be more precisely designated *Vedic Aryans*, or *Indo-Aryans*.

In the nineteenth century, *Aryan* was the term applied to the widespread language group known more commonly today as *Indo-European*. To this widely distributed family belong Greek, Latin, and the Romance languages, the Germanic languages, the Slavic tongues, and the Indo-Iranian languages of Persian and Sanskrit and their derivatives. The common basis of all these Indo-European tongues is evident in similar names for both family relations *(father, mother,* and so on) and divine beings (for example, Latin *deus,* and Sanskrit *deva,* "god"). The perverse misuse of *Aryan* in Nazi Germany referred to a white "master race." This term is now usually restricted to linguistic use for the Indo-Iranian branch of the Indo-

Hymn to a Rigvedic Goddess

Here we see the personification of a natural phenomenon, the night, as a goddess whom worshipers can petition. Such hymns make up the Rigveda collection and mirror the close relationship of nature and the transcendent world in the Vedic Aryan world view.

TO NIGHT

With all her eyes the goddess Night looks forth
   approaching many a spot:
She hath put all her glories on.

Immortal, she hath filled the waste, the goddess
   hath filled height and depth:
She conquers darkness with her light.

The goddess as she comes hath set the Dawn her
   sister in her place:
And then the darkness vanishes.

So favour us this night, O thou whose pathways we
   have visited
As birds their nest upon the tree.

The villagers have sought their homes, and all that
   walks and all that flies,
Even the falcons fain for prey.

Keep off the she-wolf and the wolf; O Night, keep
   the thief away:
Easy be thou for us to pass.

Clearly hath she come nigh to me who decks the
   dark with richest hues:
O morning, cancel it like debts.

These have I brought to thee like kine. O Night,
   thou child of heaven, accept
This laud as for a conqueror.

Rig Veda (10.127)

From *Hinduism,* ed. by L. Renou (New York: George Braziller, 1962), p. 71.

Hymn to Indra

This hymn celebrates especially the greatest deed ascribed to Indra, the slaying of the dragon Vritra to release the waters needed by people and livestock. Whether these are the rain or the dammed-up rivers is difficult to say. This victory also symbolizes the victory of the Aryans over the dark-skinned Dasas *and the very creation of the world from the dragon's body. Note the sexual and rain imagery. The* kadrukas *may be the bowls used for soma in the sacrifice. The* vajra *is Indra's thunderbolt; the name* Dasa *for the lord of the waters is also that used for the peoples defeated by the Aryans and for all enemies of Indra, of whom the* Pani *tribe are one.*

Indra's heroic deeds, indeed, will I proclaim, the first ones which the wielder of the vajra accomplished. He killed the dragon, released the waters, and split open the sides of the mountains.

He killed the dragon lying spread out on the mountain; for him Tvashtar fashioned the roaring vajra. Like bellowing cows, the waters, gliding, have gone down straightway to the ocean.

Showing off his virile power he chose soma; from the three *kadrukas* he drank of the extracted soma. The bounteous god took up the missile, the vajra; he killed the first-born among the dragons.

When you, O Indra, killed the first-born among the dragons and further overpowered the wily tricks (māyā) of the tricksters, bringing forth, at that very moment, the sun, the heaven and the dawn—since then, indeed, have you not come across another enemy.

Indra killed Vritra, the greater enemy, the shoulder-less one, with his mighty and fatal weapon, the vajra. Like branches of a tree lopped off with an axe, the dragon lies prostrate upon the earth. . . .

Over him, who lay in that manner like a shattered reed flowed the waters for the sake of man. At the feet of the very waters, which Vritra had [once] enclosed with his might, the dragon [now] lay [prostrate]. . . .

With the Dāsa as their lord and with the dragon as their warder, the waters remained imprisoned, like cows held by the Pani. Having killed Vritra, [Indra] threw open the cleft of waters which had been closed.

You became the hair of a horse's tail, O Indra, when he [Vritra] struck at your sharp-pointed vajra— the one god (*eka deva*) though you were. You won the cows, O brave one, you won soma; you released the seven rivers, so that they should flow. . . .

Indra, who wields the vajra in his hand, is the lord of what moves and what remains rested, of what is peaceful and what is horned. He alone rules over the tribes as their king; he encloses them as does a rim the spokes. □

Rig Veda 1.32

Wm. Theodore de Bary et al., *Sources of Indian Tradition* (New York, 1963).

European family (Sanskrit, Persian, and so on), or to historical use for the particular peoples who invaded northern India and the Iranian plateau in the second millennium B.C.

THE "ARYANIZING" OF NORTH INDIA.

The Vedic Aryans were seminomadic warriors who reached India via the mountain passes of the Hindu Kush, in modern Afghanistan. Theirs was probably a gradual migration of rather small tribal groups. These Aryans were horsemen and cattle herders rather than farmers and city builders. They, like their Iranian relatives, left their mark not in their material culture but in the changes that their conquest of new territory brought to existing society: a new language, a new social organization, new techniques of warfare, and new religious forms and ideas.

Without documentation, we can piece together only the broad outlines of the early Aryans' gradual subjugation of northern India and their equally gradual shift from pastoral nomadism to settled agriculture and ani-

mal husbandry. We know that they penetrated first into the area of the Punjab and the Indus valley (CA. 1800–1500 B.C.), presumably in search of grazing lands for their cattle and other livestock. They would have exploited their military superiority (based on the use of horses, chariots, and copper–bronze weaponry) to overcome the Indus peoples or their successors in these regions.

Echoes of such conflict seem to occur in some Rig-vedic hymns. One thinks especially here of those in which the god Indra is hailed as the warrior who smashes the fortifications of enemies (possibly the conquest of the Indus citadels?) and slays the great serpent who had blocked the rivers (possibly the destruction of the dams used to control the rivers of the Indus area for agriculture?). Where some later Rigvedic hymns speak of human rather than divine warriors, actual historical events may lie behind the legends. An example is the late hymn that praises the king of a tribe called the *Bharatas*—whence the modern name of India, *Bharat*, "land of the Bharatas."

Hymn to the Lord of Creatures

Here we have the creation of the world depicted as a Vedic sacrifice in which the primeval male principle, Purusha, is sacrificed by the gods as priests, apparently as an offering to himself. This paradox can occur in part because the figure Purusha is a blend of aspects of the male principle (Viraj in the text was originally a female principle of creative power), the god Agni, and the power of the sacrifice itself. The hymn is a late one, and its reference to the creation of the four social classes of humankind is the first such mention in an Indian text (Brāhmans formed the priestly class; Rajānyas, the warriors; Vaishyas, the merchant or commoner groups; and Shūdras, the serf or servant class). These became and remained in later India the four major categories of the social order (note that the warriors were later called Kshatriyas).

Thousand-headed Purusha, thousand-eyed, thousand-footed—he, having pervaded the earth on all sides, still extends ten fingers beyond it.

Purusha alone is all this—whatever has been and whatever is going to be. Further, he is the lord of immortality and also of what grows on account of food.

Such is his greatness; greater, indeed, than this is Purusha. All creatures constitute but one quarter of him, his three quarters are the immortal in the heaven.

With his three quarters did Purusha rise up; one quarter of him again remains here. With it did he variously spread out on all sides over what eats and what eats not.

From him was Virāj born, from Virāj there evolved Purusha. He, being born, projected himself behind the earth as also before it.

When the gods performed the sacrifice with Purusha as the oblation, then the spring was its clarified butter, the summer the sacrificial fuel, and the autumn the oblation.

The sacrificial victim, namely, Purusha, born at the very beginning, they sprinkled with sacred water upon the sacrificial grass. With him as oblation the gods performed the sacrifice, and also the Sādhyas [a class of semidivine beings] and the rishis [ancient seers].

From that wholly offered sacrificial oblation were born the verses [*rc*] and the sacred chants; from it were born the meters (*chandas*); the sacrificial formula was born from it.

From it horses were born and also those animals who have double rows [i.e., upper and lower] of teeth; cows were born from it, from it were born goats and sheep.

When they divided Purusha, in how many different portions did they arrange him? What became of his mouth, what of his two arms? What were his two thighs and his two feet called?

His mouth became the brāhman; his two arms were made into the rājanya; his two thighs the vaishyas; from his two feet the shūdra was born.

The moon was born from the mind; from the eye the sun was born; from the mouth Indra and Agni; from the breath (prāna) the wind (vāyu) was born.

From the navel was the atmosphere created, from the head the heaven issued forth; from the two feet was born the earth and the quarters (the cardinal directions) from the ear. Thus did they fashion the worlds.

Seven were the enclosing sticks in this sacrifice, thrice seven were the fire-sticks made, when the gods, performing the sacrifice, bound down Purusha, the sacrificial victim.

With this sacrificial oblation did the gods offer the sacrifice. These were the first norms (dharma) of sacrifice. These greatnesses reached to the sky wherein live the ancient Sādhyas and gods. ❑

Rig Veda 19.90

Wm. Theodore de Bary et al., *Sources of Indian Tradition* (New York, 1963).

In what may be called the Rigvedic period (CA. 1700–1000 B.C.), the newcomers settled in the Punjab and beyond, where they took up agriculture as well as stockbreeding. The Thar desert blocked any southward expansion, so their subsequent movement was to the east. How far they penetrated before 1000 B.C. is not clear, but their main locus remained the Punjab and the plains west of the Yamuna River (northwest of modern Delhi). Then, between about 1000 and 500 B.C., these Aryan Indians (for no longer can we speak of them as a foreign people) spread across the Doab, the "two-rivers" plain formed between the Yamuna and the Ganges, and beyond. They cleared (probably by burning) the heavy forests that covered this area at that time and settled here. They also moved further northeast to the Himalayan foothills and southeast along the Ganges, in what was to be the cradle of subsequent Indian civilization. In this age, the importance of the Punjab receded sharply.

This later Vedic period (CA. 1000–500 B.C.) is often referred to as the Brahmanic age because of the dominance of the priestly religion of the Brahman class attested in later Vedic commentaries called the *Brahmanas* (CA. 1000–800 or 600 B.C.). This age is sometimes also called the *epic age*, because it provided the setting for the two classical Indian epics, the *Mahabharata* and the *Ramayana*. Both were composed much later, probably only in the period CA. 400 B.C.–A.D. 200, but they contain older materials and refer to dimly remembered events of earlier times. The *Mahabharata*, the longest epic poem in the world, centers on the power struggle of two Aryan clans in the area to the north and west of modern Delhi, perhaps around 900 B.C. The *Ramayana* tells of the legendary and dramatic adventures of King Rama, whose travels may at one level recall the movement of northern Indian culture into southern India about the end of the Brahmanic period. Both epics evidence the complex cultural mixing of Aryan, Indus, and other earlier subcontinent peoples.

By about A.D. 200, this mixing would give rise to a distinguishable "Indian" civilization over most of the subcontinent. Its basis was clearly Aryan, but its language, society, and religion had assimilated much that was non-Aryan. Harappan culture vanished, but elements of it and other regional cultures played their part in the formation of Indian culture as we know it.

VEDIC ARYAN SOCIETY. The Aryans brought with them a society apparently characterized by patrilineal family descent and inheritance. The masculine orientation of the society is reflected in its overwhelmingly male gods. The patriarchal family was the basic unit of society. Marriage seems to have been monogamous, and widows could remarry.

Related families formed larger kin groups. The largest social grouping was the tribe, which was ruled by a tribal leader, or *raja* ("king" in Sanskrit, and a cognate of the latin *rex*), whose power was shared with a tribal council. In early Vedic days, the ruler was chosen for his prowess and was never a priest-king. His chief function was to lead in battle; he had originally no sacred authority. Alongside him was a chief priest, who looked after the often elaborate sacrifices on which religious life centered. We do not know if the king originally acted as the judge in legal matters, although by late Vedic, or Brahmanic, times he performed this function with the help of the priests. In the Brahmanic period, the power of the priestly class increased along with that of the king, who was now a heredity ruler claiming divine qualities sanctioned by the priestly establishment.

Although there were probably identifiable groups of warriors and priests, Aryan society seems originally to have distinguished only two basic grades of society: the noble and the common. The *Dasas*, the darker, conquered peoples, came to form a third group (together with those who intermarried with them) of the socially excluded. Over time, a more rigid set of social classes, four in number, evolved. By the late Rigvedic period, these four divisions, or *varnas*, had become so basic as to be sanctioned explicitly in religious theory. These four classes (excluding the non-Aryan *Dasas*) were the priestly *(brahman)*, the warrior/noble *(Kshatriya)*, the peasant/tradesman *(Vaishya)*, and the servant *(Shudra)* groups, a division that has continued in theory to the present as a general way of organizing the far more numerous subgroups known as *castes* (see Chapter 7). It was, of course, only the members of the three upper classes who were full participants in the various spheres of social, political, and religious life. This isolation of the lowest groups foreshadowed the rigidity of caste distinctions that would later become a basic element in Indian life.

MATERIAL CULTURE. The early, seminomadic Aryans had little in the way of impressive material culture. They did not build cities or even monuments as far as we know. A gray-painted pottery is one of the few physical remains of their culture. They lived simply in wood and thatch or, later, mud-walled dwellings, measured wealth in cattle (presaging the later importance of the cow in Hindu India?), and had developed craftsmanship in carpentry and bronze metalworking. Iron probably was not known in India before 1000 B.C. Gold was used for ornamentation. Wool provided the basic textiles, and alongside stockbreeding, some cultivation, especially of grains, was practiced. Intoxicating drink was well known, both the *soma* used in religious rites and a kind of mead.

Music seems to have been a highly developed art and pastime; singing and dancing are mentioned in the texts, as are various musical instruments. Gambling appears to have been a popular and frequent vice. Betting on chariot racing may have attracted the more affluent, but it is dicing above all that we hear of in Vedic and epic texts. One of the few secular pieces among the Vedic hymns is a "Gambler's Lament," which closes with a plea to the dice: "Take pity on us. Do not bewitch us with your fierce magic. . . . Let no one be trapped by the brown dice!"

The Brahmanic age has left us only a few more material remains. It was still not a time of developed urban culture, even in the mud-brick towns that now were growing up as new lands were burned clear for cultivation and village settlements. There were now established kingdoms with fixed capitals, and trade was growing, especially along the Ganges, although we have no mention of a true coinage system. Specialized groups of craftsmen—goldsmiths, basketmakers, weavers, potters, and entertainers—are mentioned in the later texts.

We do not know when writing was introduced or developed. To judge from references to its common use by around 500 B.C. it may have been about 700 B.C.

The evidence shows that Indian goods were again finding their way to Mesopotamia in this period. This suggests that writing may have been reintroduced in the subcontinent through this trade connection. Yet so highly developed was the oral tradition of Veda transmission among the Brahman class, that writing continued to be scorned as an unworthy medium for the sacred texts of the Veda.

RELIGION. The most important contributions of Vedic India to later history were religious. In the Vedas, we can glimpse the broad outlines and development of Vedic-Brahmanic religion over the thousand years following the arrival of the first Aryans in the subcontinent. However, they tell us only about the public cult and domestic rituals of the Aryan upper classes, not about popular traditions of the masses. We can surmise that among the latter, many Harappan and other non-Aryan practices and ideas continued to flourish. Apparently non-Aryan elements are visible occasionally even in the Vedic texts themselves—especially later ones such as the Upanishads (after CA. 800 B.C.)—in their emphasis on fertility and female deities, ritual pollution and ablutions, and the transmigration of the soul after death.

The central Vedic cult, which was controlled by priests serving a military aristocracy, was dominant until the middle of the first millennium B.C. By this time other, perhaps older, religious forms were evidently asserting themselves among the populace.

The increasing ritual formalism of Brahmanic religion generated challenges in both religious practice and speculative thought. It culminated in the rise and spread of the Buddhist, Jain, and Hindu traditions (see Chapter 2).

The earliest Indo-Aryans seem to have worshiped numerous gods, who most often embodied or were associated with powers of nature. We see vestiges of this in the Rigvedic hymns, which are addressed to anthropomorphic gods. Despite their human form, these gods are commonly linked to one or more natural phenomena: the sky, the clouds, or the sun. Whether the human aspect of what may once have been deified natural forces was due to a gradual divinizing or mythologizing of the ancient human heroes, we cannot say. But the deities we encounter in the Rig Veda are comparable to those of Greek religion. They are also probably distantly related to the latter; note, for example, the similar names of the Aryan father-god Dyaus and the Greek father-god Zeus, which point to a common Indo-European source. In Vedic India, however, unlike in Greece, the father-god had receded in importance before the rising cult of his children. Chief among them was Indra, god of war and the storm. A rowdy god not unlike the old Norse Thor, he led his heavenly warriors across the sky to slay dragons or other enemies with his thunderbolt in his hand.

Also of major importance was Varuna, who may have connections with the later Iranian god Ahura Mazda and Uranus, Greek god of the heavens. Varuna was more remote from human affairs than Indra. He was depicted as an imperial or regal figure who sat on his heavenly throne and guarded the cosmic order, *Rta*, which is both the law of nature and the universal moral law or truth. As the god whose great holiness commanded awe and demanded righteous behavior, Varuna had characteristics of a supreme, omnipresent divinity.

Another god whose central place in the Vedas stands out is Agni, the god of fire (his name, which is the word for "fire" in Sanskrit, is related to Latin *ignis*, "fire," and thus to our *ignite*). He had diverse roles. He was the god who mediated between earth and heaven through the offering of the fire sacrifice; thus, he was the god of the sacrifice and the priests; and he was also the god of the hearth and hence the home. Like the elusive flame, he was a mysterious deity about whose form and presence in all earthly fires there is much speculation in the Rig Veda.

Many other gods could be mentioned: Soma, the god of the hallucinogenic soma plant and drink; Ushas, the goddess of dawn (one of very few feminine deities); Yama, god of the dead; Rudra, the archer and storm god; Vishnu, a solar deity; and the sun god Surya. A major characteristic of the Vedic hymns is that when any single god is addressed, he or she is praised as possessing a wide variety of powers. Many of these powers may normally have been associated with other deities, but this did not bar attributing them also to the god the worshiper was addressing.

The focus of Vedic religious life was sacrifice to the gods. In the sacrificial ritual, the sacrificers seem to have experienced the presence of the gods to whom they made their offering.

The drinking of soma juice was a prominent sacrificial ritual that greatly enhanced the subjective experience of the participants. There seems to have been no emphasis on thanksgiving or expiation of guilt through sacrifice. The recurring theme is the desire for the good things of this life: prosperity, health, victory, and the like. Fire sacrifices were particularly important, on both a large, public and private, domestic scale. There were also exclusively royal rituals, such as that of the elaborate and seldom-performed horse sacrifice.

By Brahmanic times, there had emerged considerable mystical and speculative interpretation of the sacrifice in which sacrificer, sacrificial animal, and god were all identified with one another. Even the creation of the world is described in one Rigvedic hymn as the sacrifice of a primordial being to himself by the lesser gods. The late Vedic texts also emphasize magical and

CA. 2250–1750 B.C. (2500–1500?)	Indus (Harappan) civilization
CA. 1800–1500 B.C.	Aryan peoples invade northwest India
CA. 1500–1000 B.C.	Rigvedic period: Composition of Rigvedic hymns; Punjab as center of Indo-Aryan civilization
CA. 1000–500 B.C.	Later Vedic period: Doab as center of Indo-Aryan civilization
CA. 1000–800/600 B.C.	Composition of Brahmanas and other Vedic texts
CA. 800–500 B.C.	Composition of major Upanishads
CA. 700–500 B.C.	Probable introduction of writing
CA. 400 B.C.–A.D. 200	Composition of great epics, the *Mahabharata* and *Ramayana*

cosmic aspects of ritual and sacrifice. Indeed, some of the Brahmanas indicate that only through the exact performance of the sacrifice is the world order maintained.

The word *Brahman* was originally used to designate the ritual utterance, and it came to refer also to the generalized divine power present in the sacrifice. In the Upanishads, some of the latest Vedic texts and the ones most concerned with speculation about the universe, *Brahman* is extended to refer to the Absolute, the transcendent principle of reality. As the guardian of ritual and the master of the sacred word, the priest was known throughout the Vedic Aryan period by a related word, *Brahmana*, for which the English is *Brahman*. Echoes of these associations were to lend force in later Hindu tradition to the special status of the Brahman caste groups as the highest class of society. We shall see this in Chapter 7 when we take up the Indian story once more.

Early Chinese Civilization

Neolithic Origins in the Yellow River Valley

Agriculture began in China about 4000 B.C. in the basin of the southern bend of the Yellow River. This is the northernmost of East Asia's four great river systems. The others are the Yangtze in central China, the West River in southern China, and the Red River in what is today northern Vietnam. All drain eastward into the Pacific Ocean. In recent millennia, the Yellow River has flowed through a deforested plain, cold in winter and subject to periodic droughts. But in 4000 B.C., its climate was warmer, with forested highlands in the west and swampy marshes to the east. The bamboo rat that today can be found only in semitropical Southeast Asia lived along the Yellow River.

The chief crop of China's agricultural revolution was millet. A second agricultural development focusing on rice may have occurred on the Huai River between the Yellow River and the Yangtze near the coast. In time, wheat entered China from the west. The early Chinese cleared land and burned its cover to plant millet and cabbage and later, rice and soybeans. When the soil became exhausted, the fields were abandoned, and sometimes early villages were abandoned, too. The tools were of stone: axes, hoes, spades, and sickle-shaped knives. The early Chinese domesticated pigs, sheep, cattle, dogs, and chickens. Game was also plentiful, and hunting continued to be important to the village economy. In excavated village garbage heaps of ancient China are found the bones of deer, wild cattle, antelopes, rhinoceros, hares, and marmots. Grain was stored in pottery painted in bold, geometric designs of red and black. This pottery gave way later to a harder, thin black pottery, made on a potter's wheel, that spread west along the Yellow River and south to the Yangtze. The tripodal shapes of Neolithic pots prefigure later Chinese bronzes.

The earliest cultivators lived in wattle-and-daub pit-dwellings with wooden support-posts and sunken, plastered floors. Their villages were located in isolated clearings along the slopes of river valleys. Archaeological finds of weapons and the remains of earthen walls suggest tribal warfare between villages. Of the religion of these people, little is known, though some evidence indicates the worship of ancestral spirits. They practiced divination by applying heat to a hole drilled in the shoulder bone of a steer or the undershell of a tortoise, and interpreting the resulting cracks in the bone. They buried their dead in cemeteries with jars of food. Tribal leaders wore rings and beads of jade.

The Early Bronze Age: The Shang

The traditional history of China tells of three ancient dynasties:

2205–1766 B.C.	Hsia
1766–1050 B.C.	Shang
1050–256 B.C.	Chou

Until early in this century, modern historians saw the first two as legendary. Then, in the 1920s, archaeological excavations at "the wastes of Yin" near present-day An Yang discovered the ruins of a walled city that had been a late Shang capital. Other Shang cities have been discovered more recently. The ruins contained the archives of the department of divination of the Shang court, with thousands on thousands of "oracle bones" incised with archaic Chinese writing. The names of kings on the bones fit almost perfectly those of the traditional historical record. The recognition that the Shang actually existed has led historians to suggest that the Hsia may also have been an actual dynasty. Perhaps the Hsia was a late Neolithic black-pottery kingdom; perhaps it already had bronze and represents the earliest, still missing stage of Chinese writing.

The characteristic political institution of Bronze Age China was the city-state. The largest was the Shang capital, which, frequently moved, lacked the monumental architecture of Egypt or Mesopotamia. The walled city contained public buildings, altars, and the residences of the aristocracy and was surrounded by a sea of Neolithic tribal villages. By late Shang times, several such cities were spotted across the north China plain. The Shang king possessed political, economic, social, and religious authority. When he died, he was sometimes succeeded by a younger brother and sometimes by a son. The rulers of other city-states acknowledged his authority.

The military aristocracy went to war in chariots, supported by levies of foot soldiers. Their weapons were spears and powerful compound bows. Accounts tell of armies of three or four thousand troops, and of a battle involving thirteen thousand. The Shang fought against barbarian tribes and, occasionally, against other city-states in rebellion against their rule. Captured prisoners were enslaved.

One feature of Shang civilization was its system of writing. Scribes at the Shang court kept records on strips of bamboo, which have not survived. But there are inscriptions on bronzes as well as on the oracle bones. Some bones contain the question put to the oracle, the answer, and the outcome of the matter. Representative questions were: Which ancestor is causing the king's earache? If the king goes hunting at Ch'i, will there be a disaster? Will the king's child be a son? If the king sends his army to attack an enemy, will

MAP 1-4 BRONZE-AGE CHINA DURING THE SHANG DYNASTY, 1766–1050 B.C. *An Yang was a capital toward the end of the Shang dynasty. Loyang was the capital of the Eastern Chou.*

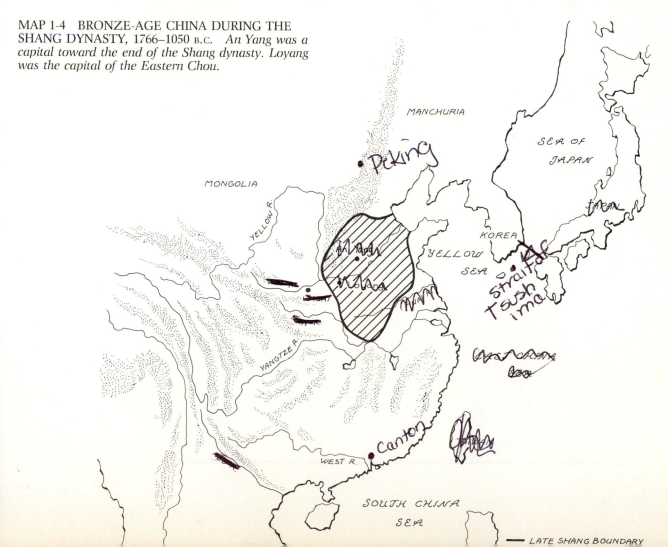

Chinese Writing

The Chinese system of writing dates back at least to the Shang dynasty (1766–1050 B.C.), when animal bones and tortoise shells (the so-called oracle bones) were incised for the purpose of divination. About half of the three thousand characters used in Shang times have been deciphered. These evolved over the centuries into the fifty thousand characters found in the largest dictionaries. But even today only about three thousand or four thousand are in common use. A scholar may know twice that number.

Characters developed from little pictures. Note the progressive stylization. By 200 B.C., the writing had become standardized and close to the modern form of the printed character.

	Shang (1400 B.C.)	Chou (600 B.C.)	Seal Script (200 B.C.)	Modern
Sun				
Moon				
Tree				
Bird				
Mouth				
Horse				

Other characters combined two pictures to express an idea. The following examples use modern characters:

Sun 日 + moon 月 = bright 明

Mouth 口 + bird 鳥 = to chirp 鳴

Woman 女 + child 子 = good 好

Tree 木 + sun 日 = east 東

It was a matter of convention that the sun behind a tree meant the rising sun in the east and not the setting sun in the west.

Characters were formed several other ways. In one, a sound element was combined with a meaning element. Chinese has many homonyms, words with the same sound. The character 台, for example, is read *tai* and means "elevation" or "to raise up." But in spoken Chinese, there are other words with the same sound that mean "moss," "trample," a "nag," and "idle." Thus

Tai 台 + grass 艹 = moss 苔

Tai 台 + foot 足 = trample 跆

Tai 台 + horse 馬 = a nag 駘

Tai 台 + heart 心 = idle 怠

In each case the sound comes from the 台, and the meaning from the other element. Note that the 台 may be at the bottom, the top, or the right. This positioning, too, is a matter of convention. ❑

Calligraphy by Teruko Craig. (Otherwise table composed by A. Craig.)

Inscribed oracle bone from the Shang Dynasty city of An Yang. [Columbia University.]

ated with cosmology. The Shang people observed the movements of the planets and stars and reported eclipses. Celestial happenings were seen as omens from the gods above. The chief cosmologists also recorded events at the court. The Shang calendar had a month of 30 days and a year of 360 days. Adjustments were made periodically by adding an extra month. The calendar was used by the king to tell his people when to sow and when to reap.

A second mark of Shang civilization was the mastery of bronze technology. Bronze appeared in China about 2000 B.C., a thousand years later than in Mesopotamia and five hundred years after India. Because Shang methods of casting were more advanced than those of Mesopotamia, and because the designs emerge directly from the preceding black-pottery culture, an independent origin is likely. Bronze was used for weapons, armor, and chariot fittings, and for a variety of ceremonial vessels of amazing fineness and beauty.

A third feature of Shang society, and indeed of all early river valley civilizations, was that as humans gained freedom from nature through agriculture and bronze technology, they abandoned the rough equality of primitive society and used their new powers to create a rigidly stratified society in which the many were compelled to serve the few. A monopoly of bronze weapons enabled aristocrats to exploit other groups. A hierarchy of class defined life in the Chinese city-state. The king and the officials of his court lived within the walled city. Their houses were spacious, built above the ground with roofs supported by rows of wooden pillars, resting on foundation stones. Their lifestyle was, for ancient times, opulent. They wore fine clothes, feasted at banquets, and drank wine from bronze vessels. In contrast, a far larger population of agricultural workers lived outside the city in cramped pit dwellings. Their life was meager and hard. Archaeological excavations of their underground hovels have uncovered only pottery pots.

Nowhere was the gulf between the royal lineage and the baseborn more apparent than in the Shang institution of human sacrifice. One Shang tomb 39 feet long, 26 feet wide, and 26 feet deep contained the de-

the deity help him? Was a sacrifice acceptable to ancestral deities? What we know of Shang religion is based on the bones.

The Shang Chinese believed in a supreme "Deity Above," who had authority over the human world. There were also lesser natural deities—the sun, moon, earth, rain, wind, and the six clouds—who served at the court of the Deity Above. Even the Shang king sacrificed not to the Deity Above, but to his ancestors, who interceded with the Deity Above on the king's behalf. Kings, while alive at least, were not divine but were the high priests of the state. In Shang times, as later, religion in China was closely associ-

The Languages of East Asia

The two main language families in East Asia today are the Sinitic and the Ural-Altaic. These are as different from each other as they are from European tongues. The Sinitic languages are Chinese, Vietnamese, Thai, Burmese, and Tibetan. Within Chinese are several mutually unintelligible dialects. Standard Chinese, based on the Peking dialect, is further from Cantonese than Spanish is from French. Ural-Altaic languages are spoken to the east, north, and west of China. They include Japanese, Korean, Manchurian, Mongolian, the Turkic languages, and, in Europe, Finnish and Hungarian.

Human Sacrifice During the Shang

By the seventh century B.C., human sacrifices were less frequent but still happened. A poem composed when Duke Mu of the state of Ch'in died in 631 casts doubt on whether religious belief or the honor of it all made the victims go gladly to the grave. Were human feelings different, Professor K. C. Chang has asked, a thousand years earlier during the Shang? Note the identification of Heaven with "that blue one," the sky.

"Kio" sings the oriole
As it lights on the thorn-bush.
Who went with Duke Mu to the grave?
Yen-hsi of the clan Tsu-chu.
Now this Yen-hsi
Was the pick of all our men;
But as he drew near the tomb-hole
His limbs shook with dread.
That blue one, Heaven,
Takes all our good men.
Could we but ransom him
There are a hundred would give their lives

"Kio" sings the oriole
As it lights on the mulberry-tree.
Who went with Duke Mu to the grave?
Chung-hang of the clan Tsu-chu.
Now this Chung-hang
Was the sturdiest of all our men;
But as he drew near the tomb-hole
His limbs shook with dread.
That blue one, Heaven,
Takes all our good men.
Could we but ransom him
There are a hundred would give their lives. ❑

The Book of Songs, trans. by Arthur Waley (New York: Grove Press, 1960).

capitated bodies of humans, horses, and dogs, as well as ornaments of bone, stone, and jade. When a king died, hundreds of slaves or prisoners of war, together, at times, with those who had served the king during his lifetime, might be buried with him. Sacrifices also were made when a palace or an altar was built.

The Later Bronze Age: The Western Chou

To the west of the area of Shang rule, in the Wei valley near the present-day city of Sian, lived the Chou people. The Wei River is a tributary of the Yellow River.

They were less civilized, closer to the Neolithic black-pottery culture, but more warlike than the Shang. According to the oracle bones, they had relations with the Shang, sometimes friendly, sometimes hostile. In 1050 B.C., the Shang were weakened by campaigns against nomads in the north and rebellious tribes in the east. According to the traditional historical record, the last Shang kings had become weak, cruel, and tyrannical. The Chou seized the opportunity, made alliances with disaffected city-states, and swept in, conquering the Shang.

In most respects, the Chou continued the Shang pattern of life and rule. The agrarian-based city-state continued to be the basic unit of society. It is estimated that there were about two hundred in the eighth century B.C. The hierarchy of classes was not unlike that of the Shang: kings and lords, officials and warriors, peasants, and slaves. Slaves were used primarily as domestic servants. Because the Chou were culturally backward, they assimilated the culture of the Shang. Ideographic writing developed without interruption. Bronze ceremonial vessels continued to be cast, though Chou vessels lack the fineness that set the Shang above the rest of the Bronze Age world.

The Chou kept their capital in the west but set up a secondary capital at Loyang, along the southern bend of the Yellow River. They appointed their kinsmen or other aristocratic allies to rule in other city-states. Blood or lineage ties were essential to the Chou pattern of rule. The Chou king was the head of the senior branch of the family. He performed the sacrifices to the Deity Above for the entire family. The rankings of the lords of other princely states—which, for want of better terms, are usually translated into the titles of English feudal nobility: duke, marquis, earl, viscount, and baron—reflected their degree of closeness to the senior line of Chou kings.

One difference between the Shang and the Chou was in the nature of political legitimacy. The Shang rulers, descended from shamanistic rulers, had an in-built religious authority and needed no theory to justify their rule. But the Chou, having conquered the Shang, needed a rationale for why they, and not the Shang, were the rightful rulers. Their argument was that Heaven (the name for the supreme being that gradually replaced the "Deity Above" during the early Chou), appalled by the wickedness of the last Shang king, had withdrawn its mandate to rule, awarding the mandate, instead, to the Chou. This concept of the mandate of Heaven was subsequently invoked by every dynasty in China down to the twentieth century.

A Chou Dynasty Bronze Bell. Hung from the ring at the top, the bell was rung with a wooden mallet. This bell has bosses, decorative panels, and is inscribed with a text. It rests on a brocade cushion. [National Palace Museum, Taiwan, R.O.C.]

In the beginning, Heaven was both cosmological and anthropomorphic. The ideograph for Heaven 天 is related to that for man 人. In the later Chou, although Heaven continued to have a moral will, it became less anthropomorphic and more a metaphysical force.

The Iron Age: The Eastern Chou

In 771 B.C., the Wei valley capital of the Western Chou was overrun by barbarians. In Chinese tradi-

tion, the event provided the equivalent of "crying wolf." The last Western Chou king was so infatuated with a favorite concubine that he repeatedly lit the bonfires that signaled a barbarian attack. His concubine would clap her hands in delight at the sight of the army assembled in martial splendor. But the army tired of the charade, and when invaders actually came, the king's beacons were ignored. The king was killed and the Chou capital sacked. The heir to the throne, with some members of the court, escaped to the secondary capital at Loyang, two hundred miles to the east and just south of the bend in the Yellow River.

The first phase of the Eastern Chou is sometimes called the Spring and Autumn period after the classic history by that name that treats the 722–481 year span. After their flight to Loyang, the Chou kings were never able to reestablish their old authority. Loyang remained a center of culture and ritual observances. But by the early seventh century B.C., its political power was nominal: Kinship and religious ties to the Chou house had worn thin, and it no longer had the military strength to reimpose its rule. During the seventh and sixth centuries in China, the political configuration was an equilibrium of many little principalities on the north-central plain surrounded by larger, wholly autonomous territorial states along the borders of northern China. The larger states consolidated the areas within their borders, absorbed tribal peoples, and expanded, conquering states on their periphery.

To defend themselves against the more aggressive territorial states, and in the absence of effective Chou authority, the smaller states entered into defensive alliances. The earliest alliance, of 681 B.C., was directed against the half-barbarian state of Ch'u (pronounced "chew"), which straddled the Yangtze in the south. Princes and lords of smaller states elected as their hegemon (or military overlord) the lord of a northern territorial state and pledged him their support. At the formal ceremony that established the alliance, a bull was sacrificed. The hegemon and then the other lords smeared its blood on their mouths and before the gods swore oaths to uphold the alliance. That the oaths were not always upheld can be surmised from the Chinese expression "to break an oath while the blood is still wet on one's lips."

During the next two centuries, alliances shifted and hegemons changed. At best, the alliances only slowed down the pace of military aggrandizement.

The second phase of the Eastern Chou is known as the Warring States period after a chronicle of the same name treating the years from 401 to 256 B.C. By the fifth century, all defensive alliances had broken down. Strong states swallowed their weaker neighbors. The border states grew in size and power. Interstate stability disappeared. By the fourth century, only eight or nine great territorial states remained as contenders.

MAP 1-5   EARLY IRON-AGE TERRITORIAL STATES
IN CHINA DURING THE SIXTH CENTURY B.C.
*After the fall of the Western Chou in 771 B.C., north
China divided into territorial states that became in-
creasingly independent of the later Chou kings.*

4000 B.C.	Neolithic agricultural villages
1766 B.C.	Bronze Age city-states, aristo-cratic charioteers, pictographic writing
771 B.C.	Iron Age territorial states
500 B.C.	Age of philosophers
221 B.C.	China is unified

of silk and precious metals as media of exchange. Rich merchants rivaled in lifestyle the landowning lower nobility. New outer walls were added to cities to provide for expanded quarters for merchants. The bronze bells and mirrors, clay figurines, lacquer boxes, and musical instruments found in late Chou tombs give ample evidence that the material and artistic culture of China leaped ahead during this period despite its endemic wars.

A third change that doomed the city-state was the rise of a new kind of army. The war chariots of the old aristocracy, practical only on level terrain, gave way to cavalry armed with crossbows. Most of the fighting was done by conscript foot soldiers. The armies of the territorial states numbered in the hundreds of thousands. The old nobility gave way to professional commanders. The old aristocratic etiquette, which governed behavior even in battle, gave way to military tactics that were bloody and ruthless. Prisoners were often massacred.

Change also affected government. The lords of the new territorial states began to style themselves as kings, taking the title that previously only the Chou royalty had enjoyed. At some courts, the hereditary nobility began to decline, supplanted by ministers appointed for their knowledge of statecraft. To survive, the new states had to transform their agricultural and commercial wealth into military strength. To collect taxes, conscript soldiers, and administer the affairs of state required records and literate officials. Academies were established to fill the need. Beneath the ministers, a literate bureaucracy developed. Its members were referred to as *shih*, a term that had once meant "warrior" but gradually came to mean "scholar-bureaucrat." The *shih* were of mixed social origins, including the petty nobility, literate members of the old warrior class, landlords, merchants, and rising commoners. From this class came the philosophers who created the "one hundred schools" and transformed the culture of China.

Suggested Readings

GENERAL PREHISTORY
V. GORDON CHILDE, *What Happened in History* (1946).
   A pioneering study of human prehistory and history

The only question was which one would defeat the others and go on to unify China.

Three basic changes in Chinese society contributed to the rise of large territorial states. One was the expansion of population and agricultural lands. The walled cities of the Shang and Western Chou had been like oases in the wilds, bounded by plains, marshes, and forests. Game was plentiful; thus, hunting, along with sheep and cattle breeding, supplemented agriculture. But in the Eastern Chou as the population grew, the wilds began to disappear, the economy became almost entirely agricultural, and hunting became an aristocratic pastime. Friction arose over boundaries as states began to abut. These changes accelerated in the late sixth century B.C. after the start of the Iron Age. Iron tools cleared new lands and plowed deeper, raising yields and increasing agricultural surpluses. Irrigation and drainage canals became important for the first time. Serfs gave way to farmers who bought and sold land. By the third century B.C., China had about twenty million people, making it the most populous country in the world, a distinction that it has never lost.

A second development was the rise of commerce. The roads built for war were used by merchants. Goods were transported by horses, oxcarts, river-boats, and by the camel, which entered China in the third century B.C. The products of one region were traded for those of another. Copper coins joined bolts before the Greeks from an anthropological point of view.

D. C. Johnson and M. R. Edey, *Lucy: The Beginning of Mankind* (New York, 1981). An account of man's African origins.

Charles L. Redman, *The Rise of Civilization* (San Francisco, 1978). An attempt to use the evidence provided by anthropology, archaeology, and the physical sciences to illuminate the development of early urban society.

NEAR EAST

Cyril Aldred, *Akhenaten, Pharaoh of Egypt: A New Study* (London, 1968). A judicious and critical biography of the enigmatic pharaoh.

Henri Frankfort, *Ancient Egyptian Religion: An Interpretation* (New York, 1948). A brief but masterful attempt to explore the religious conceptual world of ancient Egyptians in intelligible and interesting terms.

Henri Frankfort et al., *Before Philosophy* (1949). A brilliant examination of the mind of the ancients from the Stone Age to the Greeks.

Alan Gardiner, *Egypt of the Pharaohs* (Oxford, 1961). A sound narrative history.

O. R. Gurney, *The Hittites* (Harmondsworth, 1954). A good general survey.

W. W. Hallo and W. K. Simpson, *The Ancient Near East: A History* (New York, 1971). A fine survey of Egyptian and Mesopotamian history.

Thorkild Jacobsen, *The Treasures of Darkness: A History of Mesopotamia Religion* (New Haven, 1976). A superb and sensitive re-creation of the spiritual life of Mesopotamian peoples from the fourth to the first millennium B.C.

Samuel N. Kramer, *The Sumerians: Their History, Culture and Character* (Chicago, 1963). A readable general account of Sumerian history.

A. T. Olmstead, *History of Assyria* (New York, 1923). A good narrative account.

James B. Pritchard (ed.), *Ancient Near Eastern Texts Relating to the Old Testament* (Princeton, 1969). A good collection of documents in translation with useful introductory material.

G. Roux, *Ancient Iraq* (New York, 1964). A good recent account of ancient Mesopotamia.

W. F. Saggs, *The Greatness That Was Babylon* (New York, 1962). An excellent narrative account of Mesopotamian history.

W. F. Saggs, *Everyday Life in Babylonia and Assyria* (London, 1965).

K. C. Seele, *When Egypt Ruled the East* (Chicago, 1965). A study of Egypt in its imperial period.

B. G. Trigger et al., *Ancient Egypt: A Social History* (Cambridge, 1982).

John A. Wilson, *Culture of Ancient Egypt* (Chicago, 1956). A fascinating interpretation of the civilization of ancient Egypt.

INDIA

D. P. Agrawal, *The Archaeology of India* (London, 1982). A fine survey of the problems and data. Detailed, but with excellent summaries and brief general discussions of major issues.

B. and R. Allchin, *The Birth of Indian Civilization: India and Pakistan before 500 B.C.* (Harmondsworth, 1968). A one-volume summary of prehistoric India from an archaeological perspective.

W. T. de Bary et al., comp., *Sources of Indian Tradition* (1958. 2nd rev. ed. 2 vols. New York, 1988). A fine anthology of original texts in translation from all periods of Indian civilization.

A. L. Basham, *The Wonder That Was India*, 2nd rev. ed. (New York, 1963). Chapters 1 and 2 provide a readable and carefully done introduction to ancient India through the Aryan culture. Still the classic general work.

E. C. L. During Caspers, "Summer, Coastal Arabia and The Indus Valley in Protoliterate and Early Dynastic Eras," *JESHO* 22, 2 (1979): 121–35.

C. Chakraborty, *Common Life in the Rigveda and Atharvaveda–an Account of the Folklore in the Vedic Period* (Calcutta, 1977). An interesting attempt to reconstruct everyday life in the Vedic period from the principal Vedic texts.

G. L. Possehl, ed. *Harappan Civilization: A Contemporary Perspective* (New Delhi, 1982). Many helpful articles on recent developments in Indus research, including urbanization, the Indus script, trade relations, decline and demise of this culture.

D. D. Kosambi, *Ancient India: A History of its Culture and Civilization* (New York, Toronto, and London, 1965). The most readable survey history of India to the fourth century A.D. See chapters 2–4 on prehistoric, Indus, and Aryan culture.

W. D. O'Flaherty, *The Rig Veda: An Anthology* (Harmondsworth, England, 1981). An excellent selection of vedic texts of different kinds in prosaic but very careful translation with helpful notes on the texts.

J. E. Schwartzberg, ed. *A Historical Atlas of South Asia* (Chicago, 1978). The definitive reference work for matters of historical geography. Includes chronological tables and substantive essays.

R. L. Singh, ed. *India: A Regional Geography* (Banaras, 1971). An excellent reference source for each of the major regions of the subcontinent.

CHINA

K. C. Chang, *Shang Civilization* (1980).

K. C. Chang, *Art, Myth, and Ritual, The Path to Political Authority in Ancient China* (1984). A study of the relation between shamans, gods, agricultural production, and political authority during the Shang and Chou dynasties.

K. C. Chang, *The Archeology of Ancient China*, 4th ed. (1986). The standard work on the subject.

D. Hawkes, *Ch'u Tz'u, The Songs of the South* (1985). Chou poems from the southern state of Ch'u, superbly translated.

C. Y. Hsu, *Ancient China in Transition: An Analysis of Social Mobility 722–222 B.C.* (1965).

X. Q. Li, *Eastern Zhou and Qin Civilizations* (1986). This work includes fresh interpretations based on new archaeological finds.

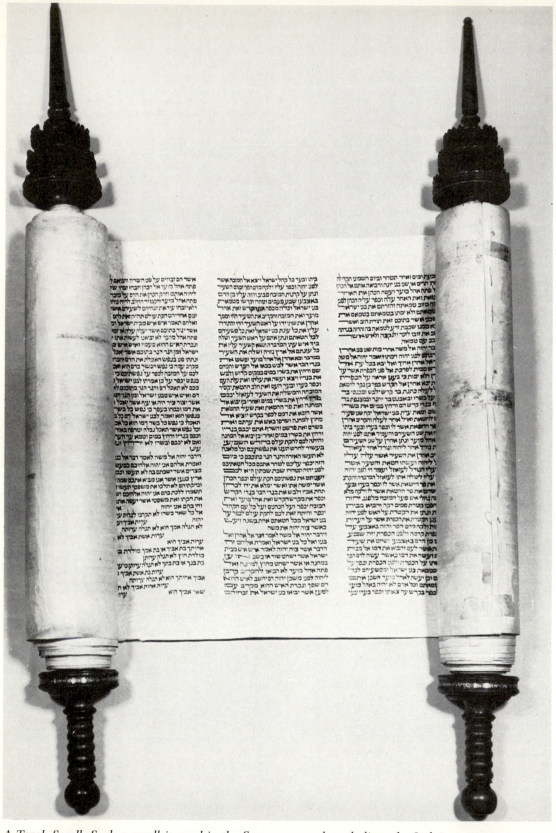

A Torah Scroll. Such a scroll is used in the Synagogue and symbolizes the Judaic commitment to the life of the Law. [Jewish Museum/Frank J. Darmstaedter.]

2 The Four Great Revolutions in Thought and Religion

Between 800 B.C. and 300 B.C., four philosophical or religious revolutions occurred that shaped the subsequent history of the world. The names of many of those involved in these revolutions are world-famous; for example, Socrates, Plato, Aristotle, the Buddha, Isaiah, and Confucius. All occurred in or near the four heartland areas in which the river valley civilizations (described in Chapter 1) had appeared one-and-a-half or more millennia earlier. The transition from the early river-valley civilizations to the intellectual and spiritual breakthroughs of the middle of the first millennium B.C. are schematized, oversimply, in the chart below.

The most straightforward case is that of China. Both geographically and culturally, its philosophical breakthrough grew directly out of the earlier river-valley civilization. There was no such continuity anywhere else in the world. The natural barrier of the central Asian steppes, mountain ranges, and deserts allowed China to develop its own unique culture relatively undisturbed and uninfluenced by outside forces.

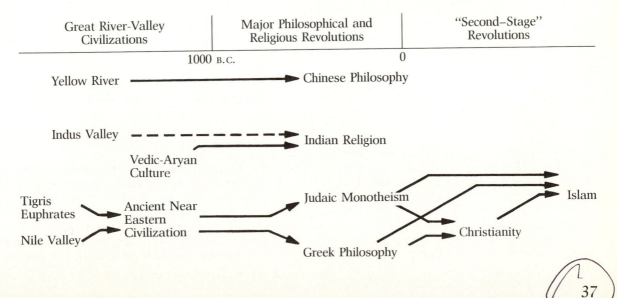

Great River-Valley Civilizations	Major Philosophical and Religious Revolutions	"Second–Stage" Revolutions

1000 B.C.　　　　　　　　0

Yellow River ⟶ Chinese Philosophy

Indus Valley ⟶ Indian Religion

Vedic-Aryan Culture

Tigris Euphrates ⟶ Ancient Near Eastern Civilization

Nile Valley

Judaic Monotheism　　　　Islam

Greek Philosophy　　Christianity

The sharpest contrast with China is the Indian sub-continent, where there was neither geographical nor cultural continuity. By the middle of the second millennium B.C., the Indus civilization had collapsed. It was replaced by the culture of the Indo-Aryan warriors who swept in from the northwest. Absorbing many particulars from the earlier tradition, they built a new civilization on the plains further east along the mighty Ganges. The great tradition of Indian thought and religion emerged after 600 B.C. from this Ganges civilization.

In southwest Asia and along the shores of the Mediterranean, the transition was more complex than in either the Chinese or the Indian case. No direct line of development can be traced from the Nile civilization of ancient Egypt or the civilization of the Tigris-Euphrates river valley to Greek philosophy or Judaic monotheism. Rather, the ancient river-valley civilizations evolved into a complex amalgam that we call ancient Near Eastern civilization. This cosmopolitan culture included diverse older religious, mythical, and cosmological traditions, as well as newer mystery cults. The Greeks and the ancient Hebrews were two among many outside peoples who invaded this region, settled down, and both absorbed and contributed to the composite civilization.

Judaic monotheism and Greek philosophy—representing very different outgrowths of this amalgam—were important in their own right. They have continued as vital elements in Western and Near Eastern civilizations. But their greatest influence occurred some centuries later when they joined to help shape, first, Christianity and then, Islam. When we talk of the major cultural zones in world history since the mid-first millennium A.D., they are the Chinese, the Indian, the Western-Christian, and the Islamic. But the latter two were formed much later than the Chinese and the Indian. They represent a second-stage formation of which the first stage was the Judaic and the Greek.

Before turning to a brief consideration of each of the original breakthroughs that occurred between 800 and 300 B.C., we might ask whether they have anything in common.

1. It is not accidental that all of the philosophical or religious revolutions occurred in the areas of the original river-valley civilizations. These contained the most advanced cultures of the ancient world. They had more sophisticated agriculture, cities, literacy, and specialized classes. In these, the material preconditions for breakthroughs in religion and thought were present.

2. Each of the revolutions in thought and ethos was born of a crisis in the ancient world. The appearance of iron meant better tools and weapons and, by extension, greater riches and more powerful armies. Old

societies began to change and then to disintegrate. Old aristocratic and priestly codes of behavior broke down, producing a demand for more universalized rules of behavior, that is to say, for ethics. The very relation of humans to nature or to the universe seemed to be changing. This predicament led to new visions of social and political order. There is more than an accidental similarity between the Jewish Messiah, the Chinese sage-king, and Plato's philosopher-king. Each was a response to a crisis in a society of the ancient world. Each would rejoin ethics to history and restore order to a troubled society.

3. It is notable how few philosophical and religious revolutions there have been. They can be counted on the fingers of one hand. The reason is not that humans' creativity dried up after 300 B.C., but that subsequent breakthroughs and advances tended to occur within the original traditions, which, absorbing new energies, continued to evolve.

4. After the first- and second-stage transformations, much of the cultural history of the world is of the spread of cultures derived from these original heartlands to ever wider spheres. Christianity spread to northern and eastern Europe, the Americas, and parts of Asia; Buddhism to central, southeastern, and eastern Asia; Confucianism to Korea, Vietnam, and Japan; and Islam to Africa, southeastern Europe, and southern, central, and southeastern Asia. Sometimes the spread occurred by movements of people; in other cases, some areas were like dry grasslands needing only the spark of the new ideas to ignite them.

5. Once a cultural pattern was set, it usually endured. Each major culture was resistant to the others and only rarely was one displaced. Even in modern times, although the culture of modern science and the learning associated with it has penetrated into every cultural zone, it has reshaped—and is reshaping, rather than displacing—the major cultures. Only Confucianism crumbled at the touch of science, and even its ethos is far from dead today. One reason for the endurance of these major cultures is that they were not only responses to particular crises, but also attempts to answer universal questions concerning the human condition: What are human beings? What is our relation to the universe? How should we relate to others?

Philosophy in China

The beauty of Shang bronzes is breathtaking, but they also have an archaic strangeness. Like Mayan stone sculpture, they are products of a culture so far removed from our own as to be almost incomprehensible. By contrast, in Confucian writings and poetry of the Eastern Chou (771–256 B.C.), we encounter a humanism that speaks to us directly. However much the philosophies of these centuries grew out of the earlier matrix of archaic culture, they mark a break with it and the beginning of what we think of today as the Chinese tradition.

The background of the philosophical revolution in China was the disintegration of the old Chou society (see Chapter 1 for details). New territorial states took the place of the many Chou city-states. Ruthless, up-start, peasant armies, augmented by an early Iron Age cavalry, began to replace the old nobles, who had gone to war in chariots. A rising merchant class disrupted the formerly stable agricultural economy. As the old etiquette crumbled, as the old rituals lost their force, a search began for new principles by which to re-create a peaceful society and new rules by which to live.

Of the four great revolutions in thought of the first millennium B.C., the Chinese was more akin, perhaps, to the Greek than to the religious transformations of India or to Judaic monotheism. Just as Greece had a gamut of philosophies, so in China there were the "one hundred schools." (When Mao Tse-tung said in 1956, "Let the one hundred flowers bloom"— encouraging a momentary easing of intellectual repression—he was referring to the creative era of Chou philosophy.) Whereas Greek thought was speculative and more concerned with the world of nature, Chinese thought was sociopolitical and more practical. Even the Taoist sages, who were inherently apolitical, found it necessary to offer a political philosophy. Chinese thought also had far greater staying power than Greek thought. Only a few centuries after the glory of Athens, Greek thought was submerged by Christianity. It became the handmaiden of theology and did not reemerge as an independent force until the Renaissance. In contrast, Chinese philosophy, though challenged for a time by Buddhism, remained dominant down to the early twentieth century. How were these early philosophies able to maintain such a grip on China when the cultures of every other part of the world fell under the sway of religions?

Part of the answer is that most Chinese philosophy was not without a religious dimension. But it was another kind of religion with assumptions quite different from those of the West. In the Christian or Islamic worldview, there is a God who, however concerned with humankind, is not of this world. This worldview leads to dualism, the distinction between an other-world, which is supernatural, and this world, which is natural.

In the Chinese worldview, the two spheres are not separate: The cosmos is seen as a single, continuous sphere, which includes heaven, earth, and man. Heaven is above. Earth is below. Man, represented by the emperor, stands in between and regulates or harmonizes the cosmological forces of heaven and earth

by the power of his virtue and by performing the sacrifices. The forms that this cosmology took under the last Manchu dynasty can be seen today in the city of Peking: The Temple of Heaven is in the south, the Temple of Earth is in the northeast, and the Imperial Palace is, symbolically at least, in between. To say that the emperor's sacrifices at the Temple of Heaven were secular (and, therefore, not religious) or religious

The Temple of Heaven. The three-storied "Temple of Prayer for a Good Harvest" is a part of the "Temple of Heaven" to the south of Peking. Once sacrosanct, it is now popular with tourists. On the second terrace, a banner proclaims that "Marxism and Leninism will endure for 10,000 years." [Magnum Photos, Inc., photograph by Rene Burri.]

(and not secular) misses the point. It projects our own dualistic assumptions onto China. Similarly, when we speak of the Taoist sage becoming one with nature, it is not the nature of a twentieth-century natural scientist; it is a nature that contains metaphysical and cosmological forces of a kind that our worldview might label as religious.

Most of the one hundred schools—if, in fact, there were that many—are unknown today. Many works disappeared in the book burning of the Ch'in dynasty (256–221 B.C.). But apart from the three major schools of Confucianism, Taoism, and Legalism, enough have survived to convey a sense of the vitality and creativity of Chou thought:

1. *Rhetoricians*. This school taught the arts of persuasion to be used in diplomatic negotiations. Its principal work instructed the rulers of territorial states by using historical anecdote. A practical work, it was popular for its humor and lively style.
2. *Logicians*. This school taught logic and relativity. For example, one proposition was "The south has no limit and has a limit." Another was "A white horse is not a horse": The concept of *horse* is not the same as the concept of *white horse*.
3. *Strategists*. *The Art of War* by Sun-tzu became the classic of military science in China and is studied today by guerrillas and in military academies around the world. It praises the general who wins victories without battles but also talks of organizing states for war, of supply, of spies, and of propaganda.
4. *Cosmologists*. This school described the functions of the cosmos in terms of *yin* and *yang*, the complementary negative and positive forces of nature, and in terms of the five elements (metal, wood, earth, fire, and water). Its ideas were later absorbed by other schools.
5. *Mohists*. Mo-tzu (470–391 B.C.) was an early critic of Confucius. His goals were peace, wealth, and the increase of population. He taught an ethic of universal love—to overcome a selfish human nature. He preached discipline and austerity and was critical of whatever lacked utility, including music, other arts, elaborate funerals, wasteful rites, and, above all, war. To achieve his goals, Mo-tzu argued for a strong state: Subjects must obey their rulers, who, in turn, must obey Heaven. Heaven would punish evil and reward good. To promote peace, Mo-tzu organized his followers into military units to aid states that were attacked.

Confucianism

Confucius was born in 551 B.C. in a minor state in northeastern China. As he received an education in

Confucius. Depicted wearing the robes of a scholar of a later age. [*National Palace Museum, Taiwan, Republic of China.*]

writing, music, and rituals, he probably belonged to the lower nobility, or the knightly class. His father died when Confucius was young, so he may have known privation. He made his living by teaching students. He traveled with his disciples from state to state, seeking a ruler who would put his ideas into practice. His ideas, however, were rejected as impractical—though he may once have held a minor position. He died in 479 B.C., honored as a teacher but a failure in his own eyes. The name Confucius is the Latinized form of K'ung Fu-tzu, or Master K'ung as he is known in China.

We know of Confucius only through the *Analects*, his sayings collected by his disciples, or perhaps by their disciples. They are mostly in the form of "The Master said," followed by his words. The picture that emerges is of a man of moderation, propriety, optimism, good sense, and wisdom. In an age of cruelty and superstition, he was humane and rational. He was upright. He demanded much of others and more of himself. Asked about death, he replied, "You do not understand even life. How can you understand

Confucius Defines the Gentleman

For over two thousand years in China, the cultural ideal was the gentleman, who combined knowledge of the ancient sages with an inner morality and outer propriety.

The Master said, "I never enlighten anyone who has not been driven to distraction by trying to understand a difficulty or who has not got into a frenzy trying to put his ideas into words.

"When I have pointed out one corner of a square to anyone and he does not come back with the other three, I will not point it out to him a second time."

The Master said, "Yu, shall I tell you what it is to know. To say you know when you know, and to say you do not when you do not, that is knowledge."

The Master said, "Is it not a pleasure, having learned something, to try it out at due intervals? Is it not a joy to have friends come from afar? Is it not gentlemanly not to take offence when others fail to appreciate your abilities?"

Someone said, "Repay an injury with a good turn. What do you think of this saying?" The Master said, "What, then, do you repay a good turn with? You repay an injury with straightness, but you repay a good turn with a good turn."

Lin Fang asked about the basis of the rites. The Master said, "A noble question indeed! With the rites, it is better to err on the side of frugality than on the side of extravagance; in mourning, it is better to err on the side of grief than on the side of formality."

The Master said, "I suppose I should give up hope. I have yet to meet the man who is as fond of virtue as he is of beauty in women."

The Master said, "The gentleman agrees with others without being an echo. The small man echoes without being in agreement."

The Master said, "The gentleman is at ease without being arrogant; the small man is arrogant without being at ease."

The Master said, "There is no point in seeking the views of a gentleman who, though he sets his heart on the Way, is ashamed of poor food and poor clothes." ❑

Confucius, *The Analects*, trans. by D. C. Lau (Penguin Books, 1979), 86, 65, 59, 129, 67, 134, 122, 123, 73.

---

death?"[1] Asked about how to serve the spirits and the gods—in which he did not disbelieve he answered, "You are not able even to serve man. How can you serve the spirits?"

Confucius described himself as a transmitter and a conservator of tradition, not an innovator. He idealized the early Shang and Chou kings as paragons of virtue. He particularly saw early Chou society as a golden age. He sought the secrets of this golden age in its writings. Some of these, along with later texts, became the Confucian classics, which through most of subsequent Chinese history had an authority not unlike Scripture in the West. Five of the thirteen classics were the following:

1. *The Book of Changes* (also known as the *Classic of Divination*). A handbook for diviners, this book was later seen as containing metaphysical truths about the universe.
2. *The Book of History*. This book contains documents and speeches from the early Chou, some au-

[1] This quotation and all quotations from Confucius in this passage are from Confucius, *The Analects*, trans. by D. C. Lau (Penguin Books, 1979).

thentic. Chinese tradition holds that it was edited by Confucius. It was interpreted as the record of sage-kings.

3. *The Book of Poetry*. This book contains some three hundred poems from the early Chou. Representing a sophisticated literary tradition, it includes love songs, as well as poems of friendship, ritual, and politics. All were given a political or moral reading in later times.
4. *The Book of Rites*. This book includes both rituals and rules of etiquette. Rites were important to Confucians, both as a support for proper behavior and because they were seen as corresponding to the forces of nature.
5. *The Spring and Autumn Annals*, a brief record of the major occurrences from 722 to 481 B.C. in the state where Confucius was born. Chinese tradition held that this book was edited by Confucius and reflected his moral judgments on past historical figures.

Basing his teachings on these writings, Confucius' solution to the turmoil of his own age was a return to the good old ways of the early Chou. When asked about government, he said, "Let the ruler be a ruler, the subject a subject, the father a father, the son a son." (The other three of the five Confucian relationships were husband–wife, older brother–younger brother, and friend–friend.) If everyone fulfilled the duties of his or her status, then harmony would prevail. Confucius understood the fundamental truth that the well-being of a society depends on the morality of its members. His vision was of an unbroken social harmony extending from the individual family member below to the monarch above.

But a return to the early Chou was impossible. China was undergoing a dynamic transition from hundreds of small city-states to a few large territorial states. New, specialized classes were appearing. Old rituals no longer worked. In this situation, it was not enough just to stress basic human relationships. The genius of Confucius was to transform the old aristocratic code into a new ethics that could be practiced by any educated Chinese. His reinterpretation of the early Chou tradition can be seen in the concept of the *chun-tzu*. This term literally meant the son of the ruler or the aristocrat. Confucius redefined it to mean a person of noble behavior, a person with the inner virtues of humanity, integrity, righteousness, altruism, and loyalty, and an outward demeanor and propriety to match.

This redefinition was not unlike the change in the meaning of *gentleman* in England from one who is gentle-born to one who is gentle-behaved. But whereas *gentleman* remained a fairly superficial category in the West, in China it went deeper. Confucius saw ethics as grounded in nature. The true gentleman was in touch with his own basic nature, which, in turn, was a part of the cosmic order. Confucius expressed this saying: "Heaven is the author of the virtue that is in me." Confucius' description of his own passage through life goes far beyond the question of good manners: "At fifteen I set my heart on learning; at thirty I took my stand; at forty I came to be free from doubts; at fifty I understood the Decree of Heaven; at sixty my ear was attuned; at seventy I followed my heart's desire without overstepping the line."

Confucius often contrasted the gentleman with the small or common person. The gentleman, educated in the classics and cultivating the Way, understands moral action. The common people, in contrast, "can be made to follow a path but not to understand it." Good government for Confucius depended on the appointment to office of good men, who would serve as examples for the multitude: "Just desire the good yourself and the common people will be good. The virtue of the gentleman is like wind; the virtue of the small man is like grass. Let the wind blow over the grass and it is sure to bend." Beyond the gentleman was the sage-king, who possessed an almost mystical virtue and

Mencius, who taught that human nature is good. [*Bettmann Archives.*]

power. For Confucius, the early Chou kings were clearly sages. But Confucius wrote, "I have no hopes of meeting a sage. I would be content if I met someone who is a gentleman."

Confucianism was not adopted as the official philosophy of China until the second century B.C., during the Han dynasty. But two other important Confucian philosophers had appeared in the meantime. Mencius (370–290 B.C.) represents the idealistic extension of Confucius' thought. His interpretation became orthodox for most of subsequent history. He is famous for his argument that humans tend toward the good just as water runs downward. All that education need do, therefore, is uncover and cultivate that innate goodness. And just as humans are good, so does Heaven possess a moral will. The will of Heaven is that a government should see to the education and the well-being of its people. The rebellion of a people against its government is the primary evidence that Heaven has withdrawn its mandate. At times in Chinese history, only lip service was paid to a concern for the people. In fact, rebellions occurred more often against weak governments than against harsh ones. But the idea that government ought to care for the people became a permanent part of the Confucian tradition.

The other influential Confucian philosopher was Hsun-tzu (300–237 B.C.), who represents a tough-minded extension of Confucius' thought. Hsun-tzu felt Heaven was amoral, indifferent to whether China was ruled by a tyrant or a sage. He felt human nature was

Taoism

bad, or, at least, that desires and emotions, if unchecked, led to social conflict. So he placed a great emphasis on etiquette and education as restraints on an unruly human nature. He emphasized good institutions, including punishments and rewards, as a means for shaping behavior. These ideas exerted a powerful influence on thinkers of the Legalist school.

Taoism

It is often said that the Chinese have been Confucian while in office and Taoist (pronounced "Dah-ohist") in their private lives. Taoism offered a refuge from the burden of social responsibilities. The classics of the school are the *Lao-tzu*, dating from the fourth century B.C., and the *Chuang-tzu*, dating from about a century later.

The central concept is the Tao, or Way. It is mysterious and cannot be named. It is the creator of the universe, the sustainer of the universe, and the process or flux of the universe. The Tao functions on a cosmic, not a human, scale. As the *Lao-tzu* put it, "Heaven and Earth are ruthless, and treat the myriad creatures as straw dogs; the sage [in accord with the Tao] is ruthless, and treats the people as straw dogs."[2]

What does it mean to be a sage? How does a human join in the rhythms of nature? The answer given by the *Lao-tzu* is by regaining or returning to an original simplicity. Various similes are used to describe this state: "to return to the infinite," "to return to being a babe," or "to return to being the uncarved block." To attain this state, one must "learn to be without learning." Knowledge is bad because it creates distinctions, because it leads to the succession of ideas and images

[2] All quotations from the *Lao-tzu* are from Lao Tzu, *Tao Te Ching*, trans. by D. C. Lau (Penguin Books, 1963).

Lao-Tzu, the founder of Taoism, as imagined by a later artist. [*Freer Gallery of Art, Washington, DC.*]

that interfere with participation in the Tao. One must also learn to be without desires beyond the immediate and simple needs of nature: "The nameless uncarved block is but freedom from desire."

If the sage treats the people as straw dogs, it would appear that he is beyond good and evil. But elsewhere in the *Lao-tzu*, the sage is described as one who "excels in saving people." If not a contradiction, this is at least a paradox. The resolution is that the sage is clearly beyond morality, but is not immoral or even amoral. Quite to the contrary, by being in harmony with the Tao the sage is impeccably moral—as one who clings to the forms of morality or makes morality a goal could never be. So in the *Lao-tzu*, it is written, "Exterminate benevolence, discard rectitude, and the people will again be filial; exterminate ingenuity, discard profit, and there will be no more thieves and bandits."

In this formulation, we also see the basis for the political philosophy of Taoism, which can be summed up as "not doing" *(wu wei).* What this means is something between "doing nothing" and "being, but not acting." In this concept, there is some overlap with Confucianism. The Confucian sage-king exerts a moral force by dint of his internal accord with nature. If a Confucian sage were perfect, he could rule without doing. Confucius said, "If there was a ruler who

achieved order without taking any action, it was, perhaps, [the sage emperor] Shun. There was nothing for him to do but to hold himself in a respectful posture and to face due south." In Taoism, all true sages had this Shun-like power to rule without action: "The way never acts yet nothing is left undone. Should lords and princes be able to hold fast to it, the myriad creatures will be transformed of their own accord." Or, says the *Lao-tzu*, "I am free from desire and the people of themselves become simple like the uncarved block." The sage acts without acting, and "when his task is accomplished and his work is done, the people will say, 'It happened to us naturally.'"

Along with the basic Taoist prescription of becoming one with the Tao are two other assumptions or principles. One is that any action pushed to an extreme will initiate a countervailing reaction in the direction of the opposite extreme. The other is that too much government, even good government, can become oppressive by its very weight. As the *Lao-tzu* put it, "The people are hungry; It is because those in authority eat up too much in taxes that the people are hungry. The people are difficult to govern; it is because those in authority are too fond of action that the people are difficult to govern." Elsewhere, the same idea was expressed in even homelier terms: "Govern a large state as you would cook small fish," that is, without too much stirring.

Legalism

The third great current in classical Chinese thought, and by far the most influential in its own age, was Legalism. Like the philosophers of other schools, the Legalists were anxious to end the wars that plagued China. True peace, they felt, required a united country, and to this end, they advocated a strong state. They favored conscription and looked on war as a means of extending state power.

The Legalists did not seek a model in the distant past. In ancient times, said one, there were fewer people and more food, so it was easier to rule; different conditions require new principles of government. Nor did the Legalists model their state on a heavenly order of values. Human nature is selfish, argued both of the leading Legalists, Han Fei-tzu (d. 233 B.C.) and Li Ssu (d. 208 B.C.). It is human to like rewards or pleasure and to dislike punishments or pain. If laws are severe and impartial, if what strengthens the state is rewarded and what weakens the state is punished, then a strong state and a good society will ensure.

Legalism

HAN FEI-TZU ARGUES FOR THE EFFICACY OF PUNISHMENTS

Now take a young fellow who is a bad character. His parents may get angry at him, but he never makes any change. The villagers may reprove him, but he is not moved. His teachers and elders may admonish him but he never reforms. The love of his parents, the efforts of the villagers, and the wisdom of his teachers and elders—all the three excellent disciplines are applied to him, and yet not even a hair on his shins is altered. It is only after the district magistrate sends out his soldiers and in the name of the law searches for wicked individuals that the young man becomes afraid and changes his ways and alters his deeds. So while the love of parents is not sufficient to discipline the children, the severe penalties of the district magistrate are. This is because men became naturally spoiled by love, but are submissive to authority. . . .

That being so, rewards should be rich and certain so that the people will be attracted by them; punishments should be severe and definite so that the people will fear them; and laws should be uniform and steadfast so that the people will be familiar with them. Consequently, the sovereign should show no wavering in bestowing rewards and grant no pardon in administering punishments, and he should add honor to rewards and disgrace to punishments—when this is done, then both the worthy and the unworthy will want to exert themselves. . . .

HAN FEI-TZU ATTACKS CONFUCIANISM

There was once a man of Sung who tilled his field. In the midst of his field stood the stump of a tree, and one day a hare, running at full speed, bumped into the stump, broke its neck, and died. Thereupon the man left his plow and kept watch at the stump, hoping that he would get another hare. But he never caught an-

other hare, and was only ridiculed by the people of Sung. Now those who try to rule the people of the present age with the conduct of government of the early kings are all doing exactly the same thing as that fellow who kept watch by the stump. . . .

Those who are ignorant about government insistently say: "Win the hearts of the people." If order could be procured by winning the hearts of the people, then even the wise ministers Yi Yin and Kuan Chung would be of no use. For all that the ruler would need to do would be just to listen to the people. Actually, the intelligence of the people is not to be relied upon any more than the mind of a baby. If the baby does not have his head shaved, his sores will recur; if he does not have his boil cut open, his illness will go from bad to worse. However, in order to shave his head or open the boil someone has to hold the baby while the affectionate mother is performing the work, and yet he keeps crying and yelling incessantly. The baby does not understand that suffering a small pain is the way to obtain a great benefit.

Now, the sovereign urges the tillage of land and the cultivation of pastures for the purpose of increasing production for the people, but they think the sovereign is cruel. The sovereign regulates penalties and increases punishments for the purpose of repressing the wicked, but the people think the sovereign is severe. Again, he levies taxes in cash and in grain to fill up the granaries and treasuries in order to relieve famine and provide for the army, but they think the sovereign is greedy. Finally, he insists upon universal military training without personal favoritism, and urges his forces to fight hard in order to take the enemy captive, but the people think the sovereign is violent. These four measures are methods for attaining order and maintaining peace, but the people are too ignorant to appreciate them. ❑

From W. T. de Bary et al., *Sources of Chinese Tradition* (New York: Columbia University Press, 1968), 146–147, 144, 142, 143.

Laws, therefore, should contain incentives for loyalty and bravery in battle, and for obedience, diligence, and frugality in everyday life. The Legalists despised merchants as parasites and approved of productive farmers. They particularly despised the purveyors of doctrines different from their own and were critical of rulers who honored the philosophers while ignoring their philosophies.

Legalism was the philosophy of the state of Ch'in, which destroyed the Chou in 256 B.C. and unified China in 221 B.C.. Because Ch'in laws were cruel and severe, and because Legalism put human laws above an ethics modeled on Heaven, later generations of Chinese have execrated its doctrines. They saw it, not without justification, as a philosophy that consumed its founders: Han Fei-tzu became an official of the Ch'in state but was eventually poisoned in a prison cell by Li Ssu, who was jealous of his growing influence. Li Ssu, too, though he became prime minister of Ch'in, was killed in 208 B.C. in a political struggle with a court eunuch. Yet, for all of the abuse heaped on the Legalist doctrines, their legacy of criminal laws became a vital part of subsequent dynastic China.

Religion in India

By the mid-first millennium B.C., new social and religious forms took shape in the Indian subcontinent. A tradition was created that drew on both the older traditions of the Aryan ruling and priestly elites, and non-Aryan ideas and practices. This tradition took its "classical" shape only much later, sometime in the early Christian era. We can call it *Indian*, as distinct from the earlier Rigvedic-Brahmanic culture (described in Chapter 1), in that its fundamental institutions and ideas came to prevail at all levels of society in virtually every part of the subcontinent.

Despite staggering internal diversity and divisions, and long periods of foreign rule, this Indian culture has survived for at least two thousand years as a coherent tradition of historical heritage, social organization, and religious worldview.

"Indian" and "Hindu"

Indian culture and tradition include more than is commonly implied by the word *Hindu* today. Earlier, *Hindu* was simply a word for *Indian*. It came from the Indo-Iranian name for the Indus and was originally the term used by outsiders, like the ancient Persians and the Greeks, to refer to the people or the land of the subcontinent. Even invading Muslims, and then invading Western Christians, used *Hindu* to characterize the most prominent religious and social institutions of India as a whole. The concept of *transmigration*, the sacredness of the Vedas and of the cow, the worship of Shiva or Vishnu, and the caste system head the list of

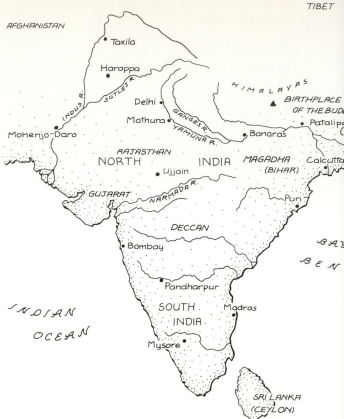

MAP 2-1 HEARTLANDS OF INDIAN CULTURE
Major ancient and modern cities of the subcontinent and their locations relative to major rivers are shown. Note that while north India is thought of as the cradle of Vedic and classical Indian religion and culture, the south was the locus, especially in the post Gupta period but also earlier, of important, long-lived regional dynasties, major religious movements, and brilliant artistic traditions.

such "Hindu" institutions. Yet not all Indians in the past twenty-five hundred years have accepted all of these and other related institutions. Most obviously, Indian Buddhists, Jains, Muslims, Sikhs, and Christians have rejected at least some of them.

We cannot say exactly when the typical aspects of Hindu society and religious life as we know it today were "in place." Some argue that it was only after A.D. 200 (or even 400), rather than sometime in the latter half of the first millennium B.C. However we date the beginning of "Hindu" religion and culture, we must remember that such usage lumps together an immense diversity of social, racial, linguistic, and religious groups. It is totally inaccurate to think of *Hindu* as a term for any single or uniform religious community.

Indian, on the other hand, commonly refers today to all the native inhabitants of the subcontinent, including Muslims, Sikhs, and Christians (who belong to traditions considerably younger than the Buddhist, Jain, or Hindu). In this book, we shall on occasion use the term *Indian* in this inclusive sense when referring to the subcontinent as a geographic or political whole, or to its peoples. However, for the period before the arrival of Muslim culture (CA. A.D. 1000), *Indian* will be used here to refer to the distinctively Indian tradition of thought and culture that began with the flowering of Upanishadic speculation and Buddhist and Jain thought around the middle of the first millennium B.C. This "Indian" tradition achieved its classical formulation in the Hindu society and religion of the first millennium A.D. However, the Jains of India and the Buddhists of wider Asia were also its legitimate heirs.

The Historical Background

We saw in Chapter 1 how, in the later Vedic or Brahmanic period, a priest-centered cult dominated among the upper classes of Aryanized northern Indian society. Apparently, by the sixth century B.C., this ritualistic cult had grown so extreme in its basically magical approach to ritual and piety that it had become an elite, esoteric cult to which most people had little or no access. The elaborate animal sacrifices on behalf of Aryan rulers were an economic burden upon the peasants of the countryside, whose livestock provided the victims. Such sacrifices were also largely irrelevant to the religious concerns of peasant and town-dweller alike. New, ascetic tendencies placed in question the basic values and practices of the older Aryan religion. Skepticism in religious matters accompanied social and political upheavals during the seventh and sixth centuries B.C.

The latest Vedic texts themselves reflect a reaction against excessive emphasis on the power of sacrifice and ritual formulas, accumulation of worldly wealth and power, and hope for an afterlife in some kind of paradise. The treatises of the Brahmanas (CA. 1000–800 B.C.) deal with the ritual application of the old Vedic texts, the explanation of Vedic rites and mythology, and the theory of the sacrifice. They had focused early on control of the sacred power *(Brahman)* present in sacrificial ritual, but now they gave ever greater attention to acquiring this power through knowledge instead of ritual acts.

This tendency became central in the Upanishads (CA. 800–500 B.C.) treatises, which proposed meditations on the meaning of ritual and the nature of Brahman. These texts carried to new levels of subtlety previous Vedic theorizing about the origin and nature of reality and the relation of thought and action to ultimate truth. The principal ideas that would guide all later Indian tradition are first clearly visible in the Upanishads, and in the thought and institutions of the

The major Hindu Gods of the cardinal directions. Hinduism has traditionally seen the absolute (Brahman) as manifest in a vast array of gods and goddesses as well as in nature. [Diana L. Eck.]

early Jain and Buddhist movements (fifth century B.C.). The Upanishadic thinkers represent the culmination of the Vedic-Brahmanic tradition in many ways. The Jain and Buddhist traditions, on the other hand, were but the most enduring of a series of sixth- and fifth-century B.C. religious movements that explicitly rejected much of the Vedic-Brahmanic tradition of sacrificial ritualism and class distinction.

Both the Upanishadic sages and the early Jains and Buddhists shared a number of ideas and concerns that signaled the "coming of age" of Indian thought. Their thinking and piety influenced not only all later Indian intellectual thought, but, through the spread of the Buddhist tradition, much of the intellectual and religious life of East and Southeast Asia as well. Thus, the middle centuries of the first millennium B.C. in India began a religious and philosophical revolution that ranks alongside those of Chinese philosophy and reli-

These sunnyasis, *or "renouncers," in the city of Benares have given up homes and families for a life of poverty, discipline, and meditation.* [Diana L. Eck.]

gion, Judaic monotheism, and Greek philosophy as a turning point in the history of civilization.

The Upanishadic Worldview

In the Upanishads, we see two new emphases. These are already evident in two sentences from the prayer of one of the earliest Upanishadic thinkers, who said, "From the unreal lead me to the Real. . . . From death lead me to immortality." The first request points to the Upanishadic focus on speculation about the nature of things, the quest for ultimate truth. Here ritual takes a back seat to meditation; knowledge, not the sacred word or act, has become the ultimate source of power.

The second new emphasis reflects a new concern with life after death. The old Vedic ideal of living a full and upright life so as to attain an afterlife in some kind of heaven of the fathers, among the gods, is no longer seen as an adequate ideal or goal. Immortality is now interpreted in terms not of afterlife but of escape from all existence—earthly, heavenly, or any other. These two Upanishadic emphases gave birth to a series of ideas that were to change the shape of Indian thought forever. Together they provide the key to its basic worldview.

THE NATURE OF REALITY. The quest for knowledge by the sages of the Upanishads concentrated on the nature of the individual self (*Atman*) and its rela-

tion to ultimate reality, or *Brahman*. The gods now take a lesser place as only one part of the total scheme of things. They are themselves subject to the laws of existence and not to be put on the same plane with the transcendent Absolute. Prayer and sacrifice to particular gods for their help is one thing; realization of Brahman is something altogether different. The latter is possible only through the action of the mind, not the bodily acts of ritual.

The culmination of the Upanishadic speculation is the recognition that the way to the Absolute is through the Self. Through contemplation, Atman-Brahman is recognized not as some divine being that can be addressed as a deity, but as the very principle of Reality itself: the unborn, unmade, unchanging Infinite. Of this Reality, all that can be said is that it is "neither this nor that," because the Ultimate cannot be conceived of nor described in finite terms. Beneath or behind the impermanence of ordinary reality is the changeless Brahman, to which the immortal self of every being belongs. The difficulty is recognizing this Self, and with it the Absolute, while one is caught in the realm of normal existence.

A second, related focus of Upanishadic inquiry was into the nature of "normal" existence. The realm of life is seen to be ultimately impermanent, ever in change. What seems such "solid" things—the physical world, our bodies and personalities, worldly success—are revealed in the Upanishads to be finally insubstantial,

Discussions of Brahman and Atman from the Upanishads

A REPORT OF THE SAGE SANDILYA'S STATEMENT ABOUT THE IDENTITY OF ATMAN AND BRAHMAN

"Verily, this whole world is Brahman. Tranquil, let one worship it as that from which he came forth, as that into which he will be dissolved, as that in which he breathes. Now, verily, a person consists of purpose. According to the purpose which a person has in this world, thus does he become on departing hence. So let him form for himself a purpose. He who consists of mind, whose body is life, whose form is light, whose conception is truth, whose soul [*atman*] is space, containing all odors, containing all tastes, encompassing this whole world, the unspeaking, the unconcerned—this Soul of mine within the heart is smaller than a grain of rice, or a barley-corn, or a mustard-seed, or a grain of millet; or the kernel of a grain of millet; this Soul of mine within the heart is greater than the earth, greater than the atmosphere, greater than the sky, greater than these worlds. Containing all works, containing all desires, containing all odors, containing all tastes, encompassing this whole world, the unspeaking, the unconcerned—this Soul of mine within the heart, this is Brahman. Into him I shall enter on departing hence. If one would believe this, he would have no more doubt."—Thus used Sandilya to say. . . .

Chandogya Upanishad 3.14

THE YOUNG BRAHMAN, SHEVETAKETU, IS INSTRUCTED IN THE IDENTITY OF ATMAN AND BRAHMAN BY HIS FATHER:

"These rivers, my dear, flow, the eastern toward the east, the western toward the west. They go just from the ocean to the ocean. They become the ocean itself. As there they know not 'I am this one,' 'I am that one'—even so, indeed, my dear, all creatures here, though they have come forth from Being, know not 'We have come forth from Being.' Whatever they are in this world, whether tiger, or lion, or wolf, or boar, or worm, or fly, or gnat, or mosquito, that they become. That which is the finest essence—this whole world has that as its soul. That is Reality. That is Atman. That art thou, Shevetaketu." ❑

Chandogya Upanishad 6.10

Selections taken with minor changes from Robert Ernest Hume (trans.), *The Thirteen Principal Upanishads*, 2nd ed. rev. (London: Oxford University Press, 1931), pp. 209–210, 246–247.

impermanent, and ephemeral. Even happiness is passing. Existence is neither satisfying nor lasting in any fundamental sense. Only Brahman is enduring, eternal, unchanging—the unmoved ground of existence. In this, there is already a marked tendency toward the eventual emphasis of the Buddhists on impermanence and suffering as the fundamental facts of existence as we know it.

LIFE AFTER DEATH. The new understanding of immortality that emerges in the Upanishads is related to these basic perceptions about the Self, the Absolute, and the world of existence. It runs, as we noted, counter to the older Vedic Aryan concept of an immortal existence either in heaven or in hell after this life is done. The Upanishadic sages developed the concept of existence as a ceaseless cycle of existence, a never-ending alternation between life and death. This idea was not only to have major implications for Indian speculative thought; it was also to become the basic assumption of all Indian thought and religious life.

The idea of the endless cycle of renewed existence, which Indians refer to as *samsara*, is only superficially to be compared to or translated as our idea of "transmigration" of souls. For Indians, it is the key to the nature of reality as we can know it. Furthermore, it is a fact that is not promising or liberating, but suffocating or burdensome. In the Indian context, *samsara* refers to the terrifying prospect of endless "redeath" as the normal lot of all beings in this world, whether animals, plants, humans, or gods. This is the fundamental problem posed for all later Indian thought. It is the problem to which the great Indian thinkers of the mid-first millennium B.C., from the sages of the Upanishads to the Buddha, addressed themselves most centrally.

KARMA. The key to the solution of the dilemma of *samsara* lies in the concept of *karma*, which in Sanskrit literally means "work" or "action." At base, it is the concept that every action has its inevitable effects, soon or later, and that as long as there is action of mind or body, there is continued effect, and hence continued existence. Good deeds bring good results, perhaps even rebirth in a heaven or as a god, and evil ones bring evil consequences, whether in this life or in rebirth in the next, whether in the everyday world or in the lower worlds of hell. Because of the fundamental impermanence of everything in existence (heavens and hells included), the good as well as the evil is temporary. The flux of existence knows only movement, change, endless cause and effect far transcending a mere human life span, or even a mere world eon.

THE SOLUTIONS. Working from the ruthless analysis of existence posed in the Upanishads and taken as the starting point of all later Indian thought, the solution to the problem of *samsara* that was worked out in the Indian tradition is of two kinds. The first alternative or strategy involves maximizing good actions and minimizing bad actions, in order to achieve the best possible rebirth in one's next round of existence. The second is different; it involves "release" (*moksha*) from existence: escaping all karmic effects by escaping action itself.

The first strategy has been followed by the great masses of Hindus, Buddhists, and Jains over the centuries. It has been characterized by Franklin Edgerton as the "ordinary norm," as opposed to the "extraordinary norm," which has been the path of only the select elite, the greatest seekers of Upanishadic truth, Jain asceticism, or the Buddhist "middle path." Essentially, the ordinary norm involves a life lived according to some code of social responsibility. The most significant codes for Indian history are those recognized by most Hindus, Buddhists, and Jains over the centuries. On the other hand, the seekers of the "extraordinary norm" are usually involved in some kind of ascetic discipline aimed at withdrawal from the karmic cycle al-

Thai monks receiving food from a Buddhist lay couple. Feeding the monks is a meritorious act. [*Magnum/ Hiraji Kubota.*]

together—and the consequent release (*moksha*) from cause and effect, good and evil, birth and rebirth. These two characteristic Indian responses to the problem posed by *samsara* show how the fundamental forms of Indian thought and piety took shape in the middle and later first millennium B.C.

SOCIAL RESPONSIBILITY: *DHARMA* AS IDEAL. The "ordinary norm" or ideal of life in the various traditions of Indian religiousness can be summarized as life lived according to *dharma*. Although *dharma* has many meanings in Indian usage, its most common is similar to that of the Vedic Aryan concept of *Rta* (see Chapter 1). In this sense, *dharma* means "the right (order of things)," "moral law," "right conduct," or even "duty." It includes the cosmic order (compare the Chinese *Tao*) as well as the right conduct of political, commercial, social, and religious affairs and individual moral responsibility. For most people—those we might call the laity, as distinguished from monks and ascetics—life according to *dharma* is the life of moral action that will lead to a better birth in the next round of existence.

Life according to *dharma* has several implications. First, it accepts action in the world of *samsara* as necessary and legitimate. Second, it demands acceptance of the responsibilities appropriate to one's sex, one's class and caste group, one's stage in life, and one's other particular circumstances. Third, it allows for legitimate self-interest: One's duty is to do those things that acquire merit for one's eternal *atman* and to avoid those that involve demerit, or evil consequences. Fourth, rebirth in heaven, in paradise, is the highest goal attainable through the life of *dharma*. However (fifth), all achievement in the world of *dharma* (which is also the world of *samsara*), even the attainment of heaven, is ultimately impermanent and is subject to change.

ASCETIC DISCIPLINE: *MOKSHA* AS IDEAL. For those who have the mental and physical capacity to abandon the world of ordinary life and to find freedom from *samsara*, the implications for living are in direct contrast to those of the "ordinary norm." First, action is viewed as negative, whether it is good or bad, for action only produces more action, more *karma*, more rebirth. Second, nonaction is achieved only by withdrawal from "normal" existence. The person seeking release (*moksha*) from *samsara* has to move beyond the usual responsibilities of family and society. Most often, this removal involves becoming some kind of "renouncer"—whether a homeless Hindu hermit, yogi, or wanderer, or a Jain or Buddhist monk. Third, this renunciation of the world and its goals demands selflessness, or absence of ego. One must give up the desires and attachments that the self normally needs to function in the world. Fourth, the highest goal is not rebirth in heaven at all, but *moksha,* "release" from all rebirth and redeath. Finally, *moksha* is lasting, permanent. Its realization means no more becoming, no more existence, no more suffering in the realm of *samsara.* Permanence, eternity, transcendence, and freedom from suffering are its attributes.

SEEKERS OF THE "EXTRAORDINARY NORM." The ideas that led persons to seek the "extraordinary norm" appeared in fullest form first in the Upanishads. These ideas were particularly congenial to an increasing number of persons who abandoned both the ritualistic religious practices and the society of class distinctions and material concerns around them. It is noteworthy that many of these seekers were of warrior-noble (*Kshatriya*), not Brahman, birth. They took up the wandering or hermit existence of the ascetic, seeking in yogic meditation and self-denial or even self-torture to gain spiritual powers. The higher seekers tried to transcend the body and bodily existence in order to realize the Absolute.

In the sixth century B.C., a number of teachers of new ideas appeared, especially in the lower Ganges basin, in the area of Magadha (modern Bihar). Most of them rejected traditional forms of religiousness as well as the authority of the Vedas in favor of one or another kind of ascetic discipline as the true spiritual path. Two of these teachers acquired sufficient followings so that their ideas and practice became the foundations of new and lasting traditions of piety and faith, those of the Jains and the Buddhists.

Mahavira and the Jain Tradition

The Jains trace their tradition to one Vardhamana, known as Mahavira ("the great hero"), who lived about 540–468 B.C. Mahavira is held by his followers to have been the final *Jina* ("victor" over *samsara*) or *Tirthankara* ("ford maker," one who finds the way across the waters of existence), in a line of twenty-four great teachers who have appeared in the latter, degenerative half of the present-world time cycle. The Jains (or *Jainas,* "adherents of the *Jina*") see in Mahavira a human teacher, not a god. He found and taught the

Jain Comments on Samsara and the Monastic Virtues

The following two selections from a later Jain writing give some idea of how vividly the suffering of the self in the many forms of existence it undergoes is conceived of (Selection 1) and how totally Jain ascetics should fight all selfishness and self-pity as they undertake the stern discipline that will rid them of karmic accretions (Selection 2).

From clubs and knives, stakes and maces, breaking my limbs,
An infinite number of times I have suffered without hope.
By keen-edged razors, by knives and shears,
Many times I have been drawn and quartered, torn apart and skinned.
Helpless in snares and traps, a deer,
I have been caught and bound and fastened, and often I have been killed. . . .
A tree, with axes and adzes by the carpenters
An infinite number of times I have been felled, stripped of my bark, cut up, and sawn into planks. . . .
Ever afraid, trembling, in pain and suffering,
I have felt the utmost sorrow and agony. . . .
In every kind of existence I have suffered
Pains which have scarcely known reprieve for a moment.
—*Uttaradhyayana* 19.61–64, 71, 74

If another insult him, a monk should not lose his temper,
For that is mere childishness—a monk should never be angry.
If he hears words harsh and cruel, vulgar and painful,
He should silently disregard them, and not take them to heart.
Even if beaten he should not be angry, or even think sinfully,
But should know that patience is best, and follow the Law.

. . . .

When his limbs are running with sweat, and grimed with dust and dirt
In the heat of summer, the wise monk will not lament his lost comfort.
He must bear it all to wear out his karma, and follow the noble, the supreme Law.
Until his body breaks up, he should bear the filth upon it. ❑
—*Uttaradhyayana* 2.24–37

From W. T. de Bary et al., *Sources of Indian Tradition* (New York: Columbia University Press, 1958), pp. 59–60, 64–65.

Jain monks honoring Bahubali, the first person in the present cosmic cycle to achieve enlightenment. The small image is a replica of the huge statue of Bahubali, the foot of which the monk in the background is touching reverently. [Magnum/Alex Webb.]

way to extricate the self, or soul, from the bonds of the material world and its accumulations of karma.

In the Jain view, there is no beginning or end to phenomenal existence, only innumerable, ceaseless cycles of generation and degeneration. The universe is alive from end to end with an infinite number of souls, all of which are immortal, omniscient, and pure in their essence. But all are caught in the web of *samsara*, whether as animals, gods, humans, plants, or even inanimate stones or fire. *Karma* here takes on a quasi-material form: Any thought, word, or deed attracts karmic matter that clings to and encumbers the soul. The greatest amounts come from evil acts, especially those done out of hate, greed, or cruelty to any other being.

Mahavira's path to release focused on the elimination of evil thoughts and acts, especially those harmful to others. His radical ascetic practice aimed at destroying one's karmic defilements and, ultimately, all actions leading to further karmic bondage. At the age of thirty, Mahavira entered on the radical self-denial

of a wandering ascetic and eventually gave up even clothing altogether (the latter a practice followed today by a relatively small sect of Jain mendicants). After a dozen years of self-deprivation and yogic meditative discipline, he attained enlightenment. Then, for some thirty years, he went about teaching his discipline to others. At the age of seventy-two, he chose to fast to death in order to burn out the last karmic residues, an action that has been emulated by some of the most advanced of Jain ascetics down to the present day.

It would, however, be very wrong to think of the entire Jain tradition in terms only of the extreme ascetic practices of some Jain mendicants. (Such practices can involve the attempt to avoid hurting even the tiniest organisms by wearing cloth masks and drinking only strained water.) Monks are bound basically by the five great vows that they share with other monastic traditions like the Buddhist and the Christian: not to kill, steal, lie, engage in sexual activity, or own anything.

Most Jains are not monks. Today, as in earlier centuries, there is a thriving lay community of perhaps three million Jains, most in western India (Gujarat and Rajasthan). Laypersons of both sexes have close ties to the monks (also of both sexes), whom they support with gifts and food. Many Jain laypersons spend some time during their life as a monk or in retreat with monks.

Jains tend to be merchants because of their aversion to farming and other occupations that involve harming plants or animals. They are vegetarians and regard *ahimsa*, "noninjury" to any being, as the paramount rule. In this latter emphasis, they have had great influence on Indian values. For example, Mahatma Gandhi, who came from a Jain area, seems to have been influenced by them in his adoption of *ahimsa* as a central tenet of his thought. Jains are known, in addition, for their hospitals—not only for humans, but also for animals. Compassion is for them, as for Buddhists, the great virtue. The merit of serving the "extraordinary-norm" seekers who adopt the mendicant life and of living a life according to the high standards of the community provides a goal even for those who as laypersons are following the "ordinary norm."

The Buddha

It can be argued that India's greatest contribution to world civilization was precisely the tradition of faith that eventually withered away in the subcontinent itself. The Buddhist tradition remains one of the greatest universalist forms of faith in the world today, but numbers only small minorities in India proper. Yet that is where it was born, where it received its fundamental shape, and where it left its mark on Hindu and Jain religion and culture. Like the two other great universalist traditions, Christianity and Islam, it traces its origins to a single figure who has loomed larger than life in the community of the faithful over the centuries.

This figure is Siddhartha Gautama, known as the "sage of the Shakya tribe" and, above all, as the Buddha, or the "enlightened/awakened one." A contemporary of Mahavira, Gautama was also born of a *Kshatriya* family (CA. 566 B.C.) in apparently comfortable if not, as the legend has it, royal circumstances. His people lived near the border of modern Nepal in the Himalayan foothills. The traditional story of how Gautama came to be the teacher of the "Middle Path" to release from *samsara* begins with his sheltered life of ease as a young married prince.

At the age of twenty-nine, Gautama suddenly realized the reality of aging, sickness, and death as the human lot. Revolted at his previous delight in sensual pleasures and even his wife and child, he abandoned his home and family to seek an answer to the dilemma of the endless cycle of mortal existence. After this "Great Renunciation," he studied first with renowned

teachers and then took up extreme ascetic disciplines of penance and self-mortification. Still finding no answer, Gautama turned finally to intense yogic meditation under a pipal tree in the place near Varanasi (Banaras) known as Gaya. In one historic night, he moved through different levels of trance, during which he realized all of his past lives, the reality of the cycle of existence of all beings, and how to stop the karmic outflows that fuel suffering existence. At this point, he became the Buddha; that is, he achieved full enlightenment—the omniscient consciousness of reality as it is. Having realized the truth of suffering existence, he committed himself to the goal of gaining release for all beings.

From the time of the experience under the Bodh Tree, or "enlightenment tree," Gautama devoted the last of his earthly lives before his final release to teaching others his "Middle Path" between asceticism and sensual indulgence. This path has been the core of

An early Indian carving showing the chakra, *or wheel of the Dharma, the Buddha's teaching, adored by humans and gods. The tree is the Bo-tree under which Gautama attained enlightenment and became the Buddha. [Diana L. Eck.]*

Buddhist faith and practice ever since. It begins with realizing the "four noble truths"—(1) all life is *dukkha*, or suffering; (2) the source of suffering is desiring; (3) the cessation of desiring is the way to end suffering; (4) and the path to this end is eightfold: right understanding, thought, speech, action, livelihood, effort, mindfulness, and concentration. The key idea of the Buddhist teaching, or *dharma*, is that everything in the world of existence is causally linked. The essential fact of existence is *dukkha*: All existing is suffering; for no pleasure, however great, is permanent (here we see the Buddhist variation on the central Indian theme of

The "Turning of the Wheel of the Dharma": Basic Teachings of the Buddha

The following are selections from the sermon said to have been the first preached by the Buddha. It was directed at five of his former companions, with whom he had practiced extreme austerities. When he had abandoned asceticism to mediate under the Bodh Tree, they had left him. This sermon is said to have made them the first to follow him. Because it set in motion the Buddha's teaching, or dharma, *on earth, it is usually described as "Setting in Motion the Wheel of* Dharma." *The text is from the* Dhammacakkappavattana-sutta.

Thus have I heard. The Blessed One was once living in the Deer Park at Isipatana (the Resort of Seers) near Bārānasi (Benares). There he addressed the group of five bhikkhus.

"Bhikkhus, these two extremes ought not to be practiced by one who has gone forth from the household life. What are the two? There is devotion to the indulgence of sense-pleasures, which is low, common, the way of ordinary people, unworthy and unprofitable; and there is devotion to self-mortification, which is painful, unworthy and unprofitable.

"Avoiding both these extremes, the Tathāgata has realized the Middle Path: it gives vision, it gives knowledge, and it leads to calm, to insight, to enlightenment, to Nibbāna. And what is that Middle Path . . . ? It is simply the Noble Eight-fold Path, namely, right view, right thought, right speech, right action, right livelihood, right effort, right mindfulness, right concentration. This is the Middle Path realized by the Tathāgata, which gives vision, which gives knowledge, and which leads to calm, to insight, to enlightenment, to Nibbāna. . . .

"The Noble Truth of suffering *(Dukkha)* is this: Birth is suffering; aging is suffering; sickness is suffering; death is suffering; sorrow and lamentation, pain, grief and despair are suffering; association with the unpleasant is suffering; dissociation from the pleasant is suffering; not to get what one wants is suffering—in brief, the five aggregates of attachment are suffering.

"The Noble Truth of the origin of suffering is this: It is this thirst (craving) which produces re-existence and re-becoming, bound up with passionate greed. It finds fresh delight now here and now there, namely, thirst for non-existence (self-annihilation).

"The Noble Truth of the Cessation of suffering is this: It is the complete cessation of that very thirst, giving it up, renouncing it, emancipating oneself from it, detaching oneself from it.

"The Noble Truth of the Path leading to the Cessation of suffering is this: It is simply the Noble Eightfold Path. . . .

"'This is the Noble Truth of Suffering (Dukkha)': such was the vision, the knowledge, the wisdom, the science, the light, that arose in me with regard to things not heard before. 'This suffering, as a noble truth, should be fully understood.' . . .

"'This is the Noble Truth of the Cessation of suffering': such was the vision . . . 'This Cessation of suffering, as a noble truth, should be realized.' . . .

"'This is the Noble Truth of the Path leading to the Cessation of suffering': such was the vision, . . . 'This Path leading to the Cessation of suffering, as a noble truth, has been followed (cultivated).' . . .

"As long as my vision of true knowledge was not fully clear . . . regarding the Four Noble Truths, I did not claim to have realized the perfect Enlightenment that is supreme in the world with its gods, . . . in this world with its recluses and brāhmanas, with its princes and men. But when my vision of true knowledge was fully clear . . . regarding the Four Noble Truths, then I claimed to have realized the perfect Enlightenment that is supreme in the world with its gods, in this world with its recluses and brāhmanas, with its princes and men. And a vision of true knowledge arose in me thus: My heart's deliverance is unassailable. This is the last birth. Now there is no more rebecoming (rebirth)."

This the Blessed One said. The group of five bhikkhus was glad, and they rejoiced at his words. ❏
(Samyutta-nikāya, LVI, II)

From Walpola Rahula, *What the Buddha Taught* (New York: Grove Press, 1974). pp. 92–94.

samsara). *Dukkha* comes from desire, from craving, from attachment to self.

Thus, Buddhist discipline focuses on the moral "eightfold path" and the cardinal virtue of compassion for all beings with the intent of eliminating the selfish desiring that is literally the root of *samsara* and its unavoidable suffering. The Buddha himself had attained this goal. When he died (CA. 486 B.C.) after a life of teaching others how to reach it, he passed from the round of existence forever. In Buddhist terminology, he attained *nirvana*, the extinguishing of continued karmic bondage. This attainment was to become the starting point for the growth and eventual spread of the Buddhist *dharma*, which was to take on diverse and far different forms in its long history.

Like the Jain movement, the Buddhist movement involved not only followers who were willing to renounce marriage and normal occupations to become part of the Buddha's communities of monks or nuns, but also laypersons who would strive to live by the high moral standards of the tradition and support those who were willing and able to strive as mendicants to realize full release. Like the Jain tradition, the Buddhist tradition encompassed from the start seekers of both the "extraordinary" and the "ordinary" norm in their present lives. This dual community has remained characteristic of all forms of Buddhism wherever it is practiced. Certainly, we shall have occasion later to see how varied these forms have been historically. But however much the essentially a-theistic, a-ritualistic, and pragmatic basic tradition was later modified and added to, so that popular Buddhism would encompass even theistic devotion to a divinized Buddha and other enlightened beings, the fundamental vision of a humanly attainable wisdom that leads to compassion and release remained.

The varying visions of Upanishadic, Jain, and Buddhist thought have proved durable, albeit in very different ways and degree in India itself, as we have noted. The emergence of "Hindu" tradition was to draw on all three of these revolutionary strands in Indian thought and to integrate their fundamental ideas about the universe, human life, morality, and society into the cultic and mythic strands of Brahmanic and popular Indian practice.

The Religion of the Jews

The world of the ancient Near East, both in Egypt and in the lands east of the Mediterranean across to the Iranian plateau, was a polytheistic world. Everywhere people worshiped local or regional gods and goddesses. Some of these deities were associated with natural places and phenomena, such as mountains or animals, the sky or the earth. For example, Shamash

in Mesopotamia and Re in Egypt were both sun gods. Others were tribal or local deities, such as Marduk in Babylonia, or Atum, the patron god of the Egyptian city of On (Heliopolis). Still others represented elemental powers of this world or the next, as was the case with Baal, the ancient fertility god of the Canaanite peoples, and Ishtar, whom the Sumerians worshiped as a goddess of love and the Assyrians as a goddess of war. Furthermore, from our perspective,

MAP 2-2 ANCIENT PALESTINE *The Hebrews established a unified kingdom in Palestine under Kings David and Solomon in the tenth century* B.C. *After the death of Solomon, however, the kingdom was divided into two parts—Israel in the north and Judah, with its capital Jerusalem, in the south. North of Israel were the great commercial cities of Phoenicia.*

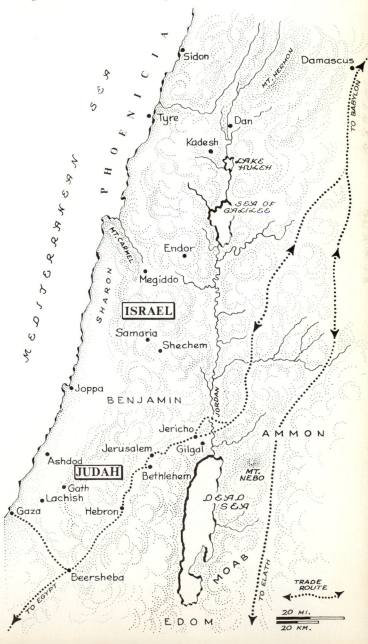

the gods were represented, by and large, as arbitrary and amoral beings who were often no more affected by the actions of human beings than were the natural forces that some of them represented.

If the gods were many and diverse, so too were the religious traditions of the ancient Near Eastern world. Even the major traditions of religious thought in Egypt and Mesopotamia did not offer comprehensive interpretations of human life that linked history and human destiny to a transcendent or eternal realm of meaning beyond this world—or at least no one such interpretation was able to spread and become dominant in this highly pluralistic, religiously fragmented world.

Out of this polytheistic and pluralistic world came the great tradition of monotheistic faith represented historically in the Jewish, Christian, and Islamic communities. This tradition traces its origin not to any of the great imperial cultures of the ancient Near Eastern world, but to the small nation of the Israelites. Although they were only a tiny tribal people whose external fortunes were at the mercy of the ebb and flow of the great dynasties and empires of the first millennium B.C., their impact on the global history of civilization was far greater than that of their giant neighbors. For all the glories of the great civilizations of the Fertile Crescent and the Nile valley, it was the Israelites, not the Babylonians or the Egyptians, who founded a tradition that significantly affected later history. This tradition was ethical monotheism.

Monotheism (faith in a single, all-powerful God who is the sole creator, sustainer, and ruler of the universe) may well be older than the Hebrews, but it made its first clear appearance with them. Their emphasis on the moral demands and ethical responsibilities placed on the individual and the community by the one God was first definitively linked to human history itself (and the Divine plan for that history). This historically based ethical and monotheistic tradition culminated later in the Jewish, Christian, and Islamic religions, but its direction had been set much earlier.

The beginnings of the tradition lie far back in the early history of an obscure tribal people whom later history knows as the Hebrews. The path from the appearance of this group as nomadic tribes in the northern Arabian peninsula, sometime after 2000 B.C., to the full flowering of Judaic monotheism in the mid-first millennium B.C. was a long one. Before we turn to the monotheistic revolution itself, we need to look briefly at the history of the Hebrews.

From Hebrew Nomads to the Israelite Nation

The history of the Hebrew people, later known as Israelites, must be pieced together from various sources. They are mentioned only rarely in the records of their ancient Near Eastern neighbors, so we must rely chiefly on their own accounts as compiled in the Hebrew Bible (or Old Testament, in Christian terminology). It was not intended as a history in our sense; rather, it is a complicated collection of historical narrative, wisdom literature, poetry, law, and religious witness. Scholars of an earlier day in the West tended to discard the Bible as a source for historians, but the most recent trend is to take it seriously while using it cautiously and critically. Although its earliest written portions go back at most only to the ninth century B.C. (it came to be fixed in the form in which it is known today only in the second century A.D.), it contains much older oral materials in its earliest parts. These allow us at least some glimpses of the earliest history of the Hebrew tribe.

We need not reject the tradition that the patriarch Abraham came from Ur in Mesopotamia and wandered west with his Hebrew clan to tend his flocks in the land along the eastern shore of the Mediterranean that became known to later history as Palestine. Such

Moses and the Burning Bush, a fresco from a synagogue in Syria from CA. A.D. 250. *The burning bush episode symbolizes divine-human encounter in Western monotheism. [Art Resource.]*

God's Purpose with Israel

In the first selection here, God, speaking through the prophet Jeremiah (fl. 626–586 B.C.), says that Jerusalem will be given over to the Babylonians. But he goes on to assure the Jews that he will also "gather them" together again and restore the "everlasting covenant" when he brings them again to Palestine. Such words provided the exiles in Babylon with an interpretation of their fate that helped them hold to their faith even in a foreign land. In the second selection, we hear the unknown prophetic voice of, so-called Second Isaiah, which dates from about 540 B.C. Here God addresses Israel as his suffering servant and promises to comfort and restore the Israelites as "a light to the nations." Such prophetic promises reflect the self-understanding of Israel with regard both to the tragedies of their history and to their special role as God's chosen instrument in his larger plan of salvation for all the nations of the earth.

The word of the LORD came to Jeremiah: "Behold, I am the LORD, the God of all flesh; is anything too hard for me? Therefore, thus says the LORD: Behold, I am giving this city into the hand of the Chalde'ans and into the hand of Nebuchadnez'zar king of Babylon, and he shall take it. . . . For the sons of Israel and the sons of Judah have done nothing but evil in my sight from their youth; the sons of Israel have done nothing but provoke me to anger by the work of their hands, says the LORD.

"Now therefore thus says the LORD, the God of Israel, concerning this city of which you say, 'It is given into the hand of the king of Babylon by sword, by famine, and by pestilence': Behold, I will gather them from all the countries to which I drove them in my anger and my wrath and in great indignation; I will bring them back to this place, and I will make them dwell in safety. And they shall be my people, and I will be their God. I will give them one heart and one way, that they may fear me for ever, for their own good and the good of their children after them. I will make with them an everlasting covenant, that I will not turn away from doing good to them; and I will put the fear of me in their hearts, that they may not turn from me. I will rejoice in doing them good, and I will plant them in this land in faithfulness, with all my heart and all my soul."

Jeremiah 32:26–41

Behold my servant, whom I uphold,
my chosen, in whom my soul delights;
I have put my Spirit upon him,
  he will bring forth justice to the nations.
He will not cry or lift up his voice, or make it
heard in the street;
a bruised reed he will not break,
  and a dimly burning wick he will not quench;
  he will faithfully bring forth justice.
He will not fail or be discouraged
  till he has established justice in the earth;
  and the coastlands wait for his law.

Isaiah 42:1–4

From *The Oxford Annotated Bible with the Apocrypha: Revised Standard Version*, ed. by H. G. May and B. M. Metzger (New York: Oxford University Press, 1965).

a movement would be in accord with what we know of a general migration of seminomadic tribes from Mesopotamia westward after about 1950 B.C. Any precise dating of the arrival of the Hebrews in the region of Palestine is impossible, but it may have been as early as 1900 B.C. or as late as 1600 B.C.

It is, however, with the patriarchal figure of Moses, at about the beginning of the thirteenth century B.C., that the Hebrews come onto the stage of history with greater clarity. Some of Abraham's people had settled down in the Palestinian area, but others apparently had wondered farther westward, into Egypt, perhaps with the Hyksos invaders (see Chapter 1). As the biblical narrative tells it, they had, by about 1400 B.C., become a settled but subject and even enslaved people there. Under the leadership of Moses, a segment of the Egyptian Israelites left the land of Egypt in search of a new homeland in the region to the east from which Abraham's descendants had come. The Children of Israel may then have wandered in the Sinai Desert and elsewhere for several decades before reaching Canaan, the province of Palestine that is described in the Bible as their promised homeland. The Bible presents this experience as the key event in Israel's history: the forging of the covenant, or mutual pact, between God, or *Yahweh*, and his people. We interpret the events of this Exodus period as the time that the Israelites emerged as a nation, a people with a sense of community and common purpose.

By about 1200 B.C., they had carved out a new Palestinian homeland for themselves at the expense of the Canaanite inhabitants of the area. After perhaps two centuries of consolidation and an existence as a loose federation of tribes, the now-settled nation reached its peak as a monarchy under kings David and Solomon in the tenth century B.C. But the sons of Solomon could not maintain the unity of the kingdom, and it split into two parts in the ninth century B.C.: Israel in the north of Palestine, and Judah, with its capital at Jerusalem, in the south.

The rise of the great empires around them brought disaster to the Israelites. The northern kingdom fell to the Assyrians in 722 B.C.; its people were scattered and, according to tradition, lost forever. These were the so-called ten lost tribes. Only the kingdom of Judah, with its seat at Jerusalem, remained, and hereafter we may call the Israelites Jews. In 586 B.C., Judah was defeated by the Neo-Babylonian king Nebuchadnezzar II. He destroyed the center of the Jewish cult, the great temple built by Solomon, and carried off the cream of the Jewish nation as exiles to be resettled in Babylon. There, in the "Babylonian Captivity" of the Exile, without a temple, the Jews managed still to cling to their traditions and faith. After the new Persian dynasty of the Achaemenids defeated the Babylonians in 539 B.C., they were allowed to return and resettle in their homeland. Many, but not all, of the exiles did return, and by about 516 B.C., a second temple was erected in a restored Jerusalem after the Exile.

The new Judaic state continued to be dominated by foreign peoples in the following centuries, but it was able to maintain its religious and national identity and occasionally to assert itself. However, it was again destroyed and its people dispersed after the destruction of Jerusalem by the Romans, in A.D. 70 and again in A.D. 132. By this time, however, the Jews had developed a religious worldview that would far exceed and long outlive that of any Judaic national state.

The Monotheistic Revolution

The fate of this small nation would be of little interest were it not for its unique religious achievement. It developed a tradition of faith that amounted to a revolution in ways of thinking about the human condition, the meaning of life and history, and the nature of the divine. It was not the overt history of the Judaic state down to its catastrophic end in A.D. 132 that was to have lasting historical importance, but what the Jews made of that history and how they interpreted it. The revolutionary character of this interpretation lay in its uniquely moralistic understanding of human life and history and the uncompromising monotheism on which this understanding was based.

At the root of this monotheistic tradition stands the figure of Abraham. Not only Jews but also Christians and Muslims look to him as the symbolic founder of their monotheistic faith. It is likely that the Hebrews in Abraham's time were much like other primitive tribal peoples in their religious attitudes. For them, the world must have been alive with many supernatural or divine powers: ancestral spirits, personifications or masters of the forces of nature, and divinities associated with particular places. Abraham probably conceived of his Lord simply as the most powerful of many divinities whom people might worship. But for the strength of his faith in God, the later biblical account recognizes him as the "Father of the Faithful," the first of the Hebrew patriarchs to enter into a covenant, or mutual pact, with God. In this covenant, Abraham promised to serve only this God, and this God prom-

A highly speculative reconstruction of Solomon's Temple, based on biblical accounts of its construction. [Bettmann Archive.]

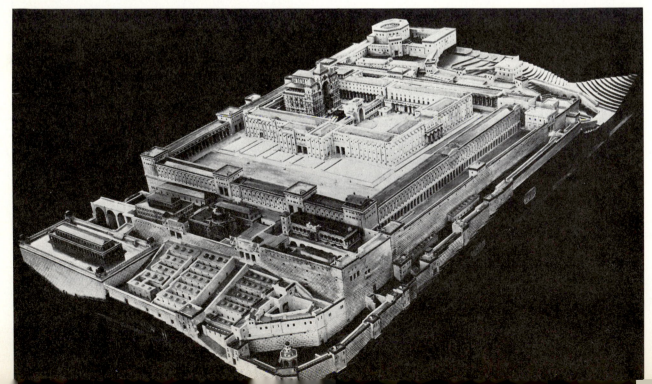

"The Wailing Wall" of Temple Mount, Jerusalem. This site is believed to be the remains of the Temple and is a focal point for Jewish pilgrimage and prayer. [James Casson.]

ised in turn to bless Abraham's descendants and guide them as his special people.

As is the case with the faith of Abraham, it is difficult to say how much the Mosaic covenant at Sinai actually represented the achievement of an exclusively monotheistic faith. A notion of the supremacy of Yahweh is reflected in the biblical emphasis on the Israelites' rejection of all other gods at this time—and on their subsequent victory, through Yahweh's might, over the Canaanites. Certainly, the covenant event was the decisive one in making of the Israelites a people united and identified by their special relationship to God. At Sinai, they received both God's holy Law (the Torah) and his promise of protection and guidance as long as they kept the law. This covenant was the necessary first step in the monotheistic revolution that came to full fruition several hundred years later. From Sinai forward, the Israelites looked on themselves as God's chosen people among the nations, and on their history as the history of the mighty acts of God.

The monotheistic revolution may thus be said to have begun with Abraham or Moses. Historically, we can trace it primarily from the division of the Israelite kingdom into two parts in 922 B.C. After this there arose men and women who were known as the *prophets*. Inspired messengers of God, prophets were sent to call people back from the worship of false gods to the worship of the one true God, and from increasing immorality and injustice to obedience to God's commandments.

Here we cannot trace the colorful history of the great and lesser prophets of Israel. The important point is that their activity was directly tied to the crucial events of Israelite history in the middle centuries of the first millennium B.C. In the biblical interpretation of these events, we can see the consolidation of the Judaic religious tradition in process. This consolidation, even amidst the political disintegration of the Israelite kingdom, was largely the result of the activities of the prophets. Their concern with purifying the faith and the morality of their people focused in particular on two ideas that proved central to Judaic monotheism.

The first was the significance of history in the Divine plan. Calling on the Jews' awareness of the covenant made at Sinai, the prophets saw in Israel's past and present troubles the hand of God punishing them for failing in their covenant duties. Their prophecies of coming disaster at the hands of enemies were based on the conviction that unless Israel changed its ways, more punishment would follow. But they were not only prophets of doom. When the predicted disasters came, their vision extended to seeing Israel the "suffering servant" among the nations, the people who, by their trials, would purify other nations and bring them also eventually to God. Here the nationalistic, particularistic focus of previous Israelite religion gave way to a universal, and therefore more complete, monotheism: Yahweh is God of all, even the Babylonians or Assyrians.

The second idea, or set of ideas, centered on the nature of Yahweh. The prophets saw in him the transcendent ideal of justice and goodness. From this view followed naturally the demand for justice and goodness in his worshipers, both individually and collectively. God was a righteous God who expected righteousness from human beings. No longer could he be understood only as the object of a sacrificial cult: He was a moral God who demands fairness and goodness, not blood offerings and empty prayers. A corollary of God's goodness was his love for his people, as especially the prophet Hosea (late eighth century B.C.) emphasized. However much he might have to punish them for their sins, God would eventually lead them back to him and his favor.

In the linking of the Lord of the Universe to history and to morality lay the heart of the breakthrough to true ethical monotheism. The Almighty Creator was seen as actively concerned with the actions and fates of his human creatures as exemplified in Israel. This concern was reflected in his involvement in history; history took on transcendent meaning. God had created humankind for an ultimately good purpose: They were called upon to be just and good like their Creator, for they were involved in the fulfillment of his divine purpose. Most concretely, this would come in the restoration of Israel as a people purified of their sins: "I will put my law within them, and I will write it upon their hearts; and I will be their God, and they shall be my people" (Jeremiah 31:33).

However, even after the Exile, the full realization of the prophecied days of peace and blessedness under God's rule clearly still had not come. The Jews were scattered now from Egypt to Babylonia, and their homeland remained in the control of stronger powers. Out of this context developed the late prophetic concept that the culmination of history would come in a future Messianic age. Faith and morality were now tied to human destiny, even without the still later Jewish idea that a day of judgment would end the golden age of the Messiah. The significance of these ideas, some of which may have come from the Jews' encounter with Zoroastrian traditions in the Exile, did not stop with Judaic religion. They went on to play a key role in similar Christian and Muslim ideas of a Messianic deliverer, resurrection of the body, and a life after death.

Alongside the prophets, the other key element in the monotheistic revolution of the Jews was the Law itself. The law is embodied in the five books of Torah (the Pentateuch, or "five books" of Genesis, Exodus, Leviticus, Numbers, and Deuteronomy). The central place of the Law in Jewish life was reestablished, after a period of decline, by King Josiah of Judah shortly before the fall of Jerusalem and the Exile. Its presence and importance in Judaic faith enabled the Jews to survive the loss of the Temple and its priestly cult even in exile, thereby fixing the Torah even over Jerusalem as the ultimate earthly focus of faith in God. Its centrality for the Jewish nation was reaffirmed after the reestablishment of the Temple, by Ezra and Nehemiah, in the fifth century B.C.

In the second century B.C., the enduring role of the Torah was ensured by its physical compilation, together with the books of the prophets and other writings, into the Holy Scriptures, or the Bible. Here we have the record of the Jews' long road to the recognition of God's law for his people, as well as the actual Law of the Torah itself. A holy, authoritative, divinely revealed scripture as an element of Judaic monotheism had revolutionary consequences, not only for Jews, but also for Christians and Muslims. In many ways, it put the seal on the monotheistic revolution that had made the sovereignty and righteousness of God the focal point of faith. It thereby affirmed the meaning of human action and human history for the faithful through the tangible historical record of God's law and Israel's historical experience.

A rabbi in Jerusalem reading from Torah in morning prayer. [*Bettmann Archive.*]

In the evolution of Judaic monotheistic faith, we see the beginning of one of the major religious traditions of world civilization. For the first time, in the Jews we find a nation defined not primarily by dynastic, linguistic, or geographical considerations, but above all by shared religious faith and practice. This was something new in human history. It was to have still greater effects in later times when not only Judaic but also Christian and Muslim tradition would change the face of major portions of the world.

Greek Philosophy

Different approaches and answers to many of the same concerns were offered by ancient Greek thought. Calling attention, even this early, to some of those differences will help to point up the distinctive outlook of the Greeks and of the later cultures of Western civilization that have drawn heavily on it.

Greek ideas had much in common with the ideas of earlier peoples. The gods of the Greeks had most of the characteristics of the Mesopotamian deities; magic and incantations played a part in Greek lives; and their law was usually connected with divinity. Many, if not most, Greeks in the ancient world must have lived their lives with notions not very different from those held by other peoples. But the surprising thing is that some Greeks developed ideas that were strikingly different and, in so doing, set a part of humankind on an entirely new path. As early as the sixth century B.C., some Greeks living in the Ionian cities of Asia Minor raised questions and suggested answers about nature that produced an intellectual revolution. In speculating about the nature of the world and its origin, they made guesses that were completely naturalistic and made no reference to supernatural powers. One historian of Greek thought put the case particularly well:

In one of the Babylonian legends it says: "All the lands were sea. . . . Marduk bound a rush mat upon the face of

the waters, he made dirt and piled it beside the rush mat." What Thales did was to leave Marduk out. He, too, said that everything was once water. But he thought that earth and everything else had been formed out of water by a natural process, like the silting up of the Delta of the Nile. . . . It is an admirable beginning, the whole point of which is that it gathers together into a coherent picture a number of observed facts without letting Marduk in.[3]

Thales was the first Greek philosopher. His putting of the question of the world's origin in a naturalistic form as early as the sixth century B.C. may have been the beginning of the unreservedly rational investigation of the universe, and so the beginning of both Western philosophy and Western science.

The same relentlessly rational approach was used even in regard to the gods themselves. In the same century as Thales, Xenophanes of Colophon expressed the opinion that humans think that the gods were born and have clothes, voices, and bodies like themselves. If oxen, horses, and lions had hands and could paint like human beings, they would paint gods in their own image; the oxen would draw gods like oxen and the horses like horses. Thus black people believed in flat-nosed, black-faced gods, and the Thracians in gods with blue eyes and red hair.[4] In the fifth century B.C., Protagoras of Abdera went so far in the direction of agnosticism as to say, "About the gods I can have no knowledge either that they are or that they are not or what is their nature."[5]

This rationalistic, skeptical way of thinking carried over into practical matters as well. The school of medicine led by Hippocrates of Cos (about 400 B.C.) attempted to understand, diagnose, and cure disease without any attention to supernatural forces or beings. One of the Hippocratics wrote of the mysterious disease epilepsy: "It seems to me that the disease is no more divine than any other. It has a natural cause, just as other diseases have. Men think it divine merely because they do not understand it. But if they called everything divine which they do not understand, why, there would be no end of divine things."[6] By the fifth century B.C., too, it was possible for the historian Thucydides to analyze and explain the behavior of humans in society completely in terms of human nature and chance, leaving no place for the gods or supernatural forces.

The same absence of divine or supernatural forces characterized Greek views of law and justice. Most

[3] Benjamin Farrington, *Greek Science* (London: Penguin, 1953), p. 37.

[4] Frankfort et. al., pp. 14–16.

[5] Hermann Diels, *Fragmente der Vorsokratiker*, 5th ed., by Walther Kranz (Berlin: Weidmann, 1934–1938), Frg. 4.

[6] Ibid., Frgs. 14–16.

Greeks, of course, liked to think in a vague way that law came ultimately from the gods. In practice, however, and especially in the democratic states, they knew very well that laws were made by humans and should be obeyed because they represented the expressed consent of the citizens. Law, according to the fourth century B.C. statesman Demosthenes, is "a general covenant of the whole State, in accordance with which all men in that State ought to regulate their lives."[7]

The statement of these ideas, so different from any that came before the Greeks, opens the discussion of most of the issues that appear in the long history of civilization and that remain major concerns in the modern world: What is the nature of the universe and how can it be controlled? Are there divine powers, and if so, what is humanity's relationship to them? Are law and justice human, divine, or both? What is the place in human society of freedom, obedience, and reverence? These and many other problems were confronted and intensified by the Greeks.

Reason and the Scientific Spirit

The rational spirit characteristic of Greek geometric pottery and even of many Greek myths blossomed in the sixth century B.C. into the intellectual examination of the physical world and the place of humankind in it that we call philosophy. It is not surprising that the first steps along this path were taken in Ionia, which was on the fringe of the Greek world and therefore in touch with foreign ideas and the learning of the East. The Ionians were among the first to realize that the Greek account of how the world was created and maintained and of the place of humans in it was not universally accepted. Perhaps this realization helped spark the first attempts at disciplined philosophical inquiry.

We have already met Thales of Miletus, who lived early in the sixth century B.C. He believed that the earth floated on water and that water was the primary substance. This was not a new idea; what was new was the absence of any magical or mythical elements in the explanation. Thales observed, as any person can, that water has many forms: liquid, solid, and gaseous. He saw that it could "create" land by alluvial deposit and that it is necessary for all life. These observations he organized by reason into a single explanation that accounted for many phenomena without any need for the supernatural. The first philosopher thus set the tone for future investigations. Greek philosophers assumed that the world was knowable, rational, and simple.

The search for fundamental rational explanations of phenomena was carried forward by another

[7]Against Aristogeiton, 16.

Thales of Miletus, the first Greek philosopher. His explanation for the origin of the world was based on reason and the observation of nature without any need for the supernatural. [Bettmann Archive.]

Milesian, Anaximander. He imagined that the basic element was something undefined, "unlimited." The world emerged from it as the result of an interaction of opposite forces—wet and dry, hot and cold. He pictured the universe in eternal motion, with all sensible things emerging from the "unlimited," then decaying and returning to it. He also argued that human beings originated in water and had evolved to the present state through several stages, including that of a fish.

Anaximenes, another Milesian who flourished about 546 B.C., believed air to be primary. It took different forms because of the purely physical processes of rarefaction and condensation.

Heraclitus of Ephesus, who lived near the end of the sixth century B.C., carried the dialogue further. His famous saying, "All is motion," raised important problems. If all is constantly in motion, it would appear that nothing ever really exists. Yet Heraclitus believed that the world order was governed by a guiding principle, the Logos, and that though phenomena changed, the Logos did not. *Logos* has several meanings, among them "word," "language," "speech," and "reason." So when Heraclitus said that the physical world was governed by Logos, he implied that it could be explained by reason. In this way, speculations about the physical world, what we would call natural

The Atomists' Account of the Origin of the World Order

Leucippus and Democritus were Greek thinkers of the fifth century B.C. *who originated the theory that the world is entirely material, made up of atoms and the void, moving through space without external guidance. They provided a fundamental explanation of things that was purely natural, without divine or mythical intervention. Their view was passed on and later influenced such Renaissance scientists as Galileo.*

The world-orders arise in this way. Many bodies of all sorts of shapes "split off" from the infinite into a great void where, being gathered together, they give rise to a single vortex, in which, colliding and circling in all sorts of ways, they begin to separate apart, like to like. Being unable to circle in equilibrium any longer because of their congestion, the light bodies go off into the outer void like chaff, while the rest "remain together" and, becoming entangled, unite their motions and produce first a spherical structure.

This stands apart like a "membrane," containing in itself all sorts of bodies; and, because of the resistance of the middle, as these revolve the surrounding membrane becomes thin as contiguous bodies continually flow together because of contact with the vortex. And in this way the earth arose, the bodies which were carried to the middle remaining together. Again, the surrounding membrane increases because of the acquisition of bodies from without; and as it moves with the vortex, whatever it touches it adds to itself. Certain of these, becoming entangled, form a structure at first very watery and muddy; but afterward they dry out, being carried about with the rotation of the whole, and ignite to form the substance of the heavenly bodies.

Certainly the atoms did not arrange themselves in order by design or intelligence, nor did they propound what movements each should make. But rather myriad atoms, swept along through infinite time or myriad paths by blows and their own weight, have come together in every possible way and tried out every combination that they could possibly create. So it happens that, after roaming the world for aeons of time in making trial of every combination and movement, at length they come together—those atoms whose sudden coincidence often becomes the origin of mighty things: of earth and sea and sky and the species of living things. ☐

The first selection is from Diogenes Laertius 9.31; the second is from Lucretius, *De Rerum Naturae* 5.419–431. Both are cited in and translated by J. M. Robinson, *An Introduction to Early Greek Philosophy* (Boston: Houghton Mifflin, 1968), pp. 206, 208–209.

science, soon led the way toward even more difficult philosophical speculations about language, about the manner of human thought, and about knowledge itself.

In opposition to Heraclitus, Parmenides of Elea and his pupil Zeno argued that change was only an illusion of the senses. Reason and reflection showed that reality was fixed and unchanging because it seemed evident that nothing could be created out of nothingness. Such fundamental speculations were carried forward by Empedocles of Acragas, who spoke of four basic elements: fire, water, earth, and air. Like Parmenides, he thought that reality was permanent but not immobile, for the four elements were moved by two primary forces, Love and Strife, or, as we might be inclined to say, attraction and repulsion.

This theory was clearly a step on the road to the atomic theory of Leucippus of Miletus and Democritus of Abdera. They believed that the world consisted of innumerable tiny, solid particles that could not be divided or modified and that moved about in the void. The size of the atoms and the arrangement in which they were joined with others produced the secondary qualities that the senses could perceive, such as color and shape. These qualities—unlike the atoms themselves, which were natural—were merely conventional. Anaxagoras of Clazomenae, an older contemporary and a friend of Pericles, had previously spoken of tiny fundamental particles called *seeds*, which were put together on a rational basis by a force called *nous*, or "mind." Thus, Anaxagoras suggested a distinction between matter and mind. The atomists, however, regarded "soul," or "mind," as material and believed that everything was guided by purely physical laws. In the arguments of Anaxagoras and the atomists, we have the beginning of the philosophical debate between materialism and idealism that has continued through the ages.

These discussions interested very few, and, in fact, most Greeks were suspicious of such speculations. A far more influential debate was begun by a group of professional teachers who emerged in the mid-fifth century B.C. and whom the Greeks called *Sophists*. They traveled about and received pay for teaching practical techniques such as rhetoric, a valuable skill in democracies like Athens. Others claimed to teach wisdom and even virtue. They did not speculate about

The Sophists: From Rational Inquiry to Skepticism

The rational spirit inherent in Greek thought was carried to remarkable and dangerous extremes by the Sophists in the fifth century B.C. They questioned even the nature, the existence, and the origin of the gods, subjecting these matters to rational analysis.

Concerning the gods, I do not know whether they exist or not. For many are the obstacles to knowledge: the obscurity of the subject and the brevity of human life.

Prodicus says that the ancients worshiped as gods the sun, the moon, rivers, springs, and all things useful to human life, simply because of their usefulness—just as the Egyptians deify the Nile. For this reason bread is worshiped as Demeter, wine as Dionysus, water as Poseidon, fire as Hephaestus, and so on for each of the things that are useful to men.

There was a time when the life of man was disorderly and bestial and subject to brute force; when there was no reward for the good and no punishment for the bad. At that time, I think, men enacted laws in order that justice might be absolute ruler and have arrogance as its slave; and if anyone did wrong he was punished. Then, when the laws prohibited them from doing deeds of violence, they began to do them secretly. Then, I think, some shrewd and wise man invented fear of the gods for mortals, so that there might be some deterrent to the wicked even if they did or said or thought something in secret. Therefore he introduced the divine, saying that there is a god, flourishing with immortal life, hearing and seeing with his mind, thinking of all things and watching over them and having a divine nature; who will hear everything that is said among mortals and will be able to see all that is done. And if you plan any evil in secret it will not escape the notice of the gods, for they are of surpassing intelligence. In speaking thus he introduced the prettiest of teachings, concealing the truth under a false account. And in order that he might better strike fear into the hearts of men he told them that the gods dwell in that place which he knew to be a source of fears to mortals—and of benefits too—namely, the upper periphery where they saw lightnings and heard the dreaded rumblings of thunder and saw the starry body of the heaven, the beauteous embroidery of that wise craftsman Time, where the bright glowing mass of the sun moves and whence dark rains descend to earth. With such fears did he surround men, and by means of them he established the deity securely in a place befitting his dignity, and quenched lawlessness. Thus, I think, did some man first persuade mortals to believe in a race of gods.   ❑

The first selection is from Diogenes Laertius 9.51; the next two are from Sextus Empiricus, *Against the Schoolmasters* 9.18, 9.54. All are cited in and translated by J. M. Robinson, *An Introduction to Early Greek Philosophy* (Boston: Houghton Mifflin, 1968), pp. 269–270.

the physical universe, but applied reasoned analysis to human beliefs and institutions. This human focus was characteristic of fifth-century thought, as was the central problem that the Sophists considered: They discovered the tension and even the contradiction between nature and custom, or law. The more traditional among them argued that law itself was in accord with nature, and this view fortified the traditional beliefs of the *polis*, the Greek city-state.

Others argued, however, that laws were merely conventional and not in accord with nature. The law was not of divine origin but merely the result of an agreement among people. It could not pretend to be a positive moral force, but merely had the negative function of preventing people from harming each other. The most extreme Sophists argued that law was contrary to nature, a trick whereby the weak control the strong. Critias went so far as to say that the gods themselves had been invented by some clever man to deter people from doing what they wished. Such ideas attacked the theoretical foundations of the *polis* and helped provoke the philosophical responses of Plato and Aristotle in the next century.

Political and Moral Philosophy

Like thinkers in other parts of the world around the middle of the first millennium B.C., some Greeks were vitally concerned with the formulation of moral principles for the governance of the state and the regulation of individual life, as well as more abstract problems of the nature of existence and transcendence. Nowhere is the Greek concern with ethical, political, and religious issues clearer than in the philosophical tradition that began with Socrates in the latter half of the fifth century B.C. That tradition continued with Socrates' pupil Plato and Plato's pupil Aristotle. Aristotle also had great interest in and made great contributions to the scientific understanding of the physical world, but he is perhaps more important for his impact on later Western and Islamic metaphysics.

Portfolio I: Judaism

Monotheism, the belief in a unique God who is the creator of the universe and its all-powerful ruler, first became a central and lasting element in religion among the Hebrews, later called Israelites and also Jews. Their religion, more than the many forms of polytheistic worship that characterized the ancient world, demanded moral rectitude and placed ethical responsibilities both on individuals and on the community as a whole. Their God had a divine plan for human history and the behavior of his chosen people was linked to it. This vision of the exclusive worship of the true God, obedience to the laws governing the community that derive from Him, and a strong ethical responsibility was connected to humanity's historical experience in this world. Ultimately it gave rise to three great religions: Judaism, Christianity, and Islam.

At the beginning of this tradition stands Abraham, recognized as the founder of their faith by all three of its branches. According to the story recorded in the Torah, this first of the Hebrew patriarchs entered into a covenant with God in which Abraham promised to worship only this God, who in turn promised to make Abraham's descendants his own chosen people— chosen to worship Him, obey His laws, and to undertake a special set of moral responsibilities. The covenant was renewed with Moses at Mount Sinai. God freed the Israelites from bondage, promised them the land of Canaan (later called Palestine and part of which is now Israel), and gave them the Law (the Torah), including the ten commandments, by which they were to guide their lives. As long as they lived by his law he would give them his guidance and protection.

In time the Israelites formed themselves into a kingdom which remained unified from about 1000 B.C. to 922 B.C. In the period after its division men and women called prophets emerged. These people, thought to be inspired by God, recalled the Israelites from their lapses into idolatry and immorality. Even as the kingdom was disintegrating and the Israelites falling under the control of alien empires, the prophets preached social reform and a return to more Godly ways. At the center of their vision was the place in history, in the fulfillment of God's plan for mankind. The prophets saw Israel's misfortune as punishment for failing to keep the covenant in many ways and predicted disaster if the Israelites did not change their ways. When disasters came, the Jewish kingdoms captured, the people enslaved and exiled, they interpreted Israel's status as a chosen people to mean that their sufferings were part of a process whereby they would become "a light unto the nations" leading other nations to the true worship of God. By this time, at the latest, the God of the Israelites was understood not only as the single God worshipped by the Jews but as the universal God for all humanity.

It was the prophets, too, who gave full expression to the Jews' belief that God was righteous and demanded righteousness from his people. At the same time, he was also a God of love; although he might need to punish his people for their sins, he would one day reward them with divine favor. Traditional Jewish belief expects that the Messiah, or "Anointed One," will someday come and establish God's kingdom on earth. He will be a descendant of King David who will restore the kingdom of Israel and rebuild the sanctuary in Jerusalem destroyed, finally, by the Romans. He will introduce an age of universal brotherhood in which all nations will acknowledge the true God and the righteous of past generations will be restored to life.

The Jews are very much "the people of the Book," and the foremost of their sacred writings is the Bible, consisting of the Five Books of Moses (the Torah), the books of the prophets, and other writings. Its heart is the Torah, the source of law. Over the centuries new experiences required the interpretation of the law to fit new circumstances, and this was accomplished by the oral law, no less sacred than the written law. Compilations of interpretation and commentary by wise and learned teachers were brought together to form the Talmud.

The destruction of their temple by the Romans in A.D. 70 hastened the scattering of the Jews throughout the empire. Thereafter almost all Jews lived in the Diaspora (dispersion), without a homeland, a political community, a national or religious center until the establishment of the Jewish state of Israel in 1948. However most Jews still live in other countries. A dominant experience for modern Judaism was the Holocaust, the culmination of centuries of persecution, when Hitler and the Nazis killed some six million Jews in a deliberate attempt to destroy the entire people in Europe. In spite of that the Jewish people and their religion live on in Israel and in many other countries.

The adherents of Judaism are divided into several groups who hold significantly different views about the place of tradition and the traditional law in the modern world. Perhaps all of them, however would give assent to the saying of Hillel, the great Talmudic teacher of the first century B.C.: "What is distasteful to you do not to your fellow man. This is the Law, all the rest is commentary. Now go and study."

I-1 The Ruins of Masada. *Masada was a fortress overlooking the Dead Sea in Israel. It was the last place the Jews held out in their rebellion against the imposition of Roman rule. The 1,000 Jewish zealots—men, women and children—held out for almost two years before the capture of the stronghold in 73* A.D. *[Erich Lessing/Magnum.]*

I-2 Israel's Bondage in Egypt. *The biblical story of The Israelites' slavery in Egypt, their liberation by Moses and the renewal of Israel's covenant with God is a critical part of the history of the Jews and their religion. This scene is painted on a wall of the tomb of Rechmire in Thebes about 1450 B.C. Rechmire was the Vizier, or minister, of the pharaohs Thutmose III and Amenophis II. It shows a construction gang of slaves directed by an overseer doing the kind of work the Israelites were compelled to perform. [Erich Lessing/Magnum.]*

I-3 Exile of the Israelites. *In 722 B.C. the northern part of Jewish Palestine, the Kingdom of Israel, was conquered by the Assyrians. Its people were driven from their homeland and exiled all over the vast Assyrian Empire. This wall carving in low relief comes from the palace of the Assyrian King Sanherib at Nineveh. It shows the exiled Jews with their cattle and baggage going into exile. [Erich Lessing/Magnum.]*

I-4 Reconstruction of the Temple of Jerusalem. *This is a model of a reconstruction of the Temple at Jerusalem. It was originally erected by King Solomon in the tenth century B.C. to be the religious center of the kingdom and the symbol of Jewish unity. It was finally destroyed by Titus, the son of the Roman Emperor Vespasian in 70 A.D. as part of the crushing of a Jewish rebellion. [Art Resource.]*

I-5 The Prophet Ezekiel. *This wall painting from a Jewish synagogue in the ancient Syrian city of Dura-Europus depicts the prophet Ezekiel's vision of the valley of the dry bones. Ezekiel's prophecies of the resurrection of Israel and the restoration of the Temple encouraged the Jews during their Babylonian captivity. [Princeton University Press.]*

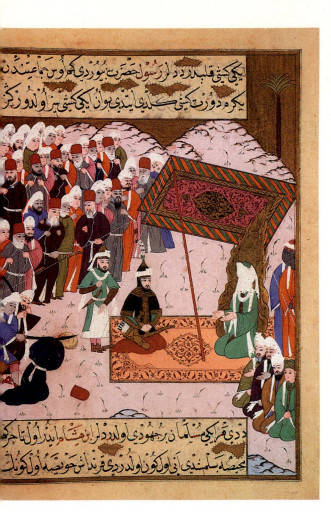

I-6 The Jews Under Islam. *This painting from an Ottoman Turkish manuscript of the late sixteenth century shows the founder of Islam, the Prophet Muhammad, ordering the execution of Jews refusing to embrace Islam. Later in the history of Islam the Jews were tolerated as a "people of the book" [the Bible]. [Chester Beatty Library, Dublin, Ireland.]*

I-7 Jews in Medieval France. *This French miniature painting from the mid-thirteenth century shows a debate between Jews and Christians, probably before the French King Saint Louis who presided over a similar debate. [Biblioteque National, Paris.]*

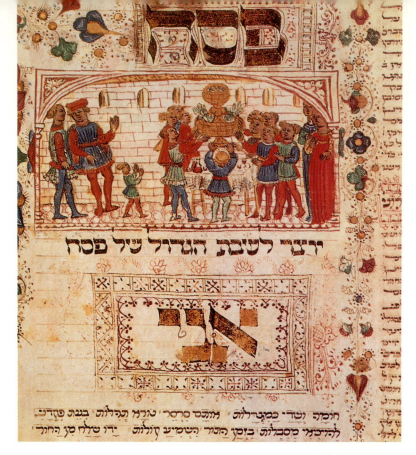

I-8 Passover in Renaissance Italy. *The Jews were scattered all over Europe by the end of the middle ages. This illumination from a Hebrew manuscript in Italy in 1466 shows a part of the Passover ceremony celebrating the escape from Egyptian bondage. [Reproduced by courtesy of the board of British Library.]*

I-9 Jews in Fifteenth Century Germany. *This illumination from a Hebrew manuscript in the State and University Library of Hamburg shows the houses of the Jewish quarter of the city. They are crowded together in the lower part of the town near the defensive walls. [Staats and Universitätsbibliothek, Hamburg.]*

C-6

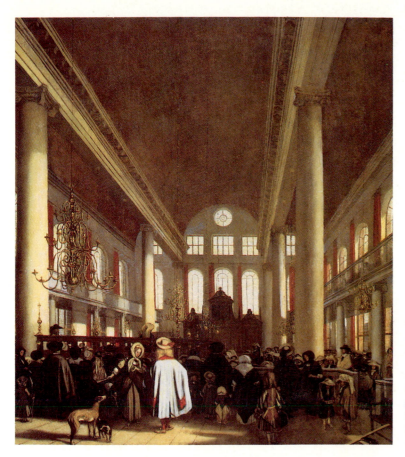

I-10 The Portuguese Synagogue in Amsterdam. *After the expulsion of the Jews from Spain and Portugal in the fifteenth century, they sought sanctuary in many countries. The Dutch Republic, extraordinarily tolerant of different religions, provided a welcome haven for many. This painting by Emanuel de Witte, done about 1680, shows the impressive interior of the Portuguese Synagogue in Amsterdam. [Rijksmuseum, Amsterdam.]*

I-11 Napoleon and the Jews. *The Enlightenment and the French Revolution brought emancipation from many of the old laws discriminating against Jews. Napoleon carried the ideas of these movements to the territories he conquered. This bit of Napoleonic propaganda shows the emperor holding out his hand to the Jews, as represented by the Jewish woman at his feet while rabbis express their thanks. He holds the new laws governing the Jews under French rule, and his arm rests on the Ten Commandments. [Bibliotheque National, Paris.]*

I-12   Russian Persecution of the Jews. *This painting,* After the Pogrom, *done by the Polish painter Maurycy Minkowski in 1910, shows a group of Jews in the aftermath of a pogrom, an organized persecution of Jews that often became a massacre. Such activities were frequently encouraged by the Russian government and were especially frightful in the late nineteenth and early twentieth centuries. [Jewish Museum/ Art Resource.]*

I-13   Nazi Anti-Jewish Propaganda. *Hitler's Nazi movement in Germany had a virulent, racist, doctrine of hostility towards the Jews as a fundamental doctrine. This propaganda poster printed during the Second World War shows the emblems of Great Britain, the United States, and the Soviet Union, the allied coalition fighting Germany and its allies. Behind them is a crude caricature of a Jew; the legend on the poster reads: "Behind the enemy the Jew." Hitler's hatred of the Jews lead to the Holocaust in which some six million Jews were murdered. [Bildarchiv Preussischer Kulturbesitz.]*

469–399 B.C.	Socrates
429–347 B.C.	Plato
384–322 B.C.	Aristotle

The starting point for all three of the philosophical giants of Hellenic political and moral philosophy was the social and political reality of the Greek city-state, or *polis*. The greatest crisis for the *polis* was the Great Peloponnesian War (435–404 B.C.), which is discussed in Chapter 4. Probably the most complicated response to this crisis may be found in the life and teachings of Socrates (469–399 B.C.). Because he wrote nothing, our knowledge of him comes chiefly from his disciples Plato and Xenophon and from later tradition. Although as a young man he was interested in speculations about the physical world, Socrates later turned to the investigation of ethics and morality. As Cicero put it, he brought philosophy down from the heavens.

Socrates was committed to the search for truth and for the knowledge about human affairs that he believed could be discovered by reason. His method was to go among men, particularly those reputed to know something, like craftsmen, poets, and politicians, to question and cross-examine them. The result was always the same: Those he questioned might have technical information and skills but seldom had any knowledge of the fundamental principles of human behavior. It is understandable that Athenians so exposed should be angry with their examiner, and it is not surprising that they thought Socrates was undermining the beliefs and values of the *polis*. Socrates' unconcealed contempt for democracy, which seemingly relied on ignorant amateurs to make important political decisions without any certain knowledge, created further hostility. Moreover, his insistence on the primacy of his own individualism and his determination to pursue philosophy even against the wishes of his fellow citizens reinforced this hostility and the prejudice that went with it.

But Socrates, unlike the Sophists, did not accept pay for his teaching; he professed ignorance and denied that he taught at all. His individualism, moreover, was unlike the worldly hedonism of some of the Sophists. It was not wealth or pleasure or power that he urged people to seek, but "the greatest improvement of the soul." He differed also from the more radical Sophists in that he denied that the *polis* and its laws were merely conventional. He thought, on the contrary, that they had a legitimate claim on the citizen, and he proved it in the most convincing fashion. In 399 B.C., he was condemned to death by an Athenian jury on the charges of bringing new gods into the city and of corrupting the youth. His dialectical inquir-

Socrates (469–399 B.C.) *changed the main focus of Greek philosophy from speculations about the physical world to the investigation of ethics and morality.* [*New York Public Library.*]

ies had angered many important people, and his criticism of democracy must have been viewed with suspicion. He was given a chance to escape, but in Plato's *Crito* we are told of his refusal because of his veneration of the laws.

Socrates' career set the stage for later responses to the travail of the *polis*; he recognized its difficulties and criticized its shortcomings. Although he turned away from an active political life, he did not abandon the idea of the *polis*. He fought as a soldier in its defense, obeyed its laws, and sought to put its values on a sound foundation by reason.

THE CYNICS. One branch of Socratic thought—the concern with personal morality and one's own soul, the disdain of worldly pleasure and wealth, and the withdrawal from political life—was developed and then distorted almost beyond recognition by the Cynic school. Antisthenes (CA. 455–CA. 360 B.C.), a follower of Socrates, is said to have been its founder, but its most famous exemplar was Diogenes of Sinope (CA. 400–CA. 325 B.C.). Socrates disparaged wealth and worldly comfort, so Diogenes wore rags and lived in a tub. He performed shameful acts in public and made his living by begging, in order to show his rejection of convention. He believed that happiness lay in satisfy-

Plato Reports the Claims of the Sophist Protagoras

Plato (CA. 429–347 B.C.) *remains to many the greatest of the ancient philosophers. Protagoras, the famous Sophist from Leontini in Sicily, came to Athens in 427 B.C. and created great excitement. In the following passage from the dialogue* Protagoras, *Plato's spokesman, Socrates, introduces a young man who wishes to benefit from Protagoras' skills.*

When we were all seated, Protagoras said: Now that the company are assembled, Socrates, tell me about the young man of whom you were just now speaking.

I replied: I will begin again at the same point, Protagoras, and tell you once more the purport of my visit: this is my friend Hippocrates, who is desirous of making your acquaintance; he would like to know what will happen to him if he associates with you. I have no more to say.

Protagoras answered: Young man, if you associate with me, on the very first day you will return home a better man than you came and better on the second day than on the first, and better every day than you were on the day before.

When I heard this, I said: Protagoras, I do not at all wonder at hearing you say this; even at your age, and with all your wisdom, if any one were to teach you what you did not know before, you would become better no doubt: but please to answer in a different way— I will explain how by an example. Let me suppose that Hippocrates, instead of desiring your acquaintance, wished to become acquainted with the young man Zeuxippus of Heraclea, who has lately been in Athens, and he had come to him as he has come to you, and had heard him say, as he heard you say, that every day he would grow and become better if he associated with him: and then suppose that he were to ask him, "In what shall I become better, and in what shall I grow?"— Zeuxippus would answer, "In painting." And suppose that he went to Orthagoas the Theban, and heard him say the same thing, and asked him, "In what shall I become better day by day?" he would reply, "In flute-playing." Now I want you to make the same sort of answer to this young man and to me, who am asking questions on his account. When you say that on the first day on which he associates with you he will return home a better man, and on every day will grow in like manner,—in what, Protagoras, will he be better? and about what?

When Protagoras heard me say this, he replied: You ask questions fairly, and I like to answer a question which is fairly put. If Hippocrates comes to me he will not experience the sort of drudgery with which other Sophists are in the habit of insulting their pupils; who, when they have just escaped from the arts, are taken and driven back into them by these teachers, and made to learn calculation, and astronomy, and geometry, and music (he gave a look at Hippias as he said this); but if he comes to me, he will learn that which he comes to learn. And this is prudence in affairs private as well as public; he will learn to order his own house in the best manner, and he will be able to speak and act for the best in the affairs of the state. ❑

Plato, *Protagoras*, trans. by Benjamin Jowett in *The Dialogues of Plato*, Vol. 1 (New York: Random House, 1937), pp. 88–89.

ing natural needs in the simplest and most direct way. Because actions to this end, being natural, could not be indecent, they could and should be done publicly.

Socrates questioned the theoretical basis for popular religious beliefs; the Cynics ridiculed all religious observances. As Plato said, Diogenes was Socrates gone mad. Beyond that, the way of the Cynics contradicted important Socratic beliefs. Socrates, unlike traditional aristocrats like Theognis, believed that virtue was not a matter of birth but of knowledge and that people do wrong only through ignorance of what is virtuous. The Cynics, on the contrary, believed that virtue is an affair of deeds and does not need a store of words and learning. Wisdom and happiness come from pursuing the proper style of life, not from philosophy. The Cynics moved even further from Socrates by abandoning the concept of the *polis* entirely. When Diogenes was asked about his citizenship, he answered that he was *kosmopolites*, a citizen of the world. The Cynics plainly had turned away from the past, and their views anticipated those of the Hellenistic Age.

PLATO. Plato (429–347 B.C.) was by far the most important of Socrates' associates and is a perfect example of the pupil who becomes greater than his master. He was the first systematic philosopher and therefore the first to place political ideas in their full philosophical context. He was also a writer of genius, leaving us twenty-six philosophical discussions. Almost all are in the form of dialogues, which somehow make the examination of difficult and complicated philosophical problems seem dramatic and entertaining.

Born of a noble Athenian family, Plato looked forward to an active political career until he was discouraged by the excesses of the Thirty Tyrants and the execution of Socrates by the restored democracy. Twice he made trips to Sicily in the hope of producing a model state at Syracuse under the tyrants Dionysius I and II, but without success. In 386 B.C., Plato founded the Academy, a center of philosophical investigation and a school for training statesmen and citizens that had a powerful impact on Greek thought and lasted until it was closed by the Emperor Justinian in the sixth century A.D.

Like Socrates, Plato firmly believed in the *polis* and its values. Its virtues were order, harmony, and justice, and one of its main objects was to produce good people. Like his master, and unlike the radical Sophists, Plato thought that the *polis* was in accord with nature. He accepted Socrates' doctrine of the identity of virtue and knowledge and made it plain what that knowledge was: *episteme*, science, a body of true and unchanging wisdom open to only a few philosophers, whose training, character, and intellect allowed them to see reality. Only such people were qualified to rule; they themselves would prefer the life of pure contemplation but would accept their responsibility and take their turn as philosopher kings. The training of such men required a specialization of function and a subordination of the individual to the community. This specialization would lead to Plato's definition of justice: that each man should do only that one thing to which his nature is best suited.

Plato saw quite well that the *polis* of his day suffered from terrible internal stress, class struggle, and factional divisions. His solution, however, was not that of some Greeks, that is, conquest and resulting economic prosperity. For Plato, the answer was in moral and political reform. The way to harmony was to destroy the causes of strife: private property, the family—anything, in short, that stood between the individual citizen and devotion to the *polis*.

The concern for the redemption of the *polis* was at the heart of Plato's system of philosophy. He began by asking the traditional questions: What is a good man, and how is he made? The goodness of a human being was a theme that belonged to moral philosophy, and when it became a function of the state, the question became part of political philosophy. Because goodness depended on knowledge of the good, it required a theory of knowledge and an investigation of what the knowledge was that was required for goodness. The answer must be metaphysical and so required a full examination of metaphysics. Even when the philosopher knew the good, however, the question remained of how the state could bring its citizens to the necessary comprehension of that knowledge. The answer required a theory of education. Even purely logical and metaphysical questions, therefore, were subordinate to the overriding political questions. In this way, Plato's need to find a satisfactory foundation for the beleaguered *polis* contributed to the birth of systematic philosophy.

ARISTOTLE. Aristotle (384–322 B.C.) was a pupil of Plato's who owed much to the thought of his master, but his very different experience and cast of mind led him in some new directions. He was born in northern Greece, the son of the court doctor of neighboring Macedon. As a young man, he came to study at the Academy, where he stayed until Plato's death. Then he joined a Platonic colony at Assos in Asia Minor, and from there, he moved to Mytilene. In both places, he carried on research in marine biology, and biological interests played a large part in all his thoughts. In 342 B.C., Philip, the king of Macedon, appointed him tutor to his son, the young Alexander (see Chapter 4). In 336, he returned to Athens, where he founded his own school, the Lyceum, or the Peripatos, as it was also called based on the covered walk within it. In later years, its members were called *Peripatetics*. On the death of Alexander in 323 B.C., the Athenians rebelled from Macedonian rule, and Aristotle found it wise to leave. He died at Chalcis in Euboea in the following year.

The Lyceum was a very different place from the Academy. Its members took little interest in mathematics and were concerned with gathering, ordering, and analyzing all human knowledge. Aristotle wrote dialogues on the Platonic model, but none survived. He and his students also prepared many collections of information to serve as the basis for scientific works, but of these only the *Constitution of the Athenians*, one of 158 constitutional treatises, remains. Almost all of what we posses is in the form of philosophical and scientific studies, whose loose organization and style suggest that they were lecture notes. The range of subjects treated is astonishing, including logic, physics, astronomy, biology, ethics, rhetoric, literary criticism, and politics.

In each field, the method is the same. Aristotle began with observation of the empirical evidence, which in some cases was physical and in others was common opinion. To this body of information he applied reason and discovered inconsistencies or difficulties. To deal with these, he introduced metaphysical principles to explain the problems or to reconcile the inconsistencies. His view on all subjects, like Plato's, was teleological; that is, both Plato and Aristotle recognized purposes apart from and greater than the will of the individual human being. Plato's purposes, however, were contained in the Ideas, or Forms—transcendental concepts outside the experience of most people. For Aristotle, the purposes of most things were easily inferred by observation of their behavior in the world. Aristotle's most striking characteristics are his moderation and common sense. His epistemology finds room for both reason and experience; his metaphysics gives meaning and reality to both mind and body; his ethics aims at the good life, which is the contemplative life, but recognizes the necessity for moderate wealth, comfort, and pleasure.

All these qualities are evident in Aristotle's political thought. Like Plato, he opposed the Sophists' assertion that the *polis* was contrary to nature and the result of mere convention. His response was to apply the teleology that he saw in all nature to politics as well. In his view, matter existed to achieve an end, and it developed until it achieved its form, which was its end. There was constant development from matter to form, from potential to actual. Therefore, human primitive instincts could be seen as the matter out of which the human's potential as a political being could be realized. The *polis* made individuals self-sufficient and allowed the full realization of their potentiality. It was therefore natural. It was also the highest point in the evolution of the social institutions that serve the human need to continue the species: marriage, household, village, and finally, *polis*. For Aristotle, the purpose of the *polis* was neither economic nor military but moral: "The end of the state is the good life" (*Politics* 1280b), the life lived "for the sake of noble actions" (1281a), a life of virtue and morality.

Characteristically, Aristotle was less interested in the best state—the utopia that required philosophers to rule it—than in the best state practically possible, one that would combine justice with stability. The constitution for that state he called *politeia*, not the best constitution, but the next best, the one most suited to and most possible for most states. Its quality was moderation, and it naturally gave power to neither the rich nor the poor but to the middle class, which must also be the most numerous. The middle class possessed many virtues: Because of its moderate wealth, it was free of the arrogance of the rich and the malice of the poor. For this reason, it was the most stable class. The stability of the constitution also came from it being a mixed constitution, blending in some way the laws of democracy and of oligarchy. Aristotle's scheme was unique because of its realism and the breadth of its vision.

All the political thinkers of the fourth century B.C. recognized that the *polis* was in danger, and all hoped to save it. All recognized the economic and social troubles that threatened it. Isocrates, a contemporary of Plato and Aristotle, urged a program of imperial conquest as a cure for poverty and revolution. Plato saw the folly of solving a political and moral problem by purely economic means and resorted to the creation of utopias. Aristotle combined the practical analysis of political and economic realities with the moral and political purposes of the traditional defenders of the *polis*. The result was a passionate confidence in the virtues of moderation and of the middle class and the proposal of a constitution that would give it power. It is ironic that the ablest defense of the *polis* came soon before its demise.

The concern with an understanding of nature in a purely rational, scientific way remained strong through the fifth century B.C., culminating in the work of the formulators of the atomic theory, Democritus and Leucippus, and in that of the medical school founded by Hippocrates of Cos. In the mid-fifth century, however, men like the Sophists and Socrates turned their attention to humankind and to ethical, political, and religious questions. This latter tradition of inquiry led, by way of Plato, Aristotle (in his metaphysical thought), and the Stoics, to Christianity and had, as well, a substantial impact on Judaic and Islamic thought. The former tradition of thought, following a line from the natural philosophers, the Sophists, Aristotle (in his scientific thought), and the Epicureans, had to wait until the Renaissance in Western Europe to exert an influence. Since the eighteenth century, this line of Greek thought has been the more influential force in Western civilization. It may not be too much to say that since the Enlightenment of that century, the Western world has been engaged in a debate between the two strands of the Greek intellectual tradition. As Western influence has spread over the world in recent times, that debate has become of universal importance, for other societies have not seen cause to separate the religious and philosophical from the scientific and physical realms as radically as has the modern West.

Suggested Readings

CHINA

W. T. deBary et al., *Sources of Chinese Tradition* (1960). A reader in China's philosophical and historical literature. It should be consulted for the later periods as well as for the Chou.

H. G. Creel, *What is Taoism? And Other Studies in Chinese Cultural History* (1970).

Y. L. Fung (D. Bodde, ed.), *A Short History of Chinese Philosophy* (1948). A survey of Chinese philosophy from its origins down to recent times.

D. C. Lau (trans.), *Lao Tzu, Tao Te Ching* (1963).

D. C. Lau (trans.), *Confucius, The Analects* (1979).

F. W. Mote, *Intellectual Foundations of China* (1971).

B. I. Schwartz, *The World of Thought in Ancient China* (1985).

A. Waley, *Three Ways of Thought in Ancient China* (1956). An easy yet sound introduction to Confucianism, Taoism, and Legalism.

B. Watson (trans.), *Basic Writings of Mo Tzu, Hsun Tzu, and Han Fei Tzu* (1963).

B. Watson (trans.), *The Complete Works of Chuang Tzu* (1968).

H. Welch, *Taoism, The Parting of the Way* (1967).

INDIA

W. T. deBary et al., *Sources of Indian Tradition* (1958). 2 vols. Vol. I: *From the Beginning to* 1800, ed. and rev. Ainslie T. Embree. (New York, 1988). Excellent selections from a wide variety of Indian texts, with good introductions to chapters and individual selections.

A. L. Basham, ed. *A Cultural History of India* (Delhi, Oxford, etc., 1975). A fine collection of historical-survey essays by a variety of scholars. Relevant here is Part I, "The Ancient Heritage" (Chapters 2–16).

A. L. Basham. *The Wonder That Was India*, rev. ed. (New York, 1963). Chapter VII, "Religion," is a superb introduction to the Vedic-Aryan, Brahmanic, Hindu, Jain, and Buddhist traditions of thought.

W. N. Brown. *Man in the Universe: Some Continuities in Indian Thought* (Berkeley, 1970). A superb and brief reflective summary of major patterns in Indian thinking.

T. J. Hopkins, *The Hindu Religious Tradition* (Belmont, CA, 1971). A first-rate, thoughtful introduction to Hindu religious ideas and practice.

W. Rahula, *What the Buddha Taught*, 2nd ed. (New York, 1974). A clear, concise, and readable introduction to Buddhist thought from a traditionalist Theravadin viewpoint, with primary-source selections.

R. H. Robinson and W. L. Johnson, *The Buddhist Religion: A Historical Introduction*, 3rd ed. (Belmont, CA, 1982). An excellent first text on the Buddhist tradition, its thought, development, and diffusion.

R. C. Zaehner, *Hinduism* (New York, 1966). One of the best general introductions to central Indian religious and philosophical ideas.

ISRAEL

J. Bright. *A History of Isreal* (1968). 2nd ed. (Philadelphia, 1972). One of the standard scholarly introductions to biblical history and literature.

W. D. Davies and L. Finkelstein, eds., *The Cambridge History of Judaism: Vol. I: Introduction; The Persian Period* (Cambridge, 1984). Excellent essays on diverse aspects of the exilic period and later.

J. Neusner, *The Way of Torah: An Introduction to Judaism* (North Scituate, MA, 1979). A sensitive introduction to the Judaic tradition and faith.

L. W. Schwarz, ed., *Great Ages and Ideas of the Jewish People* (New York, 1956). Especially interesting is the first section, "The Biblical Age," by Yehezkel Kaufmann.

GREECE

J. Burnet, *Early Greek Philosophy* (1963). Stresses the rational aspect of Greek thought and its sharp break with mythology.

F. M. Cornford, *From Religion to Philosophy* (1912). Emphasizes the elements of continuity between myth and religion on the one hand and Greek philosophy on the other.

B. Farrington, *Greek Science* (1953). A lively interpretation of the origins and character of Greek scientific thought.

G. B. Kerferd, *The Sophistic Movement* (Cambridge, 1981). An excellent description and analysis.

J. Lear, *Aristotle: the Desire to Understand* (Cambridge, 1988). A brilliant yet comprehensible introduction to the work of the philosopher.

J. M. Robinson, *An Introduction to Early Greek Philosophy* (1968). A valuable collection of the main fragments of, and ancient testimony to the works of, the early philosophers, with excellent commentary.

G. Vlastos, *The Philosophy of Socrates* (New York, 1971). A splendid collection of essays illuminating the problems presented by this remarkable man.

G. Vlastos, *Platonic Studies*, 2nd ed. (Princeton, 1981). A similar collection on the philosophy of Plato.

Empires and Cultures of The Ancient World

THE LAST five hundred years before the beginning of the Christian era and the two centuries that followed saw the appearance of great empires in Iran, India, and China, and of the Roman Empire in the West. Though each arose in response to local conditions, they had common features. Each replaced a confusion of local sovereign units, whether aristocratic family domains, smaller territorial states, tribal confederacies, or city-states, with vast centralized monarchies. Each had the large, efficient armies needed to conquer and control new lands. They all created well-organized bureaucracies to regulate their widespread empires and built extensive roads to ease communication and transportation. They all systematically imposed and collected taxes to pay for the armies and bureaucracies, for the construction of roads and defenses, and for the splendor of their imperial courts and palaces.

The military, political, and economic unification of vast territories produced considerable periods of relative peace and prosperity. There is evidence of communication and trade even between the Romans and the distant eastern empires of India and China. Imperial unification also had cultural consequences. The imposition of a single rule over different peoples in a far-flung empire encouraged the use of a common tongue, at least as a second language, which assisted the formation of a common culture. The Greeks, the Romans, the Hindus, and the Chinese produced great works in a variety of literary genres, such as epic poetry, history, and philosophy, which set a stamp on their own societies and served as the basis for later cultural developments. In all four areas, the wealth and patronage of the monarchs, the general prosperity of their empires, and the desire for splendor gave great impetus to such arts as painting, sculpture, and architecture.

The rise of these empires also brought important developments in religion. The Iranian conquests under the Achaemenid dynasty spread the religion of Zarathushtra (Zoroaster) throughout the Persian Empire, and the quasi-monotheistic faith had a powerful and broad influence before the tide of Islam swept over it in the seventh century A.D. In India in the third century B.C., under the Mauryan king Ashoka, Buddhism took on a missionary character and spread across Asia to the east and west. In the first century B.C., it came to China, where it competed not only with traditional Confucianism but also with a new form of Taoism that had taken on a more mysterious and otherworldly character during the Later Han period. In Greece, as the city-states gave way to the great empires of Philip and Alexander of Macedon and their Hellenistic successors, a largely amoral paganism gave way to such quasi-religious philosophies as Stoicism. In the Roman Empire that succeeded the

Hellenistic kingdoms, Christianity ultimately overcame all competitors to become the official religion by the end of the fourth century A.D. These religious movements stressed morality, and most of them were more otherworldly than their predecessors, placing greater emphasis on escape from the pain and troubles of this world and the search for personal immortality.

Such developments seem to have had some connection with the loss of prosperity, the increase of warfare, both internal and external, and the collapse of stability. None of the great empires could avoid a cycle of growth and decline. There was never enough wealth to sustain the cost of empire beyond a limited period of time. Taxes rose beyond the citizens' capacity to pay, and bureaucracies became bloated and ineffective. More and more depended on the central government, but talented leadership was not always available. The attractions of civilization drew the envy of vigorous barbarians outside the empires, even as internal problems and diminished willingness to fight reduced the capacity of the empires to resist. The Achaemenids fell victim to Alexander the Great, but the rule of his Hellenistic successors was brief. The Parthians, who succeeded to the old Persian Empire, were never able to impose the same imperial and cultural unity. In India, the Mauryan Empire did not long survive the death of its gentle king Ashoka, giving way to local uprisings and barbarian assaults from central Asia. Both China and Rome, weakened by internal struggles, gave way to barbarian assaults and saw the collapse of central authority. In both cases, the conquering tribes were themselves conquered by the religions of their victims, Buddhism in China and Christianity in Rome. In India, China, and Rome, moreover, the cultural achievements of the great empires would later serve as the basis for new advances in civilization. ❑

EUROPE	NEAR EAST/INDIA

3000 B.C.

ca. 2500–1100 Minoan Civilization on Crete
ca. 1600–1100 Mycenaean Civilization on Greek mainland

ca. 3000 Emergence of cililization along the Nile River
ca. 2300 Emergence of Harappan Civilization in Indus Valley
2276–2221 Sargon of Akkad creates the first Mesopotamian Empire
ca. 2000 Epic of Gilgamesh
1750 Hammurabi's Code

1500 B.C.

ca. 1100–800 Greek "Dark Ages"
800 Etruscan civilization begins in Italy
ca. 750–550 Rise of the "polis"
594 Solon's legislation at Athens
509 Foundation of the Roman Republic
508 Democracy established in Athens

ca. 1500 Aryan peoples migrate into N.W. India
960–933 Rule of Hebrew King Solomon
ca. 628–551 Traditional dates of Zarathustra
ca. 537–486 Siddhartha Gautama
559–529 Cyrus the Great creates the Persian Empire

500 B.C.

480–479 Persian invasion of Greece
478 Foundation of Delian League/Athenian Empire
431–404 Peloponnesian Wars
338 Battle of Chaeronia; Macedonian conquest of Greece
336–323 Career of Alexander the Great

ca. 540–468 Vardhamana Mahavira, founder of Jain tradition
334 Alexander begins conquest of the Near East; invades India in 327
321–181 Mauryan Empire in India
ca. 300 Foundation of Seleucid dynasty in Anatolia, Syria, and Mesopotamia; Ptolemaic dynasty in Egypt

300 B.C.

265 Rome rules all of Italy
146 Rome destroys Carthage; rules all of Western Mediterranean
44–31 Civil Wars destroy Republic
31 Rome rules Mediterranean
31 B.C.–A.D. 14 Principate of Augustus

269–232 Mauryan Emperor, Ashoka, patronizes Buddhism
247 B.C.–A.D. 224 Parthian dynasty controls Persia
180 B.C.–A.D. 320 India politically divided

A.D. 1

91–180 The Good Emperors rule Rome
180–284 Breakdown of the Pax Romana
306–337 Constantine reigned
313 Edict of Milan
325 Council of Nicaea
380 Theodosius makes Christianity the official imperial religion
ca. 400–500 The Germanic Invasions
426 The City of God, by Augustine
476 The last Western Emperor is deposed

30 Crucifixion of Jesus
70 Romans destroy the Temple at Jerusalem
ca. 224 Fall of Parthians, rise of Sasanids in Persia
ca. 320–500 Gupta Dynasty in India
ca. 400 Chandra Gupta (r. 375–415) conquers western India; increases trade with Near East and China
ca. 450 The Huns invade India

EAST ASIA	AFRICA	THE AMERICAS
ca. 3000 Neolithic cultures in China ca. 3000 Jōmon Neolithic cultures in Japan 1766 Bronze Age city-states and writing in China ca. 1600–1050 Shang Civilization in China	ca. 3000 Practice of agriculture spreads from Nile River Valley to the Sudan ca. 2000 Ivory and gold trade between Kush (Nubia) and Egypt ca. 1500 Practice of agriculture spreads from the Sudan to Abyssinia and the savannah region.	ca. 3000 Maize already domesticated in the Mexican peninsula
1027–771 Western Zhou Dynasty, China ca. 771 Iron Age territorial states in China 771–256 Chou dynasty in China ca. 551–479 Confucius in China	750 Kushite King Kashta conquers Upper Egypt; founds 25th Egyptian dynasty ca. 720 Kushite king Piankhy completes conquest of Egypt and reigns as king of Kush and Egypt ca. 600 Meroitic period of Kushan Civilization begins	ca. 1500 B.C.–A.D. 300 Olmec Civilization on Gulf Coast of Mexico ca. 1000 Practice of agriculture and village communities in American Southwest; enclosed ceremonial centers in eastern North America
ca. 500–200 Rise of Mohist, Taoist and Legalist schools of thought in China 403–321 Period of the Warring States in China ca. 300 Jōmon Neolithic Culture in Japan replaced by Yayoi Culture		
221 Ch'in Emperor unites all of China 207 End of Ch'in dynasty 206 B.C.–A.D. 8 Former Han Dynasty in China ca. 179–104 Han philosopher, Dong Zhong Shu ca. 145–90 Han historian, Sima Qian 141–187 Emperor Wu Ti of China reigned	25 Romans sack Kushite capital of Napata 100 B.C.–A.D. 1 Probable first Indonesia migrations to East African coast	ca. 300 Mexican sun temple Atetello at Teothuican ca. 164 Oldest Mayan monuments
9–25 Interregnum of Wang Mang in China 25–220 The Later Han Dynasty, China ca. 220–590 Spread of Buddhism in China 221–280 Three Kingdoms Era in China ca. 300–500 Barbarian invasions of China ca. 300–680 Archaic Yamato State in Japan	ca. 200 Camel first used for trans-Saharan transport ca. 200–900 Expansion of Bantu people ca. 250 Aksum (Ethiopia) controls the Red Sea Trade ca. 300–400 Rise of Kingdom of Ghana ca. 350 Kush ceases to exist	ca. 300 Disappearance of Olmec civilization ca. 300–1500 Mayan civilization, Central America ca. 300–900 Classic period of Teotihucacán civilization, Mexico

Olive harvest. This scene on an Attic jar from late in the sixth century B.C. shows how olives, one of Athen's most important crops, were harvested. [Reproduced by courtesy of the Trustees of the British Museum.]

3 The Rise of Greek Civilization

About 2000 B.C., Greek-speaking peoples settled the lands surrounding the Aegean Sea and established a style of life and formed a set of ideas, values, and institutions that spread far beyond the Aegean corner of the Mediterranean Sea. Preserved and adapted by the Romans, Greek culture powerfully influenced the society of Western Europe in the Middle Ages and dominated the Byzantine Empire in the same period. The civilization emerging from this experience spread across Europe and in time crossed the Atlantic to the Western Hemisphere.

At some time in their history, the Greeks of the ancient world founded cities on every shore of the Mediterranean Sea, and pushing on through the Dardanelles, they placed many settlements on the coasts of the Black Sea in southern Russia and as far east as the approaches to the Caucasus Mountains. The center of Greek life, however, has always been the Aegean Sea and the lands in and around it. This location at the eastern end of the Mediterranean very early put the Greeks in touch with the more advanced and earlier civilizations of the Near East: Egypt, Asia Minor, Syria–Palestine, and the rich culture of Mesopotamia. A character in one of Plato's dialogues says, "Whatever the Greeks have acquired from foreigners they have, in the end, turned into something finer."[1] This proud statement indicates at least that the Greeks were aware of how much they had learned from other civilizations.

The Bronze Age on Crete and on the Mainland to CA. 1150 B.C.

One source of Greek civilization was the culture of the large island of Crete in the Mediterranean. With

[1] *Epinomis*, 987 d.

Greece to the north, Egypt to the south, and Asia to the east, Crete was a cultural bridge between the older civilizations and the new one of the Greeks.

The Minoans

The Bronze Age came to Crete not long after 3000 B.C. In the third and second millenia B.C., a civilization arose that powerfully influenced the islands of the Aegean and the mainland of Greece. This civilization has been given the name *Minoan*, after Minos, the legendary king of Crete.

On the basis of pottery styles and the excavated levels where the pottery and other artifacts are found, scholars have divided the Bronze Age on Crete into three major divisions with some subdivisions. Dates for Bronze Age settlements on the Greek mainland, for which the term *Helladic* is used, are derived from the same chronological scheme.

During the Middle and Late Minoan periods in the cities of eastern and central Crete, a civilization developed that was new and unique in its character and its beauty. Its most striking feature is presented by the palaces uncovered at such sites as Phaestus, Haghia Triada, and, most important, Cnossus. The palace design and the paintings show the influence of Syria, Asia Minor, and Egypt, but the style and quality are unique to Crete.

Along with palaces, paintings, pottery, jewelry, and other valuable objects, writing of three distinct kinds was found and one of these proved to be an early form of Greek. The script was written on clay tablets like those found in Mesopotamia. They were preserved accidentally, being hardened in a great fire that destroyed the palace. They reveal an organization centered on the palace, in which the king ruled and was served by an extensive bureaucracy, which kept remarkably detailed records. This sort of organization is typical of what we find in the Near East but nothing like what we will see among the Greeks, yet the inventories were written in a form of Greek. Why should Minoans, who were not Greek, write in a language not their own? This question raises the larger one of what the relationship was between Crete and the Greek mainland in the Bronze Age. It leads us to an examination of mainland, or Helladic, culture.

The Mycenaeans

In the third millennium B.C., most of the Greek mainland, including many of the sites of later Greek cities, was settled by people who used metal, built some impressive houses, and traded with Crete and the islands of the Aegean. The names they gave to places—names that were sometimes preserved by later invaders—make it clear that they were not Greeks and that they spoke a language that was not Indo-European.

Not long after the year 2000 B.C., many of the Early Helladic sites were destroyed by fire, some were abandoned, and still others appear to have yielded peacefully to an invading people. This invasion probably signaled the arrival of the Greeks.

The invaders succeeded in establishing control of the entire mainland, and the shaft graves cut into the rock at the royal palace-fortress of Mycenae show that they prospered and sometimes became very rich. At Mycenae and all over Greece, there was a smooth transition between the Middle and Late Helladic periods. At Mycenae, the richest finds come from the period after 1600 B.C. The city's wealth and power reached their peak during this time, and the culture of the whole mainland during the Late Helladic period goes by the name *Mycenaean*.

The excavation of Mycenaean sites reveals a culture influenced by, but very different from, the Minoan culture. Mycenae and Pylos, like Cnossus, were built some distance from the sea. It is plain, however, that defense against attack was foremost in the minds of the founders. Both cities were built on hills in a position commanding the neighboring territory. The Mycenaean people were warriors, as their art, architecture, and weapons reveal. The success of their campaigns and the defense of their territory required strong central authority, and all available evidence shows that the kings provided it. Their palaces, in which the royal family and its retainers lived, were located within the walls; most of the population lived outside the walls. The palace walls were usually covered with paintings, like those on Crete, but instead of peaceful scenery and games, the Mycenaean murals depicted scenes of war and boar hunting.

About 1500 B.C., the already impressive shaft graves were abandoned in favor of *tholos* tombs. These were large, beehivelike chambers cut into the hillside, built of enormous, well-cut, fitted stones, approached by an unroofed passage (*dromos*) cut horizontally into the side of the hill. The lintel block alone of one of these tombs weighs over a hundred tons. Only a strong king whose wealth was great, whose power was unquestioned, and who commanded the labor of many could undertake such a project. His wealth had to come from plundering raids, piracy, and trade. Some of this trade went westward to Italy and Sicily, but most of it was with the islands of the Aegean, the coastal towns of Asia Minor, and the cities of Syria, Egypt, and Crete. The Mycenaeans sent pottery, olive oil, and animal hides in exchange for jewels and other luxuries.

Tablets containing Mycenaean writing have been found all over the mainland; the largest and most useful collection was found at Pylos. The tablets reveal a world very similar to the one shown by the records at Cnossus. The king, whose title was *wanax*, held a

MAP 3-1 THE AEGEAN AREA IN THE BRONZE AGE *The Bronze Age in the Aegean area lasted from about 1900 to about 1100 B.C. Its culture on Crete is called Minoan and was at its height about 1900–1400 B.C. Bronze Age Helladic culture on the mainland flourished from about 1600 to 1200 B.C.*

royal domain, appointed officials, commanded servants, and kept a close record of what he owned and what was owed to him. This evidence confirms all the rest: the Mycenaean world was made up of a number of independent, powerful, and well-organized monarchies. These Greek invaders inhabited a flourishing Crete until the end of the Bronze Age, and there is good reason to believe that at the height of Mycenaean power (1400–1200 B.C.), Crete was part of the Mycenaean world.

These were prosperous and active years for the Mycenaeans. Their cities were enlarged, their trade grew, and they even established commercial colonies in the east. They are mentioned in the archives of the Hittite kings of Asia Minor. They are also named as marauders of the Nile Delta in the Egyptian records, and sometime about 1250 B.C. they probably sacked the city of Troy on the coast of northwestern Asia Minor, giving rise to the epic poems of Homer, the *Iliad* and the *Odyssey* (see Map 3.1). Around the year

1200 B.C., however, the Mycenaean world showed signs of great trouble, and by 1100 B.C., it was gone: its palaces were destroyed, many of its cities abandoned, and its art, its pattern of life, its system of writing buried and forgotten.

The Greeks themselves believed in a legend that told of the Dorians, a rude people from the north who spoke a different Greek dialect from that of the Mycenaean peoples. The Dorians joined with one of the Greek tribes, the Heraclidae, in an attack on the southern Greek peninsula of Peloponnesus, which was repulsed. One hundred years later they returned and gained full control. This legend of "the return of the Heraclidae" has been identified by modern historians with the Dorian invasion, the incursion from the north into Greece of a less civilized Greek people speaking the Dorian dialect.

The Greek "Middle Ages" to CA. 750 B.C.

The immediate effects of the Dorian invasion were disastrous for the inhabitants of the Mycenaean world. The palaces and the kings and bureaucrats who managed them were destroyed. The wealth and organization that had supported the artists and the merchants were likewise swept away by a barbarous people who did not have the knowledge or social organization to maintain them. Many villages were abandoned and never resettled. Some of their inhabitants probably turned to a nomadic life, and many perished.

Another result of the invasion was the spread of the Greek people eastward from the mainland to the Aegean islands and the coast of Asia Minor. The Dorians themselves, after occupying most of the Peloponnesus, swept across the Aegean to occupy the southern islands and the southern part of the Anatolian coast.

These migrations made the Aegean a Greek lake, but trade with the old civilizations of the Near East was virtually ended by the fall of the advanced Minoan and Mycenaean civilizations. Nor was there much trade between different parts of Greece. The Greeks were forced to turn inward, and each community was left largely to its own devices. This happened at a time when the Near East was also in disarray, and no great power arose to impose its ways and its will on the helpless people who lived about the Aegean. These circumstances allowed the Greeks time to recover from their disaster and to create their unique style of life.

The Age of Homer

For a picture of society in these "dark ages," the best source is Homer. His epic poems, the *Iliad* and the *Odyssey*, tell of the heroes who captured Troy, men of the Mycenaean age, but the world described in those poems clearly is a different one. Homer's heroes are not buried in *tholos* tombs but are cremated; they worship gods in temples, whereas the Mycenaeans had no temples; they have chariots but do not know their proper use in warfare. The poems of Homer are the result of an oral tradition that went back into the Mycenaean age. Through the centuries, bards sang tales of the heroes who fought at Troy, using verse arranged in rhythmic formulas to aid the memory. In this way, some very old material was preserved until the poems were finally written, no sooner than the eighth century B.C., but the society these old oral poems describe seems to be that of the tenth and ninth centuries B.C.

In the Homeric poems, the power of the kings is much smaller than that of the Mycenaean rulers. The ability of the kings to make important decisions was limited by the need to consult the council of nobles. The nobles felt free to discuss matters in vigorous language and in opposition to the king's wishes. In the *Iliad*, Achilles does not hesitate to address Agamemnon, the "most kingly" commander of the Trojan expedition, in these words: "thou with face of dog and heart of deer . . . folk devouring king." Such language may have been impolite, but it was not treasonous. The king, on the other hand, was free to ignore the council's advice, but it was risky to do so.

The right to speak in council was limited to noblemen (males only), but the common people could not be ignored. If a king planned a war or a major change of policy during a campaign, he would not fail to call the common soldiers to an assembly, where they could listen and express their feelings by acclamation, even though they could not take part in the debate. The evidence of Homer shows that even in these early times the Greeks, unlike their predecessors and contemporaries, practiced some forms of limited constitutional government.

Homeric society, nevertheless, was sharply divided into classes, the most important division being the one between nobles and commoners. We do not know the origin of the distinction, but we cannot doubt that at this time Greek society was aristocratic. Birth determined noble status, and wealth usually accompanied it. Below the nobles were the peasants, the landless laborers, and the slaves. We cannot tell whether the peasants owned the land they worked outright and so were free to sell it or if they worked a hereditary plot that belonged to their clan and was therefore not theirs to dispose of as they chose. It is clear, however, that the peasants worked hard to make a living.

Far worse was the condition of the hired agricultural laborer. The slave, at least, was attached to a family household and so was protected and fed. In a

Odysseus Addresses Nobles and Commoners: Homeric Society

The Iliad *was probably composed about 750* B.C. *In this passage, Odysseus is trying to stop the Greeks at Troy from fleeing to their ships and returning to their homes. The difference in his treatment of nobles and commoners is striking.*

Whenever he found one that was a captain and a man of mark, he stood by his side, and refrained him with gentle words: "Good sir, it is not seemly to affright thee like a coward, but do thou sit thyself and make all thy folk sit down. For thou knowest not yet clearly what is the purpose of Atreus' son; now is he but making trial, and soon he will afflict the sons of the Achaians. And heard we not all of us what he spake in the council? Beware lest in his anger he evilly entreat the sons of the Achaians. For proud is the soul of heaven-fostered kings; because their honour is of Zeus, and the god of counsel loveth them."

But whatever man of the people he saw and found him shouting, him he drave with his sceptre and chode him with loud words: "Good sir, sit still and hearken to the words of others that are thy betters; but thou art no warrior, and a weakling, never reckoned whether in battle or in council. In no wise can we Achaians all be kings here. A multitude of masters is no good thing; let there be one master, one king, to whom the son of crooked-counselling Kronos hath granted it . . ." ❑

Homer, *The Iliad*, trans. by A. Lang, W. Leaf, and E. Myers (New York: Random House, n.d.), pp. 24–25.

world where membership in a settled group gave the only security, the free laborers were desperately vulnerable. Slaves were few in number and were mostly women, who served as maids and concubines. Some male slaves worked as shepherds. Few, if any, worked in agriculture, which depended on free labor throughout Greek history.

The Homeric poems hold up a mirror to this society, and they reflect an aristocratic code of values that powerfully influenced all future Greek thought. In classical times, Homer was the schoolbook of the Greeks. They memorized his text, settled diplomatic disputes by citing passages in it, and emulated the behavior and

cherished the values they found in it. Those values were physical prowess, courage; fierce protection of one's family, friends, and property; and above all, one's personal honor and reputation. Returning home after his wanderings, Odysseus ruthlessly kills all the suitors of his wife because they have used up all his wealth, wooed his wife, scorned his son, and so dishonored him. Speed of foot, strength, and, most of all, excellence at fighting in battle are what make a man great, yet Achilles leaves the battle and allows his fellow Greeks to be slain and almost defeated because Agamemnon has wounded his honor by taking away his battle prize. He returns not out of a sense of duty to

Jumpers painted on a Greek cup. Athletics were an important part of Greek culture. The Gods were honored with contests, and physical training was essential for young males. Here, the jumpers are using weights to improve their performance.

the army but because his dear friend Patroclus has been killed. In each case, the hero seeks to display the highest virtue of Homeric society, *arētē*—manliness, courage in the most general sense, and the excellence proper to a hero.

This quality was best revealed in a contest, or *agon*. Homeric battles are not primarily group combats but a series of individual contests between great champions. One of the prime forms of entertainment is the athletic contest, and the funeral of Patroclus is celebrated by such a contest. The central ethical idea in Homer can be found in the instructions that the father of Achilles gives to his son when he sends him off to fight at Troy: "Always be the best and distinguished above others." The father of another Homeric hero has given his son exactly the same orders and has added to them the injunction "do not bring shame on the family of your fathers who were by far the best in Ephyre and in wide Lycia." Here in a nutshell we have the chief values of the aristocrats of Homer's world: to vie for individual supremacy in *arētē* and to defend and increase the honor of the family. They would remain prominent aristocratic values long after Homeric society was only a memory.

The *Polis*

The characteristic Greek institution was the *polis*. The attempt to translate that word as "city-state" is misleading, for it says both too much and too little. All Greek *poleis* began as little more than agricultural villages or towns, and many stayed that way, so the word *city* is inappropriate. All of them were states, in the sense of being independent political units, but they were much more than that. The *polis* was thought of as a community of relatives; all its citizens, who were theoretically descended from a common ancestor, belonged to subgroups, such as fighting brotherhoods (*phratries*), clans, and tribes. They worshiped the gods in common ceremonies.

Aristotle argued that the *polis* was a natural growth and that man (explicitly male; Greek women were not full participants in the life on the *polis*) was by his nature "an animal who lives in a *polis*." Man alone has the power of speech and from it derives the ability to distinguish good from bad and right from wrong, "and the sharing of these things is what makes a household and a *polis*." A man who is incapable of sharing these things or who is so self-sufficient that he has no need of them is not a man at all, but either a wild beast or a god. Without law and justice, man is the worst and most dangerous of the animals. With them he can be the best, and justice exists only in the *polis*. These high claims were made in the fourth century B.C., hundreds of years after the *polis* came into existence, but they accurately reflect an attitude that was present from the first.

Development of the Polis

Originally the word *polis* referred only to a citadel, an elevated, defensible rock to which the farmers of the neighboring area could retreat in case of attack. The Acropolis in Athens and the hill called Acrocorinth in Corinth are examples. For some time, such high places and the adjacent farms comprised the *polis*. The towns grew gradually and without planning, as the narrowness and the winding, disorderly character of their streets show. For centuries, they had no city walls. Unlike the city-states of the Near East, they were not placed for commercial convenience on rivers or the sea, nor did they grow up around a temple to serve the needs of priests and to benefit from the needs of worshipers. The availability of farmland and of a natural fortress determined their location. They were placed either well inland or far enough away from the sea to avoid piratical raids. Only later and gradually did the *agora* appear. It grew to be not only a marketplace but also a civic center and the heart of the Greeks' remarkable social life, which was distinguished by conversation and argument carried on in the open air.

Some *poleis* probably came into existence early in the eighth century B.C. The institution was certainly common by the middle of that century, for all the colonies that were established by the Greeks in the years after 750 B.C. took the form of the *polis*. Once the new institution had been fully established, true monarchy disappeared. Vestigial kings survived in some places, but they were almost always only ceremonial figures without power. The original form of the *polis* was an aristocratic republic dominated by the nobility through its council of nobles and its monopoly of the magistracies.

The Hoplite Phalanx

A new military technique was crucial to the development of the *polis*. In earlier times, the brunt of the fighting had been carried on by small troops of cavalry and individual "champions" who first threw their spears and then came to close quarters with swords. Toward the end of the eighth century B.C., however, the hoplite phalanx came into being. It remained the basis of Greek warfare thereafter.

The hoplite was a heavily armed infantryman who fought with a sword and a pike about nine feet long. These soldiers were formed into a phalanx in close order, usually at least eight ranks deep. So long as the hoplites fought bravely and held their ground, there would be few casualties and no defeat, but if they gave way, the result was usually a rout. All depended on the discipline, strength, and courage of the individual

The hoplite phalanx. This vase painting from the so-called "Chigi" vase is the earliest surviving picture of the new style of close-order, heavily armed infantry adopted by the Greeks toward the end of the eighth century B.C. Notice the large circular shields, helmets, greaves, body armor, raised spears, and the close order of the soldiers. The flute player provides music to help keep the soldiers in step. [Hirmer Fotoarchiv München.]

soldier. At its best, the phalanx could withstand cavalry charges and defeat infantries not as well protected or disciplined. Until defeated by the Roman legion, it was the dominant military force in the eastern Mediterranean.

The usual hoplite battle in Greece was between the armies of two *poleis* quarreling over a piece of land. One army invaded the territory of the other at a time when the crops were almost ready for harvest. The defending army had no choice but to protect its fields. If the army was beaten, its fields were captured or destroyed and its people might starve. In every way, the phalanx was a communal effort that relied not on the extraordinary actions of the individual but on the courage of a considerable portion of the citizens.

The phalanx and the *polis* arose together, and both heralded the decline of the kings. The phalanx, however, was not made up only of aristocrats. Most of the hoplites were farmers working relatively small holdings. The immediate beneficiaries of the royal decline were the aristocrats, but because the existence of the *polis* depended on the small farmers, their wishes could not for long be wholly ignored. The rise of the hoplite phalanx created a bond between the aristocrats and the peasants who fought in it, and this bond helps to explain why class conflicts were muted for some time. It also guaranteed, however, that the aristocrats, who dominated at first, would not always be unchallenged.

Expansion of the Greek World

From the middle of the eighth century B.C. until well into the sixth, the Greeks vastly expanded the territory they controlled, their wealth, and their contacts with other peoples in a burst of colonizing activity that placed *poleis* from Spain to the Black Sea. A century earlier, a few Greeks had established trading posts in Syria. There they had learned new techniques in the art and crafts and much more from the older civilizations of the Near East. About 750 B.C., they borrowed a writing system from one of the Semitic scripts and added vowels to create the first true alphabet. The new Greek alphabet was easier to learn than any earlier writing system and made possible the widely literate society of classical Greece.

The Greek Colony

Syria and its neighboring territory were too strong to penetrate, so the Greeks settled the southern coast of Macedonia and the Chalcidic peninsula (see Map 3.2). These regions were sparsely settled, and the natives were not well enough organized to resist the Greek colonists. Southern Italy and eastern Sicily were even more inviting areas. Before long, there were so many Greek colonies in Italy and Sicily that the Romans called the whole region *Magna Graecia* ("Great Greece"). The Greeks also put colonies in Spain and southern France. In the seventh century B.C., Greek colonists settled the coasts of the northeastern Mediterranean, the Black Sea, and the straits connecting them. About the same time, they established settlements on the eastern part of the northern African coast. The Greeks now had outposts throughout the Mediterranean world.

Only powerful pressures like overpopulation and land hunger drove thousands of Greeks from their homes to found new *poleis*. Most colonies, though independent, were friendly with their mother cities. Each might ask the other for aid in time of trouble and expect to receive a friendly hearing, although neither was obliged to help.

Colonization had a powerful influence of Greek life. By relieving the pressure of a growing population, it was a safety valve that allowed the *poleis* to escape civil wars. By emphasizing the differences between the Greeks and the new peoples they met, colonization gave the Greeks a sense of cultural identity and fostered a Panhellenic ("all-Greek") spirit that led to the establishment of a number of common religious festivals. The most important ones were at Olympia, Delphi, Corinth, and Nemea.

Colonization also encouraged trade and industry. The influx of new wealth from abroad and the increased demand for goods from the homeland stimulated a more intensive use of the land and an emphasis on crops for export, chiefly the olive and the wine grape. The manufacture of pottery, tools, weapons, and fine artistic metalwork as well as perfumed oil, the soap of the ancient Mediterranean world, was likewise encouraged. New opportunities allowed some men, sometimes outside the nobility, to become wealthy and important. These newly enriched men became a troublesome element in the aristocratic *poleis*, for they had an increasingly important part in the life of their states but were barred from political power, religious privileges, and social acceptance by the ruling aristocrats. These conditions soon created a crisis in many states.

The Tyrants (CA. 700–500 B.C.)

The crisis produced by the new economic and social conditions usually led to or intensified factional divisions within the ruling aristocracy. In the years between 700 and 550 B.C., the result was often the establishment of a tyranny.

The founding tyrant was usually a member of the ruling aristocracy who either had a personal grievance or led an unsuccessful faction. He often rose to power because of his military ability and support of the politically powerless group of the newly wealthy and of the poor peasants as well. When he took power, he often expelled many of his aristocratic opponents and divided at least some of their land among his supporters. He pleased his commercial and industrial supporters by destroying the privileges of the old aristocracy and by fostering trade and colonization.

The tyrants presided over a period of population growth that saw an increase especially in the number of city-dwellers. They responded with a program of public works that included improvement of the drainage systems, care for the water supply, the construction and organization of marketplaces, the building and strengthening of city walls, and the erection of temples. They introduced new local festivals and elaborated the old ones. They were active in the patronage of the arts, supporting poets and artisans with gratifying results. All this activity contributed to the tyrant's popularity, to the prosperity of his city, and to his self-esteem.

In most cases, the tyrant's rule was secured by a personal bodyguard and by mercenary soldiers. An

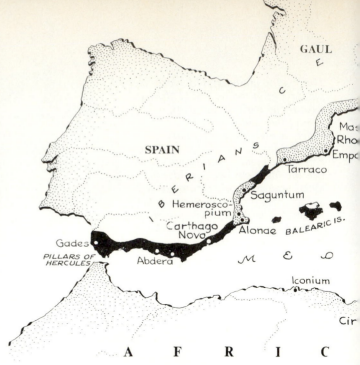

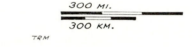

MAP 3-2 PHOENICIAN AND GREEK COLONIZATION *Most of the coast line of the Mediterranean and Black Seas was populated by Greek or Phoenician colonies. The Phoenicians were a commercial people who planted their colonies in North Africa, Spain, Sicily, and Sardinia, chiefly in the ninth century B.C. The height of Greek colonization came later, between about 750 and 550 B.C.*

armed citizenry, necessary for an aggressive foreign policy, would have been dangerous, so the tyrants usually pursued a program of peaceful alliances with other tyrants abroad and avoided war.

By the end of the sixth century B.C., tyranny had disappeared from the Greek states and did not return again in the same form or for the same reasons. The last tyrants were universally hated for the cruelty and repression they employed. They left bitter memories in their own states and became objects of fear and hatred everywhere.

From a longer perspective, however, it is clear that the tyrants made important contributions to the development of Greek civilization. They put an end, for a time, to the crippling civil wars that threatened the

survival of the aristocratic *poleis*. In general, they reduced the warfare between the states. They encouraged the economic changes that were necessary for the future prosperity of Greece. They increased the degree of communication with the rest of the Mediterranean world and made an enormous contribution to the cultivation of crafts and technology, as well as of the arts and literature. Most important of all, they broke the grip of the aristocrats and put the productive powers of the most active and talented of its citizens fully at the service of the *polis*.

Society and Culture in Archaic Greece

Styles of Life

As the "dark ages" came to an end, the features that would distinguish Greek society thereafter took

CHRONOLOGY OF THE RISE OF GREECE	
CA. 2900–1150 B.C.	Minoan period
CA. 1900 B.C.	Probable date of the arrival of the Greeks on the mainland
CA. 1600–1150 B.C.	Mycenaean period
CA. 1250 B.C.	Sack of Troy (?)
CA. 1200–1150 B.C.	Destruction of Mycenaean centers in Greece
CA. 1100–750 B.C.	Dark Ages
CA. 750–500 B.C.	Major period of Greek colonization
CA. 725 B.C.	Probable date of Homer
CA. 700 B.C.	Probable date of Hesiod
CA. 700–500 B.C.	Major period of Greek tyranny

shape. The role of the artisan and the merchant grew more important as contact with the non-Hellenic world became easier, but the great majority of people continued to make their living from the land. Wealthy aristocrats with large estates, powerful households, families, and clans, however, led very different lives from those of the poorer peasants and the independent farmers who had smaller and less fertile fields.

PEASANTS. Peasants rarely leave a record of their thoughts or activities, and we have no such record from ancient Greece. The poet Hesiod (CA. 700 B.C.), however, who presented himself as a small farmer, was certainly no aristocrat. From his *Works and Days* we get some idea of the life of such a farmer. The crops included grain, chiefly barley but also wheat; grapes for wine; olives for food, but chiefly for oil, used for

cooking, lighting, and washing; green vegetables, especially the bean; and some fruit. Sheep and goats provided milk and cheese. The Homeric heroes had great herds of cattle and ate lots of meat, but by Hesiod's time land fertile enough to provide fodder for cattle was needed to grow grain. He and small farmers like him tasted meat chiefly from sacrificial animals at festivals.

These farmers worked hard to make their living. Although Hesiod had the help of oxen and mules and one or two hired helpers for occasional labor, his life was one of continuous toil. The hardest work came in October, at the start of the rainy season, the time for the first plowing. The plow was light and easily broken, and the work of forcing the iron tip into the earth was back-breaking, though Hesiod had a team of oxen to pull his plow. Not every farmer was so fortunate,

Hesiod's Farmer's Almanac

Hesiod was a farmer and poet who lived in a village in Greece about 700 B.C. His poem Works and Days *contains wisdom on several subjects, but its final section amounts to a farmer's almanac, taking readers through the year and advising them on just when each activity is demanded. Hesiod painted a picture of a very hard life for Greek farmers. In the following passage he talks about one of the few times when the farmer is free from toil, during the hottest part of summer.*

But when House-on-Back, the snail, crawls from
    the ground up
the plants, escaping the Pleiades, it's no longer time
    for vine-digging;
time rather to put an edge to your sickles, and rout out
    your helpers.
Keep away from sitting in the shade or lying in bed till
    the sun's up
in the time of the harvest, when the sunshine scorches
    your skin dry.
This is the season to push your work and bring home
    your harvest;
get up with the first light so you'll have enough to live
    on.
Dawn takes away from work a third part of the work's
    measure.
Dawn sets a man well along on his journey, in his
    work also,
dawn, who when she shows, has numerous people
    going their ways; dawn who puts the yoke upon
    many oxen.
    But when the artichoke is in flower, and the clam-
        orous cricket
sitting in his tree lets go his vociferous singing, that
    issues
from the beating of his wings, in the exhausting season
    of summer,

then is when goats are at their fattest, when the wine
    tastes best,
women are most lascivious, but the men's strength
    fails them
most, for the star Seirios shrivels them, knees and
    heads alike,
and the skin is all dried out in the heat; then, at that
    season,
one might have the shadow under the rock, and the
    wine of Biblis,
a curd cake, and all the milk that the goats can give
    you,
the meat of a heifer, bred in the woods, who has never
    borne a calf,
and of baby kids also. Then, too, one can sit in the
    shadow
and drink the bright-shining wine, his heart satiated
    with eating
and face turned in the direction where Zephyros blows
    briskly,
make three libations of water from a spring that keeps
    running forever
and has no mud in it; and pour wine for the fourth
    libation. ❑

Hesiod, *Works and Days*, trans. by Richmond Lattimore (Ann Arbor: 1959), University of Michigan Press, pp. 87, 89.

and the cry of the crane that announced the time of year to plow "bites the heart of the man without oxen."

Autumn and winter were the time for cutting wood, building wagons, and making tools. Late winter was the time to tend to the vines, May the time to harvest the grain, July to winnow and store it. Only at the height of summer's heat did Hesiod allow for rest, but when September came, it was time to harvest the grapes. No sooner was that task done than the cycle started again. The work went on under the burning sun and in the freezing cold.

Hesiod wrote nothing of pleasure or entertainment. Less austere farmers than Hesiod gathered at the blacksmith's shop for warmth and companionship in winter, and even he must have taken part in religious rites and festivals that were accompanied by some kind of entertainment, but the life of the peasant farmers was hard and their pleasures few.

ARISTOCRATS. Most aristocrats were rich enough to employ many hired laborers, sometimes sharecroppers and sometimes even slaves, to work their extensive lands and were therefore able to enjoy leisure for other activities. The center of aristocratic social life was the drinking party, or *symposion*. This activity was not a mere drinking bout, meant to remove inhibi-

tions and produce oblivion. The Greeks, in fact, almost always mixed their wine with water, and one of the goals of the participants was to drink as much as the others without becoming drunk.

The *symposion* was a carefully organized occasion, with a "king" chosen to set the order of events and to determine that night's mixture of wine and water. Only men took part, and they ate and drank as they reclined on couches along the walls of the room. The sessions began with prayers and libations to the gods. Usually there were games, such as dice or *kottabos*, in which wine was flicked from the cups at different targets. Sometimes dancing girls or flute girls offered entertainment. Frequently, the aristocratic participants provided their own amusements with songs, poetry, or even philosophical disputes. Characteristically, these took the form of contests, with some kind of prize for the winner, for aristocratic values continued to emphasize competition and the need to excel, whatever the arena.

This aspect of aristocratic life appears in the athletic contest that became widespread early in the sixth century B.C. The games included running events; the long jump; the discus and javelin throws; the *pentathlon*, which included all of these; boxing; wrestling; and the chariot race. Only the rich could afford to raise, train, and race horses, so the chariot race was a special preserve of aristocracy. Wrestling, however, was also especially favored by the nobility, and the *palaestra* where they practiced became an important social center for the aristocracy. The contrast between the hard, drab life of the peasants and the leisured and lively one of the aristocrats could hardly be greater.

Culture

RELIGION. Like most ancient peoples, the Greeks were polytheists, and religion played an important part in their lives. A great part of Greek art and literature was closely connected with religion, as was the life of the *polis* in general. The Greek pantheon consisted of the twelve gods who lived on Mount Olympus: Zeus, the father of the gods; his wife, Hera; his brother, Poseidon, god of the seas and earthquakes; his sisters, Hestia, goddess of the hearth, and Demeter, goddess of agriculture and marriage; and his children— Aphrodite, goddess of love and beauty; Apollo, god of the sun, music, poetry, and prophecy; Ares, god of war; Artemis, goddess of the moon and the hunt; Athena, goddess of wisdom and the arts; Hephaestus, god of fire and metallurgy; and Hermes, messenger of the gods who was connected with commerce and cunning.

On the one hand, these gods were seen as behaving very much like mortals, with all the human foibles, except that they were superhuman in these as well as in their strength and immortality. On the other hand, Zeus, at least, was seen as being a source of human justice, and even the Olympians were understood to be subordinate to the Fates. Each *polis* had one of the Olympians as its guardian deity and worshiped the god in its own special way, but all the gods were Panhellenic. In the eighth and seventh centuries B.C., common shrines were established at Olympia for the worship of Zeus, at Delphi for Apollo, at the Isthmus of Corinth for Poseidon, and at Nemea once again for Zeus. Each held athletic contests in honor of its god, to which all Greeks were invited and for which a sacred truce was declared.

The worship of these deities did not involve great emotion. It was a matter of offering prayer, libations, and gifts in return for protection and favors from the god during the lifetime of the worshiper. There was no hope of immortality for the average human and little moral teaching. Most Greeks seem to have held to the commonsense notion that justice lay in paying one's debts; that civic virtue consisted of worshiping the state deities in the traditional way, performing the required public services, and fighting in defense of the state; and that private morality meant to do good to one's friends and harm to one's enemies.

In the sixth century B.C., the influence of the cult of Apollo at Delphi and of his oracle there became very great. The oracle was the most important of several that helped satisfy human craving for a clue to the future. The priests of Apollo preached moderation; their advice was exemplified in the two famous sayings identified with Apollo: "Know thyself" and "Nothing in excess." Humans need self-control (*sophrosynē*). Its opposite is arrogance (*hybris*), which is brought on by

The temple of Apollo at Delphi. The shrine of Apollo at Delphi was one of the oldest and holiest religious sites in Greece. For centuries pilgrims came from all over the Mediterranean to consult the god's oracle there. [Alinari-SCALA.]

The god Dionysus dancing with two maenads, who were female followers of him. The vase decoration is by a painter who worked between about 559 and 525 B.C. [Photograph Bibliothèque Nationale, Paris.]

excessive wealth or good fortune. *Hybris* leads to moral blindness and finally to divine vengeance. This theme of moderation and the dire consequences of its absence was central to Greek popular morality and appears frequently in Greek literature.

The somewhat cold religion of the Olympian gods and of the cult of Apollo did little to attend to human fears, hopes, and passions. For these needs, the Greeks turned to other deities and rites. Of these, the most popular was Dionysus, a god of nature and fertility, of the grape vine and drunkenness and sexual abandon. In some of his rites, the god was followed by maenads, female devotees who cavorted by night, ate raw flesh, and were reputed to tear to pieces any creature they came across.

POETRY. The great changes sweeping through the Greek world were also reflected in the poetry of the sixth century B.C. The lyric style, whether sung by a chorus or by one singer, predominated. Sappho of Lesbos, Anacreon of Teos, and Simonides of Cous composed personal poetry, often speaking of the pleasure

and agony of love. Alcaeus of Mytilene, an aristocrat driven from his city by a tyrant, wrote bitter invective.

Perhaps the most interesting poet of the century from a political point of view was Theognis of Megara. An aristocrat who lived through a tyranny, an unusually chaotic and violent democracy, and an oligarchy that restored order but that ended the rule of the old aristocracy. Theognis was the spokesman for the old, defeated aristocracy of birth. He divided everyone into two classes, the noble and the base; the former were good, the latter bad. Those nobly born had to associate only with others like themselves if they were to preserve their virtue; if they mingled with the base, they became base. Those born base, on the other hand, could never become noble. Only nobles could aspire to virtue, and only nobles possessed the critical moral and intellectual qualities, respect or honor, and judgment. These qualities could not be taught; they were innate. Even so, nobles had to be carefully guarded against corruption by wealth or by mingling with the base. Intermarriage between the noble and the base was especially condemned. These were the ideas of the unreconstructed nobility, whose power had been destroyed or reduced in most Greek states by this time. These ideas remained alive in aristocratic hearts throughout the next century and greatly influenced later thinkers, Plato, again, among them.

The Major City-States

Generalization about the *polis* becomes difficult not long after its appearance, for though the states had much in common, some of them developed in unique ways. Sparta and Athens, which became the two most powerful Greek states, had especially unusual histories.

Sparta

At first, Sparta seems not to have been strikingly different from other *poleis*, but about 725 B.C., the pressure of population and land hunger led the Spartans to launch a war of conquest against their western neighbor, Messenia. This First Messenian War gave the Spartans as much land as they would ever need, and the reduction of the Messenians to the status of serfs, or Helots, meant that the Spartans did not even have to work the land that supported them.

The turning point in Spartan history came with the Second Messenian War, a rebellion of the Helots, assisted by Argos and some other Peloponnesian cities, about 650 B.C. The war was long and bitter and at one point threatened the existence of Sparta. After the revolt had been put down, the Spartans were forced to reconsider their way of life. They could not expect to keep down the Helots, who outnumbered them perhaps ten to one, and still maintain the old free-and-easy habits typical of most Greeks. Faced with the choice of making drastic changes and sacrifices or abandoning their control of Messenia, the Spartans chose to introduce fundamental reforms that turned their city forever after into a military academy and camp.

SOCIETY. The new system that emerged late in the sixth century B.C. exerted control over each Spartan from birth, when officials of the state decided which infants were physically fit to survive. At the age of seven, the Spartan boy was taken from his mother and turned over to young instructors who trained him in athletics and the military arts and taught him to endure privation, to bear physical pain, and to live off the country, by theft if necessary. At twenty the Spartan youth was enrolled in the army and lived in barracks with his companions until the age of thirty. Marriage was permitted, but a strange sort of marriage it was, for the Spartan male could visit his wife only infrequently and by stealth. At thirty, he became a full citizen, an "equal," and was allowed to live in his own house with his wife, though he took his meals at a public mess in the company of fifteen comrades. His food, a simple diet without much meat or wine, was provided by his own plot of land, which was worked by Helots. Military service was required until the age of sixty; only then could the Spartan retire at last to his home and family.

This educational program extended to the women, too. They were not given military training, but female infants were examined for fitness to survive in the same way as males. Girls were given gymnastic training, were permitted greater freedom of movement than among other Greeks, and were equally indoctrinated with the idea of service to Sparta. The entire system was designed to change the natural feelings of devotion to wife, children, and family into a more powerful commitment to the *polis*. Privacy, luxury, and even comfort were sacrificed to the purpose of producing soldiers whose physical powers, training, and discipline made them the best in the world. Nothing that might turn the mind away from duty was permitted. The very use of coins was forbidden lest it corrupt the desires of Spartans. Neither family nor money was allowed to interfere with the only ambition permitted to a Spartan male: to win glory and the respect of his peers by bravery in war.

GOVERNMENT. The Spartan constitution was mixed, containing elements of monarchy, oligarchy, and democracy. There were two kings, whose power was limited by law and also by the rivalry that usually existed between the two royal houses.

The oligarchic element was represented by a king and a council of elders consisting of twenty-eight men over sixty, who were elected for life. These elders had important judicial functions, sitting as a court in cases involving the kings. They also were consulted before

MAP 3-3 ATTICA AND VICINITY *Citizens of all towns in Attica were also citizens of Athens. Sparta's region, Laconia, was in the Peloponnesus. Near-by states were members of the Peloponnesian League under Sparta's leadership.*

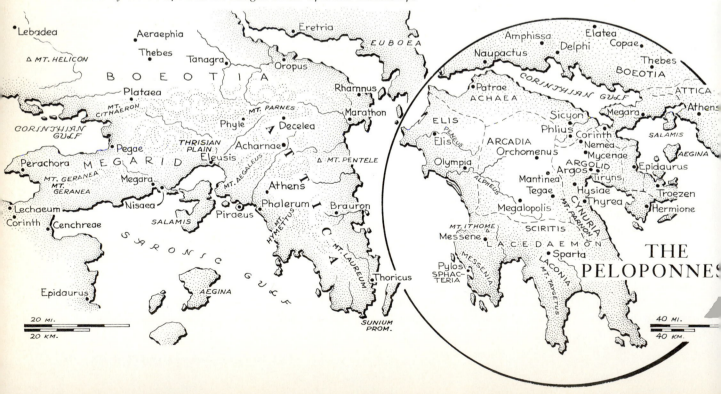

any proposal was put before the assembly of Spartan citizens. In a traditional society like Sparta's, they must have had considerable influence.

The Spartan assembly consisted of all males over thirty. Theoretically, they were the final authority, but because, in practice, debate was carried on by magis-

Tyrtaeus Describes Excellence: Code of the Citizen Soldier

The military organization of citizen soldiers for the defense of the polis *and the idea of the* polis *itself, which permeated Greek political thought, found echoes in Greek lyric poetry. A major example is this poem by Tyrtaeus, a Spartan poet who wrote about 625* B.C. *It gives important evidence on the nature of warfare in the phalanx and the values taught by the* polis.

I would not say anything for a man nor take
 account of him
  for any speed of his feet or wrestling skill he
  might have,
not if he had the size of a Cyclops and strength to
 go with it,
  not if he could outrun Bóreas, the North Wind
  of Thrace,
not if he were more handsome and gracefully
 formed than Tithónos,
  or had more riches than Midas had, or Kinyras
  too,
not if he were more of a king than Tantalid Pelops,
 or had the power of speech and persuasion
 Adrastos had,
not if he had all splendors except for a fighting
 spirit.
  For no man ever proves himself a good man in
  war unless he can endure to face the blood
  and the slaughter,
  go close against the enemy and fight with his
  hands.
Here is courage, mankind's finest possession, here
 is
  the noblest prize that a young man can
  endeavor to win,
and it is a good thing his city and all the people
 share with him
  when a man plants his feet and stands in the
  foremost spears
relentlessly, all thought of foul flight completely
 forgotten,
  and has well trained his heart to be steadfast
  and to endure,
and with words encourages the man who is
 stationed beside him.
  Here is a man who proves himself to be valiant
  in war.
With a sudden rush he turns to flight the rugged
 battalions
  of the enemy, and sustains the bearing waves
  of assault.

And he who so falls among the champions and loses
 his sweet life,
  so blessing with honor his city, his father, and
  all his people,
with wounds in his chest, where the spear that he
 was facing has transfixed
  that massive guard of his shield, and gone
  through his breastplate as well,
why, such a man is lamented alike by the young
 and the elders,
  and all his city goes into mourning and grieves
  for his loss.
His tomb is pointed out with price, and so are his
 children,
  and his children's children, and afterward all
  the race that is his.
His shining glory is never forgotten, his name is
 remembered,
  and he becomes an immortal, though he lies
  under the ground,
when one who was a brave man has been killed by
 the furious War God
  standing his ground and fighting hard for his
  children and land.
But if he escapes the doom of death, the destroyer
 of bodies,
  and wins his battle, and bright renown for the
  work of his spear,
all men give place to him alike, the youth and the
 elders,
  and much joy comes his way before he goes
  down to the dead.
Aging he has reputation among his citizens. No one
 tries to interfere with his honors or all he
 deserves;
all men withdraw before his presence, and yield
 their seats to him,
  and youth, and the men of his age, and even
  those older than he.
Thus a man should endeavor to reach this high
 place of courage
  with all his heart, and, so trying, never be
  backward in war. ❑

Greek Lyrics, trans. by Richmond Lattimore (Chicago: University of Chicago Press, 1949, 1950, 1955), pp. 14–15.

trates, elders, and kings alone, and because voting was usually by acclamation, the assembly's real function was to ratify decisions already taken or to decide between positions favored by the leading figures. In addition, Sparta had a unique institution, the board of ephors. This consisted of five men elected annually by the assembly. Originally they appear to have been intended to check the power of the kings, but gradually they acquired other important functions: they controlled foreign policy, oversaw the generalship of the kings on campaign, presided at the assembly, and guarded against rebellion by the Helots.

By about 550 B.C., the Spartan system was well established, and its limitations had been made plain. Suppression of the Helots required all the effort and energy that Sparta had. The Spartans could expand no further, but they could not allow unruly independent neighbors to cause unrest that might inflame the Helots.

When the Spartans defeated Tegea, their northern neighbor, they imposed an unusual peace. Instead of taking away land and subjecting the defeated state, Sparta left the Tegeans their land and their freedom. In exchange, they required the Tegeans to follow the Spartan lead in foreign affairs and to supply a fixed number of soldiers to Sparta on demand. This became the model for Spartan relations with the other states in the Peloponnesus, and soon Sparta was the leader of an alliance that included every Peloponnesian state but Argos; modern scholars have named this alliance the Peloponnesian League. It provided the Spartans with the security they needed, and it also made Sparta the most powerful *polis* in Hellenic history. By 500 B.C., Sparta and the league had given the Greeks a force capable of facing mighty threats from abroad.

Athens

In the seventh century B.C., Athens was a typical aristocratic *polis*. The aristocrats held the most and best land and dominated religious and political life. There was no written law, and decisions were rendered by powerful nobles on the basis of tradition and, most likely, self-interest. The state was governed by the Areopagus, a council of nobles deriving its name from the hill where it held its sessions. Annually, the council elected nine magistrates who joined the Areopagus after their year in office. Because they served for only a year, were checked by their colleagues, and looked forward to a lifetime as members of the Areopagus after their terms were ended, it is plain that the aristocratic council was the true master of the state.

In the seventh century B.C., the peaceful life of Athens experienced some disturbances, which were caused in part by quarrels within the nobility and in part by the beginnings of an agrarian crisis.

The root of Athens' troubles were agricultural. Many Athenians worked family farms, from which they obtained most of their living. It appears that they planted wheat, the staple crop, year after year without rotating fields or using sufficient fertilizer. In time, this procedure exhausted the soil and led to bad crops. To survive, the farmer had to borrow from a wealthy neighbor to get through the year. In return, he promised one sixth of the next year's crop. The arrangement was marked by the deposit of an inscribed stone on the entailed farm. Bad harvests persisted, and soon the debtor had to pledge his wife and children and himself as surety for the loans needed for survival. As bad times continued, many Athenians defaulted and were enslaved. Some were even sold abroad. Revolutionary pressures grew among the poor, who began to demand the abolition of debt and a redistribution of the land.

SOLON AND REFORM. The circumstances might easily have brought about class warfare and tyranny, but the remarkable conciliatory spirit of Athens intervened. In the year 594 B.C., as tradition has it, the Athenians elected Solon, a successful general and talented poet, with extraordinary powers to legislate and revise the constitution. Immediately, he attacked the agrarian problem by canceling current debts and forbidding future loans secured by the person of the borrower. He helped bring back many Athenians enslaved abroad as well as freeing those in Athens enslaved for debt. This program was called the "shaking off of burdens." It did not, however, solve the fundamental economic problem, and Solon did not redistribute the land. In the short run, therefore, he did not put an end to the economic crisis, but his other economic actions had profound success in the long run. He forbade the export of wheat and encouraged that of olive oil. This policy had the effect of making wheat more available in Attica and encouraging the cultivation of olive oil and wine as cash crops. By the fifth century B.C., this form of agriculture had become so profitable that much Athenian land was diverted from grain production to the cultivation of cash crops, and Athens became dependent on imported wheat.

Solon also changed the Athenian standards of weights and measures to conform with those of Corinth and Euboea and the cities of the East. This change also encouraged commerce and turned Athens in the direction that would lead to great prosperity in the fifth century. He also encouraged industry by offering citizenship to foreign artisans, and his success is reflected in the development of the outstanding Attic pottery of the sixth century.

Solon also significantly changed the constitution. All male adults whose fathers were citizens were citizens, too, and to their number he added immigrants who were offered citizenship. All these Athenian citizens were divided into four classes on the basis of wealth, measured by annual agricultural production.

Men whose property produced five hundred measures were called five-hundred-measure men, and those producing three hundred measures were called cavalry; these two classes alone could hold office and sit on the Areopagus.

Producers of two hundred measures were called owners of a team of oxen; they were allowed to serve as hoplites. They could be elected to the council of four hundred chosen by all the citizens, one hundred from each tribe. Solon seems to have meant this council to serve as a check on the Areopagus and to prepare any business that needed to be put before the assembly.

The last class, producing less than two hundred measures, were the *thetes*. They voted in the popular assembly for the magistrates and the council members and on any other business brought before them by the magistrates. They also sat on a new popular court established by Solon. At first, this court must have had little power, for most cases continued to be heard in the country by local barons and in Athens by the aristocratic Areopagus. But the new court was recognized as a court of appeal, and by the fifth century B.C., almost all cases came before the popular courts.

PISISTRATUS THE TYRANT. Solon's efforts to avoid factional strife failed. Within a few years, contention reached such a degree that no magistrates could be chosen. Out of this turmoil emerged the first Athenian tyranny. Pisistratus, a nobleman, faction leader, and military hero, seized power firmly. His rule rested on the force provided by mercenary soldiers. He engaged in great programs of public works, urban improvement, and religious piety. Temples were built and religious centers expanded and improved. New religious festivals were introduced, such as the one dedicated to Dionysus, the god of fertility, wine, and ecstatic religious worship imported from Phrygia in Asia Minor. Old ones, like the Great Panathenaic festival, were amplified and given greater public appeal. Poets and artists were supported to add cultural luster to the court of the tyrant.

Pisistratus aimed at increasing the power of the central government at the expense of the nobles. The festival of Dionysus and the Great Panathenaic festival helped fix attention on the capital city, as did the new temples and the reconstruction of the Agora as the center of public life. Circuit judges were sent out into the country to hear cases, another feature that weakened the power of the local barons. All this time, Pisistratus made no formal change in the Solonian constitution. Assembly, councils, and courts met; magistrates and councils were elected; Pisistratus merely saw to it that his supporters were chosen. The intended effect was to blunt the sharp edge of tyranny with the appearance of constitutional government, and it worked. The rule of Pisistratus was remembered as popular and mild. The unintended effect was to give the Athenians more experience in the procedures of self-government and a growing taste for it.

INVASION BY SPARTA. Pisistratus was succeeded by his oldest son, Hippias, who followed his father's ways at first. In 514 B.C., however, brother Hipparchus was murdered as a result of a private quarrel. Hippias became nervous, suspicious, and harsh. At last, one of the noble clans exiled by the sons of Pisistratus, the Alcmaeonids, won favor with the influential oracle at Delphi and used its support to persuade Sparta to attack the Athenian tyranny. Led by their ambitious king, Cleomenes I, the Spartans marched into Attica in 510 B.C. and deposed Hippias, who went into exile to the Persian court. The tyranny was over.

The Spartans must have hoped to leave Athens in friendly hands, and indeed Cleomenes' friend Isagoras held the leading position in Athens after the withdrawal of the Spartan army. However, he was not unopposed. Clisthenes of the restored Alcmaeonid clan was his chief rival who, however, lost out in the political struggle among the noble factions. Isagoras seems to have tried to restore a version of the pre-Solonian aristocratic state. As part of his plan, he carried through a purification of the citizen lists, removing those who had been enfranchised by Solon or Pisistratus and any others thought to have a doubtful claim. Clisthenes then took an unprecedented action by turning to the people for political support and won it with a program of great popular appeal. In response, Isagoras called in the Spartans again; Cleomenes arrived and allowed the expulsion from Athens of Clisthenes and a large number of his supporters. But the Athenian political consciousness, ignited by Solon and kept alive under Pisistratus, was fanned by the popular appeal of Clisthenes. The people would not hear of an aristocratic restoration and drove out the Spartans and Isagoras with them. Clisthenes and his allies returned, ready to put their program into effect.

CLISTHENES, THE FOUNDER OF DEMOCRACY. A central aim of Clisthenes' reforms was to diminish the influence of traditional localities and regions in Athenian life, for these were an important source of power for the nobility and of factions in the state.

Clisthenes immediately enrolled the disenfranchised who had supported him in the struggle with Isagoras. Ten new tribes replaced the traditional four. The composition of each tribe guaranteed that no region would dominate any of them. Because the tribes had common religious activities and fought as regimental units, the new organization would also increase devotion to the *polis* and diminish regional divisions and personal loyalty to local barons.

A new council of five hundred was invented to replace the Solonian council of four hundred. Final authority in all things rested with the assembly composed of all adult male Athenian citizens. Debate was free and open; any Athenian could submit legislation, offer amendments, or argue the merits of any question. It is fair to call Clisthenes the father of Athenian democracy. He did not alter the property qualifications of Solon, but his enlargement of the citizen rolls, his diminution of the power of the aristocrats, and his elevation of the role of the assembly, with its effective and manageable council, all give him a firm claim to that title.

As a result of the work of Solon, Pisistratus, and

Aristogeiton and Harmodius were Athenian aristocrats who were slain while assassinating Hipparchos, brother of the tyrant Hippias. After the overthrow of the Pisistratids, the Athenians erected a famous statue to honor their memory. This is a Roman Copy. [Alinari-SCALA.]

CA. 725–710 B.C.	First Messenian War
CA. 650–625 B.C.	Second Messenian War
632 B.C.	Cylon tries to establish a tyranny at Athens
621 B.C.	Draco publishes legal code at Athens
594 B.C.	Solon institutes reforms at Athens
CA. 560–550 B.C.	Sparta defeats Tegea: Beginning of Peloponnesian League
546–527 B.C.	Pisistratus reigns as tyrant at Athens (main period)
510 B.C.	Hippias, son of Pisistratus, deposed as tyrant of Athens
CA. 508–501 B.C.	Clisthenes institutes reforms at Athens

Clisthenes, Athens entered the fifth century B.C. well on the way to prosperity and democracy. It was much more centralized and united than it had been, and was ready to take its place among the major states that would lead the defense of Greece against the dangers that lay ahead.

The Persian Wars

The Greeks' period of fortunate isolation and freedom at last came to an end. In the middle of the sixth century B.C., these Greek cities of Asia Minor came under the control of Lydia and its king, Croesus (CA. 560–546 B.C.). The Lydian rule seems not to have been very harsh, but the Persian conquest of Lydia in 546 B.C. brought a subjugation that was less pleasant.

The Persians required their subjects to pay tribute and to serve in the Persian army. They ruled the Greek cities through local individuals, who governed their cities as "tyrants." The Ionians had been moving in the direction of democracy and were not pleased with monarchical rule, but most of the "tyrants" were not harsh. The Persian tribute was not excessive, and there was general prosperity.

The Ionian Rebellion

The Ionian Greeks, nevertheless, preferred to be free and when the opportunity for liberty came they seized upon it. The private troubles of the ambitious tyrant of Miletus, Aristagoras, started the Ionian rebellion of 499 B.C. He had urged a Persian expedition against the island of Naxos; when it failed, he feared the consequences and organized the rebellion. To gain support, he overthrew the tyrannies and proclaimed democratic constitutions. Then he turned to the mainland states for help. As the most powerful Greek state, Sparta was naturally the first stop, but the Spartans would have none of Aristagoras' promises of easy victory and great wealth.

Aristagoras next sought help at Athens, and there the assembly agreed and voted to send a fleet of twenty ships to help the rebels. The Athenians were related to the Ionians and had close ties of religion and tradition with the rebels. The Athenian expedition was strengthened by five ships from Eretria in Euboea, which participated out of gratitude for past favors.

In 498 B.C., the Athenians and their allies made a swift march and a surprise attack on Sardis, the old capital of Lydia and now the seat of the satrap, and burned it. This caused the revolt to spread throughout the Greek cities of Asia Minor outside Ionia, but the Ionians could not follow it up. The Athenians withdrew and took no further part, and gradually the Persians imposed their will. In 495 B.C., they defeated the Ionian fleet at Lade, and in the next year, they wiped out Miletus. Many men were killed; others were transported to the Persian Gulf, and the women and children were enslaved. The Ionian rebellion was over.

The War in Greece

In 490 B.C., the Persians launched an expedition directly across the Aegean to punish Athens, to restore Hippias, and to gain control of the Aegean Sea (see Map 3.3). The resistance was led by Miltiades, an Athenian and an outstanding soldier who had fled from Persian service after earning the anger of Darius (reigned 521–486 B.C.). His knowledge of the Persian army and his distaste for submission to Persia made him an ideal leader. He led the army to Marathon in Attica and won a decisive victory. The battle at Marathon (490 B.C.) was of enormous importance to the future of Greek civilization. A Persian victory would have destroyed Athenian freedom, and the conquest of all the mainland Greeks would have followed. The greatest achievements of Greek culture, most of which lay in the future, would have been impossible under Persian rule. The Athenian victory, on the other hand, made a positive contribution to those achievements. It instilled in the Athenians a sense of confidence and price in their *polis*, and themselves.

For the Persians, Marathon was only a small and temporary defeat, but it was annoying. Internal troubles, however, prevented swift revenge. In 481 B.C., Darius' successor, Xerxes (reigned 486–465 B.C.), gathered an army of at least 150,000 men and a navy of more than six hundred ships for the conquest of Greece. The Greeks did not make good use of the discovered a rich vein of silver in the state mines, and Themistocles persuaded them to use the profits to increase their fleet. By 480 B.C., Athens had over two hundred ships, the backbone of the navy that defeated the Persians.

As the Persian army gathered south of the Hellespont, only thirty-one Greek states out of hundreds were willing to fight. They were led by Sparta, Athen, Corinth, and Aegina. In the spring of 480 B.C., Xerxes launched his invasion. The Persian strategy was to march into Greece, destroy Athens, defeat the Greek army, and add the Greeks to the number of Persian subjects. The huge Persian army needed to keep in touch with the fleet for supplies. If the Greeks could defeat the Persian navy, the army could not remain in Greece long. Themistocles knew that the Aegean was subject to sudden devastating storms that might damage or destroy the enemy fleet. His strategy was to delay the Persian army and then to bring on the kind of naval battle he might hope to win.

The Greek League, founded specifically to resist this Persian invasion, met at Corinth as the Persians were ready to cross the Hellespont. The league chose Sparta as leader on land and sea and sent a force to Tempe to try to defend Thessaly. Tempe proved to be indefensible, so the Greeks retreated and took up new positions at Thermopylae (the "hot gates") on land and off Artemisium at sea. The opening between the mountains and the sea at Thermopylae was so narrow that it might be held by a smaller army against a much larger one. The Spartans sent their king, Leonidas, with three hundred of their own citizens and enough allies to make a total of about nine thousand. The Greeks may have intended to hold only long enough to permit the Athenians to evacuate Athens, or to force a sea battle, or they may have hoped to hold Thermopylae until the Persians were discouraged enough to withdraw. Perhaps they thought of all these possibilities, for they were not mutually contradictory.

Severe storms wrecked a large number of Persian ships while the Greek fleet waited safely in their protected harbor. Then Xerxes attacked Thermopylae, and for two days the Greeks butchered his best troops without serious loss to themselves. On the third day, however, a traitor showed the Persians a mountain trail that permitted them to attack the Greeks from behind. Many allies escaped, but Leonidas and his three hundred Spartans all died. At about the same time, the Greek and Persian fleets fought an indecisive battle, and the fall of Thermopylae forced the Greek navy to withdraw.

If an inscription discovered in 1959 is authentic, Themistocles had foreseen this possibility, and the Athenians had begun to evacuate their homeland and move to defend Salamis. The fate of Greece was decided in the narrow waters to the east of the island.

Greek hoplite attacking a Persian soldier. The contrast between the Greek's heavy metal body armor, large shield, and long spear and the cloth and leather garments of the Persian gives some indication of the reason for the ultimate Greek victory. This Attic red-figure vase is said to be from the island of Rhodes and was made about 475 B.C. [Metropolitan Museum of Art, New York; Rogers Fund, 1906.]

delay, but Athens was an exception. Themistocles had become its leading politician, and he had always wanted to turn Athens into a naval power. The first step was to build a fortified port at Piraeus during his archonship in 493 B.C. A decade later, the Athenians

CA. 560–546 B.C.	Greek cities of Asia Minor conquered by Croesus of Lydia
546 B.C.	Cyrus of Persia conquers Lydia and gains control of Greek cities
499–494 B.C.	Greek cities rebel (Ionian rebellion)
490 B.C.	Battle of Marathon
480–479 B.C.	Xerxes' invasion of Greece
480 B.C.	Battles of Thermopylae, Artemisium, and Salamis
479 B.C.	Battles of Plataea and Mycale

Themistocles persuaded the reluctant Peloponnesians to stay by threatening to remove all the Athenians and settle anew in Italy. The Spartans knew that they and the other Greeks could not hope to win without the aid of the Athenians. The Greek ships were fewer, slower, and less maneuverable than those of the Persians, so the Greeks put soldiers on their ships and relied chiefly on hand-to-hand combat. The Persians lost more than half their ships and retreated to Asia with a good part of their army, but the danger was not over yet. The Persian general Mardonius spent the winter in central Greece, and in the spring, he unsuccessfully tried to win the Athenians away from the Greek League. The Spartan regent, Pausanias, then led the largest Greek army up to that time to confront Mardonius in Boeotia. At Plataea, in the summer of 479 B.C., Mardonius died in battle, and his army fled toward home. Meanwhile, the Ionian Greeks urged King Leotychidas, the Spartan commander of the fleet, to fight the Persian fleet at Samos. At Mycale, on the coast nearby, Leotychidas destroyed the Persian camp and its fleet offshore. The Persians fled the Aegean and Ionia. For the moment, at least, the Persian threat was gone.

The Rise of Greek Civilization in World Perspective

Hellenic civilization, a unique cultural experience, is at the root of Western civilization. It has powerfully influenced the peoples of the modern world. Itself influenced by the great Bronze-Age civilization of Crete, it emerged from the collapse of the Bronze-Age civilization on the Greek mainland that we call Myce-naean. These earlier civilizations resembled others in Egypt, Mesopotamia, Palestine–Syria, China, India, and elsewhere more than they did the Hellenic version that sprang from them. They had highly developed urban lives; a system of writing; strong, centralized monarchical systems of government ruling over tightly organized, large bureaucracies; hierarchical social systems; professional standing armies—and a regular system of taxation to support all this. To a greater or lesser degree, (more in Egypt, less in China), these early civilizations tended toward cultural stability and uniformity. The striking fact about the emergence of Hellenic civilization was its sharp departure from this pattern of development. The collapse of the Myce-naean world produced a harsh drop in the level of material well-being for the Greeks. It also caused a decline in the cultural level. Cities were swept away and replaced by small farm villages. Trade was all but ended, and communications not only between the Greeks and other peoples, but even among the Greeks themselves, were sharply curtailed. The art of writing was lost for more than three centuries. The matrix of Hellenic civilization was a dark age in which a small number of poor, isolated, illiterate people were ignored by the rest of the world and let alone to develop their own kind of society.

During the three and a half centuries from about 1100 to 750 B.C., the Greeks set the foundations for their great achievements. The crucial unit in the new Greek way of life was the *polis*, the Hellenic city-state. There were hundreds of them, ranging in size from a few thousand inhabitants to hundreds of thousands. Each city-state evoked a kind of loyalty and attachment by its citizens that made the idea of dissolving one's own *polis* into a larger unit unthinkable. The result was a dynamic, many-faceted, competitive, sometimes chaotic society in which rivalry for excellence and victory had the highest value.

This competitive quality marks Greek life throughout its history. Its negative aspect was constant warfare among the states. Its positive side was its extraordinary achievement in literature and art, where competition, sometimes formal and organized, spurred on poets and artists.

The *poleis* were republics. Class distinctions were less marked and less important than in other civilizations, partly because the Greeks were so poor and the differences in wealth among them were relatively small. The introduction of a new mode of fighting, the hoplite phalanx, had further leveling effects upon a class system, for it placed the safety of the state in the hands of the average farmer. Armies were made up of unpaid citizen-soldiers, who returned to their farms after a campaign. As a result, political control was shared with a relatively large portion of the people, and participation in political life was highly valued.

Even when the art of writing was newly acquired from western Semites (perhaps the Phoenicians), there was no bureaucracy, for there were no kings, and not much economic surplus to support them. Most states imposed no regular taxation. There was no separate caste of priests and little concern with any life after death. In this varied, dynamic, secular, and remarkably free context there arose a speculative natural philosophy based on observation and reason. Greek ideas formed the root of modern natural science and philosophy.

Expanded contact and trade with the rest of the world increased the wealth of many Greek cities and brought in valuable new information and ideas. Greek art was powerfully shaped by Egyptian and Near Eastern models that were always adapted and changed rather than copied. Changes often produced social and economic strain, leading to the overthrow of traditional aristocratic regimes by tyrants. Because monarchic rule was anathema to the Greeks, these regimes were temporary. They were usually replaced by oligarchies of greater or lesser breadth, but in Athens the destruction of the tyranny brought the world's first democracy. Sparta, on the other hand, developed a uniquely stable government that avoided tyranny and impressed the other Greeks.

The Greeks' time of independent development, untroubled by external forces, came to an end in the sixth century when Iran's powerful Achaemenid dynasty conquered the Greek cities of Asia Minor. When the Persian kings tried to conquer the Greek mainland, however, the leading states managed to put their quarrels aside and unite against the common enemy. Their determination to preserve their freedom carried them to victory over tremendous odds.

Suggested Readings

A. ANDREWES, *Greek Tyrants* (New York, 1963). A clear and concise account of tyranny in early Greece.

A. ANDREWES, *The Greeks* (London, 1967). A thoughtful general survey.

JOHN BOARDMAN, *The Greeks Overseas* (Harmondsworth, England, 1964). A study of the relations between the Greeks and other peoples.

A. R. BURN, *The Lyric Age of Greece* (New York, 1960). A discussion of early Greece that uses the evidence of poetry and archaeology to fill out the sparse historical record.

A. R. BURN, *Persia and the Greeks*, 2nd ed. (London, 1984). A thorough narrative and analysis of the conflict between the Persians and the Greeks down to 479 B.C.

J. B. BURY AND R. MEIGGS, *A History of Greece*, 4th ed. (London and New York, 1975). A thorough and detailed one-volume narrative history.

J. CHADWICK, *The Mycenaean World* (Cambridge, 1976). A readable account, by a man who helped decipher Mycenaean writing.

E. R. DODDS, *The Greeks and the Irrational* (1955). An excellent account of the role of the supernatural in Greek life and thought.

V. EHRENBERG, *The Greek State* (1964). A good handbook of constitutional history.

V. EHRENBERG, *From Solon to Socrates* (1968). An interpretive history that makes good use of Greek literature to illuminate politics.

J. V. FINE, *The Ancient Greeks* (1983). An excellent survey that discusses historical problems and the evidence that gives rise to them.

M. I. FINLEY, *World of Odysseus*, rev. ed. (1965). A fascinating attempt to reconstruct Homeric society.

M. I. FINLEY, *Early Greece* (1970). A succinct interpretive study.

W. G. FORREST, *The Emergence of Greek Democracy* (1966). A lively interpretation of Greek social and political developments in the archaic period.

W. G. FORREST, *A History of Sparta*, 950–192 B.C. (1968). A brief but shrewd account.

P. GREEN, *Xerxes at Salamis* (1970). A lively and stimulating history of the Persian wars.

C. HIGNETT, *A History of the Athenian Constitution* (1952). A scholarly account, somewhat too skeptical of the ancient sources.

C. HIGNETT, *Xerxes' Invasion of Greece* (1963). A valuable account, but too critical of all sources other than Herodotus.

S. HOOD, *The Minoans* (1971). A sketch of Bronze Age civilization on Crete.

D. KAGAN, *The Great Dialogue: A History of Greek Political Thought from Homer to Polybius* (1965). A discussion of the relationship between the Greek historical experience and political theory.

G. S. KIRK, *The Songs of Homer* (1962). A discussion of the Homeric epics as oral poetry.

H. D. F. KITTO, *The Greeks* (1951). A personal and illuminating interpretation of Greek culture.

W. K. LACEY, *The Family in Ancient Greece* (Ithaca, 1984).

H. L. LORIMER, *Homer and the Monuments* (1950). A study of the relationship between the Homeric poems and the evidence of archaeology.

H. MICHELL, *Sparta* (1952). A study of Spartan institutions.

O. MURRAY, *Early Greece* (1980). A lively and imaginative account of the early history of Greece to the end of the Persian War.

D. L. PAGE, *History and the Homeric Iliad*, 2nd ed. (1966). A well-written and interesting, if debatable, attempt to place the Trojan War in a historical setting.

G. M. A. RICHTER, *Archaic Greek Art* (1949).

CARL ROEBUCK, *Ionian Trade and Colonization* (1959). An introduction to the history of the Greeks in the east.

B. SNELL, *Discovery of the Mind* (1960). An important study of Greek intellectual development.

A. M. SNODGRASS, *The Dark Age of Greece* (Chicago, 1972). A good examination of the archaeological evidence.

C. G. STARR, *Origins of Greek Civilization* 1100–650 B.C. (1961). An interesting interpretation based largely on archaeology and especially on pottery styles.

C. G. STARR, *The Economic and Social Growth of Early Greece*, 800–500 B.C. (1977).

EMILY VERMEULE, *Greece in the Bronze Age* (1972). A study of the Mycenaean period.

A. G. WOODHEAD, *Greeks in the West* (1962). An account of the Greek settlements in Italy and Sicily.

W. J. WOODHOUSE, *Solon the Liberator* (1965). A discussion of the great Athenian reformer.

D. C. YOUNG, *The Olympic Myth of Greek Athletics* (Chicago, 1984). A lively challenge to the orthodox view that Greek athletes were amateurs.

The striding god from Artemisium. This bronze statue dating about 460 B.C. was found in the sea near Artemisium, the northern tip of the large Greek island of Euboea. Exactly whom he represents is not known. Some have thought him to be Poseidon holding a trident; others believe that he is Zeus hurling a thunderbolt. In either case he is a splendid representative of the early classical period of Greek sculpture and therefore now lives at the Athens archaecological museum. [Bettmann Archive.]

4 Classical and Hellenistic Greece

Classical Greece

The Greeks' remarkable victory over the Persians in 480–479 B.C. won them another period of freedom and autonomy, a time when they carried their political and cultural achievement to its height. In Athens, especially, the victory produced a great sense of confidence and ambition. Spartan withdrawal from active leadership against the Persians left a vacuum that was filled by the Delian League, which soon turned into the Athenian Empire.

At the same time as it tightened its hold over the Greek cities in and around the Aegean Sea, Athens developed an extraordinarily democratic constitution at home. Fears and jealousies of this new kind of state and empire created a split in the Greek world that led to a series of major wars. These wars impoverished Greece and left it vulnerable to conquest. In 338 B.C. Philip of Macedon conquered the Greek states, putting an end to the age of the *polis*.

The Delian League

The unity of the Greeks had shown strain even in the life-and-death struggle against the Persians. Within two years of the Persian retreat, the unity gave way almost completely and yielded to a division of the Greek world into two spheres of influence, dominated by Sparta and Athens. The need of the Ionian Greeks to obtain and defend their freedom from Persia and the desire of many Greeks to gain revenge and financial reparation for the Persian attack brought on the split.

Sparta had led the Greeks to victory, and it was natural to look to the Spartans to continue the campaign. But Sparta was ill suited to the task, which required a long-term commitment and continuous naval action far from the Peloponnesus.

The emergence of Athens as the leader of a Greek coalition against Persia was a natural development.

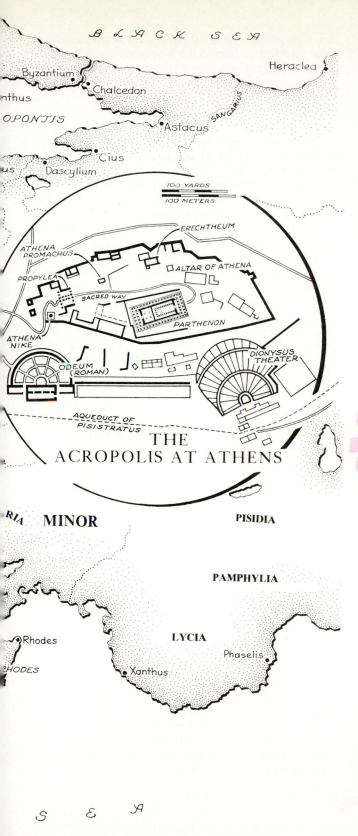

MAP 4-1 CLASSICAL GREECE *Greece in the classical period* (CA. 480–338 B.C.) *centered on the Aegean Sea. Although there were important Greek settlements in Italy, Sicily, and all around the Black Sea, the area shown in this general reference map embraced the vast majority of Greek states. The inset shows the location of the major monuments still visible on the Athenian Acropolis of the classical period.*

Athens had become the leading naval power in Greece, and the same motives that had led Athens to support the Ionian revolt moved it to try to drive the Persians from the Aegean and the Hellespont. The Ionians were at least as eager for the Athenians to take the helm as the Athenians were to accept the responsibility and opportunity.

In the winter of 478–477 B.C., the islanders, the Greeks from the coast of Asia Minor, and some from other Greek cities on the Aegean met with the Athenians on the sacred island of Delos. Here, they swore oaths of alliance. As a symbol that the alliance was meant to be permanent, they dropped lumps of iron into the sea; the alliance was to hold until these rose to the surface.

The aims of this new Delian League were to free those Greeks who were under Persian rule, to protect all against a Persian return, and to obtain compensation from the Persians by attacking their lands and taking booty. League policy was determined by a vote of the assembly, in which each state, including Athens, had one vote. Athens, however, was clearly designated leader.

From the first, the league was remarkably successful. The Persians were driven from Europe and the Hellespont, and the Aegean was cleared of pirates. Some states were forced into the league or were prevented from leaving. The members approved coercion because they believed it was necessary for the common safety. In 467 B.C., a great victory over the Persians at the Eurymedon River in Asia Minor routed the Persians and added a number of cities to the league.

Cimon, son of Miltiades, the hero of Marathon, became the leading Athenian soldier and statesman soon after the Persian war. Themistocles appears to have been driven from power by a coalition of his enemies. Ironically, the author of the Greek victory over Persia of 480 B.C. was ostracized and ended his days at the court of the Persian king. Cimon, who was to dominate Athenian politics for almost two decades, pursued a policy of aggressive attacks on Persia and friendly relations with Sparta. In domestic affairs, Cimon was conservative. He accepted the democratic constitution of Clisthenes, which appears to have become somewhat more limited after the Persian war. Defending this constitution and this foreign policy,

Cimon led the Athenians and the Delian League to victory after victory. His own popularity grew with success.

The First Peloponnesian War

In 465 B.C., the island of Thasos rebelled from the league. After a siege of more than two years Cimon forced an end to the rebellion. The revolt of Thasos had an important influence on the development of the Delian League, on Athenian politics, and on relations between Athens and Sparta. It is the first recorded instance in which Athenian interests alone seemed to have determined league policy, a significant step in the evolution of the Delian League into the Athenian empire. When Cimon returned to Athens from Thasos, he was charged with taking bribes not to conquer Macedonia, although that was not part of his assignment. He was acquitted and the trial was proved to be only a device by which his political opponents tried to reduce his influence.

The democratic opposition's program at home was to undo the gains made by the conservative council called the Areopagus and to bring about further changes in the direction of democracy. Abroad, the enemies of Cimon wanted to break with Sparta and contest its claim to leadership over the Greeks. They intended at least to establish the independence of Athens and its alliance. The head of this faction was Ephialtes. His supporter, and the man chosen to be the public prosecutor of Cimon, was Pericles, a member of a distinguished Athenian family. He was still a young man, and his defeat in court did not do lasting damage to his career.

When the Thasians began their rebellion, they asked Sparta to invade Athens the next spring. The ephors agreed. An earthquake, accompanied by a rebellion of the Helots that threatened the survival of Sparta, prevented the invasion. The Spartans asked their allies, the Athenians among them, for help. In Athens, Ephialtes urged the Athenians "not to help or restore a city that was a rival to Athens but to let Sparta lie low and be trampled underfoot." However, Cimon persuaded them to send help. The results were disastrous. The Spartans sent the Athenian troops home for fear of "the boldness and revolutionary spirit of the Athenians." While Cimon was in the Peloponnesus, helping the Spartans, Ephialtes stripped the Areopagus of almost all its power. In the spring of 461 B.C., Cimon was exiled, and Athens made an alliance with Argos, Sparta's traditional enemy. Almost overnight, Cimon's domestic and foreign policies had been overturned.

The new regime at Athens was confident and ambitious. When Megara, getting the worst of a border dispute with Corinth, withdrew from the Peloponnesian League, the Athenians accepted the Megarians as al-lies. This alliance gave Athens a great strategic advantage, for Megara barred the way from the Peloponnesus to Athens. The alliance also brought on the First Peloponnesian War, for Sparta resented the defection of Megara to Athens. The early years of the war brought Athens great success. The Athenians conquered Aegina and gained control of Boeotia. At one moment, Athens was supreme and invulnerable, controlling the states on its borders and dominating the sea (see Map 4.1).

In 454 B.C., however, the tide turned. In that year, a disastrous defeat struck an Athenian fleet that had gone to aid an Egyptian rebellion against Persia. The great loss of men, ships, and prestige caused rebellions in the empire, forcing Athens to make a truce in Greece in order to subdue Athens' allies in the Aegean. In 449 B.C., the Athenians ended the war against Persia. In 446 B.C., the war on the Greek mainland broke out again. Rebellions in Boeotia and Megara removed Athens' land defenses and brought a Spartan invasion. Rather than fight, Pericles, the commander of the Athenian army, agreed to a peace of thirty years. By the terms of the agreement, he abandoned all Athenian possessions on the continent. In return, the Spartans gave formal recognition to the Athenian empire. From then on, Greece was divided into two power blocs: Sparta and its alliance on the mainland and Athens ruling its empire in the Aegean.

The Athenian Empire

After the Egyptian disaster, the Athenians moved the Delian League's treasury to Athens and began to keep one sixtieth of the annual revenues for themselves. Because of the peace with Persia, there seemed no further reason for the allies to pay tribute. In spite of Athenian propaganda, nothing could cloak the fact that Athens was becoming the master and its allies mere subjects. By 445 B.C., only Chios, Lesbos, and Samos were autonomous and provided ships. All the other states paid tribute.

The change from alliance to empire came about because of the pressure of war and rebellion and in large measure because the allies were unwilling to see to their own defense. The empire was not universally unpopular and had many friends among the lower classes and the democratic politicians. Nevertheless, it came to be seen more and more as a tyranny. But the Athenians had come to depend on the empire for prosperity and security. The Thirty Years' Peace of 445 B.C. had recognized the empire, and the Athenians were determined to defend it at any cost.

Athenian Democracy

Even as the Athenians were tightening their control over their allies at home, they were evolving the freest government the world had ever seen. This extension of

MAP 4-2   THE ATHENIAN EMPIRE ABOUT 450 B.C.   *The Empire at its fullest extent shortly before 450 B.C. We see Athens and the independent states that provided manned ships for the imperial fleet but paid no tribute, dependent states who paid tribute, and states allied to but not actually in the Empire.*

the Athenian democracy took place chiefly under the guidance of Pericles, who succeeded to the leadership of the democratic faction after the assassination of Ephialtes in 462 B.C. Legislation was passed making the hoplite class eligible for the archonship. In practice, no adult male was thereafter prevented from serving on the basis of property class. Pericles himself proposed the law introducing pay for jury members, opening that important duty to the poor. Circuit judges were reintroduced, making swift impartial justice available even to the poorest residents in the countryside.

Finally, Pericles himself introduced a bill limiting citizenship to those who had two citizen parents. From a modern perspective, this measure might be seen as a step away from democracy, and, in fact, it would have barred Cimon and one of Pericles' ancestors. In Greek terms, however, it was quite natural. Democracy was defined in terms of those who held citizenship, and

because citizenship had become a valuable commodity, the decision to limit it must have won a large majority. Participation in government in all the Greek states was denied to slaves, resident aliens, and women.

Within the citizen body, however, the extent of the democracy was remarkable. Every decision of the state had to be approved by the popular assembly—a collection of the people, not their representatives. Every judicial decision was subject to appeal to a popular court of not fewer than 51 and as many as 1,501 citizens, chosen from an annual panel of jurors widely representative of the Athenian male population. Most officials were selected by lot, without regard to class. The main elected officials, such as the generals and the imperial treasurers, were generally nobles and almost always rich men, but the people were free to choose others. All public officials were subject to scrutiny before taking office, could be called to account and re-

Thucydides Reports Pericles on Athenian Democracy

Pericles (CA. 495–429 B.C.) *delivered this speech after the first campaigning season of the Great Peloponnesian War, probably late in the winter of 431 B.C. It is the most famous statement of the ideals of the Athenian imperial democracy.*

Our constitution does not copy the laws of neighbouring states; we are rather a pattern to others than imitators ourselves. Its administration favours the many instead of the few; this is why it is called a democracy. If we look to the laws, they afford equal justice to all in their private differences; if to social standing, advancement in public life falls to reputation for capacity, class considerations not being allowed to interfere with merit; nor again does poverty bar the way, if a man is able to serve the state, he is not hindered by the obscurity of his condition. The freedom which we enjoy in our government extends also to our ordinary life. There, far from exercising a jealous surveillance over each other, we do not feel called upon to be angry with our neighbour for doing what he likes, or even to indulge in those injurious looks which cannot fail to be offensive, although they inflict no positive penalty. But all this ease in our private relations does not make us lawless as citizens. . . . Our public men have, besides politics, their private affairs to attend to, and our ordinary citizens, though occupied with the pursuits of industry, are still fair judges of public matters; for, unlike any other nation, regarding him who takes no part in these duties not as unambitious but as useless, we Athenians are able to judge at all events if we cannot originate, and instead of looking on discussion as a stumbling-block in the way of action, we think it an indispensable preliminary to any wise action at all. . . .

In short, I say that as a city we are the school of Hellas; while I doubt if the world can produce a man, who where he has only himself to depend upon, is equal to so many emergencies, and graced by so happy a versatility as the Athenian. ❑

Thucydides, *The Peloponnesian War*, trans. by Richard Crawley (New York: Random House, 1951), pp. 104–106.

moved from office during their tenure, and were held to a compulsory examination and accounting at the end of their term. There was no standing army, no police force, open or secret, and no way to coerce the people.

If Pericles was elected to the generalship fifteen years in a row and thirty times in all, it was not because he was a dictator but because he was a persuasive speaker, a skillful politician, a respected general, an acknowledged patriot, and a man patently incorruptible. When he lost the people's confidence, they did not hesitate to depose him from office. In 443 B.C., however, after the removal of his chief rival, he stood at the height of his power. He had been persuaded by the defeat of the Athenian fleet in the Egyptian campaign and the failure of Athens' continental campaigns that its future lay in a conservative policy of retaining the empire in the Aegean and living at peace with the Spartans. It was in this direction that he led Athens' imperial democracy in the years after the First Peloponnesian War.

The Women of Athens

Greek society, like most cultures, was dominated by men. This was true of the democratic city of Athens

A klepsydra, *or juror's water clock. The Athenians used water clocks to time speeches in their law courts. The clock shown here was found in the Athenian Agora and is now in the Royal Ontario Museum, Toronto. The mark XX shows that it holds two choes (about 6.5 liters); the six minutes that it would take to empty was the time alloted for rebuttal speeches in suits of a certain magnitude. [Agora Excavations, American School of Classical Studies at Athens.]*

in the great days of Pericles, in the fifth century B.C., no less than in other Greek cities. Nonetheless, the position of women in classical Athens has been the subject of much controversy. The bulk of the evidence—coming from the law, from philosophical and moral writings, and from information about the conditions of daily life and the organization of society—shows that women were excluded from most aspects of public life. They could not vote, take part in the political assemblies, hold public office, or take any direct part in politics. Male citizens of all classes had these public responsibilities and opportunities.

The same sources show that, in the private aspects of life, women were always under the control of a male guardian: a father, a husband, or, failing these, an appropriate male relative. Women married young, usually between the ages of twelve and eighteen, whereas their husbands were typically over thirty; hence, they were always in a relationship like that of a daughter to a father. Marriages were arranged; the woman normally had no choice of husband, and her dowry was controlled by a male relative. Divorce was difficult for a woman to obtain, for she needed the approval of a male relative who was then willing to serve as her guardian after the dissolution of the marriage. In case of divorce, the dowry returned with the woman but was controlled by her father or the appropriate male relative.

The main function and responsibility of a respectable Athenian woman of a citizen family was to produce male heirs for the household (*oikos*) of her husband. If, however, her father's *oikos* lacked a male heir, the daughter became an *epikleros*, the "heiress" to the family property. In that case, she was required by law to marry the next of kin on her father's side in order to produce the desired male offspring. In the Athenian way of thinking, women were "lent" by one household to another for purposes of bearing and raising a male heir to continue the existence of the *oikos*.

Because the pure and legitimate lineage of the offspring was important, women were carefully segregated from men outside the family and were confined to the women's quarters in the house. Men might seek sexual gratification outside the house with prostitutes of high or low style, frequently recruited from abroad. But respectable women stayed home to raise the children, cook, weave cloth, and oversee the management of the household. The only public function of women was an important one in the various rituals and festivals of the state religion. Apart from these activities, Athenian women were expected to remain home, quiet and unnoticed. Pericles told the widows and mothers of the Athenian men who died in the first year of the Peloponnesian War only this: "Your great glory is not to fall short of your natural character, and the greatest glory of women is to be least talked about by men, whether for good or bad."

The picture derived from these sources is largely accurate, but it does not fit well with what we learn from the evidence of the pictorial art, the tragedy and

Medea Bemoans the Condition of Women

In 431 B.C., Euripides (CA. 485–406 B.C.) presented his play Medea *at the Dionysiac festival in Athens. The heroine is a foreign woman who has unusual powers, but in the speech that follows, she describes the fate of women in terms that appear to give an accurate account of the condition of women in fifth-century B.C. Athens.*

Of all things which are living and can form a
    judgment
We women are the most unfortunate creatures.
Firstly, with an excess of wealth it is required
For us to buy a husband and take for our bodies
A master; for not to take one is even worse.
And now the question is serious whether we take
A good or bad one; for there is no easy escape
For a woman, nor can she say no to her marriage.
She arrives among new modes of behavior and
    manners,
And needs prophetic power, unless she has learned
    at home,
How best to manage him who shares the bed with her.
And if we work out all this well and carefully,

And the husband lives with us and lightly bears his
    yoke,
Then life is enviable. If not, I'd rather die.
A man, when he's tired of the company in his
    home,
Goes out of the house and puts an end to his
    boredom
And turns to a friend or companion of his own age.
But we are forced to keep our eyes on one alone.
What they say of us is that we have a peaceful time
Living at home, while they do the fighting in war.
How wrong they are! I would very much rather
    stand
Three times in the front of battle than bear
    one child. ❑

Euripides, *Medea* in *Four Tragedies*, trans. by Rex Warner, (Chicago: University of Chicago Press, 1955), pp. 66–67.

to men accords well with much of the evidence, but we must take note of the fact that the woman who complains of women's lot is the powerful central figure in a tragedy bearing her name. This tragedy was produced at state expense before most of the Athenian population, and was written by a man who was one of Athens' greatest poets and dramatists. Medea is a cause of terror to the audience and, at the same time, an object of their pity and sympathy as a victim of injustice. She is anything but the creature "least talked about by men, whether for good or for bad." There is reason to believe that the role played by Athenian women may have been more complex than their legal status might suggest.

The Great Peloponnesian War

In the decade after the Thirty Years' Peace of 445 B.C., the willingness of each side to respect the new arrangements was tested and not found wanting.

About 435 B.C., however, a dispute arose in a remote and unimportant part of the Greek world, plunging the Greeks into a long and disastrous war that shook the foundations of their civilization. On one side stood Sparta and the Peloponnesian League, on the other Athens and its Empire.

The Spartan strategy was traditional: to invade the enemy's country and threaten the crops, forcing the enemy to defend them in a hoplite battle. Such a battle the Spartans were sure to win, because they had the better army and they and their allies outnumbered the Athenians at least two to one. Any ordinary *polis* would have yielded or fought and lost, but Athens had an enormous navy, an annual income from the empire, a vast reserve fund, and long walls that connected the fortified city with the fortified port of Piraeus.

comedy, and the mythology of the Athenians. These often show women as central characters and powerful figures in both the public and the private spheres. The Clytemnestra in Aeschylus' tragedy *Agamemnon* arranges the murder of her royal husband and establishes the tyranny of her lover, whom she dominates. The terrifying and powerful Medea negotiates with kings. We are left with an apparent contradiction clearly revealed by a famous speech in Euripides' tragedy *Medea*. (See the document on page 105.)

The picture that Medea paints of women subjected

A foundry is depicted on an Attic vase of the fifth century B.C. Greek skill in metal work reached a high level of achievement by the fifth century. The major practical use for the skill was in weapons of war, but artistic applications, especially in bronze, were also important. Here we see an artisan stroking a furnace to maintain the high but carefully controlled temperature needed in his work.

The Athenians' strategy was to allow devastation of the land to prove that Athens was invulnerable. At the same time, the Athenians launched seaborne raids on the Peloponnesian coast to show that the allies of Sparta could be hurt. Pericles expected that within a year or two, three at most, the Peloponnesians would become discouraged and make peace, having learned their lesson. If the Peloponnesians held out, Athenian resources were inadequate to continue for more than four or five years without raising the tribute in the empire and running an unacceptable risk of rebellion. The plan required restraint and the leadership only a Pericles could provide.

Ten years of war (431–421 B.C.) led to a stalemate concluded by the Peace of Nicias. The peace was for fifty years and guaranteed the status quo, with a few exceptions. Neither side carried out all its commitments, and several of Sparta's allies refused to ratify the peace.

In 415 B.C. Alcibiades, a young and ambitious leader, persuaded the Athenians to attack Sicily to bring it under their control. In 413 B.C., the entire expedition was destroyed. The Athenians lost some two hundred ships, about forty-five hundred of their own men, and almost ten times as many allies. It was a disaster perhaps greater than the defeat of the Athenian fleet in the Egyptian campaign some forty years earlier. It shook Athenian prestige, reduced the power of Athens, provoked rebellions, and brought the wealth and power of Persia into the war on Sparta's side.

It is remarkable that the Athenians were able to continue fighting in spite of the disaster. They survived a brief oligarchic coup in 411 B.C. and won several important victories at sea as the war shifted to the Aegean. As their allies rebelled, however, and were sustained by fleets paid for by Persia, the Athenians saw their financial resources shrink and finally disappear. When their fleet was caught napping at Aegospotami in 405 B.C., they could not build another. The Spartans—under Lysander, a clever and ambitious general who was responsible for obtaining Persian support—cut off the food supply through the Hellespont, and the Athenians were starved into submission. In 404 B.C., they surrendered unconditionally; the city walls were dismantled, Athens was permitted no fleet, and the empire was gone. The Great Peloponnesian War was over.

The Struggle for Greek Leadership

THE HEGEMONY OF SPARTA. The collapse of the Athenian empire created a vacuum of power in the Aegean and opened the way for Spartan leadership, or hegemony. Fulfilling the contract that had brought them the funds to win the war, the Spartans handed the Greek cities of Asia Minor back to Persia. Under the leadership of Lysander, the Spartans went on to make a complete mockery of their promise to free the Greeks by stepping into the imperial role of Athens in the cities along the European coast and the islands of the Aegean. In most of the cities, Lysander installed a board of ten local oligarchs loyal to him and supported them with a Spartan garrison. Tribute brought in an annual revenue almost as great as that which the Athenians had collected.

Limited manpower, the Helot problem, and traditional conservatism all made Sparta less than an ideal state to rule a maritime empire. Some of Sparta's allies, especially Thebes and Corinth, were alienated by the increasing arrogance of Sparta's policies. In 404 B.C., Lysander installed an oligarchic government in Athens whose outrageous behavior earned them the title "Thirty Tyrants." Democratic exiles took refuge in Thebes and Corinth and created an army to challenge the oligarchy. Sparta's conservative king, Pausanias, replaced Lysander, arranging a peaceful settlement and ultimately the restoration of democracy. Thereafter, Athenian foreign policy remained under Spartan control, but otherwise Athens was free.

In 405 B.C., Darius II of Persia (reigned 424–405 B.C.) died and was succeeded by Artaxerxes II. His younger brother, Cyrus, contested his rule and received Spartan help in recruiting a Greek mercenary army to help him win the throne. They marched inland as far as Mesopotamia, where they defeated the Persians at Cunaxa in 401 B.C., but Cyrus was killed. The Greeks were able to march back to the Black Sea and safety; their success revealed the potential weakness of the Persian Empire.

The Greeks of Asia Minor had supported Cyrus and were now afraid of Artaxerxes' revenge. The Spartans accepted their request for aid and sent an army into Asia, attracted by the prospect of prestige, power, and money. In 396 B.C., the command was given to Sparta's new king, Agesilaus (444–360 B.C.). His personality and policy dominated Sparta throughout its period of hegemony and until his death in 360 B.C. Hampered by his lameness and his disputed claim to the throne, he seems to have compensated for both by always ad-

THE GREAT PELOPONNESIAN WAR

435 B.C.	Civil war at Epidamnus
432 B.C.	Sparta declares war on Athens
431 B.C.	Peloponnesian invasion of Athens
421 B.C.	Peace of Nicias
415–413 B.C.	Athenian invasion of Sicily
405 B.C.	Battle of Aegospotami
404 B.C.	Athens surrenders

vocating aggressive policies and providing himself with opportunities to display his bravery in battle.

Agesilaus collected much booty and frightened the Persians. They sent a messenger with money and promises of further support to friendly factions in all the likely states. By 395 B.C., Thebes was able to organize an alliance that included Argos, Corinth, and a resurgent Athens. The result was the Corinthian War (395–387 B.C.), which put an end to Sparta's Asian adventure. In 394, the Persian fleet destroyed Sparta's maritime empire. Meanwhile the Athenians took advantage of events to rebuild their walls, enlarge their navy, and even to recover some of their lost empire in the Aegean. The war ended when the exhausted Greek states accepted a peace dictated by the Great King of Persia.

The Persians, frightened by the recovery of Athens, turned the management of Greece over to Sparta. Agesilaus broke up all alliances except the Peloponnesian League. He interfered with the autonomy of other *poleis* by using the Spartan army, or the threat of its use, to put friends in power within them. Sparta reached a new level of lawless arrogance in 382 B.C., when it seized Thebes during peacetime without warning or pretext. In 379, a Spartan army made a similar attempt on Athens. That action persuaded the Athenians to join with Thebes, which had rebelled from Sparta a few months earlier, to wage war on the Spartans. In 371 B.C., the Thebans, led by their great generals Pelopidas and Epaminondas, defeated the Spartans at Leuctra. The Thebans encouraged the Arcadian cities of the central Peloponnesus to form a federal league, freed the Helots, and helped them found a city of their own. They deprived Sparta of much of its farmland and of the men who worked it and hemmed it in with hostile neighbors. Sparta's population had shrunk so that it could put fewer than two thousand men into the field at Leuctra. Sparta's aggressive policies had led to ruin. The Theban victory brought the end of Sparta as a power of the first rank.

THEBAN HEGEMONY. Victorious Thebes had a democratic constitution, control over Boeotia, and two outstanding and popular generals. These were the basis for Theban power after Leuctra. Pelopidas died in a successful attempt to gain control of Thessaly. Epaminondas consolidated his work, and Thebes was soon dominant over all Greece north of Athens and the Corinthian Gulf. The Thebans challenged the reborn Athenian empire in the Aegean.

All this activity provoked resistance, and by 362 B.C., Thebes faced a Peloponnesian coalition as well as Athens. Epaminondas once again led a victorious Boeotian army into the Peloponnesus at Mantinea but he died in the fight, and the loss of its two great leaders ended Thebes' dominance.

THE SECOND ATHENIAN EMPIRE. Athens had organized the Second Athenian Confederation in 378 B.C. It was aimed at resisting Spartan aggression in the Aegean, and its constitution was careful to avoid the abuses of the Delian League. But the Athenians soon began to repeat those abuses, although this time they did not have the power to put down resistance. When the collapse of Sparta and Thebes and the restraint of Persia removed any reason for voluntary membership, Athens' allies revolted. By 355 B.C., Athens had to abandon most of the empire. After two centuries of almost continuous warfare, the Greeks returned to the chaotic disorganization of the time before the founding of the Peloponnesian League.

THE SPARTAN AND THEBAN HEGEMONIES

404–403 B.C.	Thirty Tyrants rule at Athens
401 B.C.	Expedition of Cyrus, rebellious prince of Persia; Battle of Cunaxa
400–387 B.C.	Spartan War against Persia
398–360 B.C.	Reign of Agesilaus at Sparta
395–387 B.C.	Corinthian War
382 B.C.	Sparta seizes Thebes
378 B.C.	Second Athenian Confederation founded
371 B.C.	Thebans defeat Sparta at Leuctra; end of Spartan hegemony
362 B.C.	Battle of Mantinea; end of Theban hegemony

The Culture of Classical Greece

The repulse of the Persian invasion released a flood of creative activity in Greece rarely if ever matched anywhere at any time.

The Fifth Century B.C.

The century and a half between the Persian retreat and the conquest of Greece by Philip of Macedon (479–338 B.C.) produced achievements of such quality as to justify that era's designation as the Classical Period. Ironically, we often use the term *classical* to suggest calm and serenity, but the word that best describes the common element present in Greek life, thought, art, and literature in this period is *tension*. It was a time in which conflict among the *poleis* continued and intensified as Athens and Sparta gathered most of them into two competing and menacing blocs.

The Parthenon at Athens. This temple to Athena Parthenos (Athena the Maiden) was built under the direction of Pericles between 447 and 432 B.C., using funds from the treasury of the Delian League. It is generally thought to be the finest of all Greek temples. Built in the Doric order, with many subtle refinements, and crowning the Acropolis, it gave visible evidence of the greatness of Athens. [Greek National Tourist Organization, New York.]

The victory over the Persians brought a sense of exultation in the capacity of humans to accomplish great things and of confidence in the divine justice that brought arrogant pride low. But these feelings conflicted with a sense of unease as the Greeks recognized that the fate that had met Xerxes awaited all those who reached too far. Another source of tension was the conflict between the soaring hopes and achievements of individuals and the claims and limits put on them by their fellow citizens in the *polis*. These forces were at work throughout Greece, but we know them best and they had the most spectacular results in Athens in its Golden Age, the time between the Persian and Peloponnesian wars.

ATTIC TRAGEDY. Nothing reflects these concerns better than the appearance of Attic tragedy as the major form of Greek poetry in the fifth century B.C. The tragedies were presented as part of public religious observations in honor of the god Dionysus.

The whole affair was very much a civic occasion. Each poet who wished to compete submitted his work to the archon. Each offered three tragedies, which might or might not have a common subject, and a satyr play (a comic choral dialogue with Dionysus) to close. The archon chose the best three competitors and awarded them each three actors and a chorus. The actors were paid by the state, and the chorus was provided by a wealthy citizen selected by the state to perform this service as *choregos*, for the Athenians had no direct taxation to support such activities. Most of the tragedies were performed in the theater of Dionysus on the south side of the Acropolis, and as many as thirty thousand Athenians could attend. Prizes and honors were awarded to the author, the actor, and the *choregos* voted best by a jury of Athenians chosen by lot. On rare occasions, the subject of the play might be a contemporary or historical event, but almost always it was chosen from mythology. Before Euripides, it always dealt solemnly with serious questions of religion, politics, ethics, morality, or some combination of these.

ARCHITECTURE AND SCULPTURE. The great architectural achievements of Periclean Athens, just as much as Athenian tragedy, illustrate the magnificent

The porch of the maidens on the Erechtheum. This is a uniquely designed Ionic temple built on the Athenian Acropolis near the Parthenon between about 421 and 409 B.C. It housed the shrines of three different gods and presented special architectures in the porch facing the Parthenon. In place of the usual fluted columns it uses statues of young girls taking part in a religious festival as columns. (Columns made from the draped female figure are called caryatids.) [Greek National Tourist Organization, New York.]

results of the union and tension between religious and civic responsibilities on the one hand and the transcendent genius of the individual artist on the other. Beginning in 448 B.C. and continuing down to the outbreak of the Great Peloponnesian War, Pericles undertook a great building program on the Acropolis. The funds were provided by the income from the empire. The buildings were temples to honor the city's gods and a fitting gateway to the temples.

Pericles' main purpose seems to have been to represent visually the greatness and power of Athens, but in such a way as to emphasize intellectual and artistic achievement, civilization rather than military and naval power. It was as though these buildings were tangible proof of Pericles' claim that Athens was "the school of Hellas," that is, the intellectual center of all Greece.

HISTORY. The fifth century B.C. produced the first prose literature in the form of history. Herodotus, born shortly before the Persian wars, deserves his title of the "father of history," for his account of the Persian wars goes far beyond all previous chronicles, genealogies, and geographical studies. His history attempts to explain human actions and to draw instruction from them.

Herodotus accepted the evidence of legends and oracles, although not uncritically, and often explained human events in terms of divine intervention. Human arrogance and divine vengeance are key forces that help explain the defeat of Croesus by Cyrus as well as Xerxes' defeat by the Greeks. Yet the History is typical of its time in celebrating the crucial role of human intelligence as revealed by Miltiades at Marathon and Themistocles at Salamis. Nor was Herodotus unaware of the importance of institutions. There is no mistaking his pride in the superiority of the Greek *polis* and the discipline it inspired in its citizen soldiers and his pride in the superiority of the Greeks' voluntary obedience to law over the Persians' fear of punishment.

Thucydides, the historian of the Peloponnesian wars, was born about 460 B.C. and died a few years after the end of the Great Peloponnesian War. He was very much a product of the late fifth century, reflecting the influence of the scientific attitude of the Hippocratic school of medicine as well as the secular, human-centered, skeptical rationalism of the Sophists. Hippocrates of Cos was a contemporary of Thucydides who was part of a school of medical writers and practitioners. They did important pioneer work in medicine and scientific theory, placing great emphasis on the need to combine careful and accurate observation with reason to make possible the understanding, prognosis, treatment, and cure of a disease.

In the same way, Thucydides took great pains to achieve factual accuracy and tried to use his evidence to discover meaningful patterns of human behavior. He believed that human nature was essentially unchanging, so that a wise person equipped with the understanding provided by history might accurately foresee events and thus help to guide them. He believed, however, that only a few had the ability to understand history and put its lessons to good use. He thought that even the wisest could be foiled by the intervention of chance, which played a great role in human affairs. Thucydides focused his interest on politics, and in that area, his assumptions about human nature do not seem unwarranted. His work has proved to be, as he had hoped, "a possession forever." Its

The theater at Epidaurus. This theater, built in the fourth century B.C., is one of the best preserved of ancient Greek theaters. Epidaurus, a city in the eastern Peloponnesus, was the site of the Sanctuary of Asclepius, the hero and god of healing. The sick and crippled came there, as to Lourdes in modern times, to be healed. The religious festivals there included theatrical performances that drew large crowds. [Greek National Tourist Organization, New York.]

description of the terrible civil war between the two basic kinds of *polis* is a final and fitting example of the tension that was the source of both the greatness and the decline of classical Greece.

The Fourth Century B.C.

Historians often speak of the Great Peloponnesian War as the crisis of the *polis* and of the fourth century as the period of its decline. But the Greeks of the fourth century B.C. did not know that their traditional way of life was on the verge of destruction. Some looked to the past and tried to shore up the weakened structure of the *polis*; others tended toward despair and looked for new solutions; and still others averted their gaze from the public arena altogether. All of these responses are apparent in the literature, philosophy, and art of the period.

DRAMA. The tendency of some to avert their gaze from the life of the *polis* and to turn inward to everyday life, the family, and their own individuality is apparent in the poetry of the fourth century B.C. Tragedy proved to be a form whose originality was confined to the fifth century B.C.. No tragedies written in the fourth century B.C. have been preserved, and it was common to revive the great plays of the previous century. Some of the late plays of Euripides (CA. 484–406 B.C.), in fact, seem less like the tragedies of Aeschylus and Sophocles than forerunners of later forms such as the New Comedy (CA. 325–260 B.C.). Plays of Euripides like *Helena*, *Andromeda*, and *Iphigenia in Tauris* are more like fairy tales, tales of adventure, or love stories than tragedies. Euripides was less interested in cosmic confrontations of conflicting principles than in the psychology and behavior of individual human beings. His plays, which rarely won first prize when first produced for Dionysian festival competitions, became increasingly popular in the fourth century B.C. and after.

Comedy was introduced into the Dionysian festival early in the fifth century B.C. Such poets as Cratinus, Eupolis, and the great master of the genre called Old Comedy, Aristophanes (CA. 450–CA. 385 B.C.), the only one from whom we have complete plays, wrote political comedies filled with scathing invective and satire against such contemporary figures as Pericles, Cleon, Socrates, and Euripides. The fourth century B.C., however, produced what is called Middle Comedy, which turned away from political subjects and personal invective toward a comic-realistic depiction of daily life, plots of intrigue, and mild satire of domestic situations. Significantly, the role of the chorus, which in some way represented the *polis*, was very much diminished. These trends all continued and were carried even further in the New Comedy, whose leading playwright, Menander (342–291 B.C.), completely abandoned mythological subjects in favor of domestic

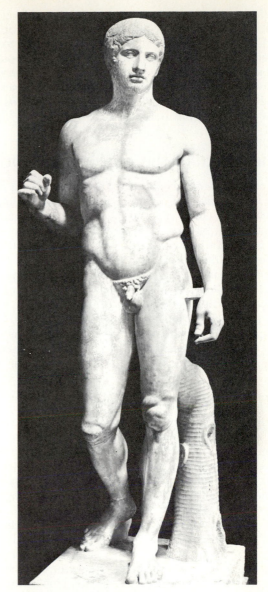

The Doryphorus ("The spear-bearer"). The young man portrayed is an athlete prepared to throw a javelin. The original, of which this is a Roman copy, was a bronze statue by the great Greek sculptor Polycleitus, who worked during the middle of the fifth century B.C. This statue was found at Pompeii and is now in the museum at Naples. [Alinari/SCALA.]

tragicomedy. His gentle satire of the foibles of ordinary people and his tales of lovers temporarily thwarted before a happy and proper ending would not be unfamiliar to viewers of modern situation comedies.

SCULPTURE. The same movement away from the grand, the ideal, and the general and toward the ordinary, the real, and the individual is apparent in the development of Greek sculpture. To see these developments, one has only to compare the statue of the *Striding God of Artemisium* (CA. 460 B.C.), thought to be either Zeus on the point of releasing a thunderbolt or Poseidon about to throw his trident or the *Doryphoros* of Polycleitus (CA. 450–440 B.C.) with the *Hermes* of Praxiteles (CA. 340–330 B.C.) or the *Apoxyomenos* attributed to Lysippus (CA. 330 B.C.).

Emergence of the Hellenistic World

The term *Hellenistic* was coined in the nineteenth century to describe the period of three centuries during which Greek culture spread far from its homeland to Egypt and far into Asia. The new civilization formed in this expansion was a mixture of Greek and Oriental elements, although the degree of mixture varied from time to time and place to place. The Hellenistic world was larger than the world of classical Greece, and its major political units were much larger than the city-states, though these persisted in different forms. The new political and cultural order had its roots in the rise to power of a Macedonian dynasty that conquered Greece and the Persian Empire in the space of two generations.

The Macedonian Conquest

The quarrels among the Greeks brought on defeat and conquest by a new power that suddenly rose to eminence in the fourth century B.C., the kingdom of Macedon. The Macedonians inhabited the land to the north of Thessaly, and through the centuries, they had unknowingly served the vital purpose of protecting the Greek states from barbarian tribes further to the north. By Greek standards, Macedon was a backward, semibarbaric land. It had no *poleis* and was ruled loosely by a king in a rather Homeric fashion. He was chosen partly on the basis of descent, but the acclamation of the army gathered in assembly was required to make him legitimate. Quarrels between pretenders to the throne and even murder to achieve it were not uncommon. A council of nobles checked the royal power and could reject a weak or incompetent king.

Hampered by constant wars with the barbarians, internal strife, loose organization, and lack of money, Macedon played no great part in Greek affairs up to the fourth century B.C. The Macedonians were of the same stock as the Greeks and spoke a Greek dialect, and the nobles, at least, thought of themselves as Greeks. The kings claimed descent from Heracles and the royal house of Argos. They tried to bring Greek culture into their court and won acceptance at the Olympic games. If a king could be found with the ability to unify this nation, it was bound to play a greater part in Greek affairs.

PHILIP OF MACEDON. That king was Philip II (359–336 B.C.), who, while still under thirty, took advantage of his appointment as regent to overthrow his infant nephew and make himself king. Like many of his predecessors, he admired Greek culture. Between 367 and 364 B.C., he had been a hostage in Thebes, where he learned much about Greek politics and warfare under the tutelage of Epaminondas. His natural talents for war and diplomacy and his boundless ambition made him the ablest king in Macedonian history. Using both diplomatic and military means, he was able to pacify the tribes on his frontiers and to make his own hold on the throne firmer. Then he began to undermine Athenian control of the northern Aegean. He took Amphipolis, which gave him control of the Strymon valley and of the gold and silver mines of Mount Pangaeus. The income allowed him to found new cities, to bribe politicians in foreign towns, and to reorganize his army into the finest fighting force in the world.

THE INVASION OF GREECE. So armed, Philip turned south toward central Greece. His conquests

Mosaic of a lion hunt from Pella, which became the royal capital of Macedon at the end of the fifth century B.C. The city developed rapidly under Philip II. [Bettmann Archive.]

Demosthenes Denounces Philip of Macedon

Demosthenes (384–322 B.C.) was an Athenian statesman who urged his fellow citizens and other Greeks to resist the advance of Philip of Macedon (CA. 358–317 B.C.). The following is from the speech we call the First Philippic, delivered probably in 351 B.C.

Do not imagine, that his empire is everlastingly secured to him as a god. There are those who hate and envy him, Athenians, even among those that are most friendly; and all feelings that are in other men belong, we may assume, to his confederates. But now they are cowed, having no refuge through your tardiness and indolence, which I say you must abandon forthwith. For you see, Athenians, the case, to what pitch of arrogance the man has advanced, who leaves you not even the choice of action or inaction, but threatens and uses (they say) outrageous language, and, unable to rest in possession of his conquests, continually widens their circle, and whilst we dally and delay, throws his net all around us. When then, Athenians, when will ye act as becomes you? In what event? In that of necessity, I suppose. And how should we regard the events happening now? Methinks, to freemen the strongest necessity is the disgrace of their condition. Or tell me, do ye like walking about and asking one another:—is there any news? Why, could there be greater news than a man of Macedonia subduing Athenians, and directing the affairs of Greece? Is Philip dead? No, but he is sick. And what matters it to you? Should anything befall this man, you will soon create another Philip, if you attend to business thus. For even he has been exalted not so much by his own strength, as by our negligence. ❑

Demosthenes, *The Olynthiac and Other Public Orations of Demosthenes*, trans. by C. R. Kennedy (London: George Bell and Sons, 1903), pp. 62–63.

---

threatened the vital interest of Athens, which still had a formidable fleet of three hundred ships.

The Athens of 350 B.C. was not the Athens of Pericles. It had neither imperial revenue nor allies to share the burden of war on land or sea, and its own population was smaller than in the fifth century. The Athenians, therefore, were reluctant to go on expeditions themselves or even to send out mercenary armies under Athenian generals, for they must be paid out of taxes or contributions from Athenian citizens.

The leading spokesman against these tendencies and the cautious foreign policy that went with them was Demosthenes (384–322 B.C.), one of the greatest orators in Greek history. He was convinced that Philip was a dangerous enemy to Athens and the other Greeks and spent most of his career urging the Athenians to resist Philip's encroachments. He was right, for beginning in 349 B.C., Philip attacked several cities in northern and central Greece and firmly planted Macedonian power in those regions. The king of "barbarian" Macedon was elected president of the Pythian Games at Delphi, and the Athenians were forced to concur in the election.

The years between 346 B.C. and 340 B.C. were spent in diplomatic maneuvering, each side trying to win strategically useful allies. At last, Philip attacked Perinthus and Byzantium, the life line of Athenian commerce, and in 340, he besieged both cities and declared war. The Athenian fleet saved both, so in the following year Philip marched into Greece. Demosthenes performed wonders in rallying the Athenians and winning Thebes over to the Athenian side, but in 338, Philip defeated the allied forces at Chaeronea in Boeotia in a great battle whose decisive blow was a cavalry charge led by the eighteen-year-old son of Philip, Alexander.

THE MACEDONIAN GOVERNMENT OF GREECE. The Macedonian settlement of Greek affairs was not as harsh as many had feared, although in some cities the friends of Macedon came to power and killed or exiled their enemies. Demosthenes continued to be free or engage in politics, and Athens was not attacked on the condition that it give up what was left of its empire and follow the lead of Macedon. The rest of Greece was arranged in such a way as to remove all dangers to Philip's rule. To guarantee his security, Philip placed garrisons at Thebes, Chalcis, and Corinth; these came to be known as the fetters of Greece. In 338 B.C., Philip called a meeting of the Greek states to form the federal league of Corinth. The constitution provided for autonomy, freedom from tribute and garrisons, and suppression of piracy and civil war. The league delegates would make foreign policy, in theory without consulting their home governments or Philip. All this was a facade; not only was Philip of Macedon president of the league, but he was its ruler. The defeat at Chaeronea meant the end of Greek freedom and autonomy. Though its form and internal life continued for some time, the *polis* had lost control of its own affairs and the special conditions that had made it unique.

Philip's choice of Corinth as the seat of his new confederacy was not made out of convenience or by accident. It was at Corinth that the Greeks had gathered to resist a Persian invasion almost 150 years earlier, and

it was there in 337 B.C. that Philip announced his intention to invade Persia in a war of liberation and revenge as leader of the new league. In the spring of 336 B.C., as he prepared to begin the campaign, Philip was assassinated.

In 1977, a mound was excavated at the Macedonian village of Vergina. The extraordinarily rich finds and associated buildings have led many scholars to conclude that this is the royal tomb of Philip II. If they are right, and the evidence seems persuasive, Philip richly deserved so distinguished a resting place. He found Macedon a disunited kingdom of semibarbarians, despised and exploited by the Greeks; at his death, Macedon was a united kingdom, master and leader of the Greeks, rich, powerful, and ready to undertake the invasion of Asia. The completion of this task was left to Philip's first son, Alexander III (356–323 B.C.), later called Alexander the Great, who came to the throne at the age of twenty.

Alexander the Great

Along with his throne, the young king Alexander inherited his father's plan to invade Persia. The idea was daring, for Persia's empire was vast and its re-

MAP 4-3   ALEXANDER'S CAMPAIGNS   *The route taken by Alexander the Great in his conquest of the Persian Empire, 334–323 B.C. Starting from the Macedonian capital at Pella, he reached the Indus valley before being turned back by his own restive troops. He died of fever in Mesopotamia.*

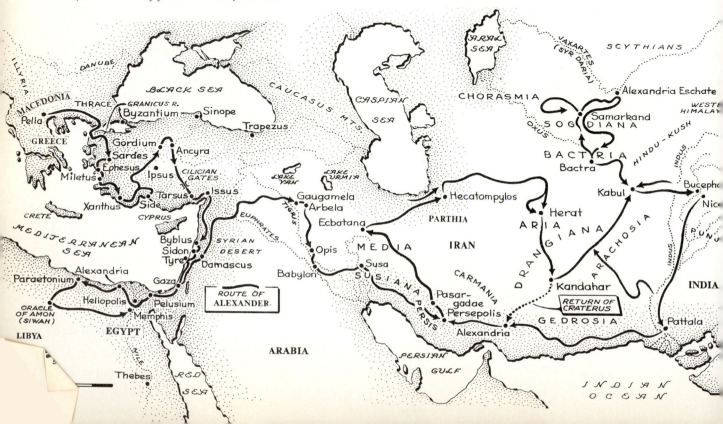

sources enormous, but the usurper Cyrus and his Greek mercenaries had shown its vulnerability by penetrating deep into the Persian Empire at the beginning of the fourth century B.C.

THE CONQUEST OF PERSIA AND BEYOND. In 334 B.C., Alexander crossed the Hellespont into Asia. His army consisted of about thirty thousand infantry and five thousand cavalry; he had no navy and little money. These facts determined his early strategy: he aimed to seek quick and decisive battles to gain money and supplies from the conquered territory. He moved along the coast so as to neutralize the Persian navy by depriving it of ports.

Alexander met the Persian forces of Asia Minor at the Granicus River, where he won a smashing victory in characteristic style (see Map 4.3). He led a cavalry charge across the river into the teeth of the enemy on the opposite bank, almost losing his life in the process and winning the devotion of his soldiers. That victory

Arrian Describes Alexander's Actions at a Tragic Drinking Party

Arrian lived in the second century A.D., *almost five hundred years after Alexander the Great, but his* Anabasis *is the best ancient source of information about Alexander's career. In 328* B.C., *Alexander's expedition had reached Samarkand. By now he had adopted a number of Persian customs and had begun to reduce the distinction between Macedonians and Persians. The older Macedonians, in particular, were resentful, and the following passage describes a drinking bout in which a quarrel arose between Alexander and one of the most distinguished Macedonian veterans.*

When the drinking-party on this occasion had already gone on too long (for Alexander had now made innovations even in regard to drinking, by imitating too much the custom of foreigners), and in the midst of the carouse a discussion had arisen about the Dioscuri, how their procreation had been taken away from Tyndareus and ascribed to Zeus, some of those present, in order to flatter Alexander, maintained that Polyleuces and Castor were in no way worthy to compare with him and his exploits. Such men have always destroyed and will never cease to ruin the interests of those who happen to be reigning. In their carousal they did not even abstain from comparing him with Heracles, saying that envy stood in the way of the living receiving the honours due to them from their associates. It was well known that Clitus had long been vexed at Alexander for the change in his style of living in excessive imitation of foreign customs, and at those who flattered him with their speech. At that time also, being heated with wine, he would not permit them either to insult the deity or, by depreciating the deeds of the ancient heroes, to confer upon Alexander this gratification which deserved no thanks. He affirmed Alexander's deeds were neither in fact at all so great or marvellous as they represented in their laudation; nor had he achieved them by himself, but for the most part they were the deeds of the Macedonians. The delivery of this speech annoyed Alexander; and I do not commend it, for I think, in such a drunken bout, it would have been sufficient if, so far as he was personally concerned, he had kept silence, and not committed the error of indulging in the same flattery as the others. But when some even mentioned Philip's actions without exercising a just judgment, declaring that he had performed nothing great or marvellous, they herein gratified Alexander; but Clitus being then no longer able to contain himself, began to put Philip's achievements in the first rank, and to depreciate Alexander and his performances. Clitus being now quite intoxicated, made other depreciatory remarks and even vehemently reviled him, because after all he had saved his life, when the cavalry battle had been fought with the Persians at the Granicus. Then indeed, arrogantly stretching out his right hand, he said, "This hand, O Alexander, preserved you on that occasion." Alexander could now no longer endure the drunken insolence of Clitus; but jumped up against him in a great rage. He was however restrained by his boon companions. As Clitus did not desist from his insulting remarks, Alexander shouted out a summons for his shield-bearing guards to attend him; but when no one obeyed him, he said that he was reduced to the same position as Darius, when he was led about under arrest by Bessus and his adherents, and that he now possessed the mere name of king. Then his companions were no longer able to restrain him; for according to some he leaped up and snatched a javelin from one of his confidential body-guards; according to others, a long pike from one of his ordinary guards, with which he struck Clitus and killed him. ❑

Arrian, *The Anabasis of Alexander*, trans. by E. J. Chinnock in *The Greek Historians*, ed. by F. R. B. Godolphin, Vol. 2 (New York: Random House, 1942), pp. 507–508.

left the coast of Asia Minor open, and Alexander captured the coastal cities, thus denying them to the Persian fleet.

In 333 B.C., Alexander marched inland to Syria, where he met the main Persian army under King Darius at Issus. Alexander himself led the cavalry charge that broke the Persian line and sent Darius fleeing into central Asia Minor. He continued along the coast and captured previously impregnable Tyre after a long and ingenious siege, putting an end to the threat of the Persian navy. He took Egypt with little trouble and was greeted as liberator, pharaoh, and son of Re (the Egyptian god whose Greek equivalent was Zeus). At Tyre, Darius sent Alexander a peace offer, yielding his entire empire west of the Euphrates River and his daughter in exchange for an alliance and an end to the invasion. But Alexander aimed at conquering the whole empire and probably whatever lay beyond that.

In the spring of 331 B.C., Alexander marched into Mesopotamia. At Gaugamela, near the ancient Assyrian city of Nineveh, he met Darius, ready for a last stand. Once again, Alexander's tactical genius and personal leadership carried the day. The Persians were broken and Darius fled once more. Alexander entered Babylon, again hailed as liberator and king. In January of 330 B.C., he came to Persepolis, the Persian capital, which held splendid palaces and the royal treasury. This bonanza ended his financial troubles and put a vast sum of money into circulation, with economic consequences that lasted for centuries. After a stay of several months, Alexander burned Persepolis to dramatize the completion of Hellenic revenge for the Persian invasion and the destruction of the native Persian dynasty.

The new regime could not be secure while Darius lived, so Alexander pursued him eastward. Just south of the Caspian Sea, he came upon the corpse of Darius, killed by Darius' relative Bessus. The Persian nobles around Darius had lost faith in him and had joined in the plot. The murder removed Darius from Alexander's path, but now had to catch Bessus, who proclaimed himself successor to Darius. The pursuit of Bessus (who was soon caught), a great curiosity, and a longing to go as far as he could and see the most distant places took Alexander to the frontier of India.

Near Samarkand, in the land of the Scythians, he founded the city of Alexandria Eschate ("Furthest Alexandria"), one of the many cities bearing his name that he founded as he traveled. As a part of his grand scheme of amalgamation and conquest, he married the Bactrian princess Roxane and enrolled thirty thousand young Bactrians for his army. These were to be trained and sent back to the center of the empire for use later.

In 327 B.C., Alexander took his army through the Khyber Pass in an attempt to conquer the lands around

THE RISE OF MACEDON

359–336 B.C.	Reign of Philip II
338 B.C.	Battle of Chaeronea; Philip conquers Greece
338 B.C.	Founding of League of Corinth
336–323 B.C.	Reign of Alexander III, the Great
334 B.C.	Alexander invades Asia
333 B.C.	Battle of Issus
331 B.C.	Battle of Gaugamela
330 B.C.	Fall of Persepolis
327 B.C.	Alexander reaches Indus Valley
323 B.C.	Death of Alexander

the Indus River (modern Pakistan). He reduced its king, Porus, to vassalage but pushed on in the hope of reaching the river called Ocean that the Greeks believed encircled the world. Finally, his weary men refused to go on. By the spring of 324 B.C., the army was back at the Persian Gulf and celebrated in the Macedonian style, with a wild spree of drinking.

THE DEATH OF ALEXANDER. Alexander was filled with plans for the future: for the consolidation and organization of his empire; for geographical exploration; for building new cities, roads, and harbors; perhaps even for further conquests in the west. There is even some evidence that he asked to be deified and worshiped as a god, although we cannot be sure if he really did so or what he had in mind if he did. In June of 323 B.C., he was overcome by a fever and died in Babylon at the age of thirty-three. His memory has never faded, and he soon became the subject of myth, legend, and romance. From the beginning, estimates of him have varied. Some have seen in him a man of grand and noble vision who transcended the narrow limits of Greek and Macedonian ethnocentrism and aimed at the brotherhood of humankind in a great world state. Others have seen him as a calculating despot, given to drunken brawls, brutality, and murder.

The truth is probably in between. Alexander was one of the greatest generals the world has seen; he never lost a battle or failed in a siege, and with a modest army, he conquered a vast empire. He had rare organizational talents, and his plan for creating a multinational empire was the only intelligent way of proceeding. He established many new cities—seventy, according to tradition—mostly along trade routes. These cities had the effect of encouraging commerce and prosperity as well as introducing Hellenic civilization into new areas. It is hard to know if the vast new empire could have been held together, but Alexander's death proved that only he could have succeeded.

Nobody was prepared for Alexander's sudden death in 323 B.C., and affairs were further complicated by a weak succession: Roxane's unborn child and Alexander's weak-minded half-brother. His able and loyal Macedonian generals at first hoped to preserve the empire for the Macedonian royal house, and to this end, they appointed themselves governors of the various provinces of the empire. However, the conflicting ambitions of these strong-willed men led to prolonged warfare among various combinations of them, in which three of the original number were killed, and all of the direct members of the Macedonian royal house were either executed or murdered. With the murder of Roxane and her son in 310 B.C., there was no longer any focus for the enormous empire, and in 306 and 305, the surviving governors proclaimed themselves kings of their various holdings.

Three of these Macedonian generals founded dynasties of significance in the spread of Hellenistic culture:

Ptolemy I (367?–283 B.C.)	Founder of the Thirty-first Dynasty in Egypt, the Ptolemies, of whom Cleopatra, who died in 30 B.C., was the last
Seleucus I (358?–280 B.C.)	Founder of the Seleucid dynasty in Mesopotamia
Antigonus I (382–301 B.C.)	Founder of the Antigonid dynasty in Asia Minor and Macedon

For the first seventy-five years or so after the death of Alexander, the world ruled by his successors enjoyed considerable prosperity. The vast sums of money he and they put into circulation greatly increased the level of economic activity. The opportunities for service and profit in the east attracted many Greeks and relieved their native cities of some of the pressure of the poor. The opening of vast new territories to Greek trade, the increased demand for Greek products, and the new availability of things wanted by the Greeks, as well as the conscious policies of the Hellenistic kings, all helped the growth of commerce. The new prosperity, however, was not evenly distributed. The urban Greeks, the Macedonians, and the hellenized natives who made up the upper and middle classes lived lives of comfort and even luxury, but the rural native peasants did not. During prosperous times, these distinctions were bearable, although even then there was tension between the two groups.

After a while, however, the costs of continuing wars, inflation, and a gradual lessening of the positive effects of the introduction of Persian wealth all led to economic crisis. The kings bore down heavily on the middle classes, who, however, were skilled in avoiding their responsibilities. The pressure on the peasants and the city laborers became great, too, and they responded by slowing down their work and even by striking. In Greece, economic pressures brought clashes between rich and poor, demands for the abolition of debt and the redistribution of land, and even, on occasion, civil war.

These internal divisions, along with the international wars, weakened the capacity of the Hellenistic kingdoms to resist outside attack, and by the middle of the second century B.C., they were all gone, except for Egypt. The two centuries between Alexander and the Roman conquest, however, were of great and lasting importance. They saw the formation into a single political, economic, and cultural unit of the entire eastern Mediterranean coast and of Greece, Egypt, Mesopotamia, and the old Persian Empire. The period also saw the creation of a new culture that took root, at least in the urban portions of that vast area, one that deserves to be differentiated from the earlier one of the Greek city-states: Hellenistic culture.

Hellenistic Culture

The career of Alexander the Great marked a significant turning point in the thought of the Greeks as it was represented in literature, philosophy, religion, and art. His conquests and the establishment of the successor kingdoms put an end once and for all to the central role of the *polis* in Greek life and thought.

Deprived of control of their foreign affairs, their important internal arrangements determined by a foreign monarch, the postclassical cities lost the kind of political freedom that was basic to the old outlook. They were cities, perhaps—in a sense, even city-states—but not *poleis*. As time passed, they changed from sovereign states to municipal towns merged in military empires. Never again in antiquity would there be either a serious attack on or a defense of the *polis*, for its importance was gone. For the most part, the Greeks after Alexander turned away from political solutions for their problems and sought instead personal responses to their hopes and fears, particularly in religion, philosophy, and magic. The confident, sometimes arrogant, humanism of the fifth century B.C. gave way to a kind of resignation to fate, a recognition of helplessness before forces too great for humans to manage.

Philosophy

These developments are noticeable in the changes that overtook the established schools of philosophy as well as in the emergence of two new and influential groups of philosophers, the Epicureans and the Stoics. Athens' position as the center of philosophical studies was reinforced, for the Academy and the Lyceum continued in operation, and the new schools were also located in Athens. The Lyceum turned gradually away from the universal investigations of its founder, Aristotle, even from his scientific interests, to become a center chiefly of literary and especially historical studies.

The Academy turned even further away from its tradition. It adopted the systematic Skepticism of Pyrrho of Elis, and under the leadership of Arcesilaus and Carneades, the Skeptics of the Academy became skilled at pointing out fallacies and weaknesses in the philosophies of the rival schools. They thought that nothing could be known and so consoled themselves and their followers by suggesting that nothing mattered. It was easy for them, therefore, to accept conventional morality and the world as it was. The Cynics, of course, continued to denounce convention and to advocate the crude life in accordance with nature, which some of them practiced publicly to the shock and outrage of respectable citizens. Neither of these views had much appeal to the middle-class city-dweller of the third century B.C., who sought some basis for choosing a way of life now that the *polis* no longer provided one ready-made.

THE EPICUREANS. Epicurus of Athens (342–271 B.C.) formulated a new teaching, which was embodied in the school he founded in his native city in 306. His philosophy conformed to the new mood in that its goal was not knowledge but human happiness, which he believed could be achieved if one followed a style of life based on reason. He took sense perception to be the basis of all human knowledge. The reality and reliability of sense perception rested on the acceptance of the physical universe described by the atomists, Democritus and Leucippus, in which atoms were continually falling through the void and giving off images that were in direct contact with the senses. These falling atoms could swerve in an arbitrary, unpredictable way to produce the combinations seen in the world; Epicurus thereby removed an element of determinism that existed in the Democritean system. When a person died, the atoms that composed the body dispersed so that the person had no further existence or perception and therefore nothing to fear after death. Epicurus believed that the gods existed but that they took no interest in human affairs. This belief amounted to a practical atheism, and Epicureans were often thought to be atheists.

The purpose of Epicurean physics was to liberate people from their fear of death, the gods, and all non-material or supernatural powers. Epicurean ethics were hedonistic, that is, based on the acceptance of pleasure as true happiness. But pleasure for Epicurus was chiefly negative: the absence of pain and trouble. The goal of the Epicureans was *ataraxia*, the condition of being undisturbed, without trouble, pain, or responsibility. Ideally, a man should have enough means to allow him to withdraw from the world and avoid business and public life; Epicurus even advised against marriage and children. He preached a life of genteel, restrained selfishness, which might appeal to intellectual men of means, but was not calculated to be widely attractive.

THE STOICS. Soon after Epicurus began teaching in his garden in Athens, Zeno of Citium in Cyprus (335–263 B.C.) established the Stoic school, which derived its name from the *Stoa Poikile*, or Painted Portico, in the Athenian Agora, where Zeno and his disciples walked and talked beginning about 300 B.C.

Like the Epicureans, the Stoics sought the happiness of the individual. Quite unlike them, the Stoics held a philosophy almost indistinguishable from religion. They believed that humans must live in harmony within themselves and in harmony with nature; for the Stoics, god and nature were the same. The guiding principle in nature was divine reason (Logos), or fire. Every human had a spark of this divinity, and after death, it returned to the eternal divine spirit. From time to time, the world was destroyed by fire, from which a new world arose. The aim of humans, and the definition of human happiness, was the virtuous life, life lived in accordance with natural law, "when all actions promote the harmony of the spirit dwelling in the individual man with the will of him who orders the universe."[1] To live such a life required the knowledge possessed only by the wise, who knew what was good, what was evil, and what was neither, but "indifferent." Good and evil were dispositions of the mind or soul: prudence, justice, courage, temperance, and so on were good, whereas folly, injustice, cowardice, and the like were evil. Life, health, pleasure, beauty, strength, wealth, and so on were neutral, morally indifferent, for they did not contribute either to happiness or to misery. Human misery came from an irrational mental contraction, from passion, which was a disease of the soul. The wise sought freedom from passion (*apatheia*), because passion arose from things that were morally indifferent.

[1] Diogenes Laertius, *Life of Zeno*

Politically, the Stoics fit well into the new world. They thought of it as a single *polis* in which all men were children of god. Although they did not forbid political activity, and many Stoics took part in political life, withdrawal was obviously preferable because the usual subjects of political argument were indifferent. Because the Stoics aimed at inner harmony of the individual, because their aim was a life lived in accordance with the divine will, and because their attitude was fatalistic and their goal a form of apathy, they fit in well with the reality of post-Alexandrian life. In fact, the spread of Stoicism made simpler the task of creating a new political system that relied not on the active participation of the governed, but merely on their docile submission.

Literature

The literature of the Hellenistic period reflects the new intellectual currents and, even more, the new conditions of literary life and the new institutions created in that period. The center of literary production in the third and second centuries B.C. was the new city of Alexandria in Egypt. There the Ptolemies, the kings of Egypt during that time, founded the museum, a great research institute where scientists and scholars were supported by royal funds, and the library, which contained almost half a million volumes, or papyrus scrolls. In the library were the works making up the great body of past Greek literature of every kind, much of which has since been lost. The Alexandrian scholars saw to it that what they judged to be the best works were copied; they edited and criticized these works from the point of view of language, form, and content and wrote biographies of their authors. Much of their work was valuable and is responsible for the preservation of most of ancient literature. Some of it is dry, petty, quarrelsome, and simply foolish. At its best, however, it is full of learning and perception.

The scholarly atmosphere of Alexandria naturally gave rise to work in the field of history and its ancillary discipline, chronology. Eratosthenes (CA. 275–195 B.C.) established a chronology of important events dating from the Trojan War, and others undertook similar tasks. Contemporaries of Alexander, such Ptolemy I, Aristobulus, and Nearchus, wrote what were apparently sober and essentially factual accounts of his career. Most of the work done by Hellenistic historians is known to us only in fragments cited by later writers, but it seems in general to have emphasized sensational and biographical detail rather than the rigorous impersonal analysis of a Thucydides.

Architecture and Sculpture

The opportunities open to architects and sculptors were greatly increased by the advent of the Hellenistic monarchies. There was plenty of money, the royal

The stoa of Attalus, Athens. Many Hellenistic kings sought to glorify their reigns by embellishing Athens in recognition of the city's intellectual fame. This two-story gallery of colonnaded shops was built by Attalus II, king of Pergamum (160–138 B.C.) in the Athenian agora, or marketplace. It was reconstructed by American archaelogists and is now a museum. [AHM.]

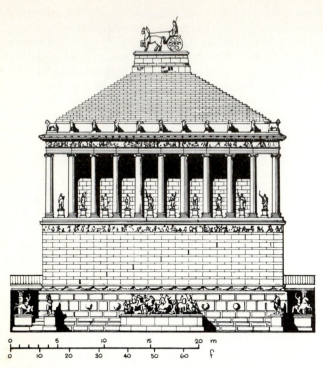

The Mausoleum. This is a conjectural reconstruction of the tomb of King Mausolus of Caria in Asia Minor, which gave us the word "mausolem." It was built at Halicarnassus in 353 B.C. by the widow, Queen Artemisia, and later made its way into Hellenistic lists of wonders of the world. [World Architecture; An Illustrated History, Trewin Copplestone, General Editor (London: Hamlyn, 1963), p. 54.]

need for conspicuous display, the need to build and beautify new cities, and a growing demand from the well-to-do for objects of art. The new cities were usually laid out on the gridiron plan introduced in the fifth century by Hippodamus of Miletus. Temples were built on the classical model, and the covered portico or *stoa* became a very popular addition to the *agoras* of the Hellenistic towns.

Sculpture reflected the cosmopolitan nature of the Hellenistic world, for leading sculptors accepted commissions wherever they were attractive, and the result was a certain uniformity of style, although Alexandria, Rhodes, and the kingdom of Pergamum in Asia Minor developed their own characteristic styles. For the most part, Hellenistic sculpture carried forward the tendencies of the fourth century B.C., moving away from the balanced tension and idealism of the fifth century toward a sentimental, emotional, and realistic mode. These qualities are readily apparent in the statue of the *Dying Gaul* dedicated by Attalus I, king of Pergamum, in about 225 B.C.

Mathematics and Science

Among the most spectacular and remarkable intellectual developments of the Hellenistic age were those that came in mathematics and science. It is not too much to say that the work done by the Alexandrians formed the greater part of the scientific knowledge available to the Western world until the scientific revolution of the sixteenth and seventeenth centuries A.D.

Euclid's *Elements* (written early in the third century B.C.) remained the textbook of plane and solid

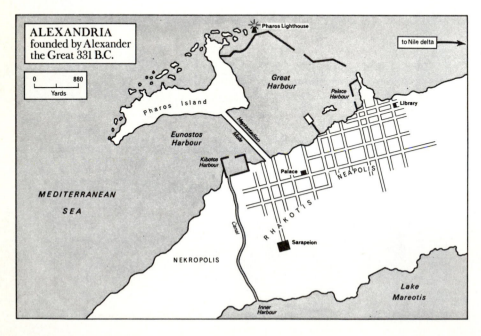

Map of Alexandria. Alexander the Great was given to founding new cities along the major trade routes in his newly conquered provinces, and several of these he allowed to be named for himself, but this one in Egypt was the only one to remain a place of consequence. His Macedonian successors, the Ptolemies, made it the capital of their Egyptian kingdom and also a center of Hellenistic culture; its library and museum were famous centers of learning and scholarship, and its lighthouse, the Pharos, was a marvel of construction to the ancient world. [Michael Grant, Ancient History Atlas (New York: Macmillan, 1971),p. 42.]

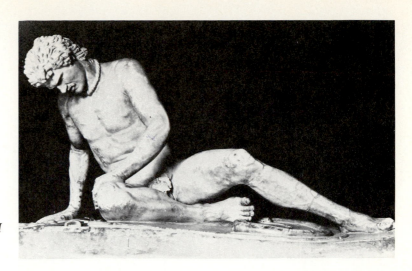

The Dying Gaul. This is a Roman copy of one of a group originally dedicated at the temple of Athena at Pergamum by Attalus I about 230 B.C. It is now in the Museo Capitolino, Rome. [Bettmann Archive.]

geometry until just recently. Archimedes of Syracuse (CA. 287–212 B.C.) made further progress in geometry, as well as establishing the theory of the lever in mechanics and inventing hydrostatics. The advances in mathematics, when added to the availability of Babylonian astronomical tables, allowed great progress in the field of astronomy. As early as the fourth century, Heraclides of Pontus (CA. 390–310 B.C.) had argued that Mercury and Venus circulate around the sun and not the earth, and he appears to have made other suggestions leading in the direction of a heliocentric theory of the universe. Most scholars, however, give credit for that theory to Aristarchus of Samos (CA. 310–230 B.C.), who asserted that the sun, along with the other fixed stars, did not move and that the earth revolved around the sun in a circular orbit and rotated on its axis while doing so.

The heliocentric theory ran contrary not only to the traditional view codified by Aristotle but to what seemed to be common sense. However, Hellenistic technology was not up to proving the theory, and, of course, the planetary orbits are not circular. The helio-

Plutarch Cites Archimedes and Hellenistic Science

Archimedes (CA. 287–211 B.C.) was one of the great mathematicians and physicists of antiquity. He was a native of Syracuse in Sicily and a friend of its king. Plutarch discusses him in the following selection and reveals much about the ancient attitude toward applied science.

Archimedes, however, in writing to King Hiero, whose friend and near relation he was, had stated that given the force, any given weight might be moved, and even boasted, we are told, relying on the strength of demonstration, that if there were another earth, by going into it he could remove this. Hiero being struck with amazement at this, and entreating him to make good this problem by actual experiment, and show some great weight moved by a small engine, he fixed accordingly upon a ship of burden out of the king's arsenal, which could not be drawn out of the dock without great labour and many men; and, loading her with many passengers and a full freight, sitting himself the while far off, with no great endeavour, but only holding the head of the pulley in his hand and drawing the cords by degrees. . . . Yet Archimedes possessed so high a spirit, so profound a soul, and such treasures of scientific knowledge, that though these inventions had now obtained him the renown of more than human sagacity, he yet would not deign to leave behind him any commentary or writing on such subjects; but, repudiating as sordid and ignoble the whole trade of engineering, and every sort of art that lends itself to mere use and profit, he placed his whole affection and ambition in those purer speculations where there can be no reference to the vulgar needs of life. . . . ❑

Plutarch, "Marcellus," in *Lives of the Noble Grecians and Romans*, trans. by John Dryden, revised by A. H. Clough (New York: Random House, n.d.), pp. 376–378.

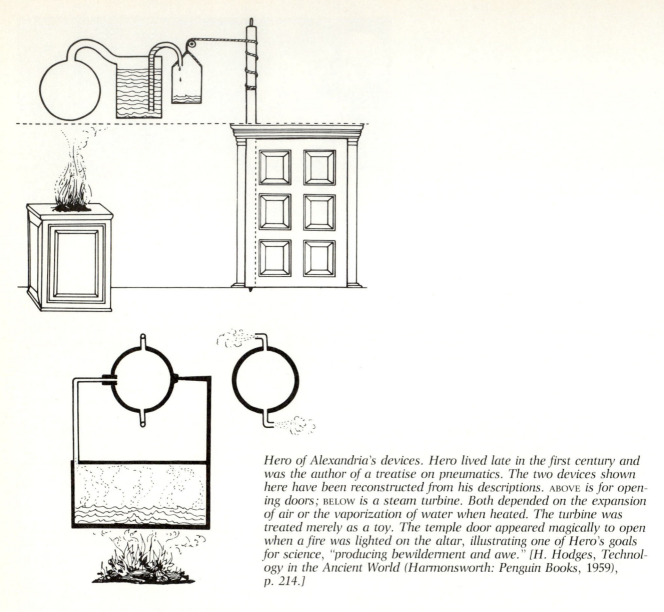

Hero of Alexandria's devices. Hero lived late in the first century and was the author of a treatise on pneumatics. The two devices shown here have been reconstructed from his descriptions. ABOVE *is for opening doors;* BELOW *is a steam turbine. Both depended on the expansion of air or the vaporization of water when heated. The turbine was treated merely as a toy. The temple door appeared magically to open when a fire was lighted on the altar, illustrating one of Hero's goals for science, "producing bewilderment and awe." [H. Hodges, Technology in the Ancient World (Harmonsworth: Penguin Books, 1959), p. 214.]*

centric theory did not, therefore, take hold. Hipparchus of Nicaea (b. CA. 190 B.C.) constructed a model of the universe on the geocentric theory, employing an ingenious and complicated model that did a very good job of accounting for the movements of the sun, the moon, and the planets. Ptolemy of Alexandria (second century A.D.) adopted Hipparchus' system with a few improvements, and it remained dominant until the work of Copernicus, in the sixteenth century A.D.

Hellenistic scientists made progress in mapping the earth as well as the sky. Eratosthenes of Cyrene (CA. 275–195 B.C.) was able to calculate the circumference of the earth within about two hundred miles and wrote a treatise on geography based on mathematical and physical reasoning and the reports of travelers. In spite of the new data that were available to later geographers, Eratosthenes' map (see Map 4.4) was in many ways more accurate than the one constructed by Ptolemy that became standard in the Middle Ages.

The Achievement of the Classical and Hellenistic Ages in World Perspective

The Classical Age of Greece was a period of unparalleled achievement. It carried forward the tradition of rational, secular speculation in natural philosophy and science, but turned its attention more to human questions in medicine and ethical and political philosophy.

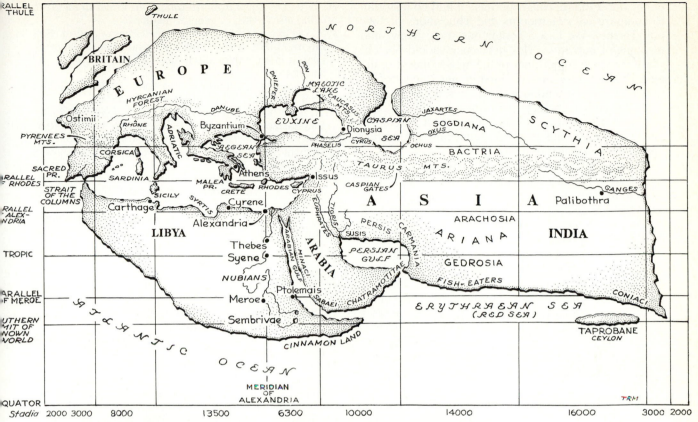

MAP 4-4 THE WORLD ACCORDING TO ERATOSTHENES *Eratosthenes of Alexandria (CA. 275–195 B.C.) was a Hellenistic geographer. His map, reconstructed here,
was remarkably accurate for its time. The world was divided by lines of "latitude" and
"longitude," thus anticipating our global divisions.*

While the rest of the world continued to be characterized by monarchical, hierarchical, command societies,
in Athens democracy was carried as far as it would go
before modern times. Although limited to adult males
of native parentage, Athenian citizenship granted full
and active participation in every decision of the state
without regard to wealth or class. Democracy disappeared with the end of Greek autonomy late in the
fourth century B.C. When it returned in the modern
world more than two millennia later, it was broader
but shallower. Democratic citizenship did not again
imply the active direct participation of every citizen in
the government of the state.

It was in this democratic imperial Athens that the
greatest artistic, literary, and philosophical achievements took place. Many of the literary genres and
forms that are vital in the modern world arose and
were developed during this time. Analytical, secular
history, tragedy and comedy, the philosophical dialogue, an organized system of logic, and logical philosophical treatise on almost every aspect open to

human thought, were among the achievements of the
Classical Age. A naturalistic style of art evolved that
placed human beings, first as they ideally might look,
and then as they really looked. This approach dominated Greek and Roman art until the fall of the Roman
Empire when it largely disappeared. It rose again to
have a powerful effect on the Italian Renaissance and,
through it, on the modern world.

These Hellenic developments, it should be clear,
diverge sharply from the experience of previous cultures and of contemporary ones in the rest of the
world. To a great degree, they sprang from the unique
political experience of the Greeks, which avoided monarchies and great, extended, land empires but was
based on independent city states. That unique experience came to an end with the Macedonian conquest,
which ultimately made the Greeks subject to or part of
some great national state or empire and brought an
end to the Classical period.

The Hellenistic Age speaks to us less fully and vividly than that of classical Greece or of the Roman Re-

public and Empire, chiefly because it had no historian to compare with Herodotus and Thucydides or Livy and Tacitus. We lack a continuous, rich, lively, and meaningful narrative. This deficiency should not obscure the great importance of the achievements of the age. The literature, art, scholarship, and science of the period deserve attention in their own right. In addition, the Hellenistic Age performed a vital civilizing function. It spread the Greek culture over a remarkably wide area and made a significant and lasting impression on much of it.

Greek culture also adjusted to its new surroundings to a degree, unifying and simplifying its cultural cargo so as to make it more accessible to outsiders. The various Greek dialects gave way to a version of the Attic tongue, the *koinē*, or common language. In the same way, the scholarship of Alexandria established canons of literary excellence and the scholarly tools with which to make the great treasures of Greek culture understandable to later generations. The union of thought and belief introduced in this period also made understanding and accord more likely among peoples who were very different. When the Romans came into contact with Hellenism, they were powerfully impressed by it, and when they conquered the Hellenistic world, they became, as Horace said, captives of its culture.

The conquests of Alexander and the Hellenistic civilization that came with them greatly affected the conquered societies and their neighbors. The Seleucid successors of Alexander ruled some parts of the old Persian Empire for almost two centuries after his death, and Hellenistic culture continued to influence the urban upper classes for some time.

The Hellenistic influence reached even further under another group of Greeks who broke away from the Seleucids to form the Indo-Greek people of Bactria. By the second century B.C., they controlled parts of northern India. The legacy of Hellenism in the East can be seen reflected in art as far as China. In the West, of course, the legacy was more complete and influential, powerfully shaping the nature of the Roman culture that would ultimately dominate the entire Mediterranean world and make important contacts beyond it.

Suggested Readings

M. Austin and P. Vidal-Naquet, *The Economic and Social History of Classical Greece* (Berkeley, 1977). A combination of documents and explanation.

E. Barker, *Political Philosophy of Plato and Aristotle* (1959). A sober and reliable account.

H. I. Bell, *Egypt from Alexander the Great to the Arab Conquest* (1948). A general history.

P. Cartledge, *Agesilaus and the Crisis of Sparta* (Baltimore, 1987). More than a biography of the Spartan king, it is a complex discussion of Spartan history and society.

G. Cawkwell, *Philip of Macedon* (London, 1978). A brief but learned account of Philip's career.

J. K. Davies, *Democracy and Classical Greece* (1978). Emphasizes archeological evidence and social history.

V. Ehrenberg, *The People of Aristophanes* (1962). A study of Athenian society as reveled by the comedies of Aristophanes.

J. R. Ellis, *Philip II and Macedonian Imperialism* (London, 1976). A study of the career of the founder of Macedonian power.

J. R. Lane Fox, *Alexander the Great* (1973). An imaginative account that does more justice to the Persian side of the problem than is usual.

Peter Green, *Alexander the Great* (1972). A lively biography.

N. G. L. Hammond and G. T. Griffith, *A History of Macedonia*, vol. 2, 550–336 B.C. (1979). A thorough account of Macedonian history that focuses on the careers of Philip and Alexander.

W. Jaeger, *Demosthenes* (1938). A good biography of the Athenian statesman.

D. Kagan, *The Outbreak of the Peloponnesian War* (1969). A study of the period from the foundation of the Delian League to the coming of the Peloponnesian War that argues that war could have been avoided.

D. Kagan, *The Archidamian War* (1974). A history of the first ten years of the Peloponnesian War.

D. Kagan, *The Peace of Nicias and the Sicilian Expedition* (1981). A history of the middle period of the Peloponnesian War.

D. Kagan, *The Fall of the Athenian Empire* (Ithaca, 1987). The last period of the war.

H. D. F. Kitto, *Greek Tragedy* (1966). A good introduction.

B. M. W. Knox, *The Heroic Temper: Studies in Sophoclean Tragedy* (1964). A brilliant analysis of tragic heroism.

D. M. Lewis, *Sparta and Persia* (Leiden, 1977). A valuable discussion of relations between Sparta and Persia in the fifth and fourth centuries B.C.

G. E. R. Lloyd, *Greek Science After Aristotle* (1974).

A. A. Long, *Hellenistic Philosophy: Stoics, Epicureans, Sceptics* (1974). An account of Greek science in the Hellenistic and Roman periods.

R. Meiggs, *The Athenian Empire* (1972). A fine study of the rise and fall of the empire, making excellent use of inscriptions.

H. W. Parke, *Festivals of the Athenians* (Ithaca, 1977). A fine discussion of the religious practices of the Athenians.

J. J. Pollitt, *Art and Experience in Classical Greece* (1972). A scholarly and entertaining study of the relationship between art and history in classical Greece, with excellent illustrations.

J. J. POLLITT, *Art in the Hellenistic Age* (Cambridge, 1986). An extraordinary analysis that places the art in its historical and intellectual context.

M. I. ROSTOVTZEFF, *Social and Economic History of the Hellenistic World*, 3 vols. (1941). A masterpiece of synthesis by a great historian.

D. M. SCHAPS, *Economic Rights of Women in Ancient Greece* (Edinburgh, 1981).

B. S. STRAUSS, *Athens After the Peloponnesian War* (Ithaca, 1987). An excellent discussion of Athens' recovery and of the nature of Athenian society and politics in the fourth century B.C.

W. W. TARN, *Alexander the Great*, 2 vols. (1948). The first volume is a narrative account; the second a series of detailed studies.

W. W. TARN AND G. T. GRIFFITH, *Hellenistic Civilization* (1961). A survey of Hellenistic history and culture.

A. E. TAYLOR, *Socrates* (1953). A good, readable account.

V. TCHERIKOVER, *Hellenistic Civilization and the Jews* (1970). A fine study of the impact of Hellenism on the Jews.

F. W. WALBANK, *The Hellenistic World* (1981).

T. B. L. WEBSTER, *Hellenistic Poetry and Art* (1961). A clear survey.

A. E. ZIMMERN, *The Greek Commonwealth* (1961). A study of political, social, and economic conditions in fifth-century Athens.

A patrician with portraits of his ancestors. Roman patricians took great pride in their lineage and would not marry outside their own group. [German Archaelogical Institute, Rome.]

5 Rome: From Republic to Empire

The achievement of the Romans was one of the most remarkable accomplishments in human history. The descendants of the inhabitants of a small village in central Italy ruled the entire Italian peninsula, then the entire Mediterranean coastline. They conquered most of the Near East and finally much of continental Europe. They ruled this vast empire under a single government that provided considerable peace and prosperity for centuries. At no time before the Romans or since has that area been united, and rarely, if ever, has it enjoyed a stable peace. But Rome's legacy was not merely military excellence and political organization. The Romans adopted and transformed the intellectual and cultural achievements of the Greeks and combined them with their own outlook and historical experience. They produced the Graeco-Roman tradition in literature, philosophy, and art that served as the core of learning for the Middle Ages and the inspiration for the new paths taken in the Renaissance. That tradition remains at the heart of Western civilization to this day.

Prehistoric Italy

The culture of Italy developed late. Paleolithic settlements gave way to the Neolithic mode of life only about 2500 B.C. The Bronze Age came about 1500 B.C., and about 1000 B.C., Italy began to be infiltrated by bands of new arrivals from across the Adriatic Sea and around its northern end. The invaders were warlike people who imposed their language and social organization on almost all of Italy. Their bronze work was better than their predecessors', and soon they made weapons, armor, and tools of iron. They cremated their dead and put the ashes in tombs stocked with weapons and armor. Before 800 B.C., people living in this style occupied the highland pastures of the Apennines. These tough mountain people—Umbrians,

MAP 5-1 ANCIENT ITALY *This map of the Italian peninsula and its neighbors in antiquity shows the major cities and towns, as well as a number of geographical regions and the locations of some of the Italic and non-Italic peoples of the area.*

Etruria (now Tuscany), west of the Apennines between the Arno and Tiber rivers, about 800 B.C. (see Map 5.1). Their origin is far from clear, but their tomb architecture, resembling that of Asia Minor, and their practice of divining the future by inspecting the livers of sacrificial animals point to an eastern origin.

The Etruscans brought civilization with them. Their settlements were self-governing, fortified city-states, of which twelve formed a loose religious confederation. At first, these cities were ruled by kings, but they were replaced by an aristocracy of the agrarian nobles, who ruled by means of a council and elected annual magistrates. The Etruscans were a military ruling class that dominated and exploited the native Italians, who worked their land and mines and served as infantry in their armies. This aristocracy accumulated considerable wealth through agriculture, industry, piracy, and a growing commerce with the Carthaginians and the Greeks.

The Etruscans' influence on the Romans was greatest in religion. They imagined a world filled with gods and spirits, many of them evil. To deal with such demons, the Etruscans evolved complicated rituals and powerful priesthoods. Divination by sacrifice and omens in nature helped discover the divine will, and careful attention to precise rituals directed by priests helped please the gods. After a while, the Etruscans,

Terracotta figures from an Etruscan sarcophagus of the late sixth century B.C. The dead couple are shown reclining as for a banquet. Museo de Villa Giulia, Rome. [Photo by Robert Emmett Bright. Rapho Guilumette.]

Sabines, Samnites, Latins, and others—spoke a set of closely related languages that we call *Italic.*

They soon began to challenge the earlier settlers for control of the tempting western plains. Other peoples lived in Italy in the ninth century B.C., but the Italic speakers and three peoples who had not yet arrived—the Etruscans, the Greeks, and the Celts—would shape its future.

The Etruscans

The Etruscans exerted the most powerful external influence on the Romans. Their civilization arose in

128

The Tiber island at Rome. This island in the Tiber made the river fordable at its location and therefore helped determine the location of the city of Rome. Later bridges kept the crossing a popular one, as shown in this eighteenth-century etching by G.B. Piranesi.

influenced by the Greeks, worshiped gods in the shape of humans and built temples for them.

The Etruscan aristocracy remained aggressive and skillful in the use of horses and war chariots. In the seventh and sixth centuries B.C., they expanded their power in Italy and across the sea to Corsica and Elba. They conquered Latium (a region that included the small town of Rome) and Campania, where they became neighbors of the Greeks of Naples.

Royal Rome

In the sixth century B.C., Rome came under Etruscan control. Led by their Etruscan kings, the Roman army, equipped and organized like the Greek phalanx, gained control of most of Latium. They achieved this success under an effective political and social order that gave extraordinary power to the ruling figures in both public and private life.

Government

To their kings, the Romans gave the awesome power of *imperium*, the right to issue commands and to enforce them by fines, arrests, and corporal or even capital punishment. The kingship was elective and the office appears to have tended to remain in the same family. The Senate, however, had to approve the candidate, and the *imperium* was formally granted by a vote of the people in assembly. The basic character of Roman government was already clear: Great power was granted to executive officers, but it had to be approved by the Senate and was derived ultimately from the people. Ostensibly the Senate had neither executive nor legislative power; it met only when summoned by the king and then only to advise him. In reality, its authority was great, for the senators, like the king, served for life. The Senate, therefore, had continuity and experience, and as it was composed of the most powerful men in the state, it could not lightly be ignored.

In early Rome, citizenship required descent from Roman parents on both sides. All citizens were organized into the third branch of government, an assembly made up of thirty groups. It met only when summoned by the king; he determined the agenda, made proposals, and recognized other speakers, if any. For the most part, the assembly was called to listen and approve. Voting was not by head but by group; a majority within each group determined its vote, and the decisions were made by majority vote of the groups. Group voting was typical of all Roman assemblies in the future.

The Family

The center of Roman life was the family. At its head stood the father, whose power and authority within the family resembled those of the king within the state. Over his children, he held broad powers analogous to *imperium* in the state, for he had the right to sell his children into slavery, and he even had the power of life and death over them. Over his wife he had less power; he could not sell or kill her. As the king's power was more limited in practice than in theory, so it was with the father. His power to dispose of his children was limited by consultation with the family, by public opinion, and, most of all, by tradition. The wife could not be divorced except for stated serious offenses, and even then she had to be convicted by a court made up of her male blood relatives. The Roman woman had a respected position and the main responsibility for managing the household. The father was the chief priest of the family. He led it in daily prayers to the dead that reflected the ancestor worship central to the Roman family and state.

Clientage

Clientage was one of Rome's most important institutions. The client was "an inferior entrusted, by custom or by himself, to the protection of a stranger more powerful than he, and rendering certain services and observances in return for this protection."[1] The Romans spoke of a client as being in the *fides*, or trust, of his patron, so that the relationship always had moral implications. The patron provided his client with protection, both physical and legal; he gave him economic assistance in the form of a land grant, the opportunity to work as a tenant farmer or a laborer on the patron's land, or simply handouts. In return, the client would fight for his patron, work his land, and support him politically. These mutual obligations were enforced by public opinion and tradition. When early custom was codified in the mid-fifth century B.C., one of the twelve tablets of laws announced: "Let the patron who has defrauded his client be accursed."

In the early history of Rome, patrons were rich and powerful whereas clients were poor and weak. But as time passed, it was not uncommon for rich and powerful members of the upper classes to become clients of even more powerful men, chiefly for political purposes.

[1] E. Badian, *Foreign Clientelae* (264–70 B.C.) (Oxford: 1958), p. 1.

Because the client–patron relationship was hereditary and sanctioned by religion and custom, it was to play a very important part in the life of the Roman Republic.

Patricians and Plebeians

In the royal period, Roman society was divided in two by a class distinction based on birth. The upper class was composed of the patricians, the wealthy men who held a monopoly of power and influence. They alone could conduct the religious ceremonies in the state, sit in the Senate, or hold office, and they formed a closed caste by forbidding marriage outside their own group. The plebeians must originally have been the poor and dependent men who were small farmers, laborers, and artisans, the clients of the nobility.

As Rome and its population grew in various ways, families who were rich but outside the charmed circle gained citizenship. From very early times, therefore, there were rich plebeians, and incompetence and bad luck must have produced some poor patricians. The line between the classes and the monopoly of privileges remained firm, nevertheless, and the struggle of the plebeians to gain equality occupied more than two centuries of republican history.

The Republic

Roman tradition tells us that the republic replaced the monarchy at Rome suddenly in 509 B.C. as the result of a revolution sparked by the outrageous behavior of the last kings and led by the noble families.

Its Constitution

The Roman constitution was an unwritten accumulation of laws and customs that had won respect and the force of law over time. The Romans were a conservative people, so they were never willing to deprive their chief magistrates of the great powers exercised by the monarchs.

THE CONSULS. The Romans elected two patricians to the office of consul and endowed them with *imperium*. They were assisted by two financial officials called *quaestors*, whose number ultimately reached eight. Like the kings the consuls led the army, had religious duties, and served as judges. They retained the visible symbols of royalty—the purple robe, the ivory chair, and the lictors (minor officials) bearing rods and axe who accompanied them—but their power was limited legally and institutionally as well as by custom.

The vast power of the consulship was granted not for life but only for a year. Each consul could prevent any action by his colleague by simply saying no to his proposal, and the religious powers of the consuls were shared with others. Even the *imperium* was limited,

Polybius Summarizes the Roman Constitution

Polybius (CA. 203–120 B.C.) *was a Greek from the city of Megalopolis, an important member of the Achaean League. As a hostage in Rome, he became a friend of influential Romans and later wrote a history of Rome's conquest of the Mediterranean lands. He praised the Roman constitution as an excellent example of a "mixed constitution" and as a major source of Roman success.*

As for the Roman constitution, it had three elements, each of them possessing sovereign powers: and their respective share of power in the whole state had been regulated with such a scrupulous regard to equality and equilibrium, that no one could say for certain, not even a native, whether the constitution as a whole were an aristocracy or democracy or despotism. . . .

. . . .

The result of this power of the several estates for mutual help or harm is a union sufficiently firm for all emergencies, and a constitution than which it is impossible to find a better. For whenever any danger from without compels them to unite and work together, the strength which is developed by the State is so extraordinary, that everything required is unfailingly carried out by the eager rivalry shown by all classes to devote their whole minds to the need of the hour, and to secure that any determination come to should not fail for want of promptitude; while each individual works, privately and publicly alike, for the accomplishment of the business in hand. Accordingly, the peculiar constitution of the State makes it irresistible, and certain of obtaining whatever it determines to attempt. . . . For when any one of the three classes becomes puffed up, and manifests an inclination to be contentious and unduly encroaching, the mutual interdependency of all the three, and the possibility of the pretensions of any one being checked and thwarted by the others, must plainly check this tendency: and so the proper equilibrium is maintained by the impulsiveness of the one part being checked by its fear of the other. . . . ❏

Polybius, *Histories*, Vol. 1, trans. by E. S. Shuckburgh (Bloomington: Indiana University Press, 1962), pp. 468, 473–474.

---

for though the consuls had full powers of life and death while leading an army, within the sacred boundary of the city of Rome the citizens had the right to appeal to the popular assembly all cases involving capital punishment. Besides, after their one year in office, the consuls would spend the rest of their lives as members of the Senate. It was a most reckless consul who failed to ask the advice of the Senate or who failed to follow it when there was general agreement.

The many checks on consular action tended to prevent initiative, swift action, and change, but this was just what a conservative, traditional, aristocratic republic wanted. Only in the military sphere did divided counsel and a short term of office create important problems. The Romans tried to get around the difficulties by sending only one consul into the field or, when this was impossible, allowing the consuls sole command on alternate days. In really serious crises, the consuls, with the advice of the Senate, could appoint a single man, the *dictator*, to the command and could retire in his favor. The *dictator's* term of office was limited to six months, but his own *imperium* was valid both inside and outside the city without appeal. These devices worked well enough in the early years of the republic, when Rome's battles were near home, but longer wars and more sophisticated opponents revealed the system's weaknesses and required significant changes.

Long campaigns prompted the invention of the proconsulship in 325 B.C., whereby the term of a consul serving in the field was extended. This innovation contained the seeds of many troubles for the constitution.

The introduction of the office of *praetor* also helped provide commanders for Rome's many campaigns. The basic function of the praetors was judicial, but they also had *imperium* and served as generals. By the end of the republic, there were eight praetors, whose annual terms, like the consuls', could be extended for military commands when necessary.

At first, the consuls classified the citizens according to age and property, the bases of citizenship and assignment in the army. After the middle of the fifth century B.C., two censors were elected to perform this duty. They conducted a census and drew up the citizen rolls, but this was no job for clerks. The classification fixed taxation and status, so that the censors had to be men of reputation, former consuls. The censors soon acquired additional powers. By the fourth century, they compiled the roll of senators and could strike senators from that roll not only for financial reasons but for moral reasons as well. As the prestige of the office grew, becoming a censor came to be considered the ultimate prize of a Roman political career.

THE SENATE AND THE ASSEMBLY. The end of the monarchy increased the influence and power of the Senate. It became the single continuous deliberative body in the Roman state. Its members were leading patricians, often leaders of clans and patrons of many clients. The Senate soon gained control of finances and of foreign policy. Its formal advice was not lightly ignored either by magistrates or by popular assemblies.

The most important assembly in the early republic was the centuriate assembly. In a sense, it was the Roman army acting in a political capacity, and its basic unit was the century, theoretically 100 fighting men classified according to their weapons, armor, and equipment. Because each man equipped himself, the organization was by classes according to wealth.

THE STRUGGLE OF THE ORDERS. The laws and constitution of the early republic clearly reflected the class structure of the Roman state, for they gave to the patricians almost a monopoly of power and privilege. The plebeians undertook a campaign to achieve political, legal, and social equality, and this attempt, which succeeded after two centuries of intermittent effort, is called the *struggle of the orders*.

The most important source of plebeian success was the need for their military service. Rome was at war almost constantly, and the patricians were forced to call on the plebeians to defend the state. According to tradition, the plebeians, angered by patrician resistance to their demands, withdrew from the city and camped on the Sacred Mount. There they formed a plebeian tribal assembly and elected plebeian tribunes to protect them from the arbitrary power of the magistrates. They declared the tribune inviolate and sacrosanct, and anyone laying violent hands on him was accursed and liable to death without trial. By extension of his right to protect the plebeians, the tribune gained the power to veto any action of a magistrate or any bill in a Roman assembly or the Senate. The plebeian assembly voted by tribe, and a vote of the assembly was binding on plebeians. They tried to make their decisions binding on all Romans but could not do so until 287 B.C.

The next step was for the plebeians to obtain access to the laws, and by 450 B.C., the Twelve Tables codified early Roman custom in all its harshness and simplicity. In 445 B.C., plebeians gained the right to marry patricians. The main prize was consulship. The patricians did not yield easily, but at last, in 367 B.C., the Licinian-Sextian Laws provided that at least one consul could be a plebeian. Before long plebeians held other offices, even the dictatorship and the censorship. In 300 B.C., they were admitted to the most important priesthoods, the last religious barrier to equality. In 287 B.C., the plebeians completed their triumph. They once again withdrew from the city and secured the passage of a law whereby decisions of the plebeian assembly bound all Romans and did not require the approval of the Senate.

It might seem that the Roman aristocracy had given

THE RISE OF THE PLEBEIANS TO EQUALITY IN ROME

509 B.C.	Kings expelled—republic founded
450–449 B.C.	Laws of the Twelve Tables published
445 B.C.	Plebeians gain right of marriage with patricians
367 B.C.	Licinian-Sextian Laws open consulship to plebeians
300 B.C.	Plebeians attain chief priesthoods
287 B.C.	Laws passed by Plebeian Assembly made binding on all Romans

way under the pressure of the lower class, but the victory of the plebeians did not bring democracy. An aristocracy based strictly on birth had given way to an aristocracy more subtle, but no less restricted, based on a combination of wealth and birth. The significant distinction was no longer between patrician and plebeian but between the *nobiles*—a relatively small group of wealthy and powerful families, both patrician and plebeian, whose members attained the highest offices in the state—and everyone else.

These same families dominated the Senate, whose power became ever greater. It remained the only continuous deliberative body in the state, and the pressure of warfare gave it experience in handling public business. Rome's success brought the Senate prestige and increased its control of policy and confidence in its capacity to rule. The end of the struggle of the orders brought domestic peace under a republican constitution dominated by a capable, if narrow, senatorial aristocracy. This outcome satisfied most Romans outside the ruling group because Rome conquered Italy and brought many benefits to its citizens.

The Conquest of Italy

Not long after the fall of the monarchy in 509 B.C., a coalition of Romans, Latins, and Italian Greeks defeated the Etruscans and drove them out of Latium for good.

GALLIC INVASION OF ITALY. At the beginning of the fourth century B.C., the Romans were the chief power in central Italy, but a disaster struck. In 387 B.C., the Gauls, barbaric Celtic tribes from across the Alps, defeated the Roman army and captured, looted, and burned Rome. The Gauls sought plunder, not conquest, so they extorted a ransom from the Romans and returned to their homes in the north. Rome's power appeared to have been wiped out.

When the Gauls left, some of Rome's allies and old enemies tried to take advantage of its weakness, but by about 350 B.C., the Romans had recovered their leadership of central Italy and were more dominant than ever. Their success in turning back new Gallic raids added still more to their power and prestige. As the Romans tightened their grip on Latium, the Latins became resentful. In 340 B.C., they demanded independence from Rome or full equality, and when the Romans refused, they launched a war of independence that lasted until 338. The victorious Romans dissolved the Latin League, and their treatment of the defeated opponents provided a model for the settlement of Italy.

ROMAN POLICY TOWARD THE CONQUERED. The Romans did not destroy any of the Latin cities or their people, nor did they treat them all alike. Some in the vicinity of Rome received full Roman citizenship; others farther away gained municipal status, which gave them the private rights of intermarriage and com-

merce with Romans but not the public rights of voting and holding office in Rome. They retained the rights of local self-government and could obtain full Roman citizenship if they moved to Rome. They followed Rome in foreign policy and provided soldiers to serve in the Roman legions.

Still other states became allies of Rome on the basis of treaties, which differed from city to city. Some were given the private rights of intermarriage and commerce with Romans and some were not; the allied states were always forbidden to exercise these rights with one another. Some, but not all, were allowed local autonomy. Land was taken from some but not from others, nor was the percentage always the same. All the allies supplied troops to the army, in which they fought in auxiliary battalions under Roman officers, but they did not pay taxes to Rome.

On some of the conquered land, the Romans placed colonies, permanent settlements of veteran soldiers in the territory of recently defeated enemies. The colo-

The Via Latina, here shown not far outside Rome, is one of the network of military roads that went from Rome into the Italian country. They enabled Roman legions to move swiftly to enforce their control of the peninsula—and, conversely, also served as convenient avenues of invasion. The Via Latina is thought to be the earliest of these great roads, dating to the fourth century B.C *[Fototeca Unione.]*

nists retained their Roman citizenship and enjoyed home rule, and in return for the land they had been given, they served as a kind of permanent garrison to deter or suppress rebellion. These colonies were usually connected to Rome by a network of military roads built as straight as possible and so durable that some are used even today. They guaranteed that a Roman army could swiftly reinforce an embattled colony or put down an uprising in any weather.

The Roman settlement of Latium reveals even more clearly than before the principles by which Rome was able to conquer and dominate Italy for many centuries. The excellent army and the diplomatic skill that allowed Rome to separate its enemies help explain its conquests. The reputation for harsh punishment of rebels and the sure promise that such punishment would be delivered, made unmistakably clear by the presence of colonies and military roads, help account for the slowness to revolt. But the positive side, represented by Rome's organization of the defeated states, is at least as important. The Romans did not regard the status given each newly conquered city as permanent. They held out to loyal allies the prospect of improving their status, even of achieving the ultimate prize, full Roman citizenship. In so doing, the Romans gave their allies a stake in Rome's future and success and a sense of being colleagues, though subordinate ones, rather than subjects. The result, in general, was that most of Rome's allies remained loyal even when put to the severest test.

DEFEAT OF THE SAMNITES. The next great challenge to Roman arms came in a series of wars with a tough mountain people of the southern Appennines, the Samnites. Some of Rome's allies rebelled, and soon the Etruscans and Gauls joined in the war against Rome. But most of the allies remained loyal. In 295 B.C., at Sentinum, the Romans defeated an Italian coalition, and by 280, they were masters of central Italy. Their power extended from the Po valley south to Apulia and Lucania.

The victory over the Samnites brought the Romans into direct contact with the Greek cities of southern Italy, which they soon conquered. By 265 B.C., Rome ruled all Italy as far north as the Po River, an area of 47,200 square miles.

Rome and Carthage

Rome's acquisition of coastal territory and its expansion to the toe of the Italian boot brought it face to face with the great naval power of the western Mediterranean, Carthage (see Map 5.2). Late in the ninth century B.C., the Phoenician city of Tyre had planted a colony on the coast of northern Africa near modern Tunis, calling it the New City, or Carthage. In the sixth century B.C., the conquest of Phoenicia by the Assyri-

ans and the Persians made Carthage independent and free to exploit its very advantageous situation.

The city was located on a defensible site and commanded an excellent harbor that encouraged commerce. The coastal plain grew abundant grain, fruits, and vegetables. An inland plain allowed sheep herding. The Phoenician settlers conquered the native inhabitants and used them to work the land. Beginning in the sixth century B.C., the Carthaginians expanded their domain to include the coast of northern Africa west beyond the Straits of Gibraltar and eastward into Libya. Overseas, they came to control the southern part of Spain, Sardinia, Corsica, Malta, the Balearic Islands, and western Sicily. The people of these territories, though originally allies, were all reduced to subjection like the natives of the Carthaginian home territory; and they all served in the Carthaginian army or navy and paid tribute. Carthage also profited greatly from the mines of Spain and from the absolute monopoly of trade Carthage imposed on the western Mediterranean.

Early contacts between Rome and Carthage had been few but not unfriendly, but Rome's new proximity to Sicily brought conflict. Roman intervention in the Sicilian city of Messana in 264 B.C. produced the first Punic War (the Romans called the Carthaginians by their ancestral name, Phoenicians; in Latin the name is *Poeni* or *Puni*).

THE FIRST PUNIC WAR (264–241 B.C.). The war in Sicily soon settled into a stalemate. At last, the Romans built a fleet to cut off supplies to the besieged Carthaginian cities at the western end of Sicily. When Carthage sent its own fleet to raise the siege, the Romans destroyed it. In 241 B.C., Carthage signed a treaty giving up Sicily and the islands between Italy and Sicily and agreed to pay a war indemnity in ten annual installments, to keep its ships out of Italian waters, and not to recruit mercenaries in Italy. Neither side was to attack the allies of the other. Rome had earned Sicily, and Carthage could well afford the indemnity.

The treaty did not bring peace to Carthage, even for the moment. A rebellion broke out among the Carthaginian mercenaries, newly recruited from Sicily and demanding their pay. In 238 B.C., while Carthage was still in danger, Rome seized Sardinia and Corsica and demanded that Carthage pay an additional indemnity. This was a harsh and cynical action by the Romans; even the historian Polybius, a great champion of Rome, could find no justification for it. The Romans were moved, no doubt, by the fear of giving Carthage a base so near Italy, but their action was unwise. It undid the calming effects of the peace of 241 B.C. and angered the Carthaginians without preventing them from recovering their strength to seek vengeance in the future.

The harbor of the ancient city of Carthage, near modern Tunis in North Africa, as reconstructed by an artist. [Radio Times Hulton Picture Library.]

THE SECOND PUNIC WAR (218–202 B.C.). After 241 B.C., Carthage recovered strength by building a rich empire in Spain while Rome looked on with some concern. In 221 B.C. Hannibal (247–182 B.C.) took command of Carthaginian forces in Spain while still a young man of twenty-five. A few years before his accession, Rome had received an offer from the people of the Spanish town of Saguntum to become the friends of Rome. The Romans accepted, thereby taking on the responsibilities of friendship with a foreign state. At first, Hannibal was careful to avoid interfering with the friends of Rome, but the Saguntines, confident of Rome's protection, began to interfere with some of the Spanish tribes allied with Hannibal.

Finally, the Romans sent an embassy to Hannibal, warning him to let Saguntum alone and repeating the injunction not to cross the Ebro. The Romans probably expected Hannibal to yield as his predecessors had, but they misjudged their man. Hannibal ignored Rome's warning, besieged Saguntum, and took the town.

MAP 5-2   THE WESTERN MEDITERRANEAN AREA DURING THE RISE OF ROME   *This map covers the theater of the conflicts between the growing Roman dominions and those of Carthage in the third century B.C. The Carthaginian empire stretched westward from the city (in modern Tunisia) along the North African coast and into southern Spain.*

On hearing of Saguntum's fall, the Romans sent an ultimatum to Carthage demanding the surrender of Hannibal. Carthage refused, and Rome declared war in 218 B.C. Rome's policy between the wars had been the worst possible combination of approaches. Rome had insulted and injured Carthage by the annexation of Sardinia in 238 B.C., and had repeatedly provoked and insulted Carthage by interventions in Spain. But Roman policy took no measures to prevent the construction of a powerful and dangerous Punic Empire or even to build defenses against a Punic attack from Spain. Hannibal saw to it that the Romans paid the price for their blunders. By September of 218 B.C., he was across the Alps. His army was weary, bedraggled, and greatly reduced, but he was in Italy and among the friendly Gauls.

Hannibal defeated the Romans at the Ticinus River and crushed the joint consular armies at the Trebia River. In 217 B.C., he outmaneuvered and trapped another army at Lake Trasimene. Hannibal's first victory brought him reinforcements of fifty thousand Gauls, and his second confirmed that his superior generalship could defeat the Roman army. The key to success, however, would be defection by Rome's allies.

Sobered by their defeats, the Romans elected Quintus Fabius Maximus (CA. 275–203 B.C.) dictator. He understood that Hannibal could not be beaten by the usual tactics and that the Roman army, decimated and demoralized, needed time to recover. His strategy was to avoid battle while following and harassing Hannibal's army. When the Roman army had recovered and Fabius could fight Hannibal on favorable ground, only then would the Romans fight.

In 216 B.C., Hannibal marched to Cannae in Apulia to tempt the Romans into another open fight. The Romans could not allow him to ravage the country freely, so they sent off an army of some eighty thousand men to meet him. Almost the entire Roman army was killed or captured. It was the worst defeat in Roman history; Rome's prestige was shattered, and most of its allies in southern Italy, as well as Syracuse in Sicily, now went over to Hannibal. In 215 B.C., Philip V, king of Macedon, made an alliance with Hannibal and launched a war to recover his influence on the Adriatic. For more than a decade, no Roman army would dare face Hannibal in the open field, and he was free to roam over all Italy and do as he pleased.

Hannibal had neither the numbers nor the supplies to besiege such walled cities as Rome and the major allies, nor did he have the equipment to take them by assault. To win the war in Spain, the Romans appointed Publius Cornelius Scipio (237–183 B.C.), later called Scipio Africanus, to the command in Spain with proconsular *imperium*. This was such a breach of tradition as to be almost unconstitutional, for Scipio was not yet twenty-five and had held no high office. But he

Portrait of Hannibal (247–183 B.C), *the great Carthaginian general from a bust in the National Museum in Naples. [Erving Galloway.]*

was a general almost as talented as Hannibal. In 209 B.C., he captured the main Punic base in Spain, New Carthage. His skillful and tactful treatment of the native Iberians won them away from the enemy and over to his own army. Within a few years, young Scipio had conquered all Spain and had deprived Hannibal of hope of help from that region.

In 204 B.C., Scipio landed in Africa, defeated the Carthaginians, and forced them to accept a peace

THE PUNIC WARS

264–241 B.C.	First Punic War
238 B.C.	Rome seizes Sardinia and Corsica
221 B.C.	Hannibal takes command of Punic army in Spain
218–202 B.C.	Second Punic War
216 B.C.	Battle of Cannae
209 B.C.	Scipio takes New Carthage
202 B.C.	Battle of Zama
149–146 B.C.	Third Punic War
146 B.C.	Destruction of Carthage

whose main clause was the withdrawal of Hannibal and his army from Italy. Hannibal had won every battle but lost the war, for he had not counted on the determination of Rome and the loyalty of its allies. Hannibal's return inspired Carthage to break the peace and to risk all in battle. In 202 B.C., Scipio and Hannibal faced each other at the battle of Zama. The generalship of Scipio and the desertion of Hannibal's mercenaries gave the victory to Rome. The new peace terms reduced Carthage to the status of a dependent ally of Rome. The Second Punic War ended the Carthaginian command of the western Mediterranean and Carthage's term as a great power. Rome ruled the seas and the entire Mediterranean coast from Italy westward.

THE NEW IMPERIAL SYSTEM. The Roman conquest of territory overseas presented a new problem. Instead of following the policy they had pursued in Italy, the Romans made Sicily a province and Sardinia and Corsica another. It became common to extend the term of the governors of these provinces beyond a year. The governors were unchecked by colleagues and exercised full *imperium*. New magistracies, in effect, were thus created free of the limits put on the power of officials in Rome. The new populations were neither Roman citizens nor allies; they were subjects who did not serve in the army but paid tribute instead. The old practice of extending citizenship and with it loyalty to Rome stopped at the borders of Italy. Rome collected the new taxes by "farming" them out at auction to the highest bidder. At first, the tax collectors were natives from the same province, later Roman allies, and finally Roman citizens below senatorial rank who became powerful and wealthy by squeezing the provincials hard. These innovations were the basis for Rome's imperial organization in the future; in time they strained the constitution and traditions of Rome to such a degree as to threaten the existence of the republic.

After the First Punic War, Carthage sent the general Hamilcar to Spain where he built a strong and profitable colony. He befriended the local Iberians and enrolled their men in his army.

Hamilcar's successor, his son-in-law Hasdrubal, pursued the same policies. His success alarmed the Romans, and they imposed a treaty in which he promised not to take an army north across the Ebro River in Spain, although Punic expansion in Spain was well south of that river at the time of the treaty. Even though the agreement preserved the appearance of Rome's giving orders to an inferior, the treaty gave equal benefits to both sides. If the Carthaginians agreed to accept the limit of the Ebro to their expansion in Spain, the Romans would not interfere with that expansion.

The Republic's Conquest of the Hellenistic World

THE EAST. By the middle of the third century B.C., the eastern Mediterranean had reached a condition of stability. It was based on a balance of power among the three great kingdoms, and even lesser states had an established place. That equilibrium was threatened by the activities of two aggressive monarchs, Philip V of Macedon (221–179 B.C.), and Antiochus III of the Seleucid kingdom (223–187 B.C.). Philip and Antiochus moved swiftly, the latter against Syria and Palestine, the former against cities in the Aegean, in the Hellespontine region, and on the coast of Asia Minor.

The threat that a more powerful Macedon might pose to Rome's friends and, perhaps, even to Italy was enough to persuade the Romans to intervene. In 200 B.C., the Romans sent an ultimatum to Philip, ordering him not to attack any Greek city and to pay reparations to Pergamum. These orders were meant to provoke, not prevent, war, and Philip refused to obey. Two years later, the Romans sent out a talented young general, Flaminius, who demanded that Philip withdraw from Greece entirely. In 197 B.C., with Greek support, he defeated Philip in the hills of Cynoscephalae in Thessaly, bringing an end to the Second Macedonian War (the first had been fought while the Romans were still occupied with Carthage, from 215 to 205 B.C.). The Greek cities freed from Philip were made autonomous, and in 196 B.C., Flaminius proclaimed the freedom of the Greeks.

Soon after the Romans withdrew from Greece, they came into conflict with Antiochus, who was expanding his power in Asia and on the European side of the Hellespont. On the pretext of freeing the Greeks from Roman domination, he landed an army on the Greek mainland. The Romans routed Antiochus at Thermopylae and quickly drove him from Greece, and in 189 B.C., they crushed his army at Magnesia in Asia Minor. The peace of Apamia in the next year deprived Antiochus of his elephants and his navy and imposed a huge indemnity on him. Once again, the Romans took no territory for themselves and left a number of Greek cities in Asia free. They continued their policy of regarding Greece, and now Asia Minor, as a kind of protectorate in which they could intervene or not as they chose.

In 179 B.C., Perseus succeeded Philip V as king of Macedon. He tried to gain popularity in Greece by favoring the democratic and revolutionary forces in the cities. The Romans, troubled by this threat to stability, launched the Third Macedonian War (172–168 B.C.), and in 168, Aemilius Paullus defeated Perseus at Pydna. The peace imposed by the Romans reveals a change in policy and a growing harshness. It divided

Macedon into four separate republics, whose citizens were forbidden to intermarry or even to do business across the new national boundaries.

The new policy reflected a change in Rome from the previous relatively gentle one to the stern and businesslike approach favored by the conservative censor Cato (234–149 B.C.). The new harshness was applied to allies and bystanders as well as to defeated opponents. Leaders of anti-Roman factions in the Greek cities were punished severely.

When Aemilius Paullus returned from his victory, he celebrated a triumph that lasted three days, during which the spoils of war, royal prisoners, and great wealth were paraded through the streets of Rome behind the proud general. The public treasury benefited to such a degree that the direct property tax on Roman citizens was abolished. Part of the booty went to the general and part to his soldiers. New motives were thereby introduced into Roman foreign policy, or, perhaps, old motives were given new prominence. Foreign campaigns could bring profit to the state, rewards to the army, and wealth, fame, honor, and political power to the general.

THE WEST. Harsh as the Romans had become toward the Greeks, they were even worse in their treatment of the people of the Iberian Peninsula, whom they considered barbarians. The Romans committed dreadful atrocities, lied, cheated, and broke treaties in their effort to exploit and pacify the natives, who fought back fiercely in guerrilla style. From 154 to 133 B.C., the fighting waxed, and it became hard to recruit Roman soldiers to fight in the increasingly ugly war. At last, in 134, Scipio Aemilianus took the key city of Numantia by siege, burned it to the ground, and put an end to the war in Spain.

Roman treatment of Carthage was no better. Although Carthage lived up to its treaty with Rome faithfully and posed no threat, some Romans refused to abandon their hatred and fear of the traditional enemy. Cato is said to have ended all his speeches in

the Senate with the same sentence, "Ceterum censeo delendam esse Carthaginem" ("Besides, I think that Carthage must be destroyed"). At last, the Romans took advantage of a technical breach of the peace to destroy Carthage. In 146 B.C., Scipio Aemilianus took the city, plowed up its land, and put salt in the furrows as a symbol of the permanent abandonment of the site. The Romans incorporated it as the province of Africa, one of six Roman provinces, including Sicily, Sardinia–Corsica, Macedonia, Hither Spain, and Further Spain.

Civilization in the Early Roman Republic: The Greek Influence

Among the most important changes wrought by Roman expansion overseas were those in the Roman style of life and thought brought about by close and continued association with the Greeks of the Hellenistic world. Attitudes toward the Greeks themselves ranged from admiration for their culture and history to contempt for their constant squabbling, their commercial practices, and their weakness. Such Roman aristocrats as the Scipios surrounded themselves with Greek intellectuals, like the historian Polybius and the philosopher Panaetius. Conservatives such as Cato might speak contemptuously of the Greeks as "Greeklings" (*Graeculi*), but even he learned Greek and absorbed Greek culture.

Before long, the education of the Roman upper classes was bilingual. In addition to the Twelve Tables, young Roman nobles studied Greek rhetoric, literature, and sometimes philosophy. These studies even had an effect on education and the Latin language. As early as the third century B.C., Livius Andronicus, a liberated Greek slave, translated the *Odyssey* into Latin. It became a primer for young Romans and put Latin on the road to becoming a literary language.

Religion

Roman religion was influenced by the Greeks almost from the beginning; the Romans identified their own gods with Greek equivalents and incorporated Greek mythology into their own. For the most part, however, Roman religious practice remained simple and Italian, until the third century B.C. brought important new influences from the east. In 205, the Senate approved the public worship of Cybele, the Great Mother goddess from Phrygia. Hers was a fertility cult accompanied by ecstatic, frenzied, and sensual rites that shocked and outraged conservative Romans to such a degree that they soon banned the cult to Romans. Similarly, the Senate banned the worship of Dionysus, or Bacchus, in 186 B.C. In the second century B.C., interest in Babylonian astrology also grew,

ROMAN ENGAGEMENT OVERSEAS

215–205 B.C.	First Macedonian War
200–197 B.C.	Second Macedonian War
196 B.C.	Proclamation of Greek freedom by Flaminius at Corinth
189 B.C.	Battle of Magnesia; Antiochus defeated in Asia Minor
172–168 B.C.	Third Macedonian War
168 B.C.	Battle of Pydna
154–133 B.C.	Roman wars in Spain
134 B.C.	Numantia taken

Plutarch Describes a Roman Triumph

In 168 B.C., Lucius Aemilius Paullus defeated King Perseus in the battle of Pydna, bringing an end to the Third Macedonian War. For his great achievement, the Senate granted Paullus the right to celebrate a triumph, the great honorific procession granted only for extraordinary victories and eagerly sought by all Roman generals. Plutarch described the details of Paullus' triumph.

The people erected scaffolds in the forum, in the circuses, as they call their buildings for horseraces, and in all other parts of the city where they could best behold the show. The spectators were clad in white garments; all the temples were open, and full of garlands and perfumes; the ways were cleared and kept open by numerous officers, who drove back all who crowded into or ran across the main avenue. This triumph lasted three days. On the first, which was scarcely long enough for the sight, were to be seen the statues, pictures, and colossal images which were taken from the enemy, drawn upon two hundred and fifty chariots. On the second was carried in a great many wagons the finest and richest armour of the Macedonians, both of brass and steel, all newly polished and glittering; the pieces of which were piled up and arranged purposely with the greatest art, so as to seem to be tumbled in heaps carelessly and by chance. . . .

. . . .

On the third day, early in the morning, first came the trumpeters, who did not sound as they were wont in a procession or solemn entry, but such a charge as the Romans use when they encourage the soldiers to fight. Next followed young men wearing frocks with ornamented borders, who led to the sacrifice a hundred and twenty stalled oxen, with their horns gilded, and their heads adorned with ribbons and garlands; and with these were boys that carried basins for libation, of silver and gold.

. . . .

After his children and their attendants came Perseus himself, clad all in black, and wearing the boots of his country, and looking like one altogether stunned and deprived of reason, through the greatness of his misfortunes. Next followed a great company of his friends and familiars, whose countenances were disfigured with grief, and who let the spectators see, by their tears and their continual looking upon Perseus, that it was his fortune they so much lamented, and that they were regardless of their own.

. . . .

. . . After these were carried four hundred crowns, all made of gold, sent from the cities by their respective deputations to Aemilius, in honour of his victory. Then he himself came, seated on a chariot magnificently adorned (a man well worthy to be looked at, even without these ensigns of power), dressed in a robe of purple, interwoven with gold, and holding a laurel branch in his right hand. All the army, in like manner, with boughs of laurel in their hands, divided into their bands and companies, followed the chariot of their commander; some singing verses, according to the usual custom, mingled with raillery; others, songs of triumph and the praise of Aemilius's deeds; who, indeed, was admired and accounted happy by all men, and unenvied by every one that was good; except so far as it seems the province of some god to lessen that happiness which is too great and inordinate, and so to mingle the affairs of human life that no one should be entirely free and exempt from calamities; but, as we read in Homer, that those should think themselves truly blessed whom fortune has given an equal share of good and evil. ❑

Plutarch, "Aemilius Paullus," in *Lives of the Noble Grecians and Romans*, trans. by John Dryden, revised by A. H. Clough (New York: Random House, n.d.), pp. 340–341.

---

and the Senate's attempt in 139 to expel the "Chaldaeans," as the astrologers were called, did not prevent the continued influence of their superstition.

Education

Human society depends on the passing on from generation to generation of the knowledge, skills, and values needed for life in any particular community. A system of education, whether formal or informal, is essential to each culture and reveals its character even as it tries to stamp that character on its children. The education provided in the early centuries of the Roman Republic reflected the limited, conservative, and practical nature of that community of plain farmers and soldiers.

Education was entirely the responsibility of the family, the father teaching his own son at home. It is not clear whether in early times girls received any education, though they certainly did later on. The boys learned to read, write, and calculate, and they learned the skills of farming. They memorized the laws of the Twelve Tables, Rome's earliest code of law; learned how to perform religious rites; heard stories of the great deeds of early Roman history and particularly those of their ancestors; and engaged in the physical training appropriate for potential soldiers. This course of study was practical, vocational, and moral. It aimed at making the boys moral, pious, patriotic, law-abiding, and respectful of tradition.

In the third century B.C., the Romans came into contact with the Greeks of southern Italy, and this contact produced momentous changes in Roman education. Greek teachers came to Rome and introduced the study of language, literature, and philosophy, as well as the idea of a liberal education, or what the Romans called *humanitas*, the root of our concept of the humanities. The aim of education changed from the practical, vocational goals of earlier times to an emphasis on broad intellectual training, critical thinking, an interest in ideas, and the development of a well-rounded person.

The first need was to learn Greek, for Rome did not yet have a literature of its own. For this purpose, schools were established where the teacher, called a *grammaticus*, taught his students the Greek language and its literature, especially the poets and particularly Homer. Hereafter, educated Romans were expected to be bilingual. After the completion of this elementary education, Roman boys of the upper classes studied rhetoric—the art of speaking and writing well—with Greeks who were expert in those arts. For the Greeks, rhetoric was a subject of less importance than philosophy. But the more practical Romans took to it avidly,

for it was of great use in legal disputes and was becoming ever more valuable in political life.

Some Romans, however, were powerfully attracted to Greek literature and philosophy. The Roman aristocrat Scipio Aemilianus, who finally defeated and destroyed Carthage, surrounded himself and his friends with such Greek thinkers as the historian Polybius and the philosopher Panaetius. Other Romans, such as Cato the Elder, were more conservative and opposed the new learning on the grounds that it would weaken Roman moral fiber. They were able on more than one occasion to pass laws expelling philosophers and teachers of rhetoric. But these attempts to go back to older ways failed. The new education suited the needs of the Romans of the second century B.C., who found themselves changing from a rural to an urban society, and who were being thrust into the sophisticated world of Hellenistic Greeks.

By the last century of the Roman Republic, the new Hellenized education had become dominant. Latin literature had come into being along with Latin translations of Greek poets, and these formed part of the course of study, but Roman gentlemen were expected to be bilingual, and Greek language and literature were still central to the curriculum. Many schools were established, and the number of educated people grew, extending beyond the senatorial class to the equestrians and outside Rome to the cities of Italy.

Though the evidence is limited, we can be sure that girls of the upper classes were educated similarly to boys, at least through the earlier stages. They were

Cato Educates His Son

Marcus Porcius Cato (234–149 B.C.) was a remarkable Roman who rose from humble origins to the highest offices in the state. He stood as the firmest defender of the old Roman traditions at a time when Hellenic ideas were strongly influential. In the following passage, Plutarch tells how Cato attended to his son's education.

After the birth of his son, no business could be so urgent, unless it had a public character, as to prevent him from being present when his wife bathed and swaddled the babe. For the mother nursed it herself, and often gave suck also to the infants of her slaves, that so they might come to cherish a brotherly affection for her son. As soon as the boy showed signs of understanding, his father took him under his own charge and taught him to read, although he had an accomplished slave, Chilo by name, who was a schoolteacher, and taught many boys. Still, Cato thought it not right, as he tells us himself, that his son should be scolded by a slave, or have his ears tweaked when he was slow to

learn, still less that he should be indebted to his slave for such a priceless thing as education. He was therefore himself not only the boys' reading-teacher, but his tutor in law, and his athletic trainer, and he taught his son not merely to hurl the javelin and fight in armour and ride the horse, but also to box, to endure heat and cold, and to swim lustily through the eddies and billows of the Tiber. His History of Rome, as he tells us himself, he wrote with his own hand and in large characters, that his son might have in his own home an aid to acquaintance with his country's ancient traditions. ❑

Plutarch, *Cato Major*, 20, trans. by Bernadotte Perrin (London and New York: Loeb Classical Library, William Heinemann, 1914).

probably taught by tutors at home rather than going to school, as was the increasing fashion among boys in the late republic. Young women did not study with philosophers and rhetoricians, for they were usually married by the age the men were pursuing their higher education. Still, some women found ways to continue their education. Some became prose writers and others poets. By the first century A.D., there were apparently enough learned women to provoke the complaints of a crotchety and conservative satirist:

Still more exasperating is the woman who begs as soon as she sits down to dinner, to discourse on poets and poetry, comparing Virgil with Homer; professors, critics, lawyers, auctioneers—even another woman—can't get a word in. She rattles on at such a rate that you'd think that all the pots and pans in the kitchen were crashing to the floor or that every bell in town was clanging. All by herself she makes as much noise as some primitive tribe chasing away an eclipse. She should learn the philosopher's lesson: "moderation is necessary even for intellectuals." And, if she still wants to appear educated and eloquent, let her dress as a man, sacrifice to men's gods and bathe in the men's baths. Wives shouldn't try to be public speakers; they shouldn't use rhetorical devices; they shouldn't read all the classics—there should be some things women don't understand. I myself cannot understand a woman who can quote the rules of grammar and never make a mistake and cites obscure, long-forgotten poets—as if men cared about such things. If she has to correct somebody let her correct her girl friends and leave her husband alone.[2]

In the late republic, Roman education, though still entirely private, became more formal and organized. From the ages of seven to twelve, boys went to elementary school accompanied by a Greek slave called a *paedagogus* (whence our term *pedagogue*) who looked after his physical well-being and his manners, and who improved his ability in Greek conversation. At school, the boy learned to read and write, using a wax tablet and a stylus, and to do simple arithmetic with the aid of an abacus and pebbles *(calculi)*. Discipline was harsh and corporal punishment frequent. From twelve to sixteen, boys went to a higher school, where the *grammaticus* undertook to provide a liberal education, using Greek and Latin literature as his subject matter. In addition, he taught dialectic, arithmetic, geometry, astronomy, and music. Sometimes he included the elements of rhetoric, especially for those boys who would not go on to a higher education.

At sixteen, some boys went on to advanced study in rhetoric. The instructors were usually Greek, and they trained their charges by requiring them to study models of fine speech of the past and by having them write, memorize, and declaim speeches suitable for different occasions. Sometimes the serious student attached himself to some famous public speaker and followed him about to learn what he could.

Sometimes a rich and ambitious Roman would support a Greek philosopher in his own home so that his son could converse with him and acquire the learning and polish thought necessary for the fully cultured gentleman. Some, like the great orator Cicero (106–43 B.C.), undertook what we might call postgraduate study by traveling abroad to study with great teachers of rhetoric and philosophy in the Greek world. One consequence of this whole style of education was to broaden the Romans' understanding through the careful study of a foreign language and culture. It made them a part of the older and wider culture of the Hellenistic world, a world that they had come to dominate and needed to understand.

Roman Imperialism

Rome's expansion in Italy and overseas was accomplished without a grand general plan. The new territories were acquired as a result of wars that the Romans believed were either defensive or preventive. Their foreign policy was aimed at providing security for Rome on Rome's terms, but these terms were often unacceptable to other nations and led to continued conflict. Whether intended or not, Rome's expansion brought the Romans an empire, and with it, power, wealth, and responsibilities.

The republican constitution, which had served Rome well during its years as a city-state and had been well adapted to the mastery of Italy, would be severely tested by the need to govern an empire beyond the seas. Roman society and the Roman character had maintained their integrity through the period of expansion in Italy. But these would be tested by the temptations and strains presented by the wealth and the complicated problems presented by an overseas empire.

The Aftermath of Conquest

War and expansion changed the economic, social, and political life of Italy. Before the Punic wars, most Italians owned their own farms, which provided most of the family's needs. Some families owned larger holdings, but their lands chiefly grew grain, and they used the labor of clients, tenants, and hired workers rather than slaves. Fourteen years of fighting in the Second Punic War did terrible damage to much Italian farmland. Many veterans returning from the wars found it impossible or unprofitable to go back to their

[2]Juvenal, *Satires* 6.434–456, trans. by Roger Killian, Richard Lynch, Robert J. Rowland, and John Sims, cited by Sarah B. Pomeroy in *Goddesses, Whores, Wives, and Slaves* (New York: Schocken Books, 1975), p. 172.

MAP 5-3 ROMAN DOMINIONS OF THE LATE REPUBLIC *The Roman Republic's conquest of Mediteranean lands—and beyond—until the death of Julius Caesar is shown here. Areas conquered before Tiberius Gracchus (ca. 133 B.C.) are distinguished from later ones and from client areas owing allegiance to Rome.*

farms. Some moved to Rome, where they could find work as occasional laborers, but most stayed in the country to work as tenant farmers or hired hands. No longer landowners, they were also no longer eligible for the army. Often the land they abandoned was gathered into large parcels by the wealthy. They converted these large units, later called *latifundia*, into large plantations for growing cash crops—grain, olives, and grapes for wine—or into cattle ranches.

The upper classes had plenty of capital to stock and operate these estates because of profits from the war and from exploiting the provinces. Land was cheap, and slaves conquered in war provided cheap labor. By fair means and foul, large landholders obtained large quantities of public land and forced small farmers from it. These changes separated the people of Rome and Italy more sharply into rich and poor, landed and landless, privileged and deprived. The result was political, social, and ultimately constitutional conflict that threatened the existence of the republic.

The Gracchi

By the middle of the second century B.C., the problems caused by Rome's rapid expansion troubled perceptive Roman nobles. The fall in status of the peasant farmers made it harder to recruit soldiers and came to present a political threat as well. The patron's traditional control over his clients was weakened by their flight from their land. Even those former landowners who worked on the land of their patrons as tenants or hired hands were less reliable. The introduction of the secret ballot in the 130s made them even more independent.

In 133 B.C., Tiberius Gracchus tried to solve these problems. He became tribune for 133 B.C. on a program of land reform. The program aroused great hostility. When Tiberius put it before the tribal assembly, one of the tribunes interposed his veto. Unwilling to give up, he put his bill before the tribal assembly again. Again it was vetoed, so Tiberius, strongly supported by the people, had the offending tribune removed from office, thereby violating the constitution.

Tiberius then proposed a second bill, harsher than the first and more appealing to the people, for he had given up hope of conciliating the Senate. There could be no compromise: Either Tiberius or the Roman constitution must go under.

Tiberius understood the danger that he would face

if he stepped down from the tribunate, so he announced his candidacy for a second successive term, another blow at tradition. At the elections, a riot broke out, and a mob of senators and their clients killed Tiberius and some three hundred of his followers and threw their bodies into the Tiber River. The Senate had put down the threat to its rule, but at the price of the first internal bloodshed in Roman political history.

The tribunate of Tiberius Gracchus brought a permanent change to Roman politics. Heretofore, Roman political struggles had generally involved struggles for honor and reputation between great families or coalitions of such families. Fundamental issues were rarely at stake. The revolutionary proposals of Tiberius, however, and the senatorial resort to bloodshed created a new situation. Tiberius' use of the tribunate to challenge senatorial rule encouraged imitation in spite of his failure. From then on, Romans could pursue a political career that was not based solely on influence within the aristocracy; pressure from the people might be an effective substitute. In the last century of the republic, such politicians were called *populares*, whereas those who supported the traditional role of the Senate were called *optimates* ("the best men").

The tribunate of Gaius Gracchus (brother of Tiberius) was much more dangerous than that of Tiberius

Appian Discusses Rome's Agrarian Crisis and the Proposal of Tiberius Gracchus

The changes that the second century B.C. had brought to Rome produced economic, social, political, and constitutional problems that demanded attention. The senatorial government was slow to move toward their solution, and the first major attempt at reform was undertaken in 133 B.C. by the tribune Tiberius Gracchus. Appian, a historian who lived in the second century A.D., described the situation.

The Romans, as they subdued the Italian nations successively in war, seized a part of their lands and built towns there, or established their own colonies in those already existing, and used them in place of garrisons. Of the land acquired by war they assigned the cultivated part forthwith to settlers, or leased or sold it. Since they had no leisure as yet to allot the part which then lay desolated by war (this was generally the greater part), they made proclamation that in the meantime those who were willing to work it might do so for a share of the yearly crops—a tenth of the grain and a fifth of the fruit. From those who kept flocks was required a share of the animals, both oxen and small cattle. They did these things in order to multiply the Italian race, which they considered the most laborious of peoples, so that they might have plenty of allies at home. But the very opposite thing happened; for the rich, getting possession of the greater part of the undistributed lands, and being emboldened by the lapse of time to believe that they would never be dispossessed, and adding to their holdings the small farms of their poor neighbors, partly by purchase and partly by force, came to cultivate vast tracts instead of single estates, using for this purpose slaves as laborers and herdsmen, lest free laborers should be drawn from agriculture into the army. The ownership of slaves itself brought them great gain from the multitude of their progeny, who increased because they were exempt from military service. Thus the powerful ones became enormously rich and the race of slaves multiplied throughout the country, while the Italian people dwindled in numbers and strength, being oppressed by penury, taxes, and military service. If they had any respite from these evils they passed their time in idleness, because the land was held by the rich, who employed slaves instead of freemen as cultivators.

. . . .

At length Tiberius Sempronius Gracchus, an illustrious man, eager for glory, a most powerful speaker, and for these reasons well known to all, delivered an eloquent discourse, while serving as tribune, concerning the Italian race, lamenting that a people so valiant in war, and blood relations to the Romans, were declining little by little in pauperism and paucity of numbers without any hope of remedy. He inveighed against the multitude of slaves as useless in war and never faithful to their masters, and adduced the recent calamity brought upon the masters by their slaves in Sicily, where the demands of agriculture had greatly increased the number of the latter; recalling also the war waged against them by the Romans, which was neither easy nor short, but long-protracted and full of vicissitudes and dangers. After speaking thus he again brought forward the law, providing that nobody should hold more than 500 jugera of the public domain. But he added a provision to the former law, that the sons of the present occupiers might each hold one-half that amount, and that the remainder should be divided among the poor by triumvirs, who should be changed annually. ❑

Appian, *Roman History*, trans. by Horace White (London and New York: William Heinemann and the Macmillan Company, 1913), pp. 5–7.

because all the tribunes of 123 B.C. were Gaius' supporters, so there could be no veto, and a recent law permitted the reelection of tribunes. Gaius developed a program of such breadth as to appeal to a variety of groups. First, he revived the agrarian commission, which had been allowed to lapse. Because there was not enough good public land left to meet the demand, he proposed to establish new colonies: two in Italy and one on the old site of Carthage. Among other popular acts, he put through a law stabilizing the price of grain in Rome, which involved building granaries to guarantee an adequate supply.

Gaius broke new ground in appealing to the equestrian order in his struggle against the Senate. The equestrians (so called because they served in the Roman cavalry) were neither peasants nor senators. A highly visible minority of them were businessmen who supplied goods and services to the Roman state and collected its taxes. Almost continuous warfare and the need for tax collection in the provinces had made many of them rich. Most of the time, these wealthy men had the same outlook as the Senate; generally they used their profits to purchase land and to try to reach senatorial rank themselves. Still, they had a special interest in Roman expansion and in the exploitation of the provinces. Toward the latter part of the second century B.C., they came to have a clear sense of group interest and they began to exert political influence.

In 129 B.C., Pergamum became a new Roman province called Asia. Gaius put through a law turning over to the equestrian order the privilege of collecting its revenue. The equestrians were now given reality as a class, as a political unit that might be set against the Senate, and they might be formed into a coalition to serve Gaius' purposes.

Gaius easily won reelection as tribune for 122 B.C. He aimed at giving citizenship to the Italians, both to solve the problem that their dissatisfaction presented and to add them to his political coalition. But the common people did not want to share the advantages of Roman citizenship, and the Senate seized on this proposal as a way of driving a wedge between Gaius and his supporters.

The Romans did not reelect Gaius in 121 B.C., and he stood naked before his enemies. A hostile consul provoked an incident that led to violence. The Senate invented an extreme decree ordering the consuls to see to it that no harm came to the republic; in effect, this decree established martial law. Gaius was hunted down and killed, and a senatorial court condemned and, without trial, put to death some three thousand of his followers.

Marius and Sulla

For the moment, the senatorial oligarchy had fought off the challenge to its traditional position. Be-fore long, however, it faced more serious dangers arising from troubles abroad. The first grew out of a dispute over the succession to the throne of Numidia, a client kingdom of Rome's near Carthage. The victory of Jugurtha (d. 104 B.C.), who became king of Numidia, and his massacre of Roman and Italian businessmen in Numidia gained Roman attention. Although the Senate was reluctant to become involved, pressure from the equestrians and the people forced the declaration of what became known as the Jugurthine War in 111 B.C.

As the war dragged on, the people, sometimes with good reason, suspected the Senate of taking bribes from Jugurtha. They elected Gaius Marius (157–86 B.C.) to the consulship for 107, and the assembly, usurping the role of the Senate, assigned him to the province of Numidia. This action was significant in several ways: Marius was a *novus homo*, a "new man," that is, the first in the history of his family to reach the consulship. Although a wealthy equestrian, he had been born in the town of Arpinum and was outside the closed circle of the old Roman aristocracy. His earlier career had won him a reputation as an outstanding soldier and something of a political maverick.

Marius quickly defeated Jugurtha, but Jugurtha escaped and guerrilla warfare continued. Finally, Marius' subordinate, Lucius Cornelius Sulla (138–78 B.C.), trapped Jugurtha and brought the war to an end. Marius celebrated the victory, but Sulla, an ambitious but impoverished descendant of an old Roman family, resented being cheated of the credit he thought he deserved. Soon rumors circulated crediting Sulla with the victory and diminishing Marius' role. Thus were the seeds planted for a personal rivalry and mutual hostility that would last until Marius' death.

While the Romans were fighting Jugurtha, a far greater danger threatened Rome from the north. In 105 B.C., two barbaric tribes, the Cimbri and the Teutones, had come down the Rhone valley and crushed a Roman army at Arausio (Orange). To meet the danger, the Romans elected Marius to his second consulship when these tribes threatened again. From 104, he served five consecutive terms until 100 B.C., when the crisis was over.

While the barbarians were occupied elsewhere, Marius used the time to make important changes in the army. He began using volunteers for the army, mostly the dispossessed farmers and rural proletarians whose problems had not been solved by the Gracchi. They enlisted for a long term of service and looked on the army not as an unwelcome duty but as an opportunity and a career. They became semiprofessional clients of their general and sought guaranteed food, clothing, shelter, and booty from victories. They came to expect a piece of land as a form of mustering-out pay or veteran's bonus when they retired. Volunteers

Sculptured portrait of Sulla, the first Roman to seize control of the republic by force. [Staatliche Antikensammlungen und Glyptothek, Munich. Studio Koppermann.]

were most likely to enlist with a man who was a capable soldier and who was influential enough to obtain what he needed for them. They looked to him rather than to the state for their rewards. He, on the other hand, had to obtain these favors from the Senate if he was to maintain his power and reputation.

Marius' innovation created both the opportunity and the necessity for military leaders to gain enough power to challenge civilian authority. The promise of rewards won these leaders the personal loyalty of their troops, and that loyalty allowed them to frighten the Senate into granting their demands.

The War against the Italian Allies (90–88 B.C.)

For a decade, Rome took no action to deal with Italian discontent. In frustration, the Italians revolted and established a separate confederation with its own capital and its own coinage.

Employing the traditional device of divide and conquer, the Romans immediately offered citizenship to those cities that remained loyal and soon made the same offer to the rebels if they laid down their arms.

Even then, hard fighting was needed to put down the uprising, and by 88 B.C., the war against the allies was over. All the Italians became Roman citizens with the protections that citizenship offered, but they retained local self-government and a dedication to their own municipalities that made Italy flourish. The passage of time blurred the distinction between Romans and Italians and forged them into a single nation.

Sulla's Dictatorship

During the war against the allies, Sulla had performed well, and he was elected consul for 88 B.C. A champion of senatorial control, he fought and won a civil war against Marius and his friends. He now held all power and had himself appointed dictator, not in the traditional sense, but for the express purpose of reconstituting the state. He had enough power and influence to make himself the permanent ruler of Rome. Yet, he was traditional enough to want a restoration of senatorial government, reformed in such a way as to prevent the misfortunes of the past.

Sulla retired to a life of ease and luxury in 79 B.C. He could not, however, undo the effect of his own example: a general using the loyalty of his own troops to take power and to massacre his opponents, as well as innocent people. These actions proved to be more significant than his constitutional arrangements.

The Fall of the Republic

Pompey, Crassus, Caesar, and Cicero

Within a year of Sulla's death, his constitution came under assault. To deal with armed threats to its powers, the Senate violated the constitution by ignoring Sulla's rigid rules for holding office, which had been meant to guarantee experienced, loyal, and safe commanders.

Crassus and Pompey were ambitious men whom the Senate feared. Both demanded special honors and election to the consulship for the year 70 B.C. They both won election and repealed most of Sulla's constitution. This opened the way for further attacks on senatorial control and for collaboration between ambitious generals and demagogic tribunes.

In 67 B.C., a special law gave Pompey *imperium* for three years over the entire Mediterranean and fifty miles in from the coast. He also was given the power to raise great quantities of troops and money to rid the area of pirates. His power was then extended to fight a war that had broken out in Asia Minor. When he returned to Rome in 62 B.C., he had more power, prestige, and popular support than any Roman in history. The Senate and his personal enemies had reason to fear that he might emulate Sulla and establish his own rule.

Rome had not been quiet in Pompey's absence. Crassus was the foremost among those who had reason to fear Pompey's return. Although rich and influential, he did not have the confidence of the Senate, a firm political base of his own, or the kind of military glory needed to rival Pompey. During the 60s, therefore, he allied himself with various popular leaders. The ablest of these men was Gaius Julius Caesar (100–44 B.C.), a descendant of an old but politically obscure patrician family that claimed descent from the kings and even from the goddess Venus.

The chief opposition to Crassus' candidates for the consulship for 63 B.C. came from Cicero (106–43 B.C.), a "new man" from Marius' home town of Arpinum. He had made a spectacular name as the leading lawyer in Rome. He wanted to unite the stable elements of the state—the Senate and the equestrians—in a harmony of the orders. This program did not appeal to the senatorial oligarchy, but the Senate preferred him to Catiline, a dangerous popular politician thought to be linked with Crassus. Cicero and Antonius were elected consuls for 63 B.C., Catiline running third.

Cicero soon learned of a plot hatched by Catiline. Catiline had run in the previous election on a platform of cancellation of debts, which appealed to discontented elements in general but especially to the heavily indebted nobles and their many clients. Made desperate by defeat, Catiline planned to stir up rebellions around Italy, to cause confusion in the city, and to take it by force. Quick action by Cicero defeated Catiline.

The First Triumvirate

Toward the end of 62 B.C., Pompey landed at Brundisium and, to general surprise, disbanded his army, celebrated a great triumph, and returned to private life. He had achieved amazing things for Rome and simply wanted the Senate to approve his excellent arrangements in the east and to make land allotments to his veterans. But the Senate was jealous and fearful of overmighty individuals and refused his requests. In this way, Pompey was driven to an alliance with his natural enemies, Crassus and Caesar, because all three found the Senate standing in the way of what they wanted.

In 60 B.C. Caesar returned to Rome from his governorship of Spain. He wanted the privilege of celebrating a triumph but the Senate refused. Caesar then performed a political miracle: He reconciled Crassus with Pompey and gained the support of both for his own ambitions. So was born the First Triumvirate, an informal agreement among three Roman politicians, each seeking his private goals, that further undermined the future of the republic.

Portrait bust of Pompey the Great. This portrait, like others, illustrates the Roman preference for realistic portrayal of public figures. [Frank Brown Collection.]

Portrait of Julius Caesar. The sculpture is in the Naples museum. [Alinari/SCALA.]

Suetonius Describes Caesar's Dictatorship

Suetonius (CA. A.D. 69–CA.140) *wrote a series of biographies of the emperors, from Julius Caesar to Domitian. In the following selection, he described some of Caesar's actions during his dictatorship in the years 46–44* B.C.

His other words and actions, however, so far outweigh all his good qualities, that it is thought he abused his power, and was justly cut off. For he not only obtained excessive honours, such as the consulship every year, the dictatorship for life, and the censorship, but also the title of emperor, and the surname of Father of His Country, besides having his statue amongst the kings, and a lofty couch in the theatre. He even suffered some honours to be decreed to him, which were unbefitting the most exalted of mankind; such as a gilded chair of state in the senate-house and on his tribunal, a consecrated chariot, and banners in the Circensian procession, temples, altars, statues among the gods, a bed of state in the temples, a priest, and a college of priests dedicated to himself, like those of Pan; and that one of the months should be called by his name. There were, indeed, no honours which he did not either assume himself, or grant to others, at his will and pleasure. In his third and fourth counsulship, he used only the title of the office, being content with the power of dictator, which was conferred upon him with the consulship; and in both years he substituted other consuls in his room, during the last three months; so that in the intervals he held no assemblies of the people, for the election of magistrates, excepting only tribunes and ediles of the people; and appointed officers, under the name of præfects, instead of the prætors, to administer the affairs of the city during his absence. The office of consul having become vacant, by the sudden death of one of the consuls the day before the calends of January [the 1st Jan.], he conferred it on a person who requested it of him, for a few hours. Assuming the same license, and regardless of the customs of his country, he appointed magistrates to hold their offices for terms of years. He granted the insignia of the consular dignity to ten persons of prætorian rank. He admitted into the senate some men who had been made free of the city, and even natives of Gaul, who were semi-barbarians. He likewise appointed to the management of the mint, and the public revenue of the state, some servants of his own household; and entrusted the command of three legions, which he left at Alexandria, to an old catamite of his, the son of his freed-man Rufinus.

He was guilty of the same extravagance in the language he publicly used, as Titus Ampius informs us; according to whom he said, "The republic is nothing but a name, without substance or reality. Sulla was an ignorant fellow to abdicate the dictatorship. Men ought to consider what is becoming when they talk with me, and look upon what I say as a law." ❑

Suetonius, *The Lives of the Twelve Caesars*, trans. by Alexander Thompson, revised by T. Forster (London: George Bell and Sons, 1903), pp. 45–47.

The Dictatorship of Julius Caesar

Caesar's efforts were retarded with election to the consulship for 59 B.C. The triumvirate program was quickly enacted, and Caesar got the extraordinary command that would give him a chance to earn the glory and power with which to rival Pompey: the governship of Illyricum and Gaul for five years.

Caesar was now free to seek the military success he craved. By 56 B.C., he had conquered most of Gaul, but he had not yet consolidated his victories firmly. He therefore sought an extension of his command, but quarrels between Crassus and Pompey so weakened the Triumvirate that the Senate was prepared to order Caesar's recall. To prevent the dissolution of his base of power, Caesar persuaded Crassus and Pompey to meet with him at Luca in northern Italy to renew the coalition. Caesar was now free to return to Gaul and finish the job.

By the time he was ready to return to Rome, however, the Triumvirate had dissolved, and a crisis was at hand. At Carrhae, in 53 B.C., Crassus died trying to conquer the Parthians, successors to the Persian Empire. Soon, Pompey broke with Caesar and joined the Senate in opposing him.

Early in January of 49 B.C., the more extreme faction in the Senate had its way and ordered Pompey to defend the state and Caesar to lay down his command by a specified day. For Caesar, this meant exile or death, so he ordered his legions to cross the Rubicon River, the boundary of his province. This action was the first act of the civil war.

In 45 B.C., Caesar defeated the last of the enemy forces under Pompey's sons at Munda in Spain. The war was over, and Caesar, in Shakespeare's words, bestrode "the narrow world like a Colossus."

Caesar's innovations generally sought to make rational and orderly what was traditional and chaotic. Another general tendency of his reforms in the political area was the elevation of the role of Italians and even provincials at the expense of the old Roman families, most of whom were his political enemies.

Caesar made few changes in the government of Rome, but his own monopoly of military power made the whole structure a sham. He treated the Senate as his creature, sometimes with disdain. His enemies were quick to accuse him of aiming at monarchy. A senatorial conspiracy gathered strength under the leadership of Gaius Cassius Longinus and Marcus Junius Brutus and included some sixty senators in all. On March 15, 44 B.C., Caesar entered the Senate, characteristically without a bodyguard, and was stabbed to death. The assassins regarded themselves as heroic tyrannicides and did not have a clear plan of action after the tyrant was dead. No doubt they simply expected the republic to be restored in the old way, but things had gone too far for that. There followed instead thirteen years of more civil war, at the end of which the republic received its final burial.

The Second Triumvirate and the Emergence of Octavian

Caesar's heir was his grandnephew, Octavian, a youth of eighteen. He joined Marcus Antonius and Lepidus, two of Caesar's officers, in the Second Triumvirate to fight the assassins, who called themselves "tyrannicides." The new triumvirs defeated the enemy in a great battle at Philippi in 42 B.C., but they soon quarreled among themselves. Octavian gained control of the western part of the empire. Antonius, together with Cleopatra, queen of Egypt, ruled the east. In 31 B.C., the forces of Octavian crushed the fleet and army of Antony and Cleopatra at Actium, putting an end to the conflict.

THE FALL OF THE ROMAN REPUBLIC

133 B.C.	Tribunate of Tiberius Gracchus
123–122 B.C.	Tribunate of Gaius Gracchus
111–105 B.C.	Jugurthine War
104–100 B.C.	Consecutive consulships of Marius
90–88 B.C.	War against the Italian allies
70 B.C.	Consulship of Crassus and Pompey
60 B.C.	Formation of First Triumvirate
58–50 B.C.	Caesar in Gaul
53 B.C.	Crassus killed in Battle of Carrhae
49 B.C.	Caesar crosses Rubicon; civil war begins
46–44 B.C.	Caesar's dictatorship
45 B.C.	End of civil war
43 B.C.	Formation of Second Triumvirate
42 B.C.	Triumvirs defeat Brutus and Cassius at Philippi
31 B.C.	Octavian and Agrippa defeat Antony at Actium

The civil wars were over, and at the age of thirty-two, Octavian was absolute master of the Mediterranean world. His power was enormous, but so too was the task before him. He had to restore peace, prosperity, and confidence, and all of these required the establishment of a constitution that would reflect the new realities without offending unduly the traditional republican prejudices that still had so firm a grip on Rome and Italy.

Rome: From Republic to Empire in World Perspective

The history of the Roman republic reflects almost as sharp a departure from the common experience of ancient civilizations as that of the Greek city-states. A monarchy in its earliest known form, Rome quite early expelled its king, abandoned the institution of monarchy, and established an aristocratic republic somewhat like the *poleis* of the Greek dark ages. Unlike the Greeks, however, the Romans continued to be in touch with foreign neighbors, including the far more civilized urban monarchies of the Etruscans, but they clung faithfully to their republican institutions. For a long time, the Romans remained a nation of farmers and herdsmen, to whom trade was relatively unimportant, especially outside Italy.

Over time, the caste distinctions between patricians and plebeians became unimportant, giving way to distinctions based on wealth. Distinctions led to an aristocracy of noble families, who held the highest elected offices in the state. The nobles enhanced their power by their military service. The Roman republic from the first found itself engaged in almost continuous warfare with its neighbors. Wars were waged either in defense of its own territory, in fights over disputed territory, or in defense of other cities or states who were friends and allies of Rome.

In both their domestic and foreign relations, the Romans were a very legalistic people who placed great importance on traditional behavior encoded into laws. Although backed by the powerful authority of the magistrates at home and the potent Roman army abroad, the laws were based on experience, common sense, and equity. Aimed at stability and fairness, Roman law succeeded well enough that few people who lived under it wanted to do away with it. Roman law grew during the imperial period and even beyond. During the European Middle Ages, it played an important part in the revival of the West and continued to exert an influence into modern times.

The force of Roman arms, the high quality of Roman roads and bridges, and the pragmatic character of Roman law helped create something unique: an empire ruled by a republic, first a large one including all of Italy, and later one that commanded the shores of the entire Mediterranean (and quite a distance inland in many places). Rome controlled an area comparable to some of the empires of the east with an effective power equal to those of the kings and emperors of China, India, and Iran. It acquired that territory, wealth, and power in a state managed by annual magistrates elected by the male Roman citizens and by an aristocratic senate, which recognized popular assemblies and a published, impersonal code of law. Rome achieved its greatness with an army of citizens and allies, without a monarchy or a regular bureaucracy.

The temptations and responsibilities of governing a vast and rich empire, however, finally proved too much for the republican constitution. Trade grew, and with it a class of merchants and financiers called equestrians, which was neither aristocratic nor agricultural but increasingly powerful. The influx of masses of slaves captured in war undermined the small farmers who had been the backbone of the Roman state and its army. As many of them were forced to leave their farms, they moved to the cities, chiefly to Rome, where they had no productive role.

Conscripted armies of farmers serving relatively short terms gave way to volunteer armies of landless men serving as professionals and expecting to be rewarded with gifts of land or money. The generals of these armies were not annual magistrates controlled by the Senate and the constitution but ambitious military leaders seeking glory and political advantage. The result was civil war and the destruction of the republic. The conquest of a vast empire moved the Romans away from their unusual historical traditions toward the more familiar path of empire trodden by rulers in Egypt, Mesopotamia, China, India, and Iran.

Suggested Readings

F. E. ADCOCK, *The Roman Art of War Under the Republic* (1940). An analysis of Roman military procedures.

E. BADIAN, *Foreign Clientelae* (1958). A brilliant study of the Roman idea of a client–patron relationship extended to foreign affairs.

E. BADIAN, *Roman Imperialism in the Late Republic*, 2nd ed. (1968).

A. H. BERNSTEIN, *Tiberius Sempronius Gracchus: Tradition and Apostacy* (1978). A new interpretation of Tiberius' place in Roman politics.

R. BLOCH, *Origins of Rome* (1960). A good account of the most generally accepted point of view.

P. A. BRUNT, *Social Conflicts in the Roman Republic* (1971).

B. CAVEN, *The Punic Wars* (1980).

T. CORNELL AND J. MATTHEWS, *Atlas of the Roman World* (1982). Much more than the title indicates, this book presents a comprehensive view of the Roman world in its physical and cultural setting.

D. C. EARL, *The Moral and Political Tradition of Rome* (1967).

R. M. ERRINGTON, *The Dawn of Empire: Rome's Rise to Power* (1972). An account of Rome's conquest of the Mediterranean.

M. GELZER, *Caesar: Politician and Statesman*, trans. by P. Needham (1968). The best biography of Caesar.

E. GJERSTAD, *Legends and Facts of Early Roman History* (1962). An unorthodox but interesting account of early Rome.

E. S. GRUEN, *The Last Generation of the Roman Republic* (1973). An interesting but controversial interpretation of the fall of the republic.

E. S. GRUEN, *The Hellenistic World and the Coming of Rome* (1984). A new interpretation of Rome's conquest of the eastern Mediterranean.

W. V. HARRIS, *War and Imperialism in Republican Rome*, 327–70 B.C. (Oxford, 1975). An analysis of Roman attitudes and intentions concerning imperial expansion and war.

L. P. HOMO, *Primitive Italy and the Beginning of Roman Imperialism* (1967). A study of early Roman relations with the peoples of Italy.

F. B. MARSH, *A History of the Roman World from 146 to 30 B.C.*, 3rd ed., rev. by H. H. Scullard (1963). An excellent narrative account.

J. C. MEYER, *Pre-Republican Rome* (1983).

C. NICOLET, *The World of the Citizen in Republican Rome* (1980).

M. PALLOTTINO, *The Etruscans*, 6th ed. (1974). Makes especially good use of archaeological evidence.

E. T. SALMON, *Roman Colonization Under the Republic* (1970).

E. T. SALMON, *The Making of Roman Italy* (1980). The story of Roman expansion on the Italian peninsula.

H. H. SCULLARD, *A History of the Roman World 753–146 B.C.*, 4th ed. (1980). An unusually fine narrative history with useful critical notes.

H. H. SCULLARD, *From the Gracchi to Nero*, 5th ed. (1982). A work of the same character and quality.

A. N. SHERWIN-WHITE, *Roman Citizenship* (1939). A useful study of the Roman franchise and its extension to other peoples.

R. E. SMITH, *Cicero the Statesman* (1966). A sound biography.

D. STOCKTON, *Cicero: A Political Biography* (1971). A readable and interesting study.

D. STOCKTON, *The Gracchi* (1979). An interesting analytic narrative.

L. R. TAYLOR, *Party Politics in the Age of Caesar* (1949). A fascinating analysis of Roman political practices.

B. H. WARMINGTON, *Carthage* (1960). A good survey.

G. WILLIAMS, *The Nature of Roman Poetry* (1970). An unusually graceful and perceptive literary study.

Equestrian statue of Emperor Marcus Aurelius in a setting in Rome arranged in the sixteenth century by Michelangelo. This is the only remaining equestrian statue of an emperor and had enormous influence on sculptors after it was discovered during the Renaisance. [Copyright by Leonard von Matt.]

6 Imperial Rome

The fall of the Roman Republic put an end to an unusual chapter in the history of civilization. Examples of nonmonarchical governments lasting for more than a relatively short time are few. And the experience of a republic lasting for almost five hundred years, as well as ruling a vast empire, has no parallel. The transition toward the more typical organization of vast territories into an imperial monarchy was difficult. The early generations of Romans after the collapse of the old order continued to think in republican terms; many of their members longed simply for a restoration of the republic.

The years of Augustus' rule were crucial in making the transition, because he skillfully maintained the appearance of republican institutions that helped mask the monarchical reality. The passage of time made such deception less necessary. Hard times and chaos in the third century revealed more clearly the basically military foundations of the rule of the increasingly autocratic emperors. In the first century, emperors began to be declared divine upon their deaths, and by the second century they were worshipped as gods during their lifetime, just like the rulers of ancient Egypt, China, Japan, and most other early empires. The basis for all this, however, was established during the years in which Augustus ruled Rome.

The Augustan Principate

If the problems facing Octavian after the Battle of Actium were great, so too were his resources for addressing them. He was the master of a vast military force, the only one in the Roman world, and he had loyal and capable assistants. Yet the memory of Julius Caesar's fate was still clear in Octavian's mind, and its lesson was that it was dangerous to flaunt unprecedented powers and to disregard all republican traditions.

Octavian's constitutional solution proved to be successful and lasting, subtle and effective. Behind all the republican trappings and the apparent sharing of authority with the Senate, the government of Octavian, like that of his successors, was a monarchy. All real power, both civil and military, lay with the ruler, whether he was called by the unofficial title of "first citizen" *(princeps)*, like Octavian, who was the founder of the regime, or "emperor" *(imperator)*, like those who followed.

On January 13, 27 B.C., he put forward a new plan in dramatic style, coming before the Senate to give up all his powers and provinces. In what was surely a rehearsed response, the Senate begged him to reconsider, and at last he agreed to accept the provinces of Spain, Gaul, and Syria with proconsular power for military command and to retain the consulship in Rome. The other provinces would be governed by the Senate as before. Because his were the border provinces containing twenty of the twenty-six legions, his true power was undiminished, but the Senate responded with almost hysterical gratitude, voting him many honors. Among them was the semireligious title "Augustus," which carried implications of veneration, majesty, and holiness. From this time on, historians speak of Rome's first emperor as Augustus and of his regime as the Principate. This would have pleased him, for it helps conceal the novel, unrepublican nature of the regime and the naked power on which it rested.

Administration

Augustus made important changes in the government of Rome, Italy, and the provinces. Most of these had the effect of reducing inefficiency and corruption, eliminating the threat to peace and order by ambitious individuals, and reducing the distinction between Romans and Italians, senators and equestrians. Augustus controlled the elections and saw to it that promising young men, whatever their origin, served the state as administrators and provincial governors. In this way, equestrians and Italians who had no connection with the Roman aristocracy entered the Senate in great numbers. For all his power, Augustus was careful always to treat the Senate with respect and honor.

The Augustan period was one of great prosperity, based on the wealth that Augustus had brought in by the conquest of Egypt, on the great increase in commerce and industry made possible by general peace and a vast program of public works, and on a strong return to successful small farming on the part of Augustus' resettled veterans.

The union of political and military power in the hands of the *princeps* made it possible for him to in-

Emperor Augustus (27 B.C.–A.D. 14). *This statue, now in the Vatican, stood in the villa of Augustus's wife Livia. The figures on the elaborate breastplate are all of symbolic significance. At the top, for example, Dawn in her chariot brings in a new day under the protective mantle of the sky god; in the center Tiberius, Augustus's future successor, accepts the return of captured Roman standards from a barbarian prince; and at the bottom is Mother Earth with a horn of plenty. [Copyright by Leonard von Matt.]*

stall rational, efficient, and stable government in the provinces for the first time.

The Army and Defense

The main external problem facing Augustus—and one that haunted all his successors—was the northern frontier. In A.D. 9, a revolt broke out, led by the German tribal leader Herrmann, or Arminius, as the Romans called him. He ambushed and destroyed three Roman legions under the general Varus as they marched through the Teutoburg Forest. The aged Au-

The Emperor Augustus Writes His Testament

Emperor Augustus wrote a record of his achievements to be read, engraved, and placed outside his mausoleum after his death. The following selections are from that document.

13. The temple of Janus Quirinus, which our ancestors desired to be closed whenever peace with victory was secured by sea and by land throughout the entire empire of the Roman people, and which before I was born is recorded to have been closed only twice since the founding of the city, was during my principate three times ordered by the senate to be closed.

. . . .

34. In my sixth and seventh consulships, after I had put an end to the civil wars, having attained supreme power by universal consent, I transferred the state from my own power to the control of the Roman senate and people. For this service of mine I received the title of Augustus by decree of the senate, and the doorposts of my house were publicly decked with laurels, the civic crown was affixed over my doorway, and a golden shield was set up in the Julian senate house, which, as the inscription on this shield testifies, the Roman senate and people gave me in recognition of my valor, clemency, justice, and devotion. After that time I excelled all in authority, but I possessed no more power than the others who were my colleagues in each magistracy.

35. When I held my thirteenth consulship, the senate, the equestrian order, and the entire Roman people gave me the title of "father of the country" and decreed that this title should be inscribed in the vestibule of my house, in the Julian senate house, and in the Augustan Forum on the pedestal of the chariot which was set up in my honor by decree of the senate. At the time I wrote this document I was in my seventy-sixth year. ❑

Augustus, *Res Gestae*, trans. by N. Lewis and M. Reinhold, in *Roman Civilization*, Vol. 2 (New York: Columbia University Press, 1955), pp. 13, 19.

gustus abandoned the campaign, leaving a problem of border defense that caused great trouble for his successors.

Under Augustus, the armed forces achieved true professional status. Enlistment, chiefly by Italians, was for twenty years, but the pay was relatively good and there were occasional bonuses and the promise of a pension on retirement in the form of money or a plot of land. Together with the auxiliaries from the provinces, these forces formed a frontier army of about 300,000 men. In normal times, this number was barely enough to hold the line. The Roman army permanently based in the provinces played a vital role in bringing Roman culture to the natives. The soldiers spread their language and customs, often marrying local women and settling down in the area of their service. They attracted merchants, who often became the nuclei of new towns and cities that became centers of Roman civilization. As time passed, the provincials on the frontiers became Roman citizens and helped strengthen Rome's defenses against the barbarians outside.

Soldiers of the élite Praetorian Guard, which was originally formed by Augustus into the personal bodyguard of the princeps. They numbered nine thousand and earned twice the salary of legionary soldiers. [Musée du Louvre, Paris. Giraudon.]

Religion and Morality

A century of political strife and civil war had undermined many of the foundations of traditional Roman society. Augustus thought it desirable to try to repair the damage, and he undertook a program aimed at preserving and restoring the traditional values of the family and religion in Rome and Italy. He introduced laws curbing adultery and divorce and encouraging early marriage and the procreation of legitimate children.

Augustus also worked at restoring the dignity of formal Roman religion, building many temples, reviving old cults, and reorganizing and invigorating the priestly colleges, and he banned the worship of newly introduced foreign gods. During his lifetime, he did not accept divine honors, though he was deified after his death, and as with Julius Caesar, a state cult was dedicated to his worship.

Civilization of the Ciceronian and Augustan Ages

The high point of Roman culture came in the last century of the republic and during the Principate of Augustus. Both periods reflected the dominant influence of Greek culture, especially in its Hellenistic mode. The education of Romans of the upper classes was in Greek rhetoric, philosophy, and literature, which also served as the models for Roman writers and artists. Yet in spirit and sometimes in form, the art and writing of both periods show uniquely Roman qualities, though each in different ways.

The Late Republic

CICERO. The towering literary figure of the late republic was Cicero. He is most famous for his orations delivered in the law courts and in the Senate. Together with a considerable body of his private letters, these orations provide us with a clearer and fuller insight into his mind than into that of any other figure in antiquity. We see the political life of his period largely through his eyes. He also wrote treatises on rhetoric, ethics, and politics that put Greek philosophical ideas into Latin terminology and at the same time changed them to suit Roman conditions and values.

Cicero's own views combined the teachings of the Academy, the Stoa, and other Greek schools to provide support for his moderate and conservative practicality. He believed in a world governed by divine and natural law that human reason could perceive and human institutions reflect. He looked to law, custom, and tradition to produce both stability and liberty. His literary style, as well as his values and ideas, was an

important legacy for the Middle Ages and, reinterpreted, for the Renaissance.

HISTORY. The last century of the republic produced some historical writing, much of which is lost to us. Sallust (86–35 B.C.) wrote a history of the years 78–67 B.C., but only a few fragments remain to remind us of his reputation as the greatest of republican historians. His surviving work consists of two pamphlets on the Jugurthine War and on the Catilinarian conspiracy of 63 B.C. They reveal his Caesarean and antisenatorial prejudices and the stylistic influence of Thucydides.

Julius Caesar (100–44 B.C.) wrote important treatises on the Gallic and civil wars. They are not fully rounded historical accounts but chiefly military narratives written from Caesar's point of view and with propagandist intent. Their objective manner (Caesar always referred to himself in the third person) and their direct, simple, and vigorous style make them persuasive even today, and they must have been most effective with their immediate audience.

LAW. The period from the Gracchi to the fall of the republic was important in the development of Roman law. Before that time, Roman law was essentially national and had developed chiefly by means of juridical decisions, case by case, but contact with foreign peoples and the influence of Greek ideas forced a change. From the last century of the republic on, the edicts of the praetors, which interpreted and even changed and added to existing law, had increasing importance in developing the Roman legal code. Quite early, the edicts of the magistrates who dealt with foreigners developed the idea of the *jus gentium*, or law of peoples, as opposed to that arising strictly from the experience of the Romans. In the first century B.C., the influence of Greek thought made the idea of *jus gentium* identical with that of the *jus naturale*, or natural law, taught by the Stoics. It was this view of a world ruled by divine reason that Cicero enshrined in his treatise on the laws, *De Legibus*.

POETRY. The time of Cicero was also the period of two of Rome's greatest poets, Lucretius and Catullus, each representing a different aspect of Rome's poetic tradition. The Hellenistic poets and literary theorists saw two functions for the poet, as entertainer and as teacher. They thought the best poet combined both roles, and the Romans adopted the same view. When Naevius and Ennius wrote epics on Roman history, they combined historical and moral instruction with pleasure. Lucretius (CA. 99–CA. 55 B.C.) pursued a similar path in his epic poem *De Rerum Natura (On the Nature of Things)*. In it, he set forth the scientific and philosophical ideas of Epicurus and Democritus with the zeal of a missionary trying to save society from fear and superstition. He knew that his doctrine might be bitter medicine to the reader: "That is why I have tried to administer it to you in the dulcet strain of poesy, coated with the sweet honey of the Muses."[1]

Catullus (CA. 84–CA. 54 B.C.) was a poet of a thoroughly different kind. He wrote poems that were personal, even autobiographical. In imitation of the Alexandrians, he wrote short poems filled with learned allusions to mythology, but he far surpassed his models in intensity of feeling. He wrote of the joys and pains of love, he hurled invective at important contemporaries like Julius Caesar, and he amused himself in witty poetic exchanges with others. He offered no moral lessons and was not interested in Rome's glorious history and in contemporary politics. In a sense, he is an example of the proud, independent, pleasure-seeking nobleman who characterized part of the aristocracy at the end of the republic.

The Age of Augustus

The spirit of the Augustan Age, the Golden Age of Roman literature, was quite different, reflecting the new conditions of society. The old aristocratic order, with its system of independent nobles following their own particular interests, was gone. So was the world of poets of the lower orders, receiving patronage from any of a number of individual aristocrats. Augustus replaced the complexity of republican patronage with a simple scheme in which all patronage flowed from the *princeps*, usually through his chief cultural adviser, Maecenas (d. 8 B.C.).

The major poets of this time, Vergil and Horace, had lost their property during the civil wars. The patronage of the *princeps* allowed them the leisure and the security to write poetry and at the same time made them dependent on him and limited their freedom of expression. They wrote on subjects that were useful for his policies and that glorified him and his family, but they were not mere propagandists. It seems evident that for the most part they were persuaded of the virtues of Augustus and his reign and sang its praises with some degree of sincerity. Because they were poets of genius, they were also able to maintain a measure of independence in their work.

VERGIL. Vergil (70–19 B.C.) was the most important of the Augustan poets. His first important works, the *Eclogues* or *Bucolics*, are pastoral idylls in a somewhat artificial mode. The subject of the *Georgics*, however, was suggested to Vergil by Maecenas. The model here was the early Greek poet Hesiod's *Works and Days*, but the mood and purpose of Vergil's poem are far different. It is, to be sure, a didactic account of

A mosaic showing Vergil reading from the Aenead to the Muses of Epic and Tragedy. [Giraudon.]

the agricultural life, but it is also a paean to the beauties of nature and a hymn to the cults, traditions, and greatness of Italy. All this, of course, served the purpose of glorifying Augustus' resettlement of the veterans of the civil wars on Italian farms and his elevation of Italy to special status in the empire.

Vergil's greatest work is the *Aeneid*, a long national epic that succeeded in placing the history of Rome in the great tradition of the Greeks and the Trojan War. Its hero, the Trojan warrior Aeneas, personifies the ideal Roman qualities of duty, responsibility, serious purpose, and patriotism. As the Roman's equivalent of Homer, Vergil glorified not the personal honor and excellence of the Greek epic heroes but the civic greatness represented by Augustus and the peace and prosperity that he and the Julian family had given to imperial Rome.

HORACE. Horace (65–8 B.C.) was the son of a freed man and fought on the republican side until its defeat at Philippi. He was won over to the Augustan cause by the patronage of Maecenas and by the attractions of the Augustan reforms. His *Satires* are genial and humorous. His great skills as a lyric poet are best revealed in his *Odes*, which are ingenious in their adaptation of Greek meters to the requirements of Latin verse. Two of the *Odes* are directly in praise of Augustus, and many of them glorify the new Augustan order, the imperial family, and the empire.

OVID. The darker side of Augustan influence on the arts is revealed by the career of Ovid (43 B.C.–

---

[1] I, Lucretius, *De Rerum Natura*, lines 93lff.

A.D. 18). He wrote light and entertaining love elegies that reveal the sophistication and the loose sexual code of a notorious sector of the Roman aristocracy. Their values and way of life were contrary to the seriousness and family-centered life that Augustus was trying to foster. Ovid's *Ars Amatoria*, a poetic textbook on the art of seduction, angered Augustus and was partly responsible for the poet's exile in A.D. 8 to Tomi on the Black Sea.

Ovid tried to recover favor, especially with his *Fasti*, a poetic treatment of Roman religious festivals, but to no avail. His most popular work is the *Metamorphoses*, a kind of mythological epic that turns Greek myths into charming stories in a graceful and lively style. Ovid's fame did not fade with his exile and death, but his fate was an effective warning to later poets.

HISTORY. The achievements of Augustus and his emphasis on tradition and on the continuity of his regime with the glorious history of Rome encouraged both historical and antiquarian prose works. A number of Augustan writers wrote scholarly treatises on history and geography in Greek. By far the most important and influential prose writer of the time, however, was Livy (59 B.C.–A.D. 17), an Italian from Padua. His *History of Rome* was written in Latin and treated the period from the legendary origins of Rome until 9 B.C. Only a fourth of his work is extant; of the rest, we have only pitifully brief summaries. He based his history on earlier accounts, chiefly the Roman annalists, and made no effort at original research. His great achievement was in telling the story of Rome in a continuous and impressive narrative. Its purpose was moral—setting up historical models as examples of good and bad behavior—and, above all, patriotic. He glorified Rome's greatness and connected it with Rome's past, just as Augustus tried to do.

ARCHITECTURE AND SCULPTURE. The visual arts revealed the same tendencies as other aspects of Roman life under Augustus. Augustus was the great patron of the visual arts, as he was of literature. He embarked on a building program that beautified Rome, glorified his reign, and contributed to the general prosperity and his own popularity. He filled the Campus Martius with beautiful new buildings, theaters, baths, and basilicas; the Roman Forum was rebuilt; and Augustus built a forum of his own. At its heart was the temple of Mars the Avenger to commemorate Augustus' victory and the greatness of his ancestors. On Rome's Palatine Hill, he built a splendid tem-

Aerial view of Pompeii, an Italian town on the Bay of Naples destroyed by the volcanic eruption of nearby Mt. Vesuvius which buried it in volcanic ash. This eruption was witnessed by the Younger Pliny and is described in his letters. The ruins of Pompeii were accidentally rediscovered in the 18th century and have now been largely excavated, revealing a propserous and pleasant town of moderate size with an active local political life. [Fotocielo.]

Tacitus Gives a Provincial View of the Imperial Peace

Tacitus (A.D. 55–CA. 115) *was a Roman senator. He is most famous as historian of Rome for the period* A.D. 14–68, *but the following selection comes from a eulogy for his father-in-law, Agricola* (A.D. 40–93). *It gives an insight into the Roman Empire viewed critically.*

The Britons, . . . convinced at length that a common danger must be averted by union, had, by embassies and treaties, summoned forth the whole strength of all their states. More than 30,000 armed men were now to be seen, and still there were pressing in all the youth of the country, with all whose old age was yet hale and vigorous, men renowned in war and bearing each decorations of his own. Meanwhile, among the many leaders, one superior to the rest in valour and in birth, Galgacus by name, is said to have thus harangued the multitude gathered around him and clamouring for battle:—

"Whenever I consider the origin of this war and the necessities of our position, I have a sure confidence that this day, and this union of yours, will be the beginning of freedom to the whole of Britain. To all of us slavery is a thing unknown; there are no lands beyond us, and even the sea is not safe, menaced as we are by a Roman fleet. And thus in war and battle, in which the brave find glory, even the coward will find safety. Former contests, in which, with varying fortune, the Romans were resisted, still left in us a last hope of succour, inasmuch as being the most renowned nation of Britain, dwelling in the very heart of the country and out of sight of the shores of the conquered, we could keep even our eyes unpolluted by the contagion of slavery. To us who dwell on the uttermost confines of the earth and of freedom, this remote sanctuary of Britain's glory has up to this time been a defence. Now, however, the furthest limits of Britain are thrown open, and the unknown always passes for the marvellous. But there are no tribes beyond us, nothing indeed but waves and rocks, and the yet more terrible Romans, from whose oppression escape is vainly sought by obedience and submission. Robbers of the world, having by their universal plunder exhausted the land, they rifle the deep. If the enemy be rich, they are rapacious; if he be poor, they lust for dominion; neither the east nor the west has been able to satisfy them. Alone among men they covet with equal eagerness poverty and riches. To robbery, slaughter, plunder, they give the lying name of empire; they make a solitude and call it peace." ❑

Tacitus, *Agricola*, in *Complete Works of Tacitus*, trans. by A. J. Church and W. Brodribb (New York: Random House, 1942), pp. 694–695.

ple to his patron god, Apollo. This was one of the many temples he constructed in pursuit of his religious policy.

Most of the building was influenced by the Greek classical style, which aimed at serenity and the ideal type. The same features were visible in the portrait sculpture of Augustus and his family. The greatest monument of the age is the Altar of Peace *(Ara Pacis)* dedicated in 9 B.C. Set originally in an open space in the Campus Martius, its walls still carry a relief. Part of it shows a procession in which Augustus and his family appear to move forward, followed in order by the magistrates, the Senate, and the people of Rome. There is no better symbol of the new order.

Peace and Prosperity: Imperial Rome (A.D. 14–180)

The central problem for Augustus' successors was the position of the ruler and his relationship to the ruled. Augustus tried to cloak the monarchical nature of his government, but his successors soon abandoned all pretense. The rulers came to be called *imperator*—from which comes our word *emperor*—as well as *Caesar*. The latter title signified connection with the imperial house, and the former indicated the military power on which everything was based. Because Augustus was ostensibly only the "first citizen" of a restored republic and his powers were theoretically voted him by the Senate and the people, he could not legally name his successor. In fact, he plainly designated his heirs by favors lavished on them and by giving them a share in the imperial power and responsibility.

Tiberius (emperor A.D. 14–37),[2] his immediate successor, was at first embarrassed by the ambiguity of his new role, but soon the monarchical and hereditary nature of the regime became patent. Gaius (Caligula, A.D. 37–41), Claudius (A.D. 41–54), and Nero (A.D. 54–68) were all descended from either Augustus or his wife, Livia, and all were elevated because of that fact.

[2]Dates for the emperors give the years of each reign.

WALL OF
ANTONINUS

WALL OF
HADRIAN

NORTH

SEA

BRITAIN

HIBERNIA

ELBE

ODER

VISTULA

RHINE

Cologne

GERMANIA
(INF.)

G E R M A N I A

A T L A N T I C

S A R M

LUGDUNENSIS

SEINE

O C E A N

LOIRE

GAUL

GERMANIA (SUP.)

RAETIA

NOR-
ICUM

DNIESTER

PRUTH

AQUITANIA

CISALPINE
GAUL

(SUP.)

PANNONIA
(INF.)

DANUBE

DACIA

TARRACONENSIS

NARBONENSIS

PO

DUERO

RHÔNE

EBRO

CORSICA

ITALY

DALMATIA

(SUP.)

DANUBE

MOESIA

(INF.)

B L

LUSITANIA

SPAIN

Rome

Apollonia

THRACE

Byzantiu

BAETICA

BALEARIC IS.

SARDINIA

MACEDONIA

ILLYRIA

GREECE

ASIA

M E D

ACHAEA

P

I

MAURETANIA

Carthage

S

SICILY

N

E

A

N

S

E

A

A

CRETE

A F R I C A

NUMIDIA

AFRICA

CYRENAICA

LIBYA

14 A.D. – *DEATH OF AUGUSTUS*

14–98 A.D. – *ACQUISITIONS,*
AUGUSTUS TO TRAJAN

98–117 A.D. – *ACQUISITIONS*
DURING THE REIGN OF TRAJAN

T R MILLER

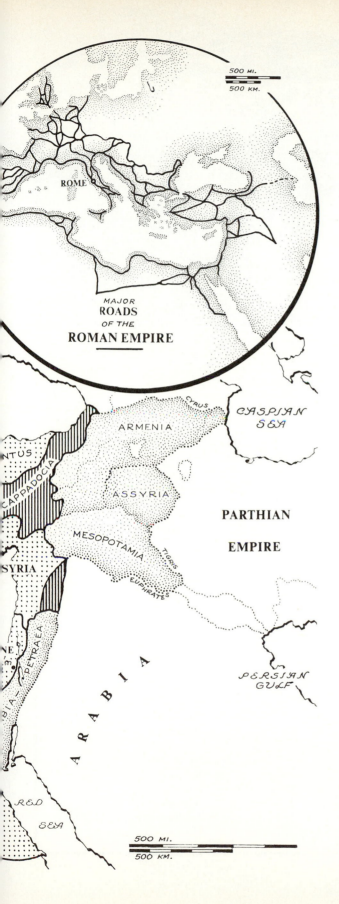

MAP 6-1 PROVINCES OF THE ROMAN EMPIRE TO A.D. 117 *The growth of the Empire to its greatest extent is here shown in three states—at the death of Augustus in B.C. 14, at the death of Nerva in 98, and at the death of Trajan in 117. The division into provinces is also indicated. The inset outlines the main roads that tied the far-flung empire together.*

In A.D. 41, the naked military basis of imperial rule was revealed when the Praetorian Guard dragged the lame, stammering, and frightened Claudius from behind a curtain and made him emperor. In A.D. 68, the frontier legions learned what the historian Tacitus called "the secret of Empire . . . that an emperor could be made elsewhere than at Rome." Nero's incompetence and unpopularity, and especially his inability to control his armies, led to a serious rebellion in Gaul in A.D. 68. The year 69 saw four different emperors assume power in quick succession as different Roman armies took turns placing their commanders on the throne.

Vespasian (A.D. 69–79) emerged victorious from the chaos, and his sons, Titus (A.D. 79–81) and Domitian (A.D. 81–96), carried forward his line, the Flavian dynasty. Vespasian was the first emperor who did not come from the old Roman nobility. He was a tough soldier who came from the Italian middle class. A good administrator and a hard-headed realist of rough wit, he resisted all attempts by flatterers to find noble ancestors for him. On his deathbed, he is said to have ridiculed the practice of deifying emperors by saying, "Alas, I think I am becoming a god."

The assassination of Domitian put an end to the Flavian dynasty. Because Domitian had no close relative who had been designated as successor, the Senate put Nerva (A.D. 96–98) on the throne to avoid chaos. He was the first of the five "good emperors," who included Trajan (A.D. 98–117), Hadrian (A.D. 117–138), Antoninus Pius (A.D. 138–161), and Marcus Aurelius (A.D. 161–180). Until Marcus Aurelius, none of these emperors had sons, so they each followed the example set by Nerva of adopting an able senator and establishing him as successor. This rare solution to the problem of monarchical succession was, therefore, only a historical accident. The result, nonetheless, was almost a century of peaceful succession and competent rule, which ended when Marcus Aurelius allowed his incompetent son, Commodus (A.D. 180–192), to succeed him, with unfortunate results.

There was, of course, some real opposition to the imperial rule. It sometimes took the form of plots against the life of the emperor. Plots and the suspicion of plots led to repression, the use of spies and paid informers, book burning, and executions. The opposition consisted chiefly of senators who looked back to republican liberty for their class and who found justifi-

Masada. In A.D. *70, Titus, the son of Emperor Vespasian, crushed the Jewish rebellion against Roman occupation of Palestine that had been raging since 66. He destroyed the Temple, plundered Jerusalem, and killed many survivors of the siege. The most determined resisters fled to the rocky fortress of Masada where they held out for years. When the Romans finally built a rampart that brought them to the summit, the resisters committed suicide rather than yield to them. [Israel Government Tourist Office, New York.]*

cation in the Greek and Roman traditions of tyrannicide as well as in the precepts of Stoicism. Plots and repression were most common under Nero and Domitian. From Nerva to Marcus Aurelius, however, the emperors, without yielding any power, again learned to enlist the cooperation of the upper class by courteous and modest deportment.

The Administration of the Empire

From an administrative and cultural standpoint, the empire was a collection of cities and towns that had little to do with the countryside. Roman policy during the Principate was to raise urban centers to the status of Roman municipalities with the rights and privileges attached to them. The Romans enlisted the upper classes of the provinces in their own government, spread Roman law and culture, and won the loyalty of the influential people.

As the efficiency of the bureaucracy grew, so did the number and scope of its functions and therefore its size. The importance and autonomy of the municipalities shrank as the central administration took a greater part in local affairs. The provincial aristocracy came to regard public service in their own cities as a burden rather than an opportunity; the price paid for the increased efficiency offered by centralized control was the loss of the vitality of the cities throughout the empire.

Augustus' successors, for the most part, accepted his conservative and defensive foreign policy. Trajan was the first emperor to take the offensive in a sustained way. Between A.D. 101 and 106, he crossed the Danube and, after hard fighting, established the new

RULERS OF THE EARLY EMPIRE

27 B.C.–A.D. 14	Augustus
	The Julio-Claudian Dynasty
A.D. 14–37	Tiberius
A.D. 37–41	Gaius (Caligula)
A.D. 41–54	Claudius
A.D. 54–68	Nero
A.D. 69	Year of the Four Emperors
	The Flavian Dynasty
A.D. 69–79	Vespasian
A.D. 79–81	Titus
A.D. 81–96	Domitian
	The "Good Emperors"
A.D. 96–98	Nerva
A.D. 98–117	Trajan
A.D. 117–138	Hadrian
A.D. 138–161	Antoninus Pius
A.D. 161–180	Marcus Aurelius

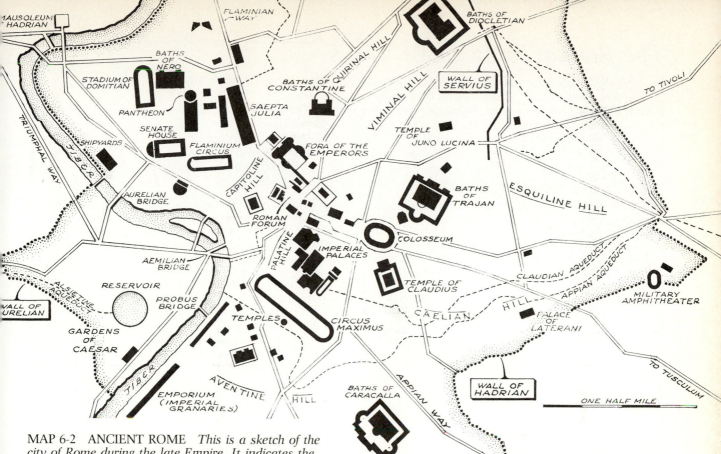

MAP 6-2 ANCIENT ROME *This is a sketch of the city of Rome during the late Empire. It indicates the seven hills on and around which the city was built, as well as the major walls, bridges, and other public sites and buildings. The Forum is between the Capitoline and Palatine hills.*

province of Dacia between the Danube and the Carpathian Mountains. He was tempted, no doubt, by its important gold mines, but he probably was also pursuing a new general strategy: to defend the empire more aggressively by driving wedges into the territory of threatening barbarians. The same strategy dictated the invasion of the Parthian Empire in the east (A.D. 113–117). Trajan's early success was astonishing, and he established three new provinces in Armenia, Assyria, and Mesopotamia, but his lines were overextended. Rebellions sprang up, and the campaign crumbled. Trajan was forced to retreat and died before getting back to Rome.

Hadrian returned to the traditional policy, keeping Dacia but abandoning the eastern provinces. Hadrian's reign marked an important shift in Rome's frontier policy. The Roman defense became rigid, and initiative passed to the barbarians. Marcus Aurelius was compelled to spend most of his reign resisting dangerous attacks in the east and on the Danube frontier, and these attacks put enormous pressure on the human and financial resources of the empire.

The Culture of the Early Empire

LITERATURE. In Latin literature, the years between the death of Augustus and the time of Marcus Aurelius are known as the Silver Age, and as the name implies, work of high quality—although probably not of so high a quality as in the Augustan era—was produced. In contrast to the hopeful, positive optimists of the Augustans, the writers of the Silver Age were gloomy, negative, and pessimistic. In the works of the former period, praise of the emperor, his achievements, and the world abound; in the latter, criticism and satire lurk everywhere.

Some of the most important writers of the Silver Age came from the Stoic opposition and reflected its hostility to the growing power and personal excesses of the emperors.

The writers of the second century appear to have turned away from contemporary affairs and even recent history. Historical writing was about remote periods, so there was less danger of irritating imperial sensibilities. Scholarship was encouraged, but we hear little of poetry, especially about any dealing with dangerous subjects.

In the third century A.D., romances written in Greek became popular and provide further evidence of the

The Roman Baths: Two Views

Public baths played an important part in the lives of the Romans of the imperial period. The finest architects built them, beautifully and expensively, for the citizens not only of Rome, but of most of the major cities in the empire. The baths served as vast community centers for social life and recreation. The first selection was written by Lucian, a writer of the second century A.D., *who described the magnificence of the baths. The second selection presents a more jaundiced view of the people who used them. It was written by Lucius Annaeus Seneca (*CA. 4 B.C.–A.D. 65*), who was Nero's tutor and a leading Roman representative of the Stoic school of philosophy.*

The building suits the magnitude of the site, accords well with the accepted idea of such an establishment, and shows regard for the principles of lighting. The entrance is high, with a flight of broad steps of which the tread is greater than the pitch, to make them easy to ascend. On entering, one is received into a public hall of good size, with ample accommodations for servants and attendants. On the left are the lounging rooms, also of just the right sort for a bath, attractive, brightly lighted retreats. Then, besides them, a hall, larger than need be for the purposes of a bath, but necessary for the reception of richer persons. Next, capacious locker rooms to undress in, on each side, with a very high and brilliantly lighted hall between them, in which are three swimming pools of cold water; it is finished in Laconian marble, and has two statues of white marble in the ancient style, one of Hygeia, the other of Aesculapius.

On leaving this hall, you come into another which is slightly warmed instead of meeting you at once with fierce heat; it is oblong, and has an apse on each side. Next to it, on the right, is a very bright hall, nicely fitted up for massage, which has on each side an entrance decorated with Phrygian marble, and receives those who come in from the exercising floor. Then near this is another hall, the most beautiful in the world, in which one can stand or sit with comfort, linger without danger, and stroll about with profit. It also is refulgent with Phrygian marble clear to the roof. Next comes the hot corridor, faced with Numidian marble. The hall beyond it is very beautiful, full of abundant light and aglow with color like that of purple hangings. It contains three hot tubs.

When you have bathed, you need not go back through the same rooms, but can go directly to the cold room through a slightly warmed chamber. Everywhere there is copious illumination and full indoor daylight. . . . Why should I go on to tell you of the exercising floor and of the cloak rooms? . . . Moreover, it is beautiful with all other marks of thoughtfulness—with two toilets, many exits, and two devices for telling time, a water clock that makes a bellowing sound and a sundial. ❑

Lucian, *Hippias, or the Bath*, in N. Lewis and M. Reinhold, *Roman Civilization*, Vol. 2 (New York: Columbia University Press, 1955), pp. 227–228.

I live over a bathing establishment. Picture to yourself now the assortment of voices, the sound of which is enough to sicken one. When the stronger fellows are exercising and swinging heavy leaden weights in their hands, when they are working hard or pretending to be working hard, I hear their groans; and whenever they release their pent-up breath, I hear their hissing and jarring breathing. When I have to do with a lazy fellow who is content with a cheap rubdown, I hear the slap of the hand pummeling his shoulders, changing its sound according as the hand is laid on flat or curved. If now a professional ball player comes along and begins to keep score, I am done for. Add to this the arrest of a brawler or a thief, and the fellow who always likes to hear his own voice in the bath, and those who jump into the pool with a mighty splash as they strike the water. In addition to those whose voices are, if nothing else, natural, imagine the hair plucker keeping up a constant chatter in his thin and strident voice, to attract more attention, and never silent except when he is plucking armpits and making the customer yell instead of yelling himself. It disgusts me to enumerate the varied cries of the sausage dealer and confectioner and of all the peddlers of the cook shops, hawking their wares, each with his own peculiar intonation. ❑

Seneca, *Moral Epistles*, in N. Lewis and M. Reinhold, *Roman Civilization*, Vol. 2 (New York: Columbia University Press, 1955), p. 228.

tendency of writers of the time to seek and provide escape from contemporary realities.

ARCHITECTURE. The prosperity and relative stability of the first two centuries of imperial Rome allowed for the full development of the Roman contribution to architecture. To the fundamental styles of buildings developed by the Greeks, the Romans added little; the great public bath and a new, free-standing kind of amphitheater were the main innovations.

The main contribution of the Romans lay in the great size of the structures they could build and in the advances in engineering that made these large structures possible. While keeping the basic post-and-lintel construction used by the Greeks, the Romans added to it the principle of the semicircular arch, borrowed from the Etruscans. They also made good use of concrete, a building material first used by the Hellenistic Greeks and fully developed by the Romans. The new principle, sometimes combined with the new material, allowed progress over the old style. The arch combined with the post and lintel produced the great Colosseum built by the Flavian emperors. When used internally in the form of vaults and domes, the arch permitted great buildings like the baths, of which the most famous and best preserved are those of the later emperors Caracalla and Diocletian.

One of Rome's most famous buildings, the Pantheon, begun by Augustus' friend Agrippa and rebuilt by Hadrian, is a good example of the combination of all these elements. Its portico of Corinthian columns is of Greek origin, but its rotunda of brick-faced concrete with its domed ceiling and relieving arches is thoroughly Roman. The new engineering also made possible the construction of more mundane but more useful structures like bridges and aqueducts.

The Colosseum at Rome. The Romans called this building the Flavian Amphitheatre because it was built by three successive emperors of the Flavian family—begun by Vespasian, dedicated in A.D. 80 by his son Titus, and finished by his younger son Domitian. How it acquired its present name is uncertain; this may derive either from its enormous size or from its proximity to a colossal statue of Emperor Nero. It is said to have been built by prisoners taken in the Jewish War, and could seat 50,000 spectators for the animal hunts, gladiatorial combats, mock sea battles, and other spectacles that took place in it. [Fototeca Unione.]

The Pantheon at Rome. A temple, with baths and water gardens, was built on this spot by Agrippa in 27–25 B.C. Destroyed by fire, it was rebuilt in its present form by Emperor Hadrian between A.D. 117 and 125 and then repaired by Septimus Severus in about 200. [Italian Government Travel Office, New York.]

SOCIETY. Seen from the harsh perspective of human history, the first two centuries of the Roman Empire deserve their reputation of a "golden age," but by the second century, troubles had arisen, troubles that foreshadowed the difficult times ahead. The literary efforts of the time reveal a flight from the present and from reality and the public realm to the past, to romance, and to private pursuits. Some of the same aspects may be seen in the more prosaic world of everyday life, especially in the decline of vitality in local government.

In the first century A.D., members of the upper classes vied with one another for election to municipal office and for the honor of doing service to their communities. By the second century, much of their zeal had disappeared, and it became necessary for the emperors to intervene to correct abuses in local affairs and even to force unwilling members of the ruling classes to accept public office. The reluctance to serve was caused largely by the imperial practice of holding magistrates and councilmen personally and collectively responsible for the revenues due. There were even some instances of magistrates' fleeing to avoid their office, a practice that became widespread in later centuries.

All of these difficulties reflected the presence of more basic problems. The prosperity brought by the end of civil war and the influx of wealth from the east, especially Egypt, could not sustain itself beyond the first half of the second century. There also appears to have been a decline in population for reasons that remain mysterious. The cost of government kept rising as the emperors were required to maintain a costly standing army, to keep the people in Rome happy with "bread and circuses," to pay for an increasingly numerous bureaucracy, and, especially in the reign of Marcus Aurelius, to wage expensive wars to defend the frontiers against dangerous and determined barbarian enemies.

The ever-increasing need for money compelled the emperors to raise taxes, to press hard on their subjects, and to bring on inflation by debasing the coinage. These were the elements that were to bring on the desperate crises that ultimately destroyed the empire, but under the able emperors, from Trajan to Marcus Aurelius, the Romans met the challenge successfully.

Life in Imperial Rome: The Apartment House

The civilization of the Roman Empire depended on the vitality of its cities, of which no more than three or four had a population of more than 75,000, the typical city having about 20,000 inhabitants. The population of Rome, however, was certainly greater than 500,000, and some scholars think it was more than a million. People coming to it for the first time found it overwhelming and were either thrilled or horrified by its size, bustle, and noise.

The rich lived in elegant homes called *domus*, single-storied houses with plenty of space, an open central courtyard, and several rooms designed for specific and different purposes, such as dining, sitting, or sleeping, in privacy and relative quiet. Though only a small portion of Rome's population lived in them, these houses took up as much as a third of the city's space. Public space for temples, markets, baths, gymnasiums, theaters, forums, and governmental buildings took up another quarter of Rome's territory.

This left less than half of Rome's area to house the mass of its inhabitants. Inevitably, as the population grew, it was squeezed into multiple dwellings that grew increasingly tall. Most Romans during the imperial period lived in apartment buildings called *insulae* ("islands") that rose to a height of five or six stories and sometimes even more. The most famous of them, the Insula of Febiala, seems to have "towered above the Rome of the Antonines like a skyscraper."[3]

These buildings were divided into separate apartments (*cenicula*) of undifferentiated rooms, the same plan on each floor. The apartments were cramped and uncomfortable. They had neither central heating nor an open fireplace; heat and fire for cooking came from small, portable stoves or braziers. The apartments were hot in summer, cold in winter, and stuffy and smoky when the stoves were lit. There was no plumbing, so tenants needed to go into the streets to wells or fountains for water and to public baths and latrines, or to less well-regulated places, to perform some natural functions. The higher up one lived, the more difficult these trips, so chamber pots and commodes were kept in the rooms. These receptacles were emptied into vats on the staircase landings or in the alleys outside, or on occasion, the contents, and even the containers, were tossed out the window. Roman satirists complained of the discomforts and dangers of walking the streets beneath such windows, and Roman law tried to find ways to assign responsibility for the injuries done to dignity and person.

In spite of these difficulties, the attractions of the city and the shortage of space caused rents to rise, making life in these buildings expensive as well as uncomfortable. Conditions were also dangerous. The houses were lightly built of concrete and brick, far too high for the limited area of their foundations, so they often collapsed. Laws limiting the height of buildings were not always obeyed and did not, in any case, always prevent disaster. The satirist Juvenal did not exaggerate much when he wrote, "We inhabit a city held up chiefly by slats, for that is how the landlord patches up the cracks in the old wall, telling the tenants to sleep peacefully under the ruin that hangs over their heads."

Even more serious was the threat of fire. The floors were supported by wooden beams, and the rooms were lit by torches, candles, and oil lamps. They were heated by braziers. Fires broke out easily and, without running water, were not easily put out; once started, they usually led to disaster.

[3] J. Carcopino, *Daily Life in Ancient Rome* (New Haven, 1940), p. 26.

When we consider the character of these apartments and compare them with the attractive public places in the city, we can easily understand why the people of Rome spent most of their time out of doors.

The Rise of Christianity

The story of how Christianity emerged, spread, survived, and ultimately conquered the Roman Empire is one of the most remarkable in history. Its origin among poor people from an unimportant and remote province of the empire gave little promise of what was to come. Christianity faced the hostility of the established religious institutions of its native Judaea and had to compete not only against the official cults of Rome and the highly sophisticated philosophies of the educated classes but also even against other "mystery" religions like the cults of Mithra, Isis, and Osiris, and many others. The Christians also faced the opposition of the imperial government and suffered formal persecution, yet Christianity achieved toleration and finally exclusive command as the official religion of the empire.

Jesus of Nazareth

An attempt to understand this amazing outcome must begin with a discussion of Jesus of Nazareth, though there are many problems in arriving at a clear picture of his life and teachings. The most important evidence is in the Gospel accounts. The authors of the Gospels believed that Jesus was the son of God and that he came into the world to redeem humanity and to bring immortality to those who believed in him and followed his way; to the Gospel writers, Jesus' resurrection was striking proof of his teachings. At the same time, the Gospels regard Jesus as a figure in history, and they recount events in his life as well as his sayings.

There is no reason to doubt that Jesus was born in the province of Judaea in the time of Augustus and that he was a most effective teacher in the tradition of the Jewish prophets. This tradition promised the coming of a Messiah (in Greek, *christos*—so *Jesus Christ* means "Jesus the Messiah"), the redeemer who would make Israel triumph over its enemies and establish the kingdom of God on earth. In fact, Jesus seems to have insisted that the Messiah would not establish an earthly kingdom but, at the Day of Judgment, would bring an end to the world as human beings knew it. On that day, God would reward the righteous with immortality and happiness in heaven and condemn the wicked to eternal suffering in hell. Until that day, which his followers believed would come very soon, Jesus taught the faithful to abandon sin and worldly concerns; to follow him and his way; to follow the moral code de-

Mark Describes the Resurrection of Jesus

Belief that Jesus rose from the dead after his crucifixion (about A.D. 30) was and is central to traditional Christian doctrine. The record of the Resurrection in the Gospel of Mark, written a generation later (toward A.D. 70), is the earliest we have. The significance to most Christian groups revolves about the assurance given them that death and the grave are not final and that, instead, salvation for a future life is possible. The appeal of these views was to be nearly universal in the West during the Middle Ages. The Church was commonly thought to be the means of implementing the promise of salvation; hence the enormous importance of the Church's sacramental system, its rules, and its clergy.

And when evening had come, since it was the day of Preparation, that is, the day before the sabbath, Joseph of Arimathea, a respected member of the council, who was also himself looking for the kingdom of God, took courage and went to Pilate, and asked for the body of Jesus. And Pilate wondered if he were already dead; and summoning the centurion, he asked him whether he was already dead. And when he learned from the centurion that he was dead, he granted the body to Joseph. And he bought a linen shroud, and taking him down, wrapped him in the linen shroud, and laid him in a tomb which had been hewn out of the rock; and he rolled a stone against the door of the tomb. Mary Magdalene and Mary the mother of Jesus saw where he was laid.

And when the sabbath was past, Mary Magdalene, and Mary the mother of James, and Salome, bought spices, so that they might go and anoint him. And very early on the first day of the week they went to the tomb when the sun had risen. And they were saying to one another, "Who will roll away the stone for us from the door of the tomb?" And looking up, they saw that the stone was rolled back; for it was very large. And entering the tomb, they saw a young man sitting on the right side, dressed in a white robe; and they were amazed. And he said to them, "Do not be amazed; you seek Jesus of Nazareth, who was crucified. He has risen, he is not here, see the place where they laid him. But go, tell his disciples and Peter that he is going before you to Galilee; there you will see him, as he told you." And they went out and fled from the tomb; for trembling and astonishment had come upon them; and they said nothing to any one, for they were afraid. □

Gospel of Mark 15:42–47; 16:1–8, *Revised Standard Version of the Bible* (New York: Thomas Nelson and Sons, 1946 and 1952).

---

scribed in the Sermon on the Mount, which preached love, charity, and humility; and to believe in him and his divine mission.

Jesus had success and won a considerable following, especially among the poor. This success caused great suspicion among the upper classes. His novel message and his criticism of the current religious practices connected with the temple at Jerusalem and its priests provoked the hostility of the religious establishment. A misunderstanding of the movement made it easy to convince the Roman governor that Jesus and his followers might be dangerous revolutionaries. He was put to death in Jerusalem by the cruel and degrading device of crucifixion, probably in A.D. 30. His followers believed that he was resurrected on the third day after his death, and that belief became a critical element in the religion that they propagated throughout the Roman Empire and beyond.

Although the new belief spread quickly to the Jewish communities of Syria and Asia Minor, there is reason to believe that it might have had only a short life as a despised Jewish heresy had it not been for the conversion and career of Saint Paul.

Paul of Tarsus

Paul (A.D. ?5–?67) was born Saul, a citizen of the Cilician city of Tarsus in Asia Minor. Even though he was trained in Hellenistic culture and was a Roman citizen, he was a zealous member of the Jewish sect known as the Pharisees, the group that was most strict in its insistence on adherence to the Jewish law. He took a vigorous part in the persecution of the early Christians until his own conversion outside Damascus about A.D. 35. The great problem facing the early Christians was their relationship to Judaism. If the new faith was a version of Judaism, then it must adhere to the Jewish law and seek converts only among Jews. James, called the brother of Jesus, was a conservative who held to that view, whereas the Hellenist Jews tended to see it as a new and universal religion.

Paul, converted and with his new name, supported the position of the Hellenists and soon won many converts among the gentiles. Paul believed it important that the followers of Jesus be evangelists (messengers), to spread the gospel ("good news") of God's gracious gift. He taught that Jesus would soon return for the

Day of Judgment, and it was important that all should believe in him and accept his way. Faith in Jesus as the Christ was necessary but not sufficient for salvation, nor could good deeds alone achieve it. That final blessing of salvation was a gift of God's grace that would be granted to some but not to all.

Organization

Paul and the other apostles did their work well, and the new religion spread throughout the Roman Empire and even beyond its borders. It had its greatest success in the cities and for the most part among the poor and uneducated. The rites of the early communities appear to have been simple and few. Baptism by water removed original sin and permitted participation in the community and its activities. The central ritual was a common meal called the *agape* ("love feast"), followed by the ceremony of the *eucharist* ("thanksgiving"), a celebration of the Lord's Supper in which unleavened bread was eaten and unfermented wine

The Catacomb of the Jordani in Rome. The early Christians built miles of tunnels, called catacombs, in Rome. They were used as underground cemeteries and as refuges from persecution. [Leonard von Matt.]

drunk. There were also prayers, hymns, and readings from the Gospels.

At first, the churches had little formal organization. Soon, it appears, affairs were placed in the hands of boards of *presbyters* ("elders") and *deacons* ("those who serve"). By the second century A.D., as their numbers grew, the Christians of each city tended to accept the authority and leadership of bishops (*episkopoi*, or "overseers"), who were elected by the congregation to lead them in worship and supervise funds. As time passed, bishops extended their authority over the Christian communities in outlying towns and the countryside. The power and almost monarchical authority of the bishops was soon enhanced by the doctrine of Apostolic Succession, which asserted that the powers that Jesus had given his original disciples were passed on from bishop to bishop by the rite of ordination.

The bishops kept in touch with one another, maintained communications between different Christian communities, and prevented doctrinal and sectarian splintering, which would have destroyed Christian unity. They maintained internal discipline and dealt with the civil authorities. After a time, they began the practice of coming together in councils to settle difficult questions, to establish orthodox opinion, and even to expel as heretics those who would not accept it. It seems unlikely that Christianity could have survived the travails of its early years without such strong internal organization and government.

The Persecution of Christians

The new faith soon incurred the distrust of the pagan world and of the imperial government. The Christians' refusal to worship the emperor was judged to be treason. The privacy and secrecy of Christian life and worship ran counter to a traditional Roman dislike of any private association, especially any of a religious nature, and the Christians thus earned the reputation of being "haters of humanity." Claudius expelled them from the city of Rome, and Nero tried to make them scapegoats for the great fire that struck the city in A.D. 64. By the end of the first century, "the name alone"—that is, simple membership in the Christian community—was a crime.

Most persecutions in this period, however, were instituted not by the government but by mob action. But even this adversity had its uses. It weeded out the weaklings among the Christians, brought greater unity to those who remained faithful, and provided the Church with martyrs around whom legends could grow that would inspire still greater devotion and dedication.

The Emergence of Catholicism

The great majority of Christians never accepted complex, intellectualized opinions, but held to what even then were traditional, simple, conservative beliefs. This body of majority opinion and the Church that enshrined it came to be called *Catholic*, which means "universal." Its doctrines were deemed orthodox, whereas those holding contrary opinions were heretics.

The need to combat heretics, however, compelled the orthodox to formulate their own views more clearly and firmly. By the end of the second century, an orthodox canon had been shaped that included the Old Testament, the Gospels, and the Epistles of Paul, among other writings. The process was not completed for at least two more centuries, but a vitally important start had been made. The orthodox declared the Church itself to be the depository of Christian teaching and the bishops to be its receivers. They also drew up creeds, brief statements of faith to which true Christians should adhere. In the first century, all that was required of one to be a Christian was to be baptized, to partake of the eucharist, and to call Jesus the Lord. By the end of the second century, an orthodox Christian—that is, a member of the Catholic church—was required to accept its creed, its canon of holy writings, and the authority of the bishops. The loose structure of the apostolic Church had given way to an organized body with recognized leaders able to define its faith and to exclude those who did not accept it.

Rome as a Center of the Early Church

During this same period, the Church in the city of Rome came to have special prominence. Besides having the largest single congregation of Christians, Rome also benefited from the tradition that both Jesus' apostles Peter and Paul were martyred there. Peter, moreover, was thought to be the first bishop of Rome, and the Gospel of Matthew (16:18) reported Jesus' statement to Peter: "Thou art Peter [in Greek, *Petros*] and upon this rock [in Greek, *petra*] I will build my church." Because of the city's early influence and because of the Petrine doctrine derived from the Gospel of Matthew, later bishops of Rome claimed supremacy in the Catholic church, but as the era of the "good emperors" came to a close, this controversy was far in the future.

The Crisis of the Third Century

The pressure on Rome's frontiers, already serious in the time of Marcus Aurelius, reached massive proportions in the third century A.D. In the east, the frontiers were threatened by a new power arising in the old Persian Empire. In A.D. 224, a new Iranian dynasty, the Sassanians, seized control from the Parthians and brought new vitality to Persia. They soon recovered Mesopotamia and made raids deep into Roman provinces.

Barbarian Invasions

On the western and northern frontiers, the pressure came not from a well-organized rival empire but from an ever-increasing number of German tribes. These tough barbarians were always eager for plunder and were much attracted by the civilized delights they knew existed beyond the frontier of the Rhine and Danube rivers.

The most aggressive of the Germans in the third century A.D. were the Goths. Centuries earlier, they had wandered from their ancestral home near the Baltic Sea into the area of southern Russia. In the 220s and 230s they began to put pressure on the Danube frontier, and by about A.D. 250, they were able to penetrate into the empire and overrun the Balkan provinces. The need to meet this threat and the one

Emperor Valerian (253–260) surrendering to Shapur I. This is a relief carved into a rock near the ancient Persian city of Persepolis. It commemorates the victory in 260 over the Romans by Shapur I of the Sassanid dynasty of Persian kings. Kneeling before Shapur is the chained Roman emperor, who soon died in captivity. [AHM.]

posed by the Persian Sassanids in the east made the Romans weaken their western frontiers, and other Germanic peoples—the Franks and the Alemanni—broke through in those regions. There was a considerable danger that Rome would be unable to meet this challenge.

Rome's perils were caused, no doubt, by the unprecedentedly numerous and simultaneous attacks against it, but Rome's internal weakness encouraged these attacks. The pressure on the frontiers and epidemics of plague in the time of Marcus Aurelius forced the emperor to resort to the conscription of slaves, gladiators, barbarians, and brigands.

Septimius Severus (emperor A.D. 193–211) and his successors played a crucial role in the transformation of the character of the Roman army. Septimius was a military usurper who owed everything to the support of his soldiers. He meant to establish a family dynasty, in contrast to the policy of the "good emperors" of the second century A.D., and he was prepared to make Rome into an undisguised military monarchy. Septimius drew recruits for the army increasingly from peasants of the less civilized provinces, and the result was a barbarization of Rome's military forces.

Economic Difficulties

These changes were a response to the great financial needs caused by the barbarian attacks. Inflation had forced Commodus (ruled A.D. 180–192) to raise the soldiers' pay, but the Severan emperors had to double it to keep up with prices, which increased the imperial budget by as much as 25 per cent. The emperors resorted to inventing new taxes, debasing the coinage, and even to selling the palace furniture, to raise money. Even then, it was hard to recruit troops, and the new style of military life introduced by Septimius—with its laxer discipline, more pleasant duties, and greater opportunity for advancement, not only in the army but in Roman society—was needed to attract men into the army. The policy proved effective for a short time but could not prevent the chaos of the late third century.

The same forces that caused problems for the army did great damage to society at large. The shortage of workers reduced agricultural production. As external threats distracted the emperors, they were less able to preserve domestic peace. Piracy, brigandage, and the neglect of roads and harbors all hampered trade. So, too, did the debasement of the coinage and the inflation in general. Imperial exactions and confiscations of the property of the rich removed badly needed capital from productive use.

More and more, the government was required to demand services that had been given gladly in the past. Because the empire lived on a hand-to-mouth basis, with no significant reserve fund and no system of credit financing, the emperors were led to compel the people to provide food, supplies, money, and labor. The upper classes in the cities were made to serve as administrators without pay and to meet deficits in revenue out of their own pockets. Sometimes these demands caused provincial rebellions, as in Egypt and Gaul. More typically, they caused peasants and even town administrators to flee to escape their burdens. The result of all these difficulties was to weaken Rome's economic strength when it was most needed.

The Social Order

The new conditions caused important changes in the social order. The Senate and the traditional ruling class were decimated by direct attacks from hostile emperors and by economic losses. Their ranks were filled by men coming up through the army. The whole state began to take on an increasingly military appearance. Distinctions among the classes by dress had been traditional since the republic, but in the third and fourth centuries A.D. they developed to the point where the people's everyday clothing was a kind of uniform that precisely revealed their status. Titles were assigned to ranks in society as to ranks in the army. The most important distinction was the one formally established by Septimius Severus, which drew a sharp line between the *honestiores* (senators, equestrians, the municipal aristocracy, and the soldiers) and the lower classes, or *humiliores*. Septimius gave the *honestiores* a privileged position before the law. They were given lighter punishments, could not be tortured, and alone had the right of appeal to the emperor.

As time passed, it became more difficult to move from the lower order to the higher, another example of the growing rigidity of the late Roman Empire. Peasants were tied to their lands, artisans to their crafts, soldiers to the army, merchants and shipowners to the needs of the state, and citizens of the municipal upper class to the collection and payment of increasingly burdensome taxes. Freedom and private initiative gave way before the needs of the state and its ever-expanding control of its citizens.

Civil Disorder

Commodus was killed on the last day of A.D. 192, and the succeeding year was like the year A.D. 69: Three emperors ruled in swift succession, Septimius Severus emerging, as we have seen, to establish firm rule and a dynasty. The death of Alexander Severus, the last of the dynasty, in A.D. 235 brought on a half century of internal anarchy and foreign invasion.

The empire seemed on the point of collapse, but two able soldiers, Claudius II Gothicus (A.D. 268–270) and Aurelian (A.D. 270–275), drove back the barbarians and stamped out internal disorder. The soldiers who followed Aurelian on the throne were good fighters and made significant changes in Rome's system of defense. They built heavy walls around Rome, Athens, and other cities that could resist barbarian attack. They drew back their best troops from the frontiers, relying chiefly on a newly organized heavy cavalry and a mobile army near the emperor's own residence. Hereafter, the army was composed largely of mercenaries who came from among the Germans. The officers gave personal loyalty to the emperor rather than to the empire. These officers became a foreign, hereditary caste of aristocrats that increasingly supplied high administrators and even emperors. In effect, the Roman people hired an army of mercenaries, only technically Roman, to protect them.

The Tetrarchs. This porphyry sculpture on the corner of the church of San Marco in Venice depicts Emperor Diocletian (284–305) and his three imperial colleagues. They are in battle dress and clasp one another to express solidarity. This fourth-century sculpture was part of the booty brought back by the Venetians from their capture of Constantinople during the Fourth Crusade about nine hundred years later. [AHM.]

The Late Empire

The Fourth Century and Imperial Reorganization

The period from Diocletian (A.D. 284–305) to Constantine (A.D. 306–337) was one of reconstruction and reorganization after a time of civil war and turmoil. Diocletian was from Illyria (now Yugoslavia), a man of undistinguished birth who rose to the throne through the ranks of the army. He knew that he was not a great general and that the job of defending and governing the entire empire was too great for one man. He therefore decreed the introduction of the tetrarchy, the rule of the empire by four men with power divided on a territorial basis (see Map 6.3).

DIOCLETIAN. Diocletian was recognized as the senior Augustus, but each tetrarch was supreme in his own sphere. The Caesars were recognized as successors to each half of the empire, and their loyalty was enhanced by marriages to daughters of the Augusti. It was a return, in a way, to the happy precedent of the "good emperors," who chose their successors from the ranks of the ablest men, and it seemed to promise orderly and peaceful transitions instead of assassinations, chaos, and civil war.

CONSTANTINE. In 305, Diocletian retired and compelled his coemperor to do the same. But his plan for a smooth succession failed completely. In 310, there were five Augusti and no Caesars. Out of this chaos, Constantine, son of Constantius, produced order. In 324, he defeated his last opponent and made himself sole emperor, uniting the empire once again; he reigned until 337.

The emperor was a remote figure surrounded by carefully chosen high officials. He lived in a great palace and was almost unapproachable. Those admitted to his presence had to prostate themselves before him and kiss the hem of his robe, which was purple and had golden threads going through it. The emperor was addressed as *dominus* ("lord"), and his right to rule was not derived from the Roman people but from God. All this remoteness and ceremony had a double purpose: to enhance the dignity of the emperor and to safeguard him against assassination.

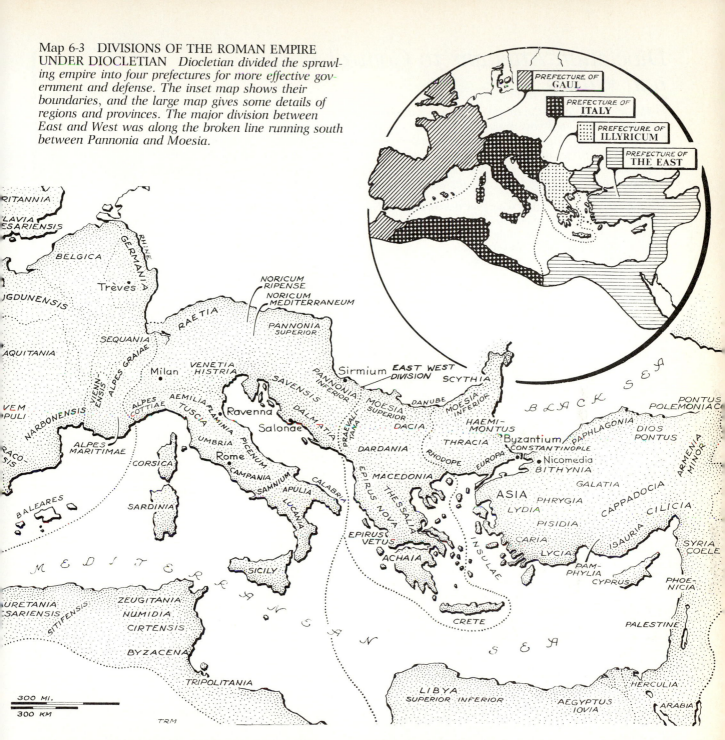

Map 6-3 DIVISIONS OF THE ROMAN EMPIRE UNDER DIOCLETIAN *Diocletian divided the sprawling empire into four prefectures for more effective government and defense. The inset map shows their boundaries, and the large map gives some details of regions and provinces. The major division between East and West was along the broken line running south between Pannonia and Moesia.*

PREFECTURE OF
GAUL

PREFECTURE OF
ITALY

PREFECTURE OF
ILLYRICUM

PREFECTURE OF
THE EAST

Constantine erected the new city of Constantinople on the site of ancient Byzantium on the Bosporus, which leads to both the Aegean and the Black seas, and made it the new capital of the empire. Its strategic location was excellent for protecting the eastern and Danubian frontiers, and, surrounded on three sides by water, it was easily defended. Until its fall to the Turks in 1453, it served as the bastion of civilization, the pre-

server of classical culture, a bulwark against barbarian attack, and the greatest city in Christendom.

The autocratic rule of the emperors was carried out by a civilian bureaucracy, which was carefully separated from the military service to reduce the chances of rebellion by anyone combining the two kinds of power.

The operation of the entire system was supervised by a vast system of spies and secret police, without

Diocletian Attempts to Control Prices and Wages

Rome's troubles in the third century A.D. caused serious economic problems. Debased currency and vast government expenditures produced a runaway inflation. In an attempt to control it, Diocletian took the unprecedented step of issuing a decree that put ceilings on prices and wages throughout the empire in the year 301. In spite of the most drastic penalties prescribed by the decree, it was widely evaded. After a time, its failure was acknowledged, and the decree was at last revoked.

Who does not know that wherever the common safety requires our armies to be sent, the profiteers insolently and covertly attack the public welfare, not only in villages and towns, but on every road? They charge extortionate prices for merchandise, not just fourfold or eightfold, but on such a scale that human speech cannot find words to characterize their profit and their practices. Indeed, sometimes in a single retail sale a soldier is stripped of his donative and pay. Moreover, the contributions of the whole world for the support of the armies fall as profits into the hands of these plunderers, and our soldiers appear to bestow with their own hands the rewards of their military service and their veterans' bonuses upon the profiteers. The result is that the pillagers of the state itself seize day by day more than they know how to hold.

Aroused justly and rightfully by all the facts set forth above, and in response to the needs of mankind itself, which appears to be praying for release, we have decided that maximum prices of articles for sale must be established. We have not set down fixed prices, for we do not deem it just to do this, since many provinces occasionally enjoy the good fortune of welcome low prices and the privilege, as it were, of prosperity. Thus, when the pressure of high prices appears anywhere—may the gods avert such a calamity!—avarice . . . will be checked by the limits fixed in our statute and by the restraining curbs of the law.

It is our pleasure, therefore, that the prices listed in the subjoined schedule be held in observance in the whole of our Empire. And every person shall take note

that the liberty to exceed them at will has been ended, but that the blessing of low prices has in no way been impaired in those places where supplies actually abound. . . . Moreover, this universal edict will serve as a necessary check upon buyers and sellers whose practice it is to visit ports and other provinces. For when they too know that in the pinch of scarcity there is no possibility of exceeding the prices fixed for commodities, they will take into account in their calculations at the time of sale the localities, the transportation costs, and all other factors. In this way they will make apparent the justice of our decision that those who transport merchandise may not sell at higher prices anywhere.

It is agreed that even in the time of our ancestors it was the practice in passing laws to restrain offenses by prescribing a penalty. For rarely is a situation beneficial to humanity accepted spontaneously; experience teaches that fear is the most effective regulator and guide for the performance of duty. Therefore it is our pleasure that anyone who resists the measures of this statute shall be subject to a capital penalty for daring to do so. And let no one consider the statute harsh, since there is at hand a ready protection from danger in the observance of moderation. . . . We therefore exhort the loyalty of all, so that a regulation instituted for the public good may be observed with willing obedience and due scruple, especially as it is seen that by a statute of this kind provision has been made, not for single municipalities and peoples and provinces but for the whole world. . . .   ❑

"Diocletian's Edict on Maximum Prices," from the *Corpus Inscriptionum Latinarum*, Vol. 3, in N. Lewis and M. Reinhold, *Roman Civilization*, Vol. 2 (New York: Columbia University Press, 1955), pp. 465–466.

whom the increasingly rigid totalitarian organization could not be trusted to perform. In spite of these efforts, the system was filled with corruption and inefficiency.

The cost of maintaining a 400,000-man army as well as the vast civilian bureaucracy, the expensive imperial court, and the imperial taste for splendid buildings put a great strain on an already weak economy. Diocletian's attempts at establishing a uniform and reliable currency failed and merely led to increased inflation. To deal with it, he resorted to price control

with his Edict of Maximum Prices in 301. For each product and each kind of labor a maximum price was set, and violations were punishable by death. The edict failed despite the harshness of its provisions.

Peasants unable to pay their taxes and officials unable to collect them tried to escape, and Diocletian resorted to stern regimentation to keep all in their places and at the service of the government. The terror of the third century had turned many peasants into *coloni*, tenant farmers who fled for protection to the *villa* ("country estate") of a larger and powerful land-

Arch of Constantine. The triumphal arch was a characteristic Roman imperial structure, and examples are found throughout the empire. This one at Rome was dedicated by Constantine in 315 in celebration of his victory over Maxentius at the Milvian Bridge.

In the distance, through the center arch, note some remaining arches of a first-century aqueduct, the Aqua Claudia.

Such structures as this arch and the aqueduct illustrate a significant point: With control of their diverse and far-flung empire continually at stake, as an adjunct of its administration, maintenance, safety, and amusement the Romans were immensely practical—almost compulsive—builders and engineers. Their bridges and aqueducts, temples and altars, triumphal arches and columns, theatres and arenas, palaces and villas, roads and government buildings, baths and public housing, harbor facilities, defensive walls, and fortresses were to be found all over the Mediterranean world and set standards that long challenged the West. [Alinari/SCALA.]

owner. They were tied to the land, as were their descendants, as the caste system hardened.

DIVISION OF THE EMPIRE. The peace and unity established by Constantine did not last long. His death was followed by a struggle for succession that was won by Constantius II (ruled 337–361). His death left the empire to his young cousin Julian (361–363), called by the Christians "the Apostate" because of his attempt to stamp out Christianity and restore paganism. Julian undertook a campaign against Persia, with the aim of putting a Roman on the throne of the Sassanids and ending the Persian menace once and for all. He penetrated deep into Persia but was killed in battle. His death put an end to the expedition and to the pagan revival.

The Germans in the west took advantage of the eastern campaign to attack along the Rhine River and the upper Danube River, but even greater trouble was brewing along the middle and upper Danube (see Map 6.4). That territory was occupied by the eastern Goths, the Ostrogoths. They were being pushed hard by their western cousins, the Visigoths, who in turn had been driven from their home in the Ukraine by the fierce Huns, a nomadic people from central Asia. The Emperor Valentinian (364–375) saw that he could not defend the empire alone and appointed his brother Valens (364–378) as coruler. Valentinian made his own headquarters at Milan and spent the rest of his life fighting successfully against the Franks and the Alemanni in the west. Valens was given control of the east. The empire was once again divided in two. The

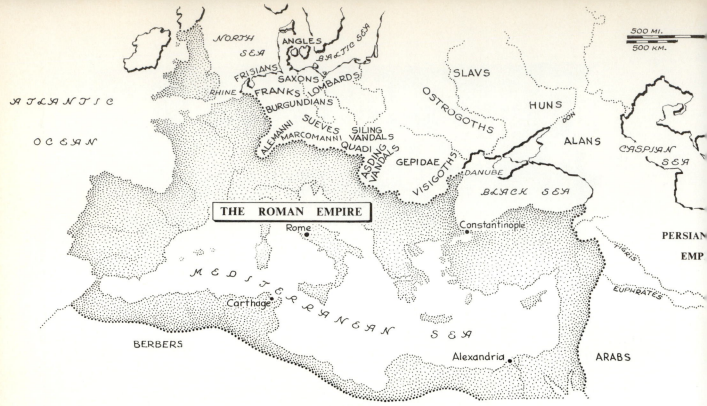

MAP 6-4 THE EMPIRE'S NEIGHBORS *In the fourth century the Roman Empire was nearly surrounded by ever more threatening neighbors. The map shows who these so-called barbarians were and where they lived before their armed contact with the Romans.*

two emperors maintained their own courts, and the two halves of the empire became increasingly separate and different. Latin was the language of the west and Greek of the east.

In 376, the hard-pressed Visigoths asked and received permission to enter the empire to escape the Huns. Contrary to the bargain, the Goths kept their weapons and began to plunder the Balkan provinces. Valens attacked the Goths and died, along with most of his army, at Adrianople in Thrace in 378. Theodosius (379–395), an able and experienced general, was named coruler in the east. He tried to unify the empire again, but his death in 395 left it divided and weak.

For the future, the two parts of the empire went their separate and different ways. The west became increasingly rural as barbarian invasions continued and grew in intensity. The *villa*, a fortified country estate, became the basic unit of life. There, *coloni* gave their services to the local magnate in return for economic assistance and protection from both barbarians and imperial officials. Many cities shrank to no more than tiny walled fortresses ruled by military commanders and bishops. The upper classes moved to the country and asserted ever greater independence of imperial authority. The failure of the central authority to maintain the roads and the constant danger from robber

bands sharply curtailed trade and communications, forcing greater self-reliance and a more primitive style of life. The new world emerging in the west by the fifth century and after was increasingly made up of isolated units of rural aristocrats and their dependent laborers. The only institution providing a high degree of unity was the Christian Church. The pattern for the early Middle Ages in the west was already formed.

In the east, the situation was quite different. Constantinople became the center of a vital and flourishing culture that we call *Byzantine* and that lasted until the fifteenth century. Because of its defensible location, the skill of its emperors, and the firmness and strength of its base in Asia Minor, it was able to deflect and repulse barbarian attacks. A strong navy allowed commerce to flourish in the eastern Mediterranean and, in good times, far beyond. Cities continued to prosper, and the emperors made their will good over the nobles in the countryside. The civilization of the Byzantine Empire was a unique combination of classical culture, the Christian religion, Roman law, and eastern artistic influences. While the west was being overrun by barbarians, the Roman Empire, in altered form, persisted in the east. While Rome shrank to an insignificant ecclesiastical town, Constantinople flourished as the seat of empire, the "New Rome," and the Byzantines called themselves "Romans." When we contemplate

Ammianus Marcellinus Describes the People Called Huns

Ammianus Marcellinus was born about A.D. *330 in Syria, where Greek was the language of his well-to-do family. After a military career and considerable travel, he lived in Rome and wrote an encyclopedic Latin history of the empire, covering the years* A.D. *96–378 and giving special emphasis to the difficulties of the fourth century. Here he described the Huns, one of the barbarous peoples pressing on the frontiers.*

The people called Huns, barely mentioned in ancient records, live beyond the sea of Azof, on the border of the Frozen Ocean, and are a race savage beyond all parallel. At the very moment of birth the cheeks of their infant children are deeply marked by an iron, in order that the hair, instead of growing at the proper season on their faces, may be hindered by the scars; accordingly the Huns grow up without beards, and without any beauty. They all have closely knit and strong limbs and plump necks; they are of great size, and low legged, so that you might fancy them two-legged beasts or the stout figures which are hewn out in a rude manner with an ax on the posts at the end of bridges.

They are certainly in the shape of men, however uncouth, and are so hardy that they neither require fire nor well-flavored food, but live on the roots of such herbs as they get in the fields, or on the half-raw flesh of any animal, which they merely warm rapidly by placing it between their own thighs and the backs of their horses.

They never shelter themselves under roofed houses, but avoid them, as people ordinarily avoid sepulchers as things not fit for common use. Nor is there even to be found among them a cabin thatched with reeds; but they wander about, roaming over the mountains and the woods, and accustom themselves to bear frost and hunger and thirst from their very cradles. . . .

There is not a person in the whole nation who cannot remain on his horse day and night. On horseback they buy and sell, they take their meat and drink, and there they recline on the narrow neck of their steed, and yield to sleep so deep as to indulge in every variety of dream.

And when any deliberation is to take place on any weighty matter, they all hold their common council on horseback. They are not under kingly authority, but are contented with the irregular government of their chiefs, and under their lead they force their way through all obstacles. . . . ❑

Ammianus Marcellinus, *Res Gestae*, trans. by C. D. Yonge (London: George Bell and Son, 1862), pp. 312–314.

the decline and fall of the Roman Empire in the fourth and fifth centuries, we are speaking only of the west. A form of classical culture persisted in the Byzantine east for a thousand years more.

The Triumph of Christianity

RELIGIOUS CURRENTS IN THE EMPIRE. In the troubled times of the fourth and fifth centuries, people sought powerful, personal deities who would bring them safety and prosperity in this world and immortality in the next. Paganism was open and tolerant, and it was by no means unusual for people to worship new deities alongside the old and even to intertwine elements of several to form a new amalgam by the device called *syncretism*.

Christianity's success owed something to the same causes as accounted for the popularity of other cults, which are often spoken of as its rivals. None of them, however, attained Christianity's universality, and none appears to have given the early Christians and their leaders as much competition as the ancient philosophies or the state religion.

IMPERIAL PERSECUTION. By the third century, Christianity had taken firm hold in the eastern provinces and in Italy. As times became bad and the Christians became more numerous and visible popular opinion blamed disasters, natural and military, on the Christians. About 250, the Emperor Decius (249–251) invoked the aid of the gods in his war against the Goths and required that all citizens worship the state gods publicly. True Christians could not obey, and Decius instituted a major persecution. Many Christians, even some bishops, yielded to threats and torture, but others held out and were killed. Valerian (253–260) resumed the persecutions, partly in order to confiscate the wealth of rich Christians. His successors, however, found other matters more pressing, and the persecution lapsed until the end of the century.

Diocletian was not generous toward unorthodox intellectual or religious movements, and his own effort to bolster imperial power with the aura of divinity boded ill for the church, yet he did not attack the Christians for almost twenty years. In 303, however, he launched the most serious persecution inflicted on the

Christians in the Roman Empire. The persecution horrified many pagans, and the plight and the demeanor of the martyrs often aroused pity and sympathy. For these reasons, as well as the incapacity of any large ancient state to carry out a program of terror with the thoroughness of modern totalitarian governments, the Christians and their church survived to enjoy what they must have considered a miraculous change of fortune. In 311, Galerius, who had been one of the most vigorous persecutors, was influenced, perhaps by his Christian wife, to issue an edict of toleration permitting Christian worship.

The victory of Constantine and his emergence as sole ruler of the empire changed the condition of Christianity from a precariously tolerated sect to the religion favored by the emperor and put it on the path to becoming the official and only legal religion in the empire.

CHRISTIANITY BECOMES THE STATE RELIGION. The sons of Constantine continued to favor the new religion, but the succession of Julian the Apostate posed a new threat. Though he refrained from persecution, he tried to undo the work of Constantine by withdrawing the privileges of the Church, removing Christians from high offices, and attempting to introduce a new form of pagan worship. His reign, however, was short, and his work did not last.

In 394, Theodosius forbade the celebration of pagan cults and abolished the pagan religious calendar. At the death of Theodosius, Christianity was the official religion of the Roman Empire.

The favored position of the Church attracted converts for the wrong reasons and diluted the moral excellence and spiritual fervor of its adherents. The problem of the relationship between church and state arose, presenting the possibility that religion would become subordinate to the state, as it had been in the classical world and in earlier civilizations. In the east, that is what happened to a considerable degree. In the west, the weakness of the emperors prevented such a development and permitted Church leaders to exercise remarkable independence. In 390, Ambrose, bishop of Milan, excommunicated Emperor Theodosius for a massacre he had carried out, and the emperor did humble penance. This act provided an important precedent for future assertions of the Church's autonomy and authority, but it did not put an end to secular interference and influence in the Church by any means.

ARIANISM AND THE COUNCIL OF NICEA. Internal divisions proved to be even more troubling as new heresies emerged. The most important and the most threatening was Arianism, founded by a priest named Arius of Alexandria (CA. 280–336) in the fourth century. Arius' view did away with the mysterious con-

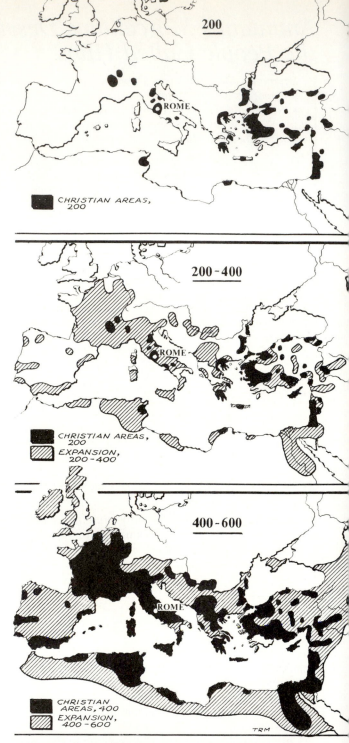

MAP 6-5 THE SPREAD OF CHRISTIANITY *Christianity grew swiftly in the third, fourth, fifth, and sixth centuries—especially after the conversion of the emperors in the fourth century. By 600, on the eve of the birth of Mohammed's new Moslem religion, Christianity was dominant throughout the Mediterranean world and most of Western Europe.*

The Council at Nicea Creates the Test of Religious Orthodoxy

In 325, Emperor Constantine called a general council of leading Christians at Nicea in Asia Minor in an attempt to end the quarreling over the question of the Trinity. The Nicene Creed was the result. Adherence to it became a test of orthodoxy, and those rejecting it were declared heretics.

We believe in one God, the Father Almighty, maker of all things visible and invisible; and in one Lord Jesus Christ, the Son of God, the only-begotten of his Father, of the substance of the Father, God of God, Light of Light; very God of very God, begotten not made, being of one substance with the Father, By whom all things were made, both which be in heaven and in earth. Who for us men and for our salvation came down [from heaven] and was incarnate and was made man. He suffered and the third day he rose again, and as-cended into heaven. And he shall come again to judge both the quick and the dead. And [we believe] in the Holy Ghost. And whosoever shall say that there was time when the Son of God was not, or that before he was begotten he was not, or that he was made of things that were not, or that he is of a different sub-stance or essence [from the Father] or that he is a crea-ture, or subject to change or conversion—all that so say, the Catholic and Apostolic Church anathematizes them. ❑

"The Nicene Creed," from *The Seven Ecumenical Councils*, trans. by A. C. McGiffort and E. C. Richardson (New York: Library of the Nicene and Post-Nicene Fathers, 2nd Series, 1900, Vol. 14), p. 3.

---

cept of the Trinity, the difficult doctrine that holds that God is three persons (the Father, the Son, and the Holy Spirit) and at the same time one in substance and essence.

Athanasius (CA. 293–373), later bishop of Alexandria, saw the Arian view as an impediment to any acceptable theory of salvation, to him the most important religious question. He adhered to the old Greek idea of salvation as involving the change of sinful mortality into divine immortality through the gift of "life." Only if Jesus were both fully human and fully God could the transformation of humanity to divinity have taken place in him and be transmitted by him to his disciples. "Christ was made man," he said, "that we might be made divine."

To deal with the growing controversy, Constantine called a council of Christian bishops of Nicea, not far from Constantinople, in 325. For the emperor, the question was essentially political, but for the disputants, salvation was at stake. At Nicea, the view expounded by Athanasius won out, became orthodox, and was embodied in the Nicene Creed. But Arianism persisted and spread. Some later emperors were either Arians or sympathetic to that view. Some of the most successful missionaries to the barbarians were Arians, with the result that many of the German tribes who overran the empire were Arians. The Christian emperors hoped to bring unity to their increasingly decentralized realms by imposing the single religion, and over time, it did prove to be a unifying force, but it also introduced new divisions where none had existed before.

REIGNS OF SELECTED LATE EMPIRE RULERS (ALL DATES ARE A.D.)

180–192	Commodus
193–211	Septimius Severus
222–235	Alexander Severus
249–251	Decius
253–260	Valerian
253–268	Gallienus
268–270	Claudius II Gothicus
270–275	Aurelian
284–305	Diocletian
306–337	Constantine
324–337	Constantine sole emperor
337–361	Constantius II
361–363	Julian the Apostate
364–375	Valentinian
364–378	Valens
379–395	Theodosius

Arts and Letters in the Late Empire

The art and literature of the late empire reflect the confluence of pagan and Christian ideas and traditions as well as the conflict between them. Much of the literature is polemical and much of the art is propaganda.

The salvation of the empire from the chaos of the third century was accomplished by a military revolution based on and led by provincials whose origins were in the lower classes. They brought with them the fresh winds of cultural change, which blew out not only the dust of classical culture but much of its substance as well. Yet the new ruling class was not interested in leveling but wanted instead to establish itself as a new aristocracy. It thought of itself as effecting a great restoration rather than a revolution and sought to restore classical culture and absorb it. The confusion and uncertainty of the times were tempered in part, of course, by the comfort of Christianity, but the new ruling class sought order and stability—ethical, literary, and artistic—in the classical tradition as well.

The Preservation of Classical Culture

One of the main needs and accomplishments of this period was the preservation of classical culture and the discovery of ways to make it available and useful to the newly arrived ruling class. The great classical authors were reproduced in many copies, and their works were transferred from perishable and inconvenient papyrus rolls to sturdier codices, bound volumes that were as easy to use as modern books. Scholars also digested long works like Livy's *History of Rome* into shorter versions and wrote learned commentaries and compiled grammars. Original works by pagan writers of the late empire were neither numerous nor especially distinguished.

Christian Writers

Of Christian writings, on the other hand, the late empire saw a great outpouring. There were many examples of Christian apologetics in poetry as well as in prose, and there were sermons, hymns, and biblical commentaries. Christianity could also boast important scholars. Jerome (348–420), thoroughly trained in both the east and the west in classical Latin literature and rhetoric, produced a revised version of the Bible in Latin, commonly called the Vulgate, which became the Bible used by the Catholic church.

Probably the most important eastern scholar was Eusebius of Caesarea (CA. 260–CA. 340). He wrote apologetics, an idealized biography of Constantine, and a valuable attempt to reconstruct the chronology of important events in the past. His most important contribution, however, was his *Ecclesiastical History*, an attempt to set forth the Christian view of history. He saw all of history as the working out of God's will. All of history, therefore, had a purpose and a direction, and Constantine's victory and the subsequent unity of empire and Church were its culmination.

The closeness and also the complexity of the relationship between classical pagan culture and that of the Christianity of the late empire is nowhere better displayed than in the career and writings of Augustine (354–430), bishop of Hippo in north Africa. He was born at Carthage and was trained as a teacher of rhetoric. His father was a pagan, but his mother was a Christian and hers was ultimately the stronger influence. He passed through a number of intellectual way stations before his conversion to Christianity. His training and skill in pagan rhetoric and philosophy made him peerless among his contemporaries as a defender of Christianity and as a theologian. His greatest works are his *Confessions*, an autobiography describing the road to his conversion, and *The City of God*. The latter was a response to the pagan charge that Rome's sack by the Goths in 410 was caused by the abandonment of the old gods and the advent of Christianity. The optimistic view held by some Christians that God's will worked its way in history and was easily comprehensible needed further support in the face of this disaster.

Augustine sought to separate the fate of Christianity from that of the Roman Empire. He contrasted the secular world, the City of Man, with the spiritual, the City of God. The former was selfish, the latter unselfish; the former evil, the latter good. Augustine argued that history was moving forward, in the spiritual sense, to the Day of Judgment, but that there was no reason to expect improvement before then in the secular sphere. The fall of Rome was neither surprising nor important, for all states, even a Christian Rome, were part of the City of Man and therefore corrupt and mortal. Only the City of God was immortal, and it, consisting of all the saints on earth and in heaven, was untouched by earthly calamities.

Augustine believed that faith is essential and primary—a thoroughly Christian view—but that it is not a substitute for reason, the foundation of classical thought. Instead, faith is the starting point for and the liberator of human reason, which continues to be the means by which people can understand what is revealed by faith. His writings constantly reveal the presence of both Christian faith and pagan reason—and the tension between them, a legacy he left to the Middle Ages.

The Problem of the Decline and Fall of the Empire in the West

Whether important to Augustine or not, the massive barbarian invasions of the fifth century put an end to effective imperial government in the West. For centuries, people have speculated about the causes of the collapse of the ancient world. Every kind of reason has been put forward, and some suggestions seem to have nothing to do with reason at all. Soil exhaustion, plague, climatic change, and even poisoning caused by lead water pipes have been suggested as reasons for Rome's decline in population, vigor, and the capacity to defend itself. Some blame the institution of slavery and the failure to make advances in science and technology that they believe resulted from it. Others blame excessive government interference in the economic life of the empire; others, the destruction of the urban middle class, the carrier of classical culture.

Perhaps a plausible explanation can be found that is more simple and obvious. It might begin with the observation that the growth of so mighty an empire as Rome's was by no means inevitable. Rome's greatness had come from conquests that provided the Romans with the means to expand still further, until there were not enough Romans to conquer and govern any more peoples and territory. When pressure from outsiders grew, the Romans lacked the resources to advance and defeat the enemy as in the past. The tenacity and success of their resistance for so long were remarkable. Without new conquests to provide the immense wealth needed for the defense and maintenance of internal prosperity, the Romans finally yielded to unprecedented onslaughts by fierce and numerous attackers.

To blame the ancients and the institution of slavery for the failure to produce an industrial and economic revolution like that of the later Western world, one capable of producing wealth without taking it from another, is to stand the problem on its head. No one yet has a satisfactory explanation for those revolutions, so it is improper to blame any institution or society for not achieving what has been achieved only once in human history, in what are still mysterious circumstances.

Imperial Rome in World Perspective

Perhaps we would do well to think of the decline of Rome as Gibbon did:

The decline of Rome was the natural and inevitable effect of immoderate greatness. Prosperity ripened the principle of decay; the cause of the destruction multiplied with the extent of conquest; and, as soon as time or accident had removed the artificial supports, the stupendous fabric yielded to the pressure of its own weight. The story of the ruin is simple and obvious; and instead of inquiring why

Imperial Rome. This is a model of a reconstruction of the city of Rome during the imperial period. At the left is the Circus Maximus; on the lower right is the Colosseum; and the Forum is just above the exact center of the picture. The model is in the Museo della Civiltà Romana. [Bettmann Archive.]

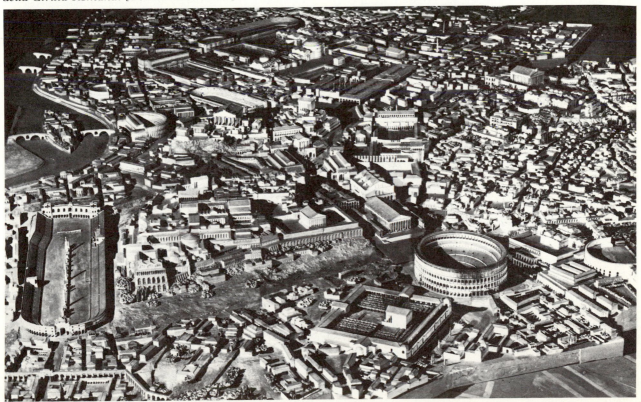

the Roman Empire was destroyed, we should rather be surprised that it had subsisted so long.[4]

This explanation allows us to see the Roman Empire as one among several great empires around the world that had similar experiences.

Out of the civil wars and chaos that brought down the republic, Augustus brought unity, peace, order, and prosperity. As a result, he was regarded with almost religious awe and attained more military and political power than any Roman before him. He ruled firmly but with moderation. He tried to limit military adventures and the costs they incurred. He supported public works that encouraged trade and communication in the empire. He tried to restore and invigorate the old civic pride, in which he had considerable success, and private morality based on family values. In this latter goal, he was less successful. He patronized the arts in such a way as to beautify Rome and glorify his reign. On his death, he was able to pass on the regime to his family, the Julio-Claudians.

For almost two hundred years, with a few brief interruptions, the empire was generally prosperous, peaceful, and well-run, but problems were growing. Management of the many responsibilities assumed by the government required the growth of a large bureaucracy. This placed a heavy and increasing burden on the treasury, required higher taxes, and stifled both civic spirit and private enterprise. Pressure from barbarian tribes on the frontiers required a large standing army, which was also very costly and led to further rises in taxation.

In the late empire, Rome's rulers resorted to many devices for dealing with their problems, which included putting down internal military rebellions led by generals from different parts of the empire. More and more, the emperors' rule and their safety depended on the loyalty of the army, so they courted the soldiers' favor with gifts of various kinds. This only increased the burden of taxes; the rich and powerful found ways to avoid their obligations, making the load on everyone else all the heavier. The government's control over the lives of its people became ever greater and the society more rigid as people tried to flee to escape the crushing load of taxes. Many measures were tried: inflating the currency, fixing farmers to the soil as serfs, building walls to keep the barbarians out, bribing barbarian tribes to fight for Rome against other barbarians; but ultimately they all failed.

It is especially instructive to look at Rome from the perspective of the historians who discern a "dynastic cycle" in China (see Chapter 8). The development of the Roman Empire, although by no means the same as the Chinese, fits the same pattern fairly well. Like the Former Han Dynasty in China, the Roman Empire in the West fell, leaving disunity, insecurity, disorder, and poverty. Like similar empires in the ancient world, it had been unable to sustain its "immoderate greatness."

Suggested Readings

J. ·P. V. D. BALSDON, *Roman Women* (1962).

T. BARNES, *The New Empire of Diocletian and Constantine* (1982).

P. BROWN, *Augustine of Hippo* (1967). A splendid biography.

P. BROWN, *The World of Late Antiquity*, A.D. 150–750 (1971). A brilliant and readable essay.

J. BURCKHARDT, *The Age of Constantine the Great* (1956). A classic work by the Swiss cultural historian.

J. CARCOPINO, *Daily Life in Ancient Rome*, trans. by E. O. Lorimer (1940).

C. M. COCHRANE, *Christianity and Classical Culture* (1957). A study of intellectual change in the late empire.

S. DILL, *Roman Society in the Last Century of the Western Empire* (1958).

E. R. DODDS, *Pagan and Christian in an Age of Anxiety* (1965). An original and perceptive study.

E. GIBBON, *The History of the Decline and Fall of the Roman Empire*, 7 vols., ed. by J. B. Bury, 2nd ed. (1909–1914). One of the masterworks of the English language.

T. RICE HOLMES, *Architect of the Roman Empire*, 2 vols. (1928–1931). An account of Augustus' career in detail.

A. H. M. JONES, *The Later Roman Empire*, 3 vols. (1964). A comprehensive study of the period.

D. KAGAN (ed.), *The End of the Roman Empire: Decline or Transformation?*, 2nd ed. (1978). A collection of essays discussing the problem of the decline and fall of the Roman Empire.

M. L. W. LAISTNER, *The Greater Roman Historians* (1963). Essays on the major Roman historical writers.

J. LEBRETON AND J. ZEILLER, *History of the Primitive Church*, 3 vols. (1962). From the Catholic viewpoint.

H. LIETZMANN, *History of the Early Church*, 2 vols. (1961). From the Protestant viewpoint.

F. LOT, *The End of the Ancient World and the Beginnings of the Middle Ages* (1961). A study that emphasizes gradual transition rather than abrupt change.

E. N. LUTTWAK, *The Grand Strategy of the Roman Empire* (1976). An original and fascinating analysis by a keen student of modern strategy.

R. MACMULLEN, *Enemies of the Roman Order* (1966). An original and revealing examination of opposition to the emperors.

R. MACMULLEN, *Paganism in the Roman Empire* (1981).

[4] Edward Gibbon, *Decline and Fall of the Roman Empire*, ed. by J. B. Bury, 2nd ed., Vol. 4 (London, 1909), pp. 173–174.

R. MacMullen, *Roman Social Relations, 50 b.c. to a.d. 284* (1981).

F. B. Marsh, *The Founding of the Roman Empire* (1959).

F. Millar, *The Roman Empire and Its Neighbors*, 2nd ed. (1981).

A. Momigliano (ed.), *The Conflict Between Paganism and Christianity* (1963). A valuable collection of essays.

H. M. D. Parker, *A History of the Roman World from a.d. 138 to 337* (1969). A good survey.

M. I. Rostovtzeff, *Social and Economic History of the Roman Empire*, 2nd ed. (1957). A masterpiece whose main thesis has been much disputed.

E. T. Salmon, *A History of the Roman World, 30 b.c. to a.d. 138* (1968). A good survey.

C. G. Starr, *Civilization and the Caesars* (1965). A study of Roman culture in the Augustan period.

R. Syme, *The Roman Revolution* (1960). A brilliant study of Augustus, his supporters, and their rise to power.

L. R. Taylor, *The Divinity of the Roman Empire* (1931). A study of the imperial cult.

A Bodhisattva statue from the Peshawar valley in India (2nd century A.D.). It probably represents the beginning of the Bodhisattva image as an important theme of Buddhist art. While the clothing is that of a contemporary Kushan or Indian nobleman, the stiff, fan-like folds of the skirt and the facial carving reflect Greco-Roman influence. [Bettmann Archive.]

7 Africa, Iran, and India before A.D. 200

After our initial look at the several birthplaces of civilization and the great revolutions in thought and religion of the first millennium B.C., we have focused on the Greek, Hellenistic, and Roman world that gave birth to Western European civilization and its modern offshoots. In Chapters 7 and 8, we take up the continuing story of ancient civilization in the world's two largest continents, Asia and Africa, during the centuries surrounding the beginning of the Christian era.

In this chapter, we shall look first at the prehistory and early history of Africa, with focus upon its principal civilized state of Kush, the successor empire to Pharaonic Egypt in ancient Nubia. Then we shall turn to the major civilizations of Iran and India from about 500 B.C. to A.D. 200. Three main themes will occupy us, all of which are primarily important in the Asian world. However, they are not wholly absent from the African scene, especially since the history of north Africa and Egypt continued to be bound up with that of the rest of the Mediterranean and western Asia.

One theme of the period from about 600 B.C. to A.D. 200 is the rise of centralized empires on a new and unprecedented scale, from the Mediterranean to China. While Africa did not produce an empire comparable to those of Rome, Iran, India, or China in this period, the vigorous Kushite kingdom of the upper Nile entered a new and lengthy phase of imperial expansion. The prosperity of this age carried on Pharaonic Egyptian culture in new ways. In Babylonia and Iran, the Achaemenids, an Aryan dynasty from the southwestern part of the Iranian plateau, founded the greatest empire yet seen in world history (CA. 539–330 B.C.). In northeast India, centered on the state of Magadha in the Ganges basin, a local dynasty known as the Mauryans founded the first great Indian empire (CA. 321–CA. 185 B.C.). Both of these empires, like their Roman and Chinese counterparts, developed sophisticated bureaucracies, professional armies, and strong communication systems.

A second theme of this period is the increasing contact and interaction of major civilizations. Africa is again something of an exception; yet, throughout this era, the peoples of its northern and eastern peripheries were in regular, largely commercial, contact with the rest of the Mediterranean-western Asian world—and to a lesser degree with the lands to the east. In Asia, these centuries saw the first sustained contact among the major centers of culture from the Mediterranean to China. These centers of civilization had already had some links of trade and travel, but the flourishing of the empires of Rome, Iran, India, and China increased and secured these links. These vast empires created new markets for diverse goods, both material and human (such as slaves, soldiers, and artisans); new security along major trade routes; new impetus for both diplomacy and conquest abroad; and a generally wider interest in the world beyond the empires' own frontiers.

The conquest (334–323 B.C.) by Alexander the Great of the Persian Empire, including modern Afghanistan and northwest India, was the most dramatic contribution of the age to new contact among diverse cultures, races, and religious traditions. His conquests ended the Achaemenid dynasty and, in the east, allowed the rising Mauryan power to extend its control over all of north India. The Hellenes and steppe peoples of northeast Iran and Central Asia, who ruled first post-Alexandrine Iran and then post-Mauryan India down to the third century A.D., inherited a world with horizons irrevocably larger than their original homelands.

A third theme of this period is the rise, spread, and consolidation of major religious traditions that would have considerable effect on later history from Africa to China. The evolution of Judaism in the Second Temple and early Diaspora periods as well as the rise and spread of early Christianity and diverse Hellenistic cults were of considerable importance to the history of north and northeast Africa and western Asia (see Chapter 6). Also important was the rise of Han Confucianism and classical Taoist thought in China (see Chapters 2, 8). Here we will emphasize the origins and growth in Iran of Zoroastrian religious practice and thought. We also take note of both the gradual emergence of an identifiable Hindu tradition and the important expansion of the Buddhist movement in India—and its spread abroad, especially into southeast Asia and China.

AFRICA

The Continent and Its Early Civilization

Africa has figured thus far only in our consideration of the ancient Mediterranean world. This belies its early importance to the history of civilization, since the origins of the human species may lie over one and one half million years ago in the Africa continent. A search for the cradle of humankind would take us first to east Africa, where archaelogical research of recent decades has given us evidence of hominid society nearly two million years ago. This has prompted the hypothesis that the other continents were peopled by dispersion from this area.

However geographically isolated the majority of the African continent was from the earliest major civilizations of Eurasia, it was never entirely cut off from the rest of the world. Most obviously, above the great divide of the Sahara, Egypt was always oriented to the Mediterranean, into which its great river emptied. In Chapter 1, we saw how the Nile valley produced one of the earliest civilized cultures as early as the fourth millennium B.C. Similarly, the north African coast was also oriented to Eurasia, and we have noted its ancient sea links across the Mediterranean in Greek, Hellenistic, and Roman times. It was a place where Berber-speaking peoples mixed with other Mediterraneans like the Phoenicians. Here a powerful Carthagenian Punic state arose that later fell prey to the imperialism of the upstart Roman state (see Chapter 5).

We turn now away from the Mediterranean to other centers of early culture in Africa in the first millennium B.C. To place these in the larger African geographical context and to introduce the continent as a whole, we must first note the special physical attributes that have controlled the history of African civilization in greater measure than that of most other continents.

Physical Considerations

Africa is huge and geologically massive. Its more than thirty million square kilometers compose one fifth of the Earth's entire land mass. It is three and one-half times the size of the continental United States and second only to Asia in total area. Its massiveness is evident in its lack of natural harbors and islands, the generally steep escarpments that surmount its narrow coasts, and its unusually high relief (the average continental elevation is 660 meters). The vast size and sharp physical variations, from high mountains to swamplands and deserts, have made rapid long-distance movement and communication difficult, consequently both were channeled along certain corridors (such as the Rift valley of East Africa, or the Niger or Zambezi river valley). The continent's high relief has made access to, as well as egress from, its interior difficult. All of Africa's major rivers (the Niger, Congo [Zaïre], Nile, Zambezi and Orange) lie largely in plateau basins and are navigable in these inland reaches but not across the cataracts and falls that they traverse before they reach the coastlands.

Africa is a continent that straddles the equator, and the special character of various regions is due in considerable part to climatic considerations. As a whole, its climate is unusually hot. North and south of the equator, dense rainforests dominate an west–east band of tropical territory from the southern coasts of West Africa across the Congo or Zaire basin to the Kenyan highlands. (Note, however, that the tropical rainforests cover only about five per cent of Africa's total surface area.) North and south of this band (and in the Kenyan highlands), the lush rainforests give way to broad grassy plains and open woodlands known as *savannah*. These in turn pass into steppeland and semidesert (the *sahel*), and finally true desert as one moves farther from the equator. Despite high rainfall and humidity in its western and central equatorial regions (except in the eastern highlands) and along its Indian-Ocean coasts, Africa contains two of the world's greatest and driest desert regions. The Sahara ("the Desert": Arabic *al-Sahra*') is the world's largest desert and has historically been the major factor hindering contact between the Mediterranean world and sub-Saharan Africa. The Kalahari is its smaller but still vast counterpart in southwest Africa. It partially cuts off the south African plateau and coastal regions from much of central Africa.

These physical factors have played a major role in the regionalization of African history. Even so, both cultural and linguistic diffusion show that, despite natural barriers, Africa's peoples have not been as internally isolated or compartmentalized as once was thought.

Other natural factors are of importance to Africa's history. The soils of Africa are typically tropical in character, which means devoid of much humus, or vegetable mold, and generally easily leached of their mineral and nutrient contents. Thus, they are easily exhausted and not highly productive for extended periods. Water shortage is also a perennial problem for agriculture in most of Africa, and a potent factor in its history past and recent. Crop pests and insects such as the tsetse fly, mosquito, and locust have also been enemies of both farming and pastoralism in Africa. On the other hand, abundant animal life has from early on made hunting or fishing an important way of survival in Africa.

The great mineral wealth of Africa has been very influential in shaping human activity throughout the continent. Salt was a very important trading commodity among Africans for centuries in various parts of the continent. For example, salt was an important focus of the trans-Sahara trade between the western Sudan and north Africa from as early as the first millennium A.D. Iron was even earlier a major trading commodity between forest and savannah zones. Copper, mined in only limited areas on the continent, was also a much-sought-after commodity. For centuries, gold was a significant trading commodity within the continent as well as an export. The ancient Egyptians sought the gold of Nubia; later, gold from west and central Africa was in demand in north Africa, the Mediterranean world, and the Indian Ocean sphere.

Finally, we should note that by convention Africa is divided into at least seven major regions:

1. north Africa, including all the Mediterranean coastal regions from modern Morocco through modern Libya and the northern regions of the Sahara;
2. Nilotic Africa (i.e., the lands of the Nile), roughly the area of the modern states of Egypt and Sudan;
3. the Sudan, the broad belt of sahel and savannah below the Sahara, which stretches from the Atlantic east across the entire continent, over the upper Nile to the Red Sea;
4. west Africa, including the desert, sahel, and savannah of the western Sudan as far east as the Lake Chad basin, and the woodland coastal regions from Cape Verde to Cameroon;
5. east Africa, from the Ethiopian highlands (a high, fertile plateau cut off by desert to its south and north) and "the Horn of Africa" south over modern Kenya and Tanzania—an area split north to south by the great Rift valley;
6. central Africa, the region north of the Kalahari, stretching from the Chad basin in the north over the Zaïre basin southeast to Lakes Tanganyika and Malawi and down to the Zambezi river (or, sometimes, the Limpopo river) in the southeast;
7. south Africa, from the Kalahari desert and Zambezi (or the Limpopo) south to the Cape of Good Hope.

Early Culture outside of Egypt

Unlike that of other continents, African history has not been one of major empires and a few major centers of cultural diffusion. This has been true especially south of the Sahara because this vast region was relatively isolated from events and cultures in Asia and

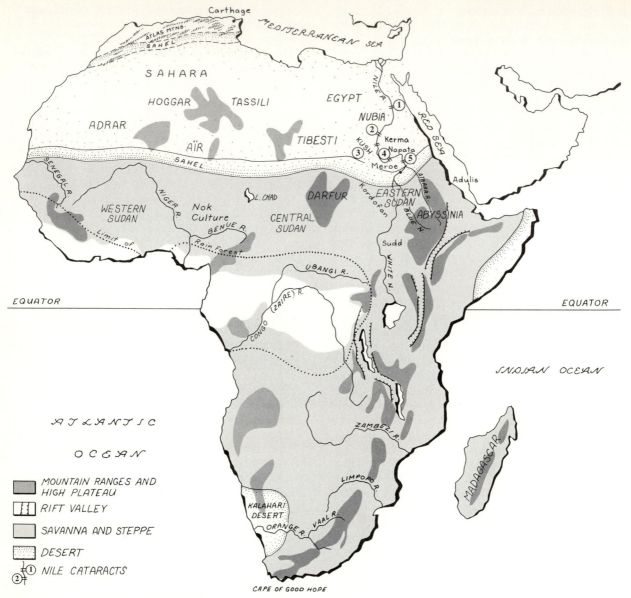

MAP 7-1 AFRICA: MAJOR PHYSICAL FEATURES. *Showing the principal physical zones and waterways of the continent, as described in the text.*

Europe until after A.D. 1000. The chief cause of this relative isolation was the increasing dessication of the once well-watered northern third of the continent from about 2500 B.C. By 1000 B.C., this process was advanced enough to make the Sahara an immense east–west expanse of largely uninhabitable desert separating the greater part of the African continent from the Mediterranean coastal rim and Near Eastern centers of early civilization.

This is not, however, to imply that regular contacts between sub-Saharan Africa and the Mediterranean world in ancient times ceased. We know, for example, that a number of north–south routes across the western and central Sahara were traversed by horses and carts or chariots long before the coming of the camel.

Well before the Christian era, the peoples of the upper Nile, the Abyssinian plateau (modern Ethiopia), and the coastal areas of East Africa below the Horn maintained contacts with Egypt, south Arabia, and likely with India and Indonesia via the Indian Ocean. We have learned from archaeology that sub-Saharan Africa had extensive settled cultures before the Christian era, most notably in the Sudanic regions below the Sahara.

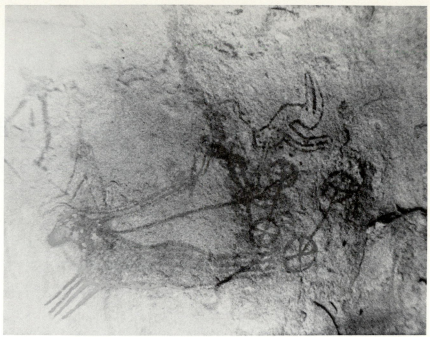

Evidence of prehistoric Saharan contact with the Sudan. The discovery of cave paintings such as this from the Tassili mountains in the western Sahara gives credence to Herodotus' report (CA. 450 B.C.) of a people called Garamantes (probably Berber), who lived in the desert oases and used horse chariots. Since such drawings have been found from the Sahara south almost to the Niger river, the Negroid peoples of the Sudan may have had contacts with the Caucasoid peoples of North Africa much earlier than even the Nok culture of the first millennium B.C. [Douglas Mazonowica.]

NEOLITHIC SUDANIC CULTURES. In the first millennium B.C., the very advanced civilization of the Kushites occupied the Nile basin on the eastern end of the great sub-Saharan belt of the Sudan. Other less advanced and preliterate, but still complex, agricultural communities of neolithic and early iron-age culture dotted its central and western reaches. Scholars surmise that these sub-Saharan peoples had once been spread farther north, in the formerly arable Saharan lands that they apparently shared with the largely nomadic Berber-speaking peoples of contemporary west-Saharan and north Africa.

Evidence for previously settled cultures in what is now uninhabitable desert comes from archaeological finds in the southwestern Sahara; they have revealed an ancient agricultural civilization with as many as two hundred towns in modern Mauritania. The most popular theory is that these towns may have been associated with trade in commodities such as salt, and that progressive dessication forced the trading centers and the agriculturalists south. They took with them the techniques of settled agriculture, especially those based on cereal grains, and of animal husbandry, as they spread into the savannah below the desert and sahel. They also domesticated new crops using their old techniques. Augmented ultimately by the knowledge of ironworking (whether passed on from north Africa or from the Nilotic kingdom of Kush), these people were able to effect an agricultural revolution. This led to considerable population growth in the more fertile of the Sudanic regions—notably those regions near the great river basins of the Niger and Senegal—and the Lake Chad basin. (A similar spread of agricultural techniques and cattle and sheep raising seems to have occurred down the Rift Valley of the east African highlands.) This agricultural revolution, effected by some time in the first millennium B.C., provided the basis for the growth of new culture centers in the sub-Saharan regions.

RACIAL DIFFERENTIATION. The changes in African food production, the subsequent development of local settled cultures, and even larger patterns of civilization have been linked by some to the apparent differences in appearance of African populations. In historical times, lighter skinned, Caucasoid African peoples have predominated in the Sahara, north Africa, and Egypt, while darker skinned, Negroid peoples have been the majority in the rest of Africa.[1] (The Greeks called all of the black peoples of Africa of whom they knew *Ethiopians*, "those with burnt skins." The Arabs termed all of Africa south of the Sahara and of Egypt *Bilad al-Sudan*, "the Land of the Blacks," and from this we get the term *Sudan*.) Other, yellowish-brown

---

[1] Note, however, that actual distribution of skin color in the past is very hard to determine; there is even sharp disagreement as to whether the ancient Egyptians were more "white" or more "black." See the discussions in G. Mokhtar, ed., *Ancient Civilizations of Africa*, vol. 2 of UNESCO General History of Africa (London, 1981), pp. 27–83.

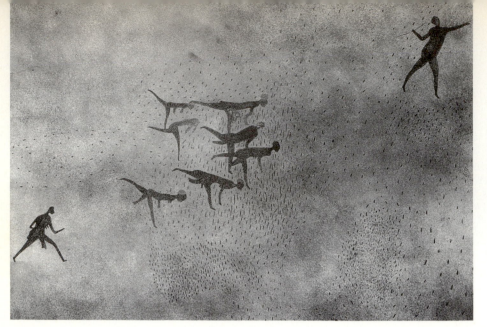

A Stone Age Saharan rock painting. *One scholar believes this strikingly beautiful painting represents women gathering grain (represented by the dots, presumably). If so, it would have likely been wild grain unless cereal crops were cultivated very early here— something for which we have no evidence. Whether gathering grain or engaged in graceful dance, the figures here remind us of the ancient human presence in the once-green Saharan regions.*

peoples occur in smaller numbers in sub-Saharan, especially southern, Africa, largely as more isolated, small herding or hunter-gatherer groups. These peoples are known as the Khoikhoi and San—the "Hottentots" and "Bushmen" of traditional European usage—or, collectively, the Khoisan; they survive in greatest number in the Kalahari region today.

Some theories have attempted to link differences of color or racial type to the development and spread of everything from agriculture or cattle herding to iron-working or state-building in Africa. However, none of these theories is tenable, if only because the concept of race itself is a problematic one. As many scholars have pointed out, long periods of relative isolation of different human populations in prehistory led to differing common gene pools in different areas. Yet always, especially in more recent times, the mixing of different gene pools produced constant change. In Africa, the various populations were so mixed that most Africans might even best be considered to belong to one large race, regardless of color or other physical attributes.[2] Thus, one should not make too much out of the obvious color differences in Africa. These differences have resulted from differing gene pools and, perhaps, some climatic adaptation. We do not know at what point in prehistory such factors led to differentiation between the Caucasoid peoples of northern Africa, the Negroid peoples of the Sudan and regions further south, and the "brown" peoples of the more southern areas. All these types are found in an infinite variety of mixtures in most areas of Africa today.

[2] Philip Curtin, et al., *African History* (London, 1978), pp. 14–16.

THE NOK CULTURE. Whatever their earlier history, we know that in the first millennium B.C. the Negroid peoples of the Sudan developed and refined techniques for settled agriculture. The result changed the face of sub-Saharan Africa, where previously small groups of hunter-gatherers had predominated. With the advent of early iron technology, these settled peoples were able to develop societies larger and more complex than had existed before.

One of the most impressive neolithic cultures in the Sudanic regions was located in west Africa on the central Nigerian plateau of Jos. Archaeological digs have yielded evidence of the agriculturalist and cattle-herding Nok culture, named for the village of the first find. Stone tools, iron implements, and highly artistic terracotta sculpture dated between 900 B.C. and A.D. 200 have been found here. Two aspects of this culture are of particular interest. The first is the fact that the Nok people had entered the Iron Age. They had learned the relatively difficult art of smelting iron as early as 500 B.C. and thus represent perhaps the earliest iron-age culture in west Africa. A major unanswered question is whether this technique reached the Jos plateau from the Kushite culture of the upper Nile (see below) via the central and eastern Sudan, or from the north African world via the Sahara. In either case, we have here evidence of contacts among early identifiable cultures in the African continent.

The second distinctive aspect is their extraordinarily highly developed sculptural art, most vividly seen in the magnificent burial or ritual masks they produced. The apparent continuities of Nok sculptural traditions with those of other, later west African cultures to the south suggest that this culture had an important impact on later west African life. These continuities pro-

Prehistoric West African sculpture from Nok. Magnificent terra-cotta heads recovered from Nok culture sites such as Igbo-Ukwu reveal that the prehistoric civilization of the western Sudan had highly developed artistic tastes and techniques. The style of the head shown here suggests that such terra-cotta castings may have had wooden prototypes. [National Museum of African Art, Smithsonian Institution.]

vide good indication that ancient communities of some sophistication laid a basis upon which later, better-known Sudanic civilizations must have built. We shall return to these in Chapter 11.

The Successor to Egyptian Empire: The Kingdom of Kush

When we move east across the Sudan to the upper Nile basin, just above the first cataract, we find the land of Kush, in lower Nubia. By comparison with the western or central Sudan, this eastern region had earlier and more frequent contact with ancient Near Eastern culture through its intercourse with Pharaonic Egypt down the Nile valley. It was here that an Egyptianized segment of the Negroid peoples of Nubia built the earliest-known literate and politically unified civilization in Africa outside of Egypt.

THE NAPATAN EMPIRE. As early as 2000 B.C., Kerma, a Kushite town above the third cataract, was a major trading outpost for the Middle-Kingdom Egyptians. From this and other Sudanic settlements, a stream of building materials, ivory, slaves, mercenaries, and especially gold flowed north down the Nile. After the Hyksos invasions, in New Kingdom times, Kush came under stronger Egyptian cultural influence as well as political and military domination. By the tenth century B.C., as the later Pharaonic dynasties grew weak, Kush went from being a provincial border territory of the Egyptian state to emergence as a virtually independent kingdom. Nonetheless, the royal line that ruled at the new Kushite capital of Napata was culturally heavily Egyptian; indeed, they saw themselves as Egyptian. Their kings practiced the Pharaohs' custom of marrying their own sisters—a practice known to many kingship institutions around the world. They buried their royalty embalmed in pyramids in traditional Egyptian style. They used Egyptian protocol and titles. In the eighth century B.C., they conquered Egypt proper and ruled it for about a century as the Twenty-fifth pharaonic Dynasty. This Kushite dynasty was driven out of Egypt only by the iron-equipped military might of Assyria around the middle of the seventh century B.C.

THE MEROITIC EMPIRE. Forced back above the lower cataracts of the Nile by the Assyrians and kept there by the Persians, the Kushite kingdom became increasingly isolated from Egypt and the Mediterranean world and developed in its own distinctive ways. Invaded by an Egyptian army in 591 B.C., Napata itself was sacked. This led to a relocation of the capital farther south in the prosperous city of Meroe, bringing the seat of rule closer to the geographical center of the Kushite domains. By this time, the Kushite kings had extended their sway westward into Kordofan, south above the confluence of the Blue and the White Nile, and southeast to the edges of the Abyssinian plateau. Meroe now became the kingdom's densely populated political and cultural capital. In the sixth century B.C. Meroe was the center of a flourishing iron industry, from which iron smelting may first have been dispersed west and south to the sub-Saharan world. Certainly the Kushites traded widely to the west across the Sudan. The Meroitic empire enjoyed a long and

The Kushite Conquest of Memphis

The following text is taken from a granite pillar that the Kushite king Piankhi had erected near Napata to commemorate his conquest of Egypt in the decade before 750 B.C. It describes the siege and capture of Memphis.

When day broke, at early morning, his majesty reached Memphis. When he had landed on the north of it, he found that the water had approached to the walls, the ships mooring at (the walls of) Memphis. Then his majesty saw that it was strong, and that the wall was raised by a new rampart, and battlements manned with mighty men. There was found no way of attacking it. Every man told his opinion among the army of his majesty, according to every rule of war. Every man said: "Let us besiege it—; lo, its troops are numerous." Others said: "Let a causeway be made against it; let us elevate the ground to its walls. Let us bind together a tower; let us erect masts and make the spars into a bridge to it. We will divide it on this (plan) on every side of it, on the high ground and ——— on the north of it, in order to elevate the ground at its walls, that we may find a way for our feet."

Then his majesty was enraged against it like a panther; he said: "I swear, as Re loves me, as my father, Amon (who fashioned me), favors me, this shall befall it, according to the command of Amon . . . I will take it like a flood of water. I have commanded . . . " Then he sent forth his fleet and his army to assault the harbor of Memphis; they brought to him every ferryboat, every (cargo) boat, every (transport), and the ships, as many as there were, which had moored in the harbor of Memphis, with the bow-rope fastened among its houses. (There was not) a citizen who wept, among all the soldiers of his majesty.

His majesty himself came to line up the ships, as many as there were. His majesty commanded his army: "Forward against it! Mount the walls! Penetrate the houses over the river. If one of you gets through upon the wall, let him not halt before it (so that) the (hostile) troops may not repulse you . . . "

Then Memphis was taken as (by) a flood of water, a multitude of people were slain therein, and brought as living captives to the place where his majesty was. ❑

From J. H. Breasted, *Ancient Records of Egypt* (Chicago: 1906), vol. 4, pars, 861 ff. Reprinted in Basil Davidson, *The African Past* (New York: Grosset and Dunlap, 1964, 1967), pp. 51–52.

prosperous life before it began to decline, apparently about A.D. 100. It came to an end in the fourth century at the hands of the rival trading state of Aksum on the Abyssinian plateau (see Chapter 11).

CULTURE AND ECONOMY. The heyday of Meroitic [i.e., of Meroe] culture was from about the middle of the third century B.C. to the first century A.D. The kingdom was middleman for the varied African goods in demand in the Mediterranean and Near East: animal skins, ebony and ivory, gold, oils and perfumes, and slaves. The Kushites traded with the Hellenistic-Roman world, south Arabia, and India, and in this regard were truly a part of the larger international world. Economically, the Kushite lands between the Nile and the Red Sea were a major source of gold for Egypt and the ancient Mediterranean world. They shipped quality iron to Aksum and the Red Sea. Cattle breeding and other forms of animal husbandry were of special importance, while agriculture along the banks of the Nile and more widely afield by irrigation was the other mainstay of the economy. Cotton cultivation in Kush preceded that of Egypt and may well have been an early export product of the kingdom.

Pyramid tombs of the kings of Kush. These pyramids at Gebel Barkal in Upper Nubia, the heartland of Kush, date from the first century B.C. The Meroites may have transferred the royal cemetery here from Meroe, which is farther south along the Nile, when they became increasingly active in the northern part of their realm, which stretched beyond Aswan in Ptolemaic times. For example, they inflicted a substantial, if temporary, defeat on the Romans in the Aswan area in 24 B.C. [Oriental Institute, University of Chicago]

A Temple Ram of Ancient Meroe. *This finely chiseled granite statue stands before the ruins of a Meroitic temple at the site of Naqa. Such statues were apparently associated with temples dedicated especially to the worship of Amun Re, who, like the god Khnum, is commonly depicted as a Ram-headed deity.*

This was an era of prosperity. Many monuments were built, including royal pyramids and the storied palace and walls of the capital. Fine pottery and jewelry were produced. Meroitic culture is especially renowned for its two kinds of pottery: one turned on wheels was the product of an all-male industry attuned apparently to market demands, and another made exclusively by hand by women was used largely domestically. This latter kind of pottery seems to have come out of an older tradition of African pottery craft that is found well outside the region of Kush—an indication of ancient traditions shared in varied regions of Africa.

RULE AND ADMINISTRATION. The political system of the Meroitic empire, like the Pharaonic, was apparently traditionalist and stable over many centuries. The system did, however, have features that distinguished it from its Egyptian models. The king seems to have ruled strictly by customary law, presumably as interpreted by the priests. His actions were limited by firm taboos; according to some Greek accounts, violation of those taboos could lead to enforced royal suicide. There was also a royal election system, commented on by Herodotus and other Greek authors. Diodorus of Sicily says that the priests would present several outstanding candidates for king, and from this group the god would choose the new sacred king (by what oracular mechanism, we are not told). The priests apparently considered the king to be a living god—a practice known both in ancient Egypt and many other African societies. A Kushite inscription on the coronation of a new king tells us, however, that King Aspelta (reigned 593–568 B.C.) was elected to succeed his brother from among his other royal brothers by twenty-four high officials and military leaders.

From this we see that royal succession was not from father to son, but within the royal family. Other inscriptions tell us that the succession was often through the maternal rather than the paternal line. The role of the queen mother in the election appears to have been crucial—another parallel if not a direct link to African practices elsewhere. Indeed, the queen mother seems to have adopted formally her son's wife upon his succession. By the second century B.C., a woman had become sole monarch, initiating a long line of queens, or "Candaces" (*Kandake*, from the Meroitic word for queen mother).

We know very little of Meroitic administration. The empire seems to have been under the autocratic rule of the royal sovereign, perhaps on the Egyptian model. He or she presided over a central administration run by a number of high officials: chiefs of the treasury, seal bearers, chiefs of granaries, army commanders, and chiefs of scribes and archives. The various provinces had to be delegated to princes who must have functioned with considerable autonomy, given the likely slow communication over the vast and difficult terrain of the upper Nile and eastern Sudanic region.

SOCIETY AND RELIGION. We know little of the social structure outside the circle of the palace—the ruling class of monarch and relatives, priests, courtiers, and provincial nobility. We do find mention of slaves, most commonly female domestics, but also male laborers who were drawn largely from prisoners of war. We can presume that cattle breeders, farmers, traders, craftsmen, and minor government functionar-

Herodotus Mentions "the Ethiopians" of Meroitic Kush

[CA. 430 B.C.] I went as far as Elephantine [Aswan] to see what I could with my own eyes, but for the country still further south I had to be content with what I was told in answer to my questions. The most I could learn was that beyond Elephantine the country rises steeply; and in that part of the river boats have to be hauled along by the ropes—one rope on each side—much as one drags an ox. If the rope parts, the boat is gone in a moment, carried away by the force of the stream. These conditions last over a four days' journey, the river all the time winding greatly, like the Maeander, and the distance to be covered amounting to twelve *schoeni*. After this one reaches a level plain, where the river is divided by an island named Tachompso.

South of Elephantine the country is inhabited by Ethiopians who also possess half of Tachompso, the other half being occupied by Egyptians. Beyond the island is a great lake, and round its shores live nomadic tribes of Ethiopians. After crossing the lake one comes again to the stream of the Nile, which flows into it. At this point one must land and travel along the bank of the river for forty days, because sharp rocks, some showing above the water and many just awash, make the river impracticable for boats. After the forty days' journey on land one takes another boat and in twelve days reaches a big city named Meroë, said to be the capital city of the Ethiopians. The inhabitants worship Zeus and Dionysus alone of the Gods, holding them in great honor. There is an oracle of Zeus there, and they make war according to its pronouncements, taking from it both the occasion and the object of their various expeditions. ❏

From the translation of *The Histories* of Herodotus by Aubrey de Sélincourt, Penguin Books, 1954, as cited by Basil Davidson, *The African Past* (New York: Grosset and Dunlap, 1964, 1967), pp. 52–53.

EARLY AFRICAN CIVILIZATIONS

CA. 10,000 B.C.	Dessication of Saharan region begins
CA. 3000–2000 B.C.	Relatively rapid dessication of Saharan region
CA. 2000–1000 B.C.	Increasing Egyptian influence in Nubia
CA. 1000–900 B.C.	Kushite kingdom with capital at Napata becomes independent of Egypt
751–663 B.C.	Kushite kings Piankhy and Taharqa rule all Egypt
CA. 600–500 B.C.	Meroe becomes new Kushite capital
CA. 500 B.C.–A.D. 330	Meroitic kingdom of Kush (height of Meroitic Kushite power CA. 250 B.C.–A.D. 50)
CA. 500 B.C.–A.D. 500(?)	Nok Culture flourishes on Jos plateau in western Sudan (modern central Nigeria)
CA. A.D. 1–100	Rise of Aksum as trading power on Ethiopian (Abyssinian) plateau
CA. A.D. 330	Kush conquered by Aksumites

ies formed an intermediate class or classes between the slaves and the rulers.

In religious matters, we have no direct records of actual Kushite practices, but it is clear that they closely followed Egyptian traditions in their worship for a number of centuries. To judge from the great temples dedicated to him, Amon seems to have been the highest god for the earlier kings; and his priests had considerable influence. By the third century B.C., however, gods unknown to Egypt rose in importance alongside Amon and other Egyptian gods. Most notable was Apedemak, a warrior god with a lion's head. The many lion temples associated with him (as many as forty-six have been identified) reflect the great importance of this Kushite god. Such gods likely represented local deities who gradually rose to take their place alongside the highest Egyptian gods. However, some scholars have speculated about Iranian or Indian influences (via the Indian Ocean–Red Sea trade link) in the non-Egyptian elements of the Kushite cult.

In sum, we find many evidences of numerous neolithic and early iron-age African cultures above the equator in the first millennium B.C. However, urban, literate civilization and large-scale empires were made possible only in the north, with the Punic empire of Carthage, and in the east, with the Egyptian and Kushite kingdoms, through sustained contact with the main kingdoms and cultures of the ancient world.

Portfolio II: Hinduism

The term "Hinduism" is simply our modern word for the majority of the diverse religious traditions of India taken as a whole. Until the word was coined in the nineteenth century, it (like "Buddhism") was not even a concept in the West, let alone in India itself. In contemporary usage, however, it has become a catch-all term used for all the Indian religious communities that look upon the texts of the Vedas (see Chapter 1) as eternal, perfect truth.

The historical beginnings of the varied Hindu traditions can be traced to the ancient Aryan migrations into south Asia in the second millenium before our common era. This was the age in which the Vedic hymns were composed. In them we find a pantheon of gods not unlike that found among other Indo-European peoples, the Greeks, and the Romans. Centered on a sacrificial cult of these gods, Vedic religion became more and more the preserve of the Brahmin priestly class of early Indian society. The Brahmins gradually elaborated a cult characterized by complex rituals of sacrifice, involved purificatory rules, and increasingly fixed distinctions of birth upon which the later caste system was based. These developments are mirrored in the later Vedic, or Brahmanical, texts (ca. 1000–500 B.C.) that provide commentary on and instructions for ritual use of the Vedic hymns.

After about 700 B.C., new developments set in. North India produced a series of religious reformers, most of whom championed knowledge and ascetic discipline rather than purity and ritual action. Some of these reformers broke with the Vedic tradition. Of these, Siddhartha Gautama (the Buddha; born ca. 563) and Mahavira Vardhamana (founder of the Jain tradition; born ca. 550) were the two most famous. Other thinkers reinterpreted the older sacrifice as an inner activity and deepened its spiritual dimensions. They further tried to link or to identify Transcendence, or Ultimate Being (*Brahman*) with the inmost self (*atman*). Their thinking is represented especially in the Upanishads, which many Hindus consider the most sublime philosophical texts in the Indian tradition.

First developed so long ago, such notions have been part of the complex but logically compelling vision of existence that lies behind the myriad forms of religious life known to us as "Hinduism." In this vision, the immortal part of each human being, the *atman*, is enmeshed in existence, but not ultimately of it. The nature of existence is *samsara*—unending becoming and change, a ceaseless round of cause and effect determined by the inescapable consequences of *karma*, or "action." The doctrine of *karma* is a kind of moral as well as physical economy in which every act has unavoidable results; so long as mental or physical action occurs, becoming and life go on repeatedly. Birth determines one's place and duties in the traditional Indian caste system. Caste is the most visible and concrete reminder of the pervasiveness of the Hindu concept of absolute causality that keeps us enmeshed in existence. The final goal is to transcend at some point in this or another lifetime the endless round of rebirth, or *samsara*, in which we are all caught. Release, or *moksha*, is the only way out of this otherwise endless becoming and rebirth. *Moksha* may be gained through knowledge, action, or devotion.

On the popular level, the period after about 500 B.C. is most notable in Indian religious life for two developments. Both took place alongside the ever deeper intrenchment in society of caste distinctions and a supporting ethic of obligations and privileges. The first was the elaboration of ascetic traditions of inner quest and self-realization, such as that of yoga. The second was the rise of devotional worship of specific gods and goddesses who are seen by their worshipers as identical with the Ultimate—in other words, as supreme deities for those who serve them. The latter development was of particular importance for popular religion in India. Evident in the famous and beloved Hindu devotional text, the *Bhagavad Gita*, it reached its highest level after A.D. 500 in the myriad movements of fervent, loving devotionalism, or *bhakti*, many of which remain important today. A striking aspect of Hindu piety has been its willingness to accomodate the focus on one "chosen deity" who is worshiped as supreme to a worldview that holds that the Divine can and does take many forms. Thus most Hindus worship one deity, but they do so in the awareness that faith in other deities can also lead one to the Ultimate.

The period between about 500 B.C. and A.D. 1000

saw the rise of two gods in particular, Vishnu and Shiva, to special prominence as the primary forms in which the supreme Lord is worshiped. Along with the mother-goddess figure, who takes various names and forms (Kali, Durga, for example), Vishnu and Shiva have remained to the present day the most important manifestations of the divine in India. Their followers are known as Vaishnavas and Shaivas, respectively. Countless differing traditions of devotion are practiced among Vaishnavas and Shaivas, as well as other groups. However, a few recurring phenomena and ideas can suggest something of Indian religiousness in practice.

Hindu practice is characterized especially by temple worship *(puja)*, in which offerings of flowers, food, and the like are brought by the worshipers. The temple images are especially sought out by the faithful for the blessing that the sight of them brings. Recitation of sacred texts, many of which are vernacular hymns of praise to a particular deity, are another important part of Hindu devotionalism. *Mantras*, or special recitative texts from the Vedas, are also used by many Hindus in their original Sanskrit form. These texts are thought to have extraordinary power. A prominent feature of Hindu life is preoccupation with purity and pollution, most evident in the food taboos associated with caste groupings.

The ascetic tendency in India is also highly developed. Although they are influential, only a tiny minority relative to the great masses of Indians take up a life of full renunciation. In this life, the ascetic worshiper does not settle in one place, take on possessions, or perform regular worship. He or she rather wanders about in search of teachers and devotes himself or herself to meditation and self-realization. Even though the majority of Hindus have families and work at their salvation through merit gained by *puja* and moral living, the ascetic ideal has an important place in the overall Indian worldview. This ideal is seen even by householders as valid and worthy of respect; it stands as a constant reminder of the deeper reality beyond the everyday world and any individual life.

II-2 A Hindu Ascetic in Nepal. *The* sadhu, *or ascetic, shown here is a devotee, of Shiva. He is mediating and fasting in observance of the annual celebration of Shivaratri, the holy night of Shiva. Shiva in his ascetic manifestation is the model for the ascetic life of the sadhu. [Judith Aronson/Peter Arnold, Inc.]*

II-1 [opposite] The Birla Mandir Temple with Sacred Cows. *In India, cows are allowed to roam free. They are considered sacred because of their powerful symbolic connotation, which include the virtue of generosity, the bounty of nature, and the sanctity of all forms of life. [Bernard Pierre Wolff/ Magnum.]*

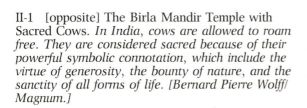

II-3 Purification Rituals in the Waters of the Holy Ganges. *Purification rituals are part of the obligatory daily rituals of all "twice-born" Hindus. The morning rituals performed by the women here in the Ganges include greeting the sun with recitation and prayer and purification by bathing. [Ian Berry/Magnum.]*

II-4   Garlanded Statue of Hanuman in a Mysore Temple. *This statue of the monkey-god Hanuman in a niche of the Chamundi Hill Temple has been draped with yellow garlands by worshippers at the shrine. Hanuman, known as "the beautiful one," is a famous figure in the great epic of the Ramayana. As a monkey servant and friend of Lord Rama, he used his miraculous powers to help his master regain his abducted wife, Sita, from Sri Lanka, where she was held hostage by the demon king, Ravana. As a folk deity, he is worshipped for his magical powers, especially against evil spirits. He is also a model of devotion to Lord Rama. [Bernard Pierre Wolff/Magnum.]*

II-5   Krishna Holding up Govardhana. *The beloved cycle of Krishna myths is popular not only among worshipers of Lord Krishna but most Indians. In this Bikaner painting of circa 1690, we see him using the entire mountain of Govardhana as an umbrella to protect his homeland and sacred territory of Brindavan from the deluge sent down by the great god Indra. Indra appears on his elephant in the upper right hand distance. The women gathered around Lord Krishna are the cowherdesses, or gopis, famous from other tale of the Dark Lord. [Scala/Art Resource.]*

II-6 Krishna Dancing with the Gopis. *This seven-teenth-century opaque watercolor with gold depicts one of the most frequent motifs of Indian art, namely the play and dancing of Lord Krishna with the cowherdesses of Brindavan. He lures them away from their homes to sport with him in the moonlight as his consorts. This sexual motif expresses the ideas of the intense love between Krishna and his devotees and the consequent willingness of the latter to forsake all else for their Lord. [Philadelphia Museum of Art, Gift of Mr. and Mrs. Lessing J. Rosenwald.]*

II-7 Lord Vishnu Reclining on the Serpent of Eternity, Ananta. *Here Krishna, in his form as Lord Vishnu, is depicted in the act of creation of the world, which emerges in the form of the four-faced god Brahma from the lotus blossom that in turn arises from Vishnu's navel. On the left, Krishna's consort, Radha (or Lakshmi), serves her Lord. The serpent, Ananta (which means "without end," or eternal), rests upon the cosmic waters that existed before creation. [Michael Holford.]*

II-8, II-9   Kajuraho, Temple of Kandariyo Mahadeva. *This famous eleventh-century Hindu temple sacred to the worship of Shiva as supreme Lord is built in the form of a mountain. All the way up to its main spire, or shikara its exterior teems with subsidiary peaks or "spires" and is literally covered with images of mythical and royal figures, as seen in the detail photograph. The interior takes the form of a cave/womb sanctuary in which the image of Shiva is kept. [Frontal view: Borromeo, EPA/Art Resource. Detail of facade: Scala/Art Resource.]*

II-10   Shiva Nataraja, "Dancing Shiva." *This magnificent tenth-century Chola bronze statue from South India shows Shiva dancing upon the body of a fallen demon. The Lord of Dancers bearing the emblems of creation and destruction that signify his mythic role, is dancing the world in and out of existence, defeating death, and transcending time. [Borromeo, EPA/Art Resource.]*

II-11 "Kali Killing the Ashuras." *This eighteenth-century painting imaginatively portrays the Goddess, Kali, riding her tiger as she destroys with her trident the larger of two demons, or ashuras. The depiction of Kali garlanded with bodies and in a hideous manifestation belies the fact that she is fervently worshipped by her devotees as mother goddess. Like Shiva, her horrific form is part of her power to destroy demons and evil and hence can comfort as well as inspire fear and awe. [Cleveland Museum of Art, Edward L. Whittemore Fund.]*

II-12 Rama Destroys the Ten-headed Demon King, Ravana. *In another episode from the* Ramayana *epic cycle, Ravana, the king of Sri Lanka, is finally destroyed by Rama's arrow after the rescue of Sita. This death scene is told in great detail in the great epic of the* Ramayana. *[Bury Peerless.]*

The First Iranian Empire
(550–330 B.C.)

The Land

Iran is the name given to the huge expanse of southwest Asia that lies between the Caspian and the Arabian seas; it is bounded by Transoxiana to the northeast, the Indus valley to the southeast, the Tigris-Euphrates basin to the southwest, and Armenia and the Caucasus to the northwest. The region is dominated by the vast expanse of the high central Iranian plateau at its center. It is cut off on all sides by mighty mountain ranges, principally the Hindu Kush, the Sulaiman chain, the Zagros, and the Elburz. In its central reaches, it contains two large, empty, and uninhabitable salt deserts whose desolation is a more formidable barrier to travel than most of the great mountain chains themselves.

Population in Iran early clustered in the plains, the lower mountain reaches, and the many fertile oases, wherever rainfall or ground water was plentiful and communication with outside areas easiest. Foremost among these areas have been Persis, Media, Hyrcania, and Parthia. The great trade routes of Asian history have put Iran at the heart of east–west interchange. But these routes and the subsequent location of major cities and towns have been determined more by the mountain passes and traversable stretches of the Iranian plateau than by the distances involved.

The Ancient Iranian Background

The oldest texts in ancient Persian dialects show that the Aryan peoples who settled on the Iranian plateau itself, perhaps around 1100 B.C., were related to the Vedic or Indo-Aryans of north India. Presumably, both were pastoralists, horse-breeding peoples who had come originally from the Eurasian or Central Asian steppes. The most prominent of the ancient Iranian peoples were the Medes and the Persians. By the eighth century B.C., they had spread around the deserts to settle and control the western and southwestern areas of Iran to which they gave their names, Media and Persis (later Fars), respectively.

The Medes developed a tribal confederacy in western Iran. By the end of the seventh century B.C., with the Neo-Babylonians, they were able to defeat the mighty Assyrians and break their hold on the Fertile Crescent. The rise of Persian power in the seventh and sixth centuries B.C. led to the founding of the Achaemenid Empire. Many of the institutions that developed (such as the satrapy system of provincial administra-

tion) were likely continuations of Median practices, which had in turn been drawn from Babylonian and Assyrian models in many instances.

Ancient Iranian Religion

We know more about the religious tradition of ancient Iran than about other aspects of its culture, because our only preimperial texts are religious ones. These suggest that the old Iranian culture and religion were similar to those of the Vedic Aryans. The importance of water and fire, the role of sacrifice, the centrality of the cow, and the names and traits of particular divine beings and religious concepts all have their counterparts in Vedic texts. The emphasis was on moral order, or the "Right"—that is, *asha* or *arta* (equivalent to the Vedic *rta*—see Chapter 1). The supreme heavenly deity was Ahura (the equivalent of the Vedic *Varuna*) Mazda, the "Wise Lord." These facts also reflect the kinship of Vedic and Iranian tradition. Still, the Iranian religion of the early second millennium was far from monolithic. Cultural variations in ancient Iran among the southeast (Sistan), the northeast (Parthia, Herat, and Bactria), the west (Media), and the southwest (Persis) were substantial.

Zoroaster

The first person who stands out in Iranian history was not Cyrus, founder of the Achaemenid Empire, but Zarathushtra, the great prophet-reformer of Iranian religion. He is commonly known in the West by the Greek version of his name, Zoroaster. Although some scholars date his life to before 1000 B.C., according to the most common reckoning he lived from 628 to 551 B.C. in northeastern Iran. Not unlike the Hebrew prophets, the Buddha, and Confucius, Zoroaster preached a message of moral reform in an age when materialism, political opportunism, and ethical indifference were common. He found a royal protector in an eastern Iranian tribal leader said to have been converted to Zoroaster's ideas about 588 B.C.

In Zoroaster's hymns, we glimpse the values of a peasant-pastoralist society that was growing up along with early urban trade centers in northeast Iran. These values contrasted with those of the nomadic warrior peoples of the steppes. For example, Zoroaster called for a reform of traditional animal sacrifices (especially those involving the particularly sacred cow and ox) to make them more humane to the victim.

Zoroaster himself was trained as a priest in the old Iranian tradition, but his hymns, or *Gathas*, reflect the new religious vision he championed. This vision

A Hymn of Zoroaster about the Twin Spirits of Good and Evil

The focus of Zoroaster's reform was on the supremacy of Ahura Mazda (the "Wise Lord") over all the deities of the Iranian pantheon. He is pictured in the hymns, or Gathas, as the greatest of the ahuras, *the divinities associated with the good. The world is seen in terms of a moral dualism of good and evil, which is represented on the divine plane in the twin spirits created by Ahura Mazda and given the freedom to choose the Truth or the Lie. As the following selection shows, the "Most Holy Spirit" chose truth ("Righteousness"), and the "evil spirit" chose the evil of the Lie. Similarly, humans can choose with which side—the good spirit and the* ahuras, *or the evil spirit and the* daevas *("the false gods")—they will ally themselves. The struggle on the divine level between the gods is mirrored in the struggle on the human level between the righteous and the evildoers, as the hymn here emphasizes. This selection is from Yasna ("Worship") section 30 of the main Zoroastrian holy book, the Avesta. It makes vivid the dualistic bent of Zoroastrianism.*

YASNA 30

Now will I speak to those who will hear
Of the things which the initiate should remember:
The praises and prayer of the Good Mind to the
    Lord
And the joy which he shall see in the light who has
    remembered them well.

Hear with your ears that which is the sovereign
    good;
With a clear mind look upon the two sides
Between which each man must choose for himself,
Watchful beforehand that the great test may be
    accomplished in our favour.

Now at the beginning the twin spirits have declared
    their nature,
The better and the evil,
In thought and word and deed. And between the
    two
The wise ones choose well, not so the foolish.

And when these two spirits came together,
In the beginning they established life and non-life,
And that at the last the worst existence should be
    for the wicked,
But for the righteous one the Best Mind.

Of these two spirits, the evil one chose to do the
    worst things;
But the Most Holy Spirit, clothed in the most
    steadfast heavens,
Joined himself unto Righteousness;
And thus did all those who delight to please the
    Wise Lord by honest deeds.

Between the two, the *false gods* also did not choose
    rightly,

For while they pondered they were beset by error,
So that they chose the Worst Mind.
Then did they hasten to join themselves unto Fury,
That they might by it deprave the existence of man.

And to him came *Devotion,* together with
    Dominion, Good
    Mind and *Righteousness:*
She gave endurance of body and the breath of life,
That he may be thine apart from them,
As the first by the retributions through the metal.

And when their punishment shall come to these
    sinners,
Then, O Wise One, shall thy Dominion, with the
    Good Mind,
Be granted to those who have delivered Evil into
    the hands of Righteousness, O Lord!

And may we be those that renew this existence!
O Wise One, and you other Lords, and
    Righteousness, bring your alliance,
That thoughts may gather where wisdom is faint.

Then shall Evil cease to flourish,
While those who have acquired good fame
Shall reap the promised reward
In the blessed dwelling of the Good Mind, of the
    Wise One, and of Righteousness.

If you, O men, understand the commandments
    which the Wise One has given,
Well-being and suffering—long torment for the
    wicked and salvation for the righteous—
All shall hereafter be for the best. ❑

From Jacques Duchesne-Guillemin (trans.), *The Hymns of Zarathushtra,* trans. from the French by M. Henning (Boston: Beacon, 1963), pp. 103, 105, 107.

stemmed from his passionate sense of personal encounter with Ahura Mazda as the most powerful of deities. He reinterpreted the old sacrificial fire as the symbol of the supreme Lord. He called on people to abandon worship of and sacrifice to all lesser deities, or *daevas*, whom he identified as demons rather than gods. He tried to reform the morality of his people by calling on them to turn from the "Lie" *(druj)* to the "Truth" *(asha)*. He warned of a "final reckoning," when the good will be rewarded with "future glory" and the wicked punished with "long-lasting darkness, ill food, and wailing."

By the mid-fourth century B.C., the Zoroastrian reform had spread into western as well as eastern Iran. The quasi-monotheistic worship of Ahura Mazda, the "Wise Lord," was rapidly accommodated to the veneration of older Iranian gods by the interpretation of these deities as secondary gods or even different manifestations of the Wise Lord himself. What role the Iranian priestly clan known as the *Magi* played in these developments is not clear. They may have integrated Zoroastrian ideas and texts into their older, polytheistic tradition, becoming thereby architects of a reformed tradition. Certainly the name *magi* was later used for the priests of the tradition that we refer to as *Zoroastrian*.

Zoroastrianism probably influenced not only the Jewish, Christian, and Muslim ideas of the messiah, angels, and devils, the last judgment, and an afterlife, but certain Buddhist concepts as well. Zoroastrianism was wiped out as a major force by Islam in the seventh and eighth centuries A.D. However, its tradition continues in the faith and practice of the Parsis, a community today of perhaps 100,000 people, most of whom live in western India.

The Achaemenid Empire

In October A.D. 1971, the Iranian king Muhammad Reza Shah presided over a lavish pageant amidst the ruins of the ancient Persian imperial city of Persepolis. This extravagant celebration commemorated the twenty-five-hundredth anniversary of the establishment under Cyrus the Great of "the imperial glory of Iran." The shah felt he had recreated this traditional Iranian ideal since the 1950s in his modern secularist regime. Although the Iranian revolution of 1978 thwarted his attempts to kindle a secular Iranian nationalism, modern Iran does have an undeniably dual heritage: that of the rich Iranian Islamic culture of recent centuries; and that of the far older, Indo-Iranian, Zoroastrian, and imperial culture of pre-Islamic Iran.

MAP 7-2   THE ACHAEMENID EMPIRE   *The empire created by Cyrus had fullest extent under Darius when Persia attacked Greece in 490 B.C. It reached from India to the Aegean—and even into Europe—including the lands formerly ruled by Egyptians, Hittites, Babylonians, and Assyrians.*

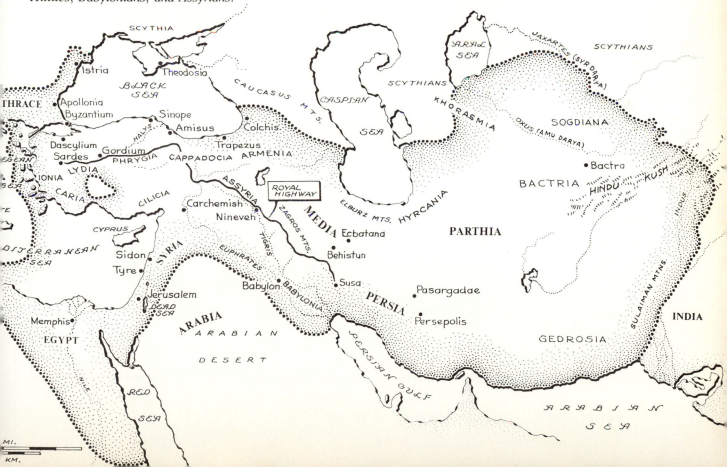

The latter culture had its beginning with the Persian dynasty of the Achaemenids.

The rise of Iran as a world power and a major civilization is usually dated from the reign of Cyrus the Great (559–530 B.C.), the ruling prince of the Achaemenid clan. His regional power in southwestern Iran (Persis) went back at least to his grandfather, Cyrus I. The empire that he founded was anticipated in many ways by the sizable but loosely controlled empire of his predecessors, the Medes, in Anatolia and western Iran. According to Babylonian and Greek sources, Cyrus defeated the last Median king about 650 B.C. Then he moved swiftly westward, winning northern Assyria and Cilicia and subduing the Anatolian kingdom of Lydia, near the Aegean coast of Asia Minor. The Lydian capital, Sardis, became a provincial capital of the growing Persian state (and the base for diplomatic intrigue against the Hellenic *poleis*). Next, Cyrus turned to Babylon and, in less than three weeks, he defeated the last Babylonian king.

This event, in 539 B.C., symbolically marks the beginning of the Achaemenid Empire, for it joined for the first time under one rule the Mesopotamian and Iranian spheres—a unity that would last for centuries. One of its immediate repercussions was the end of the Babylonian Exile of the Jews (see Chapter 2). Cyrus also extended Achaemenid rule in the east before being killed in battle with steppe tribes of Ekbatana (later Hamadan).

Better to administer the new empire, Cyrus had moved his capital to the old Median capital. He and his successors, in what was really a tribal confederation, adopted and continued Median administrative practice; and many Medes were highly placed in the new state. Thus, it is not surprising that the Achaemenid rulers are referred to in the Bible and other sources as the "Medes and Persians." What the Medes had set in motion, Cyrus and his heirs consolidated and expanded, so that the new Iranian Empire became the most powerful the world had ever seen.

After the brief reign of Cambyses (529–522 B.C.), Darius I won the contest for succession. His reign (521–486 B.C.) was one of prosperity, in which the imperial borders reached their greatest extent—from Egypt in the west to southern Russia and Sogdiana (Transoxiana) in the north and the Indus valley in the east. The next five rulers (486–359 B.C.) fared less well, and after 478 B.C., the Persians were militarily inferior to the Greeks. The former managed to keep their divided enemy at bay by clever diplomacy, but Greek cultural influence steadily grew in Anatolia. Repeated rebellions by Egypt, internal succession struggles, renewed conflict with Scythian tribes on the steppe borders, and less enlightened leadership plagued Achaemenid rule in this era. Much might have been recouped by the able, energetic Artaxerxes III (reigned 359–338 B.C.), had he not been poisoned in a palace coup just as Philip of Macedon was unifying the Greeks. When Philip's son Alexander succeeded him, the days of the Achaemenid Empire were numbered.

The Achaemenid State

Perhaps the greatest achievement of the Achaemenids was the relative stability of their rule. They

---

Inscription of Darius I

The Achaemenids, like other ancient rulers before them, used public inscriptions to underscore their victories and other accomplishments. One of the best of our sources for Darius' reign in particular comes from the monumental rock reliefs and inscriptions that he had put up on a giant cliff at Behistun, a site between Hamadan and Mesopotamia, directly on the major east–west trade road. The inscription that follows reflects the Achaemenid ruler's sense of his own special relationship to Ahura Mazda and his role as a defender of the Right.

Darius the king says: By the will of Ahuramazdā I am king. Ahuramazdā delivered the kingship to me.

Darius the king says: These are the countries which came to me. By the will of Ahuramazdā I have become king over them: Persis, . . .

[There follows a list of satrapies.]

Darius the king says: These are the countries which came to me. By the will of Ahuramazdā they became my subjects, they bore me tribute. Day and night they did what I told them.

Darius the king says: Among these countries, whatever man was loyal I treated well, (but) whomever was unruly I punished well. By the will of Ahuramazdā these countries behaved according to my law. They did as I told them.

Darius the king says: Ahuramazdā delivered this kingship to me. Ahuramazdā bore me aid until I had secured this empire. By the will of Ahuramazdā I hold this empire. ❑

From William W. Malandra, *An Introduction to Ancient Iranian Religion* (Minneapolis: University of Minnesota Press, 1983), p. 48

Darius on the throne. This relief from the treasury at Persepolis depicts Darius I granting audience to a Median nobleman. Note the incense burners before the king and the noble's gesture of respect. The sceptre and lotus blossom held by Darius symbolize his kingship; his son and heir Xerxes stands behind him. [Bettmann Archive.]

justified their title of *Shahanshah*, "king of kings," as a universal sovereignty entrusted to them by Ahura Mazda. Their inscriptions reflect their sense that their justice and uprightness earned them this trust; their elaborate court ceremony and impressive architectural monuments underscored it. They acted as priests and sacrificers in the court rituals and symbolized their role as cosmic ruler by burning a special royal fire throughout each reign. The talents and evident charisma of their early leaders strengthened the force of their claim to special, divinely sanctioned royal status among their subject peoples. Yet alongside this, they were tolerant of diversity in ways earlier empires had not been. In part, the sheer size of their realms demanded this. Even Darius' conversion to Zoroastrianism did not bring forced conformity or conversion, as his lenient treatment of the Jews vividly shows.

The Achaemenids operated a powerful army, but their rule was not simply a military despotism. Much of their success lay in their administrative abilities and their willingness to learn and to borrow from predecessors like the Medes and conquered peoples like the Babylonians. Most of their leaders showed themselves adept at conciliation and sought to establish what has been termed a *pax Achaemenica*.[3] They were able to maintain continuity even while their state evolved from the relatively simple tribal confederation to a sophisticated monarchy. The state of Cyrus, with its

[3] Richard N. Frye, *The Heritage of Persia* (New York and Toronto, 1966), p. 110.

largely Iranian troops and tribute system of revenue, was replaced by a monarchy supported by a noble class, professional armies (led by loyal Persian elite troops), an administrative system of provinces ruled by governors called satraps, and fixed-yield levies of revenue.

The excellence of their administrative skills can also be seen in their communication and propaganda systems. A courier system linked the far-flung imperial outposts with the heartlands over a system of well-kept highways, which also served to move troops at maximum speed. The greatest of these was the highway from Sardis to Susa that Herodotus called "the King's Road." A network of observers and royal inspectors kept the court abreast of activities in diverse places. An efficient chancery with large archives and numerous scribes served many administrative needs. The bureaucratic adoption of Aramaic, which had become the common language of the Near East under the Assyrians, helped link east and west. Royal proclamations were rapidly and widely distributed, often in multilingual form for different regions.

Little is known of the actual judicial system, but Achaemenid inscriptions reflect a strong emphasis on universal justice and the rule of law throughout the empire.

The choice of strategically located capitals in Western Iran, such as Ekbatana and Susa, was important to central control of the empire. In general, however, the Achaemenids moved the court as needed to one or another of their palaces, whether in Babylon or the Iranian highlands, and never fixed on a single capital.

PEOPLES

CA. 2000–1000 B.C.	Indo-Iranian (Aryan) tribes move south into the Punjab of India and the Iranian Plateau
835 B.C.	Assyrian text mentions kingdom of Medes
CA. 700–600 B.C.	Medes and Persians are settled in west and southwest Iran

RELIGION

CA. 628–551 B.C. (or before 1000? B.C.)	Zoroaster (Zarathushtra), probably in east/northeast Iran (perhaps originally in Herat?)

EMPIRES, RULERS

559–530 B.C.	Reign of Cyrus the Great as Persian Achaemenid ruler
539–330 B.C.	Achaemenid Empire
331–330 B.C.	Alexander (d. 323) conquers Achaemenid empire
312–CA. 125 B.C.	Seleucid rule in part of old Achaemenid realm
CA. 248 B.C.– A.D. 224	Parthian empire of the Arsacids in Iran, Babylonia

The ruins of the famous royal complex at Persepolis, sacked and burned by Alexander the Great in 330 B.C. The first restoration work took place in this century. [Scala/Art resource.]

the centralized power of the "king of kings" held together the diverse provinces and tribute-paying states.

The empire's overall stability for over two centuries testifies to the quality of the *pax Achaemenica*. The cosmopolitan basis for the coming hellenization of western Asia in the wake of Alexander's conquests was already in place.

The satrapy divisions usually followed those of the previous states. The satraps were powerful princes in their own right. Although some revolted on occasion,

INDIA

The First Indian Empire (321–185 B.C.)

True empire in the Indian subcontinent came only after the oriental campaigns of Alexander the Great, who conquered the Achaemenid provinces of Gandhara and the Indus valley in 327 B.C. Alexander himself made little or no impact on the subcontinent save in the extreme northwest area of Gandhara. Here, his passage opened the way for the increased Greek and

Indian cultural interpenetration that developed under the Mauryan emperors of India.

The Political Background

The basis for empire in northern India was the rise of regional states and commercial towns between the seventh and fourth centuries B.C. The most powerful of the states were the monarchies that clustered on the Ganges plains. North and northwest of the plains, in the Himalayan foothills and in the Punjab and beyond, tribal republics were more common. From two of these republics came the Buddha and Mahavira (see Chapter 2), although both spent much of their lives in the states of Kosala and Magadha, the two most powerful Ganges monarchies. In their lifetimes, Magadha emerged as the strongest state in India under Bimbisara (d. 493 B.C.).

Bimbisara was, as far as we know, the first king to build a centralized state (possibly on the Achaemenid model) strong enough for imperial expansion. He emphasized good roads, able administrators, and fair agricultural taxes. His son annexed Kosala, so that Magadha controlled the Ganges trade. Therefore, Magadha remained preeminent in the Ganges basin even under several less competent successors. A new dynasty, the Nandas, replaced the last of these as rulers of Magadha; their imperial hopes were soon dashed by the rise of the Mauryan clan.

The Mauryans

The first true Indian empire was established by Chandragupta Maurya (reigned CA. 321–297 B.C.). He seized Magadha and the Ganges basin in about 324 and made Pataliputra (the modern Patna) his capital. He next marched westward into the vacuum created by Alexander the Great's departure (326 B.C.) and brought the Indus region and much of west-central India under his control. A treaty with the invading Seleucus, Alexander's successor in Bactria, added Gandhara and Arachosia to his empire in the northwest. The Greek sources say that the treaty (303 B.C.) included a marriage alliance, possibly of a Seleucid woman to Chandragupta. If such a marriage did occur, Greek blood may flow in Indian veins to this day. Certainly there was much Seleucid-Mauryan contact thereafter.

MAP 7-3 SOUTHWEST ASIA AND INDIA IN MAURYAN TIMES. *Showing not only major cities, and regions of greater Iran and the Indian subcontinent but also the neighboring eastern Mediterranean world. While the Mediterranean was closely tied to Iran from Archaemenid times onwards, it is less often recognized how many and varied were its contacts with India in the wake of the conquests of Alexander the Great.*

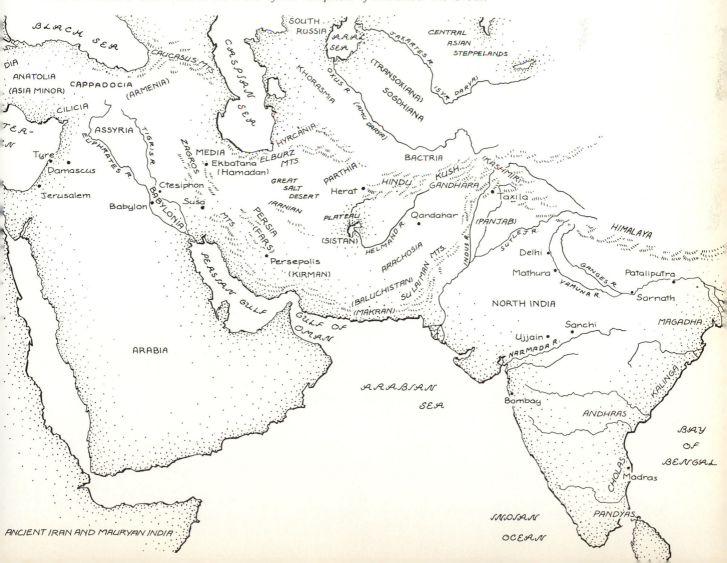

The Lion Capital of Sarnath. This famous Ashokan column capital was taken by India as its state seal after independence in 1947. It reflects both Persian and Greek influences. Originally, the capital stood atop a mighty pillar some fifty feet high and the lions supported a hugh stone wheel, the Buddhist "wheel of the Dharma," the symbol of universal law [Lauros/Giraudon.]

Chandragupta ranks as the first great Indian empire builder, although his fame is rivaled by that of his Brahman minister Kautilya. Known as the "Indian Machiavelli," Kautilya may have been the real architect of Mauryan rule. However, he was probably not the real author of the most famous Indian treatise on the art of government, the *Arthashastra*, which is ascribed to him.

Chandragupta's son and successor, Bindusara (reigned CA. 297–272 B.C.), was not long in taking up his father's imperial aspirations. He moved swiftly to conquer the Deccan, the great plateau that covers central India, dividing the far south (Tamilnad) from north India. Like his father, he had substantial contacts with the Seleucid Greeks, including Antiochus I of Syria, from whom he is said to have requested wine, figs, and a philosopher for his court!

ASHOKA. The third and greatest Mauryan emperor, Ashoka (reigned CA. 272–232 B.C.), left us numerous rock inscriptions. These are the first significant written sources in Indian history after the Indus culture. From his edicts, we can piece together much of his reign and glimpse something of the man behind the royal name as well. In his first years as king, he continued the imperial tradition by conquering Kalinga, the last independent kingdom in north India and the Deccan. He thus extended Mauryan control over the whole subcontinent except the far south.

Apparently revolted by the bloody Kalinga conquest, Ashoka underwent a religious conversion. Thereafter, he pursued the Buddhist "Middle Path" as the right course of conduct not only in personal but also in state relations. Accordingly, he forsook war, hunting, and animal flesh. Above all, he championed nonviolence *(ahimsa)*, summing up his new course in the ideal of "conquest by righteousness *(dharma)*." This is not to say that all warfare ceased however much the king may have abhorred bloodshed, but he did abandon further conquest. He also believed that by moral example he could win over others to humanitarian values. Within his realm, he looked on all his subjects as, in the words of one edict, his "children."

Ashoka's edicts show that he pursued the laity's norm of the Buddhist *dharma*, striving to attain heaven by the merit of good actions. He was not an exclusivist about his Buddhist faith, stressing tolerance for all traditions. However, he apparently sent out envoys to spread the Buddhist teaching, possibly even as far as Seleucid Macedonia in the west. Tradition has it that he was responsible for the more successful missionary work that brought the Buddhist *dharma* to Lanka (Sri Lanka, formerly Ceylon). Certainly the king of Lanka at the time was in friendly contact with Ashoka. Although Ashoka's edicts do not mention it, tradition also has it that a great Buddhist council was held at Pataliputra during Ashoka's reign (250 B.C.?). It is clear that he sought to raise standards of morality in all phases of life in his realm. For example, he appointed "*dharma* officials" under centralized control to investigate and promote public welfare and to foster just, moral government at the local level.

Ashoka evidently did ease some of the previous burdens of government and instituted many beneficial public works. However, by the end of his reign, the size of his empire had strained the limits of effective administration. His rejection of military campaigns may also have weakened imperial power in the long run, and bureaucratic corruption increased with time.

The Edicts of Ashoka

In the first of the two following excerpts from Ashokan edicts, we see the monarch's explanation of his change of heart and conversion to nonviolence after the Kalinga war and a statement of his determination to follow dharma. *"The Beloved of the Gods" was the common royal epithet used by Ashoka for himself. The second excerpt is from the end of Ashoka's reign and speaks of his efforts to better his and other people's lives by rule according to the dictates of* dharma.

FROM THE THIRTEENTH ROCK EDICT

When the king, Beloved of the Gods and of Gracious Mien, had been consecrated eight years Kalinga was conquered, 150,000 people were deported, 100,000 were killed, and many times that number died. But after the conquest of Kalinga, the Beloved of the Gods began to follow Righteousness [*dharma*], to love Righteousness, and to give instruction in Righteousness. Now the Beloved of the Gods regrets the conquest of Kalinga, for when an independent country is conquered people are killed, they die, or are deported, and that the Beloved of the Gods finds very painful and grievous. . . . The Beloved of the Gods will forgive as far as he can, and he even conciliates the forest tribes of his dominions; but he warns them that there is power even in the remorse of the Beloved of the Gods, and he tells them to reform, lest they be killed.

For all beings the Beloved of the Gods desires security, self-control, calm of mind, and gentleness. The Beloved of the Gods considers that the greatest victory is the victory of Righteousness; and this he has won here [in India] and even five hundred leagues beyond his frontiers in the realm of the Greek king Antiochus, and beyond Antiochus among the four kings Ptolemy, Antigonus, Magas, and Alexander. Even where the envoys of the Beloved of the Gods have not been sent men hear of the way in which he follows and teaches Righteousness, and they too follow it and will follow it. Thus he achieves a universal conquest, and conquest always gives a feeling of pleasure; yet it is but a slight pleasure, for the Beloved of the Gods only looks on that which concerns the next life as of great importance. . . .

FROM THE SEVENTH PILLAR EDICT

In the past kings sought to make the people progress in Righteousness, but they did not progress. . . . And I asked myself how I might uplift them through progress in Righteousness. . . . Thus I decided to have them instructed in Righteousness, and to issue ordinances of Righteousness, so that by hearing them the people might conform, advance in the progress of Righteousness, and themselves make great progress. . . . For that purpose many officials are employed among the people to instruct them in Righteousness and to explain it to them. . . .

Moreover I have had banyan trees planted on the roads to give shade to man and beast; I have planted mango groves, and I have had ponds dug and shelters erected along the roads at every eight kos. Everywhere I have had wells dug for the benefit of man and beast. But this benefit is but small, for in many ways the kings of olden time have worked for the welfare of the world; but what I have done has been done that men may conform to Righteousness. . . .

. . . I have enforced the law against killing certain animals and many others, but the greatest progress of Righteousness among men comes from exhortation in favor of noninjury to life and abstention from killing living beings.

I have done this that it may endure . . . as long as the moon and sun, and that my sons and my great-grandsons may support it; for by supporting it they will gain both this world and the next. ❏

From W. T. de Bary et al. (comps.), *Sources of Indian Tradition* (New York: Columbia University Press, 1958), pp. 146–147, 152–153.

After his death, local dynasties soon seized power from his heirs in many areas.

Ashoka's enduring influence is hard to assess, but he did provide the ideal of kingship for later Hindu and Buddhist thought—the *chakravartin*, or universal monarch who rules with righteousness, justice, and wisdom. His name lives on as a symbol of enlightened, compassionate rule that has had few if any equals in history East or West.

THE MAURYAN STATE. Mauryan bureaucracy was marked by centralization, standardization, and efficiency in long-distance communications, civil and military organization, tax collection, and information gathering (by a secret service). The fundamental unit of government, as before and ever after, was the village, with its headman and village council. Various numbers of villages formed districts within the larger provincial unit. The provinces were largely controlled through governors sent out from the capital. Some local rulers were confirmed in these positions also, much as with the Achaemenids (who very likely provided the model for much of Mauryan imperialism). The reputed pageantry and royal ceremonial of the Mauryan court must also have enhanced royal authority.

The administration of the empire depended primarily on the king himself, who did, however, have an advisory council to assist him. Each of the three great Mauryan kings was associated with one of the "new" religious movements of the age: Chandragupta with the Jains; his son with the ascetic tradition of the group known as the Ajivikas; and Ashoka with the Buddhists. Such links must have strengthened the Mauryan, especially the Ashokan, claims to righteous leadership.

Revenues came primarily from taxing the produce of the land, which was regarded as the king's property. Urban trade and production were also taxed heavily. The Mauryan economic system also involved slavery, although most of it was domestic labor, often a kind of temporary indentured service.

THE MAURYAN LEGACY. An imperial ideal and a strengthened Buddhist movement were not the Mauryans' only gifts to Indian culture. They left behind new cosmopolitan traditions of external relations and internal communication that encouraged cultural development and discouraged provincialism. The many contacts of the Mauryans with the West reflect their international perspective, as do the Ashokan edicts, which were executed in various languages and scripts. Writing and reading must have been common by this time (perhaps as a result of Buddhist monastic schooling?), or the edicts themselves would have had no purpose. The Mauryans' excellent road system facilitated internal and external contacts on an unprecedented scale, above all west to Herat and northwest to Bactria. These would later be the routes for Buddhism's spread to Central Asia and China, as well as for successive invaders of the subcontinent moving in the opposite direction.

This era also saw the flourishing of true cities across the empire: Pataliputra, Varanasi (Banaras), Ayodhya, Prayag (modern Allahabad), Ujjain, Taxila, and Qandahar. These remained centers for arts, crafts, industry, literature, and education. The architecture of the Mauryan capital, Pataliputra, has not survived intact because of its basic wood and brick construction. But Greek travelers such as Megasthenes reported that its glories surpassed those of the Achaemenid palaces. Certainly the stone building and sculpture of the Ashokan period reflect sophisticated aesthetics and technique, as well as strong Persian and Greek influences.

The Consolidation of Indian Civilization (CA. 200 B.C.–A.D. 300)

In the post-Mauryan period, the history of northwest and northern India was dominated by the influx of a variety of foreign peoples whom we shall consider in the last section of this chapter. In the rest of the subcontinent, indigenous Indian dynasties held sway. These dynasties often controlled substantial regional empires that became centers for developing Indian cultural styles. In this period, a general pattern of regional and local political autonomy arose that would be broken only by the Gupta Empire (A.D. 320–CA. 550; see Chapter 11). Religiously and culturally, the centuries between the Mauryan and the Gupta eras saw the consolidation of patterns and styles that helped to shape Indian and, through the diffusion of Buddhism, Asian civilization.

The Economic Base

Although agriculture remained, commerce flourished as the basis of the economy amidst the post-Mauryan political fragmentation. India's merchant classes prospered, as their patronage of Buddhist and Jain buildings shows. The fine Mauryan road system provided a base for trade across the length and breadth of India. Chinese and Roman demand for Indian luxury goods—jewels and semiprecious stones, sandalwood and teak, cotton and silk textiles, spices, exotic animals, and slaves—made India a center of world trade. Considerable wealth flowed in, as shown by hoards of Roman gold coins and the remains of Roman trading communities in the Tamil south. Within India, guild organizations flourished and provided technical education in skilled crafts. They were important targets of investment not only by the merchant class but by kings as well. Coin minting greatly increased after Mauryan times, and banking was a thriving concern.[4]

High Culture

In the arts, the great achievements of these centuries were primarily Buddhist in inspiration. While northwest India saw the rise of Gandharan Buddhist art, in central India as early as the first century B.C. stone-relief sculpture had developed the basic forms of what became the classical style of Indian art. The finest surviving examples of this sculpture are the stone reliefs of the great Buddhist stupas (shrines) at Bharhut and Sanchi.

Language and literature in this period rested on the sophisticated Sanskrit grammar of Panini (CA. 300 B.C.?), which remains the unsurpassed standard today. Two masterpieces of Sanskrit culture, the epics of the *Mahabharata* and the *Ramayana*, had probably taken their general shape by A.D. 200. The first of these is a composite work concerned largely with the nature of *dharma* (the moral and cosmic Law; see Chapter 2).

[4] Romila Thapar, *A History of India*, vol. 1 (Harmondsworth, 1966), pp. 105–118.

Stupa and rock-cut shrine. Figure A shows the great Stupa at Sanchi, an outstanding example of early Buddhist relic mounds. The mound, seated on an Ashokan foundation, was added to over the centuries. Its most notable art work is the magnificent carvings on the stone railings and gateways, one of which is shown in Figure B. Sanchi is located in north-central India. [American Institute of Indian Studies/Bettmann Archive.]

Included in its earlier, narrative portions are systematic treatments of *dharma* such as the Bhagavad Gita, or "Song of the Blessed Lord," the most famous and influential of all Indian religious texts. Evidence of the rise of devotional cults is seen in the importance of Krishna in the *Mahabharata* (especially in the Gita) and Rama in the *Ramayana*. Both are major incarnations, or *avataras*, of Vishnu.

Religion and Society

The post-Mauryan period saw Buddhist monasticism and lay devotionalism thrive throughout the subcontinent. However, the dominance of the Brahmans in ritual matters and Vedic learning also continued. It was also a period of diffusion for popular devotional cults of particular gods, above all Shiva and Vishnu, which were to be the mainstays of all later "Hindu" religious life. The parallel development in Buddhist tradition was the rise, along with Mahayana thought (see Chapter 11), of a cult of the person of the Buddha. It focused on pilgrimages to sites where his relics were deposited or to places associated with his life. Toward the end of this age, Buddhism in its Mahayana form began to spread from India over the trade routes to Central Asia, and eventually to China and Japan.

THE HINDU TRADITION. What we now call *Hinduism* emerged in this era. The major developments that were shaping a "Hindu" tradition were

INDIA FROM THE SIXTH CENTURY B.C. TO THE END OF MAURYAN RULE	
CA. 600–400 B.C.	Late Upanishadic age: Local/regional kingdoms and tribal republics along the Ganges, in Himalayan foothills, Panjab and northwest India
CA. 540–CA. 468 B.C.	Vardhamana Mahavira, Jain founder
CA. 537–CA. 486 B.C.	Siddhartha Gautama, the Buddha
CA. 550–324 B.C.	Regional empire of Maghadan kings
330–325 B.C.	Alexander campaigns in Indus valley, Soghdiana, Bactria, and Panjab
324–CA. 185 B.C.	Mauryan empire controls most of northern India and the Deccan
CA. 272–232 B.C.	Reign of the Mauryan emperor Ashoka

(1) the consolidation of the caste system, Brahman ascendancy, and the "high" culture of Sanskrit language and learning; (2) the increasing dominance of theistic devotionalism (especially the cults of Vishnu and Shiva); and (3) the intellectual reconciliation of these developments with the older ascetic and speculative traditions going back to the Upanishadic age. These social and religious developments would continue and solidify in the Gupta era and later times.

THE BUDDHIST TRADITION. Indian Buddhist monastic communities prospered in this period under mercantile and royal patronage—especially in or near urban centers—a trait they shared with the Jains. Merchants found both traditions attractive and strongly supported Jain and Buddhist monasteries, presumably for the merit to be gained.

Buddhist lay devotion was a prominent part of Indian religious life, especially in the Ganges basin. However, it was a very different tradition from the Buddhism of the theological texts, which focuses on the quest for *nirvana* and the "extraordinary norm" (see Chapter 2). The Buddha and the Buddhist saints were naturally identified with popular Indian deities and Buddhist worship was easily assimilated to common Indian patterns of theistic piety. Consequently, popular Buddhist practice was indistinguishable from countless other devotional cults that were coming to dominate the Indian scene. One reason that Buddhist tradition remained only one among many Indian religious paths was its absorption into the religious diversity that then and now typifies the "Hindu" religious scene.

The entrance to one of the many early Buddhist shrines, or chaitva-halls, *that were cut into the cliffs along the adjoining monastaries (viharas). Most of these rock-cut shrines are found in vertical cliffs not far from modern Bombay. [Bettmann Archive.]*

GREEK AND ASIAN DYNASTIES

The Seleucids

We have seen that the successors of Alexander the Great in the Achaemenid lands, the Greek general Seleucus and his heirs, soon lost Arachosia and Gandhara to the Maurans. They did, however, rule most of the former Achaemenid domains from about 312 to 246 B.C., and lesser portions until about 125 B.C. Alexander's policies of Greco-Persian fusion—the appointment of Iranians and Greeks as satraps, as well as large-scale Greek and Persian intermarriage—helped make the Seleucid rule of many eastern areas more viable. The new "cities"—or, more accurately, military colonies—that Alexander left behind provided bases for Seleucid control. As a foreign minority, the Seleucids had ultimately to maintain their power with mercenary troops. It was, however, the leaders of their own troops and satrapies whose imperial aspirations gradually whittled away at Seleucid rule. Always at war, neither Seleucus (reigned 311–281 B.C.; see Chapter 4) nor even the greatest of his successors, Antiochus the Great (reigned 223–187 B.C.), ever secured lasting rule on the scale of the Achaemenids.

In the end, Alexander's policy of linking Hellenes with Iranians in political power, marriage, and culture bore fruit more lasting than empire. The Seleucid emphasis on the founding and cultivation of Greek-style cities stimulated the hellenization process. During the third century B.C., Hellenistic culture and law became new ideals among the upper classes and intelligentsia of the Seleucid realms. The Seleucids did not encourage cultural mixing as had Alexander, but they did

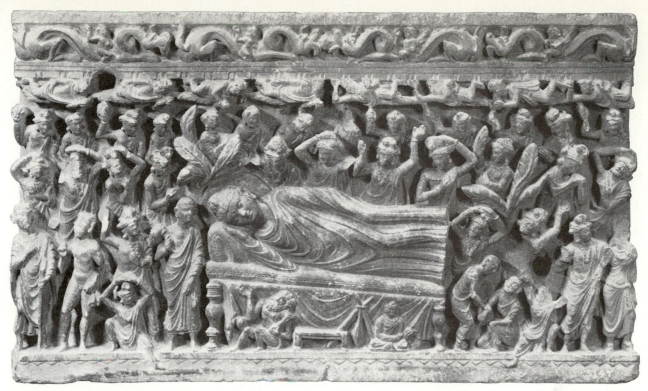

The Buddha's Nirvana. A late second or third-century A.D. *Gandharan relief which has much the style of contemporary Roman stone carvings. Here the Indian-Buddhist concept does not mesh well with the realistic Roman style and craftsmanship. Note the emotions of the bystanders at their loss of the Lord Buddha; these would not appear in native Indian style. [Art Resource/Giraudon.]*

welcome into the ruling classes those non-Hellenes willing to become hellenized. Aramaic continued to be the common language from Syria to the Hindu Kush (although it was in decline in eastern Iran). Local social and cultural forms were by no means displaced, but Greek culture did penetrate.

Zoroastrian and related Iranian religious traditions declined with the loss of their imperial-cult status. The many syncretistic cults of the Mediterranean Hellenistic world made inroads even in the east in Seleucid and Parthian times. The later Parthians probably laid the groundwork for the still later revival of the Zoroastrian tradition. Mystery and savior cults were becoming more popular in East and West. The new urban centers of the Hellenistic Age may have provided an environment in which the individual necessarily had less rootedness in the established traditions of culture and religious life. This would have enhanced the attractiveness of the focus on individual salvation common to many lesser Hellenistic cults. This was especially true of emerging traditions like the Christian, Mahayana Buddhist, Hindu devotionalist, and Manichaean that came to dominate Eurasia over the next few centuries.

The Indo-Greeks

The extreme extent of Hellenization in the east was realized not by the Seleucids, but by another line of Alexandrine successors, the Indo-Greeks of Bactria.[5] About 246 B.C., Bactria's Greek satrap broke away from the Seleucids. His successor, Euthydemus (reigned CA. 235–CA. 200 B.C.), managed to extend his sway north and southwest; he withstood a Seleucid attempt at reconquest by Antiochus the Great in 208 B.C. His son Demetrius exploited the growing Mauryan weakness. By 175 B.C. he had crossed the Hindu Kush to conquer Arachosia; then he moved up the Indus valley to take Gandhara. Demetrius and his successor, Menander, made Taxila their capital and were powerful enough to control other parts of north India. Both were thoroughly "Indianized" in their orientation. Most of the Indo-Greeks were very Indian, even in language and religion, as their coins and inscriptions show.

[5] In *The Indo-Greeks* (Oxford, 1957), A. K. Narian argues for *Indo-Greeks* as the appropriate term for these kings, who are usually called *Greco-Bactrians* or *Euthydemids*.

Before their demise at the hands of invading steppe peoples (CA. 130–100 B.C.), these Indo-Greeks left their mark on civilization in all the areas around their Bactrian center. Bactria was a crucial area of transmission, if not a major source, of the later Greco-Buddhist art of Gandhara, one of history's remarkable examples of cross-cultural influence. The Indo-Greeks probably also played a role in the early spread of Buddhism from India to Central Asia. The most famous of the Bactrian rulers, Menander, or Milinda (reigned CA. 155–130 B.C.?), is depicted as a Buddhist convert in a later Buddhist text, *The Questions of King Milinda.*

The Steppe Peoples

When we come to the Parthians, who succeeded the Seleucids in Iran, and to the steppe dynasties who succeeded the Indo-Greeks in Bactria and north India, separation of Iranian from Indian history is misleading. Both north India and the Iranian plateau were dominated from about 250 B.C. to A.D. 300 by Iranian tribal peoples originally from the Central Asian steppes. Although commonly ignored, they and other nomadic steppe peoples were the main force in Eurasian history alongside the great sedentary civilizations of the eastern Mediterranean, Mesopotamia, India, and China. These Indo-Iranian incursions were not the first (or the last) such invasions. Yet there is more tangible historical evidence of their penetration of northeastern Iran and northwest India than exists for any earlier Indo-Aryan migrations.

The Parthians

The Parni, said to be related to the Scythians, were probably the major group of Iranian steppe peoples who had first settled in the area south of the Aral Sea and Oxus. In late Achaemenid times, they moved south into Parthia and gradually adopted its dialect. Henceforth, we can call them Parthians. The independent control of Parthia by their dynastic family (the Arsacids) dates from about 247 B.C. Shortly afterward, they crossed the Elburz and began to extend their power onto the Iranian plateau. For decades only a regional power, the Parthians emerged under Mithradates I (CA. 171–138 B.C.) as a new imperial force in Eurasia. They were recognized as the true successors of the Achaemenids in Iran.

Facing weak Seleucid and Indo-Greek opposition, by CA. 140 B.C. Mithradates was able to secure a sizable empire. It covered the Iranian plateau and reached from Mesopotamia perhaps to Arachosia. Its center thereafter was his new winter capital at Ctesiphon, on the Tigris. The exact imperial borders and spheres of influence varied over time. But from the victory over the Romans at Carrhae in 53 B.C. (see Chapter 6) until their fall in A.D. 233, the Parthians were the

major power of Eurasia alongside Rome. In the end, the pressure of the Kushan empire in the east and, above all, the constant Roman wars of their last century weakened them sufficiently for a new Persian dynasty to replace them.

It is not easy to measure Parthian rule, despite its duration and successes, because of the scarcity and the bias of the available sources. For much of their long reign, the Parthians were under great pressure on all fronts, in Armenia, in Mesopotamia, and along their Indian and Central Asian frontiers. Yet, during their rule, trade in and around their domains apparently increased. In particular, there is evidence of vigorous commerce north over the Caucasus, on the "silk road" to China, and along the Indian Ocean coast (the ancient Arab's "monsoon route," used for the spice trade with the Indies).

Culturally, the Parthians were oriented toward the Hellenistic world of their Seleucid predecessors until the mid-first century A.D., after which they seem to have undergone a kind of Iranian revival. They then replaced Greek on their coins with Parthian and Aramaic, and they gave their cities their older Iranian names again. Their formerly Hellenic tastes in art turned to Iranian motifs like the hunt, the battle, and the feast. In late Parthian times the Iranian national epic took its lasting shape. Similarly, the worship of Ahura Mazda was preserved among the Magi despite the success of other Eastern and Western cults and the common assimilation of Greek gods to Iranian ones. Yet the Parthians seem to have tolerated religious diversity. In their era, a huge variety of religious cults and cultural traditions rubbed shoulders with one another and vied for supremacy in different contexts.

The Sakas and Kushans

The successors of the Indo-Greeks were steppe peoples even closer to their nomadic past than the Parthians. These peoples are often ignored by modern historians because they impinge on but do not figure centrally in Chinese, Iranian, or Indian history in our period. However, they played a major political and cultural role for several centuries, especially in the Indo-Iranian region. They reflect the cosmopolitan nature of the world of Central Asia, eastern Iran, and northwest India at this time.

Beginning about 130 B.C., Scythian (Saka) tribes from beyond the Jaxartes River (Syr Darya) overran northeast Iran, taking Sogdiana's Hellenic cities and then Bactria. Thus ended the Indo-Greek heyday, although the last Greek petty ruler lasted in the upper Indus valley until about 50 B.C. One group of Sakas soon extended their domain from Bactria into north India, as far as Mathura. Another went southwest into Herat and Sistan, where they encroached on the Parthians. In northwest India, the Sakas were, in turn,

312–CA. 125 B.C.	Seleucid rule in part of old Achaemenid realm
312–246 B.C.	Height of Seleucid imperial strength
CA. 248 B.C.– A.D. 224	Parthian empire of the Arsacids in Iran, Babylonia
246–CA. 50 B.C.	Indo-Greek ("Graeco-Bactrian," "Euthydemid") rulers of region from modern Afghanistan to Oxus
CA. 155–130 B.C.?	Reign of Indo-Greek ruler Menander (Milinda)
247 B.C.–A.D. 223	Parthian Arsacid Empire
CA. 171–138 B.C.	Reign of Arsacid king Mithradates I
CA. 140 B.C.–CA. A.D. 100	Movements west and south of Yüeh Chih (including Kushans) and Sythians (Sakas), into Sogdiana, then Bactria, then northwest India
CA. A.D. 50–CA. 250	Height of Kushan power in Oxus to Ganges region
CA. 78 [or 148?]	Accession of King Kanishka to Kushan throne in Taxila

defeated by invading Iranians known as the *Pahlavas*, who went on to rule in northwest India in the first century A.D.[6] Pahlava rule did not, however, wipe out the Sakas, for we find Saka dynasties ruling in parts of northwest and west India through the fourth century A.D.

The Sakas had been displaced earlier in Sogdiana by another steppe people, known from Chinese sources as the Yüeh Chih. They may have been driven from western China by the building of the Great Wall of China and/or drought in the steppes. These peoples, under the leadership of the Kushan tribe, next drove the Sakas out of Bactria. About a hundred years later, in the mid-first century A.D., they swept over the

---

[6]Tradition gives one of their rulers, Gondophares, the role of host to Saint Thomas, who is said to have brought Christianity to India. But since Gondophares probably ruled in the early to mid-first century A.D., this may be a confused report. Even if traditions of Thomas' mission to India are correct, some connect him instead with south India.

Standing Buddha. This Gandharan-school statue of the Buddha from the second century (A.D.) reflects the marriage of Greco-Roman statuary styles with the Indian Buddhist content. Although the head of this example has been recut in modern times, the elongated ears and sign of wisdom on the forehead (both are identifying marks of the Buddha) are typical of Gandharan sculptures. [Otto E. Nelson/The Asia Society.]

mountains into northwest India. Here they ended Pahlava rule and founded a long-lived Indian Kushan dynasty, which controlled a relatively stable empire from the upper Oxus regions over Bactria, Gandhara, and Arachosia, across the Punjab, and over the Ganges plains as far as Varanasi (Banaras). Their greatest ruler, Kanishka, reigned either at the end of the first century or the middle of the second A.D. He was the greatest patron of Buddhism since Ashoka. In their heyday (CA. the first to the third centuries A.D.), the power of the Kushans in Central Asia facilitated the missionary activity that carried Buddhism across the steppes and into China. A lasting Kushan contribution was the school of Greco-Buddhist art fostered in Gandhara by Kanishka and his successors and carried on by a later Kushan dynasty for another five hundred years.

Africa, Iran, and India before A.D. 200 in World Perspective

By the second century A.D. in Africa and in the Indo-Iranian world, we can see the development of imperial governments whose power and influence far surpassed that of any before them. In and of themselves, such empires are not the measure of progress in what we call "civilization"—that is, cited, literate culture; technological sophistication; specialized division of labor; and complex social and political structures. Yet they are indices of the security and wealth necessary to progress. This was clearly the case in the empires of the Achaemenids and Mauryans and, to a more limited degree, in that of the Kushites, and also the Carthaginians. In this respect, developments in these Afro-Asian areas paralleled those in the wider world, where the Greek, Hellenistic, and Roman empires, like the Han empire of China, provided contexts in which civilization could flourish, grow, and spread afield.

Except in the African centers of culture, this was also an era in which ultimately influential, lasting religious traditions grew up and came of age. Not all met with the same long-term success or positive response outside their homeland. The Christian, Buddhist, Confucian, and even Judaic and Hindu traditions spread abroad and took root in cultures outside their places of origin. By contrast, the Zoroastrian tradition, like the Jain in India, never had great appeal outside of its homeland, although its adherents would much later carry it with them to western India, where they continue today as the influential but small community of Parsees.

In this period, another important and portentous element for the history of civilization was the increased cross-cultural contact symbolized by the Hellenizing conquests of Alexander the Great. The central Asian reaches of Iran and India especially provided the great meeting ground of Iranian, Indian, Greek, and steppe-people's languages, customs, ideas, arts, and religious practices. In later centuries, the Iranian and Indian cultures continued to develop their own distinctive and largely independent forms, and central Asia remained a fragmented but fertile cultural melting pot. Yet the age we have briefly surveyed here set in motion cross-cultural interchanges that would continue apace in later centuries.

This matter of interchange is important for Africa, where, like Europe, the greater part of the huge continent was visibly less developed than the central axis of cited, literate culture that ran from the Mediterranean to China over roughly the region of the original river-valley cradles of civilization. This "lagging" had little to do with the character of the peoples of either sub-Saharan Africa or Europe, but was due primarily to their relative isolation from substantial, sustained interchange with the expanding older centers of civilization. In this period, we see in Rome, Iran, or India, if less so in China, increased contacts with other cultures and increased influences from abroad. These contacts and influences were manifested in new peoples, governmental structures, technological innovations, specialized skills and arts, and ethico-religious ideas. Those areas of Africa and Europe that were in sufficiently constant intercourse with the Mediterranean and western Asian civilizations of the day were precisely those in which civilization as we understand it developed first.

Suggested Readings

AFRICA

P. BOHANNAN AND P. CURTIN, *Africa and Africans*, rev. ed. (1971). Interesting topical treatment of various sectors of society, institutions, and history.

P. CURTIN, S. FEIERMANN, L. THOMPSON, AND J. VANSINA, *African History* (1978). Probably the best survey history. The relevant portions here are Chapters 1, 2, 4, 8, and 9.

J. D. FAGE, *A History of Africa* (1978). Chapters 1 and 2, on origins of society and on Africa and the ancient Mediterranean world, are relevant.

R. W. JULY, *Precolonial Africa: An Economic and Social History* (1975). Good chapters on the environment and various kinds of peoples and their livelihoods.

J. KI-ZERBO, *Methodology and African Prehistory*. Vol. I of *UNESCO General History of Africa* (1981). Useful summary and interpretive articles treat diverse topics, including sources, languages, geography, and prehistory of the various regions.

G. MOKHTAR, *Ancient Civilizations of Africa*. Vol. II of *UNESCO General History of Africa* (1981). Relevant chapters are 8–16 on Nubia, Meroe, and Aksum; 17–20 on the Saharan region in ancient times; and 22–29 on the early history of the various regions of the African subcontinent.

IRAN

M. BOYCE, *Zoroastrians: Their Religious Beliefs and Practices* (1979). The most recent survey, organized historically and based on extensive research and experience.

J. M. Cook, *The Persian Empire* (1983). A recent, solid survey of the Achaemenid period.

W. D. Davies and L. Finkelstein, ed. *The Cambridge History of Judaism*, Vol. 1 (Introduction; The Persian Period). Good articles on Iran and Iranian religion as well as on Judaism.

J. Duchesne-Guillemin, trans., *The Hymns of Zarathustra*, trans. by M. Henning (1952, 1963). The best introduction to the original texts of the Zoroastrian hymns.

R. N. Frye, *The Heritage of Persia* (1963, 1966). A first-rate survey of Iranian history to Islamic times that is readable but scholarly.

W. W. Malandra, trans. and ed., *An Introduction to Ancient Iranian Religion: Readings from the Avesta and Achaemenid Inscriptions* (1983). Helpful especially for texts of inscriptions relevant to religion.

INDIA

W. T. de Bary et al., comp., *Sources of Indian Tradition*. 1958. 2nd ed., 2 vols. Vol. I: *From the Beginning to 1800*, ed. and rev. Ainslie T. Embree. (1988). Excellent selections from a wide variety of Indian texts, with good introductions to chapters and individual selections.

A. L. Basham, ed., *A Cultural History of India* (1975). A fine collection of historical-survey essays by a variety of scholars. See Part I, "The Ancient Heritage" (Chapters 2–16).

———, *The Wonder That Was India*, rev. ed. (1963). Excellent material on Mauryan religion, society, culture, and history.

B. Rowland, *The Art and Architecture of India: Buddhist/Hindu/Jain*, 3rd rev. ed. (1970). The standard work, lucid and easy to read. Relevant here is Part Three, "Romano-Indian Art in North-West India and Central Asia."

V. A. Smith, *The Oxford History of India*, 4th rev. ed. Percival Spear et al. (1981), pp. 71–163. Perhaps the most readable survey history. Includes useful reference chronologies.

R. Thapar, *Asoka and the Decline of the Mauryas* (1973). The standard treatment of Ashoka's reign.

———, *A History of India*. Part I (1966), pp. 50–108. Contains three chapters on the period from CA. 600 B.C. to A.D. 200 that provide a basic survey.

GREEK AND ASIAN DYNASTIES

A. K. Narain, *The Indo-Greeks* (1957. Reprinted with corrections, Oxford, 1962). The most comprehensive history of the complex history of the various kings and kingdoms.

F. E. Peters, *The Harvest of Hellenism* (1970), pp. 222–308. Helpful chapters on the various Greek rulers of the eastern world, from Seleucus to the last Indo-Greeks.

J. W. Sedlar, *India and the Greek World: A Study in the Transmission of Culture* (1980). A basic work that provides a good overview.

8 China's First Empire (221 B.C.–A.D.220)

One hallmark of Chinese history is the striking continuity of culture, language, and geography. The Shang and Chou dynasties were centered along the Yellow River or its tributary, the Wei. The capitals of China's first empire were in exactly the same areas. And north China would remain China's political center down through history to the present. It was as though Western civilization had progressed from Thebes on the Nile to Athens on the Nile, to Rome on the Nile, and then, in time, to Paris, London, and Berlin on the Nile. And as though each of these centers of culture spoke Egyptian and used a single writing system based on Egyptian hieroglyphics.

But geographical, ethnic, and linguistic continuity did not mean that China was unchanging. One of the key turning points in Chinese history was the third century B.C. when the old, quasi-feudal, Chou multistate system gave way to a centralized bureaucratic government that built an empire stretching from the steppe in the north to Vietnam in the south.

What we refer to as China's first empire was composed of three segments:

256–206 B.C.	Ch'in dynasty
206 B.C.–A.D. 8	Former Han dynasty
A.D. 25–220	Later Han dynasty

The Ch'in dynasty is dated from 256 B.C., the year in which it overthrew the previous Chou dynasty. It went on to unify China in 221 B.C. The Western word *China* is derived from the name of this dynasty. In reshaping China, the Ch'in developed such momentum that it became overextended and collapsed a single generation after the unification. The Ch'in was followed by the two Han dynasties, each lasting about two hundred years. They both used the same dynastic name of

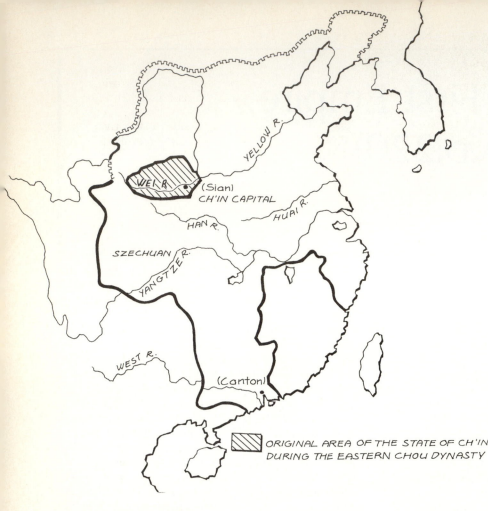

ORIGINAL AREA OF THE STATE OF CH'IN DURING THE EASTERN CHOU DYNASTY

MAP 8-1   THE UNIFICATION OF CHINA BY THE CH'IN STATE   *Between* 221 *and* 206 B.C. *the Ch'in state expanded and unified China.*

Han because the Later Han was founded by a descendant of the Former Han. Historians usually treat each of the Han as a separate period of rule, although, as they were almost back to back, they shared many institutions and cultural traits. So deep was the impression left by these two dynasties on the Chinese that even today they call themselves—in contrast to Mongols, Manchus, Tibetans, and other minorities—the "Han people," and their ideographs, "Han writing."

The Ch'in Unification of China

Of the territorial states of the late Chou era none was more innovative and ruthless than Ch'in. Its location on the Wei River in northwest China—the same area from which the Chou had launched their expansion a millennium earlier—gave it strategic advantages: it controlled the passes leading out onto the Yellow River plain and so was easy to defend and was a secure base from which to launch attacks on other states. From the late fourth century B.C., the Ch'in conquered a part of Szechwan and thus controlled two of the most fertile regions of ancient China. It welcomed Legalist administrators, who developed policies for enriching the country and strengthening its military. Despite its harsh laws, farmers moved to Ch'in from other areas, attracted by the order and stability of its society. Its armies had been forged by centuries of warfare against the nomadic raiders by whose lands it was half encircled. To counter these raiders, it adopted nomadic skills, developing cavalry in the fourth century. Other states regarded the Ch'in as tough, crude, and brutal but recognized its formidable strengths.

In 246 B.C., the man who would unify China succeeded to the Ch'in throne at the age of thirteen. He grew to be vigorous, ambitious, intelligent, and decisive. He is famous as a Legalist autocrat; but he was also well liked by his ministers, whose advice he usually followed. In 232 B.C., at the age of twenty-seven, he began the campaigns that destroyed the six remaining territorial states. On completing his conquests in 221 B.C., he adopted the glorious title we translate as "emperor"—a combination of ideographs hitherto used only for gods or mythic heroes—to raise himself above the kings of the former territorial states. He is known to history as the First Ch'in Emperor. Then, aided by officials of great talent, he set about applying to all of China the reforms that had been tried and found effective in his own realm. His accomplishments in the eleven years before his death in 210 B.C. were stupendous.

Having conquered the civilized world of north China and the Yangtze River basin, the First Emperor sent his armies to conquer new lands. They reached the northern edge of the Red River basin in what is now Vietnam. They occupied China's southeastern coast and the area about the present-day city of Canton. In the north and the northwest, the emperor's armies fought against the Hsiung Nu, Altaic-speaking Hunnish nomads organized in a tribal confederation. During the late Chou, northern border states had built long walls to protect settled lands from incursions by horse-riding raiders. The Ch'in emperor had these joined into a single Great Wall that extended fourteen hundred miles from the Pacific Ocean into central Asia. (By way of comparison, Hadrian's Wall in England was seventy-three miles long.) Its construction cost the lives of vast numbers of conscripted laborers—by some accounts, one hundred thousand; by others, as many as one million.

The most significant Ch'in reform, carried out by the Legalist minister, Li Ssu, extended the Ch'in system of bureaucratic government to the entire empire. Li Ssu divided China into forty prefectures, which were further subdivided into counties. The county heads were responsible to prefects, who, in turn, were responsible to the central government. Officials were chosen by ability. Bureaucratic administration was impersonal, based on laws to which all were subject. No one, for example, escaped Ch'in taxation. This kind of bureaucratic centralism broke sharply with the old Chou pattern of establishing dependent principalities for members of a ruler's family. Furthermore, to ensure the smooth functioning of local government offices, the former aristocracies of the territorial states were removed from their lands and resettled in the Ch'in capital, near present-day Sian. They were housed in mansions on one side of the river, from which they could gaze across at the enormous palace of the First Emperor.

Other reforms further unified the First Emperor's vast domain. Roads were built radiating out from the capital city. The emperor decreed a system of uniform weights and measures. He unified the Chinese writing system, establishing standard ideographs to replace the great variety that had hitherto prevailed. He established uniform axle lengths for carts. Even ideas did not escape the drive toward uniformity. Following the precepts of Legalism, the emperor and his advisers launched a campaign for which they subsequently have been execrated throughout Chinese history. They collected and burned the books of other schools such as Confucianism and were said to have buried alive several hundred scholars opposed to the Legalist philosophy. Only useful books on agriculture, medicine, or Legalist teachings were spared.

But the Ch'in had changed too much too quickly to pay for the roads, canals, and the Great Wall. Taxes burdened the people. Commoners hated conscription and labor service and nobles resented their loss of status. Merchants were exploited, and scholars, except for Legalists, were oppressed. A Chinese historian wrote afterward: "The condemned were an innumerable multitude; those who had been tortured and mutilated formed a long procession on the roads. From the princes and ministers down to the humblest people

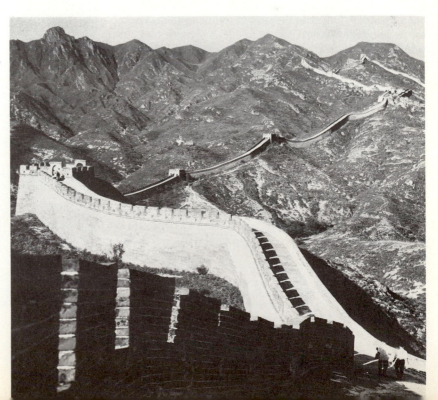

The Great Wall of China was originally built during the Ch'in dynasty (256–206 B.C.), but what we see today is the wall as it was completely rebuilt during the Ming dynasty (A.D. 1368–1644). (Photo Researchers.)

The army of life-size terra-cotta soldiers found in the tomb of the first emperor of the Ch'in dynasty (256–206 B.C.) (Liu Entai.)

Chinese archaeologists restoring warriors from the tomb of the Ch'in emperor. (Liu Entai.)

everyone was terrified and in fear of their lives."[1] When the First Emperor died in 210 B.C., intrigues broke out at court and rebellions arose in the land. At the end, the Ch'in was destroyed by the domino effect of its own legal codes. When the generals sent to quell a rebellion were defeated, they joined the rebellion rather than return to the capital and incur the severe punishment decreed for failure. The dynasty collapsed in 206 B.C.

In 1974, a farmer digging a well near Sian discovered the army of eight thousand life-sized terra-cotta horses and soldiers that guarded the tomb of the First Emperor. The historical record tells us that in the tomb itself, under a mountain of earth, is a replica of his capital, a relief model of the Chinese world with quicksilver rivers, other warriors with chariots of bronze, and the remains of horses, noblemen, and criminals sacrificed to accompany in death the emperor whose dynasty was to have lasted for ten thousand generations.

[1]C. P. Fitzgerald, *China, A Short Cultural History* (New York: Praegar, 1935), p. 147.

The Former Han Dynasty
(206 B.C.–A.D. 8)

The Dynastic Cycle

Historians of China have seen a pattern in every dynasty of long duration. They call it the *dynastic cycle.* The cycle begins with internal wars that eventually lead to the military unification of China. The fact of unification is proof that the unifier has been given the mandate of heaven. Strong and vigorous, the first ruler, in the process of consolidating his political power, restores peace and order to China. Economic growth follows, almost automatically. The peak of the cycle is marked by public works, further energetic reforms, and aggressive military expansion. During this phase, China appears invincible. But then the cycle turns downward. The costs of expansion, coupled with an increasing opulence at the court, place a heavy burden on tax revenues just as they are beginning to decline. The vigor of the monarchs wanes. Intrigues develop at the court. The central controls loosen, and provincial governors and military commanders gain autonomy. Finally, canals and other public works fall into disrepair, floods and pestilence occur, rebellions break out, and eventually the dynasty collapses. In the view of Confucian historians, the last emperors are not only politically weak but morally culpable as well.

The Early Years of the Former Han Dynasty

The first sixty years of the Han may be thought of as the early phase of its dynastic cycle. Of the several rebel generals who emerged after the collapse of the Ch'in, one gained control of the Wei basin and went on to unify China. He became the first emperor of the Han dynasty and is known by his posthumous title of Kao Tzu. He rose from plebeian origins to become emperor; only once again would this occur in Chinese history. Kao Tzu built his capital at Ch'ang-an, not far from the former capitals of the Western Chou and the Ch'in. It took many years for the early Han emperors to consolidate their power because they consciously avoided actions that would remind the populace of the hated Ch'in despotism. They made punishments less severe and reduced taxes. Good government prevailed, the economy rebounded, granaries were filled, and vast cash reserves were accumulated. Later historians often singled out the early Han rulers as model sage emperors.

MAP 8-2   THE HAN EMPIRE 206 B.C.–A.D. 220   *At the peak of the Han expansion, the Han armies advanced far out into the steppe north of the Great Wall and west into Central Asia: The silk road to Rome passed through the Tarim Basin and the Kushan Empire.*

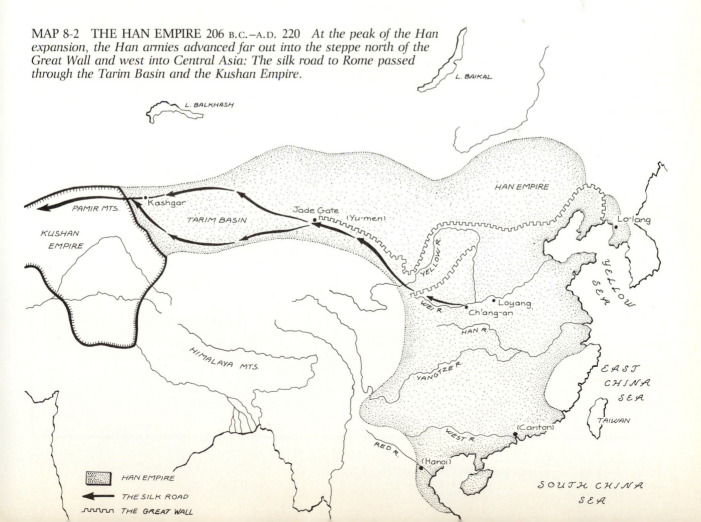

Han Wu Ti

The second phase of the dynastic cycle began with the rule of Wu Ti (the "martial emperor"), who came to the throne in 141 B.C. at the age of sixteen and remained there for fifty-four years, the second longest rule in all Chinese history. Wu Ti was daring, vigorous, and intelligent but also superstitious, suspicious, and vengeful. He wielded tremendous personal authority.

Building on the prosperity achieved by his predecessors, Wu Ti initiated new economic policies. A canal was built from the Yellow River to the capital in northwest China, linking the two major economic regions of north China. "Ever-level granaries" were established throughout the country so that bumper crops could be bought and then sold in time of scarcity. To increase revenues, taxes were levied on merchants, the currency was debased, and some offices were sold. Wu Ti also moved against merchants who had built fortunes in untaxed commodities by reestablishing government monopolies—a practice of the Ch'in—on copper coins, salt, iron, and liquor. For fear of Wu Ti, no one spoke out against the monopolies, but a few years after his death, a famous debate was held at the court. Known after the title of the chronicle as the "Salt and Iron Debate," it was frequently cited thereafter in China, and in Japan and Korea as well. On one side, quasi-Legalist officials argued that the state should enjoy the profits from the sale of salt and iron. On the other side, Confucians argued that the moral purity of officials would be sullied by dealings with merchants. The Confucian scholars who compiled the chronicle made themselves the winner in the debate; but state monopolies became a regular part of Chinese government finance.

Wu Ti also aggressively expanded Chinese borders—a policy that would characterize every strong dynasty. His armies swept south into what is today northern Vietnam and northeast across Manchuria to establish a commandery in north Korea that would last until A.D. 313.

The principal threat to the Han was from the Hsiung Nu empire to the north. Their mounted archers could raid China and flee before an army could be sent against them. To combat them, Wu Ti employed the entire repertoire of policies that would become standard thereafter. When possible he "used the barbarian to control the barbarian," making allies of border nomads against those more distant. Allies were permitted to trade with Chinese merchants; they were awarded titles and honors; and their kings were sent Chinese princesses as brides. When this method did not work, he used force. Between 129 and 119 B.C., Wu Ti sent several armies of over 100,000 troops into the steppe, destroying Hsiung Nu power south of the Gobi Desert in southern Mongolia. To establish a strategic line of defense aimed at the heart of the Hsiung Nu empire further to the west, Wu Ti then sent 700,000 Chinese colonists to the arid Kansu panhandle and

Chinese Women among the Nomads

About the year 105 B.C., Wu Ti sent a Chinese lady, Hsi-chün, to be the wife of a nomad king of the Wu-sun people of central Asia. When she got there, she found her husband to be old and decrepit. He saw her only once or twice a year, when they drank a cup of wine together. They could not converse, as they had no language in common.

My people have married me
In a far corner of Earth;
Sent me away to a strange land,
To the king of the Wu-sun.
A tent is my house,
Of felt are my walls;

Raw flesh my food
With mare's milk to drink.
Always thinking of my own country,
My heart sad within.
Would I were a yellow stork
And could fly to my old home!

Centuries later, the T'ang poet Tu Fu visited the village of another woman sent out to be the wife of a nomad king.

Ten thousand ranges and valleys approach the
   Ching Gate
And the village in which the Lady of Light was born
   and bred.
She went out from the purple palace into the desert-
   land;

She has now become a green grave in the yellow
   dusk.
Her face!—Can you picture a wind of the spring?
Her spirit by moonlight returns with a tinkling
Song of the Tartars on her jade guitar,
Telling her eternal sorrow.   ❑

Arthur Waley, *Chinese Poems* (London, George Allen and Unwin, 1946), p. 43; Witter Bynner and Kiang Kang-hsi, *The Jade Mountain* (New York, Alfred Knopf, 1929), p. 157.

The Position of Women

In the teachings of Confucius, a woman first obeyed her parents, then her husband, and finally her son—as the new family head. Descent was traced through the male line. A woman left her family and her ancestors at marriage to join those of her husband. A millennium before footbinding began in China, Fu Hsüan (A.D. 217–278) *wrote this lament.*

WOMAN

How sad it is to be a woman!
Nothing on earth is held so cheap.
Boys stand leaning at the door
Like Gods fallen out of Heaven.
Their hearts brave the Four Oceans,
The wind and dust of a thousand miles.
No one is glad when a girl is born:
By *her* the family sets no store.
When she grows up, she hides in her room
Afraid to look a man in the face.
No one cries when she leaves her home—
Sudden as clouds when the rain stops.
She bows her head and composes her face,
Her teeth are pressed on her red lips:

She bows and kneels countless times.
She must humble herself even to the servants.
His love is distant as the stars in Heaven,
Yet the sunflower bends towards the sun.
Their hearts more sundered than water and fire—
A hundred evils are heaped upon her.
Her face will follow the year's changes:
Her lord will find new pleasures.
They that were once like substance and shadow
Are now as far as Hu from Ch'in [two distant
  places]
Yet Hu and Ch'in shall sooner meet
Than they whose parting is like Ts'an and
Ch'en [two stars]. ❑

Arthur Waley, *Chinese Poems* (1946), pp. 84–85.

---

extended the Great Wall to the Jade Gate outpost at the eastern end of the Tarim basin. From this outpost, Chinese influence was extended over the rim oases of Central Asia, establishing the Silk Road that linked Ch'ang-an with Rome.

Government during the Former Han

As a token of how different they were from the Ch'in dynasty, the early Han emperors set up some Chou-like principalities: small, semiautonomous states with independent lords. But these were closely superintended and then, curtailed after several generations. So basically, despite its repudiation of the Ch'in and all its works, the Han continued the Ch'in form of centralized bureaucratic administration. Officials were organized by grades and were paid salaries in grain, plus cash or silk. They were recruited by sponsorship or recommendation: provincial officials had the duty of recommending promising candidates. A school was established at Ch'ang-an that was said to have thirty thousand students by the Later Han. The bureaucracy grew until, by the first century B.C., there were more than 130,000 officials—perhaps not too many for a population that, by that time, had reached sixty million.

During the course of the Han dynasty, this "Legalist" structure of government became partially Confucianized. It did not happen overnight. The first emperor, Kao Tzu, despised Confucians as bookish pedants—he once urinated in the hat of a scholar. But in time, Confucian ideas proved useful. The mandate

of heaven provided an ethical justification for dynastic rule. A respect for old records and the written word fitted in well with the vast bookkeeping that the empire entailed. The Confucian classics gradually were accepted as the standard for education. Confucianism was seen as shaping moral men, who as officials would be upright, even in the absence of external constraints. For Confucius had taught the transformation of self through ethical cultivation and had presented a vision of benevolent government by men who were virtuous as well as talented. No one attempted to replace laws with a code of etiquette, but increasingly laws were interpreted and applied by men with a Confucian education.

The court during the Han dynasty exhibited features that would appear in later dynasties as well. The emperor was all-powerful. He was the "son of heaven." When he was an adult and strong, his will was paramount. But when he was weak or still a child, others ruled in his name. Four contenders for this role appeared and reappeared through Chinese history. One was the officials. They had, after all, been selected to govern; they staffed the apparatus of government; and their influence was considerable. Apart from the emperor himself, they were usually the most powerful men in China. Yet the position of court officials was often precarious. Few officials escaped being removed from office or banished once or twice during their careers. Of the seven prime ministers who served Wu Ti, five were executed by his order.

A second contender for power was the empress

dowager. Of the emperor's many wives, she was the one whose child had been named as the heir to the throne. On Kao Tzu's death in 195 B.C., for example, the Empress Lu became the regent for her child, the new emperor. Aided by members of her family, she seized control of the court and murdered a rival, and when her son was about to come of age, she had him killed and a younger son made the heir in order to continue her rule as regent. When she died in 180 B.C., loyal adherents of the imperial family who had opposed her rule massacred the members of her family.

The third group of contenders for power at the court were eunuchs. Mostly from families of low social status, they were brought to the court as boys, castrated, and assigned to serve in the emperor's harem. They were thus in contact with the future emperor from the day he was born; they became his childhood confidants; and they often continued to advise him after he had gained the throne. Emperors found eunuchs useful as a counterweight to officials. But in the eyes of the scholars who wrote China's history, the eunuchs were greedy half-men, given to evil intrigues.

The fourth group of contenders were military commanders. Dynasties were founded by military figures— generals or rebels. In the later phase of most dynasties, regional military commanders often became semi-independent rulers. A few even usurped the position of the emperor. Yet they were less powerful at the Chinese court than they were, for example, in imperial Rome. This was partly because the military constituted a separate category, lower in prestige than the better educated civil officials. It was also partly because the court took great pains to prevent them from establishing a base of personal power. An appointment to command a Han army was given only for a specific campaign, and commanders were appointed in pairs so that each would check the other.

Another characteristic of government during the Han and subsequent dynasties was that its functions were limited. It collected taxes, maintained military forces, administered laws, supported the imperial household, and carried out public works that were beyond the powers of local jurisdictions. But government in a district that remained orderly and paid its taxes was left largely in the hands of local notables and large landowners. This pattern was not, to be sure, unique to China. Most premodern governments, even those that were bureaucratic, floated on top of local society and lacked the means to reach down and interfere in the everyday lives of their subjects.

Decline and Usurpation

During the last decade of Wu Ti's rule in the early first century A.D., military expenses ran ahead of revenues. His successor cut back on military costs, eased economic controls, and reduced taxes. But over the next several generations, large landowners began to use their growing influence in provincial politics to avoid paying taxes. State revenues declined. The tax burden on smaller landowners and free peasants grew heavier. In 22 B.C., rebellions broke out in several parts of the empire. At the court, too, a decline had set in. There had been a succession of weak emperors. Intrigues, nepotism, and factional struggles grew apace. Even officials began to sense that the dynasty no longer had the approval of heaven. The dynastic cycle approached its end.

Many at the court urged Wang Mang, the regent for the infant emperor and the nephew of an empress, to become the emperor and begin a new dynasty. Wang Mang refused several times—to demonstrate his lack of eagerness—and then accepted in A.D. 8. He drew up a program of sweeping reforms based on ancient texts. He was a Confucian, yet he relied on new institutional arrangements, rather than moral reform, to produce a better society. He revived ancient titles, expanded state monopolies, abolished private slavery (about 1 per cent of the population), made loans to poor peasants, and then moved to confiscate large private estates.

These reforms, however, alienated many. Merchants disliked the monopolies. Large landowners resisted the expropriation of their lands. Nature also conspired to bring down Wang Mang: the Yellow River overflowed its banks and changed its course, destroying the northern Chinese irrigation system. Several years of poor harvests produced famines. The Hsiung Nu overran China's northern borders. In A.D. 18, the Red Eyebrows, a peasant secret society, rose in rebellion. In A.D. 23, rebels attacked Ch'ang-an, and Wang Mang was killed and eaten by rebel troops. Wang Mang had tried to found a new dynasty from within a decrepit court without having an independent military base. The attempt was futile. Internal wars continued in China for two more years until a large landowner, who had become the leader of a rebel army, emerged triumphant in A.D. 25. Because he was from a branch line of the imperial family, his new dynasty was viewed as a restoration of the Han.

The Later Han (A.D. 25–220) and Its Aftermath

The First Century

The founder of the Later Han moved his capital east to Loyang. Under the first emperor and his two successors, there was a return to strong central government and a laissez-faire economy. Agriculture and population recovered from the devastation caused by war. By the end of the first century A.D., China was as prosperous as it had been during the good years of the Former Han. The shift from pacification and recuperation to military expansion came earlier than during the previous dynasty. Even during the reign of the first emperor, south China and Vietnam were retaken. Dissension within the Hsiung Nu confederation enabled the Chinese to secure an alliance with some of the southern tribes in A.D. 50, and in A.D. 89, Chinese armies crossed the Gobi Desert and defeated the northern Hsiung Nu. This defeat sparked the migrations, some historians say, that brought the Hsiung Nu to the southern Russian steppes and then, in the fifth century A.D., to Europe, where they were known as the Huns of Attila. In A.D. 97, a Chinese general led an army as far west as the shores of the Caspian Sea. The expansion to inner Asia, coupled with more lenient government policies toward merchants, facilitated the camel caravans that carried Chinese silk across the Tarim basin to Iran, Palestine, and Rome.

Decline during the Second Century

Until A.D. 88, the emperors of the Later Han were vigorous; afterward they were ineffective and short-lived. Empresses plotted to advance the fortunes of their families. Emperors turned for help to palace eunuchs, whose power at times surpassed that of officials. In A.D. 159, a conspiracy of eunuchs in the service of an emperor slaughtered the family of a scheming empress dowager and ruled at the court. When officials and students protested against the eunuch dictatorship, over a hundred were killed and over a thousand were tortured or imprisoned. In another incident in A.D. 190, a general deposed one emperor, installed another, killed the empress dowager, and massacred most of the eunuchs at the court.

In the countryside, large landowners, who had been powerful from the start of the dynasty, grew more so. They harbored private armies. Farmers on the estates of the mighty were reduced to serfs. The landowners used their influence to avoid taxes. Great numbers of free farmers fled south to avoid taxes. The remaining freeholders paid ever heavier taxes and labor services. Many peasants turned to neo-Taoist religious movements: the Yellow Turbans in the east and the Five Pecks of Rice Band in Szechwan.

In A.D. 184, rebellions organized by members of the religious sects broke out against the government. Religion provided the ideology and organization to channel their discontents. Han generals suppressed the rebellions but stayed on to rule in the provinces they had pacified. In 220 A.D., they deposed the last Han emperor.

The Aftermath of Empire

For more than three and a half centuries after the fall of the Han, China was disunited. For several gen-

A green-glazed pottery model of a Later Han Dynasty watch tower. Note the resemblence to later Chinese Buddhist pagodas. (W.R. Nelson Trust.)

erations, it was divided into three kingdoms, whose heroic warriors and scheming statesmen were made famous by wandering storytellers. These figures later peopled the *Tales of the Three Kingdoms*, a great romantic epic of Chinese literature.

Chinese history during the post-Han centuries had two characteristics. The first was the dominant role played by the great aristocratic landowning families. With vast estates, huge numbers of serfs, fortified manor houses, and private armies, they were beyond the control of most governments. Because they took over many of the functions of local government, some historians describe post-Han China as having reverted to the quasi-feudalism of the Chou. The second characteristic of these centuries was that north and south China developed in quite different ways.

In the south, there followed a succession of ever weaker dynasties with capitals at Nanking. The entire period of Chinese history from A.D. 220 to 589 is called the Six Dynasties era after these Nanking-centered states. The main developments in the south were (1) the continuing economic growth of south China and the emergence of Nanking as a thriving center of commerce; (2) the ongoing absorption of the tribal peoples of south China into Chinese society and culture; (3) large-scale immigrations of Chinese fleeing the north; and (4) the spread of Buddhism and its penetration to the heart of Chinese culture. Although called dynasties, these six southern states were in fact short-lived kingdoms, plagued by intrigues, usurpations, and coups d'état, frequently at war with northern states, and in constant fear of their own generals.

In the north, state formation depended on the interaction of nomads and Chinese. During the Han dynasty, Chinese invasions of the steppe had led to the incorporation of semi-Sinicized Hsiung Nu as the northernmost tier of the Chinese defense system—just as Germanic tribes had acted as the teeth and claws of the late Roman Empire. But as the Chinese state weakened, the highly mobile nomads broke loose, joined with other tribes, and began to invade China. The short-lived states that they formed are usually referred to as the *Sixteen Kingdoms*. One kingdom was founded by invaders of Tibetan stock. Most spoke Altaic languages: the Hsien Pi (proto-Mongols), the

Toba (proto-Turks), and the Juan Juan (who would later appear in eastern Europe as the Avars). But differences of language and stock were less important than these tribes' similarities:

1. All began as steppe nomads with a way of life different from that of agricultural China.
2. After forming states, all became at least partially Sinicized. Chinese from great families, which had preserved the Han traditions, served as their tutors and administrators.
3. Wars were endemic. Some were fought between northern courts and conservative steppe tribes that resisted Sinicization.
4. Buddhism was powerful in the north as in the south. As a universal religion, it acted as a bridge between "barbarians" and Chinese—just as Christianity was a unifying force in post-Roman Europe. The crude tribes were especially attracted to its magical side. Usually Buddhism was made the state religion. Of the northern states, the most durable was the Northern Wei (A.D. 386–534), famed for its Buddhist sculpture.

Han Thought and Religion

Poems describe the splendor of Ch'ang-an and Loyang: broad boulevards, tiled gateways, open courtyards, watchtowers, and imposing walls. Most splendid of all were the palaces of the emperors, with

Court figures painted on ceramic tile in a Han dynasty tomb. (Museum of Fine Arts, Boston.)

their audience halls, vast chambers, harem quarters, and parks containing artificial lakes and rare animals and birds. But today little remains of the grandeur of the Han. Whereas Roman ruins abound in Italy and circle the Mediterranean, in China nothing remains aboveground. Only from the pottery, bronzes, musical instruments, gold and silver jewelry, lacquerware, and clay figurines that were buried in tombs do we gain an inkling of the rich material culture of the Han period. And only from painting on the walls of tombs do we know of its art.

But there is a wealth of written records that convey the sophistication and depth of Han culture. Perhaps the two most important areas were philosophy and history.

Han Confucianism

A major accomplishment of the early Han was the recovery of texts that had been lost during the Ch'in persecution of scholars. Some were retrieved from the walls of houses where they had been hidden; others were reproduced from memory by scholars. Debate arose regarding the relative authenticity of the old and new texts—a controversy that has continued until modern times. In 51 B.C. and again in A.D. 79, councils were held to determine the true meaning of the Confucian classics. In A.D. 175, an approved, official version of the texts was inscribed on stone tablets. In about A.D. 100, the first dictionary was compiled. Containing about nine thousand characters, it helped promote a uniform system of writing. In Han times, as today, Chinese from the north could not converse with Chinese from the southeastern coast. But a common written language bridged differences of pronunciation, contributing to Chinese unity.

It was also in Han times that scholars began writing commentaries on the classics, a major activity for scholars throughout Chinese history. Scholars learned the classics by heart and used classical allusions in their writing.

Beyond the advances in scholarship, Han philosophers also extended Chou Confucianism by adding to it the teachings of cosmological naturalism. Chou Confucianists had assumed that the moral force of a virtuous emperor would not only order society but also harmonize nature. Han Confucianists explained why. Tung Chung-shu (CA. 179–104 B.C.), for example, held that all nature was a single, interrelated system. Just as summer always follows spring, so does one color, one virtue, one planet, one element, one number, and one officer of the court always take precedence over another. All reflect the systematic workings of *yang* and *yin* and the five elements. And just as one dresses appropriately to the season, so was it important for the emperor to choose policies appropriate to the se-

quences inherent in nature. If he is moral, if he acts in accord with Heaven's natural system, then all will go well. But if he acts inappropriately, then Heaven will send a portent as a warning—a blue dog, a rat holding its tail in its mouth, an eclipse, or a comet. If the portent is not heeded, wonders and then misfortunes will follow. If was the Confucian scholars, of course, who claimed to understand nature's messages and advised the emperor.

It is easy to criticize Han philosophy as pseudo-scientific, or as a mechanistic view of nature. But it represented a new effort of the Chinese mind to encompass and comprehend the interrelationships of the natural world. Spurring an interest in nature, this effort led to inventions like the seismograph and to advances in astronomy, music, and medicine. It was also during the Han that the Chinese invented paper, the

A Chinese seismograph. The suspended weight swings in the direction of the earthquake. This moves a lever and a dragon drops a ball into the mouth of one of the four waiting ceramic frogs. [New York Public Library.]

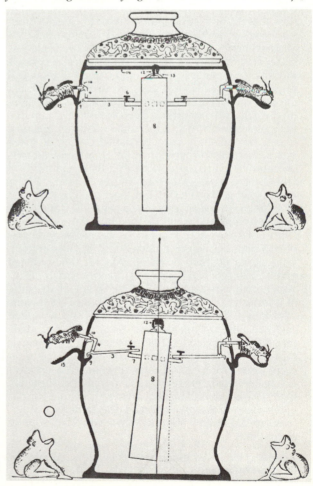

wheelbarrow, the stern-post rudder, and the compass (known as the "south-pointing chariot").

History

The Chinese were the greatest historians of the premodern world. They wrote more history than anyone else, and what they wrote was usually more accurate. Apart from the *Spring and Autumn Annals* and the scholarship of Confucius himself, history writing in China began during the Han dynasty. Why the Chinese were so history-minded has been variously explained: because the Chinese tradition is this-worldly; because Confucianists were scholarly and their veneration for the classics carried over to the written word; because history was seen as a lessonbook (the Chinese called it a mirror) for statesmen, and thus a necessity

Ssu-ma Ch'ien on the Wealthy

More than half of the chapters in Ssu-ma Ch'ien's Historical Records *(early first century* B.C.*) were biographies of extraordinary men and women. He wrote of scholars, wandering knights, diviners, harsh officials and reasonable officials, wits and humorists, doctors, and money-makers. The following is his description of the vibrant economic life of Han cities and his judgments regarding the wealthy.*

Anyone who in the market towns or great cities manages in the course of a year to sell the following items: a thousand brewings of liquor; a thousand jars of pickles and sauces; a thousand jars of sirups; a thousand slaughtered cattle, sheep, and swine; a thousand *chung* of grain; a thousand cartloads or a thousand boat-lengths of firewood and stubble for fuel; a thousand logs of timber; ten thousand bamboo poles; a hundred horse carriages; a thousand two-wheeled ox carts; a thousand lacquered wooden vessels; brass utensils weighing thirty thousand catties; a thousand piculs of plain wooden vessels, iron vessels, or gardenia and madder dyes; two hundred horses; five hundred cattle; two thousand sheep or swine; a hundred male or female slaves; a thousand catties of tendons, horns, or cinnabar; thirty thousand catties of silken fabric, raw silk, or other fine fabrics; a thousand rolls of embroidered or patterned silk; a thousand piculs of fabrics made of vegetable fiber or raw or tanned hides; a thousand pecks of lacquer; a thousand jars of leaven or salted bean relish; a thousand catties of globefish or mullet; a thousand piculs of dried fish; thirty thousand catties of salted fish; three thousand piculs of jujubes or chestnuts; a thousand skins of fox or sable; a thousand piculs of lamb or sheep skins; a thousand felt mats; or a thousand *chung* of fruits or vegetables— such a man may live as well as the master of an estate of a thousand chariots. The same applies for anyone who has a thousand strings of cash [i.e., a million cash] to lend out on interest. Such loans are made through a moneylender, but a greedy merchant who is too anxious for a quick return will only manage to revolve his working capital three times while a less avaricious merchant has revolved his five times. These are the principal ways of making money. There are various other occupations which bring in less than twenty percent profit, but they are not what I would call sources of wealth.

Thrift and hard work are without doubt the proper way to gain a livelihood. And yet it will be found that rich men have invariably employed some unusual scheme or method to get to the top. Plowing the fields is a rather crude way to make a living, and yet Ch'in Yang did so well at it that he became the richest man in his province. Robbing graves is a criminal offense, but T'ien Shu got his start by doing it. Gambling is a wicked pastime, but Huan Fa used it to acquire a fortune. Most fine young men would despise the thought of traveling around peddling goods, yet Yung Lo-ch'eng got rich that way. Many people would consider trading in fats a disgraceful line of business, but Yung Po made a thousand catties of gold at it. Vending sirups is a pretty occupation, but the Chang family acquired ten million cash that way. It takes little skill to sharpen knives, but because the Chih family didn't mind doing it, they could eat the best of everything. Dealing in dried sheep stomachs seems like an insignificant enough trade, but thanks to it the Cho family went around with a mounted retinue. The calling of a horse doctor is a rather ignominious profession, but it enabled Chang Li to own a house so large that he had to strike a bell to summon the servants. All of these men got where they did because of their devotion and singleness of purpose.

From this we may see that there is no fixed road to wealth, and money has no permanent master. It finds its way to the man of ability like the spokes of a wheel converging upon the hub, and from the hands of the worthless it falls like shattered tiles. A family with a thousand catties of gold may stand side by side with the lord of a city; the man with a hundred million cash may enjoy the pleasures of a king. Rich men such as these deserve to be called the "untitled nobility," do they not? ❑

Records of the Grand Historian of China, trans. from the *Shih chi* of Ssu-ma Ch'ien by Burton Watson (New York: Columbia University Press, 1961), pp. 494–495, 499.

The Castration of Ssu-ma Ch'ien

Why did the historian Ssu-ma Ch'ien let himself be castrated? When he incurred the wrath of the Emperor Wu Ti for defending a general defeated by the Hsiung Nu and was condemned to suffer this shame in 98 B.C., why did he not choose an honorable suicide? Read his explanation.

A man has only one death. That death may be as weighty as Mount T'ai, or it may be as light as a goose feather. It all depends upon the way he uses it. . . . It is the nature of every man to love life and hate death, to think of his relatives and look after his wife and children. Only when a man is moved by higher principles is this not so. Then there are things which he must do. . . . The brave man does not always die for honor, while even the coward may fulfill his duty. Each takes a different way to exert himself. Though I might be weak and cowardly and seek shamefully to prolong my life, yet I know full well the difference between what ought to be followed and what rejected. How could I bring myself to sink into the shame of ropes and bonds? If even the lowest slave and scullery maid can bear to commit suicide, why should not one like myself be able to do what has to be done? But the reason I have not refused to bear these ills and have continued to live, dwelling among this filth, is that I grieve that I have things in my heart that I have not been able to express fully, and I am shamed to think that after I am gone my writings will not be known to posterity.

I too have ventured not to be modest but have entrusted myself to my useless writings. I have gathered up and brought together the old traditions of the world which were scattered and lost. I have examined the deeds and events of the past and investigated the principles behind their success and failure, their rise and decay, in one hundred and thirty chapters. I wished to examine into all that concerns heaven and man, to penetrate the changes of the past and present, completing all as the work of one family. But before I had finished my rough manuscript, I met with this calamity. It is because I regretted that it had not been completed that I submitted to the extreme penalty without rancor. When I have truly completed this work, I shall deposit it in some safe place. If it may be handed down to men who will appreciate it and penetrate to the villages and great cities, then though I should suffer a thousand mutilations, what regret would I have? ❑

W. T. de Bary, W. T. Chan, and B. Watson (eds.), *Sources of Chinese Tradition* (New York: Columbia University Press, 1960), pp. 272–273.

---

for the literate men who operated the centralized Chinese state.

The practice of using actual documents and first-hand accounts of events began with Ssu-ma Ch'ien (d. 85 B.C.), who set out to write a history of the known world from the most ancient times down to the age of the Emperor Wu Ti. His *Historical Records* consisted of 130 substantial chapters (in over 700,000 characters) divided into "Basic Annals"; "Chronological Tables"; "Treatises" on rites, music, astronomy, the calendar, and so on; "Hereditary Houses"; and 70 chapters of "Biographies," including descriptions of foreign peoples.

A second great work, *The Book of the Han*, was written by Pan Ku (d. A.D. 92). It applied the analytical schema of Ssu-ma Ch'ien to a single dynasty, the Former Han, and established the pattern by which each dynasty wrote the history of its predecessor.

Neo-Taoism

As the Han dynasty waned, the effort to realize the Confucian ethic in the sociopolitical order became more and more difficult. Some scholars abandoned Confucianism altogether in favor of Neo-Taoism, or "mysterious learning," as it was called at the time. A few wrote commentaries on the classical Taoist texts that had been handed down from the Chou. The *Chuang Tzu* was especially popular. Other scholars, defining the natural as the pleasurable, withdrew from society to engage in witty "pure conversations." They discussed poetry and philosophy, played the lute, and drank wine. The most famous were the Seven Sages of the Bamboo Grove of the third century A.D. One sage was always accompanied by a servant carrying a jug of wine and a spade—the one for his pleasure, the other to dig his grave should he die. Another wore no clothes at home. When criticized, he replied that the cosmos was his home, and his house his clothes. "Why are you in my pants?" he asked a discomfited visitor. Still another took a boat to visit a friend on a snowy night, but on arriving at his friend's door, turned around and went home. When pressed for an explanation, he said that it had been his pleasure to go, and that when the impulse died, it was his pleasure to return. This story reveals a scorn for convention coupled with an admiration for an inner spontaneity, however eccentric.

Another concern of what is called Neo-Taoism was immortality. Some sought it in dietary restrictions and Yoga-like meditation; some, in sexual abstinence or orgies. Others, seeking elixirs to prolong life, dabbled

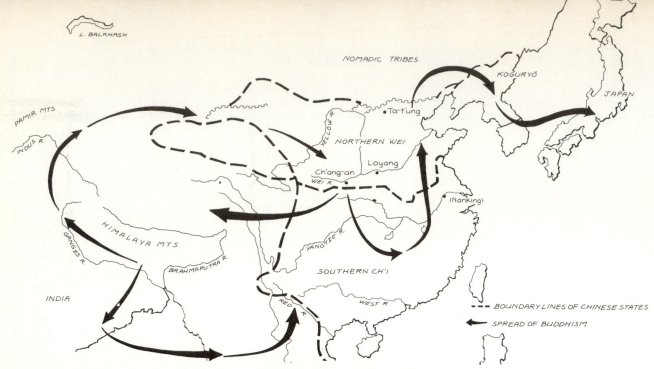

MAP 8-3   THE SPREAD OF BUDDHISM AND CHINESE STATES IN A.D. 500
Buddhism originated in a Himalayan state in northwest India. It spread in one wave south in India and on to southeast Asia as far as Java. But it also spread into northwest India, Afghanistan, Central Asia, and then to China, Korea, and Japan.

in alchemy, and although no magical elixir was ever found, the schools of alchemy to which the search gave rise are credited with the discovery of medicines, dyes, glazes, and gunpowder.

Meanwhile among the common people, there arose popular religious cults that, because they included the Taoist classics among their sacred texts, are also called Neo-Taoist. Like most folk religions, these contained an amalgam of beliefs, practices, and superstitions. They had a pantheon of gods and immortals and taught that the good or evil done in this life would be recompensed in the innumerable heavens or hells of an afterlife. This movement or cult had priests, shamans who practiced faith healing, seers, and sorceresses. For a time, it also had a hierarchical church organization, but this was smashed when the Yellow Turbans and Five Pecks of Rice rebellions were suppressed at the end of the second century A.D. Local Taoist temples and monasteries, however, continued down to modern times. With many Buddhist accretions, they furnished the religious beliefs of the bulk of the Chinese population. Even today, these sects continue in Taiwan and in Chinese communities in Southeast Asia.

Buddhism

Central Asian missionaries, following the trade routes east, brought Buddhism to China in the first century A.D. It was at first viewed as a new Taoist sect. This is not surprising because early translators used Taoist terms to render Buddhist concepts. *Nirvana*, for example, was translated as "not doing" (*wu-wei*). In the second century B.C., this led to the very Chinese view that Lao-tzu had gone to India, where the Buddha had become his disciple, and that Buddhism was the Indian form of Taoism.

Then, as the Han sociopolitical order collapsed in the third century A.D., Buddhism spread rapidly—parallel, perhaps, to the spread of Christianity at the end of the Roman Empire. Though an alien religion in China, Buddhism had some advantages over Taoism:

1. It was a doctrine of personal salvation, offering several routes to that goal;
2. It contained high standards of personal ethics;
3. It had systematic philosophies, and during its early centuries in China, it continued to receive inspiration from India;
4. It drew on the Indian tradition of meditative practices and psychologies, which were the most sophisticated in the world.

By the fifth century A.D., Buddhism had spread over all of China. Occasionally it was persecuted by Taoist emperors—in the north between A.D. 446 and 452, and again between A.D. 574 and 578. But most courts supported Buddhism. The "Bodhisattva Emperor" Wu of the southern Liang dynasty three times gave himself to a monastery and had to be ransomed back by his disgusted courtiers. Temples and monasteries abounded in both the north and the south. There were communities of women as well as of men. Chinese artists produced Buddhist painting and sculpture of surpassing beauty, and thousands of monk-scholars labored to translate sutras and philosophical treatises. Chinese monks went on pilgrimages to India. The record left by Fa Hsien, who traveled to India overland and back by sea between A.D. 399 and 413, became a prime source of Indian history. The T'ang monk Hsuan Tsang went to India from 629 until 645. Several centuries later, his pilgrimage was novelized as *Monkey*, in which faith, magic, and adventure are joined together.

A comparison of Indian and Chinese Buddhism highlights some distinctive features of its spread. Buddhism in India had begun as a reform movement. For-

get speculative philosophies and elaborate metaphysics, taught the Buddha, and concentrate on simple truths: Life is suffering, the cause of suffering is desire, death does not end the endless cycle of birth and rebirth; only the attainment of *nirvana* releases one from the "wheel of karma." Thus, in this most otherworldly of the world's religions, all of the cosmic drama of salvation is compressed into the single figure of the Buddha meditating under the Bodhi tree. Over the centuries, however, Indian Buddhism developed contending philosophies and conflicting sects and, having become virtually indistinguishable from Hinduism, was reabsorbed after A.D. 1000.

In China, there were a number of sects with different doctrinal positions. But the Chinese genius was more syncretic. It took in the sutras and meditative practices of early Buddhism. It took in the Mahayana philosophies that depicted a succession of Buddhas, cosmic and historical, past and future, all embodying a

The Peach Blossom Spring

The poet Ta'o Ch'ien wrote in A.D. 380 of a lost village without taxes and untouched by the barbarian invasions and wars of the post-Han era. The simplicity and naturalness of his utopian vision was in accord, perhaps, with certain strains of Neo-Taoist thought. It struck a chord in the hearts of Chinese, and then Koreans and Japanese, inspiring a spate of paintings, poetry, and essays.

During the T'ai-yuan period of the Ch'in dynasty a fisherman of Wuling once rowed upstream, unmindful of the distance he had gone, when he suddenly came to a grove of peach trees in bloom. For several hundred paces on both banks of the stream there was no other kind of tree. The wild flowers growing under them were fresh and lovely, and fallen petals covered the ground—it made a great impression on the fisherman. He went on for a way with the idea of finding out how far the grove extended. It came to an end at the foot of a mountain whence issued the spring that supplied the stream. There was a small opening in the mountain and it seemed as though light was coming through it. The fisherman left his boat and entered the cave, which at first was extremely narrow, barely admitting his body; after a few dozen steps it suddenly opened out onto a broad and level plain where well-built houses were surrounded by rich fields and pretty ponds. Mulberry, bamboo and other trees and plants grew there, and criss-cross paths skirted the fields. The sounds of cocks crowing and dogs barking could be heard from one courtyard to the next. Men and women were coming and going about their work in the fields. The clothes they wore were like those of ordinary people. Old men and boys were carefree and happy.

When they caught sight of the fisherman, they asked in surprise how he had got there. The fisherman told the whole story, and was invited to go to their house, where he was served wine while they killed a chicken for a feast. When the other villagers heard about the fisherman's arrival they all came to pay him a visit. They told him that their ancestors had fled the disorders of Ch'in times and, having taken refuge here with wives and children and neighbors, had never ventured out again; consequently they had lost all contact with the outside world. They asked what the present ruling dynasty was, for they had never heard of the Han, let alone the Wei and the Chin. They sighed unhappily as the fisherman enumerated the dynasties one by one and recounted the vicissitudes of each. The visitors all asked him to come to their houses in turn, and at every house he had wine and food. He stayed several days. As he was about to go away, the people said, "There's no need to mention our existence to outsiders."

After the fisherman had gone out and recovered his boat, he carefully marked the route. On reaching the city, he reported what he had found to the magistrate, who at once sent a man to follow him back to the place. They proceeded according to the marks he had made, but went astray and were unable to find the cave again. ❑

J. R. Hightower, *The Poetry of Ta'o Ch'ien* (Oxford: Clarendon Press, 1970), pp. 254–255.

single ultimate reality. It also took in the sutras and practices of Buddhist devotional sects. And then, in the T'ien-t'ai sect, the Chinese joined together these various elements as different levels of a single truth. So the monastic routine of a T'ien-tai monk would include reading sutras, sitting in meditation, and also practicing devotional exercises.

Socially, too, Buddhism adapted to China. Ancestor worship demanded that there be heirs to perform the sacrifices. In the absence of progeny, ancestors might become "hungry ghosts." Hence, the first son would marry and have a family, and the second son would become a monk. The practice also arose of holding Buddhist masses for dead ancestors. Still another difference between China and India was the more extensive regulation of Buddhism by the state in China. Just as Buddhism was not to injure the family, so Buddhism was not to reduce the taxes paid on land. As a result, limits were placed on the number of monasteries, nunneries, and monastic lands, and the requirement was made that the state must give its permission before men or women abandoned the world to enter a religious establishment. The regulations, to be sure, were not always enforced.

China's First Empire in World Perspective

Were there world-historical forces that produced at roughly the same time great empires in China, India, and the Mediterranean? Certainly there were similar features in these empires. All three came after revolutions in thought. The Han built on Chou thought (it would be hard to imagine the Han bureaucratic state without Legalism and Confucianism), just as Rome used Greek thought, and the Mauryan empire Buddhist thought. In each case, the conception of universal political authority sustaining the empire derived from the earlier philosophies. All three were Iron Age empires, joining their respective technologies with new organizational techniques to create superb military forces.

The differences between the empires are also instructive. Contrast China and Rome. In China, the pervasive culture and the only higher culture in the area was Chinese—even before the first empire arose. This culture had been slowly spreading for centuries and in places outran the polity. Even the culture of the Ch'u peoples south of the Yangtse, though viewed as "semibarbarian" by northern Chinese, was only a variation of the higher culture. Thus cultural unity had paved the way for political unity.

In contrast, the polyglot empire of Rome encompassed quite different peoples, including older civilizations. The genius of Rome, in fact, was to fashion a government and a set of laws that could contain its cultural diversity. Geographically, however, Rome had an easier time of it, for the Mediterranean offered direct access to most parts of the empire and was a thoroughfare for commerce. China, in contrast, was largely landlocked. It was composed of several regional economic units, each of which, located in a segment of a river basin separated from the others by natural barriers, looked inward. It was the genius of Chinese administration to overcome physical and spatial barriers and to integrate the country politically.

A second difference was that government in Han China was more orderly, more complex, and more competent. Government officials controlled the military almost until the end, whereas in latter Roman times, emperor after emperor was set on the throne by the army or the Praetorian Guard. The Roman empire was in no sense a dynasty.

A third salient difference was in the military dynamics of the two empires. Roman power was built over centuries. Its history is the story of one state growing in power by steady increments, imposing its will on others, and gradually piecing together an empire. Not until the early centuries A.D. was the whole empire in place. China, in contrast, remained a multistate system right up to 232 B.C. and then, in a sudden surge, was unified by one state in eleven years. The greater dynamism of China during the first empire can be explained, perhaps, by the greater military challenge it faced across its northern border: an immense Hunnish nomadic empire. Since the threat was more serious than that posed to Rome by any European barbarian enemy, the Chinese response was correspondingly massive.

Suggested Readings

D. BODDE, *China's First Unifier* (1938). A study of the Ch'in unification of China, viewed through the Legalist philosopher and statesman Li Ssu.

T. T. CH'U, *Law and Society in Traditional China* (1961). Treats the sweep of Chinese history from 202 B.C. to 1911.

T. T. CH'U, *Han Social Structure* (1972).

J. K. FAIRBANK, E. O. REISCHAUER, AND A. M. CRAIG, *East Asia: Tradition and Transformation* (1989). A widely read single-volume history covering China, Japan, and other countries in East Asia from antiquity to recent times.

J. GERNET, *A History of Chinese Civilization* (1982). An excellent survey of Chinese history.

C. Y. HSU, *Ancient China in Transition* (1965). On social mobility during the Eastern Chou era.

dom that held sway in the Zambe
and southern Africa, this age is m
diffusion of Bantu-speaking peopl
can subcontinent. In west and nor
increased commercial traffic, as w

The gradual penetration of Isla
regions was one prominent featur
undergoing even more pronounce
was also entering ever more prom
seas, which reached across the In
much of Africa was firmly caught
community.

In Iran, a state religion of Zoro
dialect assisted political centraliza
Sasanids further strengthened thei
on industries like silk and glass. F
the Byzantine Empire, and the gro
rule that they proved easy prey to
Persian language and culture deve
ever, and ultimately greatly enrich
bilities of Islamic civilization.

In India, the incursions of Hun
end the great classical era of Gup
caste system solidify, establishing
regulating the groups with whom
Hindu tradition gained the genera
led to the ascendancy of regional
1000 in north India brought an Is
before. By 1500, Islam was an im
well as its religious and political r

In the seventh century, the new
next two centuries took a variety
last in a line of monotheistic prop
immorality, and injustice in his ho
legiance, his Arab successors carr
tine realms, all of the Persian emp
within a century. Muslim traders a
culture well beyond the political b
ples in later centuries expanded tl
though split into factions, the Isla
than division and never experienc
dom suffered. Only the Mongol ir
shattering disruption to political o

Western Europe survived barba
under Carolingian and Merovingia
(768–814). Toward the end of thi
aggressor itself in Byzantium and
tween Western rulers and the Chr
became the docile friend of kings
were and Orthodox Christianity in
emperor and pope struggled with
the twelfth and thirteenth centurie
ending any possibility of a unified
lection of nation-states that remai
tive.

C. Y. Hsu, *Han Agriculture* (1980). A study of the agrarian economy of China during the Han dynasty.

M. Loewe, *Everyday Life in Early Imperial China* (1968). A social history of the Han dynasty.

J. Needham, *The Shorter Science and Civilization in China* (1978). An abridgement of the multivolume work on the same subject with the same title—minus *Shorter*—by the same author.

C. Schirokauer, *A Brief History of Chinese and Japanese Civilizations* (1978). A standard text, especially good on literature and art.

M. Sullivan, *The Arts of China* (1967). An excellent survey history of Chinese art.

D. Twitchett and M. Loewe (eds.), *The Ch'in and Han Empires*, 221 B.C.–A.D. 220 (1986). (Volume 1 of *The Cambridge History of China.*)

Z. S. Wang, *Han Civilization* (1982).

B. Watson, *Ssu-ma Ch'ien, Grand Historian of China* (1958). A study of China's premier historian.

B. Watson, *Records of the Grand Historian of China*, vols. 1 and 2 (1961). Selections from the *Shih-chi* by Ssu-ma Ch'ien.

B. Watson, *The Columbia Book of Chinese Poetry* (1986).

A. Wright, *Buddhism in Chinese History* (1959).

Y. S. Yu, *Trade and Expansion in Han China* (1967). A study of economic relations between the Chinese and their neighbors.

Consol
Interac
World

B ETWEEN 5
and cultural
Surviving
nese dynast
attained a tr
rope. In ach
cianism, wh
the technolc
dense popul
base for cor
period from
1227. Kubla
ism that had
absorb the f
looking.
In Japan,
and sixth ce
early China,
cratic status
took in the
roughly the
culture and
served a sep
partly becau
in Europe di
("those who
they were re
periods—ro
aside the Ch
military rule
Land and Ze
In Africa,
rica and Egy
notable was
enth century
major powe
the proud, c
of note was

	EUROPE	NEAR EAST/INDIA
500 A.D.	*511* Death of Clovis, Frankish ruler of Gaul *529* Benedict of Nursia founds Benedictine Order *590–604* Pontificate of Gregory I, "the Great" *768–814* Charles the Great (Charlemagne)	*529* Justinian's *Corpus Juris Civilis* *531–579* Reign of Chosroes Anosharvian *ca. 570–632* Muhammad *622* The Hijra *616–657* Reign of Harsha; neo-Gupta revival in India *651* Death of last Sasanid ruler *ca. 710* first Muslim invasion of India *661–750* Umayyad dynasty; continued expansion of Islam *680* Death of Al-Husayn at Karbala; second civil war begins *730* Iconoclastic Controversy, Byzantine Empire *750–1258* Abbasid Dynasty *786–809* Caliph Harun Al-Rashid reigned
800	*ca. 800–1000* Invasions of England and the Carolingian Empire (Vikings, Magyars, and Muslims) *843* Treaty of Verdun divides Carolingian Empire *910* Cluny Monastery founded *1019–1054* Yaroslav the Wise reigned; peak of Kievan Russia *1054* Schism between Latin and Greek churches *1066* Norman Conquest of England *1073–1085* Investiture Controversy *1096–1270* The Crusades	*800–1200* Period of "feudal" overlordship in India *900–1100* Golden Age of Muslim learning *945–1055* Buyid rule in Baghdad *994–1186* Ghaznavid rule in N.W. India, Afghanistan, and Iran *1055–1194* Seljuk rule in Baghdad *1071* Seljuk Turks capture Jerusalem *1081–1118* Byzantine Emperor Alexius Comnenus reigns *ca. 1000–1300* Turko-Afghan raids into India
1100	*1154–1158* Frederick Barbarosa invades Italy *1182–1226* St. Francis of Assisi *1198–1216* Pontificate of Innocent III *ca. 1100–1300* Growth of trade and towns *1215* Magna Carta granted *ca. 1225–1274* St. Thomas Aquinas *1265–1321* Dante Alighieri	*1174–1193* Saladin reigns *1192* Muslim conquerors end Buddhism in India *1206–1526* Delhi Sultanate in India; Indian culture divided into Hindu and Muslim *ca. 1220* Mongol invasions of Iran, Iraq, Syria, India *1258* Hulagu Khan, Mongol leader conquers Baghdad *1260–1335* Il-Khans rule Iran
1500	*1337* Hundred Years War begins *ca. 1340–1400* Geoffrey Chaucer *1347–1349* The Black Death *1375–1527* The Italian Renaissance *1485* The Battle of Bosworth Field; accession of Henry Tudor to the throne of England *1492* Columbus' first voyage to the New World	*1366–1405* Timur (Tamerlane) reigns *1405–1494* Timurids rule in Transoxiana and Iran *1453* Byzantine Empire falls to the Ottoman Turks, with capture of Constantinople

EAST ASIA	AFRICA	THE AMERICAS
589–618 Sui dynasty reunifies China *607* Japan begins embassies to China *618–907* T'ang dynasty in China *701–762* Li Po, T'ang poet *710–784* Nara court, Japan's first permanent capital *712* Records of Ancient Matters, in Japan *713–756* Emperor Hsuan Tsung reigns in China *755* An Lu-shan Rebellion in China *794–1185* Heian (Kyoto) court in Japan	*ca. 500* States of Takrur and Ghana founded *ca. 500–700* Political and commercial ascendancy of Aksum (Ethiopia) *ca. 600–1500* Extensive slave trade from Sub-Saharan Africa to Mediterranean *ca. 700–800* Ghanians begin to supply gold to Mediterranean *ca. 700–900* States of Gao and Kanem *ca. 800* Appearance of the Kanuri people around Lake Chad	*ca. 600–1000* Tiahuanaco civilization in South America
856–1086 Fujiwara dominate at Heian court *960–1279* Sung dynasty in China *ca. 1000* Pillow Book by Sei Shōnagon and Tale of Genji by Murasaki Shikibu *1037–1101* Su Tung-p'o, Sung poet	*ca. 800–900* Decline of Aksum *ca. 900–1100* Kingdom of Ghana; capital city, Kumbi Saleh *ca. 1000–1100* Islam penetrates sub-Sahara Africa *1000–1500* "Great Zimbabwe" center of Bantu Kingdom in southeast Africa	*800* City of Machu Picchu, Peru *800–1000* "Time of Troubles" in MesoAmerica *ca. 900* Second Pueblo Period in American Southwest *ca. 1000–1300* Toltic Hegemony in Mexico
1130–1200 Chu Hsi, Sung philosopher *1165–1227* Genghis Khan begins Mongol empire *1185–1333* Kamakura shogunate in Japan *1274, 1281* Mongol invasions of Japan *1279–1368* Mongol (Yuan) dynasty in China	*ca. 1100–1897* Kingdom of Benin in tropical rain forest region *1194–1221* Kanem Empire achieves greatest expansion *1203* Kingdom of Ghana falls to Sosso people *ca. 1230–1450* Kingdom of Mali *1230–1255* King Sundiata, 1st ruler of Mali Empire; Walata and Timbuktu become centers of trade and culture	*ca. 1000–1500* Inca civilization in South America *1100* Third Pueblo Period in American Southwest
1336–1467 Ashikaga shogunate in Kyoto *1368–1644* Ming dynasty in China *1405–1433* Voyages of Cheng Ho to India and Africa *1467–1568* Warring States Era in Japan *1472–1529* Wang Yang-ming, Ming philosopher	*1307–1332* Mansa Musa, greatest king of Mali; 1324, makes pilgrimage to Mecca *1490s* Europeans establish trading posts on west African coast; slave trade begins *mid-1400s* Decline of Mali Empire; creation of Songhai Empire *1468* Sonni Ali captures Timbuktu *1476–1507* King Mai Ali of Bornu reigns; Bornu becomes most powerful state in central Sudan *1493–1528* Songhai ruler, Askia Muhammed reigns; consolidates Songhai Empire; 1497, makes pilgrimage to Mecca	*ca. 1325* Aztecs arrive in Valley of Mexico *1369* City of Tenochtitlan founded on island in Lake Tezcoco

A rice-paddy scene south of the Yangtze. A farmer and his wife use their legs and feet to work the square-pallet chain pump. At left a boy drives a large water buffalo to turn a larger water-pumping device. Boy in the background fishes. [Bradly Smith/Laurie Platt Winfrey Inc.]

9 Imperial China (589–1368)

If Chinese dynasties from the late sixth to the mid-fourteenth centuries were given numbers like those of ancient Egypt, the Sui and T'ang dynasties would be called the Second Empire; the Sung, the Third; and the Yuan, the Fourth. This would be unfortunate, as each of these dynasties has a distinct personality. The T'ang (618–907) is everyone's favorite dynasty: open, cosmopolitan, expansionist, exuberant, and creative. It was the example of T'ang China that decisively influenced the formation of states and the high cultures in Japan, Korea, and Vietnam. Poetry during the T'ang reached a peak never attained in China before and never equaled since. The Sung (960–1279) rivaled the T'ang in the arts; it was China's great age of painting and was the most significant period for philosophy since the Chou, when Chinese philosophy began. Although not militarily strong, the Sung dynasty also witnessed an important commercial revolution. The Yuan (1279–1368) was a short dynasty of rule by Mongols during which China became the most important unit in the largest empire the world had yet seen.

The Reestablishment of Empire: The Sui (589–618) and T'ang (618–907) Dynasties

In the period corresponding to the European early middle ages, the most notable feature of Chinese history was the reunification of China, the recreation of a centralized bureaucratic empire consciously modeled on the earlier Han dynasty (206 B.C.–A.D. 220). The process of reunification, as usual, began in the north. The first steps were taken by the Northern Wei (386–534), the most enduring of the northern Sino-Turkic states. It moved its court south to Loyang, made Chinese the language of the court, and adopted Chinese

A Sui Dynasty A.D. *589–618 sculpture of the historical Buddha. [Fogg Art Museum, Harvard University.]*

dress and surnames. It also used the leverage of its nomadic cavalry to impose a new land tax, mobilizing resources for state use. The Northern Wei was followed by several short-lived kingdoms. Because the emperors, the officials, and the military commanders of these kingdoms all came from the same stratum of aristocratic families, the social distance between them was small, and the throne was often usurped.

The Sui Dynasty

The general of mixed Chinese-Turkic ancestry, Sui Wen-ti, who came to power in 581 and began the Sui dynasty (589–618) was no exception to this rule. But he displayed great talent, unified the north, restored the tax base, reestablished a centralized bureaucratic government, and went on to conquer south China and unify the country. During his reign, all went well. Huge palaces were built in his Wei valley capital. The Great Wall was rebuilt. The Grand Canal was constructed, linking the Yellow and Yangtze rivers. This canal enabled the northern conquerors to tap the wealth of central China. Peace was maintained with the Turkic tribes along China's northern borders. Eastern Turkic khans (chiefs) were sent Chinese princesses as brides.

The early years of the Second Sui emperor were also constructive, but then, Chinese attempts to meddle in steppe politics led to hostilities and wars. The hardships and loss of Chinese lives in campaigns against Korea and along China's northern border produced rising discontent. Natural disasters occurred. The court became bankrupt and demoralized. Rebellions broke out, and once again, there was a free-for-all among the armies of aristocratic military commanders. The winner, and the founder of the T'ang dynasty, was a relative of the Sui empress and a Sino-barbarian aristocrat of the same social background as those who had ruled before him.

Chinese historians often compare the short Sui dynasty with that of the Ch'in (256–206 B.C.). Each brought all of China under a single government after centuries of disunity. Each did too much, fell, and was replaced by a long dynasty. The T'ang built on the foundations that had been laid by the Sui, just as the Han had built on those of the Ch'in.

The T'ang Dynasty

The first T'ang emperor took over the Sui capital, renamed it Ch'ang-an, and made it his own. Within a decade or so, the T'ang dynasty had extended its authority over all of China; frugality was practiced in government; tax revenues were adequate to government needs; and Chinese armies had begun the campaigns that would push Chinese borders out further than ever before. Confucian scholars were employed at the court, Buddhist temples and monasteries flourished, and peace and order prevailed in the land. The years from 624 to 755 were the good years of the dynasty.

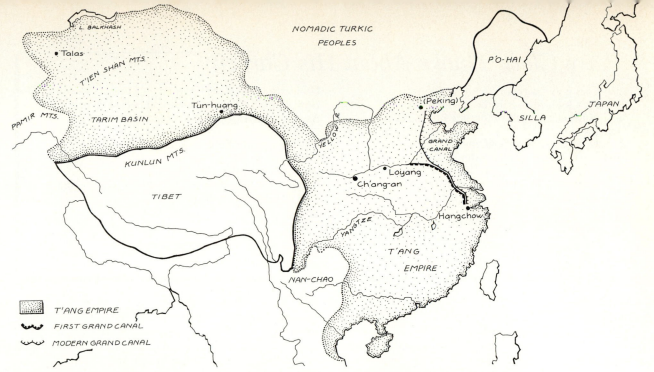

MAP 9-1   THE T'ANG EMPIRE AT ITS PEAK DURING THE EIGHTH CEN-
TURY   *The T'ang Expansion into Central Asia reopened trade routes to the Middle
East and Europe. Students from P'o-Hai, Silla (Korea) and Japan studied in the T'ang
capital of Ch'ang-an, and then returned, carrying with them T'ang books and technology.*

GOVERNMENT. The first T'ang emperor had been
a provincial governor under the Sui before he became
a rebel general. Many of those whom he appointed to
posts in the new T'ang administration were former Sui
officials who had served with him. In building the new
administration, he and his successors had to reconcile
two conflicting sets of interests. On the one hand, the
emperor wanted a bureaucratic government in which
authority was centralized in his own person. On the
other hand, he had to make concessions to the aristocrats—the dominant elements in Chinese society since
the late Han—who staffed his government and continued to dominate early T'ang society.

The degree to which political authority was centralized was apparent in the formal organization of the
bureaucracy, at right.

At the highest level were three organs: Military Affairs, the Censorate, and the Council of State. Military
Affairs supervised the T'ang armies, with the emperor,
in effect, the commander-in-chief. The Censorate had
watchdog functions: It reported instances of misgov-
ernment directly to the emperor and could also remon-
strate with the emperor when his behavior was improper. The Council of State was the most important
body. It met daily with the emperor and was made up
of the heads of the Secretariat, which drafted policies;
the Chancellery, which reviewed them; and State Af-

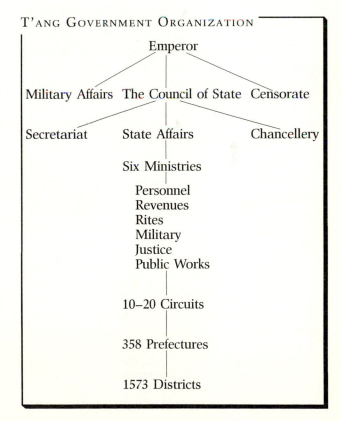

T'ANG GOVERNMENT ORGANIZATION

Emperor

Military Affairs   The Council of State   Censorate

Secretariat   State Affairs   Chancellery

Six Ministries

Personnel
Revenues
Rites
Military
Justice
Public Works

10–20 Circuits

358 Prefectures

1573 Districts

A Petty Clerk Thinks About His Career

I'm not so poor at reports and decisions—
Why can't I get ahead in the government?
The rating officials are determined to make life hard.
All they do is try to expose my faults.
Everything, I guess, is a matter of Fate;
Still, I'll try the exam again this year.
A blind boy aiming at the eye of a sparrow
Might just accidentally manage a hit.

In vain I slaved to understand the Three Histories;

Uselessly I pored over the Five Classics.
Until I'm old I'll go on checking census figures;
As in the past, a petty clerk scribbling in tax ledgers;
When I ask the Book of Changes it says there's trouble ahead;
All my life is ruled by evil stars.
If only I could be like the tree at the river's edge
Every year turning green again! ❑

Cold Mountains: 100 Poems by Han-shan, trans. by B. Watson (New York, Grove Press, 1962), pp. 37, 48.

---

fairs, which carried them out. Beneath State Affairs were the Six Ministries, which continued as the core of the central government down to the twentieth century; beneath these were the several levels of local administration.

Concessions to the interests of the aristocratic families were embodied in the tax system. All land was declared to be the property of the emperor, and was then redistributed to able-bodied cultivators, who paid taxes in labor and grain. Since all able-bodied adult males received an equal allotment of land (women and children got less), the land tax system was called the "Equal Field System." But the system was not egalitarian. Aristocrats enjoyed special exemptions and grants of "rank" and "office" lands that, in effect, confirmed their estate holdings.

Aristocrats were also favored in the recruiting of officials. Most officials were either recommended for posts or received posts because their fathers had been high officials. They were drawn almost exclusively from the aristocracy, at first from the northwestern aristocratic families that had supported the dynasty from the start, and then, in time, from the aristocracies of other areas. Only a tiny per cent were recruited by examinations. Those who passed the examinations had the highest prestige and were more likely to have brilliant careers. But as only well-to-do families could afford the years of study needed to master the Confucian classics and pass the rigorous examinations, even the examination bureaucrats were usually the able among the noble. Entrance to government schools at Ch'ang-an and the secondary capital at Loyang was restricted to the sons of nobles and officials.

THE EMPRESS WU. Women of the inner court also continued to play a role in government. For example, Wu Chao (626—CA. 706), a young concubine of the strong second emperor, had so entranced his weak heir by her charms that when he succeeded to the throne, she was recalled from the nunnery to which all the former wives of deceased emperors were routinely consigned and was installed at the court. She poisoned or otherwise removed her rivals and became his empress. She also murdered or exiled the statesmen who opposed her growing influence. When the emperor suffered a stroke in 660, she completely dominated the court. After his death in 683, she ruled for seven years as regent and then, deposing her son, became emperor herself, the only woman in Chinese history to hold the title. She moved the court to Loyang in her native area and proclaimed a new dynasty. A fervent Buddhist with an interest in magic, she saw herself as the incarnation of the Buddha Maitreya and built temples throughout the land. She patronized the White Horse Monastery, appointing one of her favorites as its abbot. Her sexual appetites were said to have been prodigious. She ruled China until 705, when at the age of eighty she lost her hold and was deposed.

After Empress Wu, no woman would ever become emperor again; yet, remarkably enough, her machinations do not appear to have seriously weakened the court. So highly centralized was power during these early years of the dynasty that the ill effects of her intrigues could be absorbed without provinces' breaking away or military commanders' becoming autonomous. In fact, a by-product of her struggle for power may have been a stronger central government, for, to overcome the old northwest China aristocrats, she turned not to members of her family but to the products of the examination system and to a group known as the Scholars of the North Gate. This policy broadened the base of government by bringing in aristocrats from other regions of China. The dynamism of a young dynasty may also explain why her rule coincided with the maximal geographical expansion of T'ang military power.

THE CH'ANG-AN OF EMPEROR HSUAN-TSUNG. Only a few years after Empress Wu was deposed—years filled with tawdry intrigues—Hsuan-tsung came to the throne. In reaction to Empress Wu, he appointed special government commissions headed by distinguished aristocrats to superintend the reform of government finances. Examination bureaucrats lost ground during his reign. The Grand Canal was repaired and extended. A new census extended the tax rolls. Wealth and prosperity returned to the court. Hsuan-tsung's reign (713–756) was also the most brilliant culturally. Years later, while in exile, Li Po wrote a poem in which memories of youthful exhilaration merged with the glory of the capital of Hsuan-tsung:

Long ago, among the flowers and willows,
We sat drinking together at Ch'ang-an.
The Five Barons and Seven Grandees were of our
　company,
But when some wild stroke was afoot
It was we who led it, yet boisterous though we were
In the arts and graces of life we could hold our own
With any dandy in the town—
In the days when there was youth in your cheeks
And I was still not old.
We galloped to the brothels, cracking our gilded whips,
We sent in our writings to the palace of the Unicorn,
Girls sang to us and danced hour by hour on tortoise-
　shell mats.
We thought, you and I, that it would be always like
　this.
How should we know the grasses would stir and dust
　rise on the wind?
Suddenly foreign horsemen were at the Hsien-ku Pass
Just when the blossom at the palace of Ch'in was
　opening on the sunny boughs. . . .[1]

Ch'ang-an was an imperial city, an administrative city that lived on taxes. It was designed to exhibit the power of the emperor and the majesty of his court. At the far north of the city, the palace faced south. The placement was traditional: Confucius, speaking of Shun, said he had only "to hold himself in a respectful posture and to face due south." In front of the palace was a complex of government offices, from which an imposing 500-foot-wide avenue led to the main southern gate. The city was laid out on a north-south, east-west grid, which one T'ang poet compared to a chessboard. Each block of the city was administered as a ward with interior streets and gates that were locked at night. Enclosed by great walls, the area of the city was 30 square miles. Its population was 1,960,186—half within the walls, the other half in suburbs—the

largest city in the world. (The population of China in the year 750 was about 50 million—less than 5 per cent of its population today.) Ch'ang-an was also a trade center from which caravans set out across central Asia. Merchants from India, Iran, Syria, and Arabia hawked the wares of the Near East and all of Asia in its two government-controlled markets.

THE T'ANG EMPIRE. A Chinese dynasty is like an accordion, first expanding into the territories of its barbarian neighbors and then contracting back to its original densely populated core area. The principal threats to the T'ang state were from Tibetans in the west, Turks in the northwest and north, and Khitan Mongols in Manchuria.

Toward these peoples, the T'ang employed a four-tier policy. When nothing else would work, the T'ang sent armies. But armies were expensive, and using them against nomads was like sweeping back an ocean tide with a broom. A victory might dissolve a confederation, but a decade or two later, it would reappear under a new tribal leader. For example, in 630, T'ang armies defeated the eastern Turks' in 648, they took the Tarim basin, opening trade routes to western Asia for almost a century; and in 657, they defeated the western Turks and extended Chinese influence across the Pamir Mountains to petty states near Samarkand. By 698, however, the Turks were back invading northeast China, and between 711 and 736, they were in control of all of the steppe from the Oxus River to China's northern frontier.

Chinese efforts against Tibet were much the same. From 670, Tibet expanded and threatened China. In 679, it was defeated. In 714, it rose again; wars were fought from 727 to 729; and a settlement was reached in 730. But wars broke out anew. In 752, Tibet entered an alliance with the state of Nan Chao in Yunnan. In 763, Tibetan forces captured and looted Ch'ang-an. They were driven out, but the point is that even during the good years of the T'ang, no final victory was possible.

The human costs of sending armies far afield was detailed in a poem by Li Po:

Last year we were fighting at the source of the Sang-
　kan;
This year we are fighting on the Onion River road.
We have washed our swords in the surf of Parthian
　seas;
We have pastured our horses among the snows of the
　T'ien Shan,
The King's armies have grown grey and old
Fighting ten thousand leagues away from home.
The Huns have no trade but battle and carnage;
They have no fields or ploughlands,

---

[1] Arthur Waley, *The Poetry and Career of Li Po* (New York: Macmillan, 1950), pp. 87–88.

A bearded "barbarian" groom tends the charger of the second T'ang emperor (reigned 626–649). This stone relief was found on the Emperor's tomb. Note the stirrup, a Chinese invention of the fourth century A.D. [University of Pennsylvania Museum.]

But only wastes where white bones lie among yellow sands.
Where the House of Ch'in built the great wall that was to keep away the Tartars.
There, in its turn, the House of Han lit beacons of war.
The beacons are always alight, fighting and marching never stop.
Men die in the field, slashing sword to sword;
The horses of the conquered neigh piteously to Heaven.
Crows and hawks peck for human guts,
Carry them in their beaks and hang them on the branches of withered trees.
Captains and soldiers are smeared on the bushes and grass;

The General schemed in vain.
Know therefore that the sword is a cursed thing
Which the wise man uses only if he must.[2]

The second tier of Chinese defenses was to use nomads against other nomads. The critical development for the T'ang was the rise to power of the Uighur Turks. From 744 to 840, the Uighurs controlled Central Asia and were staunch allies of the T'ang. Without their support, the T'ang dynasty would not have survived as long as it did.

A third tier was the defenses along China's borders, including the Great Wall. At mid-dynasty, whole fron-

[2]Waley, pp. 34–35.

tier provinces in the north and the northwest were put under military commanders who, in time, came to control the provinces' civil governments as well. The bulk of the T'ang military was in such frontier commands. At times, they were as much a threat to the T'ang as to the enemy.

Diplomacy is always cheaper than war. The fourth line of defense was to bring the potential enemy into the empire as a tributary. The T'ang defined the position of "tributary" with great elasticity. It included principalities truly dependent on China; central Asian states conquered by China; enemy states such as Tibet or the Thai state of Nan Chao in Yunnan when they were not actually at war with China; the Korean state Silla, which had unified the peninsula with T'ang aid but had then fought T'ang armies to a standstill when they attempted to impose Chinese hegemony; and wholly independent states such as Japan. All sent embassies bearing gifts to the T'ang court, which housed and fed them and sent costly gifts in return.

For some countries, these embassies had a special significance. As the only "developed nation" in eastern Asia, China was a model for countries still in the throes of forming a state. An embassy gained access to the entire range of T'ang culture and technology: its philosophy and writing, governmental and land systems, Buddhism and the arts, architecture and medicine. In 640 there were eight thousand Koreans, mostly students, in Ch'ang-an. Never again would China exert such an influence, for never again would its neighbors be at that formative stage of development.

REBELLION AND DECLINE. From the mid-eighth century, signs of decline began to appear. China's frontiers started to contract. Tribes in Manchuria became unruly. Tibetans threatened China's western border. In 751, an overextended T'ang army led by a Korean general was defeated by Arabs near Samarkand in western Asia, shutting down China's caravan trade with the West for more than five centuries. And then, in 755, a Sogdian general, An Lu-shan, who commanded three Chinese provinces on the northeastern frontier, led his 160,000 troops in a rebellion that swept across north China, capturing Loyang and then Ch'ang-an. The emperor fled to Szechwan.

The event contained an element of romance. Ten years earlier, the emperor Hsuan-tsung had taken a young woman, Yang Kuei Fei, from the harem of his son (he gave his son another in exchange). So infatuated was he that he neglected not only the other "three

Pottery figures of court ladies playing polo, seventh century, T'ang dynasty. After the T'ang, for over a millennium, participation in athletic contests was considered unfeminine. [W.R. Nelson Trust.]

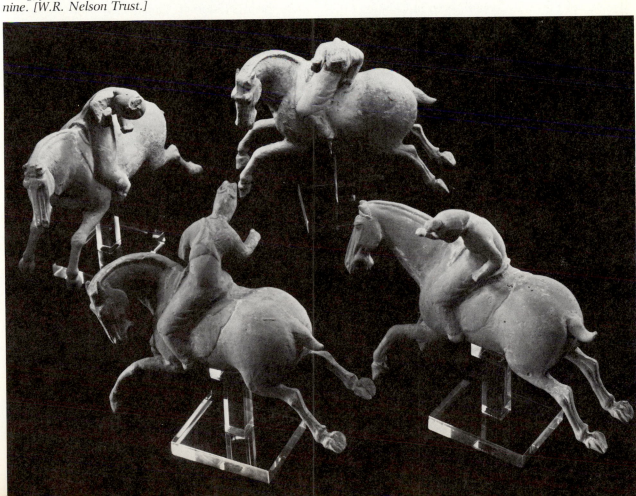

thousand beauties of his inner chambers" but the business of government as well. For a while his neglect did not matter because he had an able chief minister, but when the minister died, he appointed his concubine's second cousin to the post, initiating a train of events that resulted in rebellion. En route to Szechwan, his soldiers, blaming Yang Kuei Fei for their plight, strangled her. The event was later immortalized in a poem that described her "snow-white skin," "flowery face," and "moth eyebrows," as well as the "eternal sorrow" of the emperor, who, in fact, was seventy-two at the time.

After a decade of wars and much devastation, a new emperor restored the dynasty with the help of the Uighur Turks—who looted Ch'ang-an as a part of their reward. The recovery and the century of relative peace and prosperity that followed illustrate the resilience of T'ang institutions. China was smaller, but military governors maintained the diminished frontiers. Provincial governors were more autonomous, but taxes were still sent to the capital. Occasional rebellions were suppressed by imperial armies, sometimes led by eunuchs. Most of the emperors were weak, but three times strong emperors appeared, and reforms were carried out. Edwin O. Reischauer, after translating the diary of a Japanese monk who studied in China during the early ninth century, commented that the "picture of government in operation" that emerges "is amazing for the ninth century, even in China":

The remarkable degree of centralized control still existing, the meticulous attention to written instructions from higher authorities, and the tremendous amount of paper work involved in even the smallest matters of administration are all the more striking just because this was a period of dynastic decline.[3]

Of the reforms of this era, none was more important than that of the land system. The official census, on which land allotments and taxes were based, showed a drop in population from fifty-three million before the An Lu-shan rebellion to seventeen million afterward. Unable to put people back on the registers, the government abandoned the equal field system and replaced it with a tax collected twice a year. The new system, begun in 780, lasted until the sixteenth century. Under it, a fixed quota of taxes was levied on each province. After the An Lu-shan rebellion, government revenues from salt and iron surpassed those from land.

During the second half of the ninth century, the government weakened further. Most provinces were autonomous, often under military commanders, and re-

sisted central control. Wars were fought with the state of Nan Chao in the southwest. Bandits appeared. Droughts led to peasant uprisings. By the 880s, warlords had carved all of China into independent kingdoms, and in 907, the T'ang dynasty fell. But within half a century, a new dynasty arose. The fall of the T'ang did not lead to centuries of division of the kind that had followed the Han. Something had changed within China.

T'ANG CULTURE. The creativity of the T'ang period arose from the juxtaposition and interaction of cosmopolitan, medieval Buddhist and secular elements. The rise of each of these cultural spheres was rooted in the wealth and the social order of the recreated empire.

T'ang culture was cosmopolitan not just because of its broad contacts with other cultures and peoples but because of its openness to them. Buddhist pilgrims to India and a flow of Indian art and philosophies to China were a part of it. The voluptuousness of Indian painting and sculpture, for example, helped shape the T'ang representation of the bodhisattva. Commercial contacts were widespread. Foreign goods were vended in Ch'ang-an marketplaces. Communities of central and west Asians were established in the capital, and Arab and Iranian quarters grew up in the seaports of southeast China. Merchants brought their religions with them. Nestorian Christianity, Zoroastrianism, Manichaeism, Judaism, and Islam entered China at this time. Most would be swept away in the persecutions of the ninth century, but Islam and a few small pockets of Judaism survived until the twentieth century.

Central Asian music and musical instruments entered along the trade routes and became so popular as almost to displace the native tradition. T'ang ladies adopted foreign hairstyles. Foreign dramas and acrobatic performances by west Asians could be seen in the streets of the capital. Even among the pottery figurines customarily placed in tombs, there were representations of west Asian traders and central Asian grooms—along with those of horses, camels, and court ladies that today are so avidly sought by collectors and museums around the world. And in T'ang poetry, too, what was foreign was not shunned but judged on its own merits, or even presented as exotically attractive. Of a gallant of Ch'ang-an, Li Po wrote:

A young man of Five Barrows suburb east of the
    Golden Market,
Silver saddle and white horse cross through wind of
    spring.
When fallen flowers are trampled all under, where is it
    he will roam?

[3]E. O. Reischauer, *Ennin's Travels in T'ang China* (New York: Ronald Press, 1955), p. 7.

With a laugh he enters the tavern of a lovely Turkish wench.[4]

Later in the dynasty, another poet wrote of service on the frontier:

A Tartar horn tugs at the north wind,
Thistle Gate shines whiter than the stream.
The sky swallows the road to Kokonor.
On the Great Wall, a thousand miles of moonlight.[5]

The T'ang dynasty, though slightly less an age of faith than the preceding Six Dynasties, was the golden age of Buddhism in China nonetheless. Patronized by emperors and aristocrats, the Buddhist establishment acquired vast landholdings and great wealth. Temples and monasteries were constructed throughout China. To gain even an inkling of the beauty and sophistication of the temple architecture, the wooden sculpture, or the paintings on the temple walls, one must see Hōryūji or the ancient temples of Nara in Japan, for little of note has survived in China. The single exception is the Caves of the Thousand Buddhas at Tunhuang in China's far northwest, which were sealed during the eleventh century for protection from Tibetan raiders and were not rediscovered until the start of the twentieth century. They were found to contain stone sculptures, Buddhist frescoes, and thousands of manuscripts in Chinese and central Asian languages.

Only during the T'ang did China have a "church" establishment that was at all comparable to that of medieval Europe, and even then it was subservient to the far stronger T'ang state. Buddhist wealth and learning brought with it secular functions. T'ang temples served as schools, inns, or even bathhouses. They lent money. Priests performed funerals and dispensed medicines. Occasionally, the state moved to recapture the revenues monopolized by temples. The severest persecution, which marked a turn in the fortunes of Buddhism in China, occurred in 841–845, when an ardent Taoist emperor confiscated millions of acres of tax-exempt lands, put back on the tax registers 260,000 monks and nuns, and destroyed 4,600 monasteries and 40,000 shrines.

During the early T'ang, the principal Buddhist sect was the T'ien-t'ai, but after the mid-ninth century suppression, other sects came to the fore:

1. One devotional sect focused on Maitreya, a Buddha of the future, who will appear and create a par-

This pottery figurine from a mid-T'ang dynasty tomb depicts a Bactrian camel from west-central Asia. [Asian Art Museum of San Francisco.]

adise on earth. Maitreya (Mi Lo in Chinese and Miroku in Japanese) was a cosmic messiah, not a human figure. The messianic teachings of the sect often furnished the ideology for popular uprisings and rebellions like the White Lotus, which claimed that it was renewing the world in anticipation of Maitreya's coming.

2. Another devotional or faith sect worshipped the Amitabha (A Mi T'o in Chinese, Amida in Japanese) Buddha, the Lord of the Western Paradise or Pure Land. This sect taught that in the early centuries after the death of the historical Buddha, his teachings had been transmitted properly and people could obtain enlightenment by their own efforts, but that at present, the Buddha's teachings had become so distorted that only by reliance on Amitabha could humans obtain salvation. All who called on Amitabha with a pure heart and perfect faith would be saved. Developing a congregational form of worship, this sect became the largest in China and deeply influenced Chinese popular religion.

[4]S. Owen, *The Great Age of Chinese Poetry: The High T'ang* (New Haven, Conn.: Yale University Press, 1980), p. 130.

[5]A. C. Graham, *Poems of the Late T'ang* (Baltimore: Penguin, 1965), p. 9.

you step forward?" The psychological state of the adept attempting to deal with these problems is compared to that of "a rat pursued into a blocked pipe" or "a mosquito biting an iron ball." The discipline of meditation, combined with a Zen view of nature, profoundly influenced the arts in China, and subsequently in Korea and Japan as well.

A third characteristic of T'ang culture was the reappearance within it of secular scholarship and letters. The reestablishment of centralized bureaucratic government stimulated the tradition of learning that had been partially interrupted after the fall of the Han dynasty in the third century A.D. There emerged a scholarly-bureaucratic complex. Most men of letters, whether historians, essayists, artists, or poets, were

The T'ang poet Li Po, as imagined by the great Sung artist Liang K'ai [Tokyo National Museum.]

Stone sculpture of a Bodhisattva reflecting the full-bodied, almost voluptuous, T'ang ideal of beauty. [Bettman Archive.]

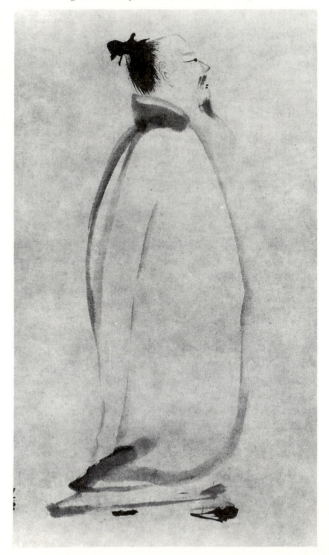

3. A third sect, and the most influential among the Chinese elites, was known in China, where it began, as *Ch'an* and is better known in the West by its Japanese name, *Zen.* Zen had no cosmic Buddhas. It taught that the historical Buddha was only a man and exhorted each person to attain enlightenment by his or her own efforts. Although its monks were often the most learned in China, Zen was anti-intellectual in its emphasis on direct intuition into one's own Buddha-nature. Enlightenment was to be obtained by a regimen of physical labor and meditation. To jolt the monk into enlightenment—after he had been readied by long hours of meditation—some Zen sects used little problems not answerable by normal ratiocination: "What was your face before you were conceived?" "If all things return to the One, what does the One return to?" "From the top of a hundred-foot pole, how do

Poems by Li Po

THE RIVER MERCHANT'S WIFE:
A LETTER

While my hair was still cut straight across my
   forehead
I played about the front gate, pulling flowers.
You came by on bamboo stilts, playing horse,
You walked about my seat, playing with blue plums.
And we went on living in the village of Chokan:
Two small people, without dislike or suspicion.

At fourteen I married My Lord you.
I never laughed, being bashful.
Lowering my head, I looked at the wall.
Called to, a thousand times, I never looked back.

At fifteen I stopped scowling,
I desired my dust to be mingled with yours
Forever and forever and forever.
Why should I climb the look out?

At sixteen you departed,
You went into far Ku-to-yen, by the river of swirling
   eddies,
And you have been gone five months.
The monkeys make sorrowful noise overhead.

You dragged your feet when you went out.
By the gate now, the moss is grown, the different
   mosses,
Too deep to clear them away!
The leaves fall early this autumn, in wind.
The paired butterflies are already yellow with
   August
Over the grass in the West garden;
They hurt me. I grow older.
If you are coming down through the narrows of the
   river Kiang,
Please let me know beforehand,
And I will come out to meet you,   ❑
                As far as Cho-fu-Sa.

Ezra Pound, Personae (New York: New Directions 1926), pp. 130–131.

also officials, and most high-ranking officials painted or wrote poems. An anthology of T'ang poetry compiled during the Ming period contained 48,900 poems by almost 2,300 authors. This secular stream of T'ang culture was not ideologically anti-Buddhist. Officials were often privately sympathetic to Buddhism. But as men involved in the affairs of government, officials became increasingly this-worldly in their values.

Court historians of the T'ang revived the Han practice of writing an official history of the previous dynasty. For the first time, scholars wrote comprehensive institutional histories and regional and local gazetteers. They compiled dictionaries and wrote commentaries on the Confucian classics. Other scholars wrote ghost stories or tales of adventure, using the literary language. (Buddhist sermons, in contrast, were often written in the vernacular.) More paintings were Buddhist than secular, but Chinese landscape painting had its origins during the T'ang. But nowhere was the growth of a secular culture more evident than in poetry, the greatest achievement of T'ang letters.

Whether Li Po (701–762) can be called wholly secular is questionable. He might better be called Taoist. But he clearly was not Buddhist. Born in Szechwan, he was exceptional among T'ang poets in never having sat for the civil service examinations, though he briefly held an official post at Ch'ang-an, given in recognition of his poetry. Large and muscular, he was a swordsman and a carouser. Of the twenty thousand poems he is said to have composed, eighteen hundred have survived, and a fair number have titles like "Bring on the Wine" or "Drinking Alone in the Moonlight." According to legend, he drowned while drunkenly attempting to embrace the reflection of the moon in a lake. His poetry is clear, powerful, passionate, and always sensitive to beauty. It also contains a sense of fantasy, as when he climbed a mountain and saw a star-goddess, "stepping in emptiness, pacing pure ether, her rainbow robes trailed broad sashes." Li Po, nearer to heaven than to earth, looked down below where

Far and wide Tartar troops were speeding,
And flowing blood mired the wild grasses
Where wolves and jackals all wore officials' caps.[6]

Life is brief and the universe is large, but this view did not lead Li Po to renounce the world. His Taoism was not of the quietistic strain close to Buddhism. Rather, he exulted, identifying with the primal flux of *yin* and *yang*:

I'll wrap this Mighty Mudball of a world all
   up in a bag
And be wild and free like Chaos itself![7]

[6] Owen, p. 134.
[7] Owen, p. 125.

Tu Fu (712–770), an equally famous T'ang poet, was from a literary family. He failed the metropolitan examination at the age of twenty-three and spent years in wandering and poverty. At thirty-nine, he received an official appointment after presenting his poetry to the court. Four years later, he was appointed to a military post. He fell into rebel hands during the An Lu-shan rebellion, escaped, and was reappointed to a civil post. But he was then dismissed and suffered further hardships. His poetry is less lyrical and more allusive than Li Po's. It also reflects more compassion for human suffering: for the mother whose sons have been conscripted and sent to war; for brothers scattered by war; for his own family, to whom he returned after having been given up for dead. Like Li Po, he felt that humans are short-lived and that nature endures. Visiting the ruins of the palace of the second T'ang emperor, he saw "Grey rats scuttling over ancient tiles" and "in its shadowed chambers ghost fires green." "Its lovely ladies are the brown soil" and only "tomb horses of stone remain." But his response to this sad scene was to

Sing wildly, let the tears cover your open hands.
Then go every onward and on the road of your travels,
Meet none who prolong their fated years.[8]

His response was unlike that of Li Po. It was close to Stoicism but it was equally un-Buddhist.

The Transition to Late Imperial China: The Sung Dynasty (960–1279)

Most traditional Chinese history was written in terms of the dynastic cycle, and for good reason: the pattern of rise and fall, of expansion and contraction, within each dynasty cannot be denied. Certainly, the Sung can be viewed from this perspective. It reunified China in 960, establishing its capital at Kaifeng on the Yellow River. Mobilizing its resources effectively, it ruled for 170 years. This period is called the Northern Sung. Then it weakened. In 1127, it lost the north, but continued to rule the south for another 150 years from a new capital at Hangchow in east central China. The Southern Sung fell before the Mongol onslaught in 1279.

But there is more to Chinese history than the inner logic of the dynastic cycle. Longer-term changes that cut across dynastic lines were ultimately more important. One such set of changes began during the late T'ang period and continued on into the Sung period,

[8]Owen, pp. 223–224.

MAP 9-2 *During the Northern Sung the Mongol Liao dynasty ruled only the extreme northern edge of China. But during the Southern Sung, half of China was ruled by the Manchurian Chin dynasty.*

THE NORTHERN SUNG AND LIAO EMPIRES—CA. A.D. 1050

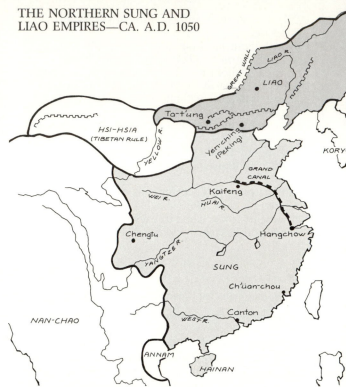

THE SOUTHERN SUNG AND CHIN EMPIRES—CA. A.D. 1150

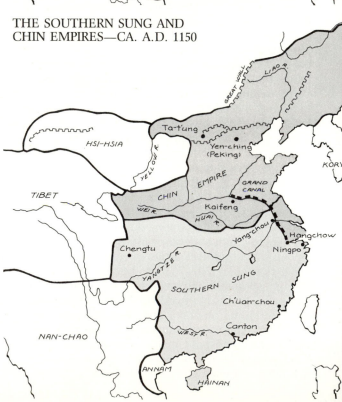

affecting its economy, society, state, and culture. Taken together, these changes help to explain why China after the T'ang did not relapse into centuries of disunity as it had after the Han, and why China would never again experience more than brief intervals of disunity. In this section, we will skip over emperors and empresses, eunuchs and generals, and focus instead on more fundamental transformations.

The Agricultural Revolution of the Sung: From Serfs to Free Farmers

Local society in China during the Sui and the T'ang periods had been dominated by landed aristocrats. The tillers of their lands were little more than serfs. Labor service was the heaviest tax, and whether performed on the office or rank lands of aristocrats or on other government lands, it created conditions of social subordination.

The aristocracy weakened, however, over the course of the T'ang and after its fall. Estates became smaller as they were divided among male children at each change of generation. Drawn to the capital, the aristocracy became less a landed, and more a metropolitan, elite. And after the fall of the T'ang, the aristocratic estates were often seized by warlords. As the aristocracy declined, the claims of those who worked the soil grew stronger, aided by changes in the land and tax systems. With the collapse of the equal field system (described earlier), farmers gained the right to buy and sell land. The ownership of land as private property gave the cultivators greater independence. They could now move about as they pleased. Taxes paid in grain gave way during the Sung to taxes in money. The commutation of the labor tax to a money tax gave the farmers more control over their own time. And conscription, the cruelest and heaviest labor tax of all, disappeared as the conscript armies of the early and middle T'ang gave way to professional armies.

Changes in technology also benefited the cultivator. New strains of an early-ripening rice permitted double cropping. In the Yangtze region, extensive water-control projects were carried out, and more fertilizers were used. New commercial crops were developed. Tea, which had been introduced during the Six Dynasties as a medicine and had been drunk by monks during the T'ang, became widely cultivated, and cotton also became a common crop. Because taxes paid in money tended to become fixed, much of the increased productivity accrued to the cultivator. Of course, not all benefited equally; there were landlords and landless tenants as well as independent small farmers.

The disappearance of the aristocrats also increased the authority of the district magistrate, who no longer had to contend with the aristocrats' interference in local affairs. The Sung magistrate became the sole representative of imperial authority in local society. But there were too many villages in his district for him to be involved regularly in their internal governance. As long as taxes were paid and order was maintained, the affairs of the village were left in the hands of the village elites. So the Sung farmer enjoyed not only a rising income and more freedom, but also a substantial measure of self-government.

One other development that began during the Sung—and became vastly more important later on—was the appearance of a scholar-gentry class. The typical gentry family contained at least one member who had passed the provincial civil-service examination and lived in the district seats or market towns. Socially and culturally, these gentry were closer to magistrates than to villagers. But they usually owned land in the villages and thus shared some interests with the local landholders. Though much less powerful than the former aristocrats, they took a hand in local affairs and at times functioned as a buffer between the village and the magistrate's office.

The Commercial Revolution of the Sung

Stimulated by changes in the countryside, and contributing to them as well, were demographic shifts, innovative technologies, the growth of cities, the spread of money, and rising trade. These developments varied by region, but overall the Sung economy reached a new level of prosperity.

THE EMERGENCE OF THE YANGTZE BASIN. Till late in the T'ang, north China had been the most populous and productive region. But from the late ninth century, the center of gravity of China's population, agricultural production, and culture shifted to the lower and eastern Yangtze region. Between 800 and 1100, the population of the region tripled as China's total population increased to about 100 million. Its rice paddies yielded more per acre than the wheat or millet fields of the north, making rice the tax base of the empire. Its wealth led to the establishment of so many schools that regional quotas for the examination system were set by the government to prevent the Yangtze region from dominating all of China. The Northern Sung capital itself was kept in the north for strategic reasons, but it was situated at Kaifeng, further east than Loyang, at the point where the Grand Canal, which carried tax rice from the south, joined the Yellow River.

NEW TECHNOLOGY. During the Northern Sung, there developed in north China a coal and iron-smelting industry that provided China with better tools and weapons. Using coke and bellows to heat furnaces to the temperatures required for carbonized steel, it was the most advanced in the world.

Printing began in China with the use of carved seals. The earliest woodblock texts, mostly on Buddhist subjects, appeared in the seventh century. By the tenth century, a complete edition of the classics had been published, and by the mid-Sung, books printed with movable type were fairly common.

Other advances during the Sung were the abacus, the use of gunpowder in grenades and projectiles, and improvements in textiles and porcelains.

THE RISE OF A MONEY ECONOMY. Exchange during the T'ang had been based on silk. Coins had been issued, but their circulation was limited. During the Northern Sung, large amounts of copper cash were coined, but the demand rose more rapidly than the supply. Coins were made with holes in the center, and 1,000 on a string constituted the usual unit for large transactions. Beginning in the Southern Sung, silver was minted to complement copper cash, ten times as much silver in the late twelfth century as in the early eleventh century. Letters of credit were used by merchants, and various kinds of paper money also were issued. The penetration of money into the village economy was such that by 1065, tax receipts paid in money had risen to thirty-eight million strings of cash—in comparison with a mere two million in mid-T'ang.

TRADE. The demand for money was spurred by the growth of trade. One may distinguish between trade within economic regions, trade between regions, and foreign trade. During the T'ang, most cities had been administrative, supported by taxes from the countryside. Official salaries and government expenditures created a demand for services and commercial products, making the cities into islands of commerce in a noncommercial hinterland. In most of China's seven or eight economic regions, this pattern continued during the Sung, but in the capital, and especially in the economically advanced regions along the Yangtze, cities became the hubs of regional commercial networks, with district seats or market towns serving as secondary centers for the local markets beneath them.

As this transition occurred, cities with more than 100,000 households almost quadrupled in number. The Northern Sung capital at Kaifeng is recorded as having had 260,000 households—probably more than one million inhabitants—and the Southern Sung capital at Hangchow had 391,000 households. Compare these to the capitals of backward Europe: London during the Northern Sung had a population of about 18,000; Rome during the Southern Sung had 35,000; and Paris even a century later had fewer than 60,000.

Furthermore, these Sung capitals, unlike Ch'ang-an with its walled wards that closed at night, were open within and spread beyond their outer walls. As in Chinese cities today, their main avenues were lined with shops. Merchant guilds replaced government officials as the managers of marketplaces. Growing wealth also led to a taste for luxury and an increasingly secular lifestyle. Restaurants, theaters, wine shops, and brothels abounded. Entertainment quarters with fortune tellers, jugglers, chess masters, acrobats, and puppeteers sprang up. These had not been absent from Ch'ang-an, but the numbers increased, and now they catered to traders and rich merchants as well as to officials.

Trade between regions during the Sung was mainly limited to luxury goods like silk, lacquerware, medicinal herbs and porcelains. Only where transport was cheap—along rivers, canals, or the coast—was interregional trade in bulk commodities economical, and even then, it was usually carried on only to make up for specific shortages.

Foreign trade also reached new heights during the Sung. In the north, Chinese traders bought horses from Tibetan, Turkic, and Mongol border states, and sold silks and tea. Along the coast, Chinese merchants took over the port trade that during the T'ang had been in the hands of Korean, Arab, and Irani merchants. The new hegemony of Chinese merchants was based on improved ships using both sail and oars and equipped with watertight compartments and better rudders. Chinese captains, navigating with the aid of the compass, came to dominate the sea routes from Japan in the north to Sumatra in the south. The content of the overseas trade reflected China's advanced economy: It imported raw materials and exported finished goods. Porcelains were sent to Southeast Asia, and then were carried by Arab ships to medieval trading centers on the Persian Gulf and down the coast of East Africa as far south as Zanzibar.

Government: From Aristocracy to Autocracy

The millennium of late imperial China after the T'ang is often spoken of as the age of autocracy or as China's age of absolute monarchy. Earlier emperors, as we have noted, were often personally powerful, but beginning with the Sung, changes occurred that made it easier for emperors to be autocrats.

One change was that Sung emperors had direct personal control over more offices than had their T'ang predecessors. For example, the Board of Academicians, an advisory office, presented the emperor with policy options separate from those presented by the Secretariat-Chancellery. The emperor could thus use the one against the other and prevent bureaucrats in the Secretariat-Chancellery from dominating the government.

A second change was that the central government was better funded than it had been previously. Revenues in 1100 were three times the peak revenues of the

T'ang, partly because of the growth of population and agricultural wealth, and partly because of the establishment of government monopolies on salt, wine, and tea, and because of various duties, fees, and taxes levied on domestic and foreign trade. During the Northern Sung, these commercial revenues rivaled the land tax; during the Southern Sung, they surpassed it. Confucian officials would continue to stress the primacy of land, but throughout late imperial China, commerce became a vital source of revenues.

A third change that strengthened the emperors was the disappearance of the aristocracy. During the T'ang, the emperor had come from the same Sino-Turkic aristocracy of northwest China as most of his principal ministers, and he was, essentially, the organ of a state that ruled on behalf of this aristocracy. Aristocrats monopolized the high posts of government. They married among themselves and with the imperial family. They called the emperor the Son of Heaven, but they knew he was one of them. During the Sung, in contrast, government officials were commoners, mostly products of the examination system. They were separated from the emperor by an enormous social gulf and saw him as a person apart.

The Sung examination system was larger than that of the T'ang, if smaller than in later dynasties. Whereas only 10 per cent of officials had been recruited by examination during the T'ang, the Sung figure rose to over 50 per cent, and these included the most important officials. The first examination was given at regional centers. The applicant took the examination in a walled cubicle under close supervision. To ensure impartiality, his answers were recopied by clerks and his name was replaced by a number before his examination was sent to the officials who would grade it. Of those who sat for the examination, only a tiny percentage passed. The second hurdle was the metropolitan examination at the national capital, where the precautions were equally elaborate. Only one in five, or about two hundred a year, passed. The average successful applicant was in his mid-thirties. The final hurdle was the palace examination, which rejected a few and assigned a ranking to the others.

To pass the examinations, the candidate had to memorize the Confucian classics, interpret selected passages, write in the literary style, compose poems on themes given by the examiners, and propose solutions to contemporary problems in terms of Confucian philosophy. The quality of the officials produced by the Sung system was impressive. A parallel might be drawn with nineteenth-century Britain, where students in the classics at Oxford and Cambridge went on to become generalist bureaucrats. The Chinese examination system that flourished during the Sung continued, with some interruptions, into the twentieth century. The continuity of Chinese government during this millennium rested on the examination elite, with its common culture and values.

The social base for this examination meritocracy was triangular, consisting of land, education, and office. Without wealth, the years of study needed to pass the examinations could not be afforded. Such an education was far beyond the means of a poor peasant or a city-dweller. Without education, official position was out of reach. And without office, family wealth could not be preserved. The Chinese pattern of inheritance, as noted earlier, led to the division of property at each change of generation. Some families were successful in passing the civil service examinations for several generations running. More often, the sons of well-to-do officials did not study as hard as those with bare means. The adage "shirt sleeves to shirt sleeves in three generations" is not inappropriate to the Sung and later dynasties. As China had an extended-family or clan system, a wealthy official often provided education for the bright children of poor relations.

How the merchants related to this system is less clear. They had wealth but were despised by scholar-officials as grubby profitseekers and were barred from taking the examinations. Some merchants avoided the system altogether—a thorough education in the Confucian classics did little to fit a merchant's son for a career in commerce. Others bought land for status and security, and their sons or grandsons became eligible. Similarly, a small peasant might build up his holdings, become a landlord, and educate a son or grandson. The system was steeply hierarchical, but it was not closed nor did it produce a new, self-perpetuating aristocracy.

Sung Culture

As society and government changed during the T'ang–Sung transition, so too did culture. Sung culture retained some of the energy of the T'ang while becoming more intensely and perhaps more narrowly Chinese. The preconditions for the rich Sung culture were a rising economy, an increase in the number of schools and higher literacy, and the spread of printing. Sung culture was less aristocratic, less cosmopolitan, and more closely associated with the officials and the scholar-gentry, who were both its practitioners and its patrons. It also was less Buddhist than had been the T'ang. Only the Zen (Ch'an) sect kept its vitality, and many Confucians were outspokenly anti-Buddhist and anti-Taoist. In sum, the secular culture of officials that had been a sidestream in the T'ang broadened and became the mainstream during the Sung.

Chinese consider the Sung dynasty as the peak of their traditional culture. It was, for example, China's greatest age of pottery and porcelains. High-firing techniques were developed, and kilns were established in every area. There was a rich variety of beautiful

An early Sung dynasty winepot. [The Metropolitan Museum of Art, Gift of Mrs. Samuel T. Peters, 1926.]

Grotto Academy, and his writings were widely distributed. Before the end of the Sung, his interpretation of Confucianism had become the orthodoxy required for the civil service examinations, and it remained so until the twentieth century.

If we search in other traditions for comparable figures, we might pick Saint Thomas Aquinas (1224–1274) of medieval Europe or the Islamic theologian al-Ghazali (1058–1111), each of whom produced a new synthesis or worldview that lasted for centuries. Aquinas joined Aristotle and Latin theology just as Chu Hsi joined Confucian philosophy and Buddhism. Because Chu Hsi used terms such as the "great ultimate" and because he emphasized a Zen-like meditation called "quiet sitting," some contemporary critics said his Neo-Confucian philosophy was a Buddhist wolf in the clothing of a Confucian sheep. This was unfair. Whereas Aquinas would make philosophy serve religion, Chu Hsi made religion serve philosophy. In his hands, the great ultimate (also known as principle or *li*) lost its otherworldly character and became a constituent of all things in the universe. We might better characterize it as innerworldly.

Later critics often argued that Chu Hsi's teachings encouraged metaphysical speculation at the expense of practical ethics. Chu Hsi's followers replied that, on the contrary, his teachings gave practical ethics a sys-

The Sung dynasty philosopher Chu Hsi (1130–1200), whose Neo-Confucian ideas remained central down to the twentieth century. [National Palace Museum, Taiwan, R.O.C.]

glazes. The shapes were restrained and harmonious. Sung pottery, like nothing produced in the world before, made ceramics a major art form in East Asia. It was also an age of great historians. Ssu-ma Kuang (1019–1086) wrote *A Comprehensive Mirror for Aid in Government*, which treated not a single dynasty but all Chinese history. His work was more sophisticated than previous histories in that it included a discussion of documentary sources and an explanation of why he chose to rely on one source rather than another. The greatest achievements of the Sung, however, were in philosophy, poetry, and painting.

PHILOSOPHY. The Sung was second only to the Chou as a creative age in philosophy. A series of original thinkers culminated in the towering figure of Chu Hsi (1130–1200). Chu Hsi studied Taoism and Buddhism in his youth, along with Confucianism. A brilliant student, he passed the metropolitan examination at the age of eighteen. During his thirties, he focused attention on Confucianism, deepening and making more systematic its social and political ethics by joining to it certain Buddhist metaphysical elements. Chu Hsi became famous as a teacher at the White Deer tematic underpinning and positively contributed to individual moral responsibility. What was discovered within by Neo-Confucian quiet sitting was just those positive ethical truths enunciated by Confucius over a thousand years earlier. The new metaphysics did not change the Confucian social philosophy.

Because Chu Hsi's teachings became a new orthodoxy that lasted until the twentieth century, historians argue, probably correctly, that it was one source of stability in late imperial China. Like the examination system, the imperial institution, the scholar-gentry class, and the land system, it contributed to continuity and impeded change. Some scholars go further and say that the emergence of the Chu Hsi orthodoxy stifled intellectual creativity. This probably is an overstatement. The need to interpret Confucianism in terms of Chu Hsi's ideas on the civil service examinations did channelize Chinese thought, but there were always other contending schools.

POETRY. Sung poets were in awe of those of the T'ang. Yet Sung poets were also among China's best. A Japanese authority on Chinese literature, wrote:

Su Tung-p'o Imagined on a Wet Day, Wearing a Rain Hat and Clogs

After Su's death, a disciple wrote:

When with tall hat and firm baton he stood in
   council,
The crowds were awed at the dignity of the
   statesman in him.
But when in cloth cap he strolled with cane and
   sandals,
He greeted little children with gentle smiles.

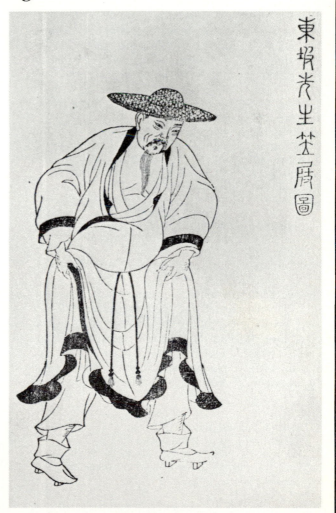

Kōjirō Yoshikawa, *An Introduction to Sung Poetry*, trans. by Burton Watson (Cambridge: Harvard University Press, Harvard-Yenching Institute Monograph Series, 1967), pp. 65 oppos., 122.

T'ang poetry could be likened to wine, and Sung poetry to tea. Wine has great power to stimulate, but one cannot drink it constantly. Tea is less stimulating, bringing to the drinker a quieter pleasure, but one which can be enjoyed more continuously.[9]

The most famous poet of the Northern Sung was Su Tung-p'o (1037–1101), a man who participated in the full range of the culture of his age: He was a painter and calligrapher, particularly knowledgeable about inks; he practiced Zen and wrote commentaries on the Confucian classics; he superintended engineering projects; and he was a connoisseur of cooking and wine. His life was shaped by politics. He was a conservative, believing in a limited role for government and social control through morality. (The other faction in the Sung bureaucracy was the reformers, who stressed law and an expanded government role.)

Passing the metropolitan examination, Su rose through a succession of posts to become the governor of a province—a position of immense power. While considering death sentences, which could not be carried over into the new year, he wrote:

New Year's Eve—you'd think I could go home early
But official business keeps me.
I hold the brush and face them with tears:
Pitiful convicts in chains,
Little men who tried to fill their bellies,
Fell into the law's net, don't understand disgrace.
And I? In love with a meager stipend
I hold on to my job and miss the chance to retire.
Do not ask who is foolish or wise;
All of us alike scheme for a meal.
The ancients would have freed them a while at
    New Year's—
Would I dare do likewise? I am silent with shame.[10]

Eight years later, when the reformers came to power, Su himself was arrested and spent one hundred days in prison, awaiting execution on a charge of slandering the emperor. Instead, he was released and sent into exile. He wrote, "Out the gate, I do a dance, wind blows in my face; our galloping horses race along as magpies cheer."[11] Arriving at his place of exile, he reflected:

Between heaven and earth I live,
One ant on a giant grindstone,
Trying in my petty way to walk to the right
While the turning of the mill wheel takes me
    endlessly left.

Though I go the way of benevolence and duty,
I can't escape from hunger and cold. . . .[12]

But exile was soon turned to art. He farmed a plot of land at the "eastern slope" from which he took his literary name, Tung-p'o. Of his work there, he wrote:

A good farmer hates to wear out the land;
I'm lucky this plot was ten years fallow.
It's too soon to count on mulberries;
My best bet is a crop of wheat.
I planted seed and within the month
Dirt on the rows was showing green.
An old farmer warned me,
Don't let seedlings shoot up too fast!
If you want plenty of dumpling flour
Turn a cow or sheep in here to graze.
Good advice—I bowed my thanks;
I won't forget you when my belly's full.[13]

After 1086, the conservatives regained control of the government, and Su resumed his official career. In 1094, another shift occurred and Su was again sent into exile on the distant southern island of Hainan. After still another shift, Su was on his way back to the capital when he died in 1101.

PAINTING. In the West, penmanship and painting are quite separate, one merely a skill and the other esteemed as an art. In China, calligraphy and painting were equally appreciated and were seen as related. A scholar spent his life with brush in hand. The same qualities of line, balance, and strength needed for calligraphy carried over to painting. Chinese calligraphy is immensely pleasing even to the untutored Western eye, and it is not difficult to distinguish between the elegant strokes of Hui-neng, the last emperor of the Northern Sung, and the powerful brushwork of the Zen monk Chang Chi-chih.

Sung painting was various—of birds or flowers; of fish or insects; of horses, monkeys, or water buffalo; of scholars, emperors, Buddhas, or Taoist immortals. But its crowning achievement was landscapes. These are quite different from Western paintings. Each stroke of the brush on silk or paper was final. Mistakes could not be covered up. Each element of a painting is presented in its most pleasing aspect; the painting is not constrained by single-point perspective. Paintings have no single source of illumination with light and shadow, but an overall diffusion of light. Space is an integral part of the painting. A typical painting might have craggy rocks or twisted pine trees in the foreground, then mist or clouds or rain to create distance,

[9] Kōjirō Yoshikawa, An Introduction to Sung Poetry, trans. by Burton Watson (Cambridge: Harvard University Press, Harvard-Yenching Institute Monograph Series, 1967), p. 37.

[10] Yoshikawa, p. 119.

[11] Yoshikawa, p. 117.

[12] Yoshikawa, p. 105.

[13] Yoshikawa, pp. 119–120.

Is the enlightened man depicted in this painting meditating or dozing? Zen paintings often have a touch of humorous ambiguity. Note the bold calligraphic brushwork in this Southern Sung or Yuan dynasty painting in the style of the Zen monk Shih Ko. [Tokyo National Museum.]

and in the background the outlines of mountains or cliffs fading into space. If the painting contains human figures at all, they are small in a natural universe that is very large. Chinese painting thus reflects the same world view as Chinese philosophy or poetry. The goal of the painter was to grasp the inner reality of the scene and not to be bound up in surface details.

In paintings by monks or masters of the Zen school, the presentation of an intuitive vision of an inner reality became even more pronounced. Paintings of Bodhidharma, the legendary founder of the Zen sect, are often dominated by a single powerful downstroke of the brush, defining the edge of his robe. Paintings of patriarchs tearing up sutras or sweeping dust with a broom from the mirror of the mind are almost as calligraphic as paintings of bamboo. A Northern Sung painting in the style of Shih K'o shows the figure of a monk or sage who is dozing or meditating. A Zen "broken ink" landscape might contain rocks, water, mountains, and clouds, each represented by a few explosive strokes of the brush.

China in the Mongol World Empire: The Yuan Dynasty (1279–1368)

The Mongols created the greatest empire in the history of the world. It extended from the Caspian Sea to the Pacific Ocean, from Russia, Siberia, and Korea in the north to Persia and Burma in the south. Invasion fleets were even sent to Java and Japan, though without success. Mongol rule in China is one chapter of this larger story.

The Rise of the Mongol Empire

The Mongols, a nomadic people, lived to the north of China on grasslands where they raised horses and herded sheep. They lived in felt tents called yurts—they sometimes called themselves "the people of the felt-tents." Women performed much of the work and were freer and more easygoing than women in China. Families belonged to clans, and related clans to tribes. Tribes would gather during the annual migration from the summer plains to winter pasturage. Chiefs were elected, most often from noble lineages, for their courage, military prowess, judgment, and leadership. Like Manchu or Turkic, the Mongol tongue was Altaic.

The Mongols believed in nature deities and in the sky god above all others. Sky blue was their sacred color. They communicated with their gods through religious specialists called *shamans*. They traded and warred with settled peoples on the borders of their vast domain.

The founder of the Mongol Empire, Temujin, was born in 1167, the son of a tribal chief. While he was still a child, his father was poisoned. He fled and after wandering for some years, returned to the tribe, avenged his father, and in time became chief himself. Through his wife's tribe, he became part of an alliance

The world conqueror, Genghis Khan (1167–1227). [National Palace Museum, Taiwan, R.O.C.]

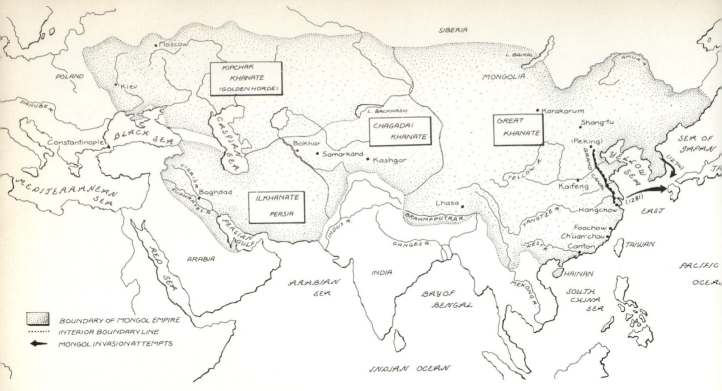

MAP 9-3   THE MONGOL EMPIRE IN THE LATE THIRTEENTH CENTURY   *Note the four khanates: the Golden Horde in Russia, the Ilkhanate in Persia, Chagadai in Central Asia, and the Great Khanate extending from Mongolia to Southern China.*

with the Ch'in empire that ruled north China. By the time he was forty, he had united all Mongol tribes and had been elected their great khan, or ruler. It is by the title *Genghis* (also spelled *Jenghiz* or *Chinggis*) *Khan* that he is known to history. Genghis possessed an extraordinary charisma, and his sons and grandsons also became wise and talented leaders. Why the Mongol tribes, almost untouched by the higher civilizations of the world, should have produced such leaders at this point in history is difficult to explain.

A second conundrum is how the Mongols, who numbered only about a million and a half, created the army that conquered vastly denser populations. Part of the answer is institutional. Genghis organized his armies into "myriads" of 10,000 troops, with decimal subdivisions of 1,000, 100, and 10. Elaborate signals were devised so that, in battle, even large units could be manipulated like the fingers of a hand. Mongol tactics were superb: units would retreat, turn, flank, and destroy their enemies. The historical record makes amply clear that Genghis' nomadic cavalry had a paralytic effect on all they encountered. Peerless horsemen, the Mongols fought with a compound bow, short enough to be used from the saddle yet more powerful than the English longbow.

They were astonishingly mobile. Each man carried his own supplies. Trailing remounts, they covered vast

distances quickly. In 1241, for example, a Mongol army had reached Hungary, Poland, and the shore of the Adriatic and was poised for a further advance into Western Europe. But when word arrived of the death of the great khan, the army turned and galloped back to Mongolia to help choose his successor.

When this army encountered walled cities, it learned the use of siege weapons from the enemies it had conquered. Chinese engineers were used in campaigns in Persia. The Mongols also used terror as a weapon. Inhabitants of cities that refused to surrender in the Near East and China were put to the sword. Large areas in north China and Szechwan were devastated and depopulated in the process of conquest. Descriptions of the Mongols by those whom they conquered dwell on their physical toughness and pitiless cruelty.

But the Mongols had strengths that went beyond the strictly military. Genghis opened his armies to recruits from the Uighur Turks, the Manchus, and other nomadic peoples. As long as they complied with the military discipline demanded of his forces, they could participate in his triumphs. In 1206, Genghis promulgated laws designed to prevent the normal wrangling and warring between tribes that would undermine his empire. Genghis also obtained thousands of pledges of personal loyalty from his followers, and he appointed these "vassals" to command his armies and staff his government. This policy gave to his forces an inner coherence that countered the divisive effect of tribal loyalties.

The Mongol conquests were all the more impressive in that, unlike the earlier Arab expansion, they lacked the unifying force of religious zeal. To be sure, at an assembly of chiefs in 1206, an influential shaman revealed that it was the sky god's will that Genghis conquer the world. Yet other unabashedly frank words attributed to Genghis may reveal a truer image of what lay behind the Mongol drive to conquest: "Man's highest joy is in victory: to conquer one's enemies, to pursue them, to deprive them of their possessions, to make their beloved weep, to ride on their horses, and to embrace their wives and daughters."[14]

Genghis divided his far-flung empire among his four sons. Trade and communications were maintained between the parts, but over several generations, each of the four khanates became independent. The khanate of Chagatai was in central Asia and remained purely nomadic. A second khanate of the Golden Horde ruled Russia from the lower Volga. The third was in Persia. The fourth, led by those who succeeded Genghis as great khans, centered first in Mongolia and then in China.

Mongol Rule in China

The standard theory used in explaining Chinese history is the dynastic cycle. A second theory explains Chinese history in terms of the interaction between the settled people of China and the nomads of the steppe. When strong states emerged in China, their wealth and population enabled them to expand militarily onto the steppe. But when China was weak, as was more often the case, the steppe peoples overran China. To review briefly:

1. During the Han dynasty (206 B.C.–A.D. 220) the most pressing problem in foreign relations was the Hsiung Nu empire to the north.
2. During the centuries that followed the Han, various nomadic peoples invaded and ruled north China.
3. The energy and institutions of these Sino-Turkic rulers of the northern dynasties shaped China's reunification during the Sui (581–618) and T'ang (618–907) dynasties. The Uighur Turks also played a major role in T'ang defense policy.
4. Northern border states became even more important during the Sung. The Northern Sung (960–1126) bought peace with payments of gold and sil-

[14]J. K. Fairbank, E. O. Reischauer, and A. M. Craig, *East Asia, Tradition and Transformation* (Boston: Houghton Mifflin, 1973), p. 164.

ver to the Liao. The South[...] all of its cultural brillian[...] tributary state of the Ch[...] panded into northern C[...]

From the very start of [...] hegemony, China was a[...] But Genghis proceede[...] leave no enemy at his b[...] Tibetan state to the northwest of Ch[...] Manchu state of Chin that ruled north China[...] forces took Peking in 1227, the year Genghis died. They went on to take Loyang and the southern reaches of the Yellow River in 1234, and all of north China by 1241. During this time, the Mongols were interested mainly in loot. Only later did Chinese advisers persuade them that more wealth could be obtained by taxation.

Kublai, a grandson of Genghis, was chosen as the great khan in 1260. In 1264, he moved his capital from Karakorum in Mongolia to Peking. It was only in 1271 that he adopted a Chinese dynastic name, the Yuan, and, as a Chinese dynasty, went to war with the Southern Sung. Once the decision was made, the Mongols swept across south China. The last Sung stronghold fell in 1279.

Kublai Khan's rule in Peking reflected the mixture of cultural elements in Mongol China. From Peking, Kublai could rule as a Chinese emperor, which would not have been possible in Karakorum. He adopted the Chinese custom of hereditary succession. He rebuilt Peking as a walled city in the Chinese style. But Peking was far to the north of any previous Chinese capital, away from centers of wealth and population; to provision it, the Grand Canal had to be extended. From Peking, Kublai could look out onto Manchuria and Mongolia and maintain ties with the other khanates. The city proper was for the Mongols. It was known to the West as *Cambulac*, "the city (*balya*) of the khan." Chinese were segregated in an adjoining walled city. The palace of the khan was designed by an Arab architect; its rooms were central Asian in style. Kublai also maintained a summer palace at Shangtu (the "Xanadu" of Samuel Taylor Coleridge's poem) in Inner Mongolia, where he could hawk and ride and hunt in Mongol style.

Early Mongol rule in north China was rapacious and exploitative, but it later shifted toward Chinese forms of government and taxation, especially in the south and at the local level. Because it was a foreign military occupation, civil administration was highly centralized. Under the emperor was a Central Secretariat, and beneath it were ten "Moving Secretariats," which became the provinces of later dynasties. These highly centralized institutions and the arbitrary style of

Kublai Khan[...] in hills at re[...]

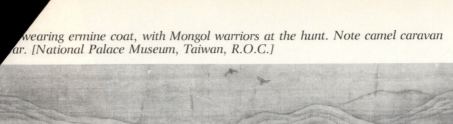

...wearing ermine coat, with Mongol warriors at the hunt. Note camel caravan ...ar. [National Palace Museum, Taiwan, R.O.C.]

Mongol decision making accelerated the trend toward absolutism that had started during the previous dynasty.

About 400,000 Mongols lived in China during the Yuan period. For such a tiny minority to control the Chinese majority, it had to stay separate. One measure was to make military service a monopoly of Mongols and their nomadic allies. Garrisons were established throughout China, with a strategic reserve on the steppe. Military officers were always regarded as more important than civil officials. A second measure was to use ethnic classifications in appointing civil officials. The highest category was the Mongols, who held the top civil and military posts. The second category included Persians, Turks, and other non-Chinese, who were given high civil posts. The third category was the northern Chinese, who included Manchus and other border peoples, and the fourth was the southern Chinese. Even when the examination system was sporadically revived after 1315, the Mongols and their allies took an easier examination; their quota was as large as that for Chinese; and they were appointed to the higher offices.

The effect of this segregated system was that most Chinese had contact only with other Chinese in low-level posts, and they did not learn Mongolian. The Mongols, concentrated in Peking or in garrisons, spoke Mongolian among themselves and usually did not bother to learn Chinese. A few exceptions wrote poetry in Chinese and painted in the Chinese style. Communication was through interpreters. When a Chinese district magistrate sent a query to the court, the ruling was made in Mongolian. (The Mongols had borrowed the alphabet of the Uighurs to transcribe their tongue.) A word-for-word translation in Chinese was written below the Mongolian and passed back down to the magistrate. As the two languages are syntactically very different, the resulting Chinese was grotesque.

Foreign Contacts and Chinese Culture

Diplomacy and trade within the greater Mongol Empire brought China into contact with other higher civilizations for the first time since the T'ang period. Persia and the Arab world were especially important. Merchants, missionaries, and diplomats voyaged from the Persian Gulf and across the Indian Ocean to seaports in south China. The Arab communities in Canton and other ports were larger than during the Sung. Camel caravans carrying silks and ceramics left Peking to pass through the central Asian oases and on to Baghdad. Although the Mongols did not favor Chinese merchants and most trade was in other hands, Chinese trade also expanded. Chinese communities became established in Tabriz, the center of trading in west Asia, and in Moscow and Novgorod. It was dur-

ing this period that knowledge of printing, gunpowder, and Chinese medicine spread to west Asia. Chinese ceramics influenced those of Persia as Chinese painting influenced Persian miniatures.

In Europe, firsthand knowledge of China was transmitted by the Venetian trader Marco Polo, who had served Kublai as an official between 1275 and 1292. His book, *A Description of the World*, was translated into most European languages. Many readers doubted that a land of such wealth and culture could exist so far from Europe, but the book excited an interest in geography. When Christopher Columbus set sail in 1492, his goal was to reach Polo's Zipangu (Japan).

Other cultural contacts were fostered by the Mongol toleration or encouragement of religion. Nestorian Christianity, spreading from Persia to Central Asia, reentered China during the Mongol era. Churches were built in the main cities. The mother of Kublai Khan was a Christian of this sect. Also, several papal missions were sent from Rome to the Mongol court. An archbishopric was established in Peking; a church was built, sermons were preached in Turkish or Mongolian, and choirboys sang hymns. Kublai sent the father and the uncle of Marco Polo with a letter to the pope asking for a hundred intelligent men acquainted with the seven arts.

Tibetan Buddhism with its magical doctrines and elaborate rites was the religion most favored by the Mongols. But Chinese Buddhism also flourished. Priests and monks of all religions were given tax exemptions. It is estimated that half a million Chinese became Buddhist monks during the Mongol century. The foreign religion that made the greatest gains was Islam, which became permanently established in central Asia and western China. Mosques were built in Peking, in the Islamic areas, and in southeastern port cities. Even Confucianism was regarded as a religion by the Mongols, its teachers being exempted from taxes. But as the scholar-gentry rarely obtained important offices, they saw the Mongol era as a time of hardship.

Despite these wide contacts with other peoples and religions, the high culture of China appears to have been influenced almost not at all—partly because China had little to learn from other areas, and partly because the centers of Chinese culture were in the south, the last area to be conquered and the area least affected by Mongol rule. Also, in reaction to the Mongol conquest, Chinese culture became conservative and turned in on itself. Scholars wrote poetry in the style of the Sung. New styles of painting developed, but the developments were from within the Chinese tradition, and the greatest Yuan paintings continued the style of the Sung. Yuan historians wrote the official history of the dynasties that preceded it. The head of the court bureau of historiography was a Mongol, but the histories produced by his Chinese staff were in the traditional mold. As the dynasty waned, unemployed scholars wrote essays expressing loyalty toward the Sung and satirizing the Mongols. Their writings were not censored: The Mongols either could not read them, did not read them, or did not care.

Marco Polo Describes the City of Hangchow

Marco Polo was a Venetian. In 1300, Venice had a population of more than 100,000 and was one of the wealthiest Mediterranean city-states. But Polo was nonetheless unprepared for what he saw in China. Commenting on Hangchow, China's capital during the Southern Sung, he first noted its size (ten or twelve times greater than that of Venice), then its many canals and bridges, its streets "paved with stones and bricks," and its location between "a lake of fresh and very clear water" and "a river of great magnitude." He spoke of "the prodigious concourse of people" frequenting its ten great marketplaces and of its "capacious warehouses . . . built of stone for the accommodation of merchants who arrive from India and other parts." He then described the life of its people:

Each of the ten market-squares is surrounded with high dwelling-houses, in the lower part of which are shops, where every kind of manufacture is carried on, and every article of trade is sold; such, amongst others, as spices, drugs, trinkets, and pearls. In certain shops nothing is vended but the wine of the country, which they are continually brewing, and serve out fresh to their customers at a moderate price. The streets connected with the market-squares are numerous, and in some of them are many cold baths, attended by servants of both sexes, to perform the offices of ablution for the men and women who frequent them, and who from their childhood have been accustomed at all times to wash in cold water, which they reckon highly conducive to health. At these bathing places, however, they have apartments provided with warm water, for the use of strangers, who from not being habituated to it, cannot bear the shock of the cold. All are in the daily practice of washing their persons, and especially before their meals.

In other streets are the habitations of the courtesans, who are here in such numbers as I dare not venture to report; and not only near the squares, which is the situation usually appropriated for their residence, but in every part of the city they are to be found, adorned with much finery, highly perfumed, occupying well-furnished houses, and attended by many female domestics. These women are accomplished, and are perfect in the arts of blandishment and dalliance, which they accompany with expressions adapted to every description of person, insomuch that strangers who have once become so enchanted by their meretricious arts, that they can never divest themselves of the impression. Thus intoxicated with sensual pleasures, when they return to their homes they report that they have been in Kin-sai [Hangchow], or the celestial city, and pant for the time when they may be enabled to revisit paradise. . . .

The inhabitants of the city are idolaters, and they use paper money as currency. The men as well as the women have fair complexions, and are handsome. The greater part of them are always clothed in silk, in consequence of the vast quantity of that material produced in the territory of Kin-sai, exclusively of what the merchants import from other provinces. Amongst the handicraft trades exercised in the place, there are twelve considered to be superior to the rest, as being more generally useful; for each of which there are a thousand workshops, and each shop furnishes employment for ten, fifteen, or twenty workmen, and in a few instances as many as forty, under their respective masters. . . .

The natural disposition of the native inhabitants of Kin-sai is pacific, and by the example of their former kings, who were themselves unwarlike, they have been accustomed to habits of tranquility. The management of arms is unknown to them, nor do they keep any in their houses. Contentious broils are never heard among them. They conduct their mercantile and manufacturing concerns with perfect candour and probity. They are friendly towards each other, and persons who inhabit the same street, both men and women, from the mere circumstance of neighbourhood, appear like one family. In their domestic manners they are free from jealousy or suspicion of their wives, to whom great respect is shown, and any man would be accounted infamous who should presume to use indecent expressions to a married woman. To strangers also, who visit their city in the way of commerce, they give proofs of cordiality, inviting them freely to their houses, showing them hospitable attention, and furnishing them with the best advice and assistance in their mercantile transactions. On the other hand, they dislike the sight of soldiery, not excepting the guards of the grand khan, as they preserve the recollection that by them they were deprived of the government of their native kings and rulers. ❑

The Travels of Marco Polo (London: J. M. Dent, 1908), pp. 290–301.

The major contribution to Chinese arts during the Yuan was by dramatists, who combined poetic arias with vaudeville theater to produce a new operatic drama. Performed by traveling troupes, the operas used few stage props. They relied for effect on makeup, costumes, pantomime, and stylized gestures. The women's roles were usually played by men. Except for the arias—the highlights of the performance—the dramas used vernacular Chinese, appealing to a popular audience. The unemployed scholars who wrote the scripts drew on the entire repertoire of the Sung storyteller. Among the stock figures in the operas were a Robin Hood–like bandit, a famous detective-judge, the T'ang monk who traveled to India, warriors and statesmen of the Three Kingdoms, and romantic heroes, villains, and ghosts. Justice always triumphed and the dramas usually ended happily. In several famous plays, the hero gets the girl, despite objections by her parents and seemingly insurmountable obstacles, by passing the civil service examinations in first place. As the examinations were not in effect during most of the Yuan, this resolution of the hero's predicament is one that looked back to the Sung pattern of government. Yuan drama continued almost unchanged in later dynasties, and during the nineteenth century, it merged with a form of southern Chinese theater to become today's Peking Opera.

The Last Years of the Yuan

Despite the Mongol military domination of China and the highly centralized institutions of the Mongol court, the Yuan was the shortest of China's major dynasties. Little more than a century elapsed between Kublai's move to Peking in 1264 and the dynasty's collapse in 1368. The rule of Kublai and his successor had been effective, but a decline set in from the start of the fourteenth century. By then, the Mongol Empire as a whole no longer lent strength to its parts. The khanates became separated by religion and culture as well as by distance. Even tribesmen in Mongolia rebelled now and then against the great khans in Peking who, in their eyes, had become too Chinese. The court at Peking, too, had never really gained legitimacy. Some Chinese officials served it loyally to the end, but most Chinese saw the government as carpetbaggers and saw Mongol rule as a military occupation. When succession disputes, bureaucratic factionalism, and pitched battles between Mongol generals broke out, the Chinese showed little inclination to rally in support of the dynasty.

Problems also arose in the countryside. Taxes were heavy and some local officials were corrupt. The government issued excessive paper money and then refused to accept it in payment for taxes. The Yellow River changed its course, flooding the canals that carried grain to the capital. At great cost and suffering, a labor force of 150,000 workers and 20,000 soldiers rerouted the river to the south of the Shantung peninsula. Further natural disasters during the 1350s led to popular uprisings. The White Lotus sect preached the coming of Maitreya. Regional military commanders, suppressing the rebellions, became independent of central control. Warlords arose. The warlord who ruled Szechwan was infamous for his cruelty. Important economic regions were devastated and, in part depopulated by rebellions. At the end, a rebel army threatened Peking, and the last Mongol emperor and his court fled on horses to Shangtu, and when that fell, they fled still deeper into the plains of Mongolia.

Imperial China in World Perspective

Rough parallels between China and Europe persisted until the sixth century A.D. Both saw the rise and fall of great empires. At first glance, the three and one half centuries that followed the Han dynasty appear remarkably similar to the comparable period after the collapse of the Roman Empire: Central authority broke down, private armies arose, and aristocratic estates were established. Barbarian tribes, once allied to the empires, invaded and pillaged large areas. Otherworldly religions entered to challenge earlier official worldviews. In China, Neo-Taoism and then Buddhism challenged Confucianism, just as Christianity challenged Roman conceptions of the sociopolitical order.

But then, from the late sixth century A.D., a fundamental divergence occurred. Europe tailed off into centuries of feudal disunity and backwardness. A ghost of empire lingered in the European memory. But the reality, even after centuries had passed, was that tiny areas like France (one seventeenth the size of China), Italy (one thirty-second), or Germany (one twenty-seventh) found it difficult to establish an internal unity, much less re-create a pan-European or pan-Mediterranean empire. This pattern of separate little states has persisted in Europe until today. In contrast, China, which is about the size of Europe and geographically no more natural a political unit, put a unified empire back together again, attaining a new level of wealth, power, and culture, and unified rule has continued down to the present in China. What is the explanation?

One reason the empire was reconstituted in China was that the victory of Buddhism in China was less complete than that of Christianity in Europe. Confucianism survived within the aristocratic families and at the courts of the Six Dynasties, and the idea of a united empire was integral to it. It is difficult even to think of Confucianism apart from the idea of a universal ruler, aided by men of virtue and ability, ruling "all under Heaven" according to Heaven's mandate. In contrast, the Roman conception of political order was not maintained as an independent doctrine. And empire was not a vital element in Christian thought—except perhaps in Byzantium, where the empire lasted longer than in Western Europe. The notion of a "Christian king" did appear in the West, but basically, the kingdom sought by Jesus was not of this world.

A second consideration was China's greater cultural homogeneity. It had a common written language that was fairly close to all varieties of spoken Chinese. Even barbarian conquerors were rapidly Sinicized. In contrast, after Rome, the Mediterranean fell apart into its component cultures. Latin became the universal language of the Western church, but for most Christians it was a foreign language, a part of the mystery of the Mass, and even in Italy it became an artificial language, separate from the living tongue. The European languages and cultures were divisive forces.

A third factor was the combination in the post-Han northern Chinese states of economic strength based on Chinese agriculture with the military striking force of a nomadic cavalry. There was nothing like it in Europe. It was by such a northern state that China was reunified in A.D. 589.

A fourth and perhaps critical factor was China's greater population density. The province (called a *circuit* at the time) of Hopei had a registered population of 10,559,728 during the eighth century A.D. Hopei was about one third the size of France, which in the eleventh century had a population of about two million. That is to say, even comparing China with France three centuries later, China's population density was fifteen times greater. (This comparison, it should be noted, is with a nonrice-producing area of China. Rice paddy areas were even more densely populated.) The far higher population density resulted in a different kind of history.

This explains why the Chinese could absorb barbarian conquerors so much more quickly than could Europe. It provided a larger agricultural surplus to the northern kingdoms than was enjoyed by comparable kingdoms in Europe. A denser population also meant better communications and a better base for commerce. To be sure, the centuries that followed the Han saw a decline in commerce and in cities. In some areas, money went out of use to be replaced by barter or the use of silk as currency. But the economic level remained higher than in early medieval Europe.

Several of the factors that explain the Sui-T'ang regeneration of a unified empire apply equally well or better to the Sung and subsequent dynasties. As schools were established and literacy rose, Confucianism and the ideal of a unified China became more widely accepted. Chinese culture was more homoge-neous and less open to outside influences in the tenth century than it had been four centuries earlier. The population was denser, with the Yangtze basin emerging as a new center of gravity.

The same cyclic regeneration of centralized bureaucratic governments—even under outside conquerors—can also be analyzed in terms of the interests it served. For the military figure who established the dynasty, the bureaucratic state was a huge tax machine that supported his armies and bestowed on him revenues beyond the imaginings of contemporary European monarchs. Government by civilian officials also offered some promise for the security of his progeny by acting as a counterweight against other military figures. For the scholar-gentry class, service to the state was the means to maintain family wealth, power, and status. Nothing was better. For merchants, a strong state was not an unmixed blessing. It might tax their profits or establish monopolies on the commodities they traded. But it also provided order and stability. More often than not, commerce expanded during such periods. For farmers, the picture was also unclear. Taxation was often exploitative, but orderly exploitation was usually preferable to rapacious warlords, bandits, or maurauding armies.

Comparisons across continents are difficult, but it seems likely that T'ang and Sung China had longer stretches of good government than any other part of the contemporary world. Not until the nineteenth century would comparable bureaucracies of talent and virtue begin to appear in the West.

Suggested Readings

GENERAL

J. CAHILL, *Chinese Painting* (1960). An excellent survey.

C. O. HUCKER, *China's Imperial Past* (1975). A superb overview of Chinese traditional history and culture by a Ming specialist.

F. A. KIERMAN, JR., AND J. K. FAIRBANK (eds.), *Chinese Ways in Warfare* (1974). Chapters by different authors on the Chinese military experience from the Chou to the Ming.

SUI AND T'ANG

P. B. EBREY, *The Aristocratic Families of Early Imperial China* (1978).

S. OWEN, *The Great Age of Chinese Poetry: The High T'ang* (1980).

E. G. PULLEYBLANK, *The Background of the Rebellion of An Lu-shan* (1955). A study of the 755 rebellion that weakened the central authority of the T'ang dynasty.

E. O. REISCHAUER, *Ennin's Travels in T'ang China* (1955). China as seen through the eyes of a ninth-century Japanese Marco Polo.

E. H. SCHAFER, *The Golden Peaches of Samarkand* (1963). A study of T'ang imagery.

D. TWITCHETT (ed.), *Sui and T'ang China, 589–906,*

Part 1 (1984). (Part 2, also in *The Cambridge History of China*, is forthcoming.)

G. W. WANG, *The Structure of Power in North China during the Five Dynasties* (1963). A study of the interim period between the T'ang and the Sung dynasties.

A. F. WRIGHT, *The Sui Dynasty* (1978).

SUNG

J. GERNET, *Daily Life in China on the Eve of the Mongol Invasion* (1962).

J. W. HAEGER (ed.), *Crisis and Prosperity in Sung China* (1975).

R. HYMES, *Statesmen and Gentlemen* (1987). On the transformation of officials into a local gentry elite during the twelfth and thirteenth centuries.

J. T. C. LIU AND P. J. GOLAS (eds.), *Change in Sung China: Innovation or Renovation?* (1969).

M. ROSSABI, *China Among Equals* (1983). A study of the Liao, Ch'in, and Sung empires and their relations.

K. YOSHIKAWA, *An Introduction to Sung Poetry*, trans. by B. Watson (1967).

YUAN

T. T. ALLSEN, *Mongol Imperialism* (1987).

J. W. DARDESS, *Conquerors and Confucians: Aspects of Political Change in Late Yuan China* (1973).

H. FRANKE AND D. TWITCHETT (eds.), *Alien Regimes and Border States, 710–1368* (to appear soon as Volume 6 of *The Cambridge History of China*).

J. D. LANGLOIS, *China Under Mongol Rule* (1981).

R. LATHAM (trans.), *Travels of Marco Polo* (1958).

H. D. MARTIN, *The Rise of Chingis Khan and His Conquest of North China* (1981).

Unlike the full-bodied T'ang ideal, this Bodhisattva from the pre-Nara Hōryūji Temple reflects the artistic influence of the earlier Northern Wei dynasty. The T'ang style entered Japan during the Nara and early Heian periods. [Tokyo National Museum.]

10 Japan: Its Early History to 1467

Japanese history has three main turning points, each marked by a major influx of an outside culture and each followed by a massive restructuring of Japanese institutions. The first turning point was in the third century B.C., when an Old Stone Age Japan became an agricultural, metalworking society, similar to those on the Korean peninsula or in northeastern Asia. This era lasted until A.D. 600. The second turning point came during the seventh century, when whole complexes of Chinese culture entered Japan directly. Absorbing these, archaic Japan made the leap to a higher historical civilization, associated with the writing system, technologies, and philosophies of China, and with Chinese forms of Buddhism. Japan would remain a part of this civilization until the third turning point, in the nineteenth century, when it encountered the West.

Japanese Origins

The antiquity of humans in Japan is hotly debated. During the ice ages, Japan was connected by land bridges to Asia. Woolly mammoths entered the northern island of Hokkaido and elephants, sabre-toothed tigers, giant elks, and other continental fauna entered the lower islands. Did not humans enter as well? Because Japan's acid volcanic soil eats up bones, there are no early skeletal remains. The earliest evidence of human habitation are finely shaped stone tools dating from about 30,000 B.C. Then, from about 10,000 B.C., there is Jōmon or "cord-pattern" pottery, the oldest in the world. Archeologists are baffled by its appearance in an Old Stone Age hunting, gathering, and fishing society—when in all other early societies pottery developed along with agriculture as an aspect of New Stone Age culture.

Along with cord-patterned pots, the hunting and gathering Jōmon people produced mysterious figurines. Is this a female deity? Why are the eyes slitted like snow goggles? [Otto E. Nelson.]

The Yayoi Revolution

After 8,000 years of Jōmon culture, the second phase of Japanese prehistory began in about 300 B.C. It is called the Yayoi culture after a place name in Tokyo where its distinctive hard, white pottery was first unearthed. There is no greater break in the entire Japanese record than that between the Jōmon and the Yayoi. For at the beginning of the third century B.C., the agricultural revolution, the bronze revolution, and the iron revolution—which in the Near East, India, and China had been separated by thousands of years, and each of which singly had wrought profound transformations—burst in upon Japan simultaneously.

The new technologies were brought to Japan by peoples moving across the Tsushima Straits from the Korean peninsula. It is uncertain whether these immigrants came as a trickle and were absorbed, or whether they came as a torrent that swept away the indigenous Jōmon people. The early Yayoi migrants, using the same seacraft by which they had crossed from Korea, spread along the coasts of northern Kyushu and western Honshu. Yayoi culture rapidly replaced Jōmon culture as far east in Japan as the

present-day city of Nagoya. After that, the Yayoi culture diffused overland into eastern Japan more slowly and with greater difficulty. Conditions were less favorable for agriculture, and a mixed agricultural-hunting economy lasted longer.

The early "frontier settlements" of the Yayoi people were located next to their fields. Their agriculture was primitive. By the first century A.D., the Yayoi population had expanded to the point where wars were fought for the best land. Excavations reveal extensive stone-axe industries, and several skulls pierced by bronze and iron arrowheads have been found. An early Chinese chronicle describes Japan as made up of "more than one hundred countries" with wars and conflicts raging on all sides. During these wars, villages were relocated in defensible positions on low hills away from the fields. From these wars emerged a more peaceful order of regional states and a ruling class of aristocratic warriors. Late Yayoi excavations reveal villages once again located by fields and far fewer stone axes.

During the third century A.D., a temporary hegemony was achieved over a number of such regional states—or, more accurately, regional tribal confederations—by a queen named Pimiko. In the Chinese chronicle, Pimiko is described as a shaman who "occupied herself with magic and sorcery, bewitching the people." She was mature but unmarried. "After she became the ruler, there were few who saw her. She had one thousand women as attendants, but only one man. He served her food and drink and acted as a medium of communication. She resided in a palace surrounded by towers and stockades with armed guards in a state of constant vigilance."[1]

After Pimiko, references to Japan disappeared from the Chinese dynastic histories for a century and a half.

Tomb Culture and the Yamato State

Emerging directly from the Yayoi culture was a period, A.D. 300–600, characterized by giant tomb mounds, which remain even today, dotting the landscape of western Japan. The early tombs—like those in Korea—were circular mounds of earth built atop megalithic burial chambers. Later tombs were sometimes keyhole-shaped. The tombs were surrounded by moats and adorned with clay cylinders and statues of warriors, scribes, musicians, houses, boats, and the like. Early tombs, like the Yayoi graves that preceded them, contained mirrors, jewels, and other ceremonial objects. From the fifth century A.D., these objects were replaced by armor, swords, spears, and military trappings. The change reflected a new wave of continental

[1] L. C. Goodrich and R. Tsunoda (trans.), *Japan in the Chinese Dynastic Histories* (South Pasadena, Calif.: Perkins Asiatic Monographs, 1951), p. 13.

Late Yayoi Japan as Presented in Chinese Histories

Weapons are spears, shields, swords, and wooden bows. . . . The arrows are sometimes tipped with bone. The men all tattoo their faces and adorn their bodies with designs. The position and size of pattern indicate the difference of rank. . . . The men's clothing is fastened breadth-wise and consists of one piece of cloth. The women tie their hair in bows, and their clothing, like our gown of one single piece of cloth, is put on by slipping it over the head. They use pink and scarlet to smear their bodies, as rice powder is used in China. . . .

The women outnumber the men, and the men of importance have four or five spouses; the rest have two or three. The women are faithful and not jealous. There is no theft, and litigation is infrequent. When men break a law, their wives and children are confiscated; when the offense is serious, the offender's family is extirpated. At death mourning lasts for more than ten days, during which time members of the family weep and lament, without much drinking and eating; while their friends sing and dance. . . .

When the lowly meet men of importance on the road, they stop and withdraw to the roadside. In conveying messages to them or addressing them, they either squat or kneel, with both hands on the ground. This is the way they show respect. When responding, they say "ah," which corresponds to the affirmative "yes. . . ."

When they go on voyages across the sea to visit China, they always select a man who does not arrange his hair, does not rid himself of fleas, lets his clothing [get as] dirty as it will, does not eat meat, and does not approach women. This man behaves like a mourner and is known as the fortune keeper. When the voyage turns out propitious, they all lavish on him slaves and other valuables. In case there is disease or mishap, they kill him, saying that he was not scrupulous in his duties. ❑

L. C. Goodrich and R. Tsunoda (trans.) *Japan in the Chinese Dynastic Histories* (South Pasadena, Calif: Perkins Asiatic Monographs, 1951), pp. 1, 2, 11, 13.

A clay statue of a warrior in armor from an ancient tomb. [Tokyo National Museum.]

influences. The flow of people and culture from Korea to Japan that had began with Yayoi was continuous into historical times.

Japan reappears in the Chinese chronicles in the fifth century A.D. This period was also covered in the earliest Japanese accounts of its own history, the *Records of Ancient Matters (Kojiki)* and the *Records of Japan (Nihongi)* compiled in 712 and 720. These records dovetail with the evidence of the tombs. The picture that emerges is of regional aristocracies under the loose hegemony of the Yamato "great kings." Historians use the geographical label "Yamato" since the courts of the great kings were located on the Yamato plain, near present-day Osaka. This was the richest agricultural region of ancient Japan. The Yamato rulers also held lands and granaries throughout Japan. The tomb of the great king Nintoku is 486 meters long and 36 meters high, with twice the volume of the Great Pyramid of Egypt. By the fifth century A.D., the great kings possessed sufficient authority to commandeer the labor for such a project.

The great kings awarded Korean-type titles to court and regional aristocrats, titles that implied a national hierarchy centering on the Yamato court. These regional rulers had the same kind of political authority

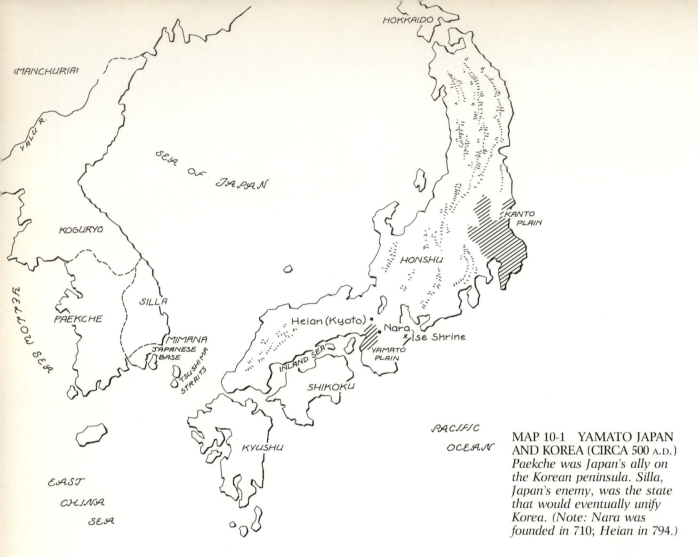

MAP 10-1 YAMATO JAPAN AND KOREA (CIRCA 500 A.D.) *Paekche was Japan's ally on the Korean peninsula. Silla, Japan's enemy, was the state that would eventually unify Korea. (Note: Nara was founded in 710; Heian in 794.)*

over their populations as is substantiated by the spread of tomb mounds to other parts of Japan.

The basic social unit of Yamato aristocratic society was the extended family (*uji*), closer in size to a Scottish clan than to a modern household. Attached to these aristocratic families were groups of specialist workers called *be*. This word was of Korean origin and was originally used to designate potters, scribes, or others with special skills who had immigrated from Korea. It was then extended to include similar groups of indigenous workers and groups of peasants as well. Yamato society had a small class of slaves, possibly captured in wars. There were also large numbers of peasants who were neither slaves nor members of aristocratic clans or specialized workers' groups.

What little is known of Yamato politics suggests that the court was the scene of incessant struggles for power between aristocratic families. There were also continuing efforts by the court to maintain control over outlying regions. Though marriage alliances were established and titles awarded, rebellions were not infre-

quent during the fifth and sixth centuries. Finally, there were constant wars with "barbarian tribes" in southern Kyushu and eastern Honshu on the frontiers of "civilized" Japan.

The Yamato Court and Korea

During the era of the Yamato court, a three-cornered military balance had emerged on the Korean peninsula between the states of Paekche in the southwest, Silla in the east, and Koguryo in the north. Japan was an ally of Paekche. Japan may also have maintained a trading base or military colony on the southern rim of Korea.

The Paekche connection was of vital importance to the Yamato court, enabling the court to expand its power within Japan. Imports of iron weapons and tools gave it military strength. The migration to Japan of Korean potters, weavers, scribes, metalworkers, and other artisans increased its wealth and influence. The significance of the immigrants from Korea can be gauged by the fact that many became established as noble families. Paekche also served as a conduit for elements of Chinese culture. Chinese writing was adopted for the transcription of Japanese names during the fifth or sixth century. Confucianism entered in 513, when Paekche sent a "scholar of the Five Classics." Buddhism first arrived in 538, when the Paekche king sent a Buddha image, sutras, and possibly a priest.

Eventually the political balance on the peninsula shifted against Japan. In 532, Paekche joined Silla in attacking Japan's southern rim colony, and by 562, Japan had been driven from Korea. But the severance of ties with Korea was less of a loss than it would have been earlier, for by this time, Japan had succeeded in establishing direct relations with China.

Religion in Early Japan

The indigenous religion of Yamato Japan was an animistic worship of the forces of nature. This was later given the name of *Shinto*, or "the way of the gods" to distinguish it from Buddhism. In all likelihood, Shinto entered Japan from the continent as a part of Yayoi culture. The underlying forces of nature might be embodied in a waterfall, a twisted tree, a strangely shaped boulder, a mountain, or in a great leader who would be worshiped as a deity after his death. Mount Fuji was holy not as the abode of a god but because the mountain itself was an upwelling of a vital natural force. Even today in Japan, a gnarled tree trunk may be circled with a straw rope and set aside as an object of veneration. The sensitivity to nature and natural beauty that pervades Japanese art and poetry owes much to Shinto. Throughout the historical period, most villages had shamans, or religious specialists who, by entering a trance, could contact directly the inner forces of nature and gain the power to foretell the future or heal sickness. The queen Pimiko was such a shaman. The sorceress is a stock figure in tales of ancient or medieval Japan. And more often than not, women, receiving the command of a god, have

Darkness and the Cave of High Heaven

The younger brother of the sun goddess was a mischief maker. Eventually the gods drove him out of heaven. On one occasion, he knocked a hole in the roof of a weaving hall and dropped in a dappled pony that he had skinned alive. One weaving maiden was so startled that she struck her genitals with the shuttle she was using and died.

The Sun Goddess, terrified at the sight, opened the door of the heavenly rock cave, and hid herself inside. Then the Plain of High Heaven was shrouded in darkness, as was the Central Land of Reed Plains [Japan]. An endless night prevailed. The cries of the myriad gods were like the buzzing of summer flies, and myriad calamities arose.

The eight hundred myriad gods assembled in the bed of the Quiet River of Heaven. They asked one god to think of a plan. They assembled the long-singing birds of eternal night and made them sing. They took hard rocks from the bed of the river and iron from the Heavenly Metal Mountain and called in a smith to make a mirror. They asked the Jewel Ancestor God to make a string of 500 curved jewels eight feet long. They asked other gods to remove the shoulder blade of a male deer and to obtain cherry wood from Mount Kagu, and to perform a divination. They uprooted a sacred tree, attaching the string of curved jewels to its upper branches, hanging the large mirror from its middle branches, and suspending offerings of white and blue cloth from its lower branches.

One god held these objects as grand offerings and another intoned sacred words. The Heavenly Hand-Strong-Male God stood hidden beside the door. A goddess bound up her sleeves with clubmoss from Mount Kagu, made a herb band from the spindle-tree, and bound together leaves of bamboo-grass to hold in her hands. Then she placed a wooden box facedown before the rock cave, stamped on it until it resounded, and, as if possessed, she exposed her breasts and pushed her shirt-band down to her genitals. The Plain of High Heaven shook as the myriad gods broke into laughter.

The Sun Goddess, thinking this strange, opened slightly the rock-cave door and said from within: "Since I have hidden myself I thought that the Plain of Heaven and the Central Land of the Reed Plains would all be in darkness. Why is it that the goddess makes merry and the myriad gods all laugh?"

The goddess replied: "We rejoice and are glad because there is here a god greater than you." While she spoke two other gods brought out the mirror and held it up before the Sun Goddess.

The Sun Goddess, thinking this stranger and stranger, came out the door and peered into the mirror. Then the Hand-Strong-Male God seized her hand and pulled her out. Another god drew a rope behind her and said: "You may not go back further than this."

So when the Sun Goddess had come forth, the Plain of High Heaven and the Central Land of the Reed Plains once again naturally shone in brightness. ❑

From the *Records of Ancient Matters* (Kojiki).

founded the "new" religions in this tradition, even down into the nineteenth and twentieth centuries.

A second aspect of early Shinto was its connection with the state and the ruling posttribal aristocracy. The more potent forces of nature such as the sea, the sun, the moon, the wind, and thunder and lightning became personified as deities. Each clan, or extended family, had its own myth centering on a nature deity (*kami*) that it claimed as its original ancestor. Aristocratic families possessed genealogies tracing their descent from the deity. A genealogy was a patent of nobility and a claim to political authority. The head of a clan was also its chief priest, who made sacrifices to its deity. When Japan was unified by the Yamato court, the myths of the several clans apparently were joined into a national composite myth. The deity of the Yamato great kings was the sun goddess, so she became the chief deity while other gods assumed lesser positions appropriate to the status of their clan.

The *Records of Ancient Matters* and *Records of Japan* tell of the creation of Japan, of the deeds and misdeeds of gods on the "plain of high heaven," and of their occasional adventures on earth or in the underworld. In mid-volume, the stories of the gods, interspersed with the genealogies of noble families, give way to stories of early emperors and early Japanese history. The Japanese emperors, the oldest royal family in the world, were viewed as the lineal descendants of the sun goddess and themselves as "living gods." And the Great Shrine of the Sun Goddess at Ise has always been the most important in Japan.

Nara and Heian Japan

The second major turning point in Japanese history was its adoption of the higher civilization of China. This is a prime example of the worldwide process by which the heartland civilizations (described in Chapter 2) spread into outlying areas. The process in Japan occurred from the seventh through the twelfth century and can best be understood in terms of three stages. The first stage was learning about China. The second stage, mostly during the eighth and ninth centuries, saw the implantation in Japan of Chinese T'ang-type institutions. The third involved the further transformation of these institutions to better fit them to conditions in Japan. By the twelfth century, this creative reworking of Chinese elements led to a distinctive Japanese culture, quite unlike that of China, yet equally unlike that of the earlier Yamato court.

The Seventh Century

The official embassies to China that began in A.D. 607, included traders, students, and Buddhist monks as well as representatives of the Yamato great kings.

Like Third-World students who study abroad today, Japanese who studied in China played key roles in their government when they returned. They brought back with them a quickening flow of technology, art, Buddhism, and knowledge of T'ang legal and governmental systems. But the difficulties of mastering Chinese and comprehending its philosophical culture were enormous for the Yamato Japanese. Large-scale institutional changes using the T'ang model actually began in the 680s with the Emperor Temmu and his successor, the Empress Jitō.

Temmu's life illustrates the interplay between court politics and the adoption of Chinese institutions. He came to the throne by leading an alliance of eastern clans in rebellion against the previous great king, his brother. The *Records of Japan* describe him as "walking like a tiger through the eastern lands." He then used Chinese systems to consolidate his power. He promulgated a Chinese-type law code, which greatly

Prince Shōtoku (574–622) *and two of his sons. Prince Shōtoku was a Buddhist and reformer who began sending regular embassies to China in 607.* [Bettmann Archive.]

augmented the powers of the ruler. He styled himself as the "heavenly emperor" (tennō), which thereafter replaced the earlier title of *great king*. He rewarded his supporters with new court ranks and with positions in a new court government, both derived from the T'ang example. He extended the authority of the court and increased its revenues by a survey of agricultural lands and a census of their population. In short, although the admiration for Chinese things must have been enormous, much of the borrowing was dictated by specific, immediate, and practical Japanese concerns.

Nara and Early Heian Court Government

Until the eighth century, the capital was usually moved each time an emperor died. Then, in 710, a new capital, intended to be permanent, was established at Nara. It was laid out on a checkerboard grid like the Chinese capital at Ch'ang-an. But then it was moved again—some say to escape the meddling in politics of powerful Buddhist temples. A final move occurred in 794 to Heian (later Kyoto) on the plain north of Nara. This site remained the capital until the move to Tokyo in 1869. Even today, Kyoto's regular geometry reflects the Chinese concepts of city planning.

The superimposition of a Chinese-type capital on a still backward Japan produced as stark a contrast as any in history. In the villages, peasants—who worshiped the forces in mountains and trees—lived in pit dwellings and either planted in crude paddy fields or used slash-and-burn techniques of dry land farming. In the capital stood pillared palaces in which dwelt the emperor and nobles, descended from the gods on high. They drank wine, wore silk, and enjoyed the paintings, perfumes, and pottery of the T'ang. Clustered about the capital were Buddhist temples, more numerous than in Nara, with soaring pagodas and sweeping tile roofs. With what awe must a peasant have viewed the city and its inhabitants!

The emperors at the Nara and Heian courts were both Confucian rulers with the majesty accorded by Chinese law and Shinto rulers descended from the Sun Goddess. Protected by an aura of the sacred, their lineage was never usurped. All Japanese history constitutes a single dynasty—though a few emperors were killed and replaced by other family members.

Beneath the emperor, the same modified Chinese pattern prevailed. Like the T'ang, Japan had a Council of State, but it was more powerful than that of China. It was the office from which leading clans manipulated the authority of an emperor who usually reigned but did not rule. Beneath this council were eight ministries—two more than in China. One of the two was a Secretariat and the other the Imperial Household Ministry. Size affected function: Where T'ang China had a population of sixty million, Nara Japan had only five

million. There were fewer people to govern in Japan; there were no external enemies to speak of; and much of local rule, in the Yamato tradition, was in the hands of local clans. Consequently, more of the business of court government was with the court itself. Of the six thousand persons in the central ministries, more than four thousand were concerned in one way or another with the imperial house itself. The Imperial Household Ministry had an official staff of 1,296, whereas the Treasury had only 305 and Military Affairs only 198.

Under the central court government were 66 provinces, which were further subdivided into districts and villages. In pre-Nara times, the regions were governed by largely autonomous regional clans; but under the new system, provincial governors were sent out from the capital. The old regional aristocrats were reduced to filling the lesser posts of district magistrates. The new system substantially increased the power of the central aristocracy.

In other respects, Japanese court government was unlike that of China. There were no eunuchs. There was little tension between the emperor and the bureaucracy—the main struggles were between clans. The T'ang movement from aristocracy toward meritocracy was also absent in Japan. Apart from clerks and monastics, only aristocrats were educated, only they took civil service examinations, and only they were appointed to important official posts. And even then, family counted more than grades.

Land and Taxes

The last Japanese embassy to China was in 838. By that time, the frenetic borrowing of Chinese culture had already slowed. The Japanese had taken in all they needed—or, perhaps, all they could handle—and were sufficiently self-confident to use Chinese ideas in innovative and flexible ways. The 350 years that followed until the end of the twelfth century were a time of assimilation and evolutionary change. Nowhere was this more evident than in the system of taxation.

The land system of Nara and early Heian Japan was the "equal field system" of the early T'ang. All land belonged to the emperor; it was redistributed every six years, and taxes were levied on people, not land. Those receiving land were liable for three taxes: a light tax in grain, a light tax in cloth, and a heavy labor tax. The system was complex, requiring land surveys, the redrawing of boundaries, and elaborate land and population registers. Even in China, with its sophisticated bureaucracy, this system broke down. In the case of Japan, the marvel is that it could be carried out at all. The evidence of old registers and recent aerial photographs suggests that it was—at least, in western Japan. Its implementation speaks of the immense energy and ability of the early Japanese, who so quickly absorbed so much of Chinese administrative technique.

Of course, as put into effect, the system was even less equal than in China. Imperial princes and high nobles received thousands or hundreds of units of rank lands, office lands, and merit lands, along with the labor to work them; local officials got much less, and the cultivators did the work.

In history, when changes are legislated or imposed from above, the results tend to be uniform. But when changes occur willy-nilly within a social system, the results are usually messy and difficult to comprehend. The evolution of the land system and taxation in late Heian Japan was of the second type.

One big change was from the equal field system to one of tax quotas payable in grain. First, the redistribution of land broke down and land holdings became hereditary. Officials discovered that peasants would not care for land they did not own. Second, the main tax of labor service was converted to a grain tax. Officials found it more efficient to hire workers and pay them in grain than to use the labor of peasants who had no incentive to work. Third, the taxes levied on provinces and districts were made over into fixed quotas. Court officials could not maintain the elaborate records needed for the equal field system. The court gave each governor a quota and he, in turn, gave one to each district magistrate. Any amount collected over the quota, they kept. The district magistrates, and other local notables and military families associated with them, gradually created a new local ruling class.

Another big change, one that affected about half of the land in late Heian Japan, was the conversion of tax-paying lands to tax-free estates. Nobles and powerful temples in Kyoto did not want to pay taxes, so they used their influence at the court to obtain *immunities*—exemptions from taxation for their lands. From the ninth century, many cultivators began to commend their small holdings to such nobles, judging that they would be better off as serfs on tax-free estates than as free farmers subject to taxation. Because of the random pattern of commendation, the typical estate in Japan was of scattered parcels of land, unlike the unified estates of Europe. The Japanese estates were managed by stewards, appointed from among the local notables. They took a share of the surplus grain for themselves, and forwarded the rest to the noble owner in Kyoto. The stewards, thus, were from the same stratum of local society as those who collected the tax quotas. Like district magistrates, they had a vital interest in upholding the local order.

The Rise of the Samurai

During the Nara period Japan experimented with a military system based on conscription. One third of all able-bodied men between the ages of twenty-one and sixty were taken. Conscript armies, however, proved inefficient, so in 792 the court abolished conscription and began a new system relying on local mounted warriors. Some were stationed in the capital and some in the provinces. They were official troops whose taxes were remitted in exchange for military service. The Japanese verb "to serve" is *samurau*, so those who served became *samurai*—the noun form of the verb. Then, from the mid-Heian period, the officially recruited local warriors were replaced by nonofficial private bands of local warriors. These constituted the military of Japan for the next half millennium or so, until the foot-soldier revolution of the fifteenth and sixteenth centuries.

Being a samurai was expensive. Horses, armor, and weapons were costly, and if they were to be used effectively, long training was required. The primary weapon was the bow and arrow, used from the saddle. Most samurai were from well-to-do local families, such as those of district magistrates or notables, or were from military families supported by the local elites or by temples or shrines. Their initial function was to preserve local order and, possibly, to help with tax collection. But at times, even early on, they contributed to disorder. From the second half of the ninth century, there are accounts of district magistrates leading local forces against provincial governors—doubtless in connection with tax disputes.

From the early tenth century, regional military coalitions or confederations began to form. They first break into history in 939, when a regional military leader, a descendant of an emperor, became involved in a tax dispute. He captured several provinces, called himself the new emperor, and appointed a government of civil and military officials. The Kyoto court responded by recruiting another military band as its champion. The rebellion was quelled, and the rebel leader died in battle. That the Kyoto court could summon a military band points up the connections that enabled it to manipulate local military leaders and maintain its political control of Japan.

The rebellion of 939 was the first of a number of conflicts between regional military bands. Many wars were fought in eastern Japan—the wild east of those days. The east was more militarized because it was the headquarters for the periodic campaigns against the tribal peoples to the north. By the middle of the twelfth century, local and regional military bands were to be found in every part of Japan.

Late Heian Court Government

Even during the Nara period, much of the elaborate apparatus of Chinese government was of little use. By the early Heian period the actual functions of government were taken over by three new offices outside the Chinese system:

1. *Audit officers.* A newly appointed provincial governor had to report on the accounts of his predecessor. Agreement was rare. So from the end of the Nara period, audit officers were sent to examine the books. By early Heian times, these auditors had come to superintend the collection of taxes and most other capital–province relationships. They tried to halt the erosion of tax revenues. But as the quota and estate systems developed, this office had less and less to do.
2. *Bureau of Archivists.* This bureau was established in 810 to record and preserve imperial decrees. Eventually it took over the executive function at the Heian court, drafting imperial decrees and attending to all aspects of the emperor's life.
3. *Police Commissioners.* Established in the second decade of the ninth century to enforce laws and prosecute criminals, the commissioners eventually became responsible for all law and order in the capital. They absorbed military functions as well as those of the Ministry of Justice and the Bureau of Impeachment.

While new institutions were evolving, there also occurred shifts in the control of the court. The key figure remained the emperor, who had the power of appointments. Until the early Heian—say, the mid-ninth century—some emperors actually ruled, or, more often, shared power with nobles of leading clans. From 856, the northern branch of the Fujiwara clan became preeminent, and from 986 to 1086, its stranglehold on the court was absolute. The administrative offices of the Fujiwara house were almost more powerful than those of the central government, and all key government posts were monopolized by members of the Fujiwara family. The Fujiwara controlled the court by marrying their daughters to the emperor, forcing the emperor to retire after a son was born, and then ruling as regents in place of the new infant emperor. At times, they even ruled as regents for adult emperors.

Fujiwara Michinaga's words were no empty boast when he said, "As for this world, I think it is mine, nor is there a flaw in the full moon."

Fujiwara rule gave way, during the second half of the eleventh century, to rule by retired emperors. The imperial family and lesser noble houses had long resented Fujiwara domination. Disputes within the Fujiwara house itself enabled an emperor to regain control. Imperial control of government was reasserted by Emperor Shirakawa, who reigned from 1072 to 1086 and, abdicating at the age of thirty-three, ruled for forty-three years as retired emperor. After his death, other retired emperors continued in the same pattern until 1156.

Ex-Emperor Shirakawa set up offices in his quarters not unlike the administrative offices of the Fujiwara family. He employed talented nobles of lesser families, and sought to reduce the number of estates by trying to confiscate those of the Fujiwara. He failed and ended, instead, by garnering huge estates for the imperial family. He developed strong ties to regional military leaders. His sense of his own power was reflected in his words—more a lament than a boast: "The only things that do not submit to my will are the waters of the Kamo River, the roll of the dice, and the soldier-monks [of the Tendai temple on Mount Hiei to the northeast of Kyoto]." But Shirakawa's powers were exercised in a capital city that was increasingly isolated from the changes in outlying regions. Even the city itself was plagued by fires, banditry, and a sense of impending catastrophe.

A momentous change occurred in 1156. The death of the ruling retired emperor precipitated a struggle for power between another retired emperor and the reigning emperor. Each called in a military confederation for backing. The House of Taira defeated the armies of the Minamoto. Taira Kiyomori had come to Kyoto to uphold an emperor, but finding himself in charge, he stayed to rule. His pattern of rule was quite Japanese: Court nobles kept their Chinese court offices; the reigning emperor, who had been supported by Kiyomori, retired and took control of the offices of the retired emperor and of the estates of the imperial family, which they managed; the head of the Fujiwara family kept the post of regent, while Taira Kiyomori married his daughter to the new emperor, and when a

WHO WAS IN CHARGE AT THE NARA AND HEIAN COURTS

710–856	Emperors or combinations of nobles
856–1086	Fujiwara nobles
1086–1156	Retired emperors
1156–1180	The military house of Taira

In the Heiji War of 1156, regional samurai bands became involved in Kyoto court politics. A scroll painting of the burning of the Sanjō Palace. [Museum of Fine Arts, Boston. Fenollosa-Weld Collection.]

son was born, Kiyomori forced the emperor to retire and ruled as the maternal grandfather of the infant emperor.

Aristocratic Culture and Buddhism in Nara and Heian Japan

If culture could be put on a scale and weighed like sugar or flour, we would conclude that the culture of Nara and early Heian Japan was overwhelmingly one of Shinto religious practices and village folkways, an extension of the culture of the late Yamato period. The aristocracy was small and was encapsulated in the routine of court life, just as the Buddhist monks were contained within the rounds of their monastic life. The early Heian aristocracy comprised one tenth of one per cent of Japan's population. Most of the court culture had only recently been imported from China. There had not been time for the commoners to ape their betters, or for the powerful force of the indigenous culture to reshape that of the elite.

The resulting cultural gap helps to explain why the aristocrats, in so far as we can tell from literature, found the commoners to be odd, incomprehensible, and, indeed, hardly human. The writings of the courtiers reflect little sympathy for the suffering and hardships of the people—except in Chinese-type poetry, where such feelings were deemed appropriate. When the fictional Prince Genji stoops to an affair with an impoverished woman, she is inevitably a princess. Sei Shōnagon was not atypical as a writer: She was offended by the vulgarity of mendicant nuns, laughed at an illiterate old man whose house had burned down,

and found lacking in charm the eating habits of carpenters, who wolfed down their food a bowl at a time.

Heian high culture resembled a hothouse plant. It was protected by the political influence of the court. It was nourished by the flow of tax revenues and income from estates. Under these conditions, the aristocrats of the never-never land of Prince Genji indulged in a unique way of life, and created canons of elegance and taste that are striking even today. The speed with which T'ang culture was assimilated and reworked was amazing. A few centuries after Mediterranean culture was introduced into northern Europe, there had appeared nothing even remotely comparable to the *Tale of Genji* or the *Pillow Book*.

The Chinese Tradition in Japan

Education at the Nara and Heian courts was largely a matter of reading Chinese books and acquiring the skills needed to compose poetry and prose in Chinese. These were enormous tasks not only because there was no prior tradition of scholarship in Japan but because the two languages were so dissimilar. To master written Chinese and use it for everyday written communications was as daunting a challenge for the Nara Japanese as it would have been for any European of the same century, but the challenge was successfully met. From the Nara period until the nineteenth century, most philosophical and legal writings, and most of the histories, essays, and religious texts in Japan, were written in Chinese. From a Chinese perspective, the writings may leave something to be desired. It would be astonishing if this were not the case, for the soul of language is the music of the spoken tongue. But the Japanese writers were competent, and

The Development of Japanese Writing

No two languages could be more different than Chinese and Japanese. Chinese is nonsyllabic, uninflected, and tonal. Japanese is polysyllabic, highly inflected, and atonal. To adopt Chinese writing for use in Japanese was thus no easy task. What the Japanese did at first—when they were not simply learning to write in Chinese—was to use certain Chinese ideographs as a phonetic script. For example, in the Man'yōshū, the eighth-century poetic anthology, shira-nami *(white wave) was written with* 之 *for* shi, 良 *for* ra, 奈 *for* na, *and* 美 *for* mi. *Over several centuries, these phonetic ideographs evolved into a uniquely Japanese phonetic script:*

	Original Chinese Ideograph	Simplified Ideograph	Phonetic Script (*kana*)
shi	之	𛀁	し
ra	良	𛁉	ら
na	奈	𛂋	な
mi	美	𛅳	み

It is apparent in the above examples how the original ideograph was first simplified according to the rules of calligraphy and was then further simplified into a phonetic script. In modern Japanese, unmodified Chinese ideographs are used for nouns and verb stems, and the phonetic script is used for inflections and particles.

学生 は 図書館 へ 行きました.

Students/as for/library/to/went.
(The students went to the library.)

In the above sentence, the Chinese ideographs are the forms with many strokes, and the phonetic script is shown in the simpler, cursive forms. ❏

---

the feelings and ideas that they expressed were authentic—when not copybook exercises in the style of a Chinese master. In 883, when Sugawara Michizane wrote a poem on the death of his son, he quite naturally wrote it in Chinese. The poem began:

> Since Amaro died I cannot sleep at night;
> if I do, I meet him in dreams and tears come
>   coursing down.
> Last summer he was over three feet tall;
> this year he would have been seven years old.
> He was diligent and wanted to know how to
>   be a good son,
> read his books and recited by heart the "Poem
>   on the Capital."[2]

The capital referred to was Ch'ang-an, and the poem, one "used in Japan as a text for little boys learning to read Chinese."

Not only were Japanese writings in Chinese a vital

[2]H. Sato and B. Watson (trans.), *From the Country of Eight Islands* (1981), p. 121.

part of the Japanese cultural tradition, but the original Chinese works themselves also became a part of the same tradition. The late T'ang poet Po Chu-i was early appreciated and widely read, and later, Tu Fu and Li Po were also read and admired. As in China itself, Chinese history was read, and its stock figures were among the heroes and villains of the Japanese historical consciousness. Chinese history became the mirror in which Japan saw itself—despite the differences in the two societies. Buddhist stories and the books of Confucianism also became Japanese classics, continuously accessible and consulted over the centuries for their wisdom and philosophy. The parallel might be the Bible, Plato, and Aristotle in England.

The Birth of Japanese Literature

Stimulated by Chinese models, the Japanese began to compose poetry in their native tongue. The first major anthology was the *Collection of Ten Thousand Leaves (Man'yōshū)*, compiled in about 760. It contained 4,516 poems. The sentiments in the poems are fresh, sometimes simple and straightforward, but

Aristocratic Taste at the Fujiwara Court: Sei Shōnagon Records Her Likes and Dislikes

Elegant Things:
A white coat worn over a violet waistcoat.
Duck eggs.
Shaved ice mixed with liana syrup and put in a new silver bowl.
A rosary of rock crystal.
Snow on wistaria or plum blossoms.
A pretty child eating strawberries.

Pleasing Things:
Someone has torn up a letter and thrown it away. Picking up the pieces, one finds that many of them can be fitted together.

A person in whose company one feels awkward asks one to supply the opening or closing line of a poem. If one happens to recall it, one is very pleased. Yet often on such occasions one completely forgets something that one would normally know.

Entering the Empress's room and finding that ladies-in-waiting are crowded round her in a tight group, I go next to a pillar which is some distance from where she is sitting. What a delight it is when Her Majesty summons me to her side so that all the others have to make way!

Hateful Things:
A lover who is leaving at dawn announces that he has to find his fan and his paper. "I know I put them somewhere last night," he says. Since it is pitch dark, he gropes about the room, bumping into the furniture and muttering, "Strange! Where on earth can they be?" Finally he discovers the objects. He thrusts the paper into the breast of his robe with a great rustling sound; then he snaps open his fan and busily fans away with it. Only now is he ready to take his leave. What charmless behavior! "Hateful" is an understatement.

A good lover will behave as elegantly at dawn as at any other time. He drags himself out of bed with a look of dismay on his face. The lady urges him on: "Come, my friend, it's getting light. You don't want anyone to find you here." He gives a deep sigh, as if to say that the night has not been nearly long enough and that it is agony to leave. Once up, he does not

often sophisticated. They reveal a deep sensitivity to nature and strong human relationships between husband and wife, parents and children. They also display a love for the land of Japan and links to a Shinto past.

An early obstacle to the development of a Japanese poetic tradition was the difficulty of transcribing Japanese sounds. In the *Ten Thousand Leaves*, Chinese characters were used as phonetic symbols. But there was no standardization, and the work soon became unintelligible. In 951, when an empress wished to read it, a committee of poets deciphered the work and put it into *kana*, the new syllabic script or alphabet that had developed during the ninth century. A second major anthology was the *Collection of Ancient and Modern Times*, compiled in 905. It was written entirely in *kana*.

The invention of *kana* opened the gate to the most brilliant developments of the Heian period. Most of the new works and certainly the greatest were by women, as most men were busy writing Chinese. One genre of writing was the diary or travel diary. An outstanding example of this genre was the *Izumi Shikibu Diary*, in which Izumi Shikibu reveals her tempestuous loves through a record of poetic exchanges.

The greatest works of the Heian period were by Sei Shōnagon and Murasaki Shikibu. Both were daughters of provincial officials serving at the Heian court. The *Pillow Book* of Sei Shōnagon contains sharp, satirical, amusing essays and literary jottings that reveal the demanding aristocratic taste of the early-eleventh-century Heian court—for which, as Sir George Sansom said, "religion became an art and art a religion."[3]

[3] G. Sansom, *Japan, A Short Cultural History* (New York: Appleton-Century-Crofts, 1962), p. 239.

instantly pull on his trousers. Instead he comes close to the lady and whispers whatever was left unsaid during the night. Even when he is dressed, he still lingers, vaguely pretending to be fastening his sash.

Presently he raises the lattice, and the two lovers stand together by the side door while he tells her how he dreads the coming day, which will keep them apart; then he slips away. The lady watches him go, and this moment of parting will remain among her most charming memories.

In Spring It Is the Dawn:
In spring it is the dawn that is most beautiful. As the light creeps over the hills, their outlines are dyed a faint red and wisps of purplish cloud trail over them.

In summer the nights. Not only when the moon shines, but on dark nights too, as the fireflies flit to and fro, and even when it rains, how beautiful it is!

In autumn the evenings, when the glittering sun sinks close to the edge of the hills and the crows fly back to their nests in threes and fours and twos; more charming still is a file of wild geese, like specks in the distant sky. When the sun has set, one's heart is moved by the sound of the wind and the hum of the insects.

In winter the early mornings. It is beautiful indeed when snow has fallen during the night, but splendid too when the ground is white with frost; or even when there is no snow or frost, but it is simply very cold and the attendants hurry from room to room stirring up the fires and bringing charcoal, how well this fits the season's mood! But as noon approaches and the cold wears off, no one bothers to keep the braziers alight, and soon nothing remains but piles of white ashes.

Things That Have Lost Their Power:
A large tree that has been blown down in a gale and lies on its side with its roots in the air.

The retreating figure of a sumō wrestler who has been defeated in a match.

A woman, who is angry with her husband about some trifling matter, leaves home and goes somewhere to hide. She is certain that he will rush about looking for her; but he does nothing of the kind and shows the most infuriating indifference. Since she cannot stay away for ever, she swallows her pride and returns. ❑

I. Morris (trans.), *The Pillow Book of Sei Shōnagon*, (New York: Columbia U. P., 1967), pp. 49, 216–217, 29–30, 1, 132.

The *Tale of Genji*, written by Murasaki Shikibu in about 1010, was the world's first novel. Emerging out of a short tradition of lesser works in which prose was a setting for poetry, *Genji* is a work of sensitivity, originality, and precise psychological delineation of character, for which there was no Chinese model. It tells of the life, loves, and sorrows of Prince Genji, the son of an imperial concubine, and, after his death, of his son Kaoru. The novel spans three quarters of a century and is historical in nature, though the court society it describes is more emperor-centered than the Fujiwara age in which Murasaki lived. Perhaps the book may be seen as having had a "definite and serious purpose." In one passage, Genji first twits a court lady whom he finds reading an extravagant romance; she is "hardly able to lift her eyes from the book in front of her." But then Genji relents and says:

I think far better of this art than I have led you to suppose. Even its practical value is immense. Without it what should we know of how people lived in the past, from the Age of the Gods down to the present day? For history books such as the *Chronicles of Japan* show us only one small corner of life; whereas these diaries and romances, which I see piled around you contain, I am sure, the most minute information about all sorts of people's private affairs.[4]

Nara and Heian Buddhism

The Six Sects of the Nara period each represented a separate philosophical doctrine within Mahayana

[4]R. Tsunoda, W. T. deBary, and D. Keene (eds.), *Sources of the Japanese Tradition* (New York: Columbia University Press, 1958), p. 181.

Buddhism. Their monks trained as religious specialists in monastic communities set apart from the larger society. They studied, read sutras, copied texts, meditated, and joined in rituals. The typical monastery was a self-contained community with a Golden Hall for worship, a pagoda that housed a relic or sutra, a belfry that rang the hours of the monastic regimen, a lecture hall, a refectory, and dormitories with monks' cells.

As in China, monasteries and temples were involved with the state. Tax revenues were assigned for their support. Monks prayed for rain in time of drought. In 741, temples were established in every province to protect the state by reading sutras. Monks prayed for the health of the emperor. The Temple of the Healing Buddha (Yakushiji) was built by an emperor when his consort fell ill. In China, in order to protect tax revenues and the family, laws were enacted to limit the number of monks and nuns. In Nara

Japan, where Buddhism spread only slowly outside the capital area, the same laws took on a prescriptive force. The figure that had been a limit in China became a goal in Japan. Thus the involvement of the state was the same as in China, but its role was far more supportive.

Japan in the seventh and eighth centuries was also far less developed culturally than China. The Japanese came to Buddhism not from the philosophical perspectives of Confucianism or Taoism, but from the magic and mystery of Shinto. The appeal of Buddhism to the early Japanese was, consequently, in its colorful and elaborate rituals; in the gods, demons, and angels of the Mahayana pantheon; and, above all, in the beauty of Buddhist art. The philosophy took longer to establish itself. The speed with which the Japanese mastered the construction of temples with elaborate wooden brackets and gracefully arching tile roofs, as well as

The Hōryūji Temple built by Prince Shōtoku in 607, contains the oldest wooden buildings in the world. They are the best surviving examples of Chinese Buddhist architecture. [Japan Information Center.]

the loveliness of Nara Buddhist sculpture, wall paintings, and lacquer temple altars, was no less an achievement than the establishment of a political system based on the T'ang codes.

Japan's cultural identity was also different. In China, Buddhism was always viewed as Indian and alien. Its earliest Buddha statues, like those of northwestern India, looked Greek. That Buddhism was part of a non-Chinese culture was one factor leading to the Chinese persecution of Buddhists during the ninth century. In contrast, Japan's cultural identity or cultural self-consciousness took shape only during the Nara and early Heian periods. One element in that identity was the imperial cult derived from Shinto. But as a religion, Shinto was no match for Buddhism. The Japanese were aware that Buddhism was foreign, but it was no more so than Confucianism and all of the rest of the T'ang culture that had helped shape the major portion of the Japanese identity, so there was no particular bias against it. Consequently, Buddhism entered deeply into Japanese culture and retained its vitality longer. It was not until the seventeenth or eighteenth centuries that Japanese elites became so Confucian as to be anti-Buddhist.

In 794, the court moved to Heian. Buddhist temples soon became as entrenched in the new capital as they had been in Nara. The two great new Buddhist sects of the Heian era were Tendai and Shingon.

Saichō (767–822) had founded a temple on Mount Hiei to the northwest of Kyoto in 785. He went to China as a student monk in 804 and returned the following year with the teachings of the Tendai sect (T'ien T'ai in Chinese; see Chapter 9). He spread in Japan the doctrine that salvation was not solely for monastic specialists but could be attained by all who led a life of contemplation and moral purity. He was a religious reformer who instituted strict monastic rules and a twelve-year training curriculum for novice monks at his mountain monastery. Over the next few centuries, the sect grew until thousands of temples had been built on Mount Hiei, and it remained a center of Japanese Buddhism until it was destroyed in the wars of the sixteenth century. Many later Japanese sects emerged from within the Tendai fold, stressing one or another doctrine within its syncretic teachings.

The Shingon sect was begun by Kūkai (774–835). He studied Confucianism, Taoism, and Buddhism at the court university. Deciding that Buddhism was superior, he became a monk at the age of eighteen. In 804, he went to China with Saichō. He returned two years later bearing the Shingon doctrines and founded a monastery on Mount Kōya to the south of the Nara plain and far from the new capital. Kūkai was an extraordinary figure. He was a bridge builder, a poet, an artist, and one of the three great calligraphers of his age. He is sometimes credited with inventing the *kana*

syllabary and with introducing tea into Japan. Shingon doctrines center on an eternal and cosmic Buddha, of whom all other Buddhas are manifestations. *Shingon* means "true word" or "mantra," a verbal formula with mystical powers. It is sometimes called *esoteric Buddhism* because it had secret teachings that were passed from master to disciple. In China, Shingon died out as a sect in the persecutions of the mid-ninth century, but it was tremendously successful in Japan. Its doctrines even spread to the Tendai center on Mount Hiei. Part of the appeal was in its air of mystery and its complex rituals involving signs, the manipulation of religious objects, and mandalas—maps of the cosmic Buddhist universe.

During the later Heian period, Buddhism began to be assimilated. In village culture, many Buddhist elements were taken into folk religion. In Japanese high culture, Shinto was almost absorbed by Buddhism. Shinto deities came to be seen as the local manifestations of universal Buddhas. The cosmic or "Great Sun Buddha" of the Shingon sect, for example, was easily identified with the sun goddess. Often, great Buddhist temples had smaller Shinto shrines on their grounds. The job of the Buddha was to watch over Japan, whereas the shrine deity had the lesser task of guarding the temple itself. Not till the mid-nineteenth century was Shinto disentangled from Buddhism, and then for political ends.

Japan's Early Feudal Age

The year 1185, or 1156 if we include Taira rule in Kyoto, marked another major turning point in Japanese history. It began the shift from centuries of rule by a civil aristocracy to centuries of rule by one that was military. It saw the formation of the *bakufu* (tent government), a completely non-Chinese type of government. It saw the emergence of the *shogun* as the *de facto* ruler of Japan, though in theory he was a military official of the emperor. It marked the beginning of new cultural forms, and initiated changes in family and social organization.

The Rise of Minamoto Yoritomo

The seizure of Kyoto by Taira Kiyomori's military band in 1156 fell far short of being a national military hegemony, for other bands still flourished elsewhere in Japan. In the decades after Kiyomori's victory, the Taira embraced the elegant lifestyle of the Kyoto court while ties to their base area along the Inland Sea weakened. They assumed that their tutelage over the court would be as enduring as had been that of the Fujiwara. In the meantime, the Minamoto were rebuilding their strength in eastern Japan. In 1180, Minamoto Yoritomo responded to a call to arms by a disaf-

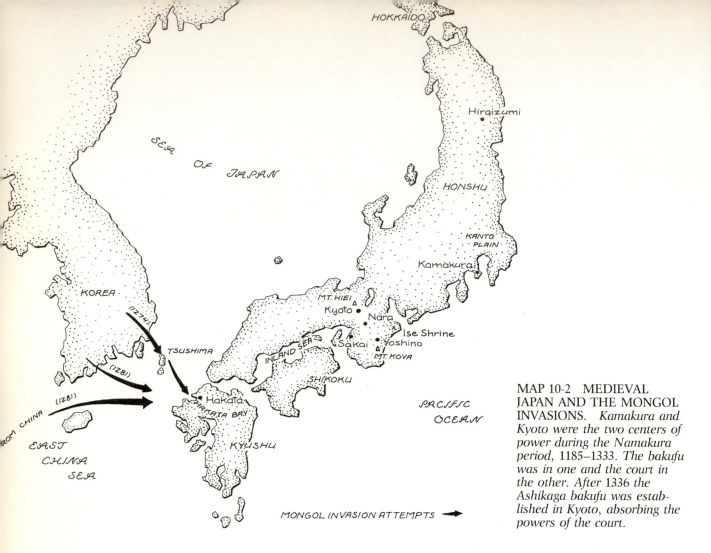

MAP 10-2 MEDIEVAL JAPAN AND THE MONGOL INVASIONS. *Kamakura and Kyoto were the two centers of power during the Namakura period, 1185–1333. The bakufu was in one and the court in the other. After 1336 the Ashikaga bakufu was established in Kyoto, absorbing the powers of the court.*

fected prince, seized control of eastern Japan (the rich Kanto plain), and began the war that ended in 1185 with the downfall of the Taira.

Yoritomo's victory in 1185 was national, for his armies had ranged over most of Japan. After his victory, warriors from every area vied to become his vassals. Wary of the blandishments of Kyoto that had weakened the Taira forces, Yoritomo set up his headquarters at Kamakura. It was thirty miles south of present-day Tokyo, at the edge of his base of power in eastern Japan. He called his government the *bakufu* (literally, "tent government") in contrast to the civil government in Kyoto. Like the house government of the Fujiwara or the "cloister government" of the retired emperors, the offices he established were few and practical: one to deal with his samurai retainers, one to administer and execute his policies, and one to hear legal suits. Each office was staffed by vassals. The decisions of these offices, built up into a body of customary law, were codified in 1232 as the Jōei Code. Yoritomo also appointed military governors in each

province and military stewards on the former estates of the Taira and others who had fought against him. These appointments carried the right to some of the income from the land. The rest of the income, as earlier, went to Kyoto as taxes or as revenues to the noble owners of the estates.

The Question of Feudalism

Scholars often contend that Yoritomo's rule marks the start of feudalism in Japan. Feudalism may be defined in terms of three criteria: lord–vassal relationships, fiefs given in return for military service, and a warrior ethic. Do these apply to Kamakura Japan?

Certainly, the mounted warriors who made up the armies of Yoritomo were his vassals, not his kin. The Minamoto and Taira houses were originally clans or extended families, very much like the Fujiwara or the earlier Yamato nobility. Yoritomo's brothers were among his generals. But after he came to power, he favored his vassals over his kin, and the lateral ties of blood gave way to the vertical and political lord–

vassal bond. On the question of fiefs, the answer is ambiguous. Kamakura vassals received rights to income from land in exchange for military service. But the income was usually a slice of the surplus from the estates of Kyoto nonmilitary aristocrats. Fiefs, as such, did not appear until the late fifteenth century.

However, there is no ambiguity regarding the warrior ethic, which had been developing among regional military bands for several centuries before 1185. The samurai prized martial qualities such as bravery, cunning, physical strength, and endurance. They gave their swords names. Their sports were hunting, hawking, and archery—loosing their arrows at the target while riding at full tilt. If the military tales of the period are to be believed, their combat was often individual, and before engaging in battle, warriors would call out their pedigrees. That is to say, warriors thought of themselves as a military aristocracy that practiced "the way of the bow and arrow," "the way of the bow and horse," "the way of the warriors," and so on. In the *Tale of Heike*, a military romance recounting the struggle between the Taira and the Minamoto, a Taira general asks a vassal from eastern Japan:

"Sanemori, in the eight eastern provinces are there many men who are as mighty archers as you are?"

"Do you then consider me a mighty archer?" asked Sanemori with a scornful smile. "I can only draw an arrow thirteen handbreadths long. In the eastern provinces there are any number of warriors who can do so. There is one famed archer who never draws a shaft less than fifteen handbreadths long. So mighty is his bow that four or five ordinary men must pull together to bend it. When he shoots, his arrow can easily pierce two or three suits of armor at once. Even a warrior from a small estate has at least five hundred soldiers. They are bold horsemen who never fall, nor do they let their horses stumble on the roughest road. When they fight, they do not care if even their parents or children are killed; they ride on over their bodies and continue the battle.

"The warriors of the western province are quite different. If their parents are killed, they retire from the battle and perform Buddhist rites to console the souls of the dead. Only after the mourning is over will they fight again. If their children are slain, their grief is so deep that they cease fighting altogether. When their rations have given out, they plant rice in the fields and go out to fight only after reaping it. They dislike the heat of summer. They grumble at the severe cold of winter. This is not the way of the soldiers of the eastern provinces."[5]

The Taira soldiers, according to the story, "heard his words and trembled."

The Kamakura military band thus pretty well fits our definition of feudalism. Nonetheless, qualifications

are in order, since Kamakura warrior bands were only a part of the total society. One qualification is that Kamakura Japan still had two political centers. The bakufu had military authority, but the Kyoto court continued the late Heian pattern of civil rule. It appointed civil governors; it received tax revenues; and it controlled the region about Kyoto. Noble families, retired emperors, and the great Buddhist temples—in control of vast estates—also contributed to Kyoto's ongoing power; and it also remained the fount of rank and honors. After his victory in 1185, Yoritomo asked the emperor for the title of *barbarian-quelling generalissimo* (*Sei i tai shōgun*, conventionally shortened to *shōgun*). He was refused, and only after the retired emperor died in 1192 did Yoritomo get the title to match his power. Yoritomo's request for the title was partly justified by the fact that he was a Minamoto offshoot of the imperial line.

The small size of Yoritomo's vassal band is an even more telling argument against viewing Japan as fully feudal at this time. Numbering about two thousand before 1221 and three thousand thereafter, most of the band were concentrated in eastern Japan. But even if as many as half were distributed about the rest of the country as military governors and stewards, there would only have been one hundred in a region the size of Massachusetts, as Japan in 1180 was about fifteen times larger than that state. Given the difficulties of transportation and communications, how could so few control such a large area? The answer is that they did not have to.

The local social order of the late Heian era continued into the Kamakura period. Governors, district magistrates, local notables—including many warriors who were not members of Yoritomo's band—were in place and continued to function more or less as they had earlier. To gain an influence on the local scene, the newly appointed Kamakura vassals had to win the cooperation of these local figures. In short, even if the Kamakura vassals themselves can be called "feudal," they were no more than a thin skim on the surface of a society constructed according to older principles.

Kamakura Rule After Yoritomo

As soon as Yoritomo died in 1199, his widow and her Hōjō kinsmen moved to usurp the power of the Minamoto house. The widow, having taken holy orders after her husband's death, was known as the Nun Shōgun. One of her sons was pushed aside. The other became shōgun but was murdered in 1219. After that, the Hōjō ruled as regents for a puppet shōgun, just as the Fujiwara had been regents for figurehead emperors. The Kyoto court tried to take advantage of the usurpation to lead an armed uprising against Kamakura in 1221, but the rebellion was quickly suppressed. New military stewards were then placed on

[5] H. Kitagawa and B. Tsuchida (trans.), *The Tale of Heike* (Tokyo, Tokyo University Press, 1975), p. 330.

Mongol invaders battling with intrepid samurai horseman. Note the bomb bursting in air at the upper right of this late thirteenth century Japanese scroll painting. [Tokyo National Museum.]

the lands of those who had joined in the uprising. Any society based on personal bonds faces the problem of how to transfer loyalty from one generation to another. In 1221, the Kamakura vassals fought for the Hōjō, despite the Hōjō usurpation of the Minamoto rule. Loyalty to the institution of the bakufu, which guaranteed their landed interests, had replaced personal loyalty.

In 1266, Kublai Khan (see Chapter 9) sent envoys demanding that Japan submit to his rule. Korea had been subjugated in 1258, and his army looked outward across the Tsushima Straits. The Kyoto court was terrified, but the Hōjō at Kamakura refused. The first Mongol invasion fleet arrived with 30,000 troops in 1274, but was destroyed by a typhoon. The Mongols again sent envoys. This time, they were beheaded. A second invasion force arrived in 1281, two years after Kublai had completed his conquest of south China. Carrying 140,000 troops, it was an amphibious operation on a scale never before seen in world history. With gunpowder bombs and phalanxes of archers protected by a forward wall of soldiers carrying overlapping shields, the Mongol forces were formidable.

The Japanese tactics of fierce individual combat were not appropriate to their foe. But a wall of stone had been erected along the curved shoreline of Hakata Bay in northwest Kyushu, and the Mongols were held off for two months until again *kamikaze*, or "divine winds," sank a portion of their fleet and forced the rest to withdraw. Preparations for a third expedition ended with Kublai's death in 1294.

The burden of repelling the Mongols fell on Kamakura's vassals in Kyushu. Non-Kamakura warriors of Kyushu also were mobilized to fight under the command of military governors. But as no land was taken, unlike in 1221, there were few rewards for those who had fought, and dissatisfaction was rife. Even temples and shrines demanded rewards, claiming that their prayers had brought about the divine winds.

Women in Warrior Society

The Nun Shōgun was one of a long line of important women in Japan. Historians no longer speak of an early matriarchal age. But the central figure of Japanese mythology was the sun goddess, who ruled the Plain of High Heaven. In the late Yayoi age the shaman ruler Pimiko was probably not an exceptional figure; she was followed by the empresses of the Yamato and Nara courts, and they, in turn, by the great women writers of the Heian period. During the era of the Kamakura bakufu, there was only one Nun Shōgun, but the daughters of warrior families, as well as the sons, often trained in archery and other military arts. Women also occasionally inherited the position of military steward. As long as society was stable, women fared relatively well. But as fighting became more common in the fourteenth century, their position began to decline, and as warfare became endemic in the fifteenth, their status plummeted. It was at this time that multigeniture gave way to male primogeniture to protect the military fief—the warrior's reward for serving his lord in battle, and the lord's guarantee that his warriors would continue their service.

The Ashikaga Era

At times, formal political institutions seem rocklike in their stability and history unfolds within the framework that they provide. Then, almost as if a kaleidoscope had been shaken, the old institutions collapse and are swept away. In their place appear new institutions and new patterns of personal relations which, often enough, had begun to take shape within the confines of the old. It is not easy to explain the timing of such upheavals, but they are easy to recognize. One occurred in Japan between 1331 and 1336.

Various tensions developed within late Kamakura society. The patrimony of a warrior was divided among his children. Over several generations, vassals became poorer, often falling into debt. High-ranking vassals of Kamakura were dissatisfied with the Hōjō monopolization of key bakufu posts. In the meantime, the ties of vassals to Kamakura were weakening, while the ties to other warriors within their region were growing stronger. New regional bands were ready to emerge.

The precipitating event was a revolt in 1331 by an emperor who thought emperors should actually rule. Kamakura sent Ashikaga Takauji, the head of a branch family of the Minamoto line, to put down the revolt. Instead, he joined it, giving a clear signal to other regional lords, who threw off Kamakura's control. The Hōjō bakufu in Kamakura collapsed.

What emerged out of the dust and confusion of the period 1331–1336 was a regional multistate system centering on Kyoto. Each region was based on a warrior band about the size of the band that had brought Yorimoto to power a century and a half earlier. In the central Kyoto region, Ashikaga Takauji (1305–1358) established his bakufu. Its offices were simple and functional: a samurai office for police and military matters, an administrative office for financial matters, a documents office for land records, and a judicial board to settle disputes. The offices were staffed by Takauji's vassals, with the most trusted vassals holding the highest posts. They were lords (now called *daimyo*) in their own right who also, usually, held appointments as military governors in the provinces surrounding Kyoto. The bakufu also appointed vassals to watch over its interests in the far north, in eastern Japan, and in Kyushu.

Government in the outlying regions was more diverse. Some lords held several provinces, some only one. Some had integrated most of the warriors in their areas into their bands. Others had several unassimilated military bands in their territories, forcing them to rely more on the authority of Kyoto. Formally, all regional lords or *daimyo* were the vassals of the shōgun. But the relationship was often nominal. Sometimes the regional lords lived on their lands; sometimes they lived in Kyoto.

The relationship between the Kyoto bakufu and the regional lords fluctuated during the period from 1336 to 1467. At times, able lords made their regions into virtually independent states. At other times, the Kyoto

GOVERNMENT BY MILITARY HOUSES	
1156–1180	Taira rule in Kyoto
1185–1333	The Kamakura Bakufu
1185	Founded by Minamoto Yoritomo
1219	Usurped by Hōjō
1221	Armed uprising by Kyoto court
1232	Formation of Jōei Legal Code
1274 and 1281	Invasion by Mongols
1336–1467	The Ashikaga Bakufu
1336	Begun by Ashikaga Takauji
1392	End of Southern Court
1467	Start of warring states

bakufu became stronger. The third shōgun, for example, tightened his grip on the Kyoto court. He even relinquished the military post of shōgun—to his son in 1394—in order to take the highest civil post of grand minister of state. He improved relations with the great Buddhist temples and Shinto shrines and established ties with Ming China. Most significant were his military campaigns, which dented the autonomy of regional lords outside of the inner Kyoto circle.

But the institution of vassalage in Japan's early feudal society contained a contradiction that even the third shōgun could not overcome. He had to rely on his vassals. To strengthen them for his campaigns, he gave them the authority to levy taxes; to unify in their own hands all judicial, administrative, and military authority in their regions; and to take on unaffiliated warriors as their direct vassals. But in doing so, he left problems for his successors. As ties of personal loyalty wore thin, local warrior bands began to form in the interstices of the Ashikaga regional states.

Agriculture, Commerce, and Medieval Guilds

Population figures for medieval Japan are rough estimations, but recent scholarship suggests six million for the year 1200 and twelve million for 1600. Much of the increase occurred during the Kamakura and Ashikaga periods when the country was fairly peaceful. The increase was brought about by land reclamation and improvements in agricultural technology: Iron-edged tools became available to all. New strains of rice were developed. Irrigation and diking improved. Double cropping began: vegetables in dry fields during fall and winter, and rice in irrigated paddies during the spring and summer.

In the Nara and early Heian periods, the economy was almost exclusively agricultural. Japan had no money, no commerce, and no cities—apart from Nara, which developed into a temple town living on assigned revenues, and Kyoto, where taxes were consumed. Following the example of China, the government had established a mint, but little money actually circulated. Taxes were paid in grain and labor. Commercial transactions were largely barter, with silk or grain as the medium of exchange. Artisans produced for the noble households or temples to which they were attached. Peasants were economically self-sufficient.

From the late Heian period, partly as a side effect of fixed tax quotas, more of the growing agricultural surplus stayed in local hands. This trend accelerated during the Kamakura and Ashikaga periods, when there was a transfer of income from the court aristocrats to the warrior class. As this occurred, artisans detached themselves from noble households and began to produce for the market. Military equipment was an early staple of commerce, but gradually *sake*, lumber, paper, vegetable oils, salt, and products of the sea also became commercialized. A demand for copper coins appeared, and as they were no longer minted in Japan, they were imported in increasingly huge quantities from China.

During the Kamakura period, independent merchants handling the products of artisans appeared as well. Some trade networks spread over all Japan. More often, artisan and merchant guilds, not unlike those of medieval Europe, paid a fee in exchange for monopoly rights in a given area. Early Kyoto guilds paid fees to powerful nobles or temples, and later to the Ashikaga bakufu. In outlying areas, guild privileges were obtained from the regional feudal lords. From the Kamakura period on, markets were held periodically in many parts of Japan—by a river or at a crossroads. Some place names in Japan today reveal such an origin. Yokkaichi, today an industrial city, means "fourth-day market." It began as a place where markets were held on the fourth, fourteenth, and twenty-fourth days of each month. During the fourteenth and fifteenth centuries, such markets were held with increasing frequency until, eventually, permanent towns were established.

Buddhism and Medieval Culture

The Nara and Heian periods are often referred to as Japan's classical age. The period that followed—say, from 1200 to 1600—is often called medieval. It was medieval in the root sense of the word in that it lay between the other two major spans of premodern Japanese history. It was also medieval in that it shared some characteristics that we label *medieval* in Europe and China. However, there is an important difference. Medieval Japan was a direct outgrowth of classical Japan; one can even say that there was some overlap during the early Kamakura. In contrast, Europe was torn by barbarian invasions, and there was a millennium separating the classical culture of Rome and high medieval culture. Even to have a Charlemagne, Europe had to wait for half a millennium. In China, the

Nobles in ox-drawn carriages and commoners on foot attend a sermon by the Pure Land monk Ippen (1239–1289). [Tokyo National Museum.]

era of political disunity and barbarian invasions lasted only four hundred years, and it was during these years that its medieval Buddhist culture blossomed.

The results of historical continuity are visible in every branch of Japanese culture. The native poetic tradition continued with great vigor. In 1205, the compilation of the *New Collection from Ancient and Modern Times (Shinkokinshū)* was ordered by the same emperor who began the 1221 rebellion against Kamakura. The flat *Yamato-e* style of painting that had reached a peak in the *Genji Scrolls* continued into the medieval era with scrolls on historical and religious themes or fairy-tale adventures. Artisan production continued without a break. The same techniques of lacquerwork with inlaid mother-of-pearl that had been used for, say, a cosmetic box for a Heian court lady were now applied to produce saddles for Kamakura warriors. In short, just as Heian estates continued on into the Kamakura era, and just as the authority of the court continued, so did Heian culture extend into medieval Japan.

Nonetheless, medieval Japanese culture had some distinctly new characteristics. First, as the leadership of the society shifted from court aristocrats to military aristocrats, changes occurred in the literature. The medieval military tales were as different from the *Tale of Genji* as the armor of the mounted warrior was from the no less colorful silken robes of the court nobility. Second, a new wave of culture entered from China. If the Nara and Heian had been shaped by T'ang culture, medieval Japan—though not its institutions—was shaped by Sung culture. This link is immediately apparent in the ink paintings of medieval Japan. Third, and most important, the medieval centuries were Japan's age of Buddhist faith. A religious revolution occurred during the Kamakura period and deepened during the Ashikaga. It fundamentally influenced the arts of Japan.

Japanese Pietism: Pure Land and Nichiren Buddhism

Among the doctrines of the Heian Tendai sect was the belief that the true teachings of the historical Buddha had been lost and that salvation could be had only by calling on the name of Amida, a cosmic Buddha who ruled over the Western Paradise (or Pure Land). During the tenth and eleventh centuries, itinerant preachers began to spread Pure Land doctrines and practices beyond the narrow circles of Kyoto. Kūya (903–972), the "saint of the marketplace," for example, preached not only in Kyoto and throughout the provinces, but even to the aboriginal Ainu in northernmost Japan. The doctrine that the world had fallen on evil times and that only faith would suffice was given credence by earthquakes, epidemics, fires, and ban-

The mid-Heian monk Kūya (903–972) preached Pure Land doctrines in Kyoto and throughout Japan. Little Buddhas emerge from his mouth. [Sekai Bunka Photo.]

ditry in the capital, as well as wars throughout the land. The deepening Buddhist coloration of the age can be read in the opening lines of the thirteenth century *Tale of the House of Taira*, written just two centuries after the *Tale of Genji* and the *Pillow Book:*

The sound of the bell of Jetavana echoes the impermanence of all things. The hue of the flowers of the teak-tree declares that they who flourish must be brought low. Yea, the proud ones are but for a moment, like an evening dream in springtime. The mighty are destroyed at the last, they are but as the dust before the wind.[6]

In the early Kamakura era, two figures stand out as religious geniuses who experienced the truth of Buddhism within themselves. Hōnen (1133–1212) was perhaps the first to say that the invocation of the name of Amida alone was enough for salvation and that only faith rather than works or rituals counted. These claims brought Hōnen into conflict with the older Buddhist establishment and marked the emergence of Pure Land as a separate sect. Hōnen was followed by Shin-

[6] A. L. Sadler (trans.), *The Tenfoot Square Hut and Tales of the Heike* (Rutland, Vt., and Tokyo: Charles E. Tuttle, 1972), p. 22.

ran (1173–1262), who taught that even a single invocation in praise of Amida, if done with perfect faith, was sufficient for salvation. But perfect faith was not solely the result of human effort: It was a gift from Amida. Pride was an obstacle to purity of heart. One of Shinran's most famous sayings is "If even a good man can be reborn in the Pure Land, how much more so a wicked man."[7]

Shinran's emphasis on faith alone led him to break many of the monastic rules of earlier Buddhism: he ate meat; he married a nun, and thereafter, the Pure Land sect had a married clergy; and he taught that all occupations were equally "heavenly" if performed with a pure heart. Exiled from Kyoto, he traveled about Japan establishing "True Pure Land" congregations. (When the Jesuits arrived in Japan in the sixteenth century, they called this sect "the devil's Christianity.")

Because of a line of distinguished teachers after Shinran, because of its doctrinal simplicity, and because of its reliance on the practice of piety, Pure Land Buddhism became the dominant form of Buddhism in Japan and remains so today. It was also the only sect in medieval Japan—apart from the Tendai sect on Mount Hiei—to develop political and military power. As a religion of faith, it developed a strong church as a protection for the saved while they were still in this world. As peasants became militarized during the fifteenth century, some Pure Land village congregations created self-defense forces. At times, they rebelled against feudal lords. In one instance, Pure Land armies ruled the province of Kaga for over a century. These congregations were smashed during the late sixteenth century, and the sect was depoliticized.

A second devotional sect was founded by Nichiren (1222–1282), who believed that the Lotus Sutra perfectly embodied the teachings of the Buddha. He instructed his adherents to chant, over and over, "Praise to the Lotus Sutra of the Wondrous Law," usually to the accompaniment of rapid drumbeats. Like the repetition of "Praise to the Amida Buddha" in the Pure Land sect or comparable verbal formulas in other religions around the world, the chanting optimally induced a state of religious rapture. The concern with an internal spiritual transformation was common to both the devotional and the meditative sects of Buddhism. Nichiren was remarkable for a Buddhist in being both intolerant and nationalistic. He blamed the ills of his age on rival sects and asserted that only his sect could protect Japan. He predicted the Mongol invasions, and his sect claimed credit for the "divine winds" that sank the Mongol fleets. Even his adopted Buddhist name, the Sun Lotus, combined the term for the rising sun of Japan with that of the flower that had become the symbol of Buddhism.

[7]Tsunoda, deBary, and Keene, p. 217.

A landscape by the Zen monk Sesshū (1420–1506). [Tokyo National Museum.]

Zen Buddhism

Meditation had long been a part of Japanese monastic practice. Zen meditation and doctrines were introduced by monks returning from study in Sung China. Eisai (1141–1215) transposed to Japan the Rinzai sect in 1191 and Dōgen (1200–1253) the Sōtō sect in 1227. Eisai's sect was patronized by the Hōjō rulers in Kamakura and the Ashikaga in Kyoto. Dōgen established his sect on Japan's western coast, far from centers of political power.

Zen in Japan was a religion of paradox. Its monks were learned, yet it stressed a return to ignorance, to the uncluttered "original mind," attained in a flash of intuitive understanding. Zen was punctiliously traditional, the most Chinese of Japanese medieval sects. The authority of the Zen master over his pupil-monks was absolute. Yet Zen was also iconoclastic. Its sages

Hakuin's Enlightenment

Hakuin (1686–1769) was a poet, a painter, and a Zen master. He wrote in colloquial Japanese as well as in Chinese. He illustrated the continuing power of the Zen tradition in postmedieval times. In an autobiographical account of his spiritual quest, he first told of his disappointments and failures, but then wrote:

In the spring of my twenty-fourth year, I was painfully struggling at the Eiganji in the province of Echigo. I slept neither day nor night, forgetting either to eat or sleep. A great doubt suddenly possessed me, and I felt as if frozen to death in the midst of an icy field extending thousands of *li*. A sense of an extraordinary purity permeated my bosom. I could not move. I was virtually senseless. What remained was only *"Mu."* Although I heard the master's lectures in the Lecture Hall, it was as though I were listening to his discourse from some sixty or seventy steps outside the Hall, or as if I were floating in the air. This condition lasted for several days until one night I heard the striking of a temple bell. All at once a transformation came over me, as though a layer of ice were smashed or a tower of jade pulled down. Instantly I came to my senses. . . . Former doubts were completely dissolved, like ice which had melted away. "How marvelous! How marvelous!" I cried out aloud. There was no cycle of birth and death from which I had to escape, no enlightenment for which I had to seek.

But Hakuin's teacher did not accept this as adequate. Hakuin's quest continued. Eight years later:

At the age of thirty-two I settled in this dilapidated temple [Shōinji]. In a dream one night my mother handed me a purple silk robe. When I lifted it I felt great weights in both sleeves. Examining it, I found in each sleeve an old mirror about five or six inches in diameter. The reflection of the right-hand mirror penetrated deep into my heart. My own mind, as well as mountains and rivers, the entire earth, became serene and bottomless. The left-hand mirror had no luster on its entire surface. Its face was like that of a new iron pan not yet touched by fire. Suddenly I became aware that the luster on the left-hand mirror surpassed that of the right by a million times. After this incident, the vision of all things was like looking at my own face. For the first time I realized the meaning of the words, "The eyes of the Tathā-gata behold the Buddha-nature." ❑

W. T. deBary (ed.), *The Buddhist Tradition in India, China, and Japan* (New York: Modern Library, 1972), pp. 384, 387–388.

A Zen garden outside the Abbot's Hall at Daitokuji in Kyoto—a "dry landscape" in which sand represents the sea and rocks represent mountains. [Japan Information Service.]

The Arts and Zen Buddhism

Zen Buddhism in Japan developed a theory of art that influenced every department of medieval culture. Put simply, it is, first, that intuitive action is better than conscious, purposive action. The best painter is one so skilled that he no longer needs to think of technique but paints as a natural act. Substitute a sword for a brush, and the same theory applies to the warrior. A swordsman who has to stop to consider his next move is at a disadvantage in battle. But to this concern with direct, intuitive action is added the Zen distinction between the deluded mind and the "original mind." The latter is also referred to as the "no mind," or the mind in the enlightened state. The highest intuitive action proceeds from such a state of being. This theory was applied, in time, to the performance of the actor, to the skill of the potter, to archery, to flower arrangement, and to the tea ceremony. Compare the following two passages, one by Seami (1363–1443), the author of many Nō plays, and the other by Takuan Sōhō (1573–1645), a famous Zen master of the early Tokugawa era (see Chapter 18).

Sometimes spectators of the Nō say, "The moments of 'no-action' are the most enjoyable." This is an art which the actor keeps secret. Dancing and singing, movements and the different types of miming are all acts performed by the body. Moments of "no-action" occur in between. When we examine why such moments without actions are enjoyable, we find that it is due to the underlying spiritual strength of the actor which unremittingly holds the attention. He does not relax the tension when the dancing or singing come to an end or at intervals between the dialogue and the different types of miming, but maintains an unwavering inner strength. This feeling of inner strength will faintly reveal itself and bring enjoyment. However, it is undesirable for the actor to permit this inner strength to become obvious to the audience. If it is obvious, it becomes an act, and is no longer "no-action." The actions before and after an interval of "no-action" must be linked by entering the state of mindlessness in which one conceals even from oneself one's intent. This, then, is the faculty of moving audiences, by linking all the artistic powers with one mind.

Where should a swordsman fix his mind? If he puts his mind on the physical movement of his opponent, it will be seized by the movement; if he places it on the sword of his opponent, it will be arrested by the sword; if he focuses his mind on the thought of striking his opponent, it will be carried away by the very thought; if the mind stays on his own sword, it will be captured by his sword; if he centers it on the thought of not being killed by his opponent, his mind will be overtaken by this very thought; if he keeps his mind firmly on his own or on his opponent's posture, likewise, it will be blocked by them. Thus the mind should not be fixed anywhere. ❑

R. Tsunoda, W. T. deBary, and D. Keene, *Sources of Japanese Tradition* (New York: Columbia U. P. 1958), p. 291.

W. T. deBary (ed.), *The Buddhist Tradition* (New York: Modern Library, 1972), p. 377.

were depicted in paintings as tearing up sutras to make the point that it is religious experience and not words that count. And within a rigidly structured monastic regimen, a vital give-and-take occurred as monks tested their understanding—gained through long hours of meditation—in encounters with their master. Buddhism stressed compassion for all sentient beings, yet in Japan, Zen was particularly involved with the samurai whose duty it was to fight and kill. Many of Japan's military saw the severe discipline of Zen as ideal training for single-minded attention to duty; a few Hōjō and Ashikaga rulers even practiced Zen themselves.

The most remarkable aspect of Zen was its influence on the arts of medieval Japan. The most beautiful gardens, for example, were in Zen temples. Many were designed by Zen masters. The most famous, at Ryōanji, consists of fifteen rocks set in white sand. Others only slightly less austere contain moss, shrubs, trees, ponds, and streams. With these elements and within a small compass, rocks become cliffs, raked sand becomes rivers or the sea, and a little world of nature emerges. If a garden may be said to possess philosophic stillness, the Zen gardens of Daitokuji and other Kyoto temples have it.

Zen monks such as Josetsu, Shūbun, and Sesshū certainly number among the masters of ink painting in East Asia. One painting by Josetsu shows a man trying to catch a catfish with a gourd. Like the sound of one hand clapping, the impossibility of catching a catfish with a gourd presents as art the kind of logical conundrum used to expound Zen teachings. Sesshū painted

"Broken ink" style painting by the Zen monk Sesshū (1420–1506). [Tokyo National Museum.]

in both the broken-ink style, in which splashlike brush strokes represent an entire mountain landscape, and in a more usual calligraphic style. Because the artist's creativity itself was seen as grounded in his experience of meditation, a painting of a waterfall or a crow on a leafless branch in winter was viewed as no less religious than a painting of the mythic Zen founder Bodhidharma.

Nō Plays

Another fascinating product of Ashikaga culture was the Nō play, a kind of mystery drama with no parallels elsewhere in East Asia. The play was performed on an almost square, bare wooden stage (often outdoors) by male actors wearing robes of great beauty and carved, painted masks of enigmatic expressions. Many such masks and robes number among Japan's National Treasures. The chorus was chanted to the accompaniment of flute and drums. The language was poetic. The action was slow and highly stylized: Circling about the stage could represent a journey, and a motion of the hand, the reading of a letter. The artistic theory of the Nō was pure Zen, though some Nō plays also drew on Pure Land doctrines for their content. At a critical juncture in most plays, the protagonist is possessed by the spirit of another and performs a dance. Spirit possession was a commonplace of Japanese folk religion and also occurs in the *Tale of Genji*. Several plays were shown in a single performance; comic skits called Crazy Words were usually interspersed between them to break the tension.

Nō plays reveal a medley of themes present in medieval Japanese culture. Some pivot on incidents in the struggle between the Taira and the Minamoto. Some are religious: A cormorant fisher is saved from the king of hell for having given lodging to a priest. Some plays pick up incidents from the *Tale of Genji* or the Heian court: The famous Heian beauty and poet Ono no Komachi is possessed by the spirit of a lover she had spurned; their conflict is left to be resolved in a Buddhist afterlife. Some plays are close to fairy tales: A fisherman takes the feather robe of an angel, but when she begins to sicken and grow wan, he returns the robe and she dances for him a dance that is only performed in heaven. Some plays have Chinese themes: A traveler dreams an entire lifetime on a magical pillow while waiting for a bowl of millet to cook. Another play reflects the Japanese ambivalence toward China: Po Chu-i, the T'ang poet most famous in Japan, rows a boat over the seas and comes to the shores of Japan, where he is met by fishermen who turn him back in the name of Japanese poetry. One fisherman speaks:

You in China make your poems and odes out of the Scriptures of India; and we have made our "uta" out of the poems and odes of China. Since then our poetry is a blend of three lands, we have named it Yamato, the great blend, and all our songs "Yamato uta."[8]

At the end, the fisherman is transformed into the Shinto god of Japanese poetry and performs the "Sea Green Dance."

---

[8] A. Waley (trans.), *The Nō Plays of Japan* (New York: Grove Press, 1957), p. 252.

Early Japanese History in World Perspective

During the first millennium A.D., the major development in world history was the spread of the civilizations that had risen out of the earlier philosophical and religious revolutions. In the West, the process began with the spread of civilization from Greece to Rome, continued with the rise of Christianity and its diffusion within the late Roman Empire, and entered a third phase when the countries of northern Europe became civilized by borrowing Mediterranean culture. The spread was slow because Rome was no longer a vital center. By contrast, in East Asia the spread of civilization from its Chinese heartland was more rapid because in the early seventh century, the T'ang empire had been reestablished—more vital, more exuberant, and more powerful than ever before. Within the East Asian culture zone, and apart from post-T'ang China itself, there were three major developing areas: Vietnam, Korea, and Japan.

All three used Chinese writing for most of their history, combined indigenous and Chinese elements to create distinctive cultures and national identities, and in premodern times built independent states. The contrast between these countries and other areas around China is interesting. Vietnam, Korea, and Japan were more Chinese in their culture than Tibet, Mongolia, or Manchuria. Yet in the modern era, the latter areas have been swallowed up by China, whereas Korea, Vietnam, and Japan have preserved their independence. These three nations used Chinese culture to forge self-identities that could resist Chinese domination—just as Third-World nations today borrow Western systems and ideas to build states that are politically anti-Western.

For all their political independence, Vietnam and Korea were nonetheless too close to China to avoid its imprint. The cultural flow was too constant. Often, there was not time for a borrowed element to evolve freely. Japan, in contrast—because it was bigger, more populous, and more distant—became the major variant to the Chinese pattern within East Asian civilization. It reflected, often brilliantly, the potentials of East Asian culture in a non-Chinese milieu.

Of particular interest to Western students are the striking parallels that developed between Japan and northwestern Europe. Both had centuries of feudalism: serfs on the estates of nobles; castles and mounted warriors, who wore armor and fought in the service of their lord; cultures in which the glorification of valor and military prowess conflicted with the gentler virtues of their religions; merchant guilds and decentralized political economies. These parallels should not be surprising since both Japan and northwestern Europe began as backward tribal or posttribal societies onto which "heartland cultures" were grafted during the first millennium A.D.

Suggested Readings

R. BORGEN, *Sugawara no Michizane and the Early Heian Court* (1986). A study of a famous courtier and poet.

D. BROWN AND E. ISHIDA, (eds.), *The Future and the Past* (1979). A translation of a history of Japan written in 1219.

M. COLLCUTT, *Five Mountains* (1980). A study of the monastic organization of medieval Zen.

P. DUUS, *Feudalism in Japan* (1969). An easy survey of the subject.

W. W. FARRIS, *Population, Disease, and Land in Early Japan*, 645–900 (1985). An innovative reinterpretation of early history.

J. W. HALL, *Government and Local Power in Japan*, 500–1700: *A Study Based on Bizen Province* (1966). The best book on Japanese history to 1700.

J. W. HALL AND J. P. MASS (eds.), *Medieval Japan* (1974). A collection of topical essays on medieval history.

J. W. HALL AND T. TOYODA, *Japan in the Muromachi Age* (1977). Another collection of essays.

D. KEENE (ed.), *Anthology of Japanese Literature from the Earliest Era to the Mid-nineteenth Century* (1955).

D. KEENE (ed.), *Twenty Plays of the Nō Theatre* (1970).

J. M. KITAGAWA, *Religion in Japanese History* (1966). A survey of religion in premodern Japan.

I. H. LEVY, *The Ten Thousand Leaves* (1981). A fine translation of Japan's earliest collection of poetry.

J. P. MASS, *The Development of Kamakura Rule*, 1180–1250 (1979).

J. P. MASS AND W. HAUSER (eds.), *The Bakufu in Japanese History* (1985). Topics in bakufu history from the twelfth to the nineteenth century.

I. MORRIS, *The World of the Shining Prince: Court Life in Ancient Japan* (1964). A study of the court during the age in which *The Tale of Genji* was written.

I. MORRIS (trans.), *The Pillow Book of Sei Shōnagon* (1967). Observations about Heian court life by the Jane Austen of ancient Japan.

S. MURASAKI, *The Tale of Genji*, trans. by E. G. Seidensticker (1976). The world's first novel and the greatest work of Japanese fiction.

S. MURASAKI, *The Tale of Genji*, trans. by A. Waley (1952).

R. J. PEARSON et al. (eds.), *Windows on the Japanese Past: Studies in Archeology and Prehistory* (1986).

D. L. PHILIPPI (trans.), *Kojiki* (1968). Japan's ancient myths.

E. O. REISCHAUER, *Japan: The Story of a Nation* (1989). A masterful introduction to Japan.

E. O. Reischauer and A. M. Craig, *Japan: Tradition and Transformation* (1989). A widely used text.

D. T. Suzuki, *Zen and Japanese Culture* (1959).

R. Tsunoda, W. T. deBary, and D. Keene (comps.), *Sources of the Japanese Tradition* (1958). A collection of original religious, political, and philosophical writings from each period of Japanese history. The best reader.

H. P. Varley, *Imperial Restoration in Medieval Japan* (1971). A study of the 1331 attempt by an emperor to restore imperial power.

A. Waley (trans.), *The Nō Plays of Japan* (1957). Medieval dramas.

A fifth-century A.D. *standing Buddha from the sculptural workshops of Mathura in north India. [Bettmann Archive.]*

Portfolio III: Buddhism

Buddhism, along with Jainism and Upanishadic Hinduism, arose out of the spiritual ferment of Vedic India during the centuries after 700 B.C. Buddhism shares a kinship with these other religions much like the relationship found further west between Judaism, Christianity, and Islam.

Siddhartha Gautama was born about 566 B.C., a prince in a petty kingdom near what is now the border of India and Nepal. He was reared amid luxury and comforts, married at sixteen, and had a child. According to legend, when at age 29 he saw an old man, a sick man, and a corpse, he suddenly realized that all humans would suffer the same fate. Gautama renounced his wealth and family and entered the life of a wandering ascetic. He visited famous teachers, practiced extremes of ascetic self-deprivation, and finally discovered the "middle path." At the age of 35, he attained *nirvana*, becoming the *Buddha*, or the "enlightened one." In early Buddhism all of the cosmic drama of religious self-transformation is compressed into the human figure of Gautama meditating under the Bodhi tree. The rest of his 80 years the Buddha spent teaching others the truths he had learned. Even during his lifetime communities of Buddhist monks and nuns (the *sangha*) developed, with a tradition of support for the monks by lay adherents.

Basic to the Buddha's understanding of the human condition were the "four noble truths:" (1) that all life is suffering—an endless karmic chain of births and rebirths; (2) that the cause of the suffering is desire—it is desire that binds humans to the wheel of *karma*; (3) that escape from the suffering and endless rebirths can only come by the cessation of desire and the attainment of *nirvana*; and, (4) that the path to nirvana is eight-fold. The eight-fold path requires; right views, thought, speech, actions, living, efforts, mindfulness, and meditation.

Ethical living combined with long periods of meditation may lead to an inner spiritual awakening or realization. Progress in the inner spiritual life may lead, eventually, to enlightenment, to liberation or release from the trammels of karmic causation. Because the goal of Buddhism is for all humans to become Bud-

dhas, some have called Buddhism the most otherworldly of the great world religions. Even for the historical Buddha the way was not easy and one lifetime was not enough. (While meditating prior to achieving enlightenment, he recalled events from his former lives. The stories of these earlier lives are told in the Jataka tales.) For others, even with the Buddha's teachings in hand, the way was hard. Monks and nuns might meditate for years and attain an inner spiritual awakening, but only a few would gain the complete release required for Buddhahood. Most could only hope for a rebirth in a higher spiritual state, to begin again closer, as it were, to the goal. For lay people the stress was on ethical living in human socity. The Buddha condemned the caste system that flourished in the India of his day. He held that poverty was a cause of immorality, and that it was futile to attempt to suppress crime with punishments. He identified with all humanity, saying "He who attends on the sick attends on me."

Buddhism spread rapidly along the Ganges River and through northern India. In the time of King Ashoka (272-232 B.C.) of the Mauryas, it spread to southern India and Ceylon. This was its great missionary age. Eventually, however, Buddhism in India was re-Hinduized: It developed schools of metaphysics and a pantheon of gods and cosmic Buddhas. It developed devotional sects. Buddhism's meditative techniques helped shape Hindu yogic exercises. As these changes occurred, Buddhism in India lost its character as a reform movement, its *raison d'etre*, and was reabsorbed into Hinduism between A.D. 500 and 1500.

India apart, two major currents of Buddhism spread out over Asia. One known as the "Way of the Elders" (*Theravada*) swept through Southeast Asia. Its teachings were close to early Indian Buddhism and it was influenced as well by other strands of Indian culture. Scenes from the great Indian epic, the *Mahabharata*, adorn the inner walls of Thai temples. Buddhism remains today the predominant religion in Burma, Thailand, Cambodia, Laos, and Vietnam, although it must contest with more recent secular ideologies. In Thailand alone it remains the state religion:

Thai kings rule as Buddhist monarchs; Thai boys spend short periods as Buddhist monks; and temples (*wats*) continue as centers of village life. Before the spread of Islam, Buddhism also flourished in what is today Malaysia and Indonesia. The temple of Borobudur in central Java remains one of the great monuments of world Buddhism; it represents in stone the Buddhist spiritual universe.

The second major current, known to its adherents as the "Greater Vehicle" (*Mahayana*) spread through northwest India to Afghanistan and Central Asia, and then to China, Korea, and Japan. This current carried with it many doctrines. One key doctrine contained the ideal of the *bodhisattva*, a being who had gone all the way to the final goal of nirvana, but held off in order to help others attain salvation. One such *bodhisattva*, who became elevated to the status of a cosmic Buddha ruling over the Western Paradise (or Pure Land), was Amitabha (or Amida). Devotion to this Buddha and to others figured prominently in East Asian Buddhism.

Another doctrine, that of the Ch'an (in China) or Zen (in Japan) sect, stressed meditation and perhaps was closer to the teachings of the historical Buddha. Buddhism in Afghanistan and Central Asia eventually gave way to Islam. In China Buddhism was weakened by the great persecution of 845. In all of East Asia there were tensions between Buddhism and the more worldly teachings of Confucius. During the modern century the struggle, as in other parts of the world, has been between religion and modern secular doctrines.

III-1   Siddhartha Gautama at Age 29. *Gautama at age 29, having renounced all worldly attachments, cuts his hair in the forest prior to setting off on his spiritual quest. Scenes from the life of the Buddha are as common in Buddhist art as those of Jesus in Christian art. This is an early nineteenth century Bangkok temple mural. [Luca Invernizzi Tettoni/Art Resource.]*

III-2 Fasting Buddha. *Before Gautama arrived at the "middle path," he practiced severe austerites for six years. According to a description in an ancient text: "My limbs became like some withered creepers with knotted joints; my buttocks like a buffalo's hoof . . . my ribs like rafters of a dilipated shed; the pupils of my eyes appeared sunk deep in their sockets as water appears shining at the bottom of a deep well. . . ." This (fourth to second century B.C.) statue of the Buddha from Gandhara (in present-day Pakistan) reflects the Greek influence on early Buddhist sculpture. [Borromeo, EPA/Art Resource.]*

III-3   Colossal Statue of Buddha. *A 175-feet-tall statue of the Buddha was carved in a cliff in the Bamian Valley of Afghanistan during second to fifth century* A.D. *It is comparable to the Lungmen Buddhas in China or the Great Buddhas of Japan. [SEF/Art Resource.]*

III-4   Buddha with Aureole. *This Buddhist sanctuary mural at Miran on the Silk Road through Central Asia shows both Indian and Greek influences. [Borromeo, EPA/Art Resource.]*

III-5   Buddha on a Throne. *This fifth-to-sixth century painting is on the walls of a cave in Ajanta, India. The Buddha, seated on a lotus throne, teaches his disciples. The lotus, like the Buddha, emerges from the floating world of mud and water, but is not defiled by it. [Borromeo, EPA/Art Resource.]*

III-6   Thai Buddha in Bronze. *This walking Buddha is from the fourteenth century. Buddhism remains the predominant religion in Thailand today. [Luca Invernizzi Tettoni/Art Resource.]*

III-7   Barbarian Royalty Worshipping the Buddha.
*This Sung or Yuan dynasty Chinese painting depicts
the peoples known to China in the thirteenth century.
That all came from afar to worship suggests the uni-
versality of his teachings. [Cleveland Museum of Art,
Gift of Mr. and Mrs. Severance A. Millikin, 57.358.]*

III-8   Bodhisattva Kneeling in Attitude of Worship. *This polychrome
bodhisattva is from a cave temple
at Tunhuang in western China.
This example of T'ang dynasty
sculpture expresses Buddhist piety.
[Arthur M. Sackler Museum, Harvard University, Cambridge, Massachusetts, First Fogg China Expedition, 1923.]*

C-22

III-9 Zen Patriarch. *The Indian Bodhidharma, the first patriarch of the Zen sect, as depicted by Itō Jakuchū (1716–1800). Bodhidharma's face reflects the fierce insight gained by years of meditation. The strong brushstrokes in his robe, however, are the focus of the painting. [Reproduced by Courtesy of the Trustees of the British Museum.]*

III-10 Zen Monks in Japan. *These Zen monks in a meditation hall are in training to become priests. Many in postwar Japan have tried Zen meditation; few have been able to integrate it with the demands of modern life. [Elliott Erwitt/Magnum.]*

III-11 Cremation Rites for a Thai Queen. *The cremation rites for a Thai Queen Rambhao Barni are conducted at the Temple of the Emerald Buddha in Bangkok in 1985. [Luca Invernizzi Tettoni/Art Resource.]*

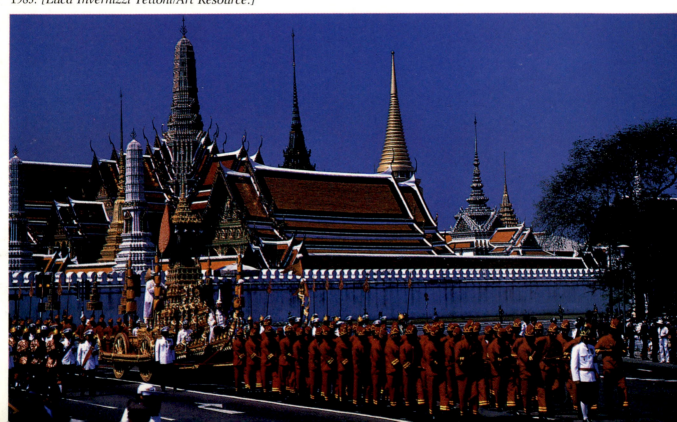

11 Africa, Iran, and India Before Islam

In this chapter, we look at civilization in sub-Saharan Africa and in south and southwest Asia before the penetration of Islam ushered in new eras and major parts of each of these regions were changed and linked culturally and religiously in new ways. The coming of Islamic civilization—with Muslim conquerors or, much more often, with Muslim traders and religious brotherhoods—took place at very different times and with differing consequences in each of these three major cultural areas.

In Africa, with the exception of north Africa, Egypt, and the east African coast, Islam as a religious tradition and sociopolitical order had its major impact only after (and sometimes long after) A.D. 1000. By contrast, in Iran, the presence of Islam in government and public life was significant from the early years of the Arab conquests in the mid-seventh century, although conversion of the masses took considerably longer. In northwest India, Arab armies penetrated the Indus region as early as 711 and the Muslims controlled the Punjab from around 1000. The establishment of the so-called Delhi Sultanate in 1205 marked the permanent arrival of Muslim ruling dynasties in the Indian heartlands. Similarly, Sufi brotherhoods made significant converts in India from about the thirteenth century. However, in earlier trading communities on the coasts of Gujarat and south India, Muslim settlers and converts provided the nuclei of Muslim communities that grew up within the larger Hindu society.

Different kinds of change had occurred in each of these vast regions in the centuries before the coming of Islam. In sub-Saharan Africa in the first millennium A.D., major movements of peoples and major changes in basic forms of subsistence were still occurring. It was an era when African peoples lived in many very different types of sociopolitical communities. Many of these still were pre- or early Iron-Age cultures, and very few were large enough or complex enough in or-

289

ganization and administration to be called states. Nonetheless, as we shall see, some sizable regional states and empires did emerge.

Iran presents another contrast. From the breakdown of Parthian rule at the beginning of the third century A.D. to the coming of Islam in the seventh, there existed a period of relative political stability under a single long-lived dynasty of Persian imperial rulers known as the Sasanids. It was a time of recovery of vitality for Zoroastrian traditions. Yet there was also entrenchment of a social and political system heavily balanced in favor of a small ruling nobility and a foreign policy centered on constant competition with the Byzantine empire. This competition finally exhausted its resources much as it did those of Byzantium. Both were ripe for defeat at the hands of the unleashed energies of the Arabs under the flag of Islam.

India experienced a similarly spectacular revival of empire under the Gupta kings, who presided over a cultural florescence of unprecedented magnificence. Then incursions of new waves of steppe peoples from about 500 on brought an era of political fragmentation. Nevertheless, regional empires emerged that lasted until the thirteenth century, when Muslim power in the north under the Delhi sultans began to forge new patterns of power and culture north and south.

For all these reasons, our attempt to trace Afro-Asian civilizations up to the coming of Islam will necessarily cover different chronological ground and focus on different kinds of change. However, in all three areas we shall see how culture, trade, and communications made great strides, even if at different stages of development, in diverse forms, and at varying paces.

AFRICA

Nilotic Africa and the Ethiopian Highlands

We begin with the African story where we left off in Chapter 7, in the upper Nile regions of the eastern Sudan. Here, the Kushite empire was apparently brought to an end about A.D. 330 by a new power to the south: the newly Christianized state of Aksum, which centered in the northern Ethiopian, or Abyssinian, highlands where the Blue Nile rises. With the ascendancy of the kingdom of Aksum, the Nubian regions of the Nile sank into two centuries of relative obscurity, until the rise of new Christian Nubian states in the mid-sixth century.

The Aksumite Empire

The peoples of Aksum were the product of a cultural and genetic mixing of African Kushitic speakers with Semitic speakers from Yemenite south Arabia. This mixing occurred after south Arabians infiltrated and settled on the Ethiopian plateau around 500 B.C. It gave to Aksum and later to Ethiopia their Semitic speech and script, which are closely related to South Arabian. Greek and Roman sources attest to the existence of an Aksumite kingdom from at least the first century A.D. By this time, the kingdom, through its chief port of Adulis, had already become the major ivory and elephant market of northeast Africa. Adulis had been important in Ptolemaic times, when it was captured by Egypt and used as a conduit for Egyptian influence in the highlands. After Egypt fell to the Romans, Aksum and its major port became an important cosmopolitan commercial center.

In the first two centuries A.D., their location on the Red Sea gave the Aksumites a strategic seat astride the increasingly important Indian Ocean trade routes. These trade routes linked India and the East Indies, Iran, Arabia, and the east African coast with the Roman Mediterranean. A further basis of Aksum's power was its key location for controlling trade between the African interior and the extra-African world, from Rome to southeast Asia—notably that centered on exports of ivory, but also of elephants, obsidian, slaves, gold dust, and other inland products.

By the third century A.D., Aksum was one of the most impressive states of its age in the African or west Asian world, as the remains of the imposing stone buildings and monuments of its major cities—Aksum, Adulis, and Matara—attest. A work attributed to the prophet Mani, CA. A.D. 216–277, describes Aksum as one of the four greatest empires in the world. From the late second century on, the Aksumites often held tributary territories across the Red Sea in South Arabia. They also gained control of all northern Ethiopia and conquered Meroitic Kush. Thus by the third and fourth century, they held sway over some of the most fertile cultivated regions of the ancient world: their own plateau, the rich Yemenite highlands of South Arabia, and much of the eastern Sudan across the upper Nile as far as the Sahara.

The resulting empire was ruled by a king of kings in Aksum through tribute-paying vassal kings in the other subject states. By the sixth century, the Aksumite king was even appointing south Arabian kings himself. The minting of its own coinage in gold, silver, and copper (it was the first tropical African state to do so) was an

A Giant Stela at Aksum. *Dating probably from the first century* A.D., *this giant carved monolith is the only one of seven giant stelae, one of which reached a height of 33 meters, that once stood in Aksum amidst numerous smaller monoliths. While the exact purpose of the stelae is not known, the generally accepted explanation is that they were commemorative funerary monuments. The immense engineering feat involved in such monouments suggests how sophisticated Aksumite engineering was.*

A Sixth-Century Account of Aksumite Trade

The following document is taken from a description of a trading voyage to Sri Lanka in A.D. *625 by a Greek-speaking monk and former merchant from Alexandria, known as Cosmas Indicopleustes. In the excerpt below, he describes what he had heard of Aksumite trading practices, including those involved with procuring gold from the interior.*

The region which produces frankincense is situated at the projecting parts of Ethiopia, and lies inland, but is washed by the ocean on the other side. Hence the inhabitants of Barbaria, being near at hand, go up into the interior and, engaging in traffic with the natives, bring back from them any kinds of spices, frankincense, cassia, calamus, and many other articles of merchandise, which they afterwards send by sea to Adule, to the country of the Homerites, to Further India, and to Persia. This very fact you will find mentioned in the Book of Kings, where it is recorded that the Queen of Sheba, that is, of the Homerite country, whom afterwards our Lord in the Gospels calls the Queen of the South, brought to Solomon spices from this very Barbaria, which lay near Sheba on the other side of the sea, together with bars of ebony, and apes and gold from Ethiopia, which, though separated from Sheba by the Arabian Gulf, lay in its vicinity. We can see again from the words of the Lord that he calls these places the ends of the earth, saying: *The Queen of the South shall rise up in judgement with this generation and shall condemn it, for she came from the ends of the earth to hear the wisdom of Solomon,* Matt. xii. 42. For the Homerites are not far distant from Barbaria, as the sea which lies between them can be crossed in a couple of days, and then beyond Barbaria is the ocean, which is there called Zingion. The country known as that of Sasu is itself near the ocean, just as the ocean is near the frankincense country, in which there are many gold mines. The king of the Axumites accordingly, every other year, through the governor of Agau, sends thither special agents to bargain for the gold, and these are accompanied by many other traders—upwards, say, of 500—bound on the same errand as themselves. They take along with them to the mining district oxen, lumps of salt, and iron, and when they reach its neighbourhood they make a halt at a certain spot and form an encampment, which they fence round with a great hedge of thorns. Within this they live, and having slaughtered the oxen, cut them in pieces, and lay the pieces on the top of the thorns, along with the lumps of salt and the iron. Then come the natives bringing gold in nuggets like peas, called *tancharas,* and lay one or two or more of these upon what pleases them—the pieces of flesh or the salt or the iron, and then they retire to some distance off. Then the owner of the meat approaches, and if he is satisfied he takes the gold away, and upon seeing this its owner comes and takes the flesh or the salt or the iron. If, however, he is not satisfied, he leaves the gold, when the native seeing that he has not taken it, comes and either puts down more gold, or takes up what he had laid down, and goes away. Such is the mode in which business is transacted with the people of that country, because their language is different and interpreters are hardly to be found. . . . ❑

J. W. McCrindle, trans., *The Christian Topography of Cosmas, an Egyptian Monk* (London, 1897), as cited in G. S. P. Freeman-Grenville, ed., *The East African Coast,* 2nd ed. (London, 1975), pp. 6–7.

index and symbol of Aksum's political as well as economic power. As a state, it enjoyed a long-lived economic prosperity. Goods of the Roman-Byzantine world and India and Sri Lanka, as well as of neighboring Meroe, flowed into Aksum. In addition to trade, vast herds and good agricultural produce gave a firm base to Aksumite prosperity.

In religion, the pre-Christian paganism of Aksum resembled the pre-Islamic paganism of south Arabia with its various gods and goddesses who were closely tied to natural phenomena such as the sun, moon, and stars, and who were served with animal sacrifices. Evidence of Jewish, Meroitic, and even Buddhist minorities living in the major cities of Aksum has also been found—an index of the cosmopolitanism of the society and of its involvement with the larger Indian Ocean, west Asian, and south Asian worlds beyond the Red Sea.

In an inscription of the powerful fourth-century ruler, King Ezana, we read of his conversion to Christianity, which led to the Christianizing of the kingdom as a whole. The conversion of Ezana and his realm was the work of Frumentius, a Syrian bishop of Aksum who also served as secretary and treasurer to the king. Subsequently, under Alexandrian influence, the Ethiopian church became Monophysite in doctrine (i.e., adhered to the dogma of the single, unitary nature of Christ; see Chapter 6). This did not cut off Aksumite trading relations with Byzantium, however much Constantinople may have persecuted Monophysites at home. In the fifth century A.D., the native language of Ge'ez began to replace Greek in the liturgy; this proved to be a major step in the unique development of the Ethiopic or Abyssinian Christian church over the succeeding centuries.

The Isolation of Christian Ethiopia

Aksumite trade continued to thrive through the sixth century, despite the decay of Rome. Strong enough at times to extend to the Yemen, Aksumite power was eclipsed in the end by the rise of Arab Islamic power. Nevertheless, the Aksumite state continued to exist long after its power had diminished. Having sheltered a refugee group of Muhammad's earliest Meccan converts, the Aksumites enjoyed relatively cordial relations with the new Muslim domains to the north in Egypt and across the Red Sea in the peninsula. But Aksum ceased to be a center of foreign trade and became more and more isolated. Its center of gravity shifted southward from the coast to the more rugged parts of the plateau. Here a Monophysite, Ge'ez-speaking culture emerged in the area of modern Ethiopia and lasted in relative isolation down to modern times, surrounded largely by Muslim peoples and Islamic states.

Ethiopia's northern neighbors, the Christian states of Maqurra and Alwa, also survived for centuries in the former Meroitic lands of the Nilotic Sudan under treaty relations with Muslim Egypt. However, incursions of the Muslim Mamluk rulers of Egypt in the fourteenth and fifteenth centuries and Arab migration from about 1300 led ultimately to the Islamization and conversion of the whole Nubian region. Ethiopia was left as the sole predominantly Christian state in Africa.

The Western and Central Sudan

In Chapter 7, we noted the apparent movements of neolithic peoples southward from the Saharan regions into the western and central Sudan and ultimately into the forests of the African equatorial regions. The rainforests were inhospitable to cows and horses, largely because of the animals' inability to survive the sleeping sickness (*trypanosomiasis*) carried by the tsetse fly. But the agriculturalists who brought their cereal grains and stone tools found particularly good conditions in the savannah just north of the west African forests. By the first or second century A.D., settled agriculture, now augmented by the use of iron tools, had become the way of life of most of the inhabitants of these western Sudanic lands. Agriculture had even made considerable progress in the forest regions farther south. The savannah areas seem to have experienced a substantial population explosion in the first few centuries A.D., especially in the areas close to the major water sup-

NILOTIC AFRICA AND THE
ETHIOPIAN HIGHLANDS

CA. 500 B.C.	Yemenites (South Arabians) enter and settle on the Ethiopian plateau
30 B.C.	Egypt becomes part of Roman empire of Octavian
CA. A.D. 1–100	Earliest mention (in Latin and Greek writers) of the kingdom of Aksum on Ethiopian plateau
CA. A.D. 330	Fall of Kushite empire to Elzana of Aksum
CA. A.D. 200–400	Heyday of Aksumite Ethiopia
CA. A.D. 500–600	Christianizing of the major Nubian states of Maqurra and Alwa
A.D. 652	Maqurra and Alwa make peace with Arab Muslim armies from Egypt

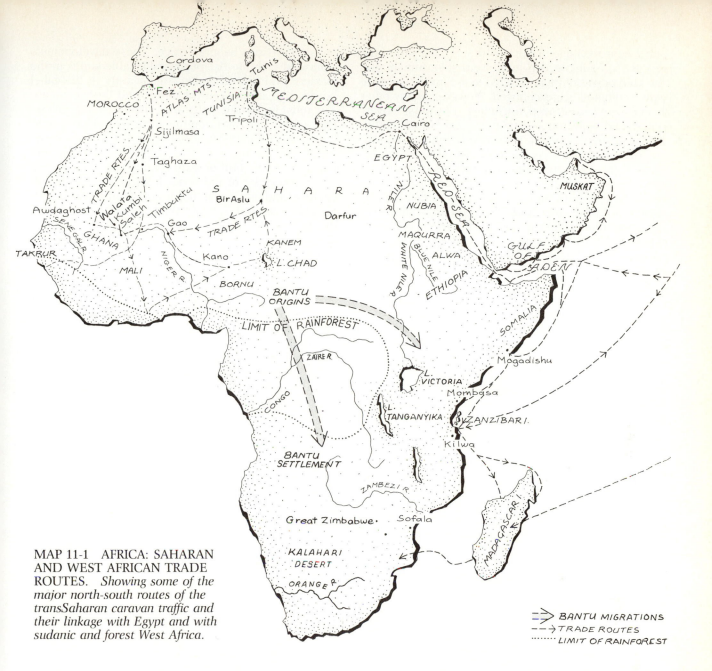

MAP 11-1 AFRICA: SAHARAN AND WEST AFRICAN TRADE ROUTES. *Showing some of the major north-south routes of the transSaharan caravan traffic and their linkage with Egypt and with sudanic and forest West Africa.*

⇒ BANTU MIGRATIONS
--→ TRADE ROUTES
······ LIMIT OF RAINFOREST

plies: along the Senegal river, around the great northern bend in the Niger river, and in the Lake Chad basin. Villages, and gradually some chiefdoms consisting of several villages, remained normally the largest political units during this period. As time went on, their growth and development provided the basis (and the need) for the eventual development of larger political units that we call true states in these areas of the western Sudan.

Trans-Saharan Trade

Another element that eventually promoted or at least accompanied the rise of larger political units in the western and central Sudan was the trans-Saharan commercial trade. As we saw earlier, contacts between the Sudanic regions and the Mediterranean were maintained throughout the first millennium B.C. over the trans-Saharan trading routes. The trans-Saharan trade became, however, much more viable with the introduction from the east (probably through north Africa) of the domesticated camel (actually the one-humped Arab camel, or dromedary), sometime around the beginning of the Christian era. By the early Christian centuries, the west African settled communities were able to develop trading centers of considerable importance on their northern peripheries, in the sahel near the edge of the true desert. The salt of the desert, so badly needed in the settled savannah, and the gold of west Africa, coveted in the north, were the prime commodities exchanged. However, many other items were also traded, including cola nuts, slaves, dates, and gum from west Africa, and horses, cattle, millet, leather, cloth, and weapons from the north.

Towns such as Awdaghast, Walata, Timbuktu, Gao, Tadmekka, and Agades have been the most famous southern terminals for this trade over the centuries. These centers allowed the largely Berber middlemen who plied the trade routes across the ever dangerous Sahara to traverse the desert via oasis stations between them and the north African coastal regions or even Egypt. Thus, some of the main routes ran as follows: (1) from the first three towns just mentioned to the major desert salt-producing center of Taghaza and thence to Morocco; (2) from Timbuktu, as from Gao over the desert direct to Morocco; and (3) from Tadmekka and Agades to the desert market town of Ghat in the north-central Sahara and on to the coasts of Libyan north Africa. Other lines went up from the region of Lake Chad; one route stretched as far east as Egypt itself, passing through the mountain massifs of the central Sahara such as that of the Tassili and Ahaggar. A typical full crossing could easily take two to three months, so this was not an easy means of transporting goods.

The Rise of States

Smaller stateless societies predominated throughout sub-Saharan Africa during most of African history. Even as late as 1880, as many as 25 per cent of all west Africans probably belonged to stateless societies. Yet because of the absence of historical records of most local cultures and regional chiefdoms, we must necessarily focus here on the rise of identifiable states—that is, larger, more complex sociopolitical entities. This is not to say that there was no "culture" in early or even in contemporary stateless tribal societies or other small communities. In Chapter 7, we noted the impressive achievements of the Nok culture, which likely was not developed under the auspices of any state organization. However, it is only very recent history of, say, the past two to five centuries, to which local or tribal oral traditions can give us valuable access. We have no other ways of identifying or tracing the development of small, stateless societies that have left no written documents, monuments, or other decipherable artifacts of their history. At least we have for them nothing comparable to the sources available for the larger societies—with known rulers, fighting forces, and towns or cities—that left their own records or that were documented by outsiders.

The first millennium A.D. saw the growth of settled agricultural populations and the development and ex-pansion of trans-Saharan trade. These developments coincided with the rise of several sizable states in the western and central Sudan, significantly in the sahel border region between the desert and the savannah. The most important states were located in the following regions: (1) Takrur on the Senegal river, from perhaps the fifth century, if not earlier; (2) Ghana, between the northern bends of the Senegal and the Niger, from the fifth or sixth century; (3) Gao, on the Niger southeast of the bend, from before the eighth century; and (4) Kanem, northeast of Lake Chad, from the eighth or ninth century. While the origins and even the full extent of major states in these regions are shrouded in obscurity, each represents only the first of a series of large political entities in its region. All continued to figure prominently in subsequent west African history.

The states developed by the Fulbe people of Takrur and the Soninke people of Ghana depended early on their ability to draw gold for the Saharan trade with Morocco from the savannah region of Bambuhu (or Bambuk), west of the upper Senegal. Of all the sub-Saharan kingdoms of the late first millennium, Ghana was the most famous outside of the region, largely because of its substantial control over the gold trade. Its people built a true empire centered at its capital of Kumbi (also known as Kumbi Saleh). Inheriting his throne by matrilineal descent, the ruler was treated as a virtually semidivine ruler whose interaction with his subjects was mediated by a hierarchy of government ministers. He is described in an eleventh-century Arabic chronicle as commanding a sizable army, including horsemen and archers, and being buried with his retainers under a dome of earth and wood. In contrast to the Soninke of Ghana, the Songhai rulers of Gao had no gold trade until the fourteenth century. Unlike its western neighbors, Gao was oriented in its forest trade toward the lower, not the upper, Niger basin and in its Saharan trade toward eastern Algeria, not Morocco.

THE WESTERN AND CENTRAL SUDAN: PROBABLE DATES FOR FOUNDING OF REGIONAL KINGDOMS

CA. 400 A.D. or earlier	Takrur (Senegal river valley)
A.D. 400–600	Ghana (in Sahel between great northern bends of the Senegal and Niger rivers)
CA. A.D. 700–800 or earlier	Gao (on the Niger river southeast of great bend)
CA. A.D. 700–900	Kanem (northeast of Lake Chad)

All of these states were built upon an agricultural base and settled populations. By contrast, the initial power of Kanem, on the northwest side of Lake Chad, originated in the borderlands of the central Sudan and the southern Sahara. Here the first state formation was a nomadic federation of black tribal peoples that persisted long enough for the separate tribes to merge and form a single people, the Kanuri. They then moved south to take over the sedentary societies of Kanem proper, just east of Lake Chad, and, later, Bornu, west of Lake Chad. By the thirteenth century, the Kanuri had themselves become sedentary; their kingdom controlled the southern terminus of perhaps the best trans-Saharan route—that running north via good watering stations to the oasis region of Fezzan in modern central Libya and thence to the Mediterranean.

Central, South, and East Africa

In the African subcontinent—that is, in central, south, and east Africa, or south of a line from roughly the Niger delta and Cameroon across to southern Somalia on the east coast—the time when human prehistory shades into history fell relatively late. Of the period before A.D. 1000, we have very little firm indigenous evidence and few outside written sources to help us write the history of the subcontinent. Some relatively certain facts and reasonable hypotheses have, however, emerged from a combination of linguistic, archaeological, and other research in this region.

The Khoisan Peoples

In the subcontinent, we find alongside the Bantu-speaking majority two smaller groups, the Khoikhoi and San peoples, both of whom are brown-skinned, usually rather short, with "peppercorn" rather than frizzy hair. Formerly and incorrectly distinguished racially, the San (long known in the West as Bushmen) and the Khoikhoi (the Hottentots of European usage) are two interrelated groups distinguished linguistically from Bantu and other language groups of Africa. Collectively, they and their language group are commonly known as Khoisan. The two groups are distinguished from each other more by their livelihood and distribution than any other characteristics.[1]

The San are likely the direct descendants of the Neolithic peoples of the south who have been traditionally hunter-gatherers as well as the authors of the striking prehistoric rock paintings of southern Africa. They do not form a single cultural group, but have developed linguistically and culturally diverse subgroups in different locales across southern Africa. Today they survive most prominently in the Kalahari region.

The more homogeneous Khoikhoi were sheep- and cattle-herding pastoralists who were also quite scattered across the south, yet who spoke closely related Khoisan tongues. Their ancestors probably originated in northern Botswana. They were hunters who relatively late—probably between A.D. 700 and 1000—learned animal herding from their Bantu-speaking south African neighbors. Thus, they became primarily pastoralists and soon expanded over the best pasturelands of western south Africa, as far south as the Cape of Good Hope. Here they flourished as pastoralist clans, sometimes united loosely as a tribe under a particularly strong chief, until their tragic encounter with the invading Dutch colonists in the mid-seventeenth century, which resulted in their demise as a distinct people.

The Bantu Migrations and Diffusion

In the African subcontinent, the vast majority of the peoples speak one of more than four hundred languages that belong to a single language group known as *Bantu*. All of these languages are as closely related as are the Germanic or Romance tongues of Europe. Although the place of origin and routes of diffusion of Bantu tongues have long been debated, today there is increasing consensus that the location of the proto-Bantu language must have been in the region south of the Benue river, in eastern Nigeria and modern Cameroon. Thence, in the course of the later centuries B.C. and the first millennium A.D., migrations of Bantu-speaking peoples must have taken their versions of this language in two basic directions: (1) south into the lower Zaïre (Congo) basin and ultimately to the southern edge of the equatorial forest in present-day northern Katanga; and (2) east around the equatorial forests into the lakes of highland east Africa.

In all these regions, Bantu tongues developed and multiplied in contact with other languages. Likewise, Bantu speakers intermixed and adapted in diverse ways, as the wide variety of physical types among Bantu peoples today demonstrates. Further migrations, some as early as the fourth century A.D. and others as late as the twelfth or thirteenth century, dispersed Bantu peoples even more widely, into south-central Africa, coastal east Africa, and south Africa. One result of this dispersion was the early civilization of Great Zimbabwe near the Zambezi river (treated in Chapter 15). The notion, however, that the Bantu or the Khoikhoi only arrived in south Africa at about the same time as the first European settlers is a fabrication used today to justify apartheid.

How the Bantu peoples managed to impose their languages upon the earlier cultures of these regions

---

[1] On the vexed problem of distinguishing San and Khoikhoi, see Richard Elphick, *Kraal and Castle: Khoikhoi and the Founding of White South Africa* (New Haven and London: 1977), pp. xxi–xxii, 3–42.

remains unexplained. The idea that they brought the knowledge of iron smelting with them and used it to dominate other peoples is not borne out by linguistic or other studies. The proto-Bantu had apparently been fishermen and hunters who also cultivated yams, date palms, and some cereals. They also raised goats and possibly sheep and some cattle, but they did not bring cattle with them in their migrations. Most of the migrating Bantu peoples seem to have been mainly cereal or grain agriculturists whose basic political and social unit was the village. Perhaps they had unusually strong social cohesion that allowed them to absorb other peoples; there is no evidence that they were military conquerors. Perhaps the Bantu brought diseases with them against which the aboriginals of the forests and the southern savannah had no immunities, much as later the European newcomers to the Cape brought the ravages of smallpox to the susceptible Khoikhoi.

In any case, their cultures became in time so fully interwoven with those of the peoples they settled among that the answers to these questions may never be known. For example, Bantu-Arab mixing on the eastern coasts produced the Swahili culture, which we shall encounter in Chapter 15. We find Bantu peoples as slash-and-burn farmers in the Zaïre river savannah, as cattle herders in the east African high plains, as perennial floodplain cultivators on the Zambezi river, and as terracing and irrigating farmers among the highland Kikuyu and Chagga peoples.

East Africa

The history of east Africa along the coast before Islam differed from that of the inland highlands. Long-distance travel was easy and common along the seashore, but less so inland.

The coast had had maritime contact with India, Arabia, and the Mediterranean via the Indian Ocean and Red Sea trade routes from at least as early as the second century B.C. By contrast, the direct contacts of the inland regions with any but adjacent areas of Africa itself were very limited or nonexistent until after A.D. 1000. Regional coastal trade is, however, also ancient. Both forms of sea trade remained important and interdependent over the centuries, since the Indian Ocean trade depended on the monsoon winds and could use only the northernmost coastal trading harbors of east Africa for round-trip voyages in the same year. The monsoon winds blow from the northeast and thus could carry sailing ships south from Iran, Arabia, and India only from December to March; they blow from the southwest only from April to August, when ships could sail from Africa northeast. Local coastal shipping thus had to haul cargoes from farther south than Zanzibar and then transfer them to other ships for the annual round-trip voyages to Arabia and beyond.

Long-distance trade came into its own in Islamic times—about the ninth century—as an Arab monopoly. However, long before the coming of Islam, trade was apparently largely in the hands of Arabs, many of whom had settled in the east African coastal towns and in Iran and India to handle this international commerce. We have documentation of Greco-Roman contact with these east African centers of the Red Sea and Indian Ocean trade from as early as the first century A.D. Most of the coastal trading towns were apparently independent, although Rhapta, the one town mentioned in the earliest Greek source, *The Periplus*, was a dependency of a south Arabian state.

The overseas trade was, however, evidently even more international than the earliest surviving sources indicate. Today, the language of Madagascar—Malagasy, an imported Malayo-Polynesian language—points graphically to the antiquity of substantial contact with the East Indies via the coastal trading routes of Asia's ancient southern rim. Evidence of an Indonesian migration even before the beginning of our era is seen in the fact that bananas, coconut palms, and other food crops indigenous to Southeast Asia spread across the entire African continent as staple foods. Further, as a result of the early regular commercial ties to distant lands of Asia, extra-African ethnic and cultural mixing has long been the rule for the east African coast; even today, its linguistic and cultural traditions are rich and varied (see Chapters 15, 22).

Other African imports included such items as Persian Gulf pottery, Chinese porcelain, and cotton cloth. The major African export good around which the east coast trade revolved was ivory, which was in perennial demand from Greece to India and, from the tenth century, even China. The slave trade was another major business. Slaves were procured, often inland, in east Africa and exported to the Arab and Persian world, as well as to India or China. Gold, that perennial lure of outsiders to Africa, became important only in Islamic times, from about the tenth century onward, as we shall see in Chapter 15. Wood and food grains must also have been shipped abroad.

The history of inland east Africa south of Ethiopia is much more difficult to trace than that of the coast, again because of the absence of written sources and the immense difficulty of access until relatively recent times. We can, however, use linguistic clues and other evidence to note some key developments that underlay more recent history in the highlands. These regions had early seen diffusion of peoples from the north, and changing conditions of subsistence over the centuries have continued to propel movements of small groups into new areas.

Of the early migrants from the north, first came Kushitic speakers, likely cattle herders and grain cultivators. Perhaps as early as 2000 B.C., they pushed from their homeland on the Ethiopian plateau south down the Rift valley as far as the southern end of Lake Tanganyika. They apparently displaced Neolithic hunter-gatherers who may have been related to the Khoisan minorities of modern east and south Africa. While Kushitic languages are spoken from east of Lake Rudolph northward in abundance, farther south only isolated remnants of Kushitic-speakers remain today, these largely in the Rift Valley in Tanzania.

Later, Nilotic peoples moved from the southwestern side of the Ethiopian plateau west over the upper Nile valley by about A.D. 1000. Then they pushed east and south, following the older Kushite paths, to spread over the Rift valley area by the fifteenth century and subsequently much of the east African highlands of modern-day Uganda, Kenya, and Tanzania. Here they all but completely supplanted their Kushite predecessors. Two of these Nilotic peoples were the Lwo and Maasai. The Lwo spread far and wide over a nine-hundred-mile-long swath of modern Uganda and parts of southern Sudan and western Kenya. They did so over a long period of time and mixed readily with various other peoples, absorbing new cultural elements and adapting to new situations wherever they went. The Maasai, on the other hand, are cattle pastoralists fiercely proud of their separate language, way of life, and cultural traditions. These features distinguish them sharply from the farming or hunting peoples whose settlements abut their pasturages at the top of the southern Rift valley in Kenya and Tanzania. Here, southwest and west of both Mt. Kenya and Mt. Kilomanjaro, the Maasai have concentrated and remained.

These migrations from the north and those of the

MOVEMENT AND CONTACT OF PEOPLES IN CENTRAL, SOUTH, AND EAST AFRICA	
CA. 1300–1000 B.C.	Kushitic-speaking peoples migrate from Ethiopian plateau south along Rift valley
CA. 400 B.C.–A.D. 1000	Probable era of major Bantu migrations into central, east, and southeast Africa
200–100 B.C. or earlier	East African coast becomes involved in Indian Ocean trade
CA. 100 B.C.	Probable time of first Indonesian immigration to east African coast
CA. A.D. 100–1500	Nilotic-speaking peoples spread over upper Nile valley; Nilotic peoples spread over Rift valley region

Bantu peoples from the west, who also entered the eastern highlands over many centuries, have made these highland regions a kind of melting pot of Kushitic, Nilotic, Bantu, and Khoisan groups. Their characteristics are visible in today's populations, with their immense diversity of languages and cultures. As much as any part of Africa, here we see the radical diversity of peoples and cultures of the entire continent mirrored in the heritages of a single major region.

IRAN

The Parthians

Parthian Arsacid rule (CA. 247 B.C.–A.D. 223) continued the Iranian imperial tradition begun by the Achaemenids (see Chapter 7). The relative Parthian tolerance of religious diversity was paralleled by the growth of regionalism in political and cultural affairs. A growing nobility built strong local power bases and became the backbone of the military power of the realm. Aramaic, the common language of the empire, gradually lost ground to regional Iranian tongues after the second century B.C.. The Parthian dialect and Greek became widely influential but could not replace Aramaic.

Despite their general religious tolerance, the Parthians still upheld such Zoroastrian traditions as the maintenance of a royal sacred fire at a shrine in their Parthian homeland and the inclusion of priestly advisers on the emperor's council. The last century or so of their rule saw increased emphasis on Iranian as opposed to foreign traditions in religious and cultural affairs. This was perhaps in reaction to the almost constant warfare with the Romans on their west flank and the Kushan threat in the east. By this time, Christianity and Buddhism were making sufficient converts in western and eastern border areas to threaten Zoroastrian tradition directly for the first time. This threat may have stimulated Parthian attempts to collect the largely oral Zoroastrian textual heritage. In this and other ways, Parthian rule laid the groundwork for the nationalistic emphases of the next few centuries, despite later Sasanid efforts to portray this era as one of decline in native Iranian traditions.

The Sasanid Empire
(A.D. 224–651)

The Sasanids were a Persian dynasty, like the Achaemenids. Claiming to be the latter's rightful heirs, the Sasanids put themselves forward as champions of Iranian legitimacy and tried to brand the Parthians as outside invaders who followed Greek and other foreign ways. Much of the lasting bad reputation of the Parthians stems from the fact that they are still known only through hostile sources.

The first Sasanid king, Ardashir (reigned A.D. 224–CA. 239), was a Persian warrior noble who had a priestly family background. The Sasanid name came from his grandfather, Sasan. Ardashir and his son, Shapur I (reigned CA. 239–272), built a strong internal administration and extended the empire abroad. While still his father's field general, Shapur took Bactria from the Kushans, thereby greatly expanding the Sasanid realm. Under his long rule, the empire grew significantly, not only in the east, but also beyond the Caucasus in the north and into Syria, Armenia, and parts of Anatolia in the west. Shapur inflicted humiliating defeats on three Roman emperors, even capturing one of them, Valerian. Thus, he could justifiably claim to be a restorer of Iranian glory and a "king of

kings," or *shahanshah*. He also centralized and rationalized taxation, the civil ministries, and the military, although neither he nor his successors could fully counterbalance the growing power of the nobility.

With the shift of the Roman Empire east to Byzantium at the beginning of the fourth century A.D., the stage of imperial conflict for the next 350 years was set: Byzantium (Constantinople) on the Bosporus and Ctesiphon on the Tigris were to be the seats of the two mightiest thrones of Eurasia until the coming of the Arabs. Each from time to time won victories over the other, and each championed a different religious orthodoxy, but neither could ever completely conquer the other. In the sixth century, each produced their greatest emperors: the Byzantine Justinian (reigned 527–565) and the Sasanid Chosroes Anosharvan ("Chosroes of the Immortal Soul," reigned 531–579). Yet, less than a century after their deaths, the new Arab power defeated one empire and destroyed the other. Byzantium survived with much reduced territory for another eight hundred years, but the Sasanid imperial order was swept away with the last of its rulers in 651. Memory of the Sasanids did not, however, entirely die. Chosroes, for example, became a legendary model of greatness for Persians and a symbol of imperial splendor even among the Arabs.

Society and Economy

Sasanid society was largely like that of earlier times. At all levels, the extended family was (as it is even today in Iran) the basic social unit. Zoroastrian orthodoxy recognized four classes: priests, warriors,

The palace of the Sasanid Shahanshahs at Ctesiphon. Built by Shapur I in the capital that the Sasanids inherited from the Arsacids, the imperial palace is only partially preserved. The gigantic, four storyed structure is said to have greatly impressed the Arab invaders in the seventh century. The massive open-vaulted hall or bay was a feature of Persian architecture which would be used later in Iranian mosques. [Bettmann Archive.]

scribes, and peasants. The great divide was between the royal house, the priesthood, and the warrior nobility on the one hand, and the common people of the cities (artisans, traders, and so on) and the rural peasantry on the other.

As before, the basis of the economy remained agriculture. The long-term trend was toward the concentration of land ownership among an ever-richer minority of the royalty, the nobility, and the priesthood. The growth of great estates was similar to that in Roman domains and was no less responsible for an increased imbalance between the rich few and the impoverished many. More and more small farmers were reduced to serfdom in the latter half of this era. The burden of land taxation, like that of conscript labor work and army duty, hit hardest those least able to afford it. It was not without eventual popular reaction, as the Mazdakite movement, which is discussed later, shows.

The Sasanids also closely oversaw and heavily taxed the lucrative caravan trade that traversed their territory, as well as export and import trade by sea. Silk and glass production increased under government monopoly, and the state controlled mining. The many urban centers of the empire and the foreign trade relied on a money system. It was from Jewish bankers in Babylonia and their Persian counterparts that Europe and the rest of the world got the use of bills of exchange (the very word *check* comes from a Pahlavi word).[2]

Sasanid aristocratic culture drew on diverse traditions, from Roman, Hellenistic, and Bactrian-Indian to Achaemenid and other native Iranian ones. Its heyday was the reign of Chosroes. Iranian legendary history and courtly literature were popular, as were translations of Indian narrative literature. Indian influences—not only religious ones, as in the case of Buddhist ideas, but also artistic and especially scientific ones—were especially strong. Indian medicine and mathematics were particularly well received. Hellenistic culture also was revived in the academy at Jundishapur in Khuzistan, where refugee scholars from Byzantium came to teach medicine and philosophy after Justinian closed the Greek academies in the west.

Religion

THE ZOROASTRIAN REVIVAL. Religion played a significant role in Sasanid life not only at the popular level but even in affairs of state. The Sasanids institutionalized Zoroastrian ritual and theology as state orthodoxy. Although they actually were simply continu-

The luxury art of the Sasanids was the culmination of the long development of earlier Iranian traditions. It was consciously Iranian and oriental, rather than Greco-Roman, although Western influence was inevitable. A popular motif was the hunt, always a favorite pastime of Persian aristocrats. The stylized figures shown at the bottom of this silver bowl are typical of the Sasanid style. [Bettmann Archive.]

ing the Arsacid patronage of Zoroastrian worship, the Sasanids claimed to be restoring the true faith after centuries of neglect. The initial architect of this propaganda and the Zoroastrian revival was the first chief priest of the empire, Tosar (or Tansar). Under Ardashir, Tosar instituted a state church organization and began the fixation of an authoritative, written canon of the Avesta, the scriptural texts that include the hymns of Zarathushtra. He may also have been the one to institute a calendar reform and to ban all images in the temples of the land, replacing them with the sacred altar fires of Zoroastrian tradition.

The greatest figure in Sasanid religious history was Tosar's successor, Kartir, or Kirdir, who served as chief priest to Shapur I and his three successors (CA. 239–293). Although his zealotry was at first kept in check by the religiously tolerant and eclectic Shapur, Kirdir gained greater power and influence after Shapur's death. He is the one figure other than a Sasanid king for whom we have personal inscriptions in the rock reliefs of the dynasty. He seems to have made numerous efforts to convert not only pagans, but also Christians, Buddhists, and other followers of foreign traditions. His chief opponents were, however, the Manichaeans, whom he considered Zoroas-

[2]R. Girshman, *Iran* (Harmondsworth, U.K., 1954), pp. 341–346. "Pahlavi" is the name of the middle Persian language that gradually replaced Aramaic as the Iranian *lingua franca* in Sasanid times.

On the Propagation of Mazda-Worship

The following excerpts are from an inscription of Kirdir, the second high priest to serve under the Sasanids. Here he proclaims his successful efforts to consolidate and spread the worship of Ahura Mazda. The time of the inscription is the reign of Vahram II, 276–293. The yazads *are beneficent divine beings, the* devs *the evil minions of the "Evil Spirit," Ahriman.*

And I was made Mobad and Judge of the whole empire, and I was made Master of Ceremonials and Warden of the Fires of Anahid-Ardashir and Anahid the Lady at Istakhr. And I was styled 'Kirder by whom Vahram's soul is saved, Mobad of Ohrmazd'. And in every province and place of the whole empire the service of Ohrmazd and the yazads was exalted, and the Mazda-worshipping religion and its priests received much honour in the land. And the yazads, and water and fire and cattle, were greatly contented, and Ahriman and the devs suffered great blows and harm. And the creed of Ahriman and the devs was driven out of the land and deprived of credence. And Jews and Buddhists and Brahmans and Aramaic and Greek-speaking Christians and Baptisers and Manichaeans were assailed in the land. And images were overthrown, and the dens of demons were (thus) destroyed, and the places and abodes of the yazads (i.e. fire temples) were established. . . . And from the first I, Kirder, underwent much toil and trouble for the yazads and the rulers, and for my own soul's sake.

And I caused many fires and priestly colleges to flourish in Iran, and also in non-Iranian lands. There were fires and priests in the non-Iranian lands which were reached by the armies of the King of kings. The provincial capital Antioch and the province of Syria, and the districts dependent on Syria; the provincial capital Tarsus and the province of Cilicia, and the districts dependent on Cilicia; the provincial capital Caesarea and the province Cappadocia, and the districts dependent on Cappadocia, up to Pontus, and the province of Armenia, and Georgia and Albania and Balasagan, up to the 'Gate of the Alans'—these were plundered and burnt and laid waste by Shabuhr, King of kings, with his armies. There too, at the command of the King of kings, I reduced to order the priests and fires which were in those lands. And I did not allow harm to be done them, or captives made. And whoever had thus been made captive, him indeed I took and sent back to his own land. And I made the Mazda-worshipping religion and its good priests esteemed and honoured in the land. . . . ❑

Mary Boyce, ed. and trans., *Textual Sources for the Study of Zoroastrianism* (Manchester: University Press, 1984), pp. 112–113.

---

trian heretics, much as they were regarded by Christian groups as Christian heretics.

MANICHAEISM. Mani (A.D. 216–277) was born of a noble Parthian family but was raised in Babylonia. A cosmopolitan who spoke Aramaic, Persian, and Greek and had traveled to India, Mani preached a message similar to, but at crucial points radically divergent from, its Zoroastrian, Judaic, and Christian forerunners. It centered on a radically dualistic and moralistic view of reality, in which good and evil, spirit and matter, always warred. His preaching was avowedly missionary, presenting itself as the culmination and restoration of the original unity of Zoroastrian, Christian, and Buddhist teachings. Mani may have been the first person in history consciously to "found" a new religious tradition or to create a "scripture" for his followers. He called his new system "Justice," although it has been known to outsiders as Manichaeism. Mani's movement proved a popular one; its popularity probably contributed to Kirdir's and later attempts to establish a Zoroastrian "orthodoxy" and scriptural canon.[3]

[3] W. C. Smith, *The Meaning and End of Religion* (New York, 1962), pp. 92–98.

Kirdir eventually won his struggle against Mani and had him executed as a heretic in 277. But Mani's movement was destined to have great consequences. It spread westward to challenge the young Christian church (Saint Augustine was once a Manichaean) and eastward along the silk route to coexist in central Asia with Nestorian Christian and Mahayana Buddhist communities as a third major universalistic tradition until after the coming of Islam. Its ideas figured even centuries later in both Christian and Islamic heresies. Its adherents probably carried the Western planetary calendar to China, where in some areas it was used for centuries.

ZOROASTRIAN ORTHODOXY. Kartir had firmly grounded Zoroastrian orthodoxy despite the persistence of such challenges to it as that of Mani. This orthodoxy became the backbone of Sasanid culture. Soon the Sasanids' Persian dialect, *Pahlavi*, became the official imperial language, displacing Parthian (although many Parthian words entered the Persian language). Eventually, the Zoroastrian sacred texts were set down in Pahlavi. In later Sasanid times, the priests produced many new writings, ranging from commen-

An angel from a Manichean mural of Central Asia (eighth–ninth century A.D.). Paintings such as this are an important source for our knowledge of Manichaean communities.

SASANID IRAN

A.D. 223–224	Ardashir (reigned 224–CA. 239) defeats the last Arsacid ruler, becomes shahanshah of Iran
CA. 225–CA. 239	Tosar chief priest (Mobad) of realm
239–272	Reign of Shapur I; expansion of the empire east and west
CA. 239–293	Kirdir chief priest (Mobad) of the realm
216–277	Mani
CA. 307–379	Reign of Shapur II
488–531	Reign of Kavad I; height of Mazdakite movement
528	Mazdak and followers massacred
531–579	Reign of Chosroes Anosharvan at Ctesiphon
651	Death of last Sasanid; Arabs conquer Persian empire

taries to myth, theology, and wisdom literature. Throughout Sasanid times, the priesthood grew in power as the jurists and legal interpreters as well as the liturgists and scholars of the land. With increasing endowments of new fire temples, the church establishment eventually controlled much of the wealth of Iran.

Later Sasanid Developments

Despite the high Zoroastrian moral intent of many of their rulers, the Sasanid ideal of justice did not include equal distribution of the empire's bounty. The radical inequalities between the aristocracy and the common folk in Sasanid lands erupted in conflict in one instance: the Mazdakite movement at the end of the fifth century. Its leader, Mazdak, seems to have drawn his ideas ultimately from Manichaeism. They included similar ascetic tendencies, were pessimistic about the

evil state of the material world, and urged vegetarianism, tolerance, and brotherly love. Mazdak's egalitarian preaching, which included a demand for a more equal distribution of society's goods, was attractive especially to the oppressed classes, and one Sasanid ruler, Kavad I (reigned 488–531), was even sympathetic for a time to Mazdak's ideas of social justice. However, in 528, Kavad's third son, the later Chosroes Anosharvan, carried out an official massacre of Mazdak and his most important followers. Although this finished the Mazdakites, the name was still used later, in Islamic times, for various Iranian popular revolts.

INDIA

The Golden Age of the Guptas

The Gupta era has always marked for Indians the high point of their civilization. Historians have seen in it the source of the "classical" norms for Hindu religion and Indian culture, the symbolic equivalent of Periclean Athens, Augustan Rome, or Han China. The Guptas ruled at a time when the various facets of Indian life took on the recognizable patterns of a single civilization which, however diverse its parts, covered all the

subcontinent. A contributing factor was the relative peace and stability that marked most of the Gupta reign.

Gupta Rule

The first Gupta king was Chandragupta (reigned A.D. 320–CA. 330; not to be confused with Chandragupta Maurya; see Chapter 7). He came to prominence first in Magadha and then the rest of the Ganges basin largely through his marriage to princess

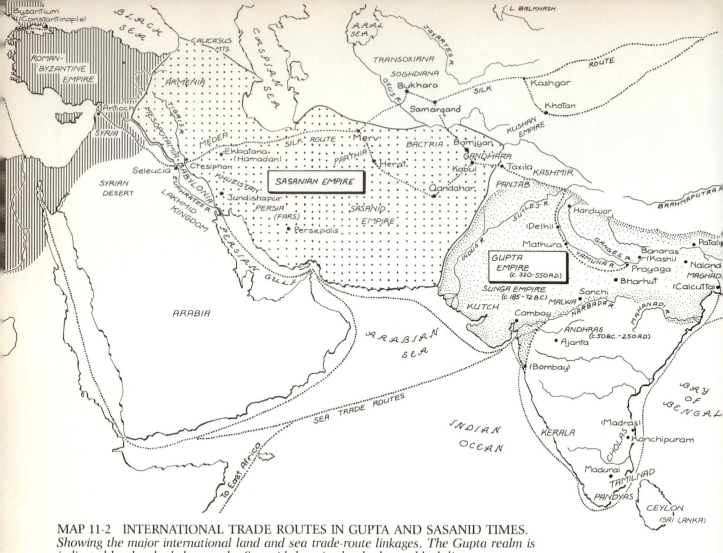

MAP 11-2 INTERNATIONAL TRADE ROUTES IN GUPTA AND SASANID TIMES.
*Showing the major international land and sea trade-route linkages. The Gupta realm is
indicated by the shaded area, the Sasanid domains by the heavy black line.*

Kumaradevi, daughter of the leader of a powerful tribe
north of the Ganges. Although their reign inaugurated
Gupta power, it was their son, Samudragupta and
especially their grandson, Chandragupta II (reigned
CA. 375–415), who turned kingdom into empire and
presided over the Gupta "golden age."

The Gupta realm became the greatest in the subcontinent, extending from the borders of the Punjab
and Kashmir south to the Narbada river in the western
Deccan and east to modern Assam. The Gupta sphere
of influence was still larger, including some of the
Kushan and Saka kingdoms of the northwest as well as
much of the eastern coast of India and possibly Ceylon
(Sri Lanka). More than the Mauryas, the Guptas were
usually ready to accept a defeated ruler as a vassal
prince rather than to try to place his kingdom under
direct central administrative control. Seated at the old
Mauryan capital of Pataliputra, Gupta splendor and
power had no rival. Under Chandragupta II, India was

arguably the most civilized and peaceful country in the
world.

Two further Gupta kings sustained this prosperity
for another half century, despite invasions by a new
wave of steppe nomads, the Huns, from about 440 on.
Various weaker kings followed until the empire collapsed around 550, but repeated Hun incursions had
already overrun western India by about 500. When
another Indian ruler did manage to break Hun control
in northwest India (530), the Guptas were too weak to
reestablish their sovereignty in the north.

Harsha, a descendant of the Guptas through his
grandmother, managed to revive some of the Gupta
splendor between 616 and 657. He ruled long and well
over a loose empire that stretched across north India.
When he died without heirs, the empire broke up
again, and the final echo of Gupta grandeur was gone.
The succeeding centuries before the arrival of Muslim
invaders in about A.D. 1000 saw several dynasties

share power in north India, but no unified rule of any duration. Outside the north, the main centers of regional empires were in the western Deccan and in Tamilnad (the extreme south), where several long-lived dynasties shared control after Gupta times. The cultural impetus of Indian civilization now shifted visibly to the Deccan and south.

Gupta Culture

With the decline of Rome in the West, from Gupta until Muslim times Indian culture experienced little new influence from outside. India's chief contacts were now with Southeast Asia and China, and most of the cultural transmission was from India eastward, not vice versa.

The Gupta period and later centuries saw massive literary and artistic productivity, of which only a few outstanding examples can be mentioned. The claim of the Gupta era to being India's golden age of culture could be sustained solely on the basis of its magnificent architecture and sculpture, the wall paintings of the Ajanta caves, and the matchless drama and verse of Kalidasa. The "Shakespeare" of Sanskrit letters, Kalidasa flourished in the time of Chandragupta II and Kumaragupta. Poetry, painting, sculpture, dance, drama, and music were popularly practiced as well as patronized in the aristocratic households of the cities that set the cultural standards.

One index of the culture was its emphasis on education, which was prominently available in Jain and Buddhist monasteries and in Brahmanical schools. Religious texts were not the only focus: Rhetoric, prose and poetic composition, grammar, logic, medicine, and metaphysics were typical subjects. Based on the

A Chinese Traveler's Report on the Gupta Realm

Fa-Hsien, a Chinese Buddhist monk, was the first of several known Chinese to travel to India to study and bring back Buddhist scriptures from the intellectual centers of Buddhist thought there. He, like later travelers of whom we know, wrote an account of his travels, first through Central Asia, then all over India, then through Ceylon and Indonesia again to China (A.D. 399–414).

On the sides of the river, both right and left, are twenty saṅghârâmas [monasteries], with perhaps 3000 priests. The law of the Buddha is progressing and flourishing. Beyond the deserts are the countries of Western India. The kings of these countries are all firm believers in the law of Buddha. They remove their caps of state when they make offerings to the priests. The members of the royal household and the chief ministers personally direct the food-giving; when the distribution of food is over, they spread a carpet on the ground opposite the chief seat (the president's seat) and sit down before it. They dare not sit on couches in the presence of the priests. The rules relating to the almsgiving of kings have been handed down from the time of Buddha till now. Southward from this is the so-called middle-country (Mâdhyadeśa). The climate of this country is warm and equable, without frost or snow. The people are very well off, without polltax or official restrictions. Only those who till the royal lands return a portion of profit of the land. If they desire to go, they go; if they like to stop, they stop. The kings govern without corporal punishment; criminals are fined, according to circumstances, lightly or heavily. Even in cases of repeated rebellion they only cut off the right hand. The king's personal attendants, who guard him on the right and left, have fixed salaries. Through-

out the country the people kill no living thing nor drink wine, nor do they eat garlic or onions, with the exception of Chandâlas [outcasts] only. The Chandâlas are named "evil men" and dwell apart from others; if they enter a town or market, they sound a piece of wood in order to separate themselves; then men, knowing who they are, avoid coming in contact with them. In this country they do not keep swine nor fowls, and do not deal in cattle; they have no shambles or wine-shops in their marketplaces. In selling they use cowrie shells. The Chandâlas only hunt and sell flesh. Down from the time of Buddha's Nirvâna, the kings of these countries, the chief men and householders, have raised vihâras [monasteries] for the priests, and provided for their support by bestowing on them fields, houses, and gardens, with men and oxen. Engraved title-deeds were prepared and handed down from one reign to another; no one has ventured to withdraw them, so that till now there has been no interruption. All the resident priests having chambers (in these vihâra) have their beds, mats, food, drink, and clothes provided without stint; in all places this is the case. The priests ever engage themselves in doing meritorious works for the purpose of religious advancement (karma—building up their religious character), or in reciting the scriptures, or in meditation. ❑

From "Buddhist Country Records," in *Si-Yu-Ki: Buddhist Records of the Western World*, trans. by Samuel Beal (London, 1884; reprint, Delhi: Oriental Books Reprint Corporation, 1969), pp. xxxvii–xxxviii.

The Bodhisattva Avalokiteshvara from Ajanta. One of the magnificent murals from the Ajanta Buddhist cave shrines. The colossal figure is that of the Bodhisattva of infinite compassion. Even through the damage of centuries, this Gupta masterpiece has an aura of serene majesty. The inclined head of Avalokiteshvara as well as the tranquil face and gesturing hands embody the compassion of this figure in what is surely one of the masterpieces of world religious art. [Government of India Tourist Office.]

still older Indian number system that came later via the Arabs to the West as the "Arabic numerals," mathematics was cultivated for theoretical as well as practical purposes.

In sculpture, the superb technique and expressive serenity of Gupta style grew out of the native Mathura and Greco-Roman schools. Hindu, Jain, and Buddhists works all shared the same style and conventions. A great center for sculpture was the monastic complex at Sarnath. Even in handwork and luxury crafts, Gupta products achieved new levels of quality and were in great demand abroad: silks, muslin, linen, ivory and other carvings, bronze metalwork, gold and silver work, and cut stones, among others. In architecture, Gupta splendor is less evident, save in the culmination of cave shrine (Chaitya hall) development at Ajanta and in the earliest surviving free-standing tem-

The Durga Temple at Aihole. This Hindu temple in the southern Deccan shows how the older Chaitya-hall of the rock-cut or cave variety, such as at Ajanta, influenced the shape of free-standing temples in Gupta times. Note the small spire that became a fixture of later Indian temple architecture. [Giraudon/Art resource.]

A Lyric Poem of Kalidasa

Perhaps the greatest lyric poet as well as dramatist of Sanskrit letters, Kalidasa represents all that was refined and aesthetically sophisticated about Gupta culture. In the following poem, he paints a picture in words from an epic tale about Kumāra, the divine offspring of Shiva, and his consort, the goddess Parvati.

KUMĀRA'S FIGHT AGAINST THE DEMON TĀRAKA

A fearful flock of evil birds,
   ready for the joy of eating the army of demons,
flew over the host of the gods,
   and clouded the sun.

A wind continually fluttered their umbrellas and
   banners,
and troubled their eyes with clouds of whirling dust,
so that the trembling horses and elephants
and the great chariots could not be seen.

Suddenly monstrous serpents, as black as powdered
   soot,
scattering poison from their upraised heads,
frightful in form,
appeared in the army's path.

The sun put on a ghastly robe
of great and terrible snakes, curling together,
as if to mark his joy
at the death of the enemy demon.

And before the very disc of the sun
jackals bayed harshly together,
as though eager fiercely to lap the blood
of the king of the foes of the gods, fallen in battle.

Lighting heaven from end to end,
with flames flashing all around,
with an awful crash, rending the heart with terror,
a thunderbolt fell from a cloudless sky.

The sky poured down torrents of red-hot ashes,
with which were mixed blood and human bones,
till the flaming ends of heaven were filled with
   smoke
and bore the dull hue of the neck of an ass.

Like the thundered threat of the angry death-god
a great crash broke the walls of the ears,
a shattering sound, tearing the tops of the
   mountains,
and wholly filling the belly of heaven.

The host of the foe was jostled together.
The great elephants stumbled, the horses fell,
and all the footmen clung together in fear,
as the earth trembled and the ocean rose to shake
   the mountains.

And, before the host of the foes of the gods,
dogs lifted their muzzles to gaze on the sun,
then, howling together with cries that rent the
   eardrums,
they wretchedly slunk away. ❑

Kumāra-sambhava, 15.14

From Louis Renou (ed.), *Hinduism* (New York: G. Braziller, 1962), pp. 181–182.

---

ples in India. The Hindu temple underwent its important development in post-Gupta times, in the eighth century and after.

The Consolidation of Indian Civilization (CA. A.D. 300–1000)

The Guptas' support of Brahmanic traditions and Vaishnava[4] devotionalism reflected the ascendancy of Hindu over Buddhist traditions as the mainstream of Indian religious life. In Gupta and subsequent times down to the advent of Muslim rule, Indian civilization

[4] *Vaishnava* or *Vaishnavite* means "related to Vishnu"; similarly, *Shaiva* or *Shaivite* refers to Shiva worship (compare with *Jaina/Jain* for devotees of the way of the *Jinas* such as Mahavira).

assumed its classical shape, its enduring "Hindu" forms of social, religious, and cultural life.

Society

In these centuries, the fundamentally hierarchical character of Hindu/Indian society solidified in practice and theory. The oldest manual of legal and ethical theory, the *Dharmashastra* of Manu, dates from about A.D. 200. Based on Vedic tradition, it treats the *dharma* appropriate to one's class and stage of life, rules for rites and study of the Veda, pollution and purification measures, dietary restrictions, royal duties and prerogatives, and other legal and moral questions.

In it, we find the classic statement of the four-class system of social hierarchy. This system rests on the basic principle that every person is born into a particular station in life (as a result of *karma* from earlier lives), and every station has its particular *dharma*, or appropriate duties and responsibilities, from the lowest servant to the highest prince or Brahman. The basic framework is the Brahmans' ancient division of Aryans into the four *varnas*, or classes, of *Brahman* (priest), *Kshatriya* (noble/warrior), *Vaishya* (tradesperson), and *Shudra* (servant). These divisions reflect an ancient attempt to fix the status and power of the upper three groups, especially the Brahmans, at the expense of the Shudras and the "fifth class" of non-Aryan "outcasts," who performed the most polluting jobs in society. Although class distinctions had already hardened before 500 B.C., the classes were, in practice, somewhat fluid. When the traditional occupation of a *varna* was closed to a member, he could often take up another, all theory to the contrary. When Brahmans, Vaishyas, or even Shudras gained political power as rulers (as was evidently the case with the Mauryas, for example), their family gradually became recognized as *Kshatriyas*, the appropriate class for princes.

Although the four classes, or *varnas*, provide the theoretical basis for caste relations, smaller subgroups, or *jatis*, are the units to which our English term *caste* refers. These basic divisions of all later Indian society were already the primary units of social distinction in Gupta times. *Jati* groupings are based essentially on principles of purity and pollution, which are expressed in three kinds of regulation: (1) commensality (one may take food only from or with persons of the same or a higher caste group); (2) endogamy (one may marry only within the group); and (3) trade or craft limitation (one must practice only the trade of one's group).[5]

As much as the caste system has been criticized, it has been the functional principle of Indian social organization for at least two millennia. It enabled Hindus to accommodate foreign cultural, racial, and religious communities within Indian society by treating them simply as new caste groups. It gave great stability and security to the individual and to society, as everyone could tell by dress and other marks how one should relate to a given person or group. It represented also the logical extension of the doctrine of *karma* into society (see Chapter 2), whether this doctrine be seen as a justification, a product, or a partial cause of the caste system itself.

Religion

HINDU RELIGIOUS LIFE. The growth of devotional cults of Vishnu, Shiva, and other deities unknown or unimportant in Vedic religion went on apace in Gupta and later times. The temple worship of a par-

ticular deity has ever since remained a basic form of Hindu piety. After Vishnu (especially in his form as the hero-savior Krishna) and Shiva (originally a fertility god identified with the Vedic deity Rudra), the chief focus of devotion came to be the goddess in one of her many forms, such as Parvati, Shakti, Durga, or Kali. Vishnu and Shiva, like Parvati, have many forms and names and have always been easily identified with other deities, who are then worshiped as one form of the Supreme Lord or Goddess. Older animal or nature deities were always part of popular Indian piety, presumably since Indus Valley days. Indian reverence for all forms of life and stress on *ahimsa*, or "non-injury" to living beings (see Chapter 2), is most vivid in the sacredness of the cow, which has always been both symbolically and economically a mainstay of life in India.

In the development of Hindu piety and practice, a major strand was the tradition of ardent theism known as *bhakti*, or "loving devotion." This was already evident, at the latest by A.D. 200, in the Bhagavad Gita's treatment of Krishna. Gupta and later times saw the rise, especially in the Tamil-speaking south, of schools of *bhakti* poetry and worship. The central *bhakti* strand in Hindu life derives in good part from the Tamil and other vernacular poets who first sang the praises of Shiva or Vishnu as Supreme Lord. Here, pre-Aryan religious sensibilities apparently reasserted themselves through the non-Aryan Dravidian peoples of the south. The great theologian of devotional Hinduism, Ramanuja (d. CA. 1137), would later come from this same Dravidian tradition. Of major importance also to devotional piety was the development in this era of the Puranas—epic, mythological, and devotional texts. They are still today the functional sacred scriptures of grassroots Hindu religious life (the Vedic texts remaining the special preserve of the Brahmans).

Whichever god or goddess a Hindu worships, there has never been any objection to paying homage on the proper occasion to other appropriate deities. Most Hindus view one deity as Supreme Lord but see others as manifestations of the Ultimate at lower levels. Hindu polytheism is not "idolatry," but a vivid affirmation of the infinite forms that transcendence takes in the created world. The sense of the presence of the divine in everything is evident at the popular level in the immense importance attached to sacred places in India. It is the land of religious pilgrimage *par excellence.* Sacred mountains, rivers, trees, and groves are all *tirthas*, or "river crossings" to the Divine.

The philosophical or theological articulation of Hindu polytheism and relativism found its finest form in post-Gupta formulations of Vedanta ("the End of the Veda"). This is one of the six major Hindu systems of thought based on the Vedas, especially the Upanishads. The major Vedantic thinker was Shan-

[5] A. L. Basham, *The Wonder That Was India* (New York, 1963), pp. 148–149.

विषाू

A

B

C

kara (d. 820). He stressed a strict "nonduality" of the Ultimate, teaching that Brahman was the only Reality behind the "illusion" *(maya)* of the world of sense experience. Yet he accepted the worship of a single lesser god or goddess as appropriate for those who could not follow his "extraordinary norm"—the intellectual realization of the formless Absolute beyond all "name and form" (see Chapter 2).

Vishnu, Shiva, and Durga. Images of three of India's most important Hindu deities, seventh to eleventh centuries A.D. *Figure A shows Vishnu seated upon the conquered Naga, or serpent deity. Figure B shows the goddess Durga standing on a defeated bull-headed demon. Her six arms hold weapons lent her for the battle by Shiva and Vishnu. Figure C is a magnificent South Indian bronze of Shiva. The fluid, balanced image depicts the so-called "dancing Shiva" engaged in his dance of simultaneous destruction and creation of the universe, an artistic-mythical rendering of the eternal flux of all worldly existence. [Diana L. Eck, Museum of Fine Arts Boston-Denman W. Ross Collection, W.R. Nelson Gallery of Art.]*

The Lord Krishna Speaks of True Devotion

In these verses (Bhagavad Gita 9.22–34), Krishna (Vishnu) tells his friend Arjuna the "supreme secret," that pure faith in and devotion to him can save a person. This is a famous expression of the bhakti *ideal of loving devotion to one's lord.*

GOD AND THE DEVOTEE

Those persons who, meditating on Me without any thought of another god, worship Me—to them, who constantly apply themselves [to that worship], I bring attainment [of what they do not have] and preservation [of what they have attained].

Even the devotees of other divinities, who worship them, being endowed with faith—they, too, O son of Kuntī [actually] worship Me alone, though not according to the prescribed rites.

For I am the enjoyer, as also the lord of all sacrifices. But those people do not comprehend Me in My true nature and hence they fall.

Worshipers of the gods go to the gods; worshipers of the manes go to the manes; those who sacrifice to the spirits go to the spirits; and those who worship Me, come to Me.

A leaf, a flower, a fruit, or water, whoever offers to Me with devotion—that same, proffered in devotion by one whose soul is pure, I accept.

Whatever you do, whatever you eat, whatever you offer in sacrifice, whatever you give away, whatever penance you practice—that, O son of Kuntī, do you dedicate to Me.

Thus will you be freed from the good or evil fruits which constitute the bondage of actions. With your mind firmly set on the way of renunciation [of fruits], you will, becoming free, come to Me.

Even-minded am I to all beings; none is hateful nor dear to Me. Those, however, who worship Me with devotion, they abide in Me, and I also in them.

Even if a person of extremely vile conduct worships Me being devoted to none else, he is to be reckoned as righteous, for he has engaged himself in action in the right spirit.

Quickly does he become of righteous soul and obtain eternal peace. O son of Kuntī, know for certain that My devotee perishes not.

For those, O son of Prithā, who take refuge in Me, even though they be lowly born, women, vaishyas, as also shūdras—even they attain to the highest goal.

How much more, then, pious brāhmans, as also devout royal sages? Having come to this impermanent, blissless world, worship Me.

On Me fix your mind; become My devotee, My worshiper; render homage unto Me. Thus having attached yourself to Me, with Me as your goal, you shall come to Me. . . . ❑

From W. T. deBary et al., *Sources of Indian Tradition* (New York: Columbia University Press, 1958), pp. 294–296.

BUDDHIST RELIGIOUS LIFE. The major developments of these centuries were (1) the solidification of what would later become the two main strands of Buddhist tradition, the Mahayana and the Theravada, and (2) the spread of Buddhism abroad from its Indian homeland.

The Mahayana ("Great Vehicle [of salvation]") arose in the first century B.C., although Mahayana ideas had been foreshadowed in divergent schools of Buddhist thought as early as the fourth century B.C. Its proponents differentiated it sharply from the older, more conservative traditions of monk-oriented piety and thought, which they called the Hinayana ("Little Vehicle"). Mahayana speculation developed in the style of Upanishadic monism: Buddhas were viewed as manifestations of a single principle of Ultimate Reality, and the Buddha Sidhartha Gautama was held to be but one Buddha among many. In the Mahayana, the model of the Buddha's infinite compassion for all beings was paramount. The highest goal was not a *nirvana* of "selfish" extinction but the enlightened status of a *bodhisattva*, or "Buddha-to-be." The *bodhisattva* postpones individual enlightenment and vows to remain in the round of existence until he has helped all other beings achieve nirvana.

What makes it possible for the bodhisattva to offer this aid is the infinite merit gained through a long career of self-sacrifice. Salvation now becomes possible not only through one's individual efforts, but through devotion to the great Buddhas and bodhisattvas. At the popular level, this idea translated into devotional cults of the transcendent Buddha and many other Buddhas and bodhisattvas similarly conceived of as divine beings. Of such cults, one of the most important was that of the Buddha Amitabha, the personification of infinite compassion. Amitabha presides over the Western Paradise, or Pure Land, to which (through his infinite compassion) all who have faith in him have access.

The older, more conservative "Way of the Elders" (Theravada) was never the totally selfish elite tradition of the few that its Mahayana critics claimed it to be. Its focus was always the monastic community, but lay devotees were needed to support this community; and their service and gifts to the monks were a major source of merit for the laity. The emphasis on gaining merit for a better rebirth through high standards of conduct was strong for monks and laity alike. Popular lay devotion to the Buddha and pilgrimage to his relics at various *stupas* also became prominent in Theravada practice. Conversely, the Mahayana also held up monastic life as the ideal. However, one of its greatest attractions was its strong devotionalism and virtually polytheistic delight in divine Buddhas and bodhisattvas to whom the average person could pray for mercy, help, and rebirth in paradise. The basis of Theravada piety and practice was the scriptural collection of traditional teachings ascribed to the Buddha as reported by his disciples. Theravadins rejected the Mahayana claim that later texts (e.g., the Lotus Sutra) contained the highest teachings of the Buddha.

The Theravada was the form of Buddhism that India gave to Ceylon, Burma, and parts of Southeast Asia. The Mahayana was the dominant form carried

The Buddha preaching his first sermon. This seated, high-relief figure of the Buddha, found in the ruins of Sarnath, is one of the finest pieces of Gupta sculpture. Both the hand gesture, which signifies the setting in motion of the eternal Dharma, and the etherealized body and head suggest the new concept of the Buddha that emerged with the Mahayana. In Gupta times, Sarnath was a thriving monastic center as well as one of the major schools for the best sculpture of the day. [Diana L. Eck.]

INDIA FROM THE GUPTA AGE TO CA. A.D. 1000	
A.D. 320–CA. 467	Gupta period
320–330	Reign of Chandragupta, first Gupta king
376–454	Reigns of Chandragupta II and Kumaragupta: Kalidasa flourishes; heyday of Gupta culture
CA. 440	Beginning of Hun invasions from Central Asia
CA. 455–467	Reign of last strong Gupta monarch, Skandagupta
399–414	Chinese Buddhist monk, Fa-Hsien, travels in India
616–657	Reign of Harsha; revival of Gupta splendor and power
820	Death of Vedantin philosopher-theologian, Shankara
550–CA. 1000	Regional Indian kingdoms in north and south; major Puranas composed; age of first great Vaishnava and Shaivite devotional poets in southern India

into central Asia and China, where it became the major form of religious practice down to the ninth century. Tantric Buddhism, an esoteric Mahayana tradition heavily influenced by Hindu Tantric speculation and ritual, entered Tibet from north India in the seventh century and became the dominant tradition there. From China, Mahayana teachings spread in the fifth to eighth centuries to fertile new fields in Korea and then Japan.

Pre-Islamic Africa, Iran, and India in World Perspective

From a European or American perspective, pre-Islamic Iran, India, and especially Africa are portrayed typically as interesting but relatively unimportant arenas of political, cultural, and religious developments. They are viewed as being on the peripheries of the late Roman and Near Eastern world of late antiquity. Such a perspective fails to recognize that the loci of major political power, cultural creativity, and religious vitality throughout most of the early centuries A.D. was not in Rome or Greece, or elsewhere in southern Europe, but in Byzantine Anatolia, Egypt, North Africa, and

The True Nature of the Buddha, According to the Lotus Sutra

The Lotus Sutra (Saddharmapundarikasutra, *"Lotus of the True* Dharma*") is one of the best-loved sacred texts of Mahayana Buddhism. Its original Sanskrit text was translated many times into Chinese (the earliest being in* A.D. *225), as well as into Tibetan and other languages. The following passage is a key one for the development of the idea of the cosmic form of the Buddha. Note that Tathagata* ("Thus Gone" [*i.e., having achieved release, or* nirvana]) *is one of the names used for a Buddha.*

Fully enlightened for ever so long, the Tathagata has an endless span of life, he lasts for ever. Although the Tathagata has not entered Nirvana, he makes a show of entering Nirvana, for the sake of those who have to be educated. And even today my ancient course as a Bodhisattva is still incomplete, and my life span is not yet ended. From today onwards still twice as many hundreds of thousands of Nayutas of Kotis of aeons must elapse before my life span is complete. Although therefore I do not at present enter into Nirvana (or extinction), nevertheless I announce my Nirvana. For by this method I bring beings to maturity. Because it might be that, if I stayed here too long and could be seen too often, beings who have performed no meritorious actions, who are without merit, a poorly lot, eager for sensuous pleasures, blind, and wrapped in the net of false views, would, in the knowledge that the Tathagata stays (here all the time), get the notion that life is a mere sport, and would not conceive the notion that the (sight of the) Tathagata is hard to obtain. In the conviction that the Tathagata is always at hand they would not exert their vigour for the purpose of escaping from the triple world, and they would not conceive of the Tathagata as hard to obtain.

Hence the Tathagata, in his skill in means, has uttered to those beings the saying that "Rarely, O monks, do Tathagatas appear in the world." Because, during many hundreds of thousands of Nayutas of Kotis of aeons those beings may have the sight of a Tathagata, or they may not. And therefore, basing my statement on this fact, I say that "Rarely, O monks, do Tathagatas appear in the world." To the extent that they understand the rarity of a Tathagata's appearance, to that extent they will wonder (at his appearance), and sorrow (at his disappearance), and when they do not see the Tathagata, they will long for the sight of him. The wholesome roots, which result from their turning their attention towards the Tathagata as towards an objective basis, will for a long time tend to their weal, benefit and happiness. Considering this, the Tathagata, although he does not actually enter Nirvana, announces his entering into Nirvana, for the sake of those to be educated. And that is a discourse on Dharma by the Tathagata himself. When he utters it, there is in it no false speech on the part of the Tathagata. ☐

15, 268–272

From Edward Conze (ed.), *Buddhist Texts through the Ages* (New York and Evanston: Harper Torchbooks, 1964), pp. 142–143.

Syria-Mesopotamia. Augustine of Hippo was, after all, an African; Christian monasticism began in Egypt; and the great doctrinal councils of the Christian church were held in Asia. Our perspective must necessarily change when we give proper recognition to the overwhelming facts: the contemporaneous importance of the Aksumite empire in Ethiopia, the Sasanid imperial culture of Iran, the Zoroastrian revival, the Manichaean movement, the compilation of the Babylonian and Palestinian Tamuds, the completion of the *Mahabharata* and *Ramayana*, Gupta imperial rule, Gupta art and literature, Indian religious thought, and the spread of Mahayana Buddhism across central Asia into China and thence to Japan.

Portions of Asia and Africa were the settings for impressive and often momentous historical developments. Consequently, simplistic notions of the progressive "rise of the West" from classical antiquity to modern times do not hold very well for the first millennium A.D., especially when we take into view the coming of Islam in the seventh century. The Western world in these centuries did not appear to hold much promise as a future center of globally important political or cultural life. Instead, progressiveness and culture seemed to be best embodied in either Sasanid or Gupta culture, or, still more in East Asia. The majesty and unity of Chinese imperial power and culture under the Han dynasty (221 B.C.–A.D. 220) and its reestablishment under the Sui (589–618) and T'ang (618–907) dynasties, or the cultural, political, and religious vibrancy of the heavily Chinese-influenced Nara (710–794) and Heian (794–1180) periods in Japan cannot be underestimated.

A revised perspective would thus see a number of important centers of cultural, religious, and political traditions around the globe, both in the Asian kingdoms and also notably in the Mediterranean imperial domains of Byzantium and in Aksumite Ethiopia. This is not to say that all the political and cultural centers, let alone the important dynasties, of these centuries would long endure. The imminent coming of the last major world religious and cultural tradition—that of Islam—would affect, redefine, or even eliminate the overt presence of many of previous centers of civilization. Nevertheless, in their heydays, these civilizations were impressive achievements.

Taken as a whole, Africa, like Europe, was still a culturally diverse and largely undeveloped region except in those areas on its peripheries that were already active commercial or political participants in the larger universe. To the east, Hindu tradition and Indian culture were undergoing important developments, while Buddhism was waning in its Indian homeland even as it found new and rich fields for conquest in central Asia, China, and Japan, as well as Southeast Asia. Zoroastrian Iran appeared well on its way into a second millennium of Iranian imperial splendor under the Sasanids. Yet it would soon face the most cataclysmic changes of all the major centers of world culture in this age. Who could have suspected in the time of Chosroes Anoshirvan how radically Persian culture would be shaken, recast, and given new life in Islamic forms within three or four centuries?

Suggested Readings

AFRICA

P. BOHANNAN AND P. CURTIN, *Africa and Africans*, rev. ed. (1971). An enjoyable and enlightening discussion of African history and prehistory, and of major African institutions (e.g., arts, family life, religion).

P. CURTIN, S. FEIERMANN, L. THOMPSON, AND J. VANSINA, *African History* (1978). Probably the best survey history. The relevant portions are Chapters 1, 2, 4, 8, and 9.

T. R. H. DAVENPORT, *South Africa: A Modern History*, 3rd rev. ed. (1987). Chapter 1 gives excellent summary coverage of prehistoric south Africa, the Khoisan peoples, and the Bantu migrations.

B. DAVIDSON, *The African Past* (1967). A combination of primary-source selections and brief secondary discussions trace sympathetically the history of the diverse parts of Africa.

J. D. FAGE, *A History of Africa* (1978). A fine general history. The relevant segment here is Part I, "The Internal Development of African Society" (Chapters 1–5).

P. GARLAKE, *The Kingdoms of Africa* (1978). A lavishly illustrated set of photographic essays that provide a helpful introduction to the various historically important areas of precolonial Africa.

R. W. JULY, *Precolonial Africa: An Economic and Social History* (1975). A very readable, topically arranged study. See especially "The Savannah Farmer," "The Bantu," "Cattlemen," and "The Traders" chapters.

R. W. JULY, *A History of the African People*, 3rd ed. (1980). Part I, "Ancient Africa" covers the precolonial centuries and offers a very readable historical introduction to African civilization.

G. MOKHTAR, *Ancient Civilizations of Africa. Vol II of UNESCO General History of Africa* (1981). Relevant chapters are 8–16 on Nubia, Meroe, and Aksum; 17–20 on the Saharan region in ancient times; and 22–29 on the early history of the various regions of the Africa subcontinent.

IRAN

M. BOYCE, ed. and trans., *Textual Sources for the Study of Zoroastrianism* (1984). An extremely valuable anthology with an important introduction that includes Boyce's arguments for a revision (to sometime between 1400 and 1200 B.C.) of the dates of Zoroaster's life.

M. BOYCE, *Zoroastrians: Their Religious Beliefs and Practices* (1979). A detailed survey by the current authority on Zoroastrian religious history. See Chapters 7–9.

R. N. FRYE, *The Heritage of Persia* (1963). Still one of the best surveys. Chapter 6 deals with the Sasanid era.

R. GHIRSHMAN, *Iran* (1954 [orig. 1951]). An introductory survey—simpler and less detailed than Frye's.

R. GHIRSHMAN, *Persian Art: The Parthian and Sasanid Dynasties* (1962). Superb photographs, and a very helpful glossary of places and names. The text is minimal and less useful.

GEO WIDENGRAN, *Mani and Manichaeism* (1965). Still the standard introductory survey of Mani's life and the later spread and development of Manichaeism.

INDIA

A. L. BASHAM, *The Wonder that Was India* (1963). Still the best accessible general survey of classical Indian religion, society, literature, art, and political organization.

S. DUTT, *Buddhist Monks and Monasteries of India* (1962). The standard work. See especially Chapters 3 ("Bhakti") and 4 ("Monasteries under the Gupta Kings").

D. G. MANDELBAUM, *Society in India*, 2 vols. (1972). The first two chapters in Vol. I of this large and interesting study of caste, family, and village relations are a good introduction to the caste system.

B. ROWLAND, *The Art and Architecture of India: Buddhist/Hindu/Jain*, 3rd ed. rev. (1970). See the excellent chapters on Sungan, Andhran, and other early Buddhist art (6–8, 14), the Gupta period (15), and the Hindu Renaissance (17–19).

V. A. SMITH, *The Oxford History of India*, 4th ed. rev. (1981). See especially pp. 164–229 (covers the Gupta period and following era to the Muslim invasions).

R. THAPAR, *A History of India*. Part I (1966), pp. 109–193. Three chapters covering the rise of mercantilism, the Gupta "classical pattern," and the southern dynasties to CA. A.D. 900.

P. YOUNGER, *Introduction to Indian Religious Thought* (1972). A sensitive attempt to delineate classical concerns of Indian religious thought and culture.

The Fatiha. A fine calligraphic rendering of the opening sura, or chapter, of the Qur'an. The first five verses of the chapter are written around the circumference of the emblem, with the vertical letters extended into an arabesque design at the center. [William Graham.]

312

12 The Formation of Islamic Civilization (622–945)

Islamic civilization arose as the last great world civilization up to now, if one excepts the post-Enlightenment modern West. On the one hand, its rise is the story of the creation, spread, and elaboration of distinctive Islamic religious, social, and political institutions within an initially Arab-dominated empire. On the other, it is the story of how, in older cultural environments, Islamic ideas and institutions evolved from their Arabian beginnings into a cosmopolitan array of cultures. Each was a different, new creation of particular circumstances, yet each was identifiably part of a larger, international Islamic civilization.

The basic ideas and ideals of the Islamic worldview derived from a single, prophetic-revelatory event, Muhammad's proclamation of the Qur'an.[1] This event galvanized the Arabs into a new kind of unity—that of the community of *Muslims*, or "submitters" to God. This community subsequently spread far beyond Arabia, and Persians, Indians, and others raised it to new heights. Arab military prowess and cultural consciousness joined with a new religious orientation to effect one of the most permanent revolutions in history. But it was the peoples of the older cultural heartlands who sustained this revolution and built a new civilization. It was their acceptance of a new vision of society (and, indeed, of reality) as more compelling than any older vision—Jewish, Greek, Iranian, Christian, Buddhist—that allowed an Islamic civilization to come into being.

Origins and Early Development

The Setting

At the beginning of the seventh century A.D., the dominant Eurasian political powers, Christian Byzan-

---

[1] The common English transliteration of this Arabic word, *Koran*, is today being replaced by the more accurate *Qur'an*; similarly, *Muhammad* is preferable to *Mohammed* and *Muslim* to *Moslem*.

The Ka'ba in Mecca. The Ka'ba is viewed in Muslim tradition as the site of the first "house of God" built by Abraham and his son Ishmael at God's command. It is held to have fallen later into idolotrous use, until Mohammad's victory over the Meccans and his cleansing of the holy cubical structure (ka'ba means cube). The Ka'ba is the geographical point toward which all Muslims face when performing ritual prayer. It and the plain of Arafat outside Mecca are the two foci of the pilgrimage or Hajj that each Muslim aspires to make at once in a lifetime.

tium and Zoroastrian Iran, or Persia, had confronted one another for over four centuries. This rivalry did not, however, continue much longer. In the wake of one final, mutually exhausting conflict (608–627), a new Arab power broke in from the southern deserts to humble the one and destroy the other.

Pre-Islamic Arabia was not just the home of desert camel nomads. In the Fertile Crescent, Byzantium and Iran had managed to keep the nomads of the Syrian and northern Arabian steppe at bay with the help of small Arab client kingdoms that served as buffer states on the edge of the desert. Settled Arab kingdoms had long existed in the agriculturally rich highlands of southern Arabia, which had direct access to the inter-

national trade that moved by land and sea along its coasts (see Chapter 11). Some of these kingdoms, including a Jewish one in the sixth century, had been independent; others had been under Persian or Abyssinian domination. Farther north, astride the major trade route through the western Arabian highland of the Hijaz, the town of Mecca was a center of the caravan trade. It was also a pilgrimage center because of its famous sanctuary, the Ka'ba (or Kaaba), where many pagan Arab tribes had their gods enshrined. The settled Arabs of Mecca formed a thriving merchant republic in which older tribal values were breaking down under the strains of urban and commercial life. But neither the Meccans nor other settled Arabs were wholly cut off from the nomads who lived on herding and raids on settlements and caravans.

The Arabic language defined and linked the Arab peoples, however divided they were by religion, blood feuds, rivalry, and open conflict. From the Yemen north to Syria–Palestine and the Euphrates, the major element of culture that the Arabs shared was their highly developed poetic idiom. Traditionally, every tribe had a poet to exhort its warriors and challenge its enemies with insults before battle. Poetry contests were also held, often in conjunction with the annual trade fairs that brought diverse tribes together under a general truce.

The popular notion of Islam as a "religion of the desert" is largely untrue. Islam began in a commercial center and first flourished in an agricultural oasis. Its first converts were settled Meccan townsfolk and date farmers of Yathrib (Medina). Most of these Arabs had been pagans, but some were Jews or Christians, or were influenced by Jews or Christians, before Islam. Caravans passed north and south through Mecca, and no merchant engaged in this traffic, as Muhammad himself was, could have been ignorant of different cultures. Early Muslim leaders used the Arabs as warriors and looked to Arab cultural ideals for roots long after the locus of Islamic power had left Arabia. But the empire and culture that they built were centered in the heartlands of Eurasian urban culture and based on settled communal existence rather than desert tribal anarchy.

Muhammad and the Qur'an

Muhammad (CA. 570–632) was raised an orphan in one of the less well-to-do commercial families of the venerable Meccan tribe of Quraysh. Later, in the midst of a successful business career made possible by his marriage to Khadija, a wealthy Meccan widow, he grew increasingly troubled by the idolatry, worldliness, and lack of social conscience around him. These traits would have been equally offensive to sensitive Jewish or Christian piety and morality, about which he certainly knew something. Yet Muhammad did not find his answers in these traditions; they remained somehow foreign to mainstream Arab culture, even though some Arab tribes were Jewish or Christian.

Muhammad's discontent with the moral status quo and older religious solutions prepared the way for a sudden religious experience that changed his life when he was about forty years old. He felt himself called by the one true God to "rise and warn" his fellow Arabs about their frivolous disregard for morality and the worship and service due their creator. On repeated occasions, revelation came to him through a figure who was gradually identified as God's messenger angel, Gabriel. It took the form of a "reciting" (qur'an) of God's word—now rendered in "clear Arabic" for

the Arabs, just as it had been given to previous prophets in Hebrew or other languages for their peoples.

The message of the Qur'an was clear: The Prophet is to warn his people against idolatrous worship of false gods and against all immorality, especially injustice to the weak and less fortunate—the poor, orphans, widows, and women in general. A judgment day at the end of time will see everyone bodily resurrected to stand alone and face eternal punishment in hellfire or eternal joy in paradise, according to how one has lived. The way to paradise lies in proper gratitude to God for the bounties of His created world, His prophetic and revelatory guidance, and His readiness to forgive the penitent. Social justice and obedient worship and service of the one Lord are demanded of every human. Everyone is to recognize his or her creatureliness and God's transcendence. The proper response is "submission" (islam) to God's will, becoming muslim ("submissive" or "surrendering") in one's worship and morality. All of creation praises and serves God by its very nature; only humans have been given a choice, either to obey or to reject Him.

In this Qur'anic message, the moral monotheism of Judaic and Christian tradition (very likely reinforced by Zoroastrian and Manichaean ideas) reached its logical conclusion in a radically theocentric vision; it de-

CA. 570	Birth of Muhammad
622	The Hijra (*Hegira*, "emigration") of Muslims to Yathrib (henceforward *al-Madina*, "The City [of the Prophet]"); beginning of Muslim calendar
632	Death of Muhammad; Abu Bakr becomes first "Successor" (*Khalifa*, caliph) to leadership, reigns 632–634
634–644	Caliphate of Umar; rapid conquests in Egypt and Iran
644–656	Caliphate of Uthman (member of Umayyad clan); more conquests; Qur'an text established; growth of sea power
656–661	Contested Caliphate of Ali; first civil war
661–680	Caliphate of Mu'awiya; founding of Umayyad dynasty (661–750); capital moved to Damascus; more expansion
680	Second civil war begins with death of al-Husayn at Karbala

manded absolute obedience to the one Lord of the Universe. The Qur'anic revelations explicitly state that Muhammad is only the last in a long line of prophets chosen to bring God's word: Noah, Abraham, Moses, Jesus, and nonbiblical Arabian figures like Salih had been sent before on similar missions. Because the

Imru l-Qais, *the Wandering Poet-Hero*

With little written or visual artistic tradition, the ancient Arabs focused on the perfection of the oral word. Each tribe had a poet who in his verse extolled the greatness and prowess of his people and their ancestry and humiliated tribal enemies with satire and polemic. Such verse reinforced the cultural ideals that sprang from the life of the camel nomads of the desert: generosity and hospitality to a fault, family pride and honor, fearless audacity in love and battle, and delight in the animals and other natural beauties of the marginal desert world. In this excerpt from a famous poem of Imru l-Qais (d. CA. 540?), we see a standard beginning of the Arabic lyric ode, or qasida: the sight of an abandoned camp that recalls some past event to the poet. There follow here boastful memories of amorous adventure and a brief segment from later in the poem about the poet's hard existence (which fell to him after his father, ruler of one of the northern desert kingdoms, banished him because he refused to give up poetry—an occupation his father felt was improper for a prince).

Here halt, and weep, for one long-remembered love, for an old
Camp at the edge of the sands that stretch from the Brakes to Floodhead,
From Clearward to the Heights. The marks are not gone yet,
For all that's blown and blown back over them, northward, southward.
Look at the white-deer's droppings scattered in the old yards
And penfolds of the place, like black pepperseeds.

. . . .

I suffered so for love, so fast the tears ran down
Over my breast, the sword-belt there was soaked with weeping.
And yet—the happy days I had of them, of women

. . . .

One day on a sandhill back she would not do my will,
And swore an oath, and swore she meant to keep her oath.

. . . .

That night I passed the wardens who watched their tents, the men
Who would have welcomed me, for the glory of murdering me,
In an hour when Pleiades glittered in the night-heaven
Like a jewelled girdle, gem and pearl and gem;
In such an hour I came; she was all doffed for sleep
But for a shift; close by the screen of the tent she lay.
God's oath on me! she whispered, but thou hast no excuse!

And now I know that thou wilt be wild for ever.
Forth we went together; I led; she trailed behind us
A robe's embroidered hem, that tracks might tell no tales.
When we were past the fenced folkyards, then we made straight
For the heart of the waste, the waves and tumbled hillocks of sand.
I pulled her head to mine by the lovelocks, and she pressed
Against me, slender, but soft even at the ankle.
Thin-waisted she was, and white, sweetly moulded about the belly,
And the skin above her breasts shone like a polished mirror,
Or a pearl of the first water, whiteness a little gilded,
Fed of a pure pool unstirred by the feet of men

. . . .

And taking a water-skin from the house, I would strap it close
Over my shoulder—how often!—and meek to such a saddle
Crossing some hollow place like the flats of Starverib Waste
Have I heard the wolf, like a spendthrift who's gambled his darlings away,
Howl! He would howl. I would answer: It's a poor trade we follow
For profit, if thou hast kept as little as I have kept;
Whatever we get, thou and I, we bolt it; and it's gone.
A man will never be fat who thrives as we two thrive. . . . ❑

From Eric Schroeder (trans.), *Muhammad's People* (Portland, Me.: Bond Wheelwright, 1955), pp. 3–5.

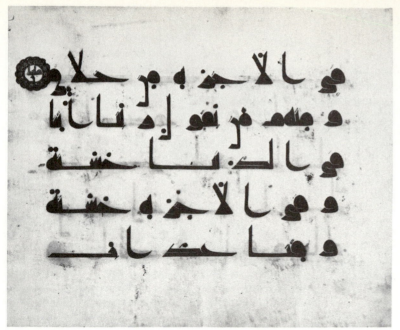

FIGURE 1

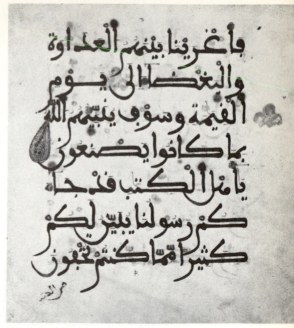

FIGURE 2

Qur'anic pages. With the Muslim aversion to images, calligraphy became a major art form in the early centuries and has continued to flourish. The Arabic script developed primarily to render the Qur'anic text as exactly as one could, and the calligraphic art developed along with it. The earliest script used widely for the Qur'an was the horizontally elongated Kufic. Figure 1 shows a page from an eighth-ninth century Qur'an written in Kufic script. The Kufic script dominated qur'anic calligraphy for three centuries. After the tenth century, other scripts began to predominate. An example of one regional script, the so-called Magribi, or North African, is shown in Figure 2. [Freer Gallery of Art.]

communities of these earlier prophets had strayed from the teachings of their scriptures or had altered them, Muhammad was given one final reiteration of God's message. Jews and Christians, like pagans, were summoned to respond to the moral imperatives of the Qur'an he recited to them.

The Prophet's preaching fell largely on deaf ears in the first years after his calling. However, a small number gradually followed the lead of his wife, Khadija, in recognizing him as a divinely chosen reformer of individual and communal life. Some prominent Meccans did join him, but the merchant aristocracy as a whole resisted. His preaching against their traditional gods and goddesses threatened not only their ancestral ways but also their Meccan pilgrimage shrine and the lucrative trade it attracted. The Muslims began to be persecuted. After the deaths of Khadija and Muhammad's uncle and protector Abu Talib, the situation worsened, and the Prophet even had to send a small band of Muslims to seek refuge in Abyssinia for a time. Then, because of his reputation as a moral and holy man, Muhammad was called to Yathrib (an agricultural oasis about 240 miles north of Mecca) as a neu-

tral arbitrator among its five quarrelsome tribes, three of which were Jewish. Having sent his Meccan followers ahead, Muhammad escaped in July 622 to Yathrib, afterward to be known as Medina (*al-Madina*, "the City [of the Prophet]"). Some dozen years later, this "emigration," or Hegira, became the starting point for the Islamic calendar. This event marked the creation of a distinctive Islamic community, or *Umma*.[2]

Muhammad quickly cemented ties between the Meccan emigrants and the Medinans, many of whom became converts. Raids on the caravans of his Meccan enemies established his leadership. They point also to the economic as well as religious dimension of the Medinan–Meccan struggle. The Jews of Medina by and large rejected his message and authority. They even had contacts with his Meccan enemies, moving

[2]The twelve-month Muslim lunar year is shorter than the Christian solar year by about eleven days, giving a difference of about three years per century. Muslim dates are reckoned from the month in 622 in which Muhammad began his Hegira [Arabic: *Hijra*]. Thus Muslims celebrated the start of their lunar year 1401 in November 1980 (A.D. 1979–1980 = A.H. [Anno Hegirae] 1400), whereas it was only 1,358 solar years from 622 to 1980.

The Qur'an, or "Recitation" of God's Word

The Qur'an has many themes, ranging from moral admonition, threats of hellfire for the ungodly, and stories of past peoples and their prophets, to praise of God, his bountiful natural world and compassion for humankind, and the joys of paradise. The following short selections touch upon (1) the qur'anic notion of revelation in both its own pages and the signs of nature; (2) praise of God the Almighty, the Creator; (3, 4) previous prophets who had testified to God's oneness and sovereignty and brought His revelations to their people.

The revelation of the Book is from God who is mighty and wise. There are signs for men of faith, in the heavens and in the earth, in your being created and in God's scattered throng of creatures—signs for people with a grasp on truth.

There are signs, too—for those with a mind to understand—in the alternation of night and day, and in the gracious rain God sends from heaven to renew the face of the parched earth, and in the veering of the winds.

These are the signs of God which truly We recite to you. Having God and His signs, in what else after that will you believe as a message?

Sura 45.1–6

He is God. There is no god but He. He knows the hidden and the evident. He is the merciful Lord of mercy.

He is God, there is no god but He. He is the King, the holy One, the Lord of peace, the Keeper of faith, the watch-Keeper, the all-strong, the ever-powerful, the Self-aware in His greatness. Glory be to God above all that idolators conceive.

Sura 59.22–23

You people of the Book, why are you so argumentative about Abraham, seeing that the Torah and the Gospel were only sent down after his time? Will you not use your reason? You are people much given to disputing about things within your comprehension: why insist on disputing about things of which you have no knowledge? Knowledge belongs to God and you lack it!

Abraham was not a Jew, nor was he a Christian. He was a man of pure worship (a *hanīf*) and a Muslim: he was not one of those pagan idolaters. The people nearest to Abraham are those who followed him and this prophet too and those who have believed. Believers are under God's care.

Sura 3.65–68

❑

From Kenneth Cragg, trans., *Readings in the Qur'ān* (London: Collins, 1988), pp. 102, 86–87, 121, 166.

Muhammad to turn on the Jews, kill or enslave some, banish others, and take their lands. Many of the continuing revelations of the Qur'an from this period pertain to communal order or to the Jews and Christians who rejected Islam.

The basic Muslim norms took shape in Medina: allegiance to the *Umma*; honesty in public and personal affairs; modesty in personal habits; abstention from alcohol and pork; fair division of inheritances; improved treatment of women, especially as to their property and other rights within marriage; careful regulation of marriage and divorce; ritual ablution before any act of worship, be it Qur'an-reciting or prayer; three (later five) daily rites of worship, facing the Meccan Ka'ba; payment of a kind of tithe to support less fortunate Muslims; daytime fasting for one month each year; and, eventually, pilgrimage to Mecca (*Hajj*) at least once in a lifetime, if one is able.

Acceptance of Islamic political authority brought a kind of tolerance. A Jewish oasis yielded to Muhammad's authority and was allowed, unlike the resistant Medinan Jews, to keep its lands, practice its faith, and receive protection in return for the payment of a head tax. This practice was followed ever after for Jews, Christians, and other "People of Scripture" who accepted Islamic rule. After long conflict, the Meccans surrendered to Muhammad, and his generosity in accepting them into the *Umma* set the pattern for the later Islamic conquests. Following an age-old practice, Muhammad cemented many of his alliances with marriage (although as long as Khadija was alive, he did not take a second wife). In the last years of the Prophet's life, the once tiny band of Muslims became the heart of an all-Arabian tribal confederation, bound together by personal allegiance to Muhammad, submission (*islam*) to God, and membership in the *Umma* of "submitters."

The Early Islamic Conquests

In 632, Muhammad died after an illness, leaving neither a son nor a named successor. The new *Umma* faced its first major crisis. A political struggle between Meccan and Medinan factions ended in a pledge of allegiance to Abu Bakr, the most senior of the early

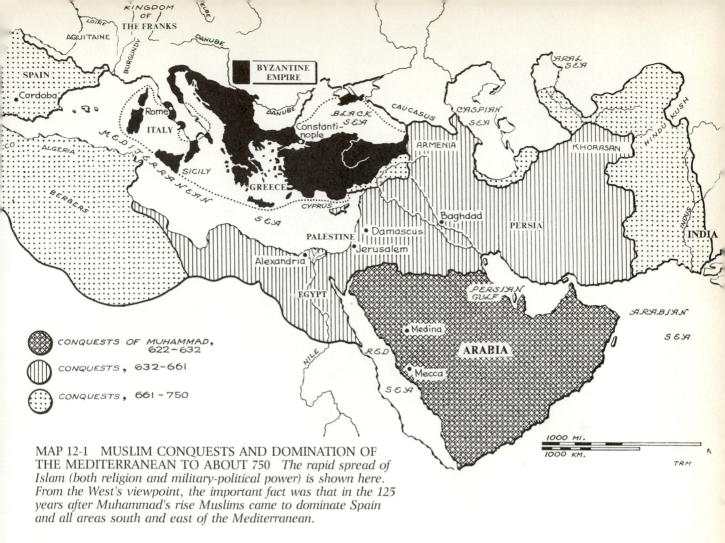

MAP 12-1   MUSLIM CONQUESTS AND DOMINATION OF
THE MEDITERRANEAN TO ABOUT 750   *The rapid spread of
Islam (both religion and military-political power) is shown here.
From the West's viewpoint, the important fact was that in the 125
years after Muhammad's rise Muslims came to dominate Spain
and all areas south and east of the Mediterranean.*

Meccan converts. Many of the naturally independent
Arab tribes renounced their allegiance to the Prophet
upon his death. Nevertheless, Abu Bakr's rule (632–
634) as Muhammad's successor, or "caliph" (Arabic,
khalifa), reestablished Medinan hegemony and at
least nominal religious conformity over the whole of
Arabia. The Arabs were forced to recognize in the
Umma a new kind of supratribal community that demanded more than allegiance to a particular leader.

The Course of Conquest

Under the next two caliphs, Umar (634–644) and
Uthman (644–656), Arab Islamic armies burst out of
the peninsula, intent on more than traditional bedouin
booty raids. In one of the most astonishing sets of military operations ever, they conquered the Byzantine
and Sasanid territories of the Fertile Crescent (by 640),
Egypt (by 642), and most of Iran (by 643). For the first
time in centuries, the lands from Egypt to Iran were
united under one rule. Finally, Arab armies swept
west over the Byzantine-controlled Libyan coast and,

in the east, pushed to the Oxus, defeating the last
Sasanid ruler by 651.

An interlude of civil war during the contested caliphate of Ali (656–661) slowed the expansion briefly.
Then, under the fifth caliph, Mu'awiya (661–680), expansion and consolidation of the new empire progressed. By 680, control of greater Iran was solidified
by permanent Arab garrisoning of Khorasan; much of
Anatolia was raided; Constantinople was besieged
(but not taken); and Armenia was brought under Islamic rule. In the Mediterranean, an Islamic fleet conquered Cyprus, plundered Sicily and Rhodes, and crippled Byzantine seapower.

Succeeding decades saw the eastern Berbers of Libyan North Africa defeated and converted in substantial
numbers, if often superficially or nominally, to Islam.
With their help, "the West" (*al-Maghrib*, modern
Morocco and Algeria), fell quickly. In 711, raids into
Spain began (the name of the Berber Muslim leader of
the first invaders, Tariq, lives on in *Gibraltar*, a corruption of *Jabal Tariq*, "Mount Tariq"). By 716, the

The Omar Mosque, or Dome of the Rock, in Jerusalem. An early example of Islamic architecture (but not a "mosque"), it dates from the seventh century, during the first wave of Arab expansion. It is built on the rock from which Muslims believe Muhammed ascended into heaven and on which Jews believe Abraham prepared to sacrifice Isaac. [Louis Goldman.]

disunited Spanish Visigoth kingdoms had fallen, and much of Iberia was under Islamic control. Pushing farther north into France, the Arabs were finally checked by a defeat at the hands of Charles Martel south of Tours (732). At the opposite end of the empire, buoyed by large-scale Arab immigration, Islamic forces consolidated their holdings as far as the Oxus river basin. In 710, Arab armies reached the Indus region of Sind. The Muslim Arabs now controlled the former Sasanid Empire and beyond. The Byzantine realm was reduced by half and Islamic power was supreme from the Atlantic to central Asia.

Factors of Success

A combination of factors contributed to this rapid expansion. Most basic was the capacity of the new Islamic vision of society and life to unite the Arabs and to attract others as well. Its corollary was the commitment among the Islamic leadership to extend "the Abode of Submission" (*Dar al-Islam*) abroad. However, too much has been made of the general Muslim zeal for martyrdom. Assurance of paradise for those engaged in *jihad*, or "struggle [in the path of God]," is less likely to have motivated the average Arab tribesman—who, at least at the beginning, was usually only nominally a Muslim—as much as promise of the booty of war.

Yet religious zeal cannot be wholly discounted, especially as time went on. The early policy of sending Qur'an-reciters among the armies' pagan tribesmen to teach the essentials of Muslim faith and practice had its effects. A major factor was certainly the leadership of the first caliphs and field generals. This leadership combined with the economic and military exhaustion of Byzantium and Iran to give Arab armies a distinct advantage. Another element was the readiness of subject populations in many areas to accept, even to welcome, Islamic rule as a relief from Byzantine or Persian oppression. Important here was the Muslim willingness to allow Christian, Jewish, and even Zoroastrian groups to continue as minorities (with their own legal systems and no military obligations) under the protection of Islamic rule. In return, they had to recognize Islamic political authority, pay a non-Muslim head tax (*jizya*), and refrain from proselytizing or interfering with Muslim religious practice.

Finally, what gave the conquests overall permanence, besides the vitality of the new faith, were the astute policies followed: relatively little bloodshed or destruction of property or economies; the adoption, with minimal changes, of existing administrative systems; the adjustment of unequal taxation; the appointment of capable governors; and the strategic siting of new Islamic garrison towns like Basra, Kufa, and Fustat (later Cairo).

Early Islamic coins. The development of early Islamic coinage reflects the evolution of Muslim self-awareness. The earliest Arab kingdom had no coinage of its own. The first Islamic caliphs and governors took over the existing Byzantine and Sasanid coinage (Figure 1: a Sasanid silver dirham with the head of the emperor), adding brief Arabic inscriptions (Figure 2), and then slightly altering previous imagery on the coins (Figure 3: "standing caliph" with sword and Arab headdress rather than Byzantine crown). It was only under Abd al-Malik, caliph from 685–705, that a reform of the coinage led to the abandonment of all imagery depicting the human form in favor of Arabic inscriptions proclaiming the basic Muslim faith (Figure 4: "There is no god but God, One, without partner"). [American Numismatic Society of New York.]

FIGURE 1

FIGURE 3

FIGURE 2

FIGURE 4

The New Islamic Order

Unlike rulers who take over an empire and continue the existing religious and cultural traditions, the Muslims brought with them a new worldview that demanded a new political, social, and cultural reality, however long it might take to effect it. Beyond the military and administrative problems they faced loomed the ultimately more important question of the nature of the Islamic state and society. Under the Prophet, a new kind of community, the *Umma*, had replaced, at least in theory and basic organization, the tribal, blood-based social and political order in Arabia. Yet, once the Arabs (most of whom became Muslims) had to rule non-Arabs and non-Muslims, new problems arose that tested the ideal of an Islamic polity. Chief among these problems were leadership and membership qualifications, social order, and religious and cultural identity.

The Caliphate

Allegiance to Muhammad had rested on his authority as a divine spokesperson and as a gifted leader. His first successors were chosen much as were Arab *shaykhs* (sheiks), or tribal chieftans, by agreement of the leaders, or elders, of the new religious "tribe" of Muslims, on the basis of superior personal qualities. Added to these qualities was now the precedence in faith conferred by piety and association with the Prophet. Their titles were "successor" (*khalifa* or caliph), "leader" (*imam*—used also for the Muslim who stands in front of Muslim worshipers to lead them in ritual prayer), and "commander (*amir*) of the faithful." These names underscored political and religious authority, both of which most Muslims were willing to recognize in the caliphs Abu Bakr and Umar, and potentially in Uthman and Ali. Unfortunately, by the time of Uthman and Ali, various dissensions had led to internal strife, then civil war. Yet the first four caliphs had all been close to Muhammad, and this closeness gave their reigns a nostalgic aura of pristine purity, especially as the later caliphal institution was based largely on sheer power and/or hereditary succession.

The nature of Islamic leadership became an issue with the first civil war (656–661) and the recognition of Mu'awiya, a kinsman of Uthman, as caliph. He founded the first dynastic caliphate, that of his Meccan clan of Umayya (661–750). Hereditary Umayyads held power until they were ousted by the Abbasid clan in 750, which based its legitimacy on descent from an uncle of the Prophet (Abbas—hence, "Abbasid"). The Umayyads had the prestige of the office held by the first four, "rightly guided" caliphs. But they also suffered by the comparison, as they were judged by many to be worldly "kings" where the earlier four had been true Muslim "successors" to Muhammad.

The Abbasids won the caliphate by open rebellion in 750, aided by their exploitation of pious dissatisfaction with Umayyad worldliness, non-Arab Muslim resentment of Arab preference (primarily in Iran), and ongoing dissension among Arab tribal factions in the garrison towns. For all their stress on the Muslim character of their caliphate, they were scarcely less worldly and continued the hereditary rule begun by the Umayyads. This they did well enough to retain control of most of the far-flung Islamic territories until 945. Thereafter, although their line continued until 1258, the caliphate was primarily a titular office representing an Islamic unity that existed politically in name only.

The Ulema

Although the caliph could exert his power, as the Abbasids did occasionally, to influence religious matters, he was never "emperor and pope rolled into one." Religious leadership in the *Umma* devolved instead on another group. The functional "successors of the Prophet" in society at large were those Muslims recognized for piety and learning and sought out as informal or even formal (as with state-appointed judges) authorities. Initially, these were the "Companions" (male and female) of Muhammad with the greatest stature in the original Medinan *Umma*—including the first four caliphs. As this generation died out, they were replaced by those younger followers most concerned with preserving, interpreting, and applying the Qur'an, and with maintaining the norms of the Prophet's *Umma*. Because the Qur'an contained very little actual legislative material, they had to draw on precedents from the practice of Medina and Mecca, as well as on oral traditions about the Prophet and Companions. In doing so, they developed an enduring pattern of education based on study under those persons highest in the chain of trustworthy Muslims linking the current age with the earliest *Umma*.

As an unofficial but generally recognized infrastructure in Islamic society, these scholars came to be known as *ulema* ("persons of right kowledge," Anglicized Arabic plural of *'alim*). Some of the most pious *ulema* refused to be judges for the Umayyads. However, their personal legal opinions and collective discussions of issues, ranging from theological doctrine to criminal punishments, established a general basis for religious and social order. By the ninth century, they had largely defined the understanding of the divine Law, or *Shari'a*, that Muslims ever after have held to be definitive for legal, social, commercial, political, ritual, and moral concerns. This understanding and the methods by which it was derived form the Muslim sci-

The ritual worship, or prayer. These illustrations show the sequence of movement prescribed for the ritual prayers that each Muslim should perform five times a day. Various words of praise, prayer, and recitation from the Qur'an accompany each position and movement. The ritual symbolizes the Muslim's complete obedience to God and recognition of God as the one, eternal, omnipotent Lord of the universe.

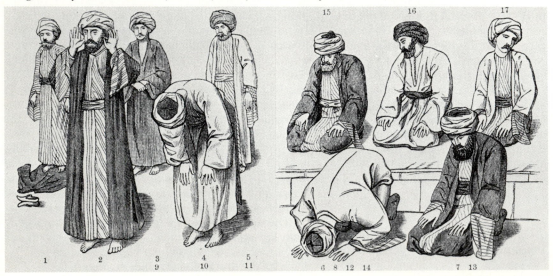

ence of jurisprudence, the core discipline of Islamic learning.

The centers of *ulema* activity were Medina, Mecca, and especially Iraq (primarily Basra and Kufa, later Baghdad), then Khorasan, Syria, North Africa and Spain, and Egypt. In Umayyad times, the *ulema* had already become the guardians of the Muslim conscience, often serving as the chief critics of caliphal rule when it departed too far from Muslim norms. In time, they became a new elite, one eventually identified with the upper class of each regional society. Caliphs and their governors regularly sought their advice, but often only for moral sanction (or legal sanction—the two are in the Muslim view the same) of a contemplated or accomplished action. Some *ulema* acquiesced in dubious sanctions and compromised themselves. Yet incorruptible *ulema* were seldom persecuted for their opinions (save when they supported sectarian rebellions), mostly because of their status and influence among rank-and-file Muslims.

Thus, without building a formal clergy, the Muslims developed a workable legal-moral system based on a formally trained if informally recognized scholarly elite and a tradition of concern with religious ideals in matters of public affairs and social order. If the caliphs and their deputies were seldom paragons of piety and often ruthless, they had at least to act with some circumspection and give compensating support for Muslim pious standards in public. Thus, the *ulema* shared the leadership in Muslim societies with the rulers, even if unequally—a pattern that has endured in Islamic states.

The Umma

A great strength of the Qur'anic message was its universalism. Although Muhammad may have conceived of his community first as an Arab one, the logical extension of the Qur'anic preaching was the acceptance into the *Umma* of anyone, of whatever race or nationality, who would submit to God and follow Muslim precepts. By the time of the first conquests, the new state was already so rooted in Muslim ideals that non-Arab converts had to be accepted, even if it meant loss of tax revenue. The social and political status of new converts was, however, clearly second to that of Arabs. Umar had organized the army register, or *diwan*, according to tribal precedence in conversion to, or (in the unique case of Christian Arab tribes) fighting for, Islam. The *diwan* served as the basis for the distribution and taxation of the new wealth, which perpetuated Arab precedence. The new garrisons, which rapidly became urban centers of Islamic rule and culture, kept the Arabs enough apart so that they were not simply absorbed into the cultural patterns or the traditions of the foreign territories. The Qur'an's centrality in Muslim life and the notion of its perfect Arabic form ensured the dominance of the Arabic language. So did the gradual implementation of Arabic in administration, where it replaced Aramaic, Greek, Middle Persian, or Coptic.

Non-Arab converts routinely attached themselves to Arab tribes as "clients." This assured protection and a place in the *diwan*, but still a permanent second-class citizenship alongside the Arabs. Although many non-Arabs, especially Persians, mastered Arabic and prospered, dissatisfaction among client Muslims was widespread and led to their participation in uprisings against caliphal authority. Persian–Arab tensions were especially strong in Umayyad and early Abbasid times. Nevertheless, a Persian cultural renaissance eventually raised the Islamicized modern Persian language to high status in Islamic culture. Consequently, it profoundly affected religion, art, and literature in much of the Islamic world.

Caliphal administration joined with the evolution of legal theory and practice and the consolidation of religious norms to give stability to the emerging Islamic society. So strong was the power of the Muslim vision of society, that when a caliph, or even a dynasty like the Umayyads, was superseded, the *Umma* and the caliphal office went on. There were, however, conflicting notions of that vision. In the course of the first three Islamic centuries, two major interpretations crystallized that reflected idealistic interpretations of the *Umma*, its leadership and membership. When neither proved viable in the practical world of society and politics, they became minority visions that continued to fire the imaginations of some but failed to win broad-based support. The third, "centrist," vision found favor with the majority; it could speak to a wide spectrum and accommodate inevitable compromises in the higher cause of Islamic unity.

THE KHARIJITES. The most radical idealists traced their political origin to the first civil war (656–661). These were the Kharijites, or "Seceders"—so named because they "seceded" from Ali's camp when, in their view, he compromised with his enemies. The Kharijite position was that the Muslim polity must be based on strict Qur'anic principles. They espoused a total egalitarianism among the faithful and held that the leadership of the *Umma* belonged to the best Muslim, whoever that might be. They took a moralistic, rigorist view of who the true members of the *Umma* were: Anyone who committed a major sin was no longer a Muslim. Extreme Kharijites called on true Muslims to join them in rebellion against the morally compromised authority of the reigning caliph. The extremist groups were constant rallying points for opposition to the Umayyads and, to a lesser degree, the Abbasids. More moderate Kharijites tempered their aversion to tolerating less-than-pious Muslims and the

The Wit and Wisdom of al-Jahiz

One of the great masters of Arabic prose, al-Jahiz (d. 869) left a number of works behind, among them his Book of Proof. *The following excerpts from this book of essays and clever sayings reflect his talent for the succinct and vivid.*

Ghailān son of Kharasha said to Ahnaf, "What will preserve the Arabs from decline?" He replied, "All will go well if they keep their swords on their shoulders and their turbans on their heads and ride horseback and do not fall a prey to the fools' sense of honour." "And what is the fools' sense of honour?" "That they regard forgiving one another as a wrong."

'Umar said, "Turbans are the crowns of the Arabs."

An Arab of the desert was asked why he did not lay aside his turban. "Surely," said he, "a thing which contains the hearing and the sight ought to be prized."

'Ali said—God be well pleased with him!—"The elegance of a man is in his bonnet, and the elegance of a woman is her boots." And Ahnaf said, "Let your shoes be fine, for shoes are to men what anklets are to women."

'Abdullah son of Ja'far said to his daughter, "O little daughter, beware of jealousy, for it is the key of divorce; and beware of chiding, for it breeds hate. Always adorn and perfume thyself, and know that the most becoming adornment is antimony and the sweetest perfume is water."

'Abdullah son of Ja'far bestowed largesse of every kind on Nusaib Abu'l-Hajīnā, who had made an ode in praise of him. "Why," they asked, "do you treat a fellow like this so handsomely—a negro and a slave?" "By God," he answered, "if his skin is black, yet his praise is white and his poem is truly Arabian. He deserves for it a greater reward than he has gotten. All he received was only some lean saddle-camels and clothes which wear out and money which is soon spent, whereas he gave an ode fresh and brilliant and praise that will never die."

Mu'āwiyah held an assembly at Kūfa to receive the oath of allegiance as Caliph. Those who swore loyalty to him were required to abjure allegiance to [the House of] 'Ali son of Abū Tālib—may God honour him! A man of the Banū Tamīm came to Mu'āwiyah, who demanded that he should repudiate 'Ali. "O Prince of the Faithful," he replied, "we will obey those of you that are living, but we will not renounce those of you that are dead." Mu'āwiyah turned to Mughīa and said, "Now, this is a man! Look after him well!"

. . . .

'Auf said on the authority of Hasan: "The feet of a son of Adam will not stir [from the place of judgment] until he be asked of three things—his youth, how he wore it away; his life, how he passed it; and his wealth, whence he got it and on what he spent it."

Yūnus son of 'Ubaid said: "I heard three sayings more than wonderful than any I have ever heard. The first is the saying of Hassān son of Abū Sinān—'Nothing is easier than abstinence from things unlawful: if aught make thee doubt, leave it alone.' The second is the saying of Ibn Sīrīn—'I have never envied any one any thing.' The third is the saying of Muwarrik al-'Ijlī—'Forty years ago I asked of God a boon which He has not granted, and I have not despaired of obtaining it.' They said to Muwarrik, 'What is it?' He replied, 'Not to meddle with that which does not concern me.'" □

From James Kritzeck (ed.), *Anthology of Islamic Literature* (New York: New American Library, Meridian Books, 1964), pp. 91–92.

rule of less-than-ideal caliphs, yet they retained a strong sense of the moral imperatives of Muslim personal and collective duty.

Kharijite ideals proved very attractive and influenced wider Muslim pietism in the long run. Although the movement declined in Abbasid times, even today moderate Kharijite groups survive in Muscat, Oman, and North Africa.

THE SHI'A. A second position was defined largely in terms of leadership in the *Umma*. Muhammad had no surviving sons, and his son-in-law and cousin Ali claimed the caliphate in 656, partly on the basis of his familial ties to the Prophet. His claim was contested by Mu'awiya in the first Islamic civil war. When Mu'awiya took over by default after a Kharijite murdered Ali in 661, many of Ali's followers felt that Islamic affairs had gone awry. Although it is difficult to date the crystallization of the developed ideology of the "partisans of Ali" (*Shi'at Ali*, or simply the *Shi'a*, or *Shi'ites*), their roots go back to Ali's murder and especially to that of his son Husayn at Karbala, in Iraq (680).

Whereas most Muslims esteemed Ali for his closeness to Muhammad, the Shi'ites believed that he was the Prophet's appointed "successor." Ali's blood tie with Muhammad was augmented in Shi'ite thinking by belief in the Prophet's designation of him as the true *imam*, or Muslim leader, after him. Numerous rebellions in Umayyad times rallied around various figures claiming descent from such a designated and related successor, whether Ali or merely any member of

Scenes of Husayn's martyrdom from a Shi'ite Passion Play in Iran. The role of the martyrdom of al-Husayn, son of Ali and grandson of Muhammed, in Shi'ite piety can hardly be exaggerated. This event and the martyrdoms of the imams after him form the basis for the Shi'ite interpretation of history, an interpretation that stresses the suffering of the Imams and of true Muslims who follow them in this world, while promising a reward beyond the grave for the faithful. The performance of passion plays about Husayn's death is unique to Shi'ite Muslim practice. [Peter Chelkowski.]

Muhammad's clan of Hashim. Even the Abbasids based their right to the caliphate on their Hashimite blood. The major Shi'ite pretenders who emerged in the ninth and tenth centuries based their claims on both the Prophet's designation and their descent from Ali and Fatima, Muhammad's daughter. They also stressed the idea of a divinely inspired knowledge passed on by Muhammad to his designated heirs. The true Muslim was the faithful follower of the *imams*, who carried both Muhammad's blood and his mantle of spiritual authority.

When Shi'ites failed to establish a true *imam* as head of the imperial state, they interpreted this failure theologically. They saw Ali's assassination by a Kharijite, and especially the brutal massacre of Husayn and his family by Umayyad troops, as proofs of the evil nature of the rulers of this world, and as rallying points for true Muslims. The martyrdom of Ali and Husayn was extended to a line of Alid *imams* that varied among different groups of Shi'ites. True Muslims, like their *imams*, must suffer. But they would be vindicated in the end by an expected *mahdi*, or "guided one," who would usher in a messianic age and a judgment day that would see the faithful rewarded.

On several occasions in later history, Shi'ite rulers did gain control of some Islamic states. But only after 1500, in Iran, did Shi'ite tradition prevail as the majority faith in a major Muslim state. The Shi'ite vision of the true *Umma* has been a powerful one, but not one that has been able to muster sufficient consensus to dominate the larger Islamic world.

THE CENTRISTS. Kharijite and Shi'ite causes were repeatedly taken up by disaffected groups in the early and later Islamic empire. But it was a third, less sharply defined position on the nature of leadership and membership in the *Umma* that gained acceptance from most Muslims. In some ways, a compromise, it proved acceptable not only to lukewarm Muslims or simple pragmatists, but also to persons of piety as intense as that of any Kharijite or Shi'ite. We may term the proponents of this position *centrists*. To emphasize the correctness of their views, they eventually called themselves *Sunnis*—followers of the tradition (*sunna*) established by the Prophet and the Qur'an. Neither they, nor the Shi'ites, nor the Kharijites, have ever been a single sect or group; they have always encompassed a wide range of reconcilable, if not always truly compatible, ideas and groups. They have comprised the broad middle spectrum of Muslims who have tended to put communal solidarity and maintenance of the Islamic polity above purist adherence to certain theological positions. They have been inclusivist rather than exclusivist, a trait that has typified the Islamic (unlike the Christian) community through most of history.

The centrist position was simply the most workable general framework for the new Islamic state. Its basic ideas were:

1. The *Umma* is a theocratic entity, a state under divine authority mediated, first, by the Qur'an and the precedent of the Prophet and, second, by the consensus of the Muslims (in practice, the *ulema*).
2. The caliph is the absolute temporal ruler, charged with administering and defending the Abode of

680–694	Second civil war
685–705	Caliphate of Abd al-Malik; second civil war (680–694); consolidation, arabization of administration
705–715	Caliphate of al-Walid; Morocco conquered, Spain invaded; Arab armies reach the Indus
CA. 750	Introduction of paper manufacture from China through Samarqand to Islamic world
750	Abbasids seize Caliphate from Umayyads, begin new dynasty (750–1258)
756	Some Umayyads escape to Spain, found new dynasty (756–1030)
762–766	New Abbasid capital built at Baghdad

Islam and protecting Muslim norms and practice and possessing no greater authority than other Muslims in matters of faith.

3. A person who professes to be Muslim by witnessing that "There is no god but God, and Muhammad is His Messenger" should be considered a Muslim (as "only God knows what is in the heart"), and not even a mortal sin excludes such a person automatically from the *Umma*.

Under increasingly influential *ulema* leadership, these and other basic premises of Muslim community came to serve as the theological underpinnings of both the caliphal state and the emerging international Islamic social order.

The High Caliphate

The consolidation of the caliphal institution began with the victory of the Umayyad caliph Abd al-Malik in 692 in a second civil war. The succeeding century and a half marks the era of the "high caliphate," the politically strong, culturally vibrant, wealthy, and centralized institution that flourished first under the Umayyads in Damascus and then in the Abbasid capital at Baghdad.[3] The height of caliphal power and splendor came only after the final Umayyad decline, in the first century of Abbasid rule, largely during the caliphates of the fabled Harun al-Rashid (786–809) and his third son al-Ma'mun (813–833).

[3] This periodization follows that of M. G. S. Hodgson, *The Venture of Islam*, 3 vols. (Chicago, 1984), I:217–236.

The Abbasid State

The Abbasids' revolution was based on non-Arab disaffection, Khorasanian regionalism, and Shi'ite religiopolitical hopes. Their victory effectively ended Arab dominance of the empire. The shift of the imperial capital from Damascus to the new "city of peace" built at Baghdad on the Tigris (762–766) symbolized the eastward shift in cultural and political orientation under the new regime. In line with this shift, more and more Persians (albeit arabicized Persians—at least in language) entered the bureaucracy. In the Abbasid heyday under Harun, the highest caliphal advisory office, that of the vizier (Arabic, *wazir*), was dominated by the Khorasanian family of the Barmakids. Religiously, the Abbasids' disavowal of Shi'ite hopes for a divinely inspired imamate reflected their determination to gain the support of a broad spectrum of Muslims, even if they still stressed their descent from Muhammad's family.

Whereas the Umayyads had relied on their Syrian Arab forces, for their main troops the Abbasids used principally Khorasanian Arabs and Iranians and, in the provinces, regional mercenaries. Beginning in the ninth century, however, they enlisted large numbers of slave soldiers (*mamluks*), mostly Turks from the northern steppes, as their personal troops. The officers of these forces, themselves slaves, soon seized the positions of power in the central and provincial bureaucracies and the army. In a matter of years, the caliphs were dominated by their *mamluk* officers. This domination led to an increasing alienation of the Muslim populace from their own rulers. This alienation was evident in Iraq itself, where unrest with his overbearing Turkish guard led the Abbasid caliph to remove the government from Baghdad to the newly built city of Samarra sixty miles up the Tigris, where it remained from 836 to 892.

Society

The division between rulers and populace, the functionally secular state and its Muslim subjects, was ever after typical of Islamic society. However, even while the independence of more and more provincial rulers reduced the power of the Abbasid state after the mid-ninth century, such rulers generally chose to recognize caliphal authority at least in name. They thereby secured legitimacy for their rule and put themselves forward as guardians of the Islamic polity, which found its actual cohesiveness in the Muslim ideals being standardized by the *ulema*.

We must remember, however, that full conversion of the diverse populace of the Islamic Empire lagged far behind the centralization of political power and the development of Islamic socioreligious institutions. It appears that Iraq and Iran (especially Khorasan,

FIGURE 1

FIGURE 2

FIGURE 3

The congregational mosque. Three examples of the finest great mosques of the classical Islamic world. Such buildings were not only designed for worship. Their large courtyards and pillared halls were intended to hold the whole population of a given city and could be used for governmental purposes or for mustering troops in time of war. Their splendor also announced the power and wealth of Islamic rule. Figure 1 shows the mosque of Ibn Tulun, built at Cairo, 876–879, Figure 2 is the great mosque at Qayrawan, in modern Tunisia (eighth-ninth centuries). Figure 3 shows the Spanish Ummayad mosque at Cordoba, built and added to from the eighth to the tenth centuries, in a series of roofed extensions (unlike the other two, which are only partially covered). [George Gerster/William Graham/ George Holton.]

which saw early large-scale Arab Muslim immigration) were the two most important areas of the early Islamization of local elites until well into the twelfth century. They were followed by Spain, North Africa, and Syria. Conversion and fuller Islamization, when it came, meant the development of a self-confident Muslim polity no longer threatened by other religious communities or political forces and a correspondingly diminished need for centralized caliphal power.[4]

[4]Richard W. Bullet, *Conversion to Islam in the Medieval Period* (Cambridge, Mass., and London, 1979), esp. pp. 7–15, 128–138.

Decline

The eclipse of the caliphal state was foreshadowed at the very outset of Abbasid rule, when one of the last Umayyads escaped the general slaughter of his family by fleeing west to Muslim Spain. Supported by Syrian, Yemenite, and some Berber tribes, he founded a Spanish Islamic state that stood for nearly three hundred years (756–1030), producing the spectacular Moorish culture of Spain. Protected by sheer distance from Abbasid control, the Spanish Umayyads even assumed the title of caliph in 929, so strong were they, and so weak were the Abbasids by this time. In all the

The mosaic floor from the bath and pleasure hall of an Umayyad palace or hunting lodge in the desert at Khirbat al-Mafjar, in modern Israel. Both the Umayyad and Abbasid caliphs built splendid palaces in the tradition of their imperial Byzantine, Roman, and Persian predecessors. [Department of Antiquities, State of Israel.]

Abbasid provinces, regional governments were always potential bases for independent states. Besides various Kharijite states among the Berbers, the earliest separate state in North Africa was set up in 801 by the governor of Harun al-Rashid in the area of modern Tunisia. A later North African regional dynasty, the Fatimids, even conquered Egypt and set up a Shi'ite caliphate there after 969.

In the East, Iran grew ever harder for Baghdad to control. Beginning in 821 in Khorasan, Abbasid governors or rebel groups set up independent dynasties repeatedly for two centuries. Because of weakness, the caliph had commonly to recognize their *de facto* sway over various parts of the Iranian plateau. Among the longest-lived of these regional Iranian dynasties were the Samanids of Khorasan and Transoxiania, who held power at Bukhara as nominal vassals of the caliph from 875 until 999. The Samanids gave northeastern Iran a long period of economic and political security from Turkish steppe invaders. Under them, Persian poetry and Arabic scientific studies started what was to become over the next centuries a Persian Islamic cultural renaissance.

Of greatest consequence for the caliphal state was, however, the rise in the mountains south of the Caspian of a Shi'ite family, the Buyids, who took over Abbasid rule in 945. Though they kept the caliph himself "in office," he and his descendants were henceforth largely puppets in the hands of Buyid "commanders" (*amirs*, or *emirs*; later *sultans*). In 1055, the Buyids were replaced by the more famous Seljuk rulers, or *sultans*. Thus, the caliphal state broke up, even though Abbasid caliphs continued as figureheads of Muslim unity until the Mongol invaders killed the last of them in 1258.

The "Classical" Culture of Abbasid Times

The pomp and splendor of the Abbasid court were grand enough to become the stuff of Islamic legend such as we find preserved much later in the tales of *The Thousand and One Nights*. Their rich cultural legacy similarly outlived the Abbasids themselves. Their power and glory was made possible by a strong army

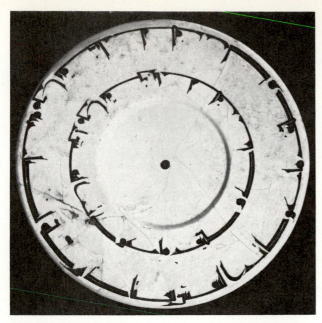

This tenth-century plate from Samarkand, decorated in Kufic script, is an example of the fine Islamic ceramic art that developed under Chinese influence beginning in early Abbasid times. [Freer Gallery of Art.]

and central government and vigorous internal and external trade. The latter may have been stimulated by the prosperous T'ang Empire of China, with which the Islamic world had much overland and sea contact. It was, for example, in the mid-eighth century that paper manufacture was introduced from China to the Islamic world through Transoxiania, at Samarkand.

Intellectual Traditions

The Abbasid heyday was marked by sophisticated tastes and an insatiable thirst for knowledge—not simply religious, but *any* knowledge. An Arab historian called Baghdad "the market to which the wares of the sciences and arts were brought, where wisdom was sought as a man seeks after his stray camels, and whose judgment of values was accepted by the whole world."[5] Older traditions continued and flourished. Contacts (primarily among intellectuals) between Muslims and Christian, Jewish, Zoroastrian, and other "protected" religious communities contributed to the cosmopolitanism of the age. Some older intellectual traditions experienced a revival in early Abbasid times, as in the case of Hellenistic learning. Philosophy, astronomy, mathematics, medicine, and other natural sciences enjoyed strong interest and support. In Islamic usage, philosophy and the sciences were subsumed under *falsafa* (from Greek *philosophia*). Is-

[5] See Oleg Grabar, *The Formation of Islamic Art* (New Haven and London, 1973), esp. pp. 1–103, 206–213.

lamic culture took over the tradition of rational inquiry from the Hellenistic world and developed as well as preserved it at a time when Europe was by comparison a cultural wasteland.

Arabic translations of Greek and Sanskrit works laid the basis for progress in astronomy and medicine. Translation reached its peak in al-Ma'mun's new academy under the guidance of a Nestorian Christian, Hunayn ibn Ishaq (d. 873), noted for his medical and Greek learning. Before, during, and after his time, there were Arabic translations of everything from Galen, Ptolemy, Euclid, Aristotle, Plato, and the Neo-Platonists to the fables that had been translated from Sanskrit originals into Middle Persian under the Sasanids. Such translations stimulated not only Arabic learning, but that of the less-advanced western European world, especially in the twelfth and thirteenth centuries.

An Egyptian crystal vase decorated with an arabesque floral design, from the early Fatimid period (late tenth century). [Freer Gallery of Art.]

The Splendor of the Abbasid Court

The following excerpts from al-Khatib's description of a visit by Byzantine ambassadors to Baghdad in 917 give some glimmer of the extravagant magnificence of the Islamic capital at the height of its opulence and power.

Then it was commanded that the ambassadors should be taken round the palace. Now there were no soldiers here, but only the eunuchs and the chamberlains and the black pages. The number of the eunuchs was seven thousand in all, four thousand of them white and three thousand black; the number of the chamberlains was also seven thousand, and the number of the black pages, other than the eunuchs, was four thousand; the flat roofs of all the palace being occupied by them, as also of the banqueting-halls. Further, the store-chambers had been opened, and the treasures therein had been set out as is customary for a bride's array; the jewels of the Caliph being arranged in trays, on steps, and covered with cloths of black brocade. When the ambassadors entered the Palace of the Tree and gazed upon the Tree, their astonishment was great. For there they saw birds fashioned out of silver and whistling with every motion, while perched on a tree of silver weighing 500 *dirhams*. Now the wonder of the ambassadors was greater at seeing these than at any of the other sights that they saw.

. . . Then at length, after the ambassadors had thus been taken round twenty-three various palaces, they were brought forth to the Court of the Ninety. Here were the pages of the Privy Chamber, full-armed, sumptuously dressed, each of admirable stature. In their hands they carried swords, small battle-axes, and maces. The ambassadors next passed down the lines formed by the black slaves; the deputy chamberlains, the soldiers, the footmen, and the sons of the chieftains, until they again came to the Presence Hall. Now there were a great number of the Slavic eunuchs in all these palaces, who during the visit were occupied in offering to all present water, cooled with snow, to drink; also sherbets and beer and some of these slaves went round with the ambassadors, to whom, as they walked or sat to take rest in some seven different places, water was thus offered, and they drank.

. . . Finally, they came again to the presence of the Caliph Muktadir, whom they found in the Palace of the Crown upon the bank of the Tigris. He was arrayed in clothes of Dabik-stuff embroidered in gold, being seated on an ebony throne overlaid with Dabik-stuff embroidered in gold likewise, and on his head was the tall bonnet called galansuwah. Suspended on the right of the throne were nine necklaces, like prayer beads and to the left were seven others, all of famous jewels, the largest of which was of such a size that its sheen eclipsed the daylight. Before the Caliph stood five of his sons, three to the right and two to the left. Then the ambassadors, with their interpreter, halted before Muktadir, and stood in the posture of humility, with their arms crossed. ❑

Oleg Grabar, *Formation of Islamic Art* (New Haven and London: Yale University Press 1973), pp. 168, 170–171.

Language and Literature

Arabic language and literature developed greatly in the wider cultural sphere of the new empire. On the secular side, there developed, largely among the secretarial class of the Abbasid bureaucracy, a significant genre of Arabic writing known as *adab*, or "manners." This genre included essays and didactic literature influenced by earlier Persian letters. As translations of different genres of writings increased the range of the original bedouin idiom, poetry was able to build on the sophisticated tradition of the Arabic ode, or *qasida*.

Grammar was central to the Qur'an interpretation that occupied the *ulema* and provided the core of an emerging curriculum of Muslim learning. A major form of Arabic writing was historical and biographical literature. It owed much to the ancient bedouin accounts of "the battle days of the Arabs." But it arose primarily to supply information about, first, the lives of the Prophet and the earliest Companions, then those of subsequent generations of Muslims. This information was crucial to judging the reliability of the "chains" of transmitters included with each traditional report, or *hadith*. The *hadith* contained words and/or deeds ascribed to Muhammad and the Companions; it became the chief source of Muslim legal and religious norms alongside the Qur'an, as well as the basic unit of history and biography. The Hadith, a collection of these reports, existed also as a separate genre that was mined by preachers and by the developing schools of legal interpretation, whose crowning glory was the work of al Shafi'i (d. 820) on the theory of legal reasoning.

Art and Architecture

In art and architecture, the Abbasid era saw the crystallization of a "classical" Islamic style by about A.D. 1000. Except for Arabic calligraphy and ceramics, there was nothing radically new about the discrete elements of Islamic art and architecture (most had clear antecedents in Greco-Roman, Byzantine, or Iranian art). What was new was the spread of such elements to new locales, generally in a movement from east (especially the Fertile Crescent) to west (Syria, Egypt, North Africa, and Spain). Sasanid stucco decoration techniques and designs turned up, for example, in Egypt and North Africa. Chronologically, urban Iraq developed an Islamic art first, then made its influence felt east and west, whether in Bukhara or in Syria and Qayrawan. Also new was the combination of discrete forms, as in the case of the colonnade (or hypostyle) mosque or the minaret tower.

The Muslims had good reason to be self-confident about their faith and culture and to want to distinguish them from others. Most monuments of the age express the distinctiveness they felt. Particular formal items, such as calligraphic motifs and inscriptions on buildings, became characteristic of Islamic architecture and defined its functions. Most striking in many ways was the avoidance of pictures or icons and overt symbols in public art. This was, of course, in line with the strong Muslim aversion both to any hint of idolatry and to the strongly iconographic traditions of Christian art. Although this iconoclasm was later eased in various strands of Islamic culture, it was a telling expression of the thrust of Muslim faith and the culture it animated. Overall, the artistic achievements of the Islamic world before the year 1000 impress us with an identifiable quality that is both distinctive and "classically" Islamic, whatever the details of a particular example.[6]

The Formation of Islamic Civilization in World Perspective

The rise of Islam as both a world religious tradition and as an international civilization is by any standard one of the great watershed events of world history. The new traditions forged first in the Arabian peninsula and then in Syria, Iraq, North Africa, Iran, and beyond were to change much of Asia and Africa and parts of Europe in major ways. Religiously, the Islamic movement was destined to become, along with the Buddhist and Christian movements, one of the three major universalist, missionary traditions of world religious history. Politically and socially, the Islamic order for government and society spread and developed in new environments far beyond even the imagination of Muhammad and his companions.

The Islamic polity was in its first three centuries the most dynamic and expansive imperial state of its day. During the same time, Chinese emperors of the T'ang were rebuilding and improving on the previous Han imperium; Charlemagne and the Carolingians were struggling to hammer out a much smaller, more homogeneous empire and a cultural renaissance in the rela-

[6] Ibid.

THE "CLASSICAL" PERIOD OF THE HIGH CALIPHATE	
786–809	Caliphate of Harun al-Rashid; apogee of caliphal power
813–833	Caliphate of al-Ma'mun; strong patronage of translations of Greek, Sanskrit, and other works into Arabic; first heavy reliance upon slave soldiers (*mamluks*)
875	Rise of Samanid power at Bukhara; patronage of Persian poetry paves way for Persian literary renaissance
909	Rise of Shi'ite Fatimid dynasty in North Africa
945–1055	Buyid amirs rules the eastern empire at Baghdad; the Abbasid caliphs continue largely as figureheads
1055	Buyid amirs replaced by Seljuk sultans as effective rulers at Baghdad and custodians of the caliphate

tively backward world of western Europe; Byzantium was struggling to survive against Islamic arms and turning inward to conserve its traditions; and post-Gupta India was divided under diverse regional kings and still subject to new forces (including those of Islam) moving into northwest India.

As different as the two were, only China compared favorably with or surpassed the Islamic world in this period in terms of political and military power, cultural unity and creativity, and cultural self-consciousness. The T'ang empire and that of the Abbasids wielded commensurate power in their heydays, although over time the Chinese held together as a centralized state much better than the Islamic did. Certainly, these were the two greatest political and cultural units in the world in their age. They each had one cultural language, although Chinese was the language of more of the masses of China's empire than was Arabic of the Islamic dominions. They also shared the central military use of nomadic cavalry as well as the adaptive ability to incorporate new peoples into their larger culture. Indeed, the great elasticity and adaptability of Islam as a religious tradition and as a social order was striking in ways that clearly give the lie to its reputation in the West today as a rigid and inflexible system of values and practices.

Nevertheless, the bases of Islamic empire were clearly different, spread as it was over vastly more culturally heterogenous and widely dispersed geographi-

Traditions from and about the Prophet

The following are the texts of three hadiths, *or traditions about the words and actions of Muhammad and his companions. Such reports were transmitted from the early days of Islam after Muhammad's death, in order to instruct or regulate Muslims in the practice of their new faith. Many such reports were forged by persons who wished to lend prophetic authority to particular practices or ideas that seemed good to them, and the* ulema *developed elaborate methods of* Hadith *criticism to identify falsified or inaccurately transmitted traditions. These examples are drawn from major* Hadith *collections compiled largely in the third century of the Hijra.*

The Apostle of God passed by a pile of grain. He put his hand into the midst of it, and his fingers encountered moisture.

He exclaimed, "O merchant, what is this?"

The owner of the grain said, "It has been damaged by the rain, O Apostle of God."

Then he replied, "If that is the case, why not put the damaged grain on top of the pile so that people can see it?"

Then he concluded, "Whoever practices fraud is not one of us."

Ibn 'Umar heard a man swear, saying, "No, I swear by the Ka'bah!" Ibn 'Umar said, "Swear by none other than God. I heard the Apostle of God say, 'Whoever swears by other than God commits blasphemy and makes someone or something an associate with God.'"

When the Prophet awoke he would say, "O God, it is you who enables us to wake up in the morning and it is you who brings us into the evening. You enable us to live. You cause us to die, and at the Resurrection we go to you." When evening came he would say, "O God, it is you who brings us into the evening, and it is you who enables us to wake up in the morning. You enable us to live. You cause us to die, and with you is the issue of our life."

Ibn 'Abbās addressed the people of Al-Basrah [a city in Iraq, founded by the Muslims in 638 A.D.] at the end of Ramadān [the month of fasting], saying, "O people of Al-Basrah, do your duty and give alms after fasting." The people looked at each other.

He said, "Who is here from Medina? Come forth and teach your brothers. Should they not know that the Apostle of God prescribed as alms to be given at the end of Ramadān, a half *sā* [a cubic measure] of wheat, or a *sā* of barley, or a *sā* of dates, to be given by every person, slave and free, man and woman?" ❑

From Kenneth Cragg and Marston Speight, eds., *Islam from Within: Anthology of a Religion* (Belmont, CA: Wadsworth, 1980), pp. 84, 89, 92–93.

cal areas than that of China. Conquest initially fueled the economy of the new Islamic state, but, in the long run, trade and urban commercial centers proved to be the backbone of Islamic prosperity, as well as the chief means of dissemination of the Muslim faith to new lands. The Islamic empire was agrarian-based, yet the overall conditions for food production were not as good as those in China or western Europe. The key element that the majority of Islamic lands were (and are) lacking was abundant water, so that supporting dense populations well was difficult. This did not stop the development of impressive Islamic states, societies, and cultures, but it did set certain limits to such development.

The Islamic achievement was different from any other in this period primarily in that it resulted from an effort to build something new rather than to recapture or resuscitate previous traditions, whether of religion, society, or government. In later centuries, the early Arabic impress of Islamic culture and religion was tempered and changed by the vast numbers of Persian- and Turkish-speaking Muslims and also the many regional groups, from Urdu- or Swahili-speakers in India or Africa to Malay and Indonesian Muslims of Southeast Asia. Nevertheless, Arabic went abroad with the holy Qur'an as the sacred language of God's final revelation. Ever since, Muslims of all the world have learned little or much of Arabic and the sacred Book, but always something.

This achievement was a new historical phenomenon, at least in terms of the scale of its occurrence. Although Muslim faith can be seen as largely a reformation of Semitic monotheism, it must be seen as more fundamentally an effort to do something new. It was an attempt to subsume older traditions of Jews or Christians in a more comprehensive vision of God's plan on earth rather than an attempt to reform earlier traditions. This is not to say that Muslims did not build on previous traditions; they adopted and adapted the traditions of the many older centers of Afro-Eurasian cultures. Yet, both as a civilization and a religious tradition, Islam developed its own strikingly recognizable stamp that persisted wherever Muslims extended the *Umma*.

Suggested Readings

A. F. L. BEESTON, T. M. JOHNSTONE, R. B. SERGEANT, AND G. R. SMITH, *Arabic Literature to the End of the Umayyad Period* (1983). The most comprehensive survey of the early Arabic historical, religious, poetic, and other literary sources.

K. CRAGG AND R. MARSTON SPEIGHT, eds., *Islam from Within: Anthology of a Religion* (1980). One of the best and most sensitive collections of selections from Islamic primary sources.

F. M. DONNER, *The Early Islamic Conquests* (1981). The introduction and first chapter are especially good for an introduction to many important issues in the origin and spread of Islam.

H. A. R. GIBB, *Mohammedanism: An Historical Survey* (1970). Despite the offensive title, still the best brief introduction to Islam as a religious tradition.

H. A. R. GIBB, *Studies on the Civilization of Islam.* Ed. S. J. Shaw and W. R. Polk (1962). This volume of selected essays by Gibb has some very helpful general studies on Islamic political order and religion.

O. GRABAR, *The Formation of Islamic Art* (1973). A critical and creative interpretation of major themes in the development of distinctively Islamic forms of art and architecture.

G. E. VON GRUNEBAUM, *Classical Islam: A History 600–1258.* Trans. K. Watson (1970), pp. 1–140. A competent, culturally oriented introductory survey of formative developments.

M. G. S. HODGSON, *The Classical Age of Islam. Vol. I of The Venture of Islam.* 3 vols. (1974). The most thoughtful and comprehensive attempt to deal with classical Islamic civilization as a whole and in relation to contemporaneous non-Islamic cultures.

B. LEWIS, ed., *Islam and the Arab World* (1976). A large-format, heavily illustrated volume with many excellent articles on diverse aspects of Islam (not simply Arab, as the misleading title suggests) civilization through the premodern period.

F. RAHMAN, *Major Themes of the Qur'an* (1980). The best introduction to the basic ideas of the Qur'an and Islam, seen through the eyes of a perceptive Muslim modernist scholar.

M. A. SHABAN, *Islamic History: A New Interpretation.* 2 vols. (1971–76). An influential reassessment of the course of Islamic history to A.D. 1055.

D. SOURDEL, *Medieval Islam* (1979). Eng. trans. W. M. Watt (1983). A brief but masterly survey of the world of medieval Islam with emphasis on social, religious, and political institutions.

An equestrian figure of Charlemagne (or perhaps one of his sons) from the early ninth century. [Musée du Louvre, Paris. Giraudon.]

13 The Early Middle Ages in the West to 1000: The Birth of Europe

The early Middle Ages mark the birth of Europe. This was the period in which a distinctive Western European culture began to emerge. In geography, government, religion, and language, Western Europe became a land distinct from both the eastern or Byzantine world and the Arab or Muslim world. It was a period of recovery from the collapse of Roman civilization, a time of forced experimentation with new ideas and institutions. Western European culture, as we know it today, was born of a unique, inventive mix of surviving Greco-Roman, new Germanic, and evolving Christian traditions.

The early Middle Ages have been called, and not with complete fairness, a "dark age" because they lost touch with classical, especially Greek, learning and science. In this period, there were fierce invasions from the north and the east by peoples that the Romans somewhat arrogantly called barbarians. To the south, the Mediterranean was transformed by Arab dominance into an inhospitable "Muslim lake." Although Western trade with the East was by no means completely cut off, Western people became more isolated than they had been before. A Europe thus surrounded and assailed from the north, east, and south understandably became somewhat insular and even stagnant. On the other hand, being forced to manage by itself, Western Europe also learned to develop its native resources. The early Middle Ages were not without a modest renaissance of antiquity during the reign of Charlemagne. And the peculiar social and political forms of this period—manorialism and feudalism—proved to be not only successful ways to cope with unprecedented chaos on local levels but also a fertile seedbed for the growth of distinctive Western institutions.

On the Eve of the Frankish Ascendancy

Germanic and Arab Invasions

As we have already seen, by the late third century A.D., the Roman Empire had become too large for a single sovereign to govern. For this reason, Emperor Diocletian (284–305) permitted the evolution of a dual empire by establishing an eastern and a western half, each with its own emperor and, eventually, imperial bureaucracy. Emperor Constantine the Great (306–337) briefly reunited the empire by conquest and was sole emperor of the east and the west after 324. (It was redivided by his sons and subsequent successors.) In 330, Constantine created the city of Constantinople as the new administrative center of the empire and the imperial residence. Constantinople gradually became a "new Rome," replacing the old, whose internal political quarrels and geographical distance from new military fronts in Syria and along the Danube River made it less appealing. Rome and the western empire were actually on the wane in the late third and fourth centuries, well before the barbarian invasions in the west began. In 286, Milan had already replaced Rome as the imperial residence; in 402, the seat of western government was moved still again, to Ravenna. When the barbarian invasions began in the late fourth century, the West was in political disarray, and the imperial power and prestige had shifted decisively to Constantinople and the East.

GERMAN TRIBES AND THE WEST. The German tribes did not burst on the West all of a sudden. They were at first a token and benign presence. Before the great invasions from the north and the east, there had been a period of peaceful commingling of the Germanic and the Roman cultures. The Romans "imported" barbarians as domestics and soldiers before the German tribes came as conquerors. Barbarian soldiers rose to positions of high leadership and fame in Roman legions. In the late fourth century, however, this peaceful coexistence came to an end because of a great influx of Visigoths (west Goths) into the empire. They were stampeded there in 376 by the emergence of a new, violent people, the Huns, who migrated from the area of modern Mongolia. The Visigoths were a Christianized (albeit unorthodox) Germanic tribe who won from the Eastern emperor Valens rights of settlement and material assistance within the empire in exchange for their defense of the frontier as *foederati*, special allies of the emperor. When in place of promised assistance the Visigoths received harsh treatment from their new allies, they rebelled, handily defeating Roman armies under Valens at the battle of Adrianople in 378.

Salvian the Priest Compares the Romans and the Barbarians

Salvian, a Christian priest writing around 440, found the barbarians morally superior to the Romans—indeed, truer to Roman virtues than the Romans themselves, whose failings were all the more serious because they, unlike the barbarians, had knowledge of Christianity.

In what respects can our customs be preferred to those of the Goths and Vandals, or even compared with them? And first, to speak of affection and mutual charity, . . . almost all barbarians, at least those who are of one race and kin, love each other, while the Romans persecute each other. . . . The many are oppressed by the few, who regard public exactions as their own peculiar right, who carry on private traffic under the guise of collecting the taxes. . . . So the poor are despoiled, the widows sigh, the orphans are oppressed, until many of them, born of families not obscure, and liberally educated, flee to our enemies that they may no longer suffer the oppression of public persecution. They doubtless seek Roman humanity among the barbarians, because they cannot bear barbarian inhumanity among the Romans. And although they differ from the people to whom they flee in manner and in language; although they are unlike as regards the fetid odor of the barbarians' bodies and garments, yet they would rather endure a foreign civilization among the barbarians than cruel injustice among the Romans.

It is urged that if we Romans are wicked and corrupt, that the barbarians commit the same sins. . . . There is, however, this difference, that if the barbarians commit the same crimes as we, yet we sin more grievously. . . . All the barbarians . . . are pagans or heretics. The Saxon race is cruel, the Franks are faithless . . . the Huns are unchaste—in short there is vice in the life of all the barbarian peoples. But are their offenses as serious as [those of Christians]? Is the unchastity of the Hun so criminal as ours? Is the faithlessness of the Frank so blameworthy as ours? ❑

Of God's Government, in James Harvey Robinson (ed.), *Readings in European History*, Vol. 1 (Boston: Athenaeum, 1904), pp. 28–30.

After Adrianople, the Romans passively permitted settlement after settlement of barbarians within the very heart of Western Europe. Why was there so little resistance to the German tribes? The invaders found a badly overextended western empire physically weakened by decades of famine, pestilence, and overtaxation, and politically divided by ambitious military commanders. In the second half of the fourth century, the Roman will to resist had simply been sapped. The Roman Empire did not fall simply because of unprecedented moral decay and materialism, but because of a combination of political mismanagement, disease, and sheer poverty.

The late fourth and early fifth centuries saw the invasion of still other tribes: the Vandals, the Burgundians, and the Franks. In 410, Visigoths revolted under Alaric (CA. 370–410) and sacked the "eternal city" of Rome. From 451 to 453, Italy suffered the invasions of Attila the Hun (D. 453), who was known to contemporaries as the "scourge of God." In 455, the Vandals overran Rome.

By the mid-fifth century, power in Western Europe had passed decisively from the hands of the Roman emperors to those of barbarian chieftains. In 476, the traditional date for the fall of the Roman Empire, the barbarian Odoacer (CA. 434–493) deposed and replaced the Western emperor Romulus Augustulus and

ruled as "king of the Romans." By the end of the fifth century, the western empire was thoroughly overrun by barbarians. The Ostrogoths settled in Italy, the Franks in northern Gaul, the Burgundians in Provence, the Visigoths in southern Gaul and Spain, the Vandals in north Africa and the Mediterranean, and the Angles and Saxons in England (see Map 13.1). Barbarians were now the western masters—but masters who were also willing to learn from the people they had conquered.

Western Europe was not transformed into a savage land. The military victories of the barbarians did not result in a great cultural defeat of the Roman Empire. The barbarians were militarily superior, but the Romans retained their cultural strength. Apart from Britain and northern Gaul, Roman language, law, and government continued to exist side by side with the new Germanic institutions. In Italy under Theodoric, Roman law gradually replaced tribal custom. Only the Vandals and the Anglo-Saxons refused to profess at least titular obedience to the emperor in Constantinople.

Behind this accommodation of cultures was the fact that the Visigoths, the Ostrogoths, and the Vandals entered the west as Christianized people. They professed, however, a religious creed that was considered heretical in the West. They were Arian Christians, that

MAP 13-1 BARBARIAN MIGRATIONS INTO THE WEST IN THE FOURTH AND FIFTH CENTURIES *The forceful intrusion of Germanic and non-Germanic barbarians into the Empire from the last quarter of the fourth century through the fifth century made for a constantly changing pattern of movement and relations. The map shows the major routes taken by the usually unwelcome newcomers and the areas most deeply affected by the main groups.*

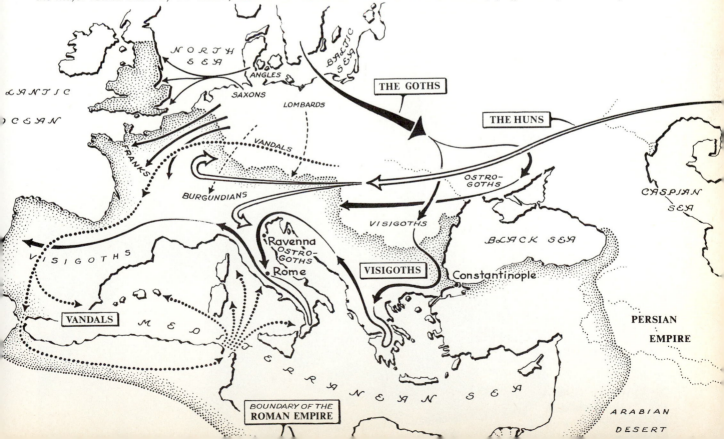

is, Christians who believed that Jesus Christ was not of one identical substance with God the Father—a point of view that had been condemned in 325 by the Council of Nicea (see Chapter 6). Later, around 500, the Franks, under their strong king, Clovis, converted to the orthodox or "Catholic" form of Christianity supported by the bishops of Rome, and they helped conquer and convert the Goths and other barbarians in Western Europe.

All things considered, rapprochement and a gradual interpenetration of two strong cultures—a creative tension—marked the period of the Germanic migrations. The stronger culture was the Roman, and it became dominant in a later fusion. Despite western military defeat, it can still be said that the Goths and the Franks became far more romanized than the Romans were germanized. Latin language, Nicene Christianity, and eventually Roman law and government were to triumph in the West during the Middle Ages.

CONTINUITY IN THE EAST. As Western Europe succumbed to the Germanic invasions, Constantinople became the sole capital of the empire, and it remained the capital until a revival of the Western empire began in the reign of Charlemagne. The Eastern empire, established in 330, was to last until May 29, 1453, when Constantinople finally fell to the Turks after centuries of unsuccessful siege.

The early Middle Ages were a period of important political and cultural achievement in the East. The

A mosaic portrait of Justinian's wife, the Empress Theodora (CA. 500-548), from the church of St. Vitale in Ravenna. She was prominent in the heated theological controversies of the time. [Bettmann Archive.]

Emperor Justinian (527–565) collated and revised Roman law. His *Code*, issued in 533, was the first codification of Roman law and became the foundation of most European law. Justinian was assisted by his brilliant and powerful wife, the empress Theodora. She favored the Monophysite teaching that Jesus had only one nature, a composite of both human and divine nature. Justinian did not share this view but supported

Byzantine church decoration consisted predominantly of rigidly stylized mosaics. A theme repeated endlessly in these church mosaics is that of Christ the Ruler of All. The stern, bearded judge is quite different from the gentle figure of Christ as the good shepherd. This example from about 1100 is from the Church of St. Savior in Istanbul. [AHM.]

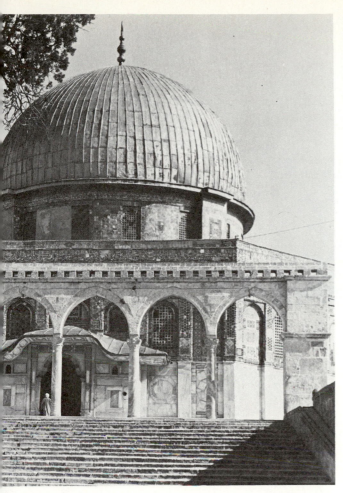

The Dome of the Rock in Jerusalem. An early example of monumental Islamic architecture, it dates from the seventh century, during the first wave of Arab expansion, and derives its name from the rock from which Muslims believe Muhammad ascended to heaven. Jews believe the rock to be the one on which Abraham prepared to sacrifice Issac. [Israel Government Tourist Office, New York.]

southern France, and Italy, which Justinian also managed to control after decades of guerrilla warfare. But a revival and reunion of the old Roman Empire was not to be. In northern Europe the Franks were becoming the dominant western power, a power Justinian's armies were not strong enough to subdue. The appearance and the firm entrenchment of the Lombards in northern Italy three years after Justinian's death created a buffer between the Franks and imperial forces that prevented what would surely have been a fatal confrontation for the reviving empire.

Islam and Its Effects on East and West

In the south, an enemy far more dangerous than the German tribes was on the march: the faith of Islam. During the lifetime of the prophet Muhammad (570–632) and thereafter, invading Arab armies absorbed the attention and resources of the emperors in Constantinople, who found themselves in a life-and-death struggle. Unlike the comparatively mild Germanic invaders, Arab armies did not encourage a creative interpenetration of cultures, although Jews and other religious minorities were tolerated within Islam. (See Chapter 12).

By the middle of the eighth century, Muslims had conquered the southern and eastern Mediterranean coastline (territories mostly still held by Islamic states today) and occupied parts of Spain, which they controlled or strongly influenced until the fifteenth century. In addition, their armies had pushed north and east through Mesopotamia and Persia and beyond (see Map 13.1). These conquests would not have been so rapid and thorough had the contemporary Byzantine and Persian empires not been exhausted by a long period of war. The Muslims struck at the conclusion of the successful campaign of Byzantine Emperor Heraclius (D. 641) against the Persian King Chosroes II. Most of the population in the conquered area spoke Semitic language and was more easily fired by hatred of the Byzantine Greek army of occupation than it was inspired to unity by a common Christian tradition. The Christian community was itself badly divided. The Egyptian (also known as *Coptic*) and Syrian churches were Monophysitic. Heraclius' efforts to impose Greek "orthodox" beliefs on these churches only increased the enmity between Greek and Semitic Christians, many of whom leaned toward Monophysitism. Many Egyptian and Syrian Christians may have looked on Arabs as deliverers from the Byzantine conquerors.

Muslims tolerated conquered Christians, whether orthodox or Monophysite, provided they paid taxes, kept their distance, and made no efforts to proselytize Muslim communities. Always anxious to maintain the

the majority view that Jesus was of two separate natures, fully human and fully divine. Despite this theological disagreement, Justinian and Theodora succeeded in imposing an imperial theology on their subjects that made the emperor supreme in religious matters. These efforts laid the foundation for a highly successful program of state control of the Church in the east.

Justinian and Theodora did not forget the West. They took advantage of the political disunity of the German tribes and papal opposition to the Arian Ostrogoths briefly to reconquer the Western empire in the mid-sixth century. Justinian's armies overcame the Vandals in Africa in 533 and marched into Spain,

Byzantine architecture—the architecture of the Roman Empire of the East after about the fifth century and of other areas strongly influenced by Byzantium—is represented here by what are probably its two grandest remaining monuments. The first one is Emperor Justinian's Hagia Sophia (Church of the Holy Wisdom) in Constantinople, which was built between 532 and 537. With its great dome, 107 feet in diameter, several half domes, and richly decorated interior of marbles and mosaics, it was enormously influential on subsequent church architecture. Its exterior is now much changed by minarets, tombs, and buttresses added at various times after the Turkish conquest of Constantinople in 1453, when the building became a mosque for nearly five hundred years. It has been a museum since 1935. [AHM.]

After Hagia Sophia, the second greatest surviving example of Byzantine architecture—from a much later period of the style—is Saint Mark's in Venice. Most of the building dates from the eleventh century and was built to house the remains of the Apostle Mark, said to have been taken from Alexandria in Egypt. The building carries the characteristic rounded arches, numerous domes, and mosaics of the Byzantine style. The ornamental pointed arches and pinnacles of the facade's upper story are later additions. [Italian Government Travel Office, New York.]

purity of their religion and culture, the Arabs forbade mixed marriages and any conscious cultural interchange. Special taxes on conquered peoples encouraged them to convert to Islam.

Assaulted on both their eastern and their western frontiers and everywhere challenged in the Mediterranean, the Europeans developed a lasting fear and suspicion of the Muslims. In the east, during the reign of the Byzantine Leo III (717–740), the Arabs were stopped after a year's siege of Constantinople (717–718). Leo and his successors in the Isaurian dynasty of Byzantine rulers created a successful defensive organization against the Arabs. It was so effective that it permitted the rulers of the following Macedonian dynasty (867–1057) to expand militarily and commercially into Muslim lands. Byzantine armies were also assisted by Muslim disunity. In 1071, the Seljuk Turks from central Asia, by way of Persia and Mesopotamia, overran Armenia at the eastern end of the empire in the first of a series of confrontations that would finally end with the fall of Constantinople in 1453 to the Seljuks' relatives, the Ottoman Turks. In 1096, the Crusaders from western Europe arrived in Constantinople in the first of a series of moves to the East that ended during the Fourth Crusade with the capture of Constantinople in 1204 and the establishment of a half century of Latin or Western rule over Byzantium.

As for the West's own dangers, the ruler of the Franks, Charles Martel, defeated a raiding party of Arabs on the western frontier of Europe near Tours (today in central France) in 732, a victory that ended any possible Arab effort to expand into Western Europe by way of Spain. From the end of the seventh century to the middle of the eleventh, the Mediterranean still remained something of a Muslim lake; although trade of the Western empire with the Orient was not cut off during these centuries, it was significantly decreased and was carried on in keen awareness of Muslim dominance.

When trade wanes, cities decline, and with them those centers for the exchange of goods and ideas that enable a society to look and live beyond itself. The Arab invasions and presence of the Mediterranean area during a crucial part of the early Middle Ages created the essential conditions for the birth of Western Europe as a distinctive cultural entity. Arab belligerency forced Western Europeans to fall back on their own distinctive resources and to develop their peculiar Germanic and Greco-Roman heritage into a unique culture. The Arabs accomplished this by diverting the attention and energies of the Eastern empire at a time of Frankish and Lombard ascendancy (thereby preventing Byzantine expansion into the West) and by greatly reducing Western navigation of the Mediterranean (thereby closing off much Eastern trade and cultural influence).

As Western shipping was reduced in the Mediterranean, coastal urban centers declined. Populations that would otherwise have been engaged in trade-related work in the cities moved in great numbers into interior regions, there to work the farms of the great landholders. The latter needed their labor and welcomed the new emigrants, who were even more in need of the employment and protection that the landholders could provide. A mild serfdom evolved both for the new landless emigrants and for the great mass of peasants on the land (perhaps 90 per cent of the population). There were free peasants, who owned their own land, and peasants who became "serfs" by surrendering their land to a more powerful landholder in exchange for assistance in time of dire need, like during periods of prolonged crop failure or foreign invasion. Basically, serfdom meant for the peasant a status of servitude to the economically and politically stronger, who provided land and dwelling in exchange for labor and goods.

As the demand for agricultural products diminished in the great urban centers and as traffic between town and country was reduced, the farming belts became regionally insular and self-contained. Production and travel adjusted to local needs, and there was little incentive for bold experimentation and exploration. The domains of the great landholders became the basic social and political units of society, and local barter economies sprang up within them. In these developments were sown the seeds of what would later come to be known as manorial and feudal society. The former was an ordering of peasant society in which land and labor were divided among lords, peasants, and serfs for the profit of some and the protection of all, whereas the latter was an ordering of aristocratic society in which a special class of warrior knights emerged as guarantors of order.

The Developing Roman Church

One institution remained firmly entrenched within the cities during the Arab invasions: the Christian church. The Church had long modeled its own structure on that of the imperial Roman administration. Like the latter, it was a centralized, hierarchical government with strategically placed "viceroys" (bishops) in European cities who looked for spiritual direction to their leader, the bishop of Rome. As the Western empire crumbled and populations emigrated to the countryside after the barbarian and Arab invasions, local bishops and cathedral chapters filled the vacuum of authority left by the removal of Roman governors. The local cathedral became the center of urban life and the local bishop the highest authority for those who remained in the cities—just as in Rome, on a larger and more fateful scale, the pope took control of the city as the Western emperors gradually departed and died out. Left to its own devices, Western Europe soon discovered that the Christian church was a rich repository of Roman administrative skills and classical culture.

The Christian church had been graced with special privileges, great lands, and wealth by Emperor Constantine and his successors. In 313, Constantine issued the Edict of Milan, giving Christians legal standing and a favored status within the empire. In 391, Emperor Theodosius I (CA. 379–395), after whose death the empire would again be divided into eastern and western parts, raised Christianity to the official religion of the empire. Both Theodosius and his predecessors acted as much for political effect as out of religious conviction; in 313, Christians composed about one fifth of the population of the empire and unquestionably composed the strongest group of the competing religions. Mithraism, the religion popular among army officers and restricted to males, was its main rival.

Challenged to become a major political force, the Church survived the period of Germanic and Arab invasions as a somewhat spiritually weakened and compromised institution, yet it was still a most potent civilizing and unifying force. It had a religious message of providential purpose and individual worth that could give solace and meaning to life at its worst. The Western church also had a ritual of baptism and a creedal confession that united people beyond the traditional barriers of social class, education, and sex. After the Germanic and Arab invasions, the Church alone possessed an effective hierarchical administration, scattered throughout the old empire, staffed by the best-educated minds in Europe, and centered in emperorless Rome. The Church also enjoyed the services of growing numbers of monks, who were not only loyal to its mission but also objects of great popular respect. Monastic culture proved again and again to be the peculiar strength of the Church during the Middle Ages.

MONASTIC CULTURE. Monks were originally hermits, who withdrew from society to pursue a more perfect way of life. They were inspired by the Christian ideal of a life of complete self-denial in imitation of Christ, who had denied himself even unto death. The popularity of monasticism began to grow as Roman persecution of Christians waned in the mid-third century. Embracing the biblical "counsels of perfection" (chastity, poverty, and obedience), the monastic life became the purest form of religious practice.

Anthony of Egypt (CA. 251–356), the father of hermit monasticism, was inspired by Jesus' command to the rich young man: "If you will be perfect, sell all that you have, give it to the poor, and follow me" (Matthew 19:21). Anthony went into the desert to pray and work,

setting an example followed by hundreds in Egypt, Syria, and Palestine in the fourth and fifth centuries. This hermit monasticism was soon joined by the development of communal monasticism. In southern Egypt in the first quarter of the fourth century, Pachomius (CA. 286–346) organized monks into a highly regimented common life. Such monastic communities grew to contain a thousand or more inhabitants, little "cities of God," separated from the collapsing Roman and the nominal Christian world. Basil the Great (329–379) popularized communal monasticism throughout the East, providing a rule that lessened the asceticism of Pachomius and directed monks beyond their enclaves of perfection into such social services as caring for orphans, widows, and the infirm in surrounding communities.

Athanasius (CA. 293–373) and Martin of Tours (CA. 315–CA. 399) introduced monasticism into the west, where the teaching of John Cassian (CA. 360–435) and Jerome (CA. 340–420) helped shape its basic values and practices. The great organizer of Western monasticism was Benedict of Nursia (CA. 480–547). In 529, Benedict founded the mother monastery of the Benedictines at Monte Cassino in Italy, the foundation on which all Western monasticism has been built. Benedict also wrote a sophisticated *Rule for Monasteries*, a comprehensive plan for every activity of the monks, even detailing how they were to sleep. The monastery was hierarchically organized and directed by an abbot, whose command was beyond question. Periods of de-

The rule of St. Benedict, followed by most medieval monasteries, required that the monks spend a third of their day at manual labor. This served to make the monastery self-sufficient and self-contained. Here monks are shown doing a variety of agricultural tasks. [Vincent Virga Archives.]

votion (about four hours each day were set aside for the "work of God," that is, regular prayers and liturgical activities) and study alternated with manual labor—a program that permitted not a moment's idleness and carefully promoted the religious, intellectual, and physical well-being of the monks.

THE DOCTRINE OF PAPAL PRIMACY.

Constantine and his successors, especially the Eastern emperors, ruled religious life with an iron hand and consistently looked on the Church as little more than a department of the state. Such "Caesaropapism"—Caesar acting as pope—involved the emperor directly in the Church's affairs, even to the point of enabling him to play the theologian and allowing him to impose conciliar solutions on doctrinal quarrels. State control of religion was the original Church–State relation in the West.

The bishops of Rome by contrast never accepted such intervention and opposed it in every way they could. In the fifth and sixth centuries, taking advantage of imperial weakness and distraction, they developed for their own defense the weaponry of the doctrine of "papal primacy." This teaching raised the Roman pontiff to an unassailable supremacy within the Church when it came to defining Church doctrine: it also put him in a position to make important secular claims. The doctrine was destined to occasion repeated conflicts between Church and State, pope and emperor, throughout the Middle Ages.

THE DIVISION OF CHRISTENDOM.

The division of Christendom into Eastern and Western churches has its roots in the early Middle Ages. From the start, there was the difference in language (Greek in the East, Latin in the West) and culture. A combination of Greek, Roman, and oriental elements had shaped Byzantine culture. The strong mystical orientation to the next world also caused the Eastern church to submit more passively than Western popes could ever do to Caesaropapism.

As in the West, Eastern church organization closely followed that of the secular state. A "patriarch" ruled over "metropolitans" and "archbishops" in the cities and provinces, and they, in turn, ruled over bishops, who stood as authorities over the local clergy.

Contrary to the evolving Western tradition of universal clerical celibacy, which Western monastic culture encouraged, the Eastern church permitted the marriage of secular priests, while strictly forbidding bishops to marry. The Eastern church also used leavened bread in the Eucharist, contrary to the Western custom of using unleavened bread. Also unliked by the West was the tendency of the Eastern church to compromise doctrinally with the politically powerful Arian and Monophysite Christians. In the background were also conflicting political claims over jurisdiction over the newly converted areas in the north Balkans.

Beyond these issues, the major factors in the religious break between East and West revolved around questions of doctrinal authority. The Eastern church

Pope Gelasius I Declares the "Weightiness" of Priestly Authority

Some see this famous letter of Pope Gelasius to Emperor Anastasius I in 494 as an extreme statement of papal supremacy. Others believe it is a balanced, moderate statement that recognizes the independence of both temporal and spiritual power and seeks their close cooperation, not the domination of Church over state.

There are two powers, august Emperor, by which this world is chiefly ruled, namely, the sacred authority of the priests and the royal power. Of these, that of the priests is the more weighty, since they have to render an account for even the kings of men in the divine judgment. You are also aware, dear son [emperor], that while you are permitted honorably to rule over humankind, yet in things divine you bow your head humbly before the leaders of the clergy and await from their hands the means of your salvation. In the reception and proper disposition of the heavenly mysteries you recognize that you should be subordinate rather than superior to the religious order, and that in these matters you depend on their judgment rather than wish to force them to follow your will. [And] if the ministers of religion, recognizing the supremacy granted you from heaven in matters affecting the public order, obey your laws, lest otherwise they obstruct the course of secular affairs . . . , with what readiness should you not yield them obedience to whom is assigned the dispensing of the sacred mysteries of religion? ❑

James Harvey Robinson (ed.), *Readings in European History*, Vol. 1 (Boston: Athenaeum, 1904), pp. 72–73.

put more stress on the authority of the Bible and of the ecumenical councils of the Church than on the counsel and decrees of the bishop of Rome. The councils and Holy Scripture were the ultimate authorities in the definition of Christian doctrine. The claims of Roman popes to a special primacy of authority on the basis of the apostle Peter's commission from Jesus in Matthew 16:18 ("Thou art Peter, and upon this rock I will build my church") were completely unacceptable to the East, where the independence and autonomy of national churches held sway. This basic issue of authority in matters of faith lay behind the mutual excommunication of Pope Nicholas I and Patriarch Photius in the ninth century and that of Pope Leo IX and Patriarch Michael Cerularius in 1054. After this time one distinguished between the Roman Catholic and the Orthodox Christian churches.

A second major issue in the separation of the two churches was the Western addition of the *filioque* clause to the Nicene-Constantinopolitan Creed—an anti-Arian move that made the Holy Spirit proceed "also from the Son" (*filioque*) as well as from the Father. This addition made clear the Western belief that Christ was "fully substantial with God the Father" and not a lesser being.

The final and most direct issue in the religious division of Christendom was the iconoclastic controversy of the first half of the eighth century. After 725, the Eastern emperor, Leo III (717–740), attempted to force Western popes to abolish the use of images in their churches. In opposing icons and images in the churches, the Eastern church was influenced by Islam. This stand met fierce official and popular resistance in the West, where images were greatly cherished.

Leo's direct challenge of the pope came almost simultaneously with still another aggressive act against the Western church: attacks by the heretofore docile Lombards of northern Italy. Assailed by both the emperor and the Lombards, the pope in Rome seemed surely doomed. But there has not been a more resilient and enterprising institution in Western history than the Roman papacy. Since the pontificate of Gregory the Great, Roman popes had eyed the Franks of northern Gaul as Europe's ascendant power and their surest protector. Imperial and Lombard aggression against the Roman pope in the first half of the eighth century provided the occasion for the most fruitful political alliance of the Middle Ages. In 754, Pope Stephen II (752–757) enlisted Pepin III and his Franks as defenders of the church against the Lombards and as a Western counterweight to the Eastern emperor. This marriage of religion and politics created a new Western church and empire: it also determined much of the course of Western history into modern times.

The Kingdom of the Franks

Merovingians and Carolingians: From Clovis to Charlemagne

A warrior chieftain, Clovis (CA. 466–511), a convert to Orthodox Christianity around 496, made the Franks and their first ruling family, the Merovingians, named for an early leader of the family Merovich, a significant force in Western Europe. Clovis and his successors subdued the pagan Burgundians and the Arian Visigoths and established within ancient Gaul the kingdom of the Franks. The Franks were a broad belt of people scattered throughout modern Belgium, the Netherlands, and western Germany, whose loyalties remained strictly tribal and local. The Merovingians attempted to govern this sprawling kingdom by pacts with landed nobility and by the creation of the royal office of count. The most persistent problem of medieval political history was the competing claims of the "one" and the "many." On the one hand, the king struggled for a centralized government and transregional loyalty, and on the other, powerful local magnates strove to preserve their regional autonomy and traditions.

The Merovingian counts were men without possessions to whom the king gave great lands in the expectation that they would be, as the landed aristocrats often were not, loyal officers of the kingdom. But like local aristocrats, the Merovingian counts also let their immediate self-interests gain the upper hand. Once established in office for a period of time, they too became territorial rulers in their own right, with the result that the Frankish kingdom progressively fragmented into independent regions and tiny principalities. This centrifugal tendency was further assisted by the Frankish custom of dividing the kingdom equally among the king's legitimate male heirs.

Rather than purchasing allegiance and unity within the kingdom, the Merovingian largess simply occasioned the rise of competing magnates and petty tyrants, who became laws unto themselves within their regions. By the seventh century, the Frankish king existed more in title than in effective executive power. Real power came to be concentrated in the office of the *mayor of the palace*, who was the spokesman at the king's court for the great landowners of the three regions into which the Frankish kingdom was divided: Neustria, Austrasia, and Burgundy. Through this office, the Carolingian dynasty rose to power.

The Carolingians (from Carolus, Charles, after Charlemagne, Charles the Great) controlled the office of the mayor of the palace from the ascent to that post of Pepin I of Austrasia (D. 639) until 751, at which time the Carolingians, with the enterprising connivance of the pope, simply expropriated the Frankish crown. Pepin II (D. 714) ruled in fact if not in title over the Frankish kingdom. His illegitimate son, Charles Martel ("the Hammer"; D. 741), created a great cavalry by bestowing lands known as *benefices* or *fiefs* on powerful nobles, who, in return, agreed to be ready to serve as the king's army. It was such an army that checked the Arab probings on the western front at Tours in 732—an important battle that helped to secure the borders of Western Europe.

The fiefs so generously bestowed by Charles Martel to create his army came in large part from landed property that he usurped from the church. His alliance with the landed aristocracy in this grand manner permitted the Carolingians to have some measure of political success where the Merovingians had failed. The Carolingians created counts almost entirely out of the landed nobility from which the Carolingians themselves had risen. The Merovingians, in contrast, had tried to compete directly with these great aristocrats by raising the landless to power. By playing to strength rather than challenging it, the Carolingians strengthened themselves, at least for the short term. Because the Church was by this time completely dependent on the protection of the Franks against the Eastern emperor and the Lombards, it gave little thought at this time to the fact that its savior had been created in part with lands to which it held claim. Later, the Franks partially compensated the Church for these lands.

THE FRANKISH CHURCH. The Church came to play a large and initially quite voluntary role in the Frankish government. By Carolingian times, monasteries were a dominant force. Their intellectual achievements made them respected repositories of culture. Their religious teaching and example imposed order on surrounding populations. Their relics and rituals made them magical shrines to which pilgrims came in great numbers. And, thanks to their many gifts and internal discipline and industry, many had become very profitable farms and landed estates, their abbots rich and powerful magnates. By Merovingian times, the higher clergy were already employed in tandem with counts as royal agents. It was the policy of the Carolingians, perfected by Charles Martel and his successor, Pepin III ("the Short"; D. 768), to use the Church to pacify conquered neighboring tribes—Frisians, Thüringians, Bavarians, and especially the Franks' archenemies, the Saxons.

Conversion to Nicene Christianity became an integral part of the successful annexation of conquered lands and people; the cavalry broke their bodies, while the clergy won their hearts and minds. The Anglo-Saxon missionary Saint Boniface (born Wynfrith; CA. 680–754) was the most important of the German clergy who served Carolingian kings in this way. Christian bishops in missionary districts and elsewhere became lords, appointed by and subject to the king—an ominous integration of secular and religious policy in which lay the seeds of the later Investiture Controversy of the eleventh and twelfth centuries.

The Church served more than Carolingian territorial expansion. Pope Zacharias (741–752) also sanctioned Pepin the Short's termination of the vestigial

A clerical scholar dictating to two of his scribes. Before the invention of the printing press at about 1450, manuscripts produced by scribes could only be duplicated, preserved, and passed on by laborious hand copying. Much of the painstaking copying was done by monks. [Bettman Archive.]

Merovingian dynasty and the Carolingian accession to outright kingship of the Franks. With the pope's public blessing, Pepin was proclaimed king by the nobility in council in 751, and the last of the Merovingians, the puppet king Childeric III, was hustled off to a monastery and dynastic oblivion. According to legend, Saint Boniface first anointed Pepin, thereby investing Frankish rule from the very start with a certain sacral character.

Zacharias' successor, Pope Stephen II (752–757), did not let Pepin forget the favor of his predecessor. Driven from Rome in 753 by the Lombards, Pope Stephen appealed directly to Pepin to cast out the invaders and to guarantee papal claims to central Italy, which was dominated at this time by the Eastern emperor. In 754, the Franks and the church formed an alliance against the Lombards and the Eastern emperor. Carolingian kings became the protectors of the Catholic church and thereby "kings by the grace of God." Pepin gained the title *patricius Romanorum*, "father-protector of the Romans," a title heretofore borne only by the representative of the Eastern emperor. In 755, the Franks defeated the Lombards and gave the pope the lands surrounding Rome, an event that created what came to be known as the *Papal States*. The lands earlier appropriated by Charles Martel and parceled out to the Frankish nobility were never returned to the Church, despite the appearance in this period of a most enterprising fraudulent document designed to win their return, the *Donation of Constantine* (written between 750 and 800), which, however, was never universally accepted in the West. This imperial parchment alleged that the Emperor Constantine had personally conveyed to the Church his palace and "all provinces and districts of the city of Rome and Italy and of the regions of the West" as permanent possessions. It was believed by many to be a genuine document until definitely exposed as a forgery in the fifteenth century by the Humanist Lorenzo Valla.

The papacy had looked to the Franks for an ally strong enough to protect it from the Eastern emperors. It is an irony of history that the Church found in the Carolingian dynasty a Western imperial government that drew almost as slight a boundary between State and Church, secular and religious policy, as did Eastern emperors. Although eminently preferable to Eastern domination, Carolingian patronage of the church proved in its own way to be no less Caesaropapist.

The False Donation of Constantine

Among the ways in which Roman ecclesiasts fought to free the Western church from political domination was to assert its own sovereign territorial and political rights. One of the most ambitious of such assertions was the so-called Donation of Constantine *(eighth century), a fraudulent document claiming papal succession to much of the old Roman Empire.*

The Emperor Caesar Flavius Constantinus in Christ Jesus . . . to the most Holy and blessed Father of fathers, Silvester, Bishop of the Roman city and Pope; and to all his successors, the pontiffs, who shall sit in the chair of blessed Peter to the end of time. . . . Grace, peace, love, joy, long-suffering, mercy . . . be with you all. . . . For we wish you to know . . . that we have forsaken the worship of idols . . . and have come to the pure Christian faith. . . .

To the holy apostles, my lords the most blessed Peter and Paul, and through them also to blessed Silvester, our father, supreme pontiff and universal pope of the city of Rome, and to the pontiffs, his successors, who to the end of the world shall sit in the seat of blessed Peter, we grant and by this present we convey our imperial Lateran palace, which is superior to and excels all palaces in the whole world; and further the diadem, which is the crown of our head; and the miter; as also the super-humeral, that is, the stole which usually surrounds our imperial neck; and the purple cloak and the scarlet tunic and all the imperial robes. . . .

And we decree that those most reverend men, the clergy of various orders serving the same most holy Roman Church, shall have that eminence, distinction, power and precedence, with which our illustrious senate is gloriously adorned; that is, they shall be made patricians and consuls. And we ordain that they shall also be adorned with other imperial dignities. Also we decree that the clergy of the sacred Roman Church shall be adorned as are the imperial officers. . . .

We convey to the oft-mentioned and most blessed Silvester, universal pope, both our palace, as preferment, and likewise all provinces, palaces and districts of the city of Rome and Italy and of the regions of the West; and, bequeathing them to the power and sway of him and the pontiffs, his successors, we do determine and decree that the same be placed at his disposal, and do lawfully grant it as a permanent possession to the holy Roman Church. ❑

Henry Bettenson (ed.), *Documents of the Christian Church* (New York: Oxford University Press, 1961), pp. 137–141.

signs: he desired to be not only king of the Germans but a universal emperor as well. He had his sacred palace city, Aachen (in French, Aix-la-Chapelle), constructed in conscious imitation of the courts of the ancient Roman and of the contemporary Eastern emperors. Although permitted its distinctiveness, the Church was looked after by Charlemagne with a paternalism almost as great as that of any Eastern emperor. He used the Church above all to promote social stability and hierarchical order throughout the kingdom—as an aid in the creation of a great Frankish Christian empire. Frankish Christians were ceremoniously baptized, professed the Nicene Creed (with the *filioque* clause), and learned in church to revere Charlemagne.

Carolingian architecture. The cathedral church at Aachen (in modern West Germany) containing the chapel of Charlemagne. The original parts were constructed between 792 and 805. [Bildarchiv Foto Marburg.]

The Reign of Charlemagne (768–814)

Charlemagne continued the role of his father, Pepin the Short, as papal protector in Italy and his policy of territorial conquest in the north. After King Desiderius and the Lombards of northern Italy were decisively defeated in 774, Charlemagne took upon himself the title "King of the Lombards" in Pavia. He widened the frontiers of his kingdom further by subjugating surrounding pagan tribes, foremost among whom were the Saxons, whom the Franks brutally Christianized and dispersed in small groups throughout Frankish lands. The Avars (a tribe related to the Huns) were practically annihilated, so that the Danubian plains were brought into the Frankish orbit. The Arabs were chased beyond the Pyrenees. By the time of his death on January 28, 814, Charlemagne's kingdom embraced modern France, Belgium, Holland, Switzerland, almost the whole of western Germany, much of Italy, a portion of Spain, and the island of Corsica—an area approximately equal to that of the modern Common Market (see Map 13.2).

THE NEW EMPIRE. Encouraged by his ambitious advisers, Charlemagne came to harbor imperial de-

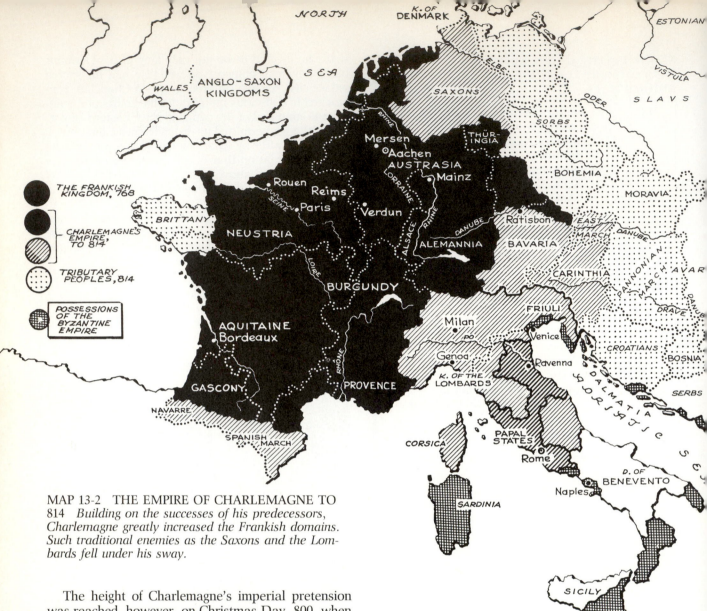

MAP 13-2 THE EMPIRE OF CHARLEMAGNE TO
814 *Building on the successes of his predecessors,
Charlemagne greatly increased the Frankish domains.
Such traditional enemies as the Saxons and the Lombards fell under his sway.*

The height of Charlemagne's imperial pretension
was reached, however, on Christmas Day, 800, when
Pope Leo III (795–816) crowned Charlemagne emperor. If the coronation benefited the Church, as it certainly did, it also served Charlemagne's imperial designs. Before Christmas Day, 800, Charlemagne had
been a minor Western potentate in the eyes of Eastern
emperors. After the coronation, Eastern emperors reluctantly recognized his new imperial dignity, and
Charlemagne even found it necessary to disclaim ambitions to rule as emperor over the East. Here began
what would come to be known as the Holy Roman
Empire, a revival, based in Germany, of the old
Roman Empire in the West.

THE NEW EMPEROR. Charlemagne stood a ma-
jestic six feet, three and one-half inches tall—a fact
secured when his tomb was opened and exact mea-
surements were taken in 1861. He was nomadic, ever

ready for a hunt. Informal and gregarious, he insisted
on the presence of friends even when he bathed and
was widely known for his practical jokes, lusty good
humor, and warm hospitality. Aachen was a festive
palace city to which people and gifts came from all
over the world. In 802, Charlemagne even received
from the caliph of Baghdad, Harun-al-Rashid, a white
elephant, the transport of which across the Alps was
as great a wonder as the creature itself.

Charlemagne had five official wives in succession,
possessed many mistresses and concubines, and sired
numerous children. This connubial variety created
special problems. His oldest son by his first marriage,
Pepin, jealous of the attention shown by his father to

the sons of his second wife, and fearing the loss of paternal favor, joined with noble enemies in a conspiracy against his father. Pepin ended his life in confinement in a monastery after the plot was exposed.

PROBLEMS OF GOVERNMENT. Charlemagne governed his kingdom through counts, of whom there were perhaps as many as 250. They were strategically located within the administrative districts into which the kingdom was divided. In Carolingian practice, the count tended to be a local magnate, one who already possessed the armed might and the self-interest to enforce the will of a generous king. He had three main duties: to maintain a local army loyal to the king, to collect tribute and dues, and to administer justice throughout his district.

This last responsibility he undertook through a district law court known as the *mallus*. The *mallus* assessed *wergeld*, or the compensation to be paid to an injured party in a feud, the most popular way of settling grievances and ending hostilities. In very difficult cases, where guilt or innocence was unclear, recourse was often had to judicial duels or to such "divine" judgments as the length of time it took a defendant's hand to heal after immersion in boiling water. In the ordeal by water, another divine test when human judgment was stymied, a defendant was thrown with his hands and feet bound into a river or pond that was first blessed by a priest; if he floated, he was pronounced guilty, because the pure water had obviously rejected him; if, however, the water received him and he sank, then he was deemed innocent.

As in Merovingian times, many counts used their official position and new judicial powers to their own advantage, becoming little despots within their districts. As the strong were made stronger, they became more independent. They looked on the land grants with which they were paid as hereditary positions rather than generous royal donations—a development that began to fragment Charlemagne's kingdom. Charlemagne tried to supervise his overseers and improve local justice by creating special royal envoys known as *missi dominici.* These were lay and clerical agents (counts and archbishops and bishops) who made annual visits to districts other than their own. But their impact was only marginal. Permanent provincial governors, bearing the title of prefect, duke, or margrave, were created in what was still another attempt to manage the counts and to organize the outlying regions of the kingdom. But as these governors became established in their areas, they proved no less corruptible than the others.

Charlemagne never solved the problem of a loyal bureaucracy. Ecclesiastical agents proved no better than secular ones in this regard. Landowning bishops had not only the same responsibilities but also the same secular lifestyles and aspirations as the royal counts. Save for their attendance to the liturgy and to church prayers, they were largely indistinguishable from the lay nobility. Capitularies, or royal decrees, discouraged the more outrageous behavior of the clergy. But Charlemagne also sensed, rightly as the Gregorian reform of the eleventh century would prove, a danger to royal government in the emergence of a distinctive and reform-minded class of ecclesiastical landowners. Charlemagne purposefully treated his bishops as he treated his counts, that is, as vassals who served at the king's pleasure.

ALCUIN AND THE CAROLINGIAN RENAISSANCE. Charlemagne accumulated a great deal of wealth in the form of loot and land from conquered tribes. He used a substantial part of this booty to attract Europe's best scholars to Aachen, where they developed court culture and education. By making scholarship materially as well as intellectually rewarding, Charlemagne attracted such scholars as Theodulf of Orleans, Angilbert, his own biographer Einhard, and the renowned Anglo-Saxon master Alcuin of York (735–804), who, at almost fifty, became director of the king's palace school in 782. Alcuin brought classical and Christian learning to Aachen and was handsomely rewarded for his efforts with several monastic estates, including that of Saint Martin of Tours, the wealthiest in the kingdom.

Although Charlemagne also appreciated learning for its own sake, this grand palace school was not created simply for love of antiquity. Charlemagne intended it to upgrade the administrative skills of the clerics and officials who staffed the royal bureaucracy. By preparing the sons of nobles to run the religious and secular offices of the realm, court scholarship served kingdom building. The school provided basic instruction in the seven liberal arts, with special concentration on grammar, logic, and mathematics, that is, training in reading, writing, speaking, and sound reasoning—the basic tools of bureaucracy. A clearer style of handwriting—the Carolingian minuscule— and accurate Latin appeared in the official documents. Lay literacy increased. Through personal correspondence and visitations, Alcuin created a genuine, if limited, community of scholars and clerics at court and did much to infuse the highest administrative levels with a sense of comradeship and common purpose.

A modest renaissance or rebirth of antiquity occurred in the palace school as scholars collected and preserved ancient manuscripts for a more curious posterity. Alcuin worked on a correct text of the Bible and made editions of the works of Gregory the Great and the monastic *Rule* of Saint Benedict. These scholarly activities aimed at concrete reforms and served official efforts to bring uniformity to Church law and liturgy, to educate the clergy, and to improve moral life within the monasteries.

THE MANOR AND SERFDOM. The agrarian economy of the Middle Ages was organized and controlled through village farms known as *manors.* Here peasants labored as farmers in subordination to a lord, that is, a more powerful landowner who gave them land and a dwelling in exchange for their services and a portion of their crops. That part of the land farmed by the peasants for the lord was the *demense,* on average about one quarter to one third of the arable land. All crops grown there were harvested for the lord.

The peasants were treated differently according to their personal status and the size of their property, all in strict accordance with custom; indeed, a social hierarchy existed among the peasantry. When a *freeman,* that is, a peasant with his own modest allodial or hereditary property (property free from the claims of a feudal overlord) became a serf by surrendering this property to a greater landowner in exchange for his protection and assistance, the freeman received it back from the lord with a clear definition of economic and legal rights that protected the freeman's self-interest.

Although the land was no longer his property, he had full possession and use of it, and the number of services and the amount of goods to be supplied the lord were often carefully spelled out. On the other hand, peasants who entered the service of a lord without any real property to bargain with (perhaps some farm implements and a few animals) ended up as *unfree* serfs and were much more vulnerable to the lord's demands, often spending up to three days a week working the lord's fields. Truly impoverished peasants who lived and worked on the manor as serfs had the lowest status and were the least protected. Weak serfs often fled to a monastery rather than continue their servitude, and therefore this avenue of escape was eventually closed by law.

By the time of Charlemagne, the moldboard plow—which was especially needed in northern Europe where the soil was heavy—and the three-field system of land cultivation were coming into use. These developments improved agricultural productivity. Unlike the older "scratch" plow, which crisscrossed the field with only slight penetration, the moldboard cut deep into the soil and turned it to form a ridge, providing a natural drainage system for the field as well as permitting the deep planting of seeds. Unlike the earlier two-

The invention of the moldboard plow greatly improved farming. The heavy plow cut deeply into the ground and furrowed it. This illustration (CA.1340) also shows that the traction harness, which lessened the strangulating effect of the yoke on the animals, had not yet been adopted. Indeed, one of the oxen seems to be on the verge on choking. [Add. MS. 42130, f. 170. Reproduced by permission of the British Board, London.]

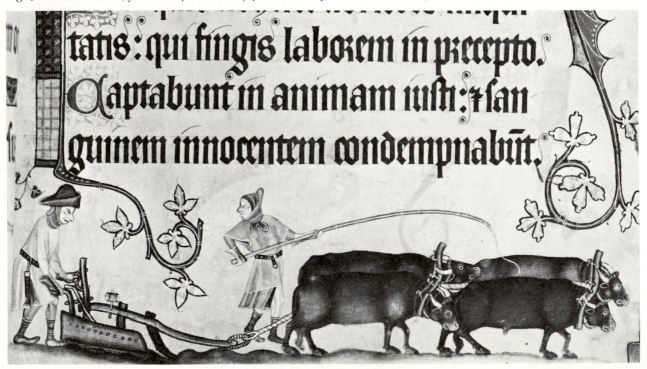

field system of crop rotation, which simply alternated fallow with planted fields each year, the three-field system increased the amount of cultivated land by leaving only one third fallow in a given year. It also better adjusted crops to seasons. In winter, one field was planted with winter crops of wheat or rye; in the summer, a second field was planted with summer crops of oats, barley, and lentils; and the third field was left fallow, to be planted in its turn with winter and summer crops.

Serfs were subject to so-called dues in kind: firewood for cutting the lord's wood, sheep for grazing their sheep on the lord's land, and the like. In this way, the lord, by furnishing shacks and small plots of land from his vast domain, created an army of servants who provided him with everything from eggs to boots. The discontent of the commoners is witnessed by the high number of recorded escapes. An astrological calendar from the period even marks the days most favorable for escaping. Escaped serfs roamed the land as beggars and vagabonds, searching for new and better masters.

RELIGION AND THE CLERGY. As owners of the churches on their lands, the lords had the right to raise chosen serfs to the post of parish priest, placing them in charge of the churches on the lords' estates. Although Church law directed the lord to set a serf free before the serf entered the clergy, lords were reluctant to do this and risk thereby a possible later challenge to their jurisdiction over the ecclesiastical property with which the serf, as priest, was invested. Lords rather preferred a "serf priest," one who not only said the mass on Sundays and holidays but who also continued to serve his lord during the week, waiting on the lord's table and tending his steeds. Like Charlemagne with his bishops, Frankish lords cultivated a docile parish clergy.

The ordinary people looked to religion for comfort and consolation. They considered baptism and confession of the Creed a surety of future salvation. They baptized their children, attended mass, tried to learn the Lord's Prayer, and received extreme unction from the priest as death approached. This was all probably done with more awe and simple faith than understanding. Religious instruction in the meaning of Christian doctrine and practice remained at a bare minimum, and the local priests on the manors were no better educated than their congregations. People understandably became particularly attached in this period to the more tangible veneration of relics and saints.

Charlemagne shared many of the religious beliefs of his ordinary subjects. He collected and venerated relics, made pilgrimages to Rome, frequented the church of Saint Mary in Aachen several times a day, and directed in his last will and testament that all but a fraction of his great treasure be spent to endow masses and prayers for his departed soul.

The Breakup of the Carolingian Kingdom

In the last years of his life, an ailing Charlemagne knew that his empire was ungovernable. The seeds of dissolution lay in regionalism, that is, the determination of each region, no matter how small, to look first—and often only—to its own self-interest. Despite his considerable skill and resolution, Charlemagne's realm became too fragmented among powerful regional magnates. Although they were his vassals, these same men were also landholders and lords in their own right. They knew that their sovereignty lessened as Charlemagne's increased and accordingly became reluctant royal servants. In feudal society, a direct relationship existed between physical proximity to authority and loyalty to authority. Local people obeyed local lords more readily than they obeyed a glorious but distant king. Charlemagne had been forced to recognize and even to enhance the power of regional magnates in order to win needed financial and military support. But as in the Merovingian kingdom so also in the Carolingian, the tail came increasingly to wag the dog. Charlemagne's major attempt to enforce subordination to royal dictates and a transregional discipline—through the institution of the *missi dominici*—proved ultimately unsuccessful.

LOUIS THE PIOUS. Carolingian kings did not give up easily. Charlemagne's only surviving son and successor was Louis the Pious (814–840), so-called because of his close alliance with the Church and his promotion of puritanical reforms. Louis had three sons by his first wife. According to Salic or Germanic law, a ruler partitioned his kingdom equally among his surviving sons. Louis, who saw himself as an emperor and no mere German king, recognized that a tripartite kingdom would hardly be an empire and acted early in his reign, in the year 817, to break this legal tradition. This he did by making his eldest son, Lothar (d. 855), coregent and sole imperial heir. To Lothar's brothers, he gave important but much lesser appanages, or assigned hereditary lands: Pepin (d. 838) became king of Aquitaine, and Louis "the German" (d. 876) became king of Bavaria, over the eastern Franks.

In 823, Louis' second wife, Judith of Bavaria, bore him still a fourth son, Charles, later called "the Bald" (d. 877). Mindful of Frankish law and custom and determined that her son should receive more than just a nominal inheritance, the queen incited the brothers Pepin and Louis to war against Lothar, who fled for refuge to the pope. More important, Judith was instrumental in persuading Louis to reverse his earlier decision and to divide the kingdom equally among his four living sons. As their stepmother and the young Charles rose in their father's favor, the three older brothers feared still further reversals, so they decided to act against their father. Supported by the pope, they joined forces and defeated their father in a battle near Colmar (833).

As the bestower of crowns upon emperors, the pope had an important stake in the preservation of the revived Western empire and the imperial title, both of which Louis' belated agreement to an equal partition of his kingdom threatened to undo. The pope condemned Louis and restored Lothar to his original inheritance. But Lothar's regained imperial dignity only stirred anew the resentments of his brothers, including his stepbrother, Charles, who resumed their war against him.

THE TREATY OF VERDUN AND ITS AFTERMATH. Peace finally came to the heirs of Louis the Pious in 843 in the Treaty of Verdun. But this agreement also brought about the disaster that Louis had originally feared: the great Carolingian empire was partitioned according to Frankish law into three equal parts, Pepin having died in 838. Lothar received a middle section, which came to be known as Lotharingia and embraced roughly modern Holland, Belgium, Switzerland, Alsace-Lorraine, and Italy. Charles the Bald received the western part of the kingdom, or roughly modern France. And Louis the German came into the eastern part, or roughly modern Germany (see Map 13.3). Although Lothar retained the imperial title, the universal empire of Charlemagne and Louis

the Pious ceased to exist after Verdun. Not until the sixteenth century, with the election in 1519 of Charles I of Spain as the Holy Roman Emperor Charles V, would the Western world again see a kingdom so vast as Charlemagne's.

The Treaty of Verdun, the oldest written document in French, proved to be only the beginning of Carolingian fragmentation. When Lothar died in 855, his middle kingdom was divided equally among his three surviving sons. This partition of the partition left the middle, or imperial, kingdom much smaller and weaker than those of Louis the German and Charles the Bald. Henceforth, Western Europe saw an eastern and a western Frankish kingdom—roughly Germany versus France—at war over the fractionalized middle kingdom, a contest that has continued into modern times.

When Charles the Bald died in 877, both the papal and the imperial thrones fell on especially hard times. Each became a pawn in the hands of powerful Italian and German magnates, respectively. Neither pope nor emperor knew dignity and power again until a new Western imperial dynasty—the Ottonians—attained dominance during the reign of Otto I (962–973). It is especially with reference to this juncture in European history—the last quarter of the ninth and the first half of the tenth century—that one may speak with some justification of a "dark age."

Simultaneously with the internal political breakdown of the empire and the papacy came new barbarian attacks, set off probably by overpopulation and famine in northern Europe. The late ninth and tenth centuries saw successive waves of Normans (Northmen), better known as Vikings, from Scandinavia;

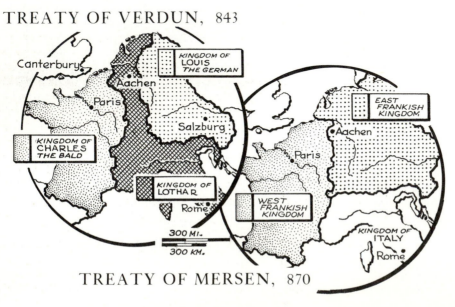

TREATY OF VERDUN, 843

Canterbury
Aachen
Paris
KINGDOM OF LOUIS THE GERMAN
Salzburg
KINGDOM OF CHARLES THE BALD
KINGDOM OF LOTHAR
Rome
300 MI.
300 KM.

EAST FRANKISH KINGDOM
Aachen
Paris
WEST FRANKISH KINGDOM
KINGDOM OF ITALY
Rome

TREATY OF MERSEN, 870

MAP 13-3 THE TREATIES OF VERDUN AND MERSEN *The Treaty of Verdun divided the kingdom of Louis the Pious among his three feuding children: Charles the Bald, Lothar, and Louis the German. After Lothar's death in 855 the middle kingdom was so weakened by division among his three sons that Charles the Bald and Louis the German divided it between themselves in the Treaty of Mersen in 870.*

Magyars, or Hungarians, the great horsemen from the eastern plains; and Muslims from the south (see Map 13.4). In the 880s, the Vikings penetrated to the imperial residence of Aachen and to Paris. Moving rapidly in ships and raiding coastal towns, they were almost impossible to defend against and kept western Europe on edge. The Franks built fortified towns and castles in strategic locations, which served as refuges. When they could, they bought off the invaders with outright grants of land (for example, Normandy) and payments of silver. In this period, local populations became more dependent than ever before on local strongmen for life, limb, and livelihood. This brute fact of life provided the essential precondition for the maturation of feudal society.

MAP 13-4 VIKING, MUSLIM, AND MAGYAR INVASIONS TO THE ELEVENTH CENTURY *Western Europe was sorely beset by new waves of outsiders from the ninth to the eleventh century. From north, east, and south a stream of invading Vikings, Magyars, and Muslims brought the West at times to near collapse and of course gravely affected institutions within Europe.*

THE CAROLINGIAN DYNASTY (751–987)

751	Pepin III "the Short" becomes king of the Franks
755	Franks drive Lombards out of central Italy; creation of Papal States
768–814	Charlemagne rules as king of the Franks
774	Charlemagne defeats Lombards in northern Italy
750–800	Donation of Constantine protests Frankish domination of Church
800	Pope Leo III crowns Charlemagne
814–840	Louis the Pious succeeds Charlemagne as "Emperor"
843	Treaty of Verdun partitions the Carolingian Empire
870	Treaty of Mersen further divides Carolingian Empire
875–950	New invasions by Vikings, Muslims, and Magyars
962	Ottonian dynasty succeeds Carolingian in Germany
987	Capetian dynasty succeeds Carolingian

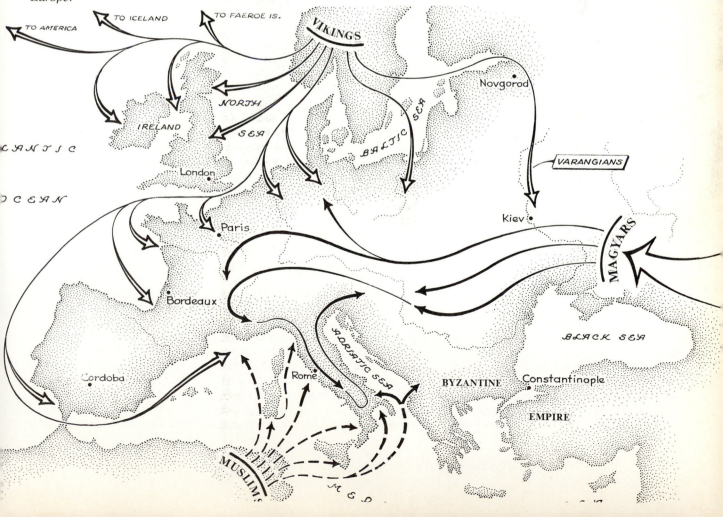

Feudal Society

A chronic absence of effective central government and the constant threat of famine, disease, and foreign invasion characterized the Middle Ages. *Feudal society* is a term used to describe the adjustment to this state of affairs as the weaker sought protection from the stronger. The term refers to the social, political, and economic system that emerged. The true lords and masters became those who could guarantee immediate protection from rapine and starvation.

A feudal society is a social order in which a regional prince or a local lord is dominant and the highest virtues are those of mutual trust and fidelity. In a feudal society, what people most need is the firm assurance that others can be depended on in time of dire need. It is above all a system of mutual rights and responsibilities.

During the early Middle Ages, the landed nobility became great lords who ruled over their domains as miniature kingdoms. They maintained their own armies and courts, regulated their area's tolls, and even minted their own coins. Large warrior groups of vassals were created by extensive bestowals of land, and they developed into a prominent professional military class with its own code of knightly conduct. In feudal society, most serfs docilely worked the land, the clergy prayed and gave counsel, and the nobility—both landed and vassal—maintained law and order by swift steed and sword.

Origins

The main features of feudal government can be found in the divisions and conflicts of Merovingian society. In the sixth and seventh centuries, there evolved the custom of individual freemen placing themselves under the protection of more powerful freemen. In this way, the latter built up armies and became local magnates, and the former solved the problem of simple survival. Freemen who so entrusted themselves to others were known as *ingenui in obsequio* ("freemen in a contractual relation of dependence"). Those who so gave themselves to the king were called *antrustiones*. All men of this type came to be described collectively as *vassi* ("those who serve"), from which evolved the term *vassalage*, meaning the placement of oneself in the personal service of another who promises protection in return.

Landed nobility, like kings, tried to acquire as many such vassals as they could, because military strength in the early Middle Ages lay in numbers. As it proved impossible to maintain these growing armies within the lord's own household, as was the original custom, or to support them by special monetary payments, the practice evolved of simply granting them land as a "tenement." Such land came to be known as a *benefice*, or a *fief*, and vassals were expected to dwell on it and maintain their steeds and other accoutrements of war in good order. Originally vassals, therefore, were little more than gangs-in-waiting.

Vassalage and the Fief

Vassalage involved "fealty" to the lord. To swear fealty was to promise to refrain from any action that might in any way threaten the lord's well-being and to perform personal services for him on his request. Chief among the expected services was military duty as a mounted knight. This could involve a variety of activities: a short or long military expedition, escort duty, standing castle guard, and/or the placement of one's own fortress at the lord's disposal, if the vassal was of such stature as to have one. Continuous bargaining and bickering occurred over the terms of service. Limitations were placed on the number of days a lord could require services from a vassal. In France in the eleventh century, about forty days of service per year were considered sufficient. It also became possible for vassals to buy their way out of military service by a monetary payment known as *scutage*. The lord, in turn, applied this payment to the hiring of mercenaries, who often proved more efficient than contract-conscious vassals. Beyond his military duty, the vassal was also expected to give the lord advice when he requested it and to sit as a member of his court when it was in session.

Beginning with the reign of Louis the Pious (814–840), bishops and abbots swore fealty and received their offices from the king as a benefice. The king formally "invested" these clerics in their offices during a special ceremony in which he presented them with a ring and a staff, the symbols of high spiritual office. Louis' predecessors had earlier confiscated Church lands with only modest and belated compensation to the Church in the form of a tithe required of all Frankish inhabitants. Long a sore point for the Church, the presumptuous practice of the lay investiture of the clergy provoked a world-shaking confrontation of Church and State in the eleventh and twelfth centuries, when reform-minded clergy rebelled against what they then believed to be involuntary clerical vassalage.

The lord's obligations to his vassals were very specific. He was, first of all, obligated to protect the vassal from physical harm and to stand as his advocate in public court. After fealty was sworn and homage paid, the lord provided for the vassal's physical maintenance by the bestowal of a benefice, or fief. The fief was simply the physical or material wherewithal to meet the vassal's military and other obligations. It could take the form of liquid wealth as well as the more common grant of real property. There were so-called money fiefs, which empowered a vassal to receive regular payments from the lord's treasury. Such

Bishop Fulbert Describes the Obligations of Vassal and Lord

Trust held the lord and vassal together. Their duties in this regard were carefully defined. Here are six general rules for vassal and lord, laid down by Bishop Fulbert of Chartres in a letter to William, Duke of Aquitaine, in 1020.

He who swears fealty to his lord ought always to have these six things in memory: what is harmless, safe, honorable, useful, easy, practicable. *Harmless*, that is to say, that he should not injure his lord in his body; *safe* that he should not injure him by betraying his secrets or the defenses upon which he relies for safety; *honorable*, that he should not injure him in his justice or in other matters that pertain to his honor; *useful*, that he should not injure him in his possessions; *easy* and *practicable*, that that good which his lord is able to do easily he make not difficult, nor that which is practicable he make not impossible to him.

That the faithful vassal should avoid these injuries is certainly proper, but not for this alone does he deserve his holding; for it is not sufficient to abstain from evil, unless what is good is done also. It remains, therefore, that in the same six things mentioned above he should faithfully counsel and aid his lord, if he wishes to be looked upon as worthy of his benefice and to be safe concerning the fealty which he has sworn.

The lord also ought to act toward his faithful vassal reciprocally in all these things. And if he does not do this, he will be justly considered guilty of bad faith, just as the former, if he should be detected in avoiding or consenting to the avoidance of his duties, would be perfidious and perjured.

James Harvey Robinson (ed.), *Readings in European History*, Vol. 1 (Boston: Athenaeum, 1904). p. 184

---

fiefs were potentially quite devilish because they made it possible for one country to acquire vassals among the nobility of another. Normally, the fief consisted of a landed estate of anywhere from a few to several thousand acres. But it could also take the form of a castle.

In Carolingian times, a benefice, or fief, varied in size from one or more small villas to several *mansi*, which were agricultural holdings of twenty-five to forty-eight acres. The king's vassals are known to have received benefices of at least thirty and as many as two hundred such holdings, truly a vast estate. Royal vassalage with a benefice understandably came to be widely sought by the highest classes of Carolingian society. As a royal policy, however, it proved deadly to the king in the long run. Although Carolingian kings jealously guarded their rights over property granted in benefice to vassals, resident vassals were still free to dispose of their benefices as they pleased. Vassals of the king, strengthened by his donations, in turn created their own vassals. These, in turn, created still further vassals of their own—vassals of vassals of vassals—in a reverse pyramiding effect that had fragmented land and authority from the highest to the lowest levels by the late ninth century.

Fragmentation and Divided Loyalty

In addition to the fragmentation brought about by the multiplication of vassalage, effective occupation of the land led gradually to claims of hereditary possession. Hereditary possession became a legally recognized principle in the ninth century and laid the basis for claims to real ownership. Fiefs given as royal donations became hereditary possessions and, with the passage of time, in some instances even the real property of the possessor. Further, vassal engagements came to be multiplied in still another way as enterprising freemen sought to accumulate as much land as possible. One man actually became a vassal to several different lords. This development led in the ninth century to the concept of a "liege lord"—one master whom the vassal must obey even to the harm of the others, should a direct conflict among them arise.

The problem of loyalty was reflected not only in the literature of the period, with its praise of the virtues of honor and fidelity, but also in the ceremonial development of the very act of "commendation" by which a freeman became a vassal. In the mid-eighth century, an "oath of fealty" highlighted the ceremony. A vassal reinforced his promise of fidelity to the lord by swearing a special oath with his hand on a sacred relic or the Bible. In the tenth and eleventh centuries, paying homage to the lord involved not only the swearing of such an oath but also the placement of the vassal's hands between the lord's and the sealing of the ceremony with a kiss.

As the centuries passed, personal loyalty and service became quite secondary to the acquisition of property. The fief overshadowed fealty; the benefice became more important than vassalage; and freemen proved themselves prepared to swear allegiance to the highest bidder.

The Early Middle Ages in World Perspective

In Western Europe, the centuries between 400 and 1000 witnessed both the decline of European classical civilization and the birth of a new European civilization. Beginning with the fifth century, the barbarian invasions separated Western Europe culturally from its classical age. Continuing for centuries, this type of separation was unknown to other world cultures. Although some important works and concepts survived from antiquity in the West (due largely to the Christian church), Western civilization would for centuries be recovering its rich classical past in "renaissances" stretching into the sixteenth century. Out of the mixture of barbarian and surviving (or recovered) classical culture, Western civilization, as we know it today, was born. Aided and abetted by the Christian church, the Carolingians created a new imperial tradition. But early medieval society remained highly fragmented in the West, probably more so than anywhere else in the world, despite a certain common religious culture. Regions were organized into institutions designed primarily to ensure that all would be fed and cared for (manorialism) and that outside predators would be successfully repulsed (feudalism). It was not a time of great cultural ambition.

In China, particularly in the seventh and eighth centuries, the T'ang dynasty also searched for ways to secure Chinese borders against foreign expansion from Turkey and Tibet. As in Western Europe, religion and philosophy served and did not compete with the state (although this would change in the West after the twelfth century). Early medieval China was, however, far more cosmopolitan and politically unified than Western Europe. China was also centuries ahead in technology. Printing with movable type existed there by the tenth century, an invention the West did not see until the fifteenth century. Chinese rulers governed effectively far beyond their immediate centers of government. The T'ang dynasty held sway over their empire in a way Carolingian rulers could only dream of doing.

In Japan, the Yamato court (300–680), much like that of the Merovingians and Carolingians, struggled to unify and control the countryside. It was also aided by a religion friendly to royalty, Shinto. As in the West, a Japanese identity evolved through struggle and accommodation with outside cultures, especially with the Chinese, the dominant influence on Japan between the seventh and twelfth centuries. But foreign cultural influence, again as in the West, never managed to eradicate the indigenous culture. By the ninth century, a distinctive Sino-Japanese culture existed. But Japan, again like Western Europe, remained a fragmented land during these centuries, despite a certain alle-

giance and willingness to pay taxes to an imperial court. Throughout Japan, the basic unit of political control consisted of those same highly self-conscious and specially devoted armed knights we saw in Western Europe. A system of lordship and vassalage evolved around bands of local mounted warriors who were known as Samurai. Through this system, local order was maintained in Japan until the fifteenth century. Like the Merovingian and Carolingian courts, the Japanese court had to tolerate strong and independent regional rulers.

In the seventh century, Islam gave birth to still another powerful new international civilization, one that reached from India to Spain by 710. Consolidated by a line of successful caliphates between 750 and 945, Islam had divided by the tenth century into more exclusive (Kharijite and Shi'ite) and more inclusive (Sunni) factions. Again as in Western Europe, its central government had broken down. But the politically strong and culturally vibrant period of the high caliphate under the Umayyads and Abbasids (Islam's "classical" period) overlapped in time the Carolingian heyday, when Western Europe witnessed the birth of a new political empire and a little cultural Renaissance of its own.

Finally, in the centuries just before the awakening of Western European civilization, India enjoyed the high point of its civilization, the Gupta Age (320–467). While Western Europeans struggled for some degree of political and social order, a vocationally and socially limiting caste system neatly imposed order on Indian society from Brahmins to outcasts. Culture, religion, and politics flourished amid this unity.

All things considered, one may say that most of the world's great civilizations were reaching a peak, when that of the West was just coming to life. This may be attributed to the fact that the other world civilizations never experienced disruptions in their cultures by foreign invaders on the magnitude known in the West during the early Middle Ages.

Suggested Readings

M. BLOCH, *Feudal Society*, Vols. 1 and 2, trans. by L. A. Manyon (1971). A classic on the topic and as an example of historical study.

P. BROWN, *Augustine of Hippo: A Biography* (1967). Late antiquity seen through the biography of its greatest Christian thinker.

H. CHADWICK, *The Early Church* (1967). Among the best treatments of early Christianity.

R. H. C. DAVIS, *A History of Medieval Europe: From Constantine to St. Louis* (1972). Unsurpassed in clarity.

K. F. DREW (ed.), *The Barbarian Invasions: Catalyst of a New Order* (1970). Collection of essays that focuses the issues.

F. Dvornik, *Byzantium and the Roman Primacy* (1966).

H. Fichtenau, *The Carolingian Empire: The Age of Charlemagne*, trans. by Peter Munz (1964). Strongest on the political history of the era.

F. L. Ganshof, *Feudalism*, trans. by Philip Grierson (1964). The most profound brief analysis of the subject.

A. F. Havighurst (ed.), *The Pirenne Thesis: Analysis, Criticism, and Revision* (1958). Excerpts from the scholarly debate over the extent of Western trade in the East during the early Middle Ages.

D. Knowles, *Christian Monasticism* (1969). Sweeping survey with helpful photographs.

M. L. W. Laistner, *Thought and Letters in Western Europe, 500 to 900* (1957). Among the best surveys of early medieval intellectual history.

J. Leclercq, *The Love of Learning and the Desire for God: A Study of Monastic Culture*, trans. by Catherine Misrahi (1962). Lucid, delightful, absorbing account of the ideals of monks.

J. Leclercq, F. Vandenbroucke, and L. Bouyer, *The Spirituality of the Middle Ages* (1968). Perhaps the best survey of medieval Christianity, East and West, to the eve of the Protestant Reformation.

R. McKitternick, *The Frankish Kingdoms under the Carolingians, 751–987* (1983).

P. Munz, *The Age of Charlemagne* (1971). Penetrating social history of the period.

H. Pirenne, *A History of Europe, I: From the End of the Roman World in the West to the Beginnings of the Western States*, trans. by Bernhard Maill (1958). Comprehensive survey, with now-controversial views on the demise of Western trade and cities in the early Middle Ages.

S. Runciman, *Byzantine Civilization* (1970). Succinct, comprehensive account by a master.

P. Sawyer, *The Age of the Vikings* (1962). The best account.

O. von Simson, *Sacred Fortress: Byzantine Art and Statecraft in Ravenna* (1948).

R. W. Southern, *The Making of the Middle Ages* (1973). Originally published in 1953, but still a fresh account by an imaginative historian.

C. Stephenson, *Medieval Feudalism* (1969). Excellent short summary and introduction.

A. A. Vasiliev, *History of the Byzantine Empire 324–1453* (1952). The most comprehensive treatment in English.

H. Waddell (ed.), *The Desert Fortress* (1957).

S. F. Wemple, *Women in Frankish Society: Marriage and the Cloister 500–900* (1981). The impact of Christian marriage customs on the Franks.

L. White, Jr., *Medieval Technology and Social Change* (1962). Often fascinating account of how primitive technology changed life.

clergy's lord and spouse. The distinctive Western separation of Church and State and the celibacy of the Catholic clergy, both of which continue today, had their definitive origins in the Cluny reform movement.

Cluny rapidly became a center from which reformers were dispatched to monasteries throughout France and Italy. It grew to embrace almost fifteen hundred dependent cloisters, each devoted to monastic and Church reform. In the last half of the eleventh century, the Cluny reformers reached the summit when the papacy embraced their reforms.

In the late ninth and early tenth centuries, the movement inspired the "Peace of God," a series of Church decrees that attempted to lessen the endemic warfare of medieval society by threatening excommunication for all who, at any time, harmed such vulnerable groups as women, peasants, merchants, and clergy. The Peace of God was subsequently reinforced by proclamations of the "Truce of God," a Church order that everyone must abstain from every form of violence and warfare during a certain part of each week (eventually from Wednesday night to Monday morning) and in all holy seasons.

Popes devoted to reforms like those urged by Cluny came to power during the reign of Emperor Henry III (1039–1056). Pope Leo IX (1049–1054) promoted regional synods in opposition to simony (that is, the selling of spiritual things, such as Church offices) and clerical concubinage. He also placed Cluniacs in key administrative posts in Rome. During the turbulent minority of Henry III's successor, Henry IV (1056–1106), reform popes began to assert themselves more openly. Pope Stephen IX (1057–1058) reigned without imperial ratification, contrary to the earlier declaration of Otto I. Pope Nicholas II (1059–1061) took the unprecedented step of establishing a College of Cardinals in 1059, and henceforth this body alone elected the pope.

THE INVESTITURE STRUGGLE: GREGORY VII AND HENRY IV. It was Pope Gregory VII (1073–1085), a fierce advocate of Cluny's reforms who had entered the papal bureaucracy a quarter century earlier during the pontificate of Leo IX, who put the Church's declaration of independence to the test. Cluniacs had repeatedly inveighed against simony. In 1075, Pope Gregory condemned under penalty of excommunication the lay investiture of clergy at any level. He had primarily in mind the emperor's well-established custom of installing bishops by presenting them with the ring and staff that symbolized episcopal office. After Gregory's ruling, bishops no more than popes were to be the creations of emperors. As popes were elected by the College of Cardinals and were not raised up by kings or nobles, so bishops would henceforth be installed in their offices by high ecclesiastical authority as empowered by the pope and none other.

Gregory's prohibition came as a jolt to royal authority. Since the days of Otto I, emperors had routinely passed out bishoprics to favored clergy. Bishops, who received royal estates, were the emperors' appointees and servants of the state. Henry IV's Carolingian and Ottonian predecessors had carefully nurtured the theocratic character of the empire in both concept and administrative bureaucracy. The church and religion were integral parts of government. Henry considered Gregory's action a direct challenge to his authority. The territorial princes, on the other hand, ever tending away from the center and eager to see the emperor weakened, were quick to see the advantages of Gregory's ruling: if the emperor did not have a bishop's ear, then a territorial prince might. In the hope of gaining an advantage over both the emperor and the clergy in their territory, the princes fully supported Gregory's edict.

The lines of battle were quickly drawn. Henry assembled his loyal German bishops at Worms in January 1076 and had them proclaim their independence from Gregory. Gregory promptly responded with the Church's heavy artillery; he excommunicated Henry and absolved all Henry's subjects from loyalty to him. The German princes were delighted by this turn of events, and Henry found himself facing a general revolt led by the duchy of Saxony. He had no recourse but to come to terms with Gregory. In a famous scene, Henry prostrated himself outside Gregory's castle retreat at Canossa on January 25, 1077. There he reportedly stood barefoot in the snow off and on for three days before the pope absolved his royal penitent. Papal power had, at this moment, reached its pinnacle. But heights are also for descending, and Gregory's grandeur, as he must surely have known when he pardoned Henry and restored him to power, was very soon to fade.

The settlement of the investiture controversy came in 1122 with the Concordat of Worms. Emperor Henry V (1106–1125) formally renounced his power to invest bishops with ring and staff. In exchange, Pope Calixtus II (1119–1124) recognized the emperor's right to be present and to invest bishops with fiefs before or after their investment with ring and staff by the Church. The old Church–State "back scratching" in this way continued, but now on very different terms. The clergy received their offices and attendant religious powers solely from ecclesiastical authority and no longer from kings and emperors. Rulers continued to bestow lands and worldly goods on high clergy in the hope of influencing them; the Concordat of Worms made the clergy more independent but not necessarily less worldly.

Pope Gregory VII Asserts the Power of the Pope

Church reformers of the high Middle Ages vigorously asserted the power of the pope within the Church and his rights against emperors and all others who might encroach on the papal sphere of jurisdiction. Here is a statement of the basic principles of the Gregorian reformers, known as the Ditatus Papae *("The Sayings of the Pope"), which is attributed to Pope Gregory VII (1073–1085).*

That the Roman Church was founded by God alone.

That the Roman Pontiff alone is rightly to be called universal.

That the Pope may depose the absent.

That for him alone it is lawful to enact new laws according to the needs of the time, to assemble together new congregations, to make an abbey of a canonry; and . . . to divide a rich bishopric and unite the poor ones.

That he alone may use the imperial insignia.

That the Pope is the only one whose feet are to be kissed by all princes.

That his name alone is to be recited in churches.

That his title is unique in the world.

That he may depose emperors.

That he may transfer bishops, if necessary, from one See to another.

That no synod may be called a general one without his order.

That no chapter or book may be regarded as canonical without his authority.

That no sentence of his may be retracted by any one; and that he, alone of all, can retract it.

That he himself may be judged by no one.

That the Roman Church has never erred, nor ever, by the witness of Scripture, shall err to all eternity.

That the Pope may absolve subjects of unjust men from their fealty. ❑

Church and State through the Centuries: A Collection of Historic Documents, trans. and ed. by S. Z. Ehler and John B. Morrall (New York: Biblo and Tannen, 1967), pp. 43–44.

The Gregorian party won the independence of the clergy at the price of encouraging the divisiveness of the political forces within the empire. The pope made himself strong by making imperial authority weak. In the end, those who profited most from the investiture controversy were the local princes.

The First Crusades

If an index of popular piety and support for the pope in the high Middle Ages is needed, the Crusades amply provide it. What the Cluny reform was to the clergy, the First Crusade to the Holy Land, proclaimed by Pope Urban II at the Council of Clermont in France in 1095, was to the laity: an outlet for the heightened religious zeal of what was Europe's most religious century prior to the Protestant Reformation. Actually, there had been an earlier Crusade of French knights, who, inspired by Pope Alexander II, had attacked Muslims in Spain in 1064. Unlike later Crusades, which were undertaken for patently mercenary as well as religious motives, the early Crusades were to a very high degree inspired by genuine religious piety and were carefully orchestrated by the revived papacy. Participants in the First Crusade to the Holy Land were promised a plenary indulgence should they die in battle, that is, a complete remission of the penance required of them for their mortal sins and hence release from suffering for them in purgatory. But this spiritual reward was only part of the crusading impulse. Other factors were the widespread popular respect for the reformed papacy and the existence of a nobility newly strengthened by the breakdown of imperial power and eager for military adventure. These elements combined to make the First Crusade a rousing success.

The Eastern emperor had petitioned both Pope Gregory VII and Pope Urban II for aid against advancing Muslim armies. The Western Crusaders did not, however, assemble for the purpose of defending Europe's borders against aggression. They freely took the offensive to rescue the holy city of Jerusalem—which had been in non-Christian hands since the seventh century—from the Seljuk Turks. To this end three great armies—tens of thousands of Crusaders—gathered in France, Germany, and Italy. Following different routes, they reassembled in Constantinople in 1097. The convergence of these spirited soldiers on the Eastern capital was a cultural shock that only deepened Eastern antipathy toward the West. The weakened Eastern emperor, Alexis I, suspected their motives, and the common people, who were forced to give them room and board, hardly considered them Chris-

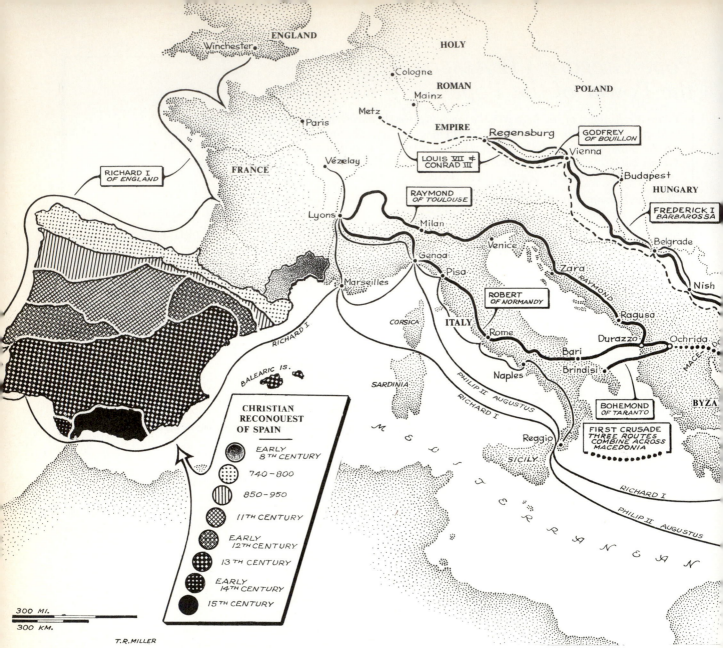

MAP 14-1 THE EARLY CRUSADES *Routes and several leaders of the crusades during the first century of the movement. Indicated names of the great nobles of the First Crusade do not exhaust the list. The even showier array of monarchs of the Second and Third still left the crusades, on balance, ineffective in achieving their ostensible goals.*

tian brothers in a common cause—especially after Rome and Constantinople had separated in 1054. Nonetheless, these fanatical Crusaders accomplished what no Eastern army had ever been able to do. They soundly defeated one Seljuk army after another in a steady advance toward Jerusalem, which fell to them on July 15, 1099.

The victorious Crusaders divided the conquered territory into the feudal states of Jerusalem, Edessa,

and Antioch, which they allegedly held as fiefs from the pope. Godfrey of Bouillon, leader of the French–German army (and after him his brother Baldwin), ruled over the kingdom of Jerusalem. However, the Crusaders remained only small islands within a great sea of Muslims, who looked on the Western invaders as hardly more than savages. Native persistence finally broke the Crusaders around mid-century, and the forty-odd-year Latin presence in the East began to

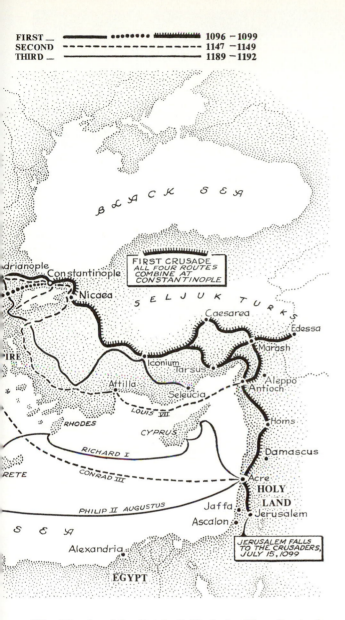

FIRST _ ●●●●●●● ▐▐▐▐▐▐▐ 1096 – 1099
SECOND _ - - - - - - - - - - - 1147 – 1149
THIRD _ ─────────── 1189 – 1192

B L A C K   S E A

Adrianople
Constantinople

**FIRST CRUSADE
ALL FOUR ROUTES
COMBINE AT
CONSTANTINOPLE**

Nicaea

S E L J U K   T U R K S

Caesarea
Edessa
Marash

Iconium
Tarsus
Attila
Aleppo
Seleucia
Antioch

LOUIS VII

RHODES
CYPRUS
Homs

RICHARD I

Damascus

CONRAD III

Acre
**HOLY
LAND**

PHILIP II AUGUSTUS

Jaffa
Jerusalem
Ascalon

S E A

Alexandria

**JERUSALEM FALLS
TO THE CRUSADERS,
JULY 15, 1099**

EGYPT

crumble. Edessa fell to Muslim armies in 1144. A Second Crusade, preached by the eminent Bernard of Clairvaux (1091–1153), Christendom's most powerful monastic leader, attempted a rescue, but it met with dismal failure. In October 1187, Jerusalem itself was reconquered by Saladin (1138–1193), king of Egypt and Syria, and, save for a brief interlude in the thirteenth century, it remained thereafter in Islamic hands until modern times.

A Third Crusade in the twelfth century (1189–1192) attempted yet another rescue, enlisting as its leaders the most powerful Western rulers: Emperor Frederick Barbarossa; Richard the Lion-Hearted, king of England; and Philip Augustus, king of France. But the Third Crusade proved a tragicomic commentary on the passing of the original crusading spirit. Frederick Barbarossa accidentally drowned in the Saleph River while en route to the Holy Land. Richard the Lion-Hearted and Philip Augustus reached the outskirts of Jerusalem, but their intense personal rivalry shattered the Crusaders' unity and chances of victory. Philip Augustus returned to France and made war on English continental territories, and Richard fell captive to the Emperor Henry VI as he was returning to England. (Henry VI suspected Richard of plotting against him with Henry's mortal enemy, Henry the Lion, the duke of Saxony, who happened also to be Richard's brother-in-law.) The English were forced to pay a handsome ransom for their king's release. Popular resentment of taxes for this ransom became part of the background of the revolt against the English monarchy that led to the royal recognition of Magna Carta in 1215.

The long-term achievement of the first three Crusades had little to do with their original purpose. Politically and religiously, they were a failure, and the Holy Land reverted as firmly as ever to Muslim hands. These Crusades were more important for the way they stimulated Western trade with the East. The merchants of Venice, Pisa, and Genoa followed the Crusader's cross to lucrative new markets. The need to

The "Castle of the Knights" (Krak-des-Chevaliers), the most magnificent of the many crusader castles built in the Holy Land in the twelfth and thirteenth centuries and whose ruins remain in modern Syria, Lebanon, and Jordan. It is situated in northern Syria a few miles from the Lebanese border. Its defense consisted of two massive walls, one overhanging the other, divided by a great moat. The Muslims of the same period used very similar military architecture. [Arab Information Center, New York.]

The Cathedral of Pisa, Italy, built in the second half of the eleventh century. Nearby is the cathedral bell tower of 1174—the "leaning Tower of Pisa"—which has settled alarmingly out of line. [Italian Government Travel Office, New York.]

resupply the new Christian settlements in the Near East not only reopened old trade routes that had long been closed by Arab domination of the Mediterranean but also established new ones. It is a commentary on both the degeneration of the original intent of the Crusades and their true historical importance that the Fourth Crusade (1202–1204) became an enterprising commercial venture manipulated by the Venetians.

Trade and the Growth of Towns (1100–1300)

During the centuries following the collapse of the Roman Empire, Western Europe became a closed and predominantly agricultural society, with small international commerce and even less urban culture. The great seaports of Italy were the exceptions. Venice, Pisa, and Genoa continued to trade actively with Constantinople and throughout the eastern Mediterranean, including Palestine, Syria, and Egypt, during the Middle Ages. The Venetians, Europe's most sober businessmen, jealously guarded their Eastern trade, attacking Western Christian competitors as quickly as Muslim predators. The latter were largely subdued by the success of the First Crusade, which proved a trade bonanza for Italian cities as the Mediterranean was opened to greater Western shipping. Venice, Pisa, and Genoa maintained major trading posts throughout the Mediterranean by the twelfth century. (See Map 14-2.)

THE NEW MERCHANT CLASS. The Western commercial revival attendant on these events repopulated the urban centers of the old Roman Empire and gave birth to new industries. Trade put both money and ideas into circulation. New riches, or the prospect of them, improved living conditions, raised hopes, and increased populations. In the twelfth century, Western Europe became a "boom-town." Among the most interesting creations were the traders themselves, who formed a new, distinctive social class. These prosperous merchants did not, as might first be suspected, spring from the landed nobility. They were, to the con-

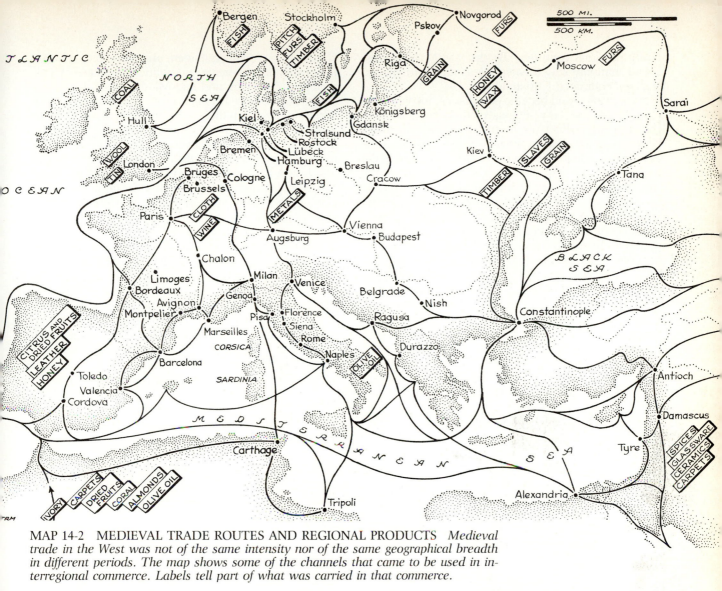

MAP 14-2 MEDIEVAL TRADE ROUTES AND REGIONAL PRODUCTS *Medieval trade in the West was not of the same intensity nor of the same geographical breadth in different periods. The map shows some of the channels that came to be used in interregional commerce. Labels tell part of what was carried in that commerce.*

trary, poor, landless adventurers who had absolutely nothing to lose and everything to gain by the risks of foreign trade. For mutual protection, they traveled together in great armed caravans, buying their products as cheaply as possible at the source and selling them as dearly as possible in Western marketplaces. They have been called the first Western capitalists, inspired by profit and devoted to little more than amassing fortunes. But their very greed and daring laid the foundations for Western urban life as we have come to know it today.

Although in power, wealth, and privilege the great merchants were destined to join and eventually eclipse the landed aristocracy, they were initially misfits in traditional medieval society. They were freemen, often possessed of great wealth, yet they neither owned land nor tilled the soil. They did not value land and farming but were persons of liquid wealth constantly on the

move. Aristocrats and clergy looked down on them as degenerates, and the commoners viewed them with suspicion. They were intruders within medieval society, a new breed who did not fit into the neat hierarchy of clergy, nobility, and serfs.

Merchants fanned out from the great Flemish and Italian trading centers: Bruges, Ghent, Venice, Pisa, Genoa, Florence. Wherever they settled in large numbers, they lobbied for the degree of freedom necessary for successful commerce, opposing tolls, tariffs, and other petty restrictions that discouraged the flow of trade. This activity brought them initially into conflict with the norms of static agricultural society. But as they demonstrated the many advantages of vigorous trade, the merchants progressively won their case. They not only remodeled city government to favor their new industries and the free flow of trade but also imparted to the cities an aura of importance unknown during previous centuries. By the late Middle Ages, cities commonly saw themselves as miniature states, even self-contained Christendoms.

As they grew and became prosperous, medieval cities also became very jealous of their good fortune. They took every measure to protect skilled industries, to expand trade, and to prevent competition from the surrounding countryside. Government remained in the hands of the rich and the few—patricians, *grandi*, the "old rich"—although wealthy merchants, aspiring to the noble style of life, increasingly found their way into the inner circles of government, as money proved early that it could talk. By the thirteenth century, city councils, operating on the basis of aristocratic constitutions and composed of patricians and wealthy merchants— the old rich *and* the new rich—internally controlled city life. These oligarchies were increasingly confronted by small artisans, who demanded improved living conditions and a role in making policy. Skilled artisans formed the far greater part of the new burgher class and organized to express their will through powerful corporations or craft guilds. These were exclusive organizations for the various skilled trades; they set

standards, certified craftsmen, and worked to enhance the economic well-being and political influence of their members. The high and late Middle Ages also saw a deepening conflict between craft masters, who were determined to keep their numbers at an absolute minimum, and journeymen, who found themselves frozen at the lower levels of their trade. The self-protectiveness and internal conflicts of medieval cities did not, however, prevent them from forming larger trade associations, such as the famous German Hanseatic League, or Hansa, which kept Baltic trade a German monopoly well into the fifteenth century.

CHANGES IN SOCIETY. The rise of a merchant class caused an important crack in the old social order. New-rich merchants, a class originally sprung from ordinary, landless people, broke into the aristocracy, and in doing so, they drew behind them the leadership of the new artisan class created by the urban industries that had grown up in the wake of growth of trade. In the late Middle Ages, the "middle classes" would firmly establish themselves.

Although from one perspective medieval towns

The English Nobility Imposes Restraints on King John

The gradual building of a sound English constitutional system in the Middle Ages was in danger of going awry if a monarch overstepped the fine line dividing necessary strength from outright despotism. The danger became acute under the rule of King John. The English nobility, therefore, forced the king's recognition of Magna Carta (1215), which reaffirmed the traditional rights and personal liberties of free men against royal authority. The document has remained enshrined in English law.

A free man shall not be fined for a small offense, except in proportion to the gravity of the offense: and for a great offense he shall be fined in proportion to the magnitude of the offense, saving his freehold; and a merchant in the same way, saving his merchandise; and the villein shall be fined in the same way, saving his wainage, if he shall be at our [i.e., the king's] mercy; and none of the above fines shall be imposed except by the oaths of honest men of the neighborhood. . . .

No constable or other bailiff of ours [i.e., the king] shall take anyone's grain or other chattels without immediately paying for them in money, unless he is able to obtain a postponement at the good will of the seller.

No constable shall require any knight to give money in place of his ward of a castle [i.e., standing guard] if he is willing to furnish that ward in his own person, or through another honest man if he himself is not able to

do it for a reasonable cause; and if we shall lead or send him into the army he shall be free from ward in proportion to the amount of time which he has been in the army through us.

No sheriff or bailiff of ours [i.e., the king], or any one else, shall take horses or wagons of any free man, for carrying purposes, except on the permission of that free man.

Neither we nor our bailiffs will take the wood of another man for castles, or for anything else which we are doing, except by the permission of him to whom the wood belongs. . . .

No free man shall be taken, or imprisoned, or dispossessed, or outlawed, or banished, or in any way injured, nor will we go upon him, nor send upon him, except by the legal judgment of his peers, or by the law of the land.

To no one will we sell, to no one will we deny or delay, right or justice. ❏

James Harvey Robinson (ed.), *Readings in European History*, Vol. 1 (Boston: Atheneaum, 1904), pp. 236–237.

were overly self-protective and "egoistic," they also became a force for innovation and change beyond their walls. This fact is all the more remarkable when it is remembered that towns at this time contained hardly more than 5 per cent of the population. Townspeople became a major force in the breakup of feudal society, aiding both kings and the peasantry at the expense of the landed nobility. Generally speaking, towns and kings tended to ally themselves against the great feudal lords. A notable exception may be seen in England, where the towns joined the barons against the oppressive monarchy of King John (1199–1216) and became a part of the parliamentary opposition. Townspeople generally, however, found their autonomy better preserved by having one distant master rather than several nearer and factious overlords. Kings, in turn, counted on the liquid wealth and administrative skills of the town-dwellers, who began to replace the clergy and the nobility in the royal bureaucracy. Urban money made it possible for kings to hire mercenary armies and thereby to decrease their dependence on the noble cavalry—an important step in the consolidation of territories divided for centuries by feudal allegiances and customs.

From the burgher ranks, kings drew the skilled lawyers who began the long process of replacing feudal custom with centralized Roman law, and towns also often had powerful militias that could be enlisted in royal service. Kings, in return, gave towns political recognition and guaranteed their constitutions (in formal charters) against territorial magnates. This was more easily done in the stronger coastal towns than in interior areas, where urban life remained less vigorous

and territorial power was on the rise. In France, towns became integrated into the royal government. In Germany and Austria, by contrast, towns fell under ever tighter control by territorial princes. In Italy, towns uniquely grew to absorb their surrounding territory, becoming city-states.

Towns also aided the peasantry, to the detriment of the landed nobility. A popular maxim of the time in German cities was: *Stadtluft macht frei*—"City air sets one free." Cities passed legislation making serfs who spent a year and a day within their walls freemen. New urban industries provided lucky peasants vocations alternative to farming. The new money economy made it possible for serfs or their urban patrons to buy their freedom from feudal services and rents as the latter became translatable into direct money payments. A serf or his patron could simply buy up the "contract." The growth of a free peasantry became especially evident in the thirteenth century.

All of this worked against the landed nobility. As urban trade and industries put more money into circulation, its value decreased (inflation). The great landowners, whose wealth was static, found themselves confronted, on the one hand, by serfs who longed to flee to the city and, on the other, by rising prices. They were losing their cheap labor supply and facing diminished productivity; at the same time, they had to pay more for their accustomed style of life. The nobility were not disciplined people, and many fell prey to money-wise urban merchants, who beat them out of their landed wealth.

The new urban economy worked, then, to free both kings and peasants from dependence on feudal lords,

The fortified city of Carcassonne in southern France, whose defenses date from the period 1240–1285, during the reigns of Louis IX and Philip the Bold. Note the protective walls and towers. [Bildarchiv Foto Marburg.]

although this was a long and complex process. As royal authority became centralized and kings were able to hire mercenary soldiers, the noble cavalry became militarily obsolescent, at most a minor part of the king's armed forces. And as towns and urban industries grew, attracting serfs from the farms, the nobility gradually lost its once all-powerful economic base. The long-term consequence: a strengthening of monarchy.

Medieval Universities and Scholasticism

Thanks to Spanish Muslim scholars, the logical works of Aristotle, the writings of Euclid and Ptolemy, the basic works of Greek physicians and Arab mathematicians, and the larger texts of Roman law became available to Western scholars in the early twelfth century. Muslim scholars preserved these works, translated portions of the Greek ones into Latin, and wrote extensive, thought-provoking commentaries on ancient texts. This renaissance of ancient knowledge, in turn, provided the occasion for the rise of universities.

BOLOGNA AND PARIS. The first important Western university was in Bologna. It received its formal grant of rights and privileges from the emperor Frederick Barbarossa in 1158. University members, like clergy, were granted royal immunity from local jurisdiction and were viewed by local townspeople as a group apart. In Bologna, we find the first formal organizations of students and professors and the first degree programs—the institutional foundations of the modern university.

The "university" was at first simply a program of study that gave the student a license to teach others. Originally, the term *university* meant no more than a group or corporation of individuals who were united by common self-interest and for mutual protection. As the local townspeople viewed both masters and students as foreigners without civil rights, such a union was necessary. It followed the model of a medieval trade guild. Bolognese students formed such a bloc in order to guarantee fair rents and prices from the townspeople and regular and high-quality teaching from their professors. Price gouging by townspeople was met with the threat to move the university to another town—a threat that could easily be carried out because the university at this time was not a great, fixed physical plant. Professors who failed to meet student expectations were boycotted. The mobility of the first universities gave them a unique independence.

Professors also formed protective associations and established procedures and standards for certification to teach within their ranks. The first academic degree was a certificate *(licentia docendi)* given by the professors' guild, which granted graduates in the liberal arts program or in the higher professional sciences of medicine, theology, and the law "the right to teach anywhere" *(ius ubique docendi)*.

Bologna was distinguished as the center for the revival of Roman law. From the seventh to the eleventh centuries, only the most rudimentary manuals of Roman law were available to be circulated. With the growth of trade and towns in the late eleventh century, Western scholars came into contact with the larger and more important parts of the Roman *Corpus Juris Civilis* of Justinian. The study and dissemination of this new material was directed by Irnerius (fl. early twelfth century). He and his students made authoritative commentaries or glosses on individual laws following their broad knowledge of the *Corpus Juris*. Around 1140, a monk named Gratian, also a resident of Bologna, created the standard legal text in church or canon law, the *Concordance of Discordant Canons*, known more commonly as Gratian's *Decretum*.

As Bologna provided the model for southern European universities and the study of law, Paris became the model for northern Europe and the study of theology. Oxford, Cambridge, and, much later, Heidelberg were among Paris's imitators. All these universities required a foundation in the liberal arts for further study in the higher sciences of medicine, theology, and law. The arts program consisted of the *trivium* (grammar, rhetoric, and logic) and the *quadrivium* (arithmetic, geometry, astronomy, and music). Before the emergence of the universities, the liberal arts had been taught in the cathedral and monastery schools, that is, schools attached to cathedrals or monasteries for the purpose of training clergy. The most famous of the cathedral schools were those of Rheims and Chartres.

The University of Paris grew institutionally out of the cathedral school of Nôtre Dame, receiving its charter in 1200 from King Philip Augustus and Pope Innocent III. Papal sanction and regulations, among them the right of the faculty to strike, were issued in 1231 in the bull *Parens scientiarum* and gave the university freedom from local church control. At this time, the University of Paris consisted of independent faculties of arts, canon law, medicine, and theology, with the masters of arts, who were grouped together in four national factions (French, Norman, English–German, and Picard), the dominant faculty.

At Paris, the college system originated. At first, colleges were no more than hospices providing room and board for poor students. But the educational life of the university rapidly expanded into these fixed buildings and began to thrive on their sure endowments. In Paris, the most famous college was the Sorbonne, founded around 1257 by Robert de Sorbon, chaplain to

The seven liberal arts of the medieval university curriculum: rhetoric, geometry, astronomy, music, natural and moral philosophy, and theology. At their feet sit the great teachers of antiquity: Cicero, Euclid, Ptolemey, Aristotle, Seneca, and Augustine. [Art Resource.]

the king, for the purpose of educating advanced theological students. In Oxford and Cambridge, the colleges became the basic unit of student life, indistinguishable from the university. By the fifteenth and sixteenth centuries, colleges had tied the universities to physical plants and fixed foundations, restricting their previous autonomy and freedom of movement.

THE CURRICULUM. Before the twelfth century the education available within the cathedral and monastic schools was quite limited. Students learned grammar, rhetoric, and elementary geometry and astronomy. They used the Latin grammars of Donatus and Priscian and studied Saint Augustine's *On Christian Doctrine*, Cassiodorus' *On Divine and Secular Learning*, and the various writings of Boethius (d. 524). Boethius was important for instruction in arithmetic and music and especially for the transmission of the small body of Aristotle's logical works known before the twelfth century. After the textual finds of the early twelfth century, Western scholars had the whole of Aristotle's logic, the astronomy of Ptolemy, the writings of Euclid, and many Latin classics. By the mid-thirteenth century the ethical, physical, and metaphysical writings of Aristotle were in circulation in the West.

In the high Middle Ages the learning process was very basic. The student wrote commentaries on authoritative texts, especially those of Aristotle. The teachers encouraged their students not to strive independently for undiscovered truth, but to organize and harmonize the accepted truths of tradition. The basic assumption was that truth already existed. It had only to be organized and elucidated. Such conviction made logic and dialectic supreme within the liberal arts.

The Scholastic program of study, based on logic and dialectic, reigned supreme in all the faculties—in law and medicine as well as in philosophy and theology. Scholasticism was a peculiar method of study. The student read the traditional authorities in his field,

Bishop Stephen Complains about the New Scholastic Learning

Scholasticism involved an intellectual, learned approach to religion and its doctrines rather than simple, uncritical piety. Many saw in it a threat to the study of the Bible and the Church Fathers, as doctrines that should simply be believed and revered were rationally dissected for their logical meaning by allegedly presumptuous and none-too-well-trained youths. Here is a particularly graphic description of the threat, replete with classical allusion, as perceived by Stephen, Bishop of Tournai, in a letter to the pope written between 1192 and 1203.

The studies of sacred letters among us are fallen into the workshop of confusion, while both disciples applaud novelties alone and masters watch out for glory rather than learning. They everywhere compose new and recent *summulae* [little summaries] and commentaries, by which they attract, detain, and deceive their hearers, as if the works of the holy fathers were not still sufficient, who, we read, expounded Holy Scripture in the same spirit in which we believe the apostles and prophets composed it. They prepare strange and exotic courses for their banquet, when at the nuptials of the son of the king of Taurus his own flesh and blood are killed and all prepared, and the wedding guests have only to take and eat what is set before them. Contrary to the sacred canons there is public disputation over the incomprehensible deity; concerning the incarnation of the Word, verbose flesh and blood irreverently litigate. The indivisible Trinity is cut up and wrangled over . . . so that now there are as many errors as doctors, as many scandals as classrooms, as many blasphemies as squares. . . . Faculties called liberal having lost their pristine liberty are sunk in such servitude that adolescents with long hair impudently usurp their professorships, and beardless youths sit in the seat of their seniors, and those who don't yet know how to be disciples strive to be named masters. And they write their *summulae* moistened with drool and dribble but unseasoned with the salt of philosophers. Omitting the rules of the arts and discarding the authentic books of the artificers, they seize the flies of empty words in their sophisms like the claws of spiders. Philosophy cries out that her garments are torn and disordered and, modestly concealing her nudity by a few specific tatters, neither is consulted nor consoles as of old. All these things, father, call for the hand of apostolic correction. . . . ❏

Lynn Thorndike, *University Records and Life in the Middle Ages* (New York: Octagon Books, 1971), pp. 22–24.

formed short summaries of their teaching, disputed it by elaborating arguments pro and con, and then drew his own modest conclusions. The twelfth century saw the rise of the "summa," a summary of all that was known about a topic, and works whose sole purpose was to conciliate traditional authorities.

Society

The Order of Life

Four basic social groups were distinguished in the Middle Ages: those who fought (the landed nobility), those who prayed (the clergy), those who labored (the peasantry), and, after the revival of towns in the eleventh century, those who traded and manufactured (the townspeople). It would be false to view each of these groups as closed and homogeneous. Throughout medieval society, like tended to be attracted to like regardless of social grouping. Barons, archbishops, rich farmers, and successful merchants had far more in common with each other than they did with the middle and lower strata of their various professions.

NOBLES. As a distinctive social group, all noblemen did not begin simply as great men with large hereditary lands. Many rose from the ranks of feudal vassals or warrior knights. The successful vassal attained a special social and legal status based on his landed wealth (accumulated fiefs), his exercise of authority over others, and his distinctive social customs—all of which set him apart from others in medieval society. By the late Middle Ages there had evolved a distinguishable higher and lower nobility living in both town and country. The higher were the great landowners and territorial magnates; the lower were petty landlords, descendants from minor knights, new-rich merchants who could buy country estates, and wealthy farmers patiently risen from ancestral serfdom.

It was a special mark of the nobility that they lived on the labor of others. Basically lord of manors, the nobility of the early and high Middle Ages neither tilled the soil like the peasantry nor engaged in the commerce of merchants—activities considered beneath their dignity. The nobleman resided in a country mansion or, if he were particularly wealthy, a castle. He was drawn to the countryside as much by personal preference as by the fact that his fiefs were usually rural manors. Arms were his profession; the nobleman's sole occupation and reason for living was waging war. His fief provided the means to acquire the expensive military equipment that his rank required, and he maintained his enviable position as he had gained it, by fighting for his chief.

The nobility accordingly celebrated the physical strength, courage, and constant activity of warfare. Warring gave them both new riches and an opportunity to gain honor and glory. Knights were paid a share in the plunder of victory, and in time of war everything became fair game. Special war wagons, designed for the collection and transport of booty, followed them into battle. Periods of peace were greeted with great sadness, as they meant economic stagnation and boredom. Whereas the peasants and the townspeople counted on peace as the condition of their occupational success, the nobility despised it as unnatural to their profession. They looked down on the peasantry as cowards who ran and hid in time of war. Urban merchants, who amassed wealth by business methods strange to feudal society, were held in equal contempt, which increased as the affluence and political power of the townspeople grew. The nobility possessed as strong a sense of superiority over these "unwarlike" people as the clergy did over the general run of laity.

The nobleman nurtured his sense of distinctiveness within medieval society by the chivalric ritual of dubbing to knighthood, a ceremonial entrance into the noble class that became almost a religious sacrament. The ceremony was preceded by a bath of purification, confession, communion, and a prayer vigil. Thereafter the priest blessed the knight's standard, lance, and sword. As prayers were chanted, the priest girded the knight with his sword and presented him his shield, enlisting him as much in the defense of the church as in the service of his lord. Dubbing raised the nobleman to a state as sacred in his sphere as clerical ordination made the priest in his. This comparison is quite legitimate. The clergy and the nobility were medieval society's privileged estates. The appointment of noblemen to high ecclesiastical office and their eager participation in the church's Crusades had strong ideological and social underpinnings as well as economic and political motives.

In peacetime, the nobility had two favorite amusements: hunting and tournaments. Because of the threat to towns and villages posed by wild animals, the great hunts actually aided the physical security of

A miniature from the Codex Manesse showing lords tilting as their ladies "ooh" and "aah." [Universitatsbibliothek, Heidelberg.]

the ordinary people, while occupying the restless noblemen. However, where they could, noblemen progressively monopolized the rights to game, forbidding the commoners from hunting in the "lord's" forests. This practice built resentment among the common people to the level of revolt. Free game, fishing, and access to wood were basic demands in the petitions of grievance and the revolts of the peasantry throughout the high and later Middle Ages.

From the repeated assemblies in the courts of barons and kings, set codes of social conduct or "courtesy" developed in noble circles. With the French leading the way, mannered behavior and court etiquette became almost as important as battlefield expertise. Knights became literate gentlemen, and lyric poets sang and moralized at court. The cultivation of a code of behavior and a special literature to eulogize it was not unrelated to problems within the social life of the nobility. Noblemen were notorious philanderers; their illegitimate children mingled openly with their legitimate offspring in their houses. The advent of courtesy was, in part, an effort to reform this situation. Although the poetry of courtly love was sprinkled with frank eroticism and the beloved in these epics were married women pursued by those to whom they were not married, the love recommended by the poet was usually love at a distance, unconsummated by sexual intercourse. It was love without touching, a kind of sex without physical sex, and only as such was it considered ennobling. Court poets depicted those who did carnally consummate their illicit love as reaping at least as much suffering as joy from it.

By the fourteenth century, several factors forced the landed nobility into a steep economic and political decline from which it never recovered. These were the great population losses of the fourteenth century brought on by the Great Plague; the changes in military tactics occasioned by the use of infantry and heavy artillery during the Hundred Years' War; and the alliance of the wealthy towns with the king. Generally, one can speak of a waning of the landed nobility after the fourteenth century. Thereafter, the effective possession of land and wealth counted far more than parentage and family tree as qualification for entrance into the highest social class.

CLERGY. Unlike the nobility and the peasantry, the clergy was an open estate. Although clerical ranks reflected the social classes from which the clergy came and a definite clerical hierarchy formed, one was still a cleric by religious training and ordination, not by the circumstances of birth or military prowess. There were two basic types of clerical vocation: the regular and the secular clergy. The former were the orders of monks, who lived according to a special ascetic rule (regula) in cloisters separated from the world. They were the spiritual elite among the clergy, and theirs was not a way of life lightly entered. Canon law required that one be at least twenty-one years of age before making a final profession of the monastic vows of poverty, chastity, and obedience. Their personal sacrifices and high religious ideals made the monks much respected in high medieval society.

Although many monks (and also nuns, who increasingly embraced the vows of poverty, obedience, and chastity without a clerical rank) secluded themselves altogether, the regular clergy were never completely cut off from the secular world. They maintained frequent contact with the laity through such charitable activities as feeding the destitute and tending the sick, through liberal arts instruction in monastic schools, through special pastoral commissions from the pope, and as supplemental preachers and confessors in parish churches during Lent and other peak religious seasons. It became the special mark of the Dominican and Franciscan friars to live a common life according to a

The Stigmatization of St. Francis (early fourteenth century) by Giotto. In a vision on Mt. Alverna, St. Francis is said to have received the wounds of Christ (the stigmata) in his own body and to have borne them for almost two years before his death in 1226. The small lower panels show Francis saving the church, receiving with his followers the Franciscans' charter from the pope, and—characteristically—preaching to the birds. [Musée du Louvre, Paris. Cliché des Musées Nationaux.]

special rule, and still to be active in worldly ministry. Some monks, because of their learning and rhetorical skills, even rose to prominence as secretaries and private confessors to kings and queens.

The secular clergy were those who lived and worked directly among the laity in the world (saeculum). They formed a vast hierarchy. There were the high prelates—the wealthy cardinals, archbishops, and bishops, who were drawn almost exclusively from the nobility—the urban priests, the cathedral canons, and the court clerks; and, finally, the great

Saint Francis of Assisi Sets Out His Religious Ideals

Saint Francis of Assisi (1182–1226) was the founder of the Franciscan Order of friars. Here are some of his religious principles as stated in the definitive Rule of the Order, approved by the pope in 1223; the rule especially stresses the ideal of living in poverty.

This is the rule and way of living of the Minorite brothers, namely, to observe the holy Gospel of our Lord Jesus Christ, living in obedience, without personal possessions, and in chastity. Brother Francis promises obedience and reverence to our lord Pope Honorius, and to his successors who canonically enter upon their office, and to the Roman Church. And the other brothers shall be bound to obey Brother Francis and his successors.

I firmly command all the brothers by no means to receive coin or money, of themselves or through an intervening person. But for the needs of the sick and for clothing the other brothers, the ministers alone and the guardians shall provide through spiritual friends, as it may seem to them that necessity demands, according to time, place, and the coldness of the temperature. This one thing being always borne in mind, that, as has been said, they receive neither coin nor money.

Those brothers to whom God has given the ability to labor shall do so faithfully and devoutly, but in such manner that idleness, the enemy of the soul, being averted, they may not extinguish the spirit of holy prayer and devotion, to which other temporal things should be subservient. As a reward, moreover, for their labor, they may receive for themselves and their brothers the necessities of life, but not coin or money; and this humbly, as becomes the servants of God and the followers of most holy poverty.

The brothers shall appropriate nothing to themselves, neither a house, nor a place, nor anything; but as pilgrims and strangers in this world, in poverty and humility serving God, they shall confidently go seeking for alms. Nor need they be ashamed, for the Lord made Himself poor for us in this world. ❑

A Source Book of Medieval History, ed. by Frederic Austin Ogg (New York: Cooper Square Publishers, 1972), pp. 375–376.

---

mass of poor parish priests, who were neither financially nor intellectually very far above the common people they served (the basic educational requirement was an ability to say the Mass). Until the Gregorian reform in the eleventh century began to reverse the trend, parish priests lived with women in a relationship akin to marriage, and their concubines and children were accepted within the communities they served. Because of their relative poverty, it was not unusual for priests to "moonlight" as teachers, artisans, or farmers, a practice also accepted and even admired by their parishioners.

During the greater part of the Middle Ages, the clergy were the "first estate," and theology was the queen of the sciences. How did the clergy come into such prominence? It was basically popular reverence for the clergy's role as mediator between God and humanity that made this superiority possible. The priest brought the very Son of God down to earth when he celebrated the sacrament of the Eucharist; his absolution released penitents from punishment for mortal sin. Theologians elaborated the distinction between the clergy and the laity very much to the clergy's benefit. The belief in the superior status of the clergy underlay the evolution of clerical privileges and immunities in both person and property. As holy persons, the clergy could not be taxed by secular rulers without special permission from the proper ecclesiastical authorities. Clerical crimes fell under the jurisdiction of special ecclesiastical courts, not the secular courts. Because churches and monasteries were deemed holy places, they too were free from secular taxation and legal jurisdiction.

By the fourteenth century, townspeople came increasingly to resent the special immunities of the clergy. They complained that it was not proper for the clergy to have greater privileges yet far fewer responsibilities than all others who lived within the town walls. Although the separation of Church and State and the distinction between the clergy and the laity have persisted into modern times, after the fifteenth century the clergy ceased to be the superior class that they had been for so much of the Middle Ages.

PEASANTS. The largest and lowest social group in medieval society was the one on whose labor the welfare of all the others depended: the agrarian peasantry. They lived on and worked the manors of the nobility, the primitive cells of rural social life, and all were to one degree or another dependent on their lords and considered their property. The manor had originally been a plot of land within a village, ranging from twelve to seventy-five acres in size, assigned to a certain member by a settled tribe or clan. This member

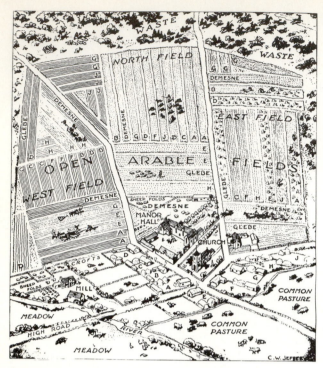

For hundreds of years and over a great part of Europe the manor was basic for much of the population. Despite regional variation and changes that came with the revival of trade and growth of towns, manors in the West had enough common features to justify this modern reconstruction of a characteristic example. Note the lord's hall and lands (demesne), *the peasant village with common grounds and services for the nine families* (a-j) *dwelling on this manor, the church and its lands* (glebe), *peasant holdings in open fields, and areas for woodcutting and hunting. [The Granger Collection.]*

and his family became lords of the land, and those who came to dwell there formed a smaller self-sufficient community within a larger village community. In the early Middle Ages, such a manor consisted of the dwellings of the lord and his family, the cottages of the peasant workers, agricultural sheds, and fields. The landowner or lord of the manor required a certain amount of produce (grain, eggs, and the like) and a certain number of services from the peasant families who came to dwell on and farm his land. The tenants were free to divide the labor as they wished, and what goods remained after the lord's levies were met were their own. A powerful lord might own many such manors, and kings later based their military and tax assessments on the number of manors owned by a vassal landlord.

There were both servile and free manors. The tenants of the latter had originally been freemen known as *coloni*, original inhabitants and petty landowners who

swapped their small possessions for a guarantee of security from a more powerful lord, who came in this way to possess their land. Unlike the pure serfdom of the servile manors, whose tenants had no original claim to a part of the land, the tenancy obligations on free manors tended to be limited and their rights more carefully defined. Tenants of servile manors were by comparison far more vulnerable to the whims of their landlords. These two types of manor tended, however, to merge; the most common situation was the manor on which tenants of greater and lesser degrees of servitude dwelt together, their services to the lord defined by their personal status and local custom.

Marc Bloch, the modern authority on manorial society, has vividly depicted the duties of tenancy:

On certain days the tenant brings the lord's steward perhaps a few small silver coins or, more often, sheaves of grain harvested on his fields, chickens from his farm yard, cakes of wax from his beehives or from the swarms of the neighboring forest. At other times he works on the arable or the meadows of the demesne [the lord's plot of land in the manoral fields, between one third and one half of that available]. Or else we find him carting casks of wine or sacks of grain on behalf of the master to distant residences. His is the labour which repairs the walls or moats of the castle. If the master has guests the peasant strips his own bed to provide the necessary extra bedclothes. When the hunting season comes round he feeds the pack. If war breaks out he does duty as a footsoldier or orderly, under the leadership of the reeve of the village.[2]

The lord also had the right to subject his tenants to exactions known as *banalities*. He could, for example, force them to breed their cows with his bull, and to pay for the privilege, as well as to grind their corn in his mill, bake their bread in his oven, make their wine in his wine press, buy their beer from his brewery, and even surrender to him the tongues or other choice parts of all animals slaughtered on his lands. He had the right to levy small taxes at will.

Exploited as the serfs may appear to have been from a modern point of view, their status was far from outright chattel slavery. It was to the lord's advantage to keep his serfs healthy and happy; his welfare, like theirs, depended on a successful harvest. Serfs had their own dwellings and modest strips of land and lived by the produce of their own labor and organization. They were permitted to market for their own profit what surpluses might remain after the harvest. They were free to choose their spouses within the local village, although the lord's permission was required if a wife or husband was sought from another village. And serfs were able to pass a goodly portion of their

[2]*Feudal Society*, trans. by L. A. Manyon (Chicago: University of Chicago Press, 1968), p. 250.

A woodcut showing wild animals damaging peasant crops. One of the greatest problems for peasants was how to protect their crops from stags and deer. Forbidden by law from hunting then, the peasants built fences and used clubs to drive the animals away. [Deutsche Fotothek, Dresden.]

property (their dwellings and field strips) and worldly goods on to their children.

Two basic changes occurred in the evolution of the manor from the early to the later Middle Ages. The first was the fragmentation of the manor and the rise to dominance of the single-family unit. As the lords parceled out their land to new tenants, their own plots became progressively smaller. The increase in the number of tenants and the decrease in the lord's fields brought about a corresponding reduction in the labor services exacted from the tenants. In France, by the reign of Louis IX (1226–1270), only a few days a year were required, whereas in the time of Charlemagne, peasants had worked the lord's fields several days a week. By the twelfth century, the manor was hopelessly fragmented. As the single-family unit replaced the clan as the basic nuclear group, assessments of goods and services fell on individual fields and households, no longer on manors as a whole. Family farms replaced manorial units. Children continued to live with their parents after marriage, and several generations of one family could be found within a single household, although nuclear families were also commonplace. The peasants' carefully nurtured communal life made possible a family's retention of its land and dwelling after the death of the head of the household. In this way, land and property remained in the possession of a single family from generation to generation.

The second change in the evolution of the manor was the translation of feudal dues into money pay-

ments, a change made possible by the revival of trade and the rise of the towns. This development, which was completed by the thirteenth century, permitted serfs to hold their land as rent-paying tenants and to overcome their servile status. Although tenants thereby gained greater freedom, they were not necessarily better off materially. Whereas servile workers had been able to count on the benevolent assistance of their landlords in hard times, rent-paying workers were left by and large to their own devices; their independence caused some landlords to treat them with indifference and even resentment.

Lands and properties that had been occupied by generations of peasants and recognized as their own were always under the threat of the lord's claim to a prior right of inheritance and even outright usurpation. As their demesnes declined, the lords were increasingly tempted to encroach on such traditionally common lands. The peasantry fiercely resisted such efforts, instinctively clinging to the little they had. In many regions, they successfully organized to win a role in the choice of petty rural officials. By the mid-fourteenth century, a declining nobility in England and France, faced with the ravages of the great plague and the Hundred Years' War, attempted to turn back the historical clock by increasing taxes on the peasantry and passing laws to restrict their migration into the cities. The peasantry responded with armed revolts in the countryside. These revolts were rural equivalents of the organization of late medieval cities in sworn communes to protect their self-interests against rulers. The revolts of the agrarian peasantry, like those of the urban proletariat, were brutally crushed. They stand out at the end of the Middle Ages as violent testimony to the breakup of medieval society. As growing national sentiment would break its political unity and heretical movements would end its nominal religious oneness, the revolts of the peasantry revealed the absence of medieval social unity.

TOWNSPEOPLE. In the eleventh century, towns and cities held only about 5 per cent of Western Europe's population. Nonetheless, one could find there the whole of medieval society: nobles visiting their townhouses, peasants living or working within the walls, resident monks and priests, university scholars, great merchants and poor journeymen, pilgrims

A medieval shoemaker. Guilds of shoemakers date back to Ancient Rome. In the Middle Ages most people wore homemade clogs or wooden shoes. Leather shoes made to order by skilled craftsmen could be quite costly and elaborate in style and were mostly for the upper classes. [Vincent Virga Archives.]

en route to shrines, and beggars passing through. By modern comparison, the great majority of medieval towns were merely small villages. Of some three thousand late medieval German towns, for example, twenty-eight hundred had populations under 1,000 and only fifteen had in excess of 10,000 inhabitants. Only London, Paris, and the great merchant capitals of Italy—Florence, Venice, and Naples—approached 100,000 by the fifteenth century.

Women appear to have slightly outnumbered men. War, the perils of long-distance travel, and illnesses resulting from immoderation in food and drink combined to reduce male ranks. The frequent remarriage of widows, whose inheritances made them attractive mates, and the church's siphoning off of an already short supply of eligible bachelors into monasteries contributed to the large number of unmarried women. Those from the upper classes entered nunneries and beguinages, and the very poor joined wandering bands of prostitutes. The great mass of lower and middle strata married women worked as virtual partners in their husbands' trade or craft. It has been speculated that the fact that unmarried women formed a large, unproductive surplus contributed to the prejudice of late medieval society against them and made them the more vulnerable targets of the great witch hunts of the fifteenth and sixteenth centuries.

The term *bourgeois* first appeared in the eleventh century to describe a new addition to the three traditional social ranks of knight (noble), cleric, and serf. The term initially designated the merchant groups, who formed new communities or "bourgs" as bases of operation in or around the old Roman towns that were governed by the landed nobility. These men, whose business was long-distance trade and commerce, were at first highly suspect within traditional medieval society. Clerics condemned the profits they gained from lending money as immoral usury, and noblemen viewed their fluid wealth and mobility as politically disruptive. The merchants in turn resented the laws and customs of feudal society that gave the nobility and the clergy special privileges. Town life was often disrupted because regional laws permitted the nobility and the clergy to live beyond the rules that governed the activities of everyone else.

Merchants especially wanted an end to the arbitrary tolls and tariffs imposed by regional magnates over the surrounding countryside. Such regulations hampered and could even bring to a standstill the flow of commerce on which both merchants and craftsmen in the growing urban export industries depended. The townspeople needed simple, uniform laws and a government sympathetic to their business interests; they wanted a government in which merchants and craftsmen had a major voice. That need created internal and external struggles with the old landed nobility. This

The vast majority of medieval women were working peasants and townswomen. This fourteenth century English manuscript shows women carrying jugs of fresh milk from the sheep pen. [Trustees of the British Museum.]

basic conflict led towns in the high and late Middle Ages to form their own independent communes and to ally themselves with kings against the nobility—developments that created a powerful challenge to feudal society.

Despite unified resistance to external domination, the medieval town was not an internally harmonious social unit. It was a collection of many selfish, competitive communities. Only families of long standing and those who owned property had the full rights of citizenship and a say in the town's government. Workers in the same trade lived together on streets that bore their name, apparently doing so as much to monitor one another's business practices as to dwell among peers. Sumptuary laws regulated not only the dress but even the architecture of the residences of the various social groups. Merchant guilds appeared in the eleventh century and were followed in the twelfth by the craft guilds (organizations of drapers, haberdashers, furriers, hosiers, goldsmiths, and so on). These organizations existed solely to advance the business interests of their members and to advance their personal well-being. They won favorable government policies and served as collection agencies for the unpaid accounts of individual members. The guilds also formed distinctive religious confraternities, close-knit associations that ministered to the needs of member families in both life and death.

The merchants and the stronger craft guilds quickly won a role in town government. "New-rich" patricians married into the old nobility and aped their social customs. Sharing the power of government in the city councils, the craft guilds used their position in the most selfish way to limit their membership, to regulate their own wages favorably, and to establish exacting standards of workmanship so that their products could not be copied by others. Trademarks first appeared in the twelfth century. So rigid and exclusive did the dominant guilds become that they stifled their own creativity and inflamed the journeymen who were excluded from joining their ranks. In the fourteenth century, unrepresented artisans and craftsmen, a true urban proletariat prevented by law from either forming their own guilds or entering the existing guilds, revolted in a number of places: Florence, Paris, and the cities of Flanders. Their main opponents were the merchant and craft guilds, which had themselves risen to prominence by opposing the antiquated laws and privileges of the old nobility.

Medieval Women

The image and the reality of medieval women are two very different things. The image, both for contemporaries and for us today, was strongly influenced by male Christian clergy, whose ideal was the celibate life of chastity, poverty, and obedience. Drawing on classical, medical, philosophical, and legal traditions that predated Christianity, as well as on ancient biblical theology, Christian theologians depicted women as physically, mentally, and morally weaker than men. On the basis of such assumptions, medieval church and society sanctioned the coercive treatment of women, including corrective wife-beating. Christian clergy generally considered marriage a debased state by comparison with the religious life, and in their writings they praised virgins and celibate widows over wives. Women, as the Bible clearly taught, were the "weaker vessel." In marriage, their role was to be subject and obedient to their husbands, who, as the stronger partners, had a duty to protect and discipline them.

This image of the medieval woman suggests that she had two basic options in life: to become either a subjugated housewife or a confined nun. In reality, the vast majority of medieval women were neither.

Both within and outside Christianity this image of women—not yet to speak of the reality of their lives—was contradicted. In chivalric romances and courtly love literature of the twelfth and thirteenth centuries, as in the contemporaneous cult of the Virgin Mary, women were presented as objects of service and devotion to be praised and admired, even put on pedestals and treated as superior to men. If the Church shared traditional misogynist sentiments, it also condemned them, as in the case of the *Romance of the Rose* (late thirteenth century) and other popular "bawdy" literature. The learned churchman Peter Lombard (1100–1169) sanctioned an image of women that was often invoked in didactic Christian literature. Why, he asked, was Eve created from Adam's rib and not instead taken from his head or his feet? The answer was clear. God took Eve from Adam's side because he wanted woman neither to rule over nor to be enslaved by man, but to stand squarely at his side, as his companion and partner in mutual aid and trust. By so insisting on the spiritual equality of men and women and their shared responsibility to one another within marriage, the Church also helped to raise the dignity of women.

Women also had basic rights under secular law that prevented them from being treated as mere chattel. All the major Germanic law codes recognized the economic freedom of women, that is, their right to inherit, administer, dispose of, and confer on their children family property and wealth. They could press charges in court against men for bodily injury and rape. Depending on the country in question, punishments for rape ranged from fines, flogging, and banishment to blinding, castration, and death.

The nunnery was an option for only a very small number of unmarried women from the uppermost classes. Entrance required a dowry *(dos)* and could be almost as expensive as a wedding, although usually it was less. Within the nunnery, a woman could rise to a position of leadership as abbess or mother superior and could exercise an organizational and administrative authority denied her in much of secular life. How-

ever, the nunneries of the established religious orders were also under male supervision, so that even abbesses had finally to answer to higher male authority.

Nunneries also provided women an escape from the debilitating effects of multiple pregnancies. When, in the ninth century, under the influence of Christianity, the Carolingians made monogamous marriage their official policy (heretofore they had practiced polygyny and concubinage and had permitted divorce), it was both a boon and a burden to women. On the one hand, the selection of a wife now became a very special event. Wives gained greater dignity and legal security. On the other hand, a woman's labor as household manager and the bearer of children greatly increased. The aristocratic wife not only ran a large household but was also the agent of her husband during his absence. In addition to these responsibilities, one wife now had sole responsibility for the propagation of heirs. Such demands clearly took their toll. The mortality rates of Frankish women increased and their longevity decreased after the ninth century. The Carolingian wife also became the sole object of her husband's wrath and displeasure. Under such conditions, the cloister could serve as a welcome refuge to women. However, the number of women in cloisters was never very great. In late medieval England, for example, there are estimated to have been no more than thirty-five hundred.

The vast majority of medieval women were neither aristocratic housewives nor nuns, but working women. Every evidence suggests that they were respected and loved by their husbands, perhaps because they worked shoulder by shoulder and hour by hour with them. Between the ages of ten and fifteen, girls were apprenticed in a trade much as were boys, and they learned to be skilled workers. If they married, they either continued their particular trade, operating their bakeshops or dress shops next to their husbands' businesses, or they became assistants and partners in the shops of their husbands. Women appeared in virtually every "blue-collar" trade, from butchers to goldsmiths, although they were especially active in the food and clothing industries. Women belonged to guilds, just like men, and they became craftmasters. In the later Middle Ages, townswomen increasingly had the opportunity to go to school and to gain vernacular literacy.

It is also true that women did not have as wide a range of vocations as men. They were excluded from the learned professions of scholarship, medicine, and law. They often found their freedom of movement within a profession more carefully regulated than a man's. Usually women performed the same work as men for a wage 25 per cent lower. And, as is still true today, they filled the ranks of domestic servants in disproportionate numbers. Still, women were as prominent and as creative a part of workaday medieval society as men.

Medieval Children

Historians have found much evidence to suggest that medieval parents remained emotionally distant from their children, showing them little interest and affection. Evidence of low parental regard for children comes from a variety of sources. First, the art and sculpture of the Middle Ages rarely portray children as distinct from adults; pictorially, children and adults look alike. Then, there was high infant and child mortality, which could only have made emotional investment in children risky. How could a medieval parent, knowing that a child had a 30–50 per cent chance of dying before age five, dare become too emotionally attached?

Also, during the Middle Ages, children directly assumed adult responsibilities. The children of peasants became laborers in the fields alongside their parents as soon as they could physically manage the work. Urban artisans and burghers sent their children out of their homes to apprentice in various crafts and trades between the ages of eight and twelve. In many, perhaps most, instances a child was placed in the home of a known relative or friend, but often he or she ended up with a mere acquaintance, even a complete stranger. That children were expected to grow up fast in the Middle Ages is also suggested by the canonical ages for marriage: twelve for girls and fourteen for boys.

Infanticide is an even more striking indication of low esteem for children. The ancient Romans exposed unwanted children at birth. In this way they regulated family size, though the surviving children appear to have been given both attention and affection. The Germanic tribes of medieval Europe, by contrast, had large families but tended to neglect their children. Infanticide appears to have been directed primarily against girls. Early medieval penance books and church synods condemned the practice outright and also forbade parents to sleep with infants and small children, as this became an occasion and an excuse (alleged accidental suffocation) for killing them.

Also, among the German tribes one paid a much lower *wergild*, or fine, for injury to a child than for injury to an adult. The *wergild* for injuring a child was only one fifth that for injuring an adult. That paid for injury to a female child under fifteen was one half that for injury to a male child—a strong indication that female children were the least esteemed members of German tribal society. Mothers appear also to have nursed boys longer than they did girls, which favored boys' health and survival. However, a woman's *wergild* increased a full eightfold between infancy and her

Children watching a puppet show. [Trustees of the British Museum.]

childbearing years, at which time she had obviously become highly prized.[3]

Despite such varied evidence of parental neglect of children, there is another side to the story. Since the early Middle Ages, physicians and theologians, at least, have clearly understood childhood to be a distinct and special stage of life. Isidore of Seville (560–636), the metropolitan of Seville and a leading intellectual authority throughout the Middle Ages, carefully distinguished six ages of life, the first four of which were infancy (between one and seven years of age), childhood (seven to fourteen), adolescence, and youth.

According to the medical authorities, infancy proper extended from birth to anywhere between six months and two years (depending on the authority) and covered the period of speechlessness and suckling. The period thereafter, until age seven, was considered a higher level of infancy, marked by the beginning of a child's ability to speak and his or her weaning. At age seven, when a child could think and act decisively and speak clearly, childhood proper began. After this point, a child could be reasoned with, could profit from regular discipline, and could begin to train for a life-long vocation. At seven a child was ready for schooling, private tutoring, or an apprenticeship in a chosen craft or trade. Until physical growth was completed, however—and that could extend to twenty-one years of age—a child or youth was legally under the guardianship of parents or a surrogate authority.

There is evidence that high infant and child mortality, rather than distancing parents from children, actually made parents look on them as all the more precious. The medical authorities of the Middle Ages were those of antiquity—Hippocrates, Galen, and Soranus of Ephesus. They dealt at length with postnatal care and childhood diseases. Both in learned and popular medicine, sensible as well as fanciful cures can be found for the leading killers of children (diarrhea, worms, pneumonia, and fever). When infants and children died, medieval parents grieved as pitiably as modern parents do. In the art and literature of the Middle Ages, we find mothers baptizing dead infants and children or carrying them to pilgrim shrines in the hope of reviving them. There are also examples of mental illness and suicide brought on by the death of a child.[4]

We also find a variety of children's toys, even devices like walkers and potty chairs, clear evidence of special attention being paid to children. The medieval authorities on child rearing widely condemned child abuse and urged moderation in the disciplining of children. In church art and drama, parents were urged to love their children as Mary loved Jesus. By the high Middle Ages, if not earlier, children were widely viewed as special creatures with their own needs and possessed of their own rights.

---

[3] David Herlihy, "Medieval Children," in *Essays on Medieval Civilization*, ed. by B. K. Lackner and K. R. Phelp (University of Texas Press, 1978), pp. 109–131.

[4] Klaus Arnold, *Kind und Gesellschaft im Mittelalter und Renaissance* (Paderborn, 1980), pp. 31, 37.

Politics

England and France: Hastings (1066) to Bouvines (1214)

WILLIAM THE CONQUEROR. The most important change in English political life was occasioned in 1066 by the death of the childless Anglo-Saxon ruler Edward the Confessor, so-named because of his reputation of piety. Edward's mother was a Norman princess, and this fact gave the duke of Normandy a hereditary claim to the English throne. Before his death, Edward, who was not a strong ruler, acknowledged this claim and even directed that his throne be given to William of Normandy (d. 1087). But the Anglo-Saxon assembly, which customarily bestowed the royal power, had a mind of its own and vetoed Edward's last wishes. It chose instead Harold Godwinsson. This defiant action brought the swift conquest of England by the powerful Normans. William's forces defeated Harold's army at Hastings on October 14, 1066. Within weeks of the invasion, William was crowned king of England in Westminster Abbey, both by right of heredity and by right of conquest.

The Norman king thoroughly subjected his noble vassals to the crown, yet he also consulted with them regularly about decisions of "state." The result was a unique blending of the "one" and the "many," a balance between monarchical and parliamentary elements that has ever since characterized English government.

For the purposes of administration and taxation, William commissioned a county-by-county survey of his new realm, a detailed accounting known as the *Domesday Book* (1080–1086). The title of the book reflects the thoroughness of the survey: just as none would escape the doomsday judgment of God, so none was overlooked by William's assessors.

HENRY II. William's son, Henry I (ruled 1100–1135), died without a male heir, throwing England into virtual anarchy until Henry II (1154–1189) mounted the throne as head of the new Plantagenet dynasty. Henry brought to the throne greatly expanded French holdings, partly by inheritance from his father (Burgundy and Anjou) and partly by his marriage to Eleanor of Aquitaine (1122–1204), a union that created the so-called Angevin or English-French empire. Eleanor married Henry while he was still the count of Anjou and not yet king of England. The marriage occurred only eight weeks after the annulment of Eleanor's fifteen-year marriage to the ascetic French king Louis VII in March 1152. Although the annulment was granted on grounds of consanguinity (blood relationship), the true reason for the dissolution of the marriage was Louis' suspicion of infidelity (according to rumor, Eleanor had been intimate with her cousin). The annulment was very costly to Louis, who lost Aquitaine together with his wife. Eleanor bore Henry eight children, five of them sons, among them the future kings Richard the Lion-Hearted and John. Not only did England, under Henry, come to control most of the coast of France, but Henry also conquered a part of Ireland and made the king of Scotland his vassal.

The French king, Louis VII, who had lost both his wife and considerable French land to Henry, saw a mortal threat to France in this English expansion. He responded by adopting what came to be a permanent French policy of containment and expulsion of the English from their continental holdings in France—a policy that did not finally succeed until the mid-fifteenth century, when English power on the Continent collapsed at the conclusion of the Hundred Years' War.

POPULAR REBELLION AND MAGNA CARTA.
As Henry II acquired new lands abroad, he became more autocratic at home. He forced his will on the clergy in the Constitutions of Clarendon (1164), measures that placed limitations on judicial appeals to Rome; subjected the clergy to the civil courts; and gave the king control over the election of bishops. The result was strong political resistance from both the nobility and the clergy. The archbishop of Canterbury, Thomas á Becket (CA. 1118–1170), once Henry's compliant chancellor, broke openly with the king and fled to Louis VII. Becket's subsequent assassination in 1170 and his canonization by Pope Alexander III at the altar in 1172 forced the king to retreat from his heavy-handed tactics, as popular resentment grew.

English resistance to the king became outright rebellion under Henry's successors, the brothers Richard the Lion-Hearted (1189–1199) and John (1199–1216). Their burdensome taxation in support of unnecessary foreign Crusades and a failing war with France left the English people little alternative. In 1209, Pope Innocent III excommunicated King John and placed England under interdict. This humiliating experience saw the king of England declare his country a fief of the pope. But it was the defeat of the English by the French at Bouvines in 1214 that proved the last straw. With the full support of the clergy and the townspeople, the English barons revolted against John. The popular rebellion ended with the king's grudging recognition of Magna Carta ("Great Charter") in 1215.

This monumental document was a victory of feudal over monarchical power in the sense that it secured the rights of the many—the nobility, the clergy, and the townspeople—over the autocratic king; it restored the internal balance of power that had been the English political experience since the Norman Conquest. The English people—at least the privileged English people—thereby preserved their right to be represented at the highest levels of government, especially in matters of taxation. The monarchy remained intact, however, and its legitimate powers and rights were duly recognized and preserved. This outcome contrasted with the experience on the Continent, where victorious nobility tended to humiliate kings and emperors and undo all efforts at centralization.

With a peculiar political genius, the English consistently refused to tolerate either the absorption of the power of the monarchy by the nobility or the abridgment of the rights of the nobility by the monarchy. Although King John continued to resist the Great Charter in every way he could, his son Henry III formally ratified it, and it has ever since remained a cornerstone of English law.

PHILIP II AUGUSTUS.
During the century and a half between the Norman Conquest (1066) and Magna Carta (1215), a strong monarchy was never in question in England. The English struggle in the high Middle Ages was to secure the rights of the many, not the authority of the king. The French faced the reverse problem in this period. Powerful feudal princes dominated France for two centuries, from the beginning of the Capetian dynasty (987) until the reign of Philip II Augustus (1180–1223). During this period, the Capetian kings wisely concentrated their limited resources on securing the royal domain, their uncontested territory round about Paris known as the Île-de-France. They did not rashly challenge the more powerful nobility. Aggressively exercising their feudal rights in this area, they secured absolute obedience and a solid base of power. By the time of Philip II, Paris had become the center of French government and culture, and the Capetian dynasty a secure hereditary monarchy. Thereafter, the kings of France were in a position to impose their will on the French nobles, who were always in law, if not in political fact, the king's sworn vassals.

The Norman conquest of England helped stir France to unity and make it possible for the Capetian kings to establish a truly national monarchy. The duke of Normandy, who after 1066 was master of the whole of England, was also among the vassals of the French king in Paris. Capetian kings understandably watched with alarm as the power of their Norman vassal grew.

Philip Augustus faced, at the same time, an internal and an international struggle, and he was successful in

Beginning in the mid-twelfth century, the Gothic style evolved from Romanesque architecture. The term itself was at first pejorative: it meant "barbaric" and was applied to the new style by its critics. Gothic was also often known in the Middle Ages as the "French style" because of its unusual popularity in France. Its most distinctive visible features are its ribbed, criss-crossing vaulting, its pointed arches rather than rounded ones and its frequent exterior buttresses. The result gives an essential impression of vertical lines. The vaulting made possible more height than the Romanesque style had sought, while the extensive addition of "flying" buttresses made even greater height possible. Because walls, therefore, did not have to carry all of a structure's weight, wide expanses of windows were possible—hence the extensive use of stained glass and the characteristic color that often floods Gothic cathedrals. Use of the windows to show stories from the Bible, saints' lives, and local events was similar to earlier use of mosaics.

This diagram shows the typical vaulting arches, and buttresses of a Gothic building. [World Architecture, Trewin Copplestone, General Editor (London: Hamlyn, 1963), p. 216.]

both. His armies occupied all the English territories on the French coast, with the exception of Aquitaine. As the showdown with the English neared on the Continent, however, the Holy Roman Emperor Otto IV (1198–1215) entered the fray on the side of the English, and the French found themselves assailed from both east and west. But when the international armies finally clashed at Bouvines on July 27, 1214, in what became the first great European battle in history, the French won handily over the English and the Germans. This victory unified France around the monarchy and thereby laid the foundation for French ascendancy in the later Middle Ages. Philip Augustus also gained control of the lucrative urban industries of Flanders. The defeat so weakened Otto IV that he fell from power in Germany.

The Hohenstaufen Empire (1152–1272)

During the twelfth and thirteenth centuries, stable governments developed in both England and France. In England, Magna Carta balanced the rights of the nobility against the authority of the king, and in France, the reign of Philip II Augustus secured the authority of the king over the competitive claims of the nobility. The experience within the Holy Roman Empire, which embraced Germany, Burgundy, and northern Italy by the mid-thirteenth century, was a very different story. There, primarily because of the efforts of the Hohenstaufen dynasty to extend imperial power into southern Italy, disunity and blood feuding remained the order of the day for two centuries and left as a legacy the fragmentation of Germany until modern times.

FREDERICK I BARBAROSSA. The investiture struggle had earlier weakened imperial authority. A new day seemed to dawn for imperial power with the accession to the throne of Frederick I Barbarossa (1152–1190), the first of the Hohenstaufens, the successor dynasty within the empire to the Franks and the Ottonians. The Hohenstaufens not only reestablished imperial authority but also initiated a new phrase in the contest between popes and emperors, one that was to prove even more deadly than the investiture struggle had been. Never have kings and popes despised and persecuted one another more than during the Hohenstaufen dynasty.

As Frederick I surveyed his empire, he saw powerful feudal princes in Germany and Lombardy and a pope in Rome who believed that the emperor was his

Salisbury cathedral, built 1220–1265, an example of English Gothic. Note the flying buttresses, which permit greater height, and the soaring towers and spire. [British Tourist Authority, New York.]

creature. There existed, however, widespread disaffection with the incessant feudal strife of the princes and the turmoil caused by the theocratic pretensions of the papacy. Popular opinion was on the emperor's side. Thus, Frederick had a foundation on which to rebuild imperial authority, and he shrewdly took advantage of it. Switzerland became Frederick's base of operation. From there he attempted to hold the empire together by stressing feudal bonds.

HENRY VI AND THE SICILIAN CONNECTION. Frederick's reign ended with stalemate in Germany and defeat in Italy. Before his death in 1190, an opportunity had opened to form a new territorial base of power for future emperors when the Norman ruler of the kingdom of Sicily, William II (1166–1189) sought an alliance with Frederick that would free him to pursue a scheme to conquer Constantinople. The alliance was sealed in 1186 by a most fateful marriage between Frederick's son—the future Henry VI (1190–1197)—and Constance, heiress to the kingdom of Sicily. This alliance proved, however, to be only another well-laid political plan that went astray. The Sicilian connection became a fatal distraction for Hohenstaufen kings, leading them repeatedly to sacrifice their traditional territorial base in northern Europe to the temptation of imperialism. Equally ominous, this union of the empire with Sicily left Rome encircled, thereby ensuring the undying hostility of a papacy already thoroughly distrustful of the emperor. The marriage alliance with Sicily proved to be the first step in what soon became a fight to the death between pope and emperor.

Henry VI died in September 1197, with chaos his immediate heir. Between English intervention in its politics and the pope's deliberate efforts to sabotage the Hohenstaufen dynasty, Germany was thrown into anarchy and civil war. England gave financial support to anti-Hohenstaufen factions. Its candidate for the imperial throne, Otto of Brunswick of the rival Welf dynasty, was crowned Otto IV by his supporters in Aachen in 1198 and later won general recognition in Germany. With England supporting Otto, the French rushed in on the side of the fallen Hohenstaufen—the beginning of periodic French fishing in troubled German waters. Meanwhile, Henry VI's four-year-old son, Frederick, was safely tucked away as a ward of Pope Innocent III (1198–1215).

Hohenstaufen support remained alive in Germany, however, and Otto reigned over a very divided kingdom. In October 1209, Pope Innocent crowned him emperor. But the pope quickly changed from benefactor to mortal enemy when, after his coronation, Otto proceeded to reconquer Sicily and once again pursue an imperial policy that left Rome encircled. Within four

MAP 14-3   GERMANY AND ITALY IN THE MIDDLE AGES   *Medieval Germany and Italy were divided lands. The Holy Roman Empire (Germany) embraced hundreds of independent territories that the emperor ruled only in name. The papacy controlled the Rome area and tried to enforce its will on Romagna. Under the Hohenstaufens (mid-12th to mid-13th century), internal German divisions and papal conflict reached new heights; German rulers sought to extend their power to southern Italy and Sicily.*

months of his papal coronation, Otto received a papal excommunication.

FREDERICK II. Pope Innocent, casting about for a counterweight to the treacherous Otto, joined the French, who had remained loyal to the Hohenstaufens against the English–Welf alliance. His new ally, Philip Augustus, impressed on Innocent the fact that a solution to their problems with Otto IV lay near at hand in Innocent's ward, Frederick of Sicily. Frederick, the son of the late Hohenstaufen Emperor Henry VI, was now of age and, unlike Otto, had an immediate hereditary claim to the imperial throne. In December 1212, the young Frederick, with papal, French, and German support, was crowned king of the Romans in Mainz, as Frederick II. Within a year and a half, Philip Augustus ended the Welf interregnum of Otto IV on the battlefield of Bouvines. Philip sent Frederick II Otto's fallen imperial banner from the battlefield, a bold gesture that suggests the extent to which Frederick's ascent to the throne was intended to be that of a French-papal puppet.

He soon disappointed any such hopes. Frederick was Sicilian and dreaded travel beyond the Alps. Only nine of his thirty-eight years as emperor were spent in Germany. Although Frederick continued to pursue royal policies in Germany through his representatives, he desired only one thing from the German princes, the imperial title for himself and his sons, and he was willing to give them what they wanted to secure it. His eager compliance with their demands laid the foundation for six centuries of German division. In 1220 he recognized the jurisdictional claims of the ecclesiastical princes of Germany, and in 1232 he extended the same recognition to the secular princes. The German princes were undisputed lords over their territories. Frederick's concessions have been characterized as a German equivalent to Magna Carta in the sense that they secured the rights of the German nobility. Unlike Magna Carta, however, they did so without at the same time securing the rights of monarchy. Magna Carta placed the king and the nobility (parliament) in England in a creative tension; the reign of Frederick II simply made the German nobility petty kings.

Frederick had an equally disastrous relationship with the pope, who excommunicated him no fewer than four times. The pope won the long struggle that ensued, although his victory proved in time to be a Pyrrhic one. In the contest with Frederick II, Pope Innocent IV (1243–1254) launched the church into European politics on a massive scale, and his wholesale secularization of the papacy made the Church highly vulnerable to the criticism of religious reformers and royal apologists. Innocent organized and led the German princes against Frederick. These princes—thanks to Frederick's grand concessions to them—had become a superior force and were in full control of Germany by the 1240s.

When Frederick died in 1250, the German monarchy died with him. The princes established an informal electoral college in 1257, which thereafter reigned supreme (it was formally recognized by the emperor in 1356). The "king of the Romans" became their puppet, this time with firmly attached strings; he was elected and did not rule by hereditary right. Between 1250 and 1272, the Hohenstaufen dynasty slowly faded into oblivion.

Independent princes now controlled Germany. Italy fell to local magnates. The connection between Germany and Sicily, established by Frederick I, was permanently broken. And the papal monarchy emerged as one of Europe's most formidable powers, soon to enter its most costly conflict with the French and the English.

The Rise of Russia

Early in the ninth century, missionaries from Byzantium had converted Russia to the Christianity of the Eastern Orthodox Church. This development meant that Russia would remain culturally separated from the Latin Christianity of Western Europe. Between the late ninth century and the mid-thirteenth century, the city of Kiev was the center of Russian political life. Although the city enjoyed fairly extensive trade relations with its neighbors, it failed to develop a political system that provided effective resistance to foreign domination.

The external threat to Kievan Russia came from the east when the Mongols moved across the vast Eurasian plains and into Russia as Genghis Khan built his empire. By 1240, the Mongols had conquered most of Russia and had turned its various cities and their surrounding countryside into dependent principalities from which tribute could be exacted. The portion of the Mongol Empire to which Russia thus stood in the relationship of a vassal was called the *Golden Horde*. It included the steppe, in what is now south Russia, with its largely nomadic population. This vassal relationship encouraged an Eastern orientation on the part of the Russians for over two centuries, although the connection of the Russian church to the Byzantine Empire remained important. During this period there was no single central political authority in Russia. The land was divided into numerous feudal principalities, each of which was militarily weak and subject in one degree or another to the Golden Horde.

The rise of Moscow as a relatively strong power eventually brought the feudal age of Russian history to an end. In the fourteenth century, under Grand Prince Ivan I, the city began to cooperate with its Mongol—

or as the Russians called them, Tatar—overlords in the collection of tribute. Ivan kept much of this tribute to himself and was soon called Ivan Kalita, or John of the Moneybag. When Mongol authority began to weaken, the princes of Moscow, who had become increasingly wealthy, filled the political power vacuum in the territory near the city. The princes extended their authority and that of the city by purchasing some territory, colonizing other areas, and conquering new lands. This slow extension of the principality of Moscow is usually known as *gathering the Russian land*.

In 1380, Grand Prince Dmitry of Moscow defeated the Mongols in battle. The result was not militarily decisive, but Moscow had demonstrated that the Mongol armies were not invincible. Conflict with the Mongols continued for another century before they were driven out. During these years, the princes of Moscow asserted their right to be regarded as the successors of the earlier Kievan rulers, and they also made Moscow the religious center of Russia.

France in the Thirteenth Century: The Reign of Louis IX

If Innocent III realized the fondest ambitions of medieval popes, Louis IX (1226–1270), the grandson of Philip Augustus, embodied the medieval view of the perfect ruler. His reign was a striking contrast to that of his contemporary, Frederick II of Germany. Coming to power in the wake of the French victory at Bouvines (1214), Louis inherited a unified and secure kingdom. Although he was also endowed with a moral character that far excelled that of his royal and papal contemporaries, he was also at times prey to naiveté. Not beset by the problems of sheer survival, and a reformer at heart, Louis found himself free to concentrate on what medieval people believed to be the business of civilization.

Magnanimity in politics is not always a sign of strength and Louis could be very magnanimous. Although in a position to drive the English from their French possessions during negotiations for the Treaty of Paris (1259), he refused to take such advantage. Had he done so and ruthlessly confiscated English territories on the French coast, he might have lessened, if not averted altogether, the conflict of the Hundred Years' War (CA. 1337–1453). Although he occasionally chastised popes for their crude ambitions, Louis remained neutral during the long struggle between Frederick II and the papacy, and his neutrality redounded very much to the pope's advantage. For their assis-

King Louis IX of France, shown in a thirteenth-century manuscript, riding off on a crusade with his knights and priests, as monks bless and bid him farewell. [Royal MS. 16G. VI, f. 404v. Reproduced by permission of the British Library Board, London.]

tance, both by action and by inaction, the Capetian kings of the thirteenth century became the objects of many papal favors.

Louis' greatest achievements lay at home. The efficient French bureaucracy, which his predecessors had used to exploit their subjects, became under Louis an instrument of order and fair play in local government. He sent forth royal commissioners (enquêteurs), reminiscent of Charlemagne's far less successful *missi dominici*, to monitor the royal officials responsible for local governmental administration. These royal ambassadors were received as genuine tributes of the people. Louis further abolished private wars and serfdom within his royal domain, gave his subjects the judicial right of appeal from local to higher courts, and made the tax system, by medieval standards, more equitable. The French people came to associate their king with justice, and national feeling, the glue of nationhood, grew very strong during his reign.

Respected by the kings of Europe, Louis became an arbiter among the world's powers, having far greater moral authority than the pope. During his reign, French society and culture became an example to all of Europe, a pattern that would continue into the modern period. Northern France became the showcase of monastic reform, chivalry, and Gothic art and architecture. Louis' reign also coincided with the golden age of Scholasticism, which saw the convergence of Europe's greatest thinkers on Paris, among them Saint Thomas Aquinas and Saint Bonaventure.

Louis' perfection remained, however, that of a medieval king. Like his father, Louis VIII (1223–1226), Louis was something of a religious fanatic. He sponsored the French Inquisition. He led two French Crusades against the Arabs, which were inspired by the purest religious motives but proved to be personal disasters. During the first (1248–1254), Louis was captured and had to be ransomed out of Egypt. He died of a fever during the second in 1270. It was especially for this selfless, but also quite useless, service on behalf of the Church that Louis IX later received the rare honor of sainthood.

The High Middle Ages in World Perspective

With its borders finally secured, Western Europe concentrated during the high Middle Ages on its political institutions and cultural development, something denied it during the early Middle Ages. In England and France, modern Western nations can be seen in formation. Within the empire, there was both revival (under Otto I) and total collapse (during the Hohenstaufen dynasty) of imperial rule. Everywhere, society successfully organized itself from noble to serf. With the flourishing of trade and the expansion of towns, a new wealthy class patronized education. Western Europe's first universities appeared and a movement called Scholasticism brought a new, and often forbidding, order to knowledge. The major disruption of the period, however, was an unprecedented conflict between former allies. The Roman Catholic church had become a monarchy in its own right, able to compete with secular states and even to dethrone (by excommunication and interdict) kings and princes. The foundation was thereby laid both for perpetual conflict between popes and rulers, which lasted well into early modern times, and for the creation of the peculiar Western separation of Church and State.

For Western Europe, the high Middle Ages were a period of clearer self-definition during which the West gained much of the shape we have come to recognize today. Other world civilizations had already become established and were beginning to depart their "classical" or "golden" periods. The best lay behind rather than before them.

Under the Sung dynasty (960–1279) before Mongol rule, China continued its technological advance. In addition to printing, the Chinese invented the abacus and gunpowder. They also enjoyed a money economy unknown in the West. But culturally, these centuries between 1000 and 1300 were closed and narrow by comparison with those of the T'ang Dynasty. Politically, the Sung was far more autocratic. In China (as also in West European lands like England and France, although not in Italy and the empire), regional aristocracies ceased to be serious obstacles to a strong centralized government.

Chinese women generally held a lower status and had fewer vocational options than in the West, as the practice of footbinding dramatically attests. As in the West, a higher degree of freedom and self-government developed in the countryside, especially by the fourteenth century, as peasants gained the right to buy and sell land and to fulfill traditional labor obligations by money payments. Intellectually, China, like the West, had a scholastic movement within its dominant philosophy; Confucianism made religious and philosophical thought more elaborate, systematic, and orthodox. Whereas Western scholasticism had the effect of making Christianity aloof, elitist, and ridiculed by its lay critics, Confucianism remained a philosophy highly adaptable and popular among laypeople.

In the late twelfth century, Japan shifted from civilian to military rule; the Kamakura Bakufu governed by mounted warriors who were paid with rights to income from land in exchange for their military services. This rise of a military aristocracy marks the beginning of Japan's "medieval," as distinct from its "classical" period. Three Mongol invasions in the thirteenth century also required a strong military. With a civilian court also in existence, Japan actually had a dual government (that is, two emperors and two courts) until the fourteenth century. However, this situation differed greatly from the deep and permanent national divisions developing at this time among the emerging states and autonomous principalities of Western Europe.

Japanese women, more like those in Western Europe than in China, traditionally played a prominent role in royal government and court culture. Nun Shogun, for example, succeeded her husband for a brief period of Kamatura rule in the late twelfth century. But the prominence of women in government would also change in Japan by the fourteenth century.

Within the many developing autonomous Islamic lands at this time, the teaching of Muhammad had created an international culture. The regular practice of religious fundamentals made it possible for Muslims to transcend their new and often very deep regional divisions. Similarly, Christianity made it possible for Englishmen, Frenchmen, Germans, and Italians to think of themselves as one people and unite in Crusades to the Holy Land. As these Crusades began in the late eleventh century, Islam too was on the march, penetrating Turkey and Afghanistan, and impinging upon India, where it gained a new challenge in Hinduism.

Suggested Readings

P. Ariès, *Centuries of Childhood: A Social History of Family Life*, trans. by Robert Baldick (1962). Provocative pioneer effort on the subject.

J. W. Baldwin, *The Scholastic Culture of the Middle Ages: 1000–1300* (1971). Best brief synthesis available.

J. W. Baldwin, *The Government of Philip Augustus* (1986). A scholarly feat.

M. W. Baldwin (ed.), *History of the Crusades, I: The First Hundred Years* (1955). Basic historical narrative.

G. Barraclough, *The Origins of Modern Germany* (1963). Penetrating political narrative.

G. Barraclough, *The Medieval Papacy* (1968). Brief, comprehensive survey, with pictures.

M. Bloch, *French Rural Society*, trans. by J. Sondheimer (1966). A classic by a great modern historian.

A. Capellanus, *The Art of Courtly Love*, trans. by J. J. Parry (1941). Documents from the court of Marie de Champagne.

M. Clagett, G. Post, and R. Reynolds (eds.), *Twelfth-Century Europe and the Foundations of Modern Society* (1966). Demanding but stimulating collection of essays.

F. C. Copleston, *Aquinas* (1965). Best introduction to Aquinas' philosophy.

F. Copleston, *A History of Philosophy, III/1: Ockham to the Speculative Mystics* (1963). The best introduction to Ockham and his movement.

R. H. C. Davis, *A History of Medieval Europe: From Constantine to St. Louis, Part 2* (1972).

G. Duby, *Rural Economy and Country Life in the Medieval West* (1968). Slice-of-life analysis.

G. Duby, *The Three Orders: Feudal Society Imagined*, trans. by Arthur Goldhammer (1981). Large, comprehensive, and authoritative.

R. Fawtier, *The Capetian Kings of France: Monarchy and Nation 987–1328*, trans. by L. Butler and R. J. Adam (1972). Detailed, standard account.

E. Gilson, *Heloise and Abelard* (1968). An analysis and defense of medieval scholarly values.

C. H. Haskins, *The Renaissance of the Twelfth Century* (1927). Still the standard account.

D. Herlihy, *Medieval Households* (1985). Sweeping survey of Middle Ages.

C. H. Haskins, *The Rise of Universities* (1972). A short, minor classic.

E. H. Kantorowicz, *The King's Two Bodies* (1957). Controversial analysis of political concepts in the high Middle Ages.

G. Leff, *Paris and Oxford Universities in the Thirteenth and Fourteenth Centuries: An Institutional and Intellectual History* (1968). Very good on Scholastic debates.

J. Le Goff, *The Birth of Purgatory* (1981).

R. S. Loomis (ed.), *The Development of Arthurian Romance* (1963). A basic study.

R. S. Lopez and I. W. Raymond (eds.), *Medieval Trade in the Mediterranean World* (1955). An illuminating collection of sources, concentrated on southern Europe.

E Mâle, *The Gothic Image: Religious Art in France in the Thirteenth Century* (1913). A classic.

P. Mandonnet, *St. Dominic and His Work* (1944). For the origins of the Dominican Order.

H. E. Mayer, *The Crusades*, trans. by John Gilligham (1972). Extremely detailed, and the best one-volume account.

J. Moorman, *A History of the Franciscan Order* (1968). The best survey.

J. B. Morrall, *Political Thought in Medieval Times* (1962). A readable and illuminating account.

J. T. Noonan, *Contraception: A History of Its Treatment by the Catholic Theologians and Canonists* (1967). A fascinating account of medieval theological attitudes toward sexuality and sex-related problems.

E. Panofsky, *Gothic Architecture and Scholasticism* (1951). A controversial classic.

C. Petit-Dutaillis, *The Feudal Monarchy in France and England from the Tenth to the Thirteenth Century*, trans. by E. D. Hunt (1964). A political narrative.

H. Pirenne, *Medieval Cities: Their Origins and the Revival of Trade*, trans. by Frank D. Halsey (1970). A minor classic.

J. M. Powell, *Innocent III: Vicar of Christ or Lord of the World* (1963). Excerpts from the scholarly debate over Innocent's reign.

F. W. Powicke, *The Thirteenth Century* (1962). An outstanding treatment of English political history.

H. Rashdall, *The Universities of Europe in the Middle Ages*, Vols. 1–3 (1936). Dated but still a standard comprehensive work.

F. Rörig, *The Medieval Town*, trans. by D. J. A. Matthew (1971). Excellent on northern Europe.

S. Shahar, *The Fourth Estate: A History of Women in the Middle Ages* (1983). Readable survey.

O. von Simson, *The Gothic Cathedral* (1956).

R. W. Southern, *Medieval Humanism and Other Studies* (1970). Provocative and far-ranging essays on topics in the intellectual history of the high Middle Ages.

B. Tierney, *The Crisis of Church and State 1050–1300* (1964). A very useful collection of primary sources on key Church–State conflicts.

W. L. Wakefield and A. P. Evans (eds.), *Heresies of the High Middle Ages* (1969). A major document collection.

S. Williams (ed.), *The Gregorian Epoch: Reformation, Revolution, Reaction* (1964). Variety of scholarly opinion on the significance of Pope Gregory's reign presented in debate form.

R. L. Wolff and H. W. Hazard (eds.), *History of the Crusades 1189–1311* (1962).

15 The Islam[ic] India, and Af[rica] (CA. 1000–150[0])

most of the Islamic heartlands. However, their culture and religion did not become dominant in the Islamic any more than in the Chinese or the Eastern Christian lands they conquered. The spread of the Turks, however, added a substantial Turkish linguistic and cultural tinge to the Islamic world. Islam impinged more and more in this age on civilization in the Indian subcontinent, Southeast Asia, and sub-Saharan Africa. Although it had not yet converted a majority in these regions, it became the major new influence in all of them.

THE ISLAMIC HEARTLANDS

Religion and Society

The notable developments of this period for the shape of Islamic society were the consolidation and institutionalization of Sunni legal and religious norms, Sufi mystical piety, and Shi'ite sectarianism.

Consolidation of Sunni Orthopraxy

The *ulema* (both Sunni and Shi'ite) gradually became an entrenched religious, social, and political elite throughout the Islamic world, especially after the breakdown of centralized power in the tenth century. Their integration into local merchant, landowning, and bureaucratic classes led to stronger identification of these groups with Islam. From the eleventh century on, the *ulema's* power and fixity as a class were expressed in the institution of the *madrasa*, or college of higher learning. On the one hand, the *madrasa* had grown up naturally as individual experts frequented a given mosque or private house and attracted students seeking to learn the Qur'an, the Hadith ("Tradition"), jurisprudence, Arabic grammar, and the like.

On the other hand, the *madrasa's* formal fixation through the endowment of buildings, scholarships, and salaried chairs was a device employed by rulers for their own as well as for pious ends. It gave them a measure of control over the *ulema* through their influence on the appointment of teachers and thus on the legal or theological slant of the curriculum. In notable contrast to the Western university with its corporate

An allegory of the mystical life. A ceramic plate [...] contemplating a bathing woman. What appears [...] be a symbolic picture of the sufi (the man) who [...] riderless horse) and progressed to contemplatin[...] male). [Freer Gallery of Art.]

The Sultan Hasan Madrasa *and Tomb-Mosque. This imposing Mamluk building (1356–1363) was built to house teachers and students, studying all four of the major traditions or "schools" of Islamic law. Living and teaching spaces are combined here in a building with a mosque and a tomb enclosure for the sultan. [William A. Graham.]*

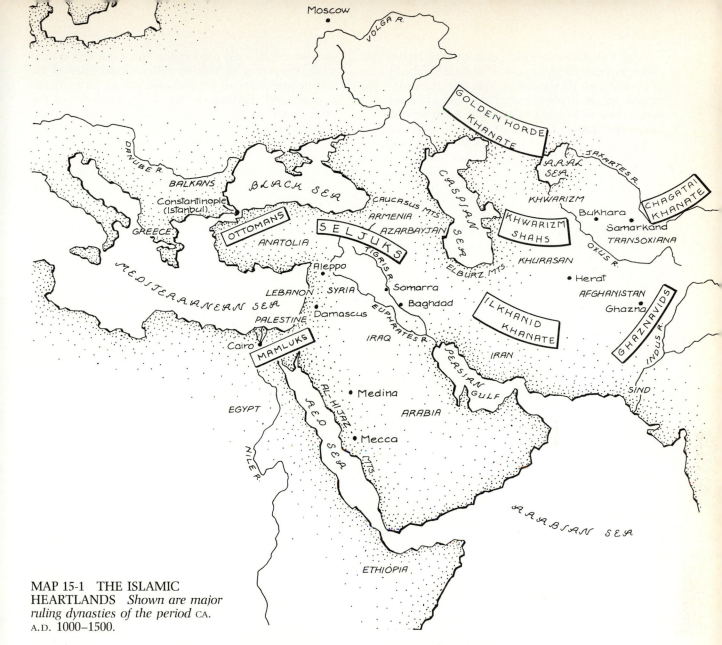

MAP 15-1 THE ISLAMIC
HEARTLANDS *Shown are major
ruling dynasties of the period* CA.
A.D. 1000–1500.

organization and granting of institutional degrees, the
madrasa was simply a support institution for individual teachers, who gave personal certification to students for the mastery of particular subjects. The absence of diplomas or degrees for a particular course of
study indicates the personalist rather than (as in Europe) corporate nature of Muslim education.[1]

Largely outside *ulema* control, popular, "unofficial" piety flourished in local pilgrimages to saints'
tombs, in folk celebrations of Muhammad's birthday
and veneration of him in song and poetry, and in the
ecstatic worship in song and dance of the Sufis. But
the shared traditions that directed family and civil law,
the daily prayer-rituals, fasting in the month of
Ramadan, and the yearly Meccan pilgrimage remained
the public bond among virtually all Muslims, even
most Kharijites or Shi'ites. In the Christian world, dogmatic theological positions (beliefs) determined sectarian identity. In contrast, the tendency in the Islamic
world, for all its many theological disputes and schools
of thought, was to define Islam in terms of the things
that Muslims do—hence by ortho*praxy* (practice)
rather than by ortho*doxy* (beliefs). The chief arbiters of
normative Sunni Islam were four mutually tolerant
schools of Muslim legal interpretation (*fiqh*), not the
various schools of theological interpretation.

[1]G. Makdisi, "Madrasa and University in the Middle Ages,"
Studia Islamica 31 (1970): 255–264.

A basic Sunni orthopraxy, discouraging further religious or social innovation, was well established by the year 1000 as the dominant Muslim tradition. The emergence of a conservative theological orientation tied to one of the four main Sunni legal schools, the Hanbalites (after Ibn Hanbal, d. 969), narrowed the scope for creative doctrinal change. The Hanbalites stressed reliance only on the Qur'an and the Hadith and a literalist reading of both. Thus, a certain orthodoxy was joined with the orthopraxy of the *Umma*, although there was no "church" to enforce either. Also, a growing social conservatism among the *ulema* reflected their places in regional social aristocracies. As often as not, the *ulema* were as committed to the status quo as were the rulers.

Sufi Piety and Organization

Sufi piety stresses the spiritual and mystical dimensions of Islam. The term *Sufi* apparently came from the Arabic *suf* ("wool") because of the old ascetic practice of wearing only a coarse woolen garment. Sufi simplicity and humility had roots with the Prophet and the Companions but developed as a distinctive tendency when, after about 700, various male and female pietists emphasized a godly life that went beyond the mere observance of Muslim duties. Some stressed the ascetic avoidance of temptations, others loving devotion to God. Psychologically, Sufi piety bridges the abyss between the human and the divine that is implied in the exalted Muslim concept of an omnipotent Creator. Socially, Sufi piety merges with folk piety, including such popular practices as saint veneration, shrine pilgrimage, ecstatic worship, and seasonal festivals. Sufi writers collected stories of the earlier saints, wrote treaties on the Sufi way, and composed some of the world's finest mystical poetry.

Some Sufis were revered as spiritual masters and saints. Their disciples formed brotherhoods that, from about the eleventh century, became both regional and international organizations. Each had its distinctive mystical teaching, Qur'anic interpretations, and devotional practice. These fraternal orders proved to be the chief instrument of the further spread of Muslim faith, as well as a locus of popular piety in almost all Islamic societies. Organized Sufism has always attracted members from the populace at large (in this, it differs from most monasticism), as well as those dedicated to poverty or other radical disciplines. Indeed, Sufi or-

A Muslim Description of Sufism

Writing at the end of the fourteenth century, the great historian and sociological commentator Ibn Khaldun prepared a massive "introduction" to history, the Muqaddima. *In it he described all aspects of Islamic civilization, including the various sectarian groups and schools of thought in the Islamic community. The following excerpts are taken from his long discussion of the Sufis.*

. . . The Sufi approach is based upon constant application to divine worship, complete devotion to God, aversion to the false splendour of the world, abstinence from the pleasure, property, and position to which the great mass aspire, and retirement from the world into solitude for divine worship. These things were general among the men around Muhammad and the early Muslims.

Then, worldly aspirations increased in the second [eighth] century and after. At that time, the special name of Sufis was given to those who aspired to divine worship.

. . . .

Very few people share the self-scrutiny of the Sufis, for negligence in this respect is almost universal. Pious people who do not get that far perform, at best, acts of obedience. The Sufis, however, investigate the results of acts of obedience with the help of mystical and ecstatic experience, in order to learn whether they are free from deficiency or not. Thus, it is evident that the Sufis' path in its entirety depends upon self-scrutiny with regard to what they do or do not do, and upon discussion of the various kinds of mystical and ecstatic experience that result from their exertions. This, then, crystallizes for the Sufi novice in a "station." From that station, he can progress to another, higher one.

. . . .

Thus, the Sufis had their special discipline, which is not discussed by other representatives of the religious law. As a consequence, the science of the religious law came to consist of two kinds. One is the special field of jurists and muftis. It is concerned with the general laws governing the acts of divine worship, customary actions, and mutual dealings. The other is the special field of the Sufis. It is concerned with pious exertion, self-scrutiny with regard to it, discussion of the different kinds of mystical experience to another, and the interpretation of the technical terminology of mysticism in use among them. ❑

From Ibn Khaldun, *The Muqaddimah*, trans. by Franz Rosenthal, ed. and abridged by N. J. Dawood (Princeton, N.J.: Princeton University Press, Bollingen Series, 1967), pp. 358–360.

ders became in this age one of the typical social institutions of everyday Muslim life in Islamic lands. Whether Sunni or Shi'ite, casually or seriously pious, large numbers of Muslims have ever since identified in some degree with one or another Sufi order.

Consolidation of Shi'ite Traditions

Shi'ite traditions crystallized between the tenth and twelfth centuries. Numerous states now came under Shi'ite rulers, some even before the Buyids took Baghdad in 945 (see Chapter 12). Yet the differences separating the diverse Shi'ite groups precluded a unified Shi'ism. Only the strongest Shi'ite state, that of the Fatimids, was able to establish an important empire in Egypt. And a substantial Shi'ite populace developed only in Iran, Iraq, and the lower Indus (Sind).

Two Shi'ite groups emerged as the most influential. The "Seveners," or "Isma'ilis," were those who recognized Isma'il (d. CA. 760), first son of the sixth Alid *imam*, as the seventh *imam* (rather than his brother). The Isma'ilis were esoterics, drawing on Gnostic and Neo-Platonic philosophy, knowledge of which they reserved for a spiritual elite. Isma'ili groups were often revolutionary, and three of them founded states that had substantial impact on the Islamic world. The other group, the Qarmatians of eastern Arabia, ruled or disrupted Iraq, Syria, and Arabia through much of the tenth century; the Fatimids conquered North Africa (909) and Egypt (969) and ruled as Shi'ite caliphs until 1171. The Nizari "Assassins" formed a radical theocracy in the Elburz mountains south of the Caspian Sea; they were at daggers drawn with other Shi'ite and Sunni states from 1090 to 1258.

By the eleventh century, however, most Shi'ites accepted a line of twelve *imams* (descended through another son of the sixth *imam*), the last of whom is said to have disappeared in Samarra (Iraq), in 873, into a concealment from which he will emerge as the Mahdi, or "guided one," who ushers in the messianic age and final judgment. Still today, the Shi'ite majority, the "Twelvers," focus on the martyrdom of the twelve *imams* and look for their intercession on the Day of Judgment. They have flourished best in Iran, the home of most Shi'ite thought, whatever the sect. The Buyids who took control of the Abbasid caliphate in 945 were Twelvers. So were the later Iranian Safavids, who made Twelver doctrine the "state religion" of Iran in the sixteenth century (see Chapter 22).

Unity and Diversity

The Islamic West

The western half of the Islamic world after the tenth century developed two regional foci: (1) in Spain, Moroccan North Africa, and to a lesser extent, west Africa; and (2) in Egypt, Syria–Palestine, Anatolia, and, to a lesser extent, Arabia and Libyan North Africa.

SPAIN AND NORTH AFRICA. The grandeur of Moorish Islamic culture is visible still in Córdoba's great mosque and the ruins of the legendary Alhambra castle. The *Chanson de Roland* preserves the echo of Charlemagne's retreat through the Pyrenees after he failed to check the first Umayyad ruler's growing power. That ruler, Abd al-Rahman I (ruled 756–788), founded the cosmopolitan tradition of Umayyad Spanish culture at Córdoba, which over the next two centuries was the cultural hub of the western world. Renowned for its medicine, science, literature, intellectual life, commercial activity, public baths and gardens, and courtly elegance, Córdoba reached its zenith under Abd al-Rahman III (912–961). He even assumed the title of caliph in 929. His absolutist but benevolent rule saw a largely unified and peaceful Islamic Spain. The mosque-university of Córdoba that

Stretching up 100 meters, the Giralda bell tower of the Seville cathedral was originally built as a Muslim minaret about 1190. Its upper portion was rebuilt in late-renaissance style by a Spanish Christian architect in the 1560s. [Art Resource.]

An Arab Biographer's Account of Maimonides

The following are excerpts from the section on Maimonides (Arabic: Musa ibn Maymun) in the biographical dictionary of learned men compiled by Ibn al-Qifti (d. 1248). In the first section omitted here, Ibn al-Qifti describes how the Spanish Jewish savant at first dissembled conversion to Islam when a new Berber ruler demanded the expulsion of Christians and Jews from Spain and North Africa in about 1133. He goes on to tell how Maimonides then made preparations and moved his family to the more tolerant Islamic world of Cairo, where he eventually became the court physician. The final section omitted concludes with mention of his marriage, death, and accomplishments. It was not at all unusual for Jews or Christians to hold high office under Muslim rulers in many places.

. . . This man was one of the people of Andalus, a Jew by religion. He studied philosophy in Andalus, was expert in mathematics, and devoted attention to some of the logical sciences. He studied medicine there and excelled in it. . . .

. . . After assembling his possessions in the time that was needed for this, he left Andalus and went to Egypt, accompanied by his family. He settled in the town of Fusṭāṭ, among its Jews, and practiced his religion openly. He lived in a district called al-Maṣīṣa and made a living by trading in jewels and suchlike. Some people studied philosophy under him. . . .

He married in Cairo the sister of a Jewish scribe called Abu'l-Ma'ālī, the secretary of the mother of Nūr al-Dīn 'Alī, known as al-Afdal, the son of Ṣalāḥ al-Dīn Yūsuf ibn Ayyūb, and he had a son by her who today is a physician in Cairo after his father. . . .

Mūsā ibn Maymūn died in Cairo in the year 605 [1208–9].[1] He ordered his heirs to carry his body, when the smell had ceased, to Lake Tiberias and bury him there, seeking to be among the graves of the ancient Israelites and their great jurists, which are there. This was done.

He was learned in the law and secrets of the Jews and compiled a commentary on the Talmud, which is a commentary and explanation of the Torah; some of the Jews approve of it. Philosophic doctrines overcame him, and he compiled a treatise denying the canonical resurrection. The leaders of the Jews held this against him, so he concealed it except from those who shared his opinion in this. He compiled an abridgement of twenty-one books of Galen, with many additions, in sixteen books. It came out very abridged and quite useless; nothing can be done with it. He edited the Kitāb al-Istikmāl [Book of Perfection] of Ibn Aflaḥ al-Andalusī, on astronomy, and improved it, for there was some confusion in the original. He also edited the Kitāb al-Istikmāl of Ibn Hūd, on mathematics. This is a fine, comprehensive book, needing some correction. He corrected and improved it. . . .

In the latter part of his life he was troubled by a man from Andalus, a jurist called Abu'l-'Arab ibn Ma'īsha, who came to Fusṭāṭ and met him. He charged him with having been a Muslim in Andalus, accused him [of apostasy] and wanted to have him punished.[2] 'Abd al-Raḥīm ibn 'Alī al-Fāḍil prevented this, and said to him, "If a man is converted by force, his Islam is not legally valid." ❑

[1] In fact, he died in 1204.

[2] The penalty for apostasy was death.

From Bernard Lewis (ed. and trans.), *Islam from the Prophet Muhammad to the Capture of Constantinople*, Vol. 2 (New York: Harper and Row, 1974), pp. 189–192.

---

he founded was the earliest institution of its kind; it attracted students from Europe as well as from the Islamic world.

An irony of this cosmopolitan world was the rigorist conservatism that dominated both Muslim and Christian thought in Spain. From time to time, it sparked Muslim–Christian conflict—a product perhaps of the uniquely close and threatening contact of the two communities. Externally, Abd al-Rahman III checked both the new Fatimid Islamic power in the Mediterranean and the Christian kingdoms in the Spanish north, making possible this golden era of Moorish power and cul-

ture. But fragmentation into warring Muslim principalities allowed a resurgence of Spain's Christian states between about 1000 and 1085, when Toledo fell permanently back into Christian hands.

There were brief Islamic revivals in Spain and North Africa under the African reform movements of the Almoravids and Almohads. The Almoravids originated as a religious-warrior brotherhood among Berber nomads in West Africa. Having subdued virtually all of northwest Africa, in 1086 they carried their zealotry from their new capital of Marrakesh into Spain and reunited its Islamic kingdoms. Under their rule,

Reading the Torah in a Spanish synagogue. A picture from a Hebrew Haggada, Spain, fourteenth century. Until their expulsion by Christian rulers at the end of the fifteenth century, Jews formed a significant minority in Spain. [The British Library.]

the arabized Christians (Mozarabs) were persecuted and many were driven out, as were some Moorish Jews. The subsequent wars in Spain with Christian rulers are best known in the West for the exploits of El Cid (d. 1099), the adventurer and mercenary who became the Spanish national hero.

A new reform movement, the Almohads, ended Almoravid rule in Morocco in 1147 and then conquered much of southern Spain. Before their demise (1225 in Spain; 1275 in Africa), they stimulated a brilliant revival of Spanish Islamic culture. In this era, paper manufacture reached Spain and then the rest of western Europe. The long westward odyssey of Indian fable literature through Iran and the Arab world ended with Spanish and Latin translations in thirteenth-century Spain. The most illustrious products of this Spanish Islamic intellectual world were a major philosopher and physician, Ibn Rushd (Averroës, d. 1198); perhaps the greatest Muslim mystical thinker, Ibn al-

The Alhambra, Patio de los Arraynes. Famed for their exquisite gardens and court-yards, the palaces of the Albambra near Granada mark the twilight of Islamic culture in Spain. Built largely in the fourteenth century by the Nasrid dynasty, the Alhambra's grandeur has been preserved well beyond its fall in 1492 to Ferdinand and Isabella. [Spanish Tourist Office.]

Arabi (d. 1240); and the famous Arab-Jewish philosopher, Maimonides (d. 1204), who was forced to spend much of his life abroad in Cairo.

EGYPT AND THE EASTERN MEDITERRANEAN WORLD. *The Fatimids.* The major Islamic presence in the Mediterranean from the tenth to the twelfth century was that of the Shi'ite Fatimids. They began as a Tunisian dynasty, then conquered Morocco, Sicily, and Egypt (969). In Egypt, they built their new capital, Cairo (*al-Qahira*, "the Victorious"), near the original garrison town of the earliest Arab conquest. They took their name from their claim to descent from Muhammad's daughter, Fatima. Their rule as Shi'ite caliphs meant that, for a time, there were three "caliphates"—in Baghdad, Córdoba, and Cairo. The Fatimids were Isma'ilis (see the earlier discussion of "Religion and Society"). Content to rule a Sunni majority in Egypt, they sought recognition as true *imams* by other Isma'ili groups. They did win the allegiance of a Shi'ite state in Yemen and were able, for a time, to take western Arabia and most of Syria from the Buyid "guardians" of the Abbasid caliphate (see Chapter 12).

The Fatimid reign spawned two splinter groups that have played visible, if minor, roles at certain points in history. The Druze of modern Lebanon and Syria originated around 1020 with a few members of the Fatimid court who professed belief in the divinity of one of the Fatimid caliphs. The tradition they founded is too far from Islam to be considered a Muslim sect. The Isma'ili "Assassins," on the other hand, were a radical movement founded by a Fatimid defector in the Elburz mountains of Iran at the beginning of the twelfth century. The name *Assassins* comes not from the political assassinations that made them infamous but from a European corruption of the Arabic *Hashishiyyin* ("users of hashish"). A local Syrian name, it was possibly connected with the story that the assassins were manipulated with drugs to undertake their usually suicidal missions. The *Assassins* were defeated by the Mongols in the thirteenth century.

The Fatimids built the Azhar mosque in Cairo as a center of learning, a role it maintains today, although for Sunni, not (as then) Shi'ite, scholarship. Fatimid rulers treated Egypt's Coptic Christians generally as well as they did their Sunni majority. Many Copts held high offices, even that of vizier. Jews, like Copts, usually fared well under the Fatimids, except for the general persecution of Jews and Christians under the apparently deranged caliph al-Hakim (d. 1021). After 1100, the Fatimids declined, falling in 1171 to their last ruler's vizier, Salah al-Din (Saladin). A Sunni, he founded a short-lived dynasty in Egypt and Syria-Palestine. Henceforward Shi'ite Islam disappeared from Egypt.

The Mamluks. The heirs of the Fatimids and

An Egyptian bronze incense burner of Copto-Arabic origin (eight-ninth century). This nearly intact piece of fine metalwork is a reminder of the constant presence of the Coptic Christian community in Egypt throughout Islamic times and down to the present day. [Freer Gallery of Art.]

Saladin in the eastern Mediterranean were the redoubtable Mamluk *sultans* ("those with authority"). As rulers of Egypt, they styled themselves after the example of the Seljuks (see below). The Mamluks alone among major Islamic dynasties withstood the Mongol invasions that closely followed their accession. The first Mamluk sultan (1250–1257), Aybak, and his successors were Turkish and Mongol slave officers, drawn originally from the bodyguard of Saladin's dynasty. Whereas the early Mamluks were often succeeded by sons or brothers, after the 1390s succession was more often a survival of the fittest; no sultan reigned more than a few years. The Mamluk state was based on a military fief system and total control by the slave-officer elite.

The Mamluk sultan Baybars (1260–1277), who took the last Crusader fortresses, has lived on in Arab legend as a larger-than-life figure. To legitimize his rule, he revived the Abbasid caliphate after its demise in the fall of Baghdad (1258; discussed later) by installing an uncle of Baghdad's last Abbasid at Cairo. He made treaties with Constantinople and Western European sovereigns, as well as with the newly converted Muslim leader—or khan, of the "Golden Horde"—of the Mongol Tatars of southern Russia. He was the first Egyptian sultan to appoint judges from each of the four law schools to administer justice, and his public works in Cairo were numerous. He extended Mamluk rule south to Nubia and west among the Berbers. The Mamluks declined after 1300, even though the Mongols in Iran conquered only Syria and never reached

756–1021	Spanish Umayyad Dynasty
912–961	Rule of Abd al-Rahman III; height of Umayyad power and civilization
969–1171	Fatimid Shi'ite Dynasty in Egypt
CA. 1020	Origin of Druze community (Egypt/Syria)
1171	Fatimids fall to Salah al-Din (Saladin), the Ayyubid lieutenant of ruler of Aleppo
1096–1291	Major European Christian crusades into Islamic lands; some European presence in Syria–Palestine
1056–1275	Almoravid and Almohad dynasties in North Africa, West Africa, and Spain
1189	Death of Ibn Rushd (Averroës), philosopher
1204	Death of Musa ibn Maymun (Maimonides), philosopher and Jewish savant
1240	Death of Ibn al-Arabi, theosophical mystic
1250–1517	Mamluk sultanate in Egypt (claim laid to Abbasid Caliphate)
1406	Death of Ibn Khaldun, historian and social philosopher
CA. 1300	Rise of Ottoman state in western Anatolia

The tomb of Qa'it Bey, Cairo (built 1472–1474), the finest example of Mamluk architecture in Cairo. [Egyptian Tourist Authority.]

Egypt itself. The dynasty did, however, survive the Ottoman conquest of Egypt (1517); it continued to rule there as the latter dynasty's governors into the nineteenth century.

Mamluk architecture, especially that of the reigns of Baybars and the extravagant Nasir (reigned 1293–1340), much of which still graces Cairo, remains their most magnificent bequest to posterity. Calligraphy, metalwork, and mosaics were among the arts and crafts of special note. The Mamluks patronized outstanding scholars, most importantly the greatest Islamic social historian and philosopher, Ibn Khaldun (d. 1406). He was born of a Spanish Muslim family in Tunis and settled in Cairo as an adult. Mamluk scholarship excelled in several areas, notably history, biography, and the sciences of astronomy, mathematics, and medicine.

The Pre-Mongol Islamic East

We noted in Chapter 12 that the Iranian dynasties of the Samanids at Bukhara (875–999) and the Buyids at Baghdad (945–1055) were the major eastern usurpers of the previously unified Abbasid rule. Their takeovers epitomized the rise of regional states that had begun to undermine the caliphate east and west by the ninth century. Similarly, the demise of each of these dynasties reflected a second important pattern already emerging before them: namely, the ascendancy of Turkish slave-rulers (like the Mamluks later in the west) and of Turkish tribal (Turkoman) peoples. With the successors of the Samanids and the Buyids, the process begun by the use of Turkish slave troops in ninth-century Baghdad ended in the permanent presence in the Islamic world of Turks. As late converts, they became typically the most zealous of Sunni Muslims.

THE GHAZNAVIDS. The rule of the Samanids in Transoxiana was finally wiped out by a Turkoman group. But they had already lost all of eastern Iran south of the Oxus in 994 to one of their own slave governors, Subuktigin (reigned 976–997). He set up his own state in modern Afghanistan, at Ghazna, whence he and his son and successor, Mahmud of Ghazna (reigned 998–1030), launched successful campaigns against his former masters. The Ghaznavids are notable for their patronage of Persian literature and culture and their conquests in northwestern India, which began a lasting Muslim presence in India. Mahmud was their greatest ruler. His name is still known in India for his booty raids and his destruction of temples in western India. His empire at its peak stretched from western Iran to the Oxus and the Indus.

The great scientist and mathematician al-Biruni (d. 1048) and the epic poet Firdawsi (d. CA. 1020) were among the scholars and artists whom he attracted to Ghazna. Firdawsi's *Shahnama* ("The Book of Kings") is the masterpiece of Persian literature, an epic of 60,000 verses that helped fix the new Persian language and revive the pre-Islamic Iranian cultural tradition. After Mahmud, the empire began to break up, although Ghaznavids ruled at Lahore until 1186.

THE SELJUKS. The Seljuks were the first major Turkish dynasty of Islam. They were a steppe clan who settled in Transoxiana, became avid Sunnis, and ex-

tended their sway over Khorasan in the 1030s. In 1055, they took Baghdad, where the nominal Abbasid caliph was happy to greet them as his deliverers from the Shi'ite Buyids. As the new guardian of the caliphate and master of an Islamic empire, the Seljuk leader Tughril Beg (reigned 1037–1063) took the title of *sultan* ("authority") to signify his temporal power and control. He was accordingly invested by the caliph as "king of east and west." He and his first successors made various Iranian cities their capitals instead of Baghdad.

New Turkish tribes joined their ranks, and Seljuk arms extended Islamic control for the first time into the central Anatolian plateau at Byzantine expense. They even captured the Byzantine emperor in a victory in Armenia in 1071. They also conquered much of Syria and wrested Mecca and Medina from the Shi'ite Fatimids. The first Turkish rule in Asia Minor (Anatolia) dates from 1077, when the Seljuk governor there

"Friday Mosque," Isfahan. Begun in the tenth century, it was rebuilt in classic four-iwan form by the Seljuk Malik Shah in 1088–1089 and remodeled by the Safavids in the fifteenth and seventeenth centuries. This view shows the large open courtyard with its ablution-pools in the center. The huge half-dome facade, or iwan, is characteristic of Iranian mosque architecture. Here is the southern iwan, behind which is the original covered area built by Malik Shah. [Diane Rawson, Photo Researchers.]

EASTERN ISLAMIC LANDS

875–999	Samanid dynasty, centered at Bukhara
945–1055	Buyid Shi'ite dynasty in Baghdad, controls caliphs
994–1186	Ghaznavid dynasty in Ghazna (modern Afghanistan) and Lahore (modern Pakistan), founded by Subuktigin (r. 976–997) and his son, Mahmud of Ghazna (r. 998–1030)
1020	Death of Firdawsi, compiler of *Shahnama*
CA. 1050	Death of al-Biruni, scientist and polyglot
1055–1194	Seljuk rule in Baghdad
1063–1092	Viziership of Nizam al-Mulk
1111	Death of al-Ghazzali, theologian and scholar
1219–1222	Gengis Khan plunders eastern Iran to Indus region
1258	Hulegu Khan conquers Baghdad
1261	Mamluk–Mongol treaty halts westward Mongol movement
1260–1335	Hulegu and his Il-Khanid successors rule Iran
1379–1405	Campaigns of Timur-i Lang (Tamerlane) devastate entire Islamic East
1405–1494	Timurids, successors of Tamerlane, rule in Transoxiana and Iran
1405–1447	Shahrukh, Timurid ruler at Herat; great patronage of the arts of philosophy

Quatrains (Ruba'iyat) *from the Pen of Umar Khayyam* (d. 1123)

Although Edward Fitzgerald's very beautiful and very free translation of Khayyam's Persian Ruba'iyat *is justly famous, the following more literal translation of three quatrains from the famous astronomer-poet also gives a good sense of the rather cynical but wry reflection evident in many of the ruba'iyat.*

Neither you nor I know the mysteries of eternity,
Neither you nor I read this enigma;
You and I only talk this side of the veil;
When the veil falls, neither you nor I will be here.

There was a water-drop, it joined the sea,
A speck of dust, it was fused with earth;
What of your entering and leaving this world?
A fly appeared, and disappeared.

Khayyam, if you are drunk on wine, enjoy it,
If you are with the tulip-cheeked, enjoy her:
Since the world's business ends in nothing,
Think that you are not and, while you are,
 enjoy it.

❑

From Peter Avery and John Heath-Stubbs, *The Ruba'iyat of Omar Khayyam* (Harmondsworth, U.K.: Penguin, 1981), pp. 48, 56, 82.

---

set up a separate sultanate of the Seljuks of Rum ("Rome"/i.e., Byzantium). These latter Seljuks were not displaced until after 1300 by the Ottomans, another, still greater Turkish dynasty (see Chapter 22).

The most notable figure of Seljuk rule was the vizier Nizam al-Mulk, who was the real power behind two sultans (1063–1092). In his era, new roads and inns (caravanserais) for trade and pilgrimage were built, canals were dug, mosques and other public buildings were founded (including the first great Sunni *madrasas*, the personal projects of Nizam al-Mulk), and science and culture were patronized. He supported an extremely accurate calendar reform and himself wrote a major work on the art of governing, the *Siyasatnamah*. Before his murder by an Isma'ili "Assassin" in 1092, he appointed as professor in his Baghdad *madrasa* Muhammad al-Ghazzali (d. 1111), probably the greatest of all Muslim religious thinkers and writers. He also patronized the poet and astronomer Umar Khayyam (d. 1123), whose Western fame rests on his "quatrains," or *Ruba'iyat*.

After declining fortunes in the early twelfth century, Iranian Seljuk rule crumbled and by 1194 was wholly wiped away by another Turkish slave dynasty from Khwarizm in the lower Oxus basin. By 1200, these Khwarizm Shahs had built a large if shaky empire and sphere of influence covering Iran and Transoxiana. In the same era, the Abbasid caliph at Baghdad, Nasir (reigned 1180–1225), tried to establish an independent caliphal state in Iraq. But neither his heirs nor the

Khwarizm Shahs were long to survive in the face of events already unfolding on the Asian steppes.

The Mongol Age

MONGOLS AND ILKHANIDS. The building of a vast Mongol empire spanning Asia from China to Po-

Genghis Khan addressing his new subjects from the pulpit (minbar) in a mosque in Bukhara. Miniature painting from a manuscript produced in the late fourteenth century. [The British Library.]

The Mongol Catastrophe

For the Muslim east, the sudden blitzkrieg of the Mongol hordes was an indescribable calamity. Something of the shock and despair of their reaction can be seen in the history of Ibn al-Athir (d. 1233), who lived during the time of their first onslaught. He writes in this selection about the year 1220–1221, when the Mongols ("Tartars") burst in upon the eastern lands.

I say, therefore, that this thing involves the description of the greatest catastrophe and the most dire calamity (of the like of which days and nights are innocent) which befell all men generally, and the Muslims in particular; so that, should one say that the world, since God Almighty created Adam until now, hath not been afflicted with the like therof, he would but speak the truth. For indeed history doth not contain aught which approaches or comes nigh unto it.

. . . .

. . . Now this is a thing the like of which ear hath not heard; for Alexander, concerning whom historians agree that he conquered the world, did not do so with such swiftness, but only in the space of about ten years; neither did he slay, but was satisfied that men should be subject to him. But these Tartars conquered most of the habitable globe and the best, the most flourishing and most populous part thereof, and that whereof the inhabitants were the most advanced in character and conduct, in about a year; nor did any country escape their devastations which did not fearfully expect them and dread their arrival.

Moreover they need no commissariat, nor the conveyance of supplies, for they have with them sheep, cows, horses, and the like quadrupeds, the flesh of which they eat, [needing] naught else. As for their beasts which they ride, these dig into the earth with their hoofs and eat the roots of plants, knowing naught of barley. And so, when they alight anywhere, they have need of nothing from without. As for their religion, they worship the sun when it arises, and regard nothing as unlawful, for they eat all beasts, even dogs, pigs, and the like; nor do they recognise the marriage-tie, for several men are in marital relations with one woman, and if a child is born, it knows not who is its father.

Therefore Islâm and the Muslims have been afflicted during this period with calamities wherewith no people hath been visited. These Tartars (may God confound them!) came from the East, and wrought deeds which horrify all who hear of them, and which thou shalt, please God, see set forth in full detail in their proper connection. . . . ❑

From Edward G. Browne, *A Literary History of Persia*, Vol. 2 (Cambridge: Cambridge University Press, 1902), pp. 427–430, passim.

---

land in the early thirteenth century proved to be momentous not only for eastern Europe and China (see Chapter 9), but also for Islamic Eurasia and India. A Khwarizm Shah massacre of Mongol ambassadors brought down the full wrath of the Great Khan, Genghis, on the hapless Islamic east. He plundered mercilessly (1219–1222) from Transoxiana and Khorasan to the Indus, razing entire cities. The death of Genghis Khan (1227) and the division of his empire into four khanates under his four sons gave the Islamic world some respite. In 1255, Hulagu Khan, a grandson of Genghis, again led a massive army across the Oxus. Constantly adding Turkish troops to his forces (Mongol armies normally included many Turks), he went from victory to victory, destroying the "Assassins" of northwestern Iran along with every other Iranian state. In 1258, when the Abbasid caliph foolishly refused to surrender, Hulagu's troops smashed Baghdad's defenses and plundered it, killing at least 80,000 men, women, and children, including the caliph and his sons.

Under the influence of his wife and many of his inner circle who were Nestorian Christians or Buddhists, Hulagu spared the Christians of Baghdad. He followed this policy in his other conquests, including the later sack of Aleppo, which, like Baghdad, resisted. When Damascus surrendered, Christians had what proved to be a vain hope of the impending fall of Mamluk Cairo and the consequent collapse of Islamic power. Hulagu's further drive west was slowed by rivalry with his kinsman Berke. A Muslim convert, Berke ruled the khanate of the "Golden Horde," the Mongol state centered in southern Russia north of the Caucasus. He was in contact with the Mamluks, and some of his Mongol troops even fought with them in their major victory over Hulagu in Palestine (1260), which stopped Mongol penetration westward. A treaty in 1261 between the Mamluk sultan and Berke established a formal alliance that confirmed the breakup of Mongol unity and of the autonomy of the four khanates: in China (the Yuan dynasty), in Iran (the Ilkhans), in Russia (the Golden Horde), and in Transoxiana (the Chagatays).

For his part, Hulagu gave allegiance to the new

The caravanserai. One of the important links in communication and commerce in the Islamic world for many centuries, the caravanserai was a building that provided shelter, food, and protection to caravans and travelers of all kinds from China to Africa. Figure above shows the exterior walls of a large Iranian caravanserai at Maragha in steppe country. In Figure below, in an Iraqui caravanserai at Feluga, north of Baghdad, we see the men and animals of a caravan taking their ease. [Bettmann Archive.]

Great Khan of China. He and his heirs ruled the old Persian Empire from Azerbaijan for some seventy-five years as the Great Khan's "viceroys" (*Il-Khans*; from which Hulagu's line is named *Ilkhanid*). Here, as elsewhere, the rule of the Mongols did not eradicate the society that they inherited. Unlike the Arabs before them, they did not convert Muslim subject populations to their own faith. Instead, both their native paganism and Buddhist and Christian leanings yielded to Muslim faith and practice, although religious tolerance remained the norm under their rule. After 1335, Ilkhanid rule fell prey to the familiar pattern of a gradual breaking away of provinces, and for fifty years, Iran was again fragmented.

TIMURIDS AND TURKOMANS. This situation prepared the way for a Turko-Mongol conquest from Transoxiana, under Timur-i Lang ("Timur the Lame," or "Tamerlane"). If Genghis Khan's invasions long before had been devastating, they could not match Timur's savage campaigns between 1379 and his death in 1405. These raids were not aimed at building up a new, centralized empire so much as at sheer conquest. Timur was a Muslim convert evidently possessed of a strong sense of his role as the protector of commerce and the punisher of the injustices of regional petty tyrants and populist—often Shi'ite—extremist groups alike. Still, whatever his ends, they hardly justified his means. In successive campaigns, he swept everything before him: all of eastern Iran (1379–1385); western Iran, Armenia, the Caucasus, and upper Mesopotamia (1385–1387); central Asia from Transoxiana to the Volga and as far as Moscow (1391–1395); southwestern Iran, Mesopotamia, and Syria (1391–1393); north India (1398); and northern Syria and Anatolia (1400–1402). Timur's sole positive contributions seem to have been the buildings he sponsored at Samarkand, his capital. He left behind him death, disease, destruction, and political chaos over the entire eastern Islamic world, which did not soon recover. His was, however,

The Gur-i-Mir, the tomb of Timur in Samarkand. Built in 1490–1501 by Timur's grandson, this tile-covered structure houses the tombs of Shahrukh, Ulug Beg, and other Timurid heirs, as well as that of Timur himself. [Bettmann Archive.]

the last great steppe invasion, for firearms soon took the steppe horsemen's advantage away forever.

Timur's sons shared his conquests with varying results in Transoxiana and Iran (1405–1494). The most successful Timurid was Shahrukh (reigned 1405–1447), who ruled a united western and eastern Iran for a time. His capital, Herat, became an important center of Persian Islamic culture and Sunni piety. He patronized the famous Herat school of miniature painting as well as Persian literature and philosophy. The Timurids had to share the control of Iran with Turkoman dynasties in western Iran, once even losing Herat to one of them. They and the Turkomans were the last Sunnis to rule Iran. Both were eclipsed at the end of the fifteenth century by the rise of the militant

Shi'ite dynasty of the Safavids, who ushered in a new era in the Iranian world (see Chapter 22).

The Spread of Islam Beyond the "Heartlands"

The period from roughly 1000 to 1500 saw the spread of Islam as a lasting religious, cultural, and political force into new areas. Not only Eurasia from the Caspian and Black Seas north to Moscow (under the "Golden Horde"), but also Greece and the Balkans, through the Ottoman Turks, came under the control of Islamic governments (see Chapter 22). In the African and Asian worlds, India, Southeast Asia (Malaysia and Indonesia), inland West Africa, and coastal East Africa all became major spheres of Islamic political or commercial power, or both. In all these areas, conversion to Islam and the absorption of Islamic cultural influences came most often at the hands of Sufi orders. Merchants, too, were major agents of Islamization in all these regions.

Conquest was a third (and demographically less important) means to the eventual conversion to Islam of significant groups in the areas in question. Conversion reached sometimes only ruling elites and sometimes wider circles of a population. In India, Southeast Asia, and sub-Saharan Africa, significant numbers of the populace (often the majority) retained their inherited religious practices and faith. Therefore, if we treat these regions from the standpoint of the spread of Islam, it is not because Islam was the only, or even the major, element in their civilization in this period. It is rather that the coming of Islam signaled truly epochal changes in all these areas.

INDIA

The Entrenchment of Islam

Islamic civilization in India, like earlier Indian civilization, was formed by the creative interaction of invading foreigners with indigenous peoples. Whereas the early Arab and Turkish invaders had been a foreign Muslim minority, later Indian Muslims were as much "Indian" as "Muslim." A new dimension was added thereby both to Indian and to Islamic civilization.

MAP 15-2   THE INDIAN SUB-CONTINENT   *Shown are major kingdoms and regions* CA. A.D. 1000–1500.

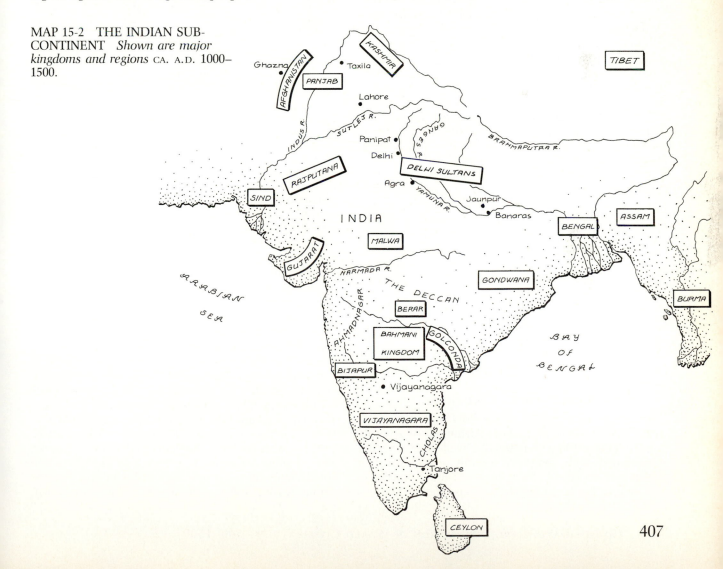

The Early Spread of Islam

Well before the Ghaznavids came to the Punjab, Muslims were to be found even outside the original Arab conquest areas in Sind. Muslim merchants had settled in the port cities of Gujarat and south India to profit from internal Indian trade as well as from trade with the Indies and China. Wherever Muslim traders went, converts to Islam were attracted by business advantages as well as by the straightforward ideology and practice of Islam and its egalitarian, supposedly "classless" ethic. Sufi orders had also gained a foothold in the south, giving today's south Indian Muslims very old roots. Sufi piety also drew converts in the north, especially when the Mongol devastation of Iran in the thirteenth century sent refugees streaming over the mountains into north India. Many of these refugee converts strengthened Islamic armies and administration as well as Muslim cultural and religious life in the subcontinent.

The Muslim–Hindu Encounter

From the beginning, Muslim leaders faced the problem of ruling a country dominated by a different culture and religion. Much as early Muslim rulers in Iran had given the Zoroastrians legal status as "People of the Book" (like Christians and Jews; see Chapter 12), the first Arab conquerors in Sind (711) had treated Hindus not as pagans but as "protected peoples" under Muslim sovereignty. These precedents gave the Ghaznavids and later Muslim rulers in India a pragmatic basis for coexistence with their Hindu subjects. These precedents did not, of course, remove Hindu resistance to Muslim rule.

The chief obstacle to Islamic expansion in India was the military prowess and tradition of a Hindu warrior class that emerged after the Hun and other Asian tribal invasions of the fifth and sixth centuries. Apparently descended from such invaders and the native warrior (Kshatriya) class of Hindus, this class was known from about the mid-seventh century as *Rajputs*. Rulers and fighters of northern Hindu society, they were a large group of clans bound together by a fierce warrior ethic and a patriotism evident in their adherence to Hindu culture and strong traditionalism. They fought the Muslim invaders with great tenacity, but their inability to unite eventually brought them under Muslim domination in the sixteenth century (see Chapter 22).

Islamic States and Dynasties

After the Ghaznavids and a brief interlude of Afghan rule, a series of Turkish–Afghan slave-generals known as the "Slave Sultans of Delhi" extended and maintained Islamic power over north India for nearly a century (1206–1290). Four later Muslim dynasties—the Khaljis, the Tughluqs, the Sayyids, and the Lodis—

Building the Castle of Khawarnaq, ca. 1494. This is one of the magnificent illustrations of the Khamsa, *or "Fire Poems" of Nizami, painted by the head of the great art academy at Herat, Bihzad (died ca. 1515). It was Shahrukh's patronage that led to this flourishing school of painting. [The British Library.]*

carried on the Delhi sultanate through the fifteenth century. Their reigns were interrupted only by several years of chaos following the infamous devastation of Delhi by Timur in 1398, from which the city took decades to recover.

In the fifteenth century, the sultanate's power was limited by the rise of independent Islamic states that shared power with Rajput kingdoms in the Deccan and north India. The most important of the independent Islamic states was that of the Bahmanids in the Deccan (1347–1527). They were famous for the intellectual life of their court and for their architecture, as well as for their role in containing the powerful southern Indian Hindu state of Vijayanagar. (A Bahmani battle with the raja of Vijayanagar in 1366 was the first documented use of firearms and gunpowder in the subcontinent.) Most of the regional capitals provided fertile ground for cultural life. Jaunpur, to the north of Benares, became, for example, an asylum for artists and intellectuals after Timur's sack of Delhi and boasted an impressive tradition of Islamic architecture. Kashmir was an independent sultanate from 1346 to 1589 and a center of literary activity where Indian works were translated into Persian.

Religious and Cultural Accommodation

Except for Timur's invasion, the Delhi sultans were able to fend off the Mongol danger, much as the Mamluks did in Egypt. They thereby provided a basic political framework within which Islam could take root. Although the ruling class remained a Muslim minority of Persianized Turks and Afghans set over a Hindu majority, conversion went on at various levels of society. Some Hindu converts came from the ruling classes who served the Muslim overlords. *Ghazis* ("warriors" for Islam), like those of the same era in Anatolia, carried Islam by force of arms to pagan groups in eastern Bengal and Assam. And Sufi orders converted numerous Hindus among the lower classes. The Muslim aristocracy, at first mostly foreigners, were usually treated in Indian society as a separate caste group or

groups. Similarly, when lower-class or other Hindus converted, they were assimilated into "Muslim castes," usually identified by occupation.

Persian was the language of intellectual and court life for all the Muslim dynasties of north India. However, Urdu began to develop well before 1500 as a Muslim military "camp language." It arose as increased contact between Hindus and Muslims required a shared medium of communication. Urdu is a form of Hindi (the medieval, Sanskrit-derived language of much of northern India) with many Persian words, written (like Persian) in Arabic script. Although its first literary use came before 1400, it was only much later that it replaced Persian as the major literary language of northern Indian and Deccan Muslims.

Indian Muslims were always susceptible to Hindu influence (in language, marriage customs, and caste consciousness). However, they were never utterly absorbed, as earlier invaders had been. The Muslims remained a group apart, conscious of their uniqueness

How the Hindus Differ from the Muslims

Al-Biruni (d. CA. 1050), *probably the greatest scholar of medieval Islam, was born in Khwarizm in northeast Iran. Much of his later life was spent at the court of Sultan Mahmud of Ghazna, and he accompanied Mahmud on various expeditions into northwest India. He learned Sanskrit and made a deep study of India and the Hindus and wrote a "History of India." The following selections from the first pages of this work show something of the reach and sophistication of his mind.*

. . . The barriers which separate Muslims and Hindus rest on different causes.

First, they differ from us in everything which other nations have in common. And here we first mention the language, although the difference of language also exists between other nations. If you want to conquer this difficulty (i.e. to learn Sanskrit), you will not find it easy, because the language is of an enormous range, both in words and inflections, something like the Arabic, calling one and the same thing by various names, both original and derived, and using one and the same word for a variety of subjects, which, in order to be properly understood, must be distinguished from each other by various qualifying epithets.

. . . .

Secondly, they totally differ from us in religion, as we believe in nothing in which they believe, and *vice versá*. On the whole, there is very little disputing about theological topics among themselves; at the utmost, they fight with words, but they will never stake their soul or body or their property on religious controversy. On the contrary, all their fanaticism is directed against those who do not belong to them—against all foreigners. They call them *mleecha*, i.e. impure, and forbid

having any connection with them, be it by intermarriage or any other kind or relationship, or by sitting, eating, and drinking with them, because thereby, they think, they would be polluted. They consider as impure anything which touches the fire and the water of a foreigner; and no household can exist without these two elements. Besides, they never desire that a thing which once has been polluted should be purified and thus recovered, as, under ordinary circumstances, if anybody or anything has become unclean, he or it would strive to regain the state of purity. They are not allowed to receive anybody who does not belong to them, even if he wished it, or was inclined to their religion. This, too, renders any connection with them quite impossible, and constitutes the widest gulf between us and them.

In the third place, in all manners and usages they differ from us to such a degree as to frighten their children with us, with our dress, and our ways and customs, and as to declare us to be devil's breed, and our doings as the very opposite of all that is good and proper. By the by, we must confess, in order to be just, that a similar depreciation of foreigners not only prevails among us and the Hindus, but is common to all nations towards each other. ❑

From Edward C. Sachau, *Alberuni's India*, Vol. 1 (London: Kegan Paul, Trench, Truebner, 1910), pp. 17, 19, 20.

A dervish and a musician of Mughal times. This fine miniature watercolor is attributed to the Mughal painter Daulat and is dated about 1610. Music has traditionally played a significant role in the practice of many Sufis. [Private Collection.]

in the Hindu world and proud to be distinct. The Muslim ruling classes saw themselves as the protectors and propagators of Islam in India. It is a measure of their sense of belonging to a larger Muslim community that, despite their independence of the rest of the Islamic world, most of the sultans of Delhi sought recognition for their rule in India from the nominal Abbasid caliphs in Baghdad or, in Mamluk times, in Cairo.

Nevertheless, reciprocal influence of Muslims and Hindus was inevitable, especially in the sphere of popular piety. Sufi devotion had an appeal similar to that of Hindu *bhakti* movements (see Chapter 11), and each at times influenced the other. Some of India's most revered Sufi and *bhakti* saints date from the fourteenth and fifteenth centuries. In this period, various theistic mystics strove to transcend the mutual antagonism and exclusivism of the more rigorous Muslims and Hindus. They typically preached devotion to a God who saves his worshipers without regard either to Hindu caste obligations or to legalistic observance of Muslim orthopraxy. The poet-saints Ramananda (d. after 1400) and Kabir (d. CA. 1518) were the two most famous of such reformers.

Other Traditions

These developments remind us that the history of India from 1000 to 1500 was not only that of the Muslims, although that is our focus here. This period was also important for the other religious communities of India. In the north, the Muslim conquests effectively ended the already greatly diminished Indian Buddhist monastic tradition. The role of the Muslim destruction of temples and monasteries in the virtual disappearance of Buddhism in this period has, however, been unduly emphasized. On the other hand, the attraction to Islam of the merchant classes, which had traditionally supported Buddhism, may have been underestimated.

Hindu religion and culture continued to flourish, even in areas of Muslim control. Both the continuing social and religious importance of the Brahmans and the popularity of *bhakti* (devotional) movements throughout India can attest the fact. In Brahmanic religious learning, it was an age of scholasticism that produced many commentaries and manuals, but few seminal works. *Bhakti* creativity was greater. The great Hindu Vaishnava Brahman, Ramanuja (d. 1137), provided a theological basis for *bhakti* devotion, reconciling its ideas with the classical Upanishadic Hindu worldview. *Bhakti* piety underlies the masterpiece of Hindu mystical love poetry, Jayadeva's *Gita Govinda* (twelfth century), which is devoted to Krishna, the most important of Vishnu's incarnations.

The south continued to be the center of Hindu cultural, political, and religious activity. Of several important dynastic states in the south in this age, the foremost was that of the Cholas (fl. CA. 900–1300). Aside from their military exploits and long political ascendency, this dynasty can claim lasting fame purely

INDIA	
CA. 900–1300	Chola dynasty in south India
1137	Death of Ramanuja
1206–1290	"Slave Sultans" of Delhi
1336–1565	Hindu dynasty of Vijayanagar
1347–1527	Muslim Bahmanid dynasty in the Deccan

Hindu Temples at Khajuraho. Here, on the central Indian plain, stand some twenty of the original eighty-five temples built by rajput princes almost 1000 years ago. The multiple spires of these spectacular structures symbolize the cosmic mountain Meru, which separated heaven and earth in Hindu mythology. In the mounting spires, the worshipper is led symbolically to union with the divine. [Diana L. Eck.]

for the school of bronze sculpture that they patronized at their capital of Tanjore. Their mightiest successor, the kingdom of Vijayanagar (1336–1565), in the fourteenth century subjugated the entire south and held out against its Muslim foes longer than had any other kingdom. Vijayanagar itself was one of India's most lavishly developed cities and a center of the cult of Shiva before its destruction by the Bahmanid sultan.

SUB-SAHARAN AFRICA

While North Africa and Egypt after 1000 were caught up in the major power struggles of the Islamic heartlands, a different situation existed in the African subcontinent, or sub-Saharan Africa. These areas developed much more strikingly according to internal African dynamics or different external influences. Nevertheless, from A.D. 1000, and largely from 1200, onward, Islam became a factor in sub-Saharan history. Thus, we allow Islamization to serve as the theme of our brief discussion of Africa in this period, even

MAP 15-3 AFRICA CA AD 1000–1500 *Shown are major cities and states referred to in the text. The circular inset provides greater detail for West Africa.*

though Islam was not in any way as important in sub-Saharan Africa as it was in North Africa and Egypt, or even India.

East Africa

The Southern Seas Trade

Along the southern rim of Asia, from the Red Sea and East Africa to Indonesia and the South China Sea, this period witnessed the gradual spread of Islamic religion and culture into new regions and among new peoples of diverse backgrounds. In port cities in Java, Sumatra, the Malaysian peninsula, South India, Gujarat, East Africa, Madagascar, and Zanzibar, Islamic traders established thriving communities. Their enclaves in these cities expanded until theirs was in many cases the dominant presence. Initially, the Muslims' economic stature attracted especially the socially and religiously mobile peoples of these cosmopolitan centers; many of them found the ideas and practices of Islam compelling as well. Typically, this first stage of conversion was followed by Islam's transmission to surrounding areas, and finally to inland centers of Hindu, Buddhist, or pagan culture and power. In this transmission, Sufi orders and their preachers and holy men played the main role. However, conquest by Muslim coastal states quickened the process later, at least in Indonesia.

The international trade network that the Muslims inherited in the southern seas went back many centuries. Before 1200, much of the trade in these waters had been dominated by Hindu or Buddhist kingdoms on the Malay Peninsula or Sumatra; Arab traders had also been active at least in the Indian Ocean. Hindu culture had been carried, along with an Indonesian language, as far as Madagascar some time in the first millennium A.D. Hindus were the chief religious group that the Muslims displaced. In the east, Islam never ousted the Indian Buddhist cultures of Burma, Thailand, and Indochina, although Muslim traders were in the port cities of all these areas. It did, however, gradually win most of Malaysia, Sumatra, Java, and the spice islands of the Moluccas—always the coastal areas first, then the inland regions.

Swahili Culture and Commerce

We saw in Chapter 11 that participation of east African port towns in the lucrative southern seas trade was ancient. Arabs, Indonesians, and at times, Indians had trafficked there for centuries. Many of them had been absorbed into what had become, from Somalia south, a predominantly Bantu-speaking east African population sometime during the first millennium A.D. From the eighth century on, Islam came along with Arab and Persian sailors and merchants to these southerly trading centers in the land of *al-Zanj*, or "the Blacks," as the Arabs called the inhabitants of Africa south of Egypt (hence "Zanzibar"). Conversion to Islam, however, went on slowly and only along the coastal perimeter. In the thirteenth century, Muslim traders from Arabia and Iran began to come in increased numbers and to dominate the coastal cities. From this time, Islamic faith and culture were influential and often predominant along the sea coast, from the port of Mogadishu south to that of Kilwa. By 1331, the traveler Ibn Battuta writes of Mogadishu as a thoroughly Islamic port and speaks of the ruler and inhabitants of Kilwa as Muslims. He also notes that there were now mosques for the faithful.[2]

By this time, a common language had developed out of the interaction of Bantu and Arabic speakers along the coast. This tongue, called *Swahili*, or *Kiswahili* (from the Arabic *sawahil*, "coastlands," a word used from ancient times for the East African coast), is Bantu in its structure, heavily Arabic in vocabulary, and written traditionally in the Arabic script, like Persian and many other languages of Islamic peoples. The

hybrid nature of this language mirrors the hybrid character of the African east-coast culture and peoples that came to be known also as Swahili.

Swahili language and culture may have developed first and most influentially in the northern towns of Manda, Lamu, and Mombasa, then further south along the coast. Today, the many coastal peoples who share them are of mixed ethnic character, joining African to Persian, Indian, Arab, and other blood. Current historical theory sees the origin of Swahili culture as basically African with a large admixture of Arab, Persian, and other extra-African elements. Nonetheless, it has ever been a source of pride for many older Swahili families to claim descent from illustrious Persian or Arab lineages of importance in Islamic history.

Swahili culture and language remained localized largely along the coast until very recent times. Likewise, the spread of Islam was largely limited to the coastal civilization and did not reach inland. The one possible exception is the Zambezi valley, where Muslim traders did penetrate some distance upriver. (This was in contrast to the lands farther north, in the Horn of Africa, where Islamic kingdoms developed in the Somali hinterland as well as on the coast.)

The height of Swahili civilization was in many ways the fourteenth and fifteenth centuries. Its centers were the harbor trading towns, most of which were on coastal islands or easily defended peninsulas. To these ports came merchants from abroad and from the African hinterlands, some to settle and stay. These towns were impressive. Beginning in the twelfth century, we can trace the development of stone-building techniques (first using coral blocks on red clay, later lime mortar). These were used for mosques, fortress-palaces, harbor fortifications, fancy private homes, and commercial buildings alike; all have their own distinctive cast that bespeaks a creative joining of African and Arabo-Persian elements.

Local states had their administrative centers in these trading towns. Today, historians are recognizing that their ruling dynasties were probably African in origin with an admixture of Arab or Persian blood from immigrants. In these coastal centers, an advanced and cosmopolitan level of culture reigned; by comparison, the majority of the populace in the small villages lived in mud and sometimes stone houses. Most of the latter earned their living either by farming or fishing, the two basic occupations of the coastal peoples besides trade. Society seems to have consisted of three principal groups: the local nobility, the commoners, and resident foreigners engaged in local commerce. Slaves constituted a fourth class of people, although the extent of their local use (as opposed to their sale) is disputed.

The trade that flourished was fed mainly by inland exports of ivory. In addition, gold, slaves, turtle shells,

[2]Ibn Battuta, *Travels in Asia and Africa*, 1325–1354, trans. and selected by H. A. R. Gibb (New York: Robert M. McBride & Co., 1929), pp. 110–113.

Ibn Battuta Visits Mogadishu and Kilwa (1331)

Ibn Battuta (d. 1369 or 1377), a native of Tangier, became one of history's most famous travelers through his voluminous and entertaining writings about his long years of relentless journeying, from Africa to India and China. In the following two excerpts from his description of his trip down the east African coast in 1331, he describes first the reception of visitors at Mogadishu and then the Sultan of Kilwa.

MOGADISHU

From there [Somalia] we sailed fifteen nights and arrived at Mogadishu, which is a very large town. The people have very many camels, and slaughter many hundreds every day. They have also many sheep. The merchants are wealthy, and manufacture a material which takes its name from the town and which is exported to Egypt and elsewhere.

Among the customs of the people of this town is the following: when a ship comes into port, it is boarded from *sanbuqs*, that is to say, little boats. Each *sanbuq* carries a crowd of young men, each carrying a covered dish, containing food. Each one of them presents his dish to a merchant on board, and calls out: 'This man is my guest.' And his fellows do the same. Not one of the merchants disembarks except to go to the house of his host among the young men, save frequent visitors to the country. In such a case they go where they like. When a merchant has settled in his host's house, the latter sells for him what he has brought and makes his purchases for him. Buying anything from a merchant below its market price or selling him anything except in his host's presence is disapproved of by the people of Mogadishu. They find it of advantage to keep to this rule.

THE SULTAN OF KILWA

When I arrived, the Sultan was Abu al-Muzaffar Hasan surnamed Abu al-Mawahib [the Father of Gifts] on account of his numerous charitable gifts. He frequently makes raids into the Zanj country, attacks them and carries off booty, of which he reserves a fifth, using it in the manner prescribed by the Koran. That reserved for the kinsfolk of the Prophet is kept separate in the Treasury, and, when Sharifs come to visit him, he gives it them. They come to him from Iraq, the Hijaz, and other countries. I found several Sharifs from the Hijaz at his court, among them Muhammad ibn Jammaz, Mansur ibn Labida ibn Abi Nami and Muhamma ibn Shumaila ibn Abi Nami. At Mogadishu I saw Tabl ibn Kubaish ibn Jammaz, who also wished to visit him. This Sultan is very humble: he sits and eats with beggars, and venerates holy men and descendants of the Prophet. ❑

G. S. P. Freeman-Grenville, *The East African Coast: Select Documents*, 2nd ed. (London: Rex Collings, 1975), pp. 27–28, 31–32.

ambergris, leopard skins, pearls, fish, sandalwood, ebony, and local cotton cloth were among the many commodities that passed through the coastal centers. The chief imports were cloth, porcelain, glassware, china, glass beads, and glazed pottery. Certain exports tended to dominate at particular ports: cloth, sandalwood, ebony, and ivory at Mogadishu; ivory at Manda; or gold at Kilwa and, farther south still, at the port of Sofala. Cowrie shells were a common medium of payment in the inland trade, but coins minted at Mogadishu and Kilwa from the fourteenth century were increasingly used in the major trading centers. The gold trade seems to have become important only in the fifteenth century.

The decline of the original Swahili civilization in the sixteenth century can be attributed primarily to the loss of much of the trade that had originally made everything possible. The arrival of the Portuguese, and their subsequent destruction of the old oceanic trade patterns and existing Islamic city-states, seem to be the chief culprits. However, some scholars point also to decreases in rainfall or invasions of Zimba peoples from inland regions as contributing factors in the decline beginning in the sixteenth century.

Southeastern Africa: "Great Zimbabwe"

At about the same time that the trading centers of the east coast were beginning to flourish, a very different kind of African civilization was enjoying its heyday inland and farther south, in the rocky, savannah-woodland watershed between the Limpopo and Zambezi rivers, in modern southern Zimbabwe. This civilization was a purely African one sited far enough inland never to have felt the impact of Islam. It was founded in the eleventh century by the ancestors of the Bantu-speaking Shona people who still inhabit the same general area of southeastern Africa. It seems to have developed into a large and prosperous state between the late thirteenth and the late fifteenth centu-

"Great Zimbabwe," so-called because it is the most impressive of 300 such stone ruins in modern Zimbabwe and neighboring countries. These sites give clear evidence of the advanced, iron-age mining, and cattle-raising culture that flourished in this region between about A.D. 1000 and 1500. Its people are thought to have been of Bantu and Negroid stock. They apparently had a highly developed trade in gold and copper with outsiders, including Arabs on the East Coast. As yet, all too little is known about this impressive society. [Bettmann Archive.]

ries. We know it only through the archaeological remains of an estimated one hundred and fifty settlements in the Zambezi-Limpopo region.

By far the most impressive of these ruins, and the apparent capital of this ancient Shona state, is that known today as "Great Zimbabwe." This is a huge, sixty-odd-acre site encompassing two different major building complexes. One is a series of stone enclosures on a high hill; it overlooks the other—a much larger enclosure that contains numerous ruins and a large circular tower, all surrounded by a massive wall some thirty-two feet high and in places as much as seventeen feet thick. The former so-called "acropolis" complex may have contained a shrine, while the latter was apparently the royal palace and fort. The impressive stonework reflects a wealthy and sophisticated society. The artifacts found there include gold and copper ornaments, soapstone carvings, and imported beads, as well as china, glass, and porcelain of Chinese, Syrian, and Persian origins.

The state itself seems to have had some degree of control of the increasing gold trade between more inland areas and the east-coast port of Sofala. Its territory lay to the east and south of substantial gold-mining enterprises that tapped both the alluvial gold of the Zambezi tributaries and the gold-ore deposits that stretched southwest in a broad band below the middle Zambezi. We can speculate that this large settlement must have been the capital city of a prosperous empire and the residence of a ruling elite. Its wider domain was made up mostly of smaller settlements of common folk who lived on subsistence agriculture and cattle raising and whose culture was considerably different from that of the capital.

We may well speculate as to reasons for the flowering of the Zimbabwe civilization. Available evidence suggests first a general population growth and increasing economic prosperity in the Zambezi-Limpopo region prior to A.D. 1500. The specific impetus for ancient Zimbabwe may have been a significant immigration around A.D. 1000 of late-Iron-Age Shona-speakers who brought with them mining techniques and/or farming innovations along with their ancestor cults. Improved farming and animal husbandry may have led to substantial population growth. Another material cause may have been an increase in the gold trade between Sofala and the inland gold mining areas, with Great Zimbabwe being the chief beneficiary through its middle-man role. This latter hypothesis would link the flourishing of Zimbabwe to the general flourishing of the east African coast from about the thirteenth century.

None of these theories are mutually exclusive, however. Without written or new archaeological sources, we shall likely never know exactly what allowed this civilization to develop so impressively and to dominate

CA. 1000–1500	"Great Zimbabwe" civilization
CA. 1200–1400	Development of Bantu Kiswahili language
CA. 1300–1600	Height of Swahili culture

the region for nearly two hundred years. Its eventual demise is also somewhat obscure. It appears that it involved primarily a splitting up of northern and southern sectors of the state and corresponding movement of the major populations away from the environs of Great Zimbabwe, likely because of exhaustion of the farming and grazing land there. The southern successor kingdom was that known as Changamire—a state that survived to become very powerful from the late 1600s until about 1830. The northern successor state was known as the kingdom ruled by the Mwene Mutapa, or "Master Pillager"—the title by which the first Portuguese sources knew first Mutota, and then his successors, as the kings of the sixteenth-century riverine empire that stretched along the middle and lower course of the Zambezi.

West Africa

The Coming of Islam

On the other side of the subcontinent, Islam penetrated south of the Sahara not by sea, but by land—south from North Africa and Egypt across the Sahara and west from the Nile south of the Sahara. Beginning as early as about 800, Islam came chiefly with Berber traders over the desert routes (mentioned in Chapter 11) to trading towns like Awdaghast on the edge of the sahel. Thence it spread south to the Niger and beyond, and west into the Senegal basin. Another source for Muslim penetration of the central and western Sudan was Egypt and Nilotic Africa. From these eastern Islamic areas, migrating Arab tribal groups came to settle in the sub-Saharan steppeland or *sahel*. Although many more Arabs followed the Mediterranean coast from Egypt to North Africa, substantial numbers sifted westward to Lake Chad and the Niger regions, from the ninth to the sixteenth centuries and beyond.

Some Muslim conversion came quite early, virtually always through the medium of Muslim traders. The year 985 marks the first time that a royal court of west Africa officially became Muslim. This was in the kingdom of Gao, east of the Niger bend (see Chapter 11). The Gao rulers did not, however, try to convert their subjects. By contrast, the rulers of Ghana clung long to their indigenous traditions of faith; but they

kept a separate township near their capital of Kumbi (or Kumbi Saleh) for the Muslim merchants with whom they dealt extensively and the Muslim advisers who helped them govern.

From the 1030s, an overt conversion campaign was begun in coastal Mauritania and Senegal and mounted in the western sahel and Sahara by the zealous militants known as Almoravids (Arabic *al-Murabitun*, after their fortified retreat centers, or *ribats*). This movement eventually swept into Ghana's territory, taking first Awdaghast and finally Kumbi in 1076. Thereafter, the forcibly converted Soninke ruling group of Ghana spread Islam among their own populace and farther south in the savannah. Here they converted Mande-speaking traders who spread it in time south into the forests as well. Farther west, the Fulbe rulers of Takrur along the Senegal had became Muslim in the 1030s and propagated their new faith among their subjects. (The Fulbe would remain important agents of the spread of Islam as they migrated gradually into new regions as far south and east as Lake Chad over the next eight centuries.) In the region of Lake Chad, as we saw in Chapter 11, the strongest ruler was Muslim from as early as about 1100—even before the Kanuri people became fully sedentarized as the ruling group of the new kingdom of Kanem.

All in all, the spread of Islam was peaceful, gradual, and partial. Typically, it never penetrated beyond the ruling or commercial classes of a region. Even among these, it tended to coexist or blend with indigenous ideas and practices. Especially in the sub-Niger region, some major groups strongly resisted Islamization altogether—notably the Mossi kingdoms founded in the Volta region at Wagadugu around 1050 and Yatenga about 1170. Thus Islamic conversion in west Africa in general was neither rapid, forcible, nor, even by 1500, widespread.

Nevertheless, Islam and its carriers were of great moment for West African history. Agents of Islam brought, on the one hand, military and commercial developments and, on the other, the Qur'an and Arabic scholarship and literate culture. In west as in east Africa, the arrival of literate culture proved to be as important an event for subsequent African history as any other development. Many innovations, from architectural techniques to intellectual and administrative traditions, depended upon writing and literacy, which are among the most important supports of the development of large-scale complex societies and cultures.

Sahelian Empires

We noted in Chapter 11 the rise, already in the first millennium, of several substantial states just south of the Sahara proper. In the period from about 1000 to

Ghana and Its People in the Mid-Eleventh Century

The following excerpt is from the geographical work of the Spanish Muslim writer al-Bakri (d. 1094). In it, he describes with great precision some customs of the ruler and the people of the capital of Ghana as he carefully gleaned them from other Arabic sources and travelers (he never visited west Africa himself, it seems).

Ghāna is a title given to their kings; the name of the region is Awkār, and their king today, namely in the year 460/1067–8, is Tankā Manīn. . . . This Tunkā Manīn is powerful, rules an enormous kingdom, and possesses great authority.

The city of Ghāna consists of two towns situated on a plain. One of these towns, which is inhabited by Muslims, is large and possesses twelve mosques, in one of which they assemble for the Friday prayer. There are salaried imams and muezzins, as well as jurists and scholars. In the environs are wells with sweet water, from which they drink and with which they grow vegetables. The king's town is six miles distant from this one and bears the name of Al-Ghāba. Between these two towns there are continuous habitations. The houses of the inhabitants are of stone and acacia (*sunt*) wood. The king has a palace and a number of domed dwellings all surrounded with an enclosure like a city wall (*sūr*). In the king's town, and not far from his court of justice, is a mosque where the Muslims who arrive at his court (*yafid 'alayh*) pray. Around the king's town are domed buildings and groves and thickets where the sorcerers of these people, men in charge of the religious cult, live. In them too are their idols and the tombs of their kings. . . .

All of them shave their beards, and women shave their heads. The king adorns himself like a woman [wearing necklaces] round his neck and [bracelets] on his forearms, and he puts on a high cap (*tartūr*) decorated with gold and wrapped in a turban of fine cotton. He sits in audience or to hear grievances against officials (*mazālim*) in a domed pavilion around which stand ten horses covered with gold-embroidered materials. Behind the king stand ten pages holding shields and swords decorated with gold, and on his right are the sons of the [vassal] kings of his country wearing splendid garments and their hair plaited with gold. The governor of the city sits on the ground before the king and around him are ministers seated likewise. . . . When the people who profess the same religion as the king approach him they fall on their knees and sprinkle dust on their heads, for this is their way of greeting him. As for the Muslims, they greet him only by clapping their hands.

Their religion is paganism and the worship of idols (*dakākīr*). When their king dies they construct over the place where his tomb will be an enormous dome of *sāj* wood. Then they bring him on a bed covered with a few carpets and cushions and place him beside the dome. At his side they place his ornaments, his weapons, and the vessels from which he used to eat and drink, filled with various kinds of food and beverages. ❑

From J. F. P. Hopkins (trans.), N. Levtzion and J. F. P. Hopkins (eds.), *Corpus of Early Arabic Sources for West African History* (Cambridge University Press, 1981), pp. 79–80.

1500, three of these sahelian kingdoms of the western and central Sudan developed into notable and relatively long-lived empires: Ghana, Mali, and Kanem.

GHANA. Ghana was the state that established the model for later west Sudanic empire. Located far north of modern Ghana (and unrelated to it), in the sahel between the Senegal and Niger, Ghana's power was built upon a solid economic base. Tribute from the empire's many chieftaincies and taxes on royal lands and crops supplemented the two major sources of income: duties levied on all incoming and outgoing trade, including imported salt, cloth, and metal goods; and profits from control of the gold trade. Although the king and court did not convert to Islam, Muslims were used to organize and administer the government, and Muslim legists advised the ruler. Ghana's society was a stratified one, ranging from slaves at the bottom through farmers and craftsmen to a merchant class and finally the nobility of king and court. A huge, well-trained army secured the king's control of his dominions. The empire was, however, vulnerable to attack from the desert fringe, as the Almoravids proved in the late tenth century. The recurring sahelian blight of drought may also have contributed to Ghana's demise just after the peak of its power in the mid-eleventh century.

MALI. After Ghana fell to the Almoravids in the late eleventh century, it was almost two centuries before another comparable empire could be reestablished in the western sahel. With Ghana's collapse and the Almoravids' failure—largely because of their greater interest in North Africa—to build a new empire in the sahel, the western Sudan broke up into various smaller kingdoms. Only in the mid-thirteenth century was one of these kingdoms able to forge a new and lasting empire; it was based in good part on improved trade along the Niger, below it into the forests, and west into the Gambia and Senegal river basins. This empire was Mali, which arose in all likelihood with the same dominant purpose and economic base as that of Ghana earlier: monopolization of the lucrative north-south gold trade through dominating enough of the sahel to control the flow of west African gold to the trans-Saharan trade routes. Mali was, however, better able than Ghana had been to control all trade on the upper Niger and to add to it that on the Gambia to the west.

Mali's new imperial power was built largely by the efforts of one leader, the Mandinke King Sundiata (or Sunjaata; reigned 1230–1255). His royal Keita dynasty had been Muslim for a century and a half before him. Probably fueled by significant population growth in the western savannah, Malian imperial rule rested upon both strong agriculture and the great commercial skills of the Mandinke people. Sundiata and his Mandinke successors exploited both to produce an even more powerful empire than its Ghanaian predecessor. Sundiata himself extended his control far beyond the former domains of Ghana, west to the Atlantic coast and beyond Timbuktu in the east. By controlling the commercial centers of Gao, Walata, and Jenne, he was able to take the Saharan trade fully in hand. He built his capital Niani, located in the savannah well south of Ghana's capital of Kumbi, into a major city.

Sundiata's and his successor's empire encompassed ultimately three major historical regions and language groups of Sudanic west Africa: (1) the Senegal region (including Takrur) with its West Atlantic languages (such as Fulbe, Tukulor, Wolof, Serer); (2) the central-Mande states and language groups of the Soninke and Mandinke, between the Senegal and Niger; and (3) the Songhai-speaking peoples of the Niger (in the region of

Mansa Musa in Cairo

The following account is by a Damascene scholar, al-Umari (d. 1349), who spent much of his life in Cairo. Here he describes what he learned of Mansa Musa's reception by the Mamluk sultan. The report reflects the respect commanded by Musa among the Cairenes, both for his piety and for his wealth and obvious power (he had a massive entourage with him).

From the beginning of my coming to stay in Egypt I heard talk of the arrival of this sultan Mūsā on his Pilgrimage and found the Cairenes eager to recount what they had seen of the Africans' prodigal spending. I asked the emir Abū 'l-ʿAbbās Aḥmad b. al-Ḥāk the *mihmandar* and he told me of the opulence, manly virtues, and piety of this sultan. "When I went out to meet him (he said), that is, on behalf of the mighty sultan al-Malik al-Nāṣir, he did me extreme honour and treated me with the greatest courtesy. He addressed me, however, only through an interpreter despite his perfect ability to speak in the Arabic tongue. Then he forwarded to the royal treasury many loads of unworked native gold and other valuables. I tried to persuade him to go up to the Citadel to meet the sultan, but he refused persistently, saying: 'I came for the Pilgrimage and nothing else. I do not wish to mix anything else with my Pilgrimage.' He had begun to use this argument but I realized that the audience was repugnant to him because he would be obliged to kiss the ground and the sultan's hand. I continued to cajole him and he continued to make excuses but the sultan's protocol demanded that I should bring him into the royal presence, so I kept on at him till he agreed.

"When we came in the sultan's presence we said to him: 'Kiss the ground!' but he refused outright saying: 'How may this be?' Then an intelligent man who was with him whispered to him something we could not understand and he said: 'I make obeisance to God who created me!' then he prostrated himself and went forward to the sultan. The sultan half rose to greet him and sat him by his side. They conversed together for a long time, then sultan Mūsā went out. The sultan sent to him several complete suits of honour for himself, his courtiers, and all those who had come with him, and saddled and bridled horses for himself and his chief courtiers. . . . He also furnished him with accommodation and abundant supplies during his stay.

"When the time to leave for the Pilgrimage came round the sultan sent to him a large sum of money with ordinary and thoroughbred camels complete with saddles and equipment to serve as mounts for him, and purchased abundant supplies for his entourage and others who had come with him. He arranged for deposits of fodder to be placed along the road and ordered the caravan commanders to treat him with honour and respect. . . . " ❑

From J. F. P. Hopkins (trans.), N. Levtzion and J. F. P. Hopkins (eds.), *Corpus of Early Arabic Sources for West African History* (Cambridge: Cambridge University Press, 1981), pp. 269–270.

Gao). The power of the rulers of Mali was always less that of a centralized bureaucratic state than that of the center of a vast sphere of influence. In their domain, individual chieftaincies and dependencies retained much of their independence, but recognized the sovereignty of the supreme, sacred *mansa*, or "emperor," of the Malian realms.

The greatest Keita king proved to be Mansa Musa (1312–1337), whose pilgrimage through Mamluk Cairo to Mecca in 1324 became famous in Egypt. He paid out or gave away so much gold in Cairo alone that he started a massive inflation that lasted over a decade. He returned from his pilgrimage with many Muslim scholars, artists, and architects in tow to grace his court. At home, he consolidated Mali's power, securing peace for most of his reign throughout his vast dominions. Musa's claimed devoutness as a Muslim translated into a positive environment for the further spread of Islam in the empire and beyond; but not all conversions of his and later reigns survived Mali's decline in the next century. Under his rule, Timbuktu became known far and wide for its madrasas and libraries, as well as its poets, scientists, and architects. During his reign, Timbuktu became the leading intellectual center of sub-Saharan Islamic religion and culture as well as one of the major trading cities of the sahel—roles that lasted far beyond the period of Mali's imperial dominance.

Mali's dominance waned after Musa's time, most sharply in the fifteenth century. A chief cause seems to have been destructive rivalries for the succession to the *mansa*'s throne. As time went on, more and more subject dependencies became independent, and the empire shrank in extent and power. In the 1430s, Berber Tuaregs wrested control from Mali of much of its sahelian dominions, including Timbuktu and Walata. The Mossi in the south made large inroads on Malian territory in the middle of the century, and thereafter the rise of a new power in Gao signaled the end of Mali's imperial authority. It marked also the beginning of the new Songhai empire that would take its place as the major west–central Sudanic power in the sixteenth century (see Chapter 22).

KANEM. Kanem represented, as we noted in Chapter 11, a very different kind of empire. It began as a southern Saharan confederation from among the black nomadic tribes known as Zaghawah, who were spread over much of the south–central and southeastern Sahara. By the twelfth century, a Zaghawah group known as the Kanuri had apparently settled in Kanem, the sahelian and Saharan region northeast of Lake Chad, and from here they set out on military expansion. Their key leader in this, Mai Dunama Dibbalemi (reigned CA. 1221–1259), was a contemporary of

Sundiata in Mali. Like Sundiata, Dibbalemi was a Muslim—indeed, probably the first Kanuri leader to embrace Islam, although there are traditions recalling a Muslim ruler in the Kanem region as early as 1085. In any case, Islam appears to have entrenched itself among the Kanuri ruling class during Dibbalemi's reign. He and his successors expanded Kanuri power north into the desert far enough to include the Fezzan in modern Libya and northeast along the sahel-Sahara fringe toward Nilotic Africa. In both directions, the Kanuri controlled important trade routes—north to Libya and east to the Nile and Egypt.

Islam was important to some of the Kanuri rulers. Dibbalemi used it as a sanction for his rule, which otherwise had the familiar African trappings of a sacred kingship. It also provided a reason for expansion through *jihad*, or holy struggle against pagans. His reign, and that of his successors through the next two centuries, saw the mixing of Kanuri and local Kanembu peoples, primarily those known as the So. There was a corresponding transformation of the Kanuri leader from a nomadic *shaykh* to a Sudanic king and a change of the Kanembu state from a nomadic to a largely sedentary kingdom replete with quasi-feudal institutions. Like Mali to the west, Kanembu dominion was both one of direct rule over and taxation of core territories and groups as well as one of tributary influence or control of a wider region of local vassal chieftaincies. Linguistic and religious (Muslim) acculturation progressed most rapidly in the core territories.

Civil strife, largely over the succession to the kingship, weakened the Kanuri state in the later fourteenth and especially the fifteenth century. In the fifteenth century, the locus of power shifted from Kanem proper westward, to the southwest of Lake Chad. Here, at the end of the fifteenth century, in the land of Bornu, a new Kanuri empire arose almost simultaneously with that of Songhai in the western Sudan (see Chapter 22).

West African Forest Kingdoms: The Example of Benin

For most of west and central Africa, we have little or no written evidence before the sixteenth century of the many states and smaller societies that flourished in the southern reaches of the Sudanic savannahs and in the forestlands to their south. However, other kinds of evidence reveal that many states, some with distinct political, religious, and cultural traditions, had developed in the southern and coastal regions of west Africa several centuries before the first Portuguese reports in 1485. Even those states like Asante or the Yoruba kingdoms of Oyo and Ife, that reached their height only after 1500, had much earlier origins. The best-known of these forest kingdoms, Benin reflects especially in its

striking developments in world history in this period; they often had cataclysmic effects upon Chinese, south and west Asian, and eastern European societies and states. These conquests and migrations did not build lasting major states or civilizations, but they did bring destruction of existing orders. They also contributed, however unintentionally, new and often significant human resources to existing civilizations like those of China and the Islamic heartlands.

In this age, Islam became truly an international tradition of religious, political, and social values and institutions. It did so by being highly adaptable and open to "indigenization" in the seemingly hostile contexts of polytheistic Hindu or African societies. Also in this age very distinct traditions of art, language, and literature, for all their local, regional, or national diversity, became intelligible and identifiable parts of a larger whole defined by a Muslim identity. Islamic civilization had nothing of the territorial contiguousness or homogeneous linguistic and cultural traditions of either Chinese or Japanese civilization. Nevertheless, the Islamic world was an international reality in which a Muslim could travel and meet other Muslims of radically diverse backgrounds with much common ground for understanding.

Indian traditional culture was not, like the Islamic, bound up with an expanding, missionary religious tradition. Yet, in this age, Hindu kingdoms throve in Indonesia. Buddhism, even while dwindling into a small minority tradition in its Indian homeland, was expanding across much of central and east Asia, thereby solidifying its place as an international missionary tradition. Christianity, by contrast, was not rapidly expanding, in Africa, Asia, or Europe; but by 1500 its western European branch was poised on the brink of internal revolution and international proselytism that began with the voyages of discovery.

In most of Africa during this period, development went on most often without interference or great influence from abroad. Only the East African coast, Egypt, and North Africa were significantly oriented to foreign societies. However, in this age, Africa did have ever increasing and ever more significant contact and interaction with other major cultural and political regions, from Europe to China. It saw the spread of Islamic patterns to new areas, and by 1500 it witnessed the beginning of European and Christian penetration. For all its diversity, Africa's change was more an extension of previous patterns than a radical divergence—at least by comparison with the transformations brewing in Western Europe.

At the beginning of this period (1000–1500) Europe was almost a backwater of culture and power by comparison with major Islamic or Hindu states, let alone those of China and Japan. At its close, however, Euro-pean civilization was riding the crest of a cultural renaissance, enjoying economic and political growth, and starting the global exploration that would turn into a flood of imperial expansion and affect most of the rest of the globe. Neither Islamic, Indian, African, Chinese, nor Japanese culture and society were so radically changed or changing in their basic ideas and institutions as were those of Western Europe over these five hundred years.

Suggested Reading

THE ISLAMIC HEARTLANDS

J. A. BOYLE, ed., *The Cambridge History of Iran*. Vol. 5: *The Saljuq and Mongol Periods* (1968). Useful and reasonably detailed articles on political, social, religious, and cultural developments.

P. K. HITTI, *History of the Arabs*, 8th ed. (1964). Still a useful English resource, largely for factual detail. See especially Part IV, "The Arabs in Europe: Spain and Sicily."

M. G. S. HODGSON, *The Expansion of Islam in the Middle Periods*. Vol. 2 of *The Venture of Islam*. 3 vols. (1964). The strongest of Hodgson's monumental three-volume survey of Islamic civilization, and the only English work of its kind to give the period 945–1500 such broad and unified coverage.

B. LEWIS, ed., *Islam and the Arab World* (1976). A large-format, heavily illustrated volume with many excellent articles on diverse aspects of Islamic (not simply Arab, as the misleading title indicates) civilization through the premodern period.

D. MORGAN, *The Mongols* (1986). A recent and readable survey history.

J. J. SAUNDERS, *A History of Medieval Islam* (1965). A brief, simple introductory survey of Islamic history to the Mongol invasions.

D. SOURDEL, *Medieval Islam*. Trans. W. M. Watt (1983). The synthetic, interpretive chapters on Islam and the political and social orders (4, 5), and on towns and art (6) are especially helpful.

B. SPULER, *The Mongols in History*. Trans. Geoffrey Wheeler (1971). A short introductory survey of Mongol history, of which Chapters 2–5 are most relevant.

B. SPULER, *The Muslim World: A Historical Survey*. Trans. F. R. C. Bagley (1960 3 vols.). Volumes I and II are handy reference volumes offering a highly condensed chronicle of Islamic history from Muhammad through the fifteenth century.

INDIA

S. M. IKRAM, *Muslim Civilization in India* (1964). The best short survey history, covering the period 711 to 1857.

R. C. MAJUMDAR, gen. ed., *The History and Culture of the Indian People*. Vol. VI: *The Delhi Sultanate*, 3rd ed. (1980). A comprehensive political and cultural account of the period in India.

M. Mujeeb, *The Indian Muslims* (1967). The best cultural study of Islamic civilization in India as a whole, from its origins onward.

V. A. Smith, *The Oxford History of India*, 4th ed. rev. Percival Spear et al. (1981). An easy-to-read historical survey with helpful chronologies. See especially Books III–V, pp. 190–319.

AFRICA

R. E. Bradbury, *Benin Studies*. Ed. P. Morton-Williams (1973). Good material on the history of the state, village life, religion, and art.

P. Curtin, S. Feierman, L. Thompson, and J. Vansina, *African History* (1978). Chapters 4 and 5 on East Africa are especially noteworthy for the present chapter's concerns.

B. Davidson, *The African Past* (1964). A combination of primary-source selections and brief secondary-study assessments trace the history of the diverse parts of Africa.

J. D. Fage, *A History of Africa* (1978). Solid survey, with some good maps. See segments on Guinea and the impact of Islam upon Africa.

R. W. July, *A History of the African People*, 3rd ed. (1980). Part I, "Ancient Africa," covers the precolonial centuries, offering an area-by-area historical introduction to African civilization.

D. T. Niane, ed., *Africa from the Twelfth to the Sixteenth Century*. UNESCO General History of Africa, Vol. 4 (1984). Contains important, up-to-date survey articles on the topics treated here.

B. A. Ogot and J. A. Kieran, eds., *Zamani: A Survey of East African History*, 2nd rev. ed. (1974). Most helpful treatment of varied aspects of history and culture by various specialists.

A. F. C. Ryder, *Benin and the Europeans*, 1485–1897 (1969). Chapter 1, on the history of the Benin kingdom, offers a good survey.

J. S. Trimingham, *A History of Islam in West Africa* (1962). Dated, but still a fundamental survey of the topic.

The World in Transition (1500–1800)

BETWEEN 1500 and 1800, the major centers of world civilization achieved political organization and stability that in some cases endured into the present century. This period also witnessed a shift in the balance of world political and economic power toward Europe. That shift was anything but inevitable. It was the result of paths taken by Europeans and not taken by the peoples and governments of other areas of the world.

Sixteenth-century Japan was torn by wars among its various small states and regions. This civil conflict eroded the manorial social structure. The adoption of the spear in place of the sword allowed the development of foot-soldier armies that displaced the samurai. By approximately 1600, however, a new political regime was establishing itself on the basis of a "feudal" society involving complex vassal–lord relationships in many, though not all, ways similar to those in medieval Europe. Tokugawa Ieyasu established his government in Edo (now Tokyo). Through a series of land transfers and confiscations, he surrounded himself with unquestionably loyal retainers and placed those of less certain loyalty at a far geographical remove from his capital. He and his successors required vassals to send their families to live as virtual hostages near the court in Edo. Finally, Tokugawa Japan imposed on itself a policy of isolation from the rest of the world. Though stable and relatively prosperous, Japan remained separated from its neighbors and the larger world from the 1630s until the middle of the nineteenth century.

Without experiencing such civil strife, China entered on an epoch of remarkable strength, expansion, and cultural achievement. The Ming and Ch'ing dynasties ruled, and only the most minimal turmoil accompanied the transfer of power in 1644. The emperors of both dynasties governed in an absolute manner. The bureaucracy — named *mandarins* by the Jesuits, who came to China in the sixteenth century — was chosen meritocratically through a complex series of examinations and governed efficiently. The population of China expanded steadily. China experienced a second commercial revolution. Chinese shipping expanded. Although a truly national economy did not emerge, China possessed several regional economies, each as large as that of a major European national state. A banking system spread through the country to foster commerce. What did not occur in China, for all its commercial enterprise, was the development of industrialism. Nonetheless, at the end of this era, China appeared to be a very strong, stable nation. As in Japan, the tradition of Confucianism had achieved vast new influence.

In 1500, over a century of continued political and military strength lay before the Islamic world. The Ottoman Empire was at the time perhaps the most powerful military state in the world. The Safavids securely governed Iran as did the Mughals India. However, by the middle of the seventeenth century, the power of all three empires was on the wane. The growing military and naval strength of Europe defeated the Ottoman Turks at the sea battle of Lepanto in 1571 and in numerous land engagements during the seventeenth century. The final Turkish siege of Vienna failed in 1683. In Iran, the intense religiosity of the Shi'ites led to the neglect of political and military structures and, consequently, to difficulty in halting aggression from the Turks. At the same time, a distinctive mode of Shi'ite pietism arose in Iran. The Mughal Empire experienced a slow but steady decline after the late seventeenth century. By the battle of Plassey in 1757, the British East India Company had established a position of strength from which, within less than a century, Britain would come to govern the entire Indian subcontinent.

Early in the sixteenth century, Western Europe began to be divided between Protestantism and Roman Catholicism. The sectarian splintering that has resulted in hundreds of modern Protestant denominations also began at this time. Even within Catholicism, deep divisions developed between Catholics who favored traditional practices and those who championed the reforms of the Counter-Reformation and the Jesuits. A century and a half of religious war and theological conflict followed. Rulers made the most of these divisions to consolidate their territories politically. Confessionalization (that is, strict enforcement of a particular "orthodox" religious belief and practice) went hand in hand with the creation of modern Western states.

Four factors largely account for this momentous shift in the cultural balance of the world. First, the new monarchies that had arisen in the late Middle Ages, particularly in France, England, and Spain, now successfully unified their realms. Between 1500 and the middle of the eighteenth century, those monarchs learned to tame their aristocracies, to collect taxes efficiently, and to build effective armies and navies. Second, in league with the commercial sectors of their national economies, the monarchs and their bureaucrats encouraged voyages of commercial expansion and discovery. Through those voyages, Europeans penetrated markets across the globe. They also conquered and colonized the American continents and thereby europeanized two vast, rich landmasses much larger than Europe itself. Third, during the seventeenth century, European thinkers carried out new intellectual explorations that culminated in the Scientific Revolution. The new knowledge and methods of rational investigation of physical nature permitted them to develop their technological skills more fully. As a consequence, the fourth factor came into play, as Europeans, and most particularly the British, achieved an early foundation of industrial manufacturing that would permit further domination of world markets with inexpensive consumer goods. ❏

	EUROPE	NEAR EAST/INDIA
1500	*1517–1555* Protestant Reformation *1533–1584* Ivan the Terrible of Russia reigns *1540* Jesuit Order founded by Ignatius Loyola *1543–1727* The Scientific Revolution *1556–1598* Philip II of Spain reigns *1558–1603* Elizabeth I of England reigns *1562–1598* French Wars of Religion *1581* The Netherlands declares its independence from the Spanish Habsburgs *1588* Defeat of the Spanish Armada *1589–1610* Henry IV, Navarre, founds Bourbon dynasty of France	*1500–1722* Safavid Shi'ite rule in Iran *1512–1520* Ottoman ruler Selim I *1520–1566* Ottoman ruler Suleiman the Magnificent *1525–1527* Babur founds Mughal dynasty in India *1540* Hungary under Ottoman rule *1556–1605* Akbar the Great of India reigns *1571* Battle of Lepanto; Ottomans defeated *ca. 1571–1640* Safavid philosopher/writer Mullah Sadra *1588–1629* Shah Abbas I of Iran reigns
1600	*1618–1648* The Thirty Years War *1640–1688* Frederick William, the Great Elector reigns in Brandenburg-Prussia *1642–1646* Puritan Revolution in England *1643–1715* Louis XIV of France reigns *1682–1725* Peter the Great of Russia reigns *1688* The Glorious Revolution in England *1690* "Second Treatise of Civil Government," by John Locke	*1605–1657* Period of religious toleration in Mughal Empire, India *1628–1657* Shah Jahan reigns; builds Taj Mahal as mausoleum for his beloved wife *1646* Founding of Maratha empire *1648* Delhi becomes capital of Mughal Empire *1658–1707* Shah Aurangzeb, the "World Conqueror," reigns in India; end of religious toleration toward Hindus; beginning of Mughal decline *1669–1683* Last military expansion by Ottomans: 1669, seize Crete; 1670s, the Ukraine; 1683, lay siege to Vienna
1700	*1701* Act of Settlement provides for Protestant succession to English throne *1702–1713* War of Spanish Succession *1740–1748* War of Austrian Succession *1756–1763* Seven Years War *ca. 1750* Industrial Revolution begins in England *1772* First partition of Poland *1793* and *1795* Last two partitions of Poland	*1700* Sikhs and Marathas bring down Mughal empire *1708* British East India Company and New East India Company merged. *1722* Last Safavid ruler forced to abdicate *1724* Rise in the Deccan of the Islamic state of Hyderabad *1725* Nadir Shah of Afghanistan becomes ruler of Persia *1739* Persian invasion of Northern India, by Nadir Shah *1748–1761* Ahmad Shah Durrani of Afghanistan invades India *1757* British victory at Plassey, in Bengal

EAST ASIA	AFRICA	THE AMERICAS
1500–1800 Commercial revolution in Ming-Ch'ing China; trade with Europe; flourishing of the novel *1543* Portuguese arrive in Japan *1568–1600* Era of unification follows end of Warring States Era in Japan *1587* Spanish arrive in Japan *1588* Hideyoshi's sword hunt in Japan *1592–1598* Ming troops battle Hideyoshi's army in Korea	*1506* East coast of Africa under Portuguese domination *1507* Mozambique founded by Portuguese *1517* Spanish crown authorizes slave trade to its South American colonies; rapid increase in importation of slaves to the New World *1554–1659* Sa'did Sultanate in Morocco *1575* Union of Bornu and Kanem by Idris Alawma (r. 1575–1610); Kanem-Bornu state the most fully Islamic in West Africa *1591* Moroccan army defeats Songhai army; Songhai Empire collapses	*1519* Conquest of the Aztecs by Cortes; Aztec ruler, Montezuma (r. 1502–1519) killed; Tenochtitlan destroyed *1529* Mexico City becomes capital of the Viceroyalty of New Spain *1533* Pizarro begins his conquest of the Incas *1536* Spanish under Mendoza arrive in Argentina *1544* Lima becomes capital of the Viceroyalty of Peru *1584* Sir Walter Raleigh sends expedition to Roanoke Island (North Carolina)
1600 Tokugawa Ieyasu wins battle of Sekigahara, completes unification of Japan *1600–1868* Tokugawa shogunate in Edo *1630s* Seclusion adopted as national policy in Japan *1644–1694* Bashō, Japanese poet *1644–1911* Ch'ing (Manchu) dynasty in China *1661–1722* K'ang Hsi reign in China *1673–1681* Revolt of southern generals in China *1699* British East India Company arrives in China	*1600s* English, Dutch, and French enter the slave trade; slaves imported to sugar plantations in the Caribbean *1619* First African slaves in North America land in Virginia *1652* First Cape Colony settlement of Dutch East India Company *1660–1856* Omani domination of East Africa; Omani state centered in Zanzibar; 1698, takes Mozambique from Portuguese	*1607* The London company establishes Jamestown Colony (Virginia) *1608* Champlain founds Quebec
1701 Forty-seven rōnin incident in Japan *1716–1733* Reforms of Tokugawa Yoshimune in Japan *1737–1795* Reign of Ch'ien Lung in China *1742* Christianity banned in China *1784* American traders arrive in China *1787–1793* Matsudaira Sadanobu reforms in Japan *1798* White Lotus Rebellion in China	*1702* Asiento Guinea Trade Company founded for slave trade between Africa and the Americas *1700s* Trans-atlantic slave trade at its height *1741–1856* United Sultanate of Oman and Zanzibar *1754–1817* Usman Dan Fodio, founder of Sultanate in northern and central Nigeria; the Fulani become the ruling class in the region *1762* End of Funj sultanate in eastern Sudanic region	*1776–1781* The American Revolution *1783–1830* Simon Bolivar, Latin American soldier, statesman *1791* First 10 Amendments to U.S. Constitution (Bill of Rights) ratified *1791* Negro slave revolt in French Santo Domingo *1791* Canada Constitution Act divides the country into Upper and Lower Canada

Michelangelo's Pieta. *This was Michelangelo's first sculpture, done when he was only eighteen in 1493–1494. Michelangelo portrayed the Madonna on a larger scale than Christ to give the effect of a mother holding her young son. The statue is now in St. Peter's in Rome. [Art Resource.]*

16 The Late Middle Ages and The Renaissance in the West (1300–1527)

The late Middle Ages and the Renaissance marked a time of unprecedented calamity and of bold new beginnings in Europe. There was the Hundred Years' War between England and France (1337–1453), an exercise in seemingly willful self-destruction, which was made even more terrible in its later stages by the introduction of gunpowder and the invention of heavy artillery. There was almost universal bubonic plague, known to contemporaries as the Black Death. Between 1348 and 1350 waves of plague killed as much as one third of the population in many regions and transformed many pious Christians into believers in the omnipotence of death. There was a great schism within the Catholic church that lasted thirty-seven years (1378–1415) and saw by 1409 the election of no fewer than three competing popes and colleges of cardinals. And there was the onslaught of the Turks, who in 1453 marched seemingly invincibly through Constantinople and toward the west. As their political and religious institutions buckled; as disease, bandits, and wolves ravaged their cities in the wake of war; and as Muslim armies gathered at their borders, Europeans beheld what seemed to be the imminent total collapse of Western civilization.

But if the late Middle Ages saw unprecedented chaos, it also witnessed a rebirth that would continue into the seventeenth century. Two modern Dutch scholars have employed the same word (*Herfsttij*, "harvesttide") with different connotations to describe the period, one interpreting the word as a "waning" or "decline" (Johan Huizinga), the other as a true "harvest" (Heiko Oberman). If something was dying away, some ripe fruit and seed grain were also being gathered in. The late Middle Ages were a creative breaking up.

It was in this period that such scholars as Marsilius of Padua, William of Ockham, and Lorenzo Valla produced lasting criticisms of medieval assumptions about the nature of God, humankind, and society. It was a period in which kings worked through parliaments and clergy through councils to place lasting limits on the pope's temporal power. The principle that sovereigns (in this case, the pope) are accountable to the bodies of which they are the head was established. The arguments used by conciliarists (advocates of the judicial superiority of a Church council over a pope) to establish papal accountability to the body of the faithful provided an example for the secular sphere. National sovereigns, who also had an independent tradition of ruler accountability in Roman law, were reminded of their responsibility to the body politic.

The late Middle Ages also saw an unprecedented scholarly renaissance. Italian Humanists made a full recovery of classical knowledge and languages and set in motion educational reforms and cultural changes that would spread throughout Europe in the fifteenth and sixteenth centuries. In the process, the Italian Humanists invented, for all practical purposes, critical historical scholarship and exploited a new fifteenth-century invention, the "divine art" of printing with movable type. It was in this period that the vernacular, the local language, began to take its place alongside Latin, the international language, as a widely used literary and political language. The independent nation-states of Europe progressively superseded the universal church as the community of highest allegiance, as patriotism and incipient nationalism became a major force. Nations henceforth "transcended" themselves not by journeys to Rome but by competitive voyages to the Far East and the Americas, as the age of global exploration opened.

A time of both waning and harvest, constriction (in the form of nationalism) and expansion (in the sense of world exploration), the late Middle Ages saw medieval culture grudgingly give way to the ages of the Renaissance and the Reformation.

Political and Social Breakdown

The Hundred Years' War and the Rise of National Sentiment

From May 1337 to October 1453, England and France periodically engaged in what was for both a futile and devastating war.

CAUSES OF THE WAR. The conflict was initiated by the English king Edward III (1327–1377), who held a strong claim to the French throne as the grandson of Philip the Fair (1285–1314). When Charles VI (1322–1328), the last of Philip the Fair's surviving sons, died, Edward, who was only fifteen at the time, asserted his

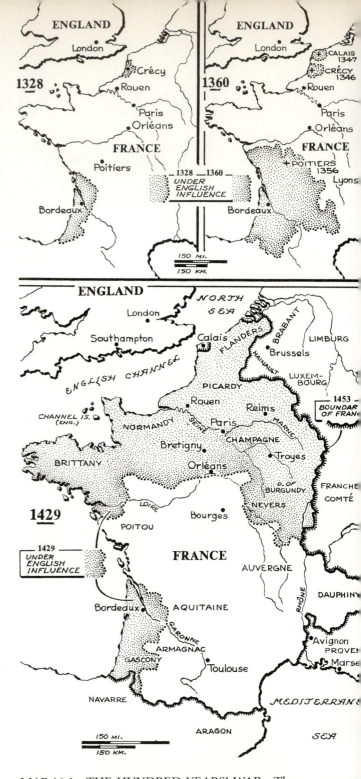

MAP 16-1   THE HUNDRED YEARS' WAR   *The Hundred Years' War went on intermittently from the late 1330s until 1453. These maps show the remarkable English territorial gains up to the sudden and decisive turning of the tide of battle in favor of the French by forces of Joan of Arc. in 1429.*

right to Capetian succession. The French barons, however, were not willing to place an English king on the French throne. They chose instead Philip VI of Valois (1328–1350), the first of a new French dynasty that was to rule into the sixteenth century.

In the background were other equally important causes. For one thing, the English king held certain French territories as fiefs from the French king. Thus he was, in law, a vassal of the French king. As Philip's vassal, Edward was, theoretically if not in fact, committed to support policies detrimental to England, if his French lord so commanded.

Still another factor that fueled the conflict was French support of the Bruces of Scotland, strong opponents of the English overlordship of Scotland who had won a victory over the English in 1314. The French and the English were also at this time quarreling over Flanders, a French fief, yet also a country whose towns were completely dependent for their livelihood on imported English wool.

Finally, there were decades of prejudice and animosity between the French and the English people, who constantly confronted one another on the high seas and in port towns. Taken together, these various factors made the Hundred Years' War a struggle to the death for national control and identity.

FRENCH WEAKNESS. Throughout the conflict, France was statistically the stronger: it had three times the population of England, was far the wealthier, and fought on its own soil. Yet, for the greater part of the conflict, until after 1415, the major battles ended in often stunning English victories. France was not as strong as it appeared. It was internally disunited by social conflict and the absence of a centralized system of taxation to fund the war. As a tool to provide him money, the king raised up a representative council of towns and nobles that came to be known in subsequent years as the *Estates General.* It convened in 1355, and although it levied taxes at the king's request, its members also used the king's plight to enhance their own regional rights and privileges. France, unlike England, still struggled in the fourteenth century to make the transition from a fragmented feudal society to a more centralized "modern" state.

Beyond this lay the clear fact of English military superiority, due to the greater discipline of its infantry and the rapid-fire and long-range capability of that ingeniously simple weapon, the English longbow, which could shoot six arrows a minute with a force sufficient to pierce an inch of wood or the armor of a knight at two hundred yards.

Finally, French weakness was related in no small degree to the comparative mediocrity of its royal leadership during the Hundred Years' War.

Progress of the War

The war had three major stages of development, each ending with a seemingly decisive victory by one or the other side.

CONFLICT DURING THE REIGN OF EDWARD III. By slapping an embargo on English wool to Flanders, Edward sparked urban rebellions by the merchants and the trade guilds. The Flemish cities, led by Ghent, revolted against the French. Having at first taken as neutral a stand as possible in the conflict, these cities, whose economies faced total collapse without imported English wool, signed a half-hearted alliance with England in January 1340, acknowledging Edward as king of France.

Edward defeated the French fleet in the first great battle of the war in the Bay of Sluys on June 23, 1340. But his subsequent effort to invade France by way of Flanders failed, largely because his allies proved undependable. As a stalemate developed, a truce was struck and was more-or-less observed until 1346. In that year, Edward attacked Normandy and won a series of easy victories that were capped by that at Crécy in August. This victory was quickly followed by the seizure of Calais, which the English held thereafter for over two hundred years. Both sides employed scorched-earth tactics and completely devastated the areas of conflict.

Exhaustion and the onset of the Black Death forced a second truce in late 1347, and the war entered a lull until 1355. On September 19, 1356, the English won their greatest victory near Poitiers, routing the noble cavalry and even taking the French king, John II the Good (1350–1364), captive back to England. After the English victory at Poitiers, there was a complete breakdown of political order in France. Disbanded soldiers from both sides became professional bandits, roaming the land, pillaging areas untouched by the war, and bringing disaster almost as great as the war itself.

Power in France lay with the privileged classes, which expressed their will through the representative assembly of the Estates General. Unlike the English Parliament, which represented the interests of a comparatively unified English nobility, the French Estates General was a many-tongued lobby, a forum for the diverse interests of the new-rich urban commercial and industrial classes, the territorial princes, and the clergy. Such a diverse body was no instrument for effective government.

On May 9, 1360, another milestone of the war was reached when England forced the Peace of Bretigny on the French. This agreement declared Edward's vassalage to the king of France ended and affirmed Edward's sovereignty over English territories in France. France also pledged to pay a ransom of three million gold crowns to win King John's release. In return, Edward renounced his claim to the French throne. Such a partition of French territorial control was completely unrealistic, and sober observers on both sides knew that it could not long continue.

FRENCH DEFEAT AND THE TREATY OF TROYES. After Edward's death, the English war effort lessened considerably, partly because of domestic problems within England. In 1396, France and England signed still another truce, this time backed up by the marriage of Richard II to the daughter of the French king, Charles VI (1380–1422). This truce lasted through the reign of Richard's successor, Henry IV of Lancaster (1399–1413). His successor, Henry V (1413–1422), reheated the war with France by taking advantage of the internal French turmoil created by the rise to power of the duchy of Burgundy under John the Fearless (1404–1419).

Henry V struck hard in Normandy, and his army routed the numerically stronger but tactically less shrewd French royal forces at Agincourt on October 25, 1415. By 1419, the Burgundians had allied with the English. With Burgundian support, France became Henry V's for the taking—at least in the short run. The Treaty of Troyes in 1420 disinherited the legitimate heir to the French throne, the dauphin (a title used by the king's oldest son), the future Charles VII, and made Henry V successor to the mad Charles VI. When Henry V and Charles VI died within months of one another in 1422, the infant Henry VI of England was proclaimed in Paris to be king of both France and England under the regency of the duke of Bedford. The dream of Edward III, the pretext for continuing the great war, was now, for the moment, realized: in 1422, an English king was the proclaimed ruler of France.

The dauphin went into retreat in Bourges, where, on the death of his father, he became Charles VII to most Frenchmen, who ignored the Treaty of Troyes.

JOAN OF ARC AND THE WAR'S CONCLUSION. Joan of Arc (1412–1431), a peasant from Domrémy, presented herself to Charles VII in March 1429. When she declared that the King of Heaven had called her to deliver besieged Orléans from the English, Charles was understandably skeptical. But the dauphin and his advisers, in retreat from what seemed to be a completely hopeless war, were desperate and were willing to try anything to reverse French fortunes on the bat-

Joan of Arc Refuses to Recant Her Beliefs

Joan of Arc, threatened with torture, refused to recant her beliefs and instead defended the instructions she received from the voices that spoke to her. Here is a part of her self-defense from the contemporary trial record.

On Wednesday, May 9th of the same year [1431], Joan was brought into the great tower of the castle of Rouen before us the said judges and in the presence of the reverend father, lord abbot of St. Cormeille de Compiegne, of masters Jean de Châtillon and Guillaume Erart, doctors of sacred theology, of André Marguerie and Nicolas de Venderes, archdeacons of the church of Rouen, of William Haiton, bachelor of theology, Aubert Morel, licentiate in canon law; Nicolas Loiseleur, canon of the cathedral of Rouen, and master Jean Massieu.

And Joan was required and admonished to speak the truth on many different points contained in her trial which she had denied or to which she had given false replies, whereas we possessed certain information, proofs, and vehement presumptions upon them. Many of the points were read and explained to her, and she was told that if she did not confess them truthfully she would be put to the torture, the instruments of which were shown to her all ready in the tower. There were also present by our instruction men ready to put her to the torture in order to restore her to the way and knowledge of truth, and by this means to procure the salvation of her body and soul which by her lying inventions she exposed to such grave perils.

To which the said Joan answered in this manner: "Truly if you were to tear me limb from limb and separate my soul from my body, I would not tell you anything more: and if I did say anything, I should afterwards declare that you had compelled me to say it by force." Then she said that on Holy Cross Day last she received comfort from St. Gabriel; she firmly believes it was St. Gabriel. She knew by her voices whether she should submit to the Church, since the clergy were pressing her hard to submit. Her voices told her that if she desired Our Lord to aid her she must wait upon Him in all her doings. She said that Our Lord has always been the master of her doings, and the Enemy never had power over them. She asked her voices if she would be burned and they answered that she must wait upon God, and He would aid her. ❑

The Trial of Jeanne D' Arc, trans. by W. P. Barrett (New York: Gotham House, 1932), pp. 303–304.

1340	English victory at Bay of Sluys
1346	English victory at Crécy and seizure of Calais
1347	Black Death strikes
1356	English victory at Poitiers
1358	*Jacquerie* disrupts France
1360	Peace of Bretigny recognizes English holdings in France
1381	English Peasants' Revolt
1415	English victory at Agincourt
1422	Treaty of Troyes proclaims Henry VI ruler of both England and France
1429	Joan of Arc leads French to victory at Orléans
1431	Joan of Arc executed as a heretic
1453	War ends; English retain only the coastal town of Calais

tlefield. Certainly the deliverance of Orléans, a city strategic to the control of the territory south of the Loire, would be a Godsend. Charles's desperation overcame his skepticism, and he gave Joan his leave to try and rescue the city.

Circumstances worked perfectly to Joan's advantage. The English force was already exhausted by its six-month siege of Orléans and actually at the point of withdrawal when Joan arrived with fresh French troops. After the English were repulsed at Orléans, there followed a succession of French victories that were popularly attributed to Joan. Joan truly deserved much of the credit, but not, however, because she was a military genius. She gave the French people and armies something that military experts could not: a unique inspiration and an almost mystical confidence in themselves as a nation. Within a few months of the liberation of Orléans, Charles VII received his crown in Rheims and ended the nine-year "disinheritance" prescribed by the Treaty of Troyes.

Charles forgot his liberator as quickly as he had embraced her. Joan was captured by the Burgundians in May 1430, and although the French king was in a position to secure her release, he did little to help her. She was turned over to the Inquisition in English-held Rouen. The Burgundians and the English wanted Joan publicly discredited, believing this would also discredit her patron, Charles VII, and might demoralize French resistance. The skilled inquisitors broke the courageous "Maid of Orléans" in ten weeks of merciless interrogation, and she was executed as a relapsed heretic on May 30, 1431. Charles reopened Joan's trial at a later date, and she was finally declared innocent of the all the charges against her on July 7, 1456, twenty-

five years after her execution. In 1920, the church declared her a saint.

Charles VII and Philip the Good made peace in 1435, and a unified France, now at peace with Burgundy, progressively forced the English back. By 1453, the date of the war's end, the English held only the coastal enclave of Calais.

During the Hundred Years' War, there were sixty-eight years of at least nominal peace and forty-four of hot war. The political and social consequences were lasting. Although the war devastated France, it also awakened the giant of French nationalism and hastened the transition in France from a feudal monarchy to a centralized state.

The Black Death

PRECONDITIONS AND CAUSES. In the late Middle Ages, nine tenths of the population were still farmers. The three-field system, in use in most areas since well before the fourteenth century, had increased the amount of arable land and thereby the food supply. The growth of cities and trade had also stimulated agricultural science and productivity. But as the food supply grew, so also did the population. It is estimated that Europe's population doubled between the years 1000 and 1300. By 1300, the balance between food supply and population was decisively tipped in favor of the latter. There were now more people than food to feed them or jobs to employ them, and the average European faced the probability of extreme hunger at least once during his or her expected thirty-five-year life span.

Famines followed the population explosion in the first half of the fourteenth century. Between 1315 and 1317, crop failures produced the greatest famine of the Middle Ages. Great suffering was inflicted on densely populated urban areas like the industrial towns of the Netherlands. Decades of overpopulation, economic depression, famine, and bad health progressively weakened Europe's population and made it highly vulnerable to the virulent bubonic plague that struck with full force in 1348. This Black Death, so called by contemporaries because of the way it discolored the body, followed the trade routes into Europe. Appearing in Sicily in late 1347, it entered Europe through the port cities of Venice, Genoa, and Pisa in 1348, and from there, it swept rapidly through Spain and southern France and into northern Europe. Areas that lay outside the major trade routes, like Bohemia, appear to have remained virtually unaffected. By the end of the fourteenth century, it is estimated that western Europe as a whole had lost as much as two fifths of its population, and a full recovery was not made until the sixteenth century. (See Map 16.2)

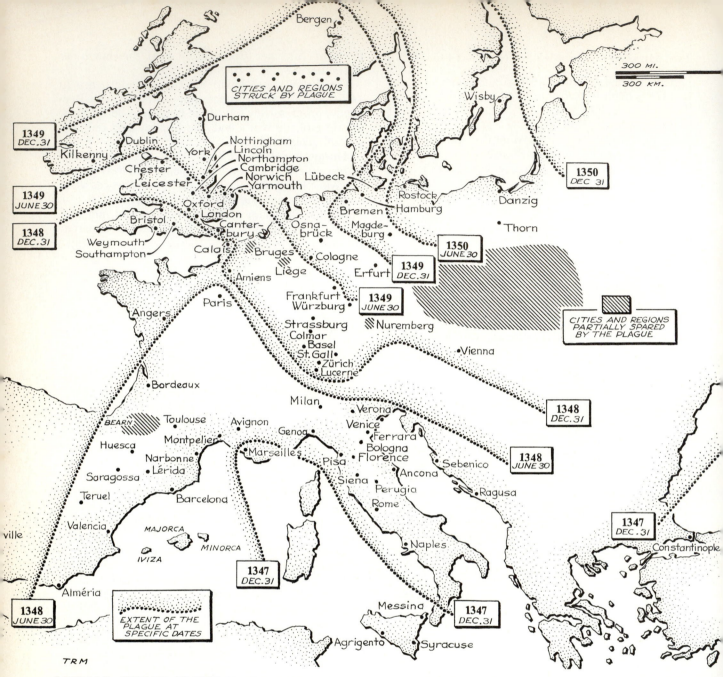

MAP 16-2 SPREAD OF THE BLACK DEATH *Apparently introduced by sea-borne rats from Black Sea areas where plague-infested rodents have long been known, the Black Death brought huge human, social, and economic consequences. One of the lower estimates of Europeans dying is 25,000,000. The map charts its spread in the mid-fourteenth century. Generally following trade routes, the plague reached Scandinavia by 1350, and some believe it then went on to Iceland and even Greenland. Areas off the main trade routes were largely spared.*

POPULAR REMEDIES. In the Black Death, people confronted a catastrophe against which they had neither understanding nor defense. Never have Western people stood so helpless against the inexplicable and the uncontrollable. Contemporary physicians did not know that the disease was transmitted by rat- or human-transported fleas, and hence the most rudimentary prophylaxis was lacking. Popular wisdom held that a corruption in the atmosphere caused the disease. Some blamed poisonous fumes released by earthquakes, and many adopted aromatic amulets as a remedy. According to the contemporary observa-

Boccaccio Describes the Ravages of the Black Death in Florence

The Black Death occasioned the poet, Humanist, and storyteller Giovanni Boccaccio (1313–1375) to assemble his great collection of tales, the Decameron. *Ten congenial men and women flee Florence to escape the plague and wile away the time telling stories. In one of the stories, Boccaccio embedded a fine clinical description of plague symptoms as seen in Florence in 1348 and of the powerlessness of physicians and the lack of remedies.*

In Florence, despite all that human wisdom and forethought could devise to avert it, even as the cleansing of the city from many impurities by officials appointed for the purpose, the refusal of entrance to all sick folk, and the adoption of many precautions for the preservation of health; despite also humble supplications addressed to God, and often repeated both in public procession and otherwise, by the devout; towards the beginning of the spring of the said year (1348) the doleful effects of the pestilence began to be horribly apparent by symptoms that shewed as if miraculous.

Not such were these symptoms as in the East, where an issue of blood from the nose was a manifest sign of inevitable death; but in men and women alike it first betrayed itself by the emergence of certain tumours in the groin or the armpits, some of which grew as large as a common apple, others as an egg, some more, some less, which the common folk called gavoccioli. From the two said parts of the body this deadly gavocciolo soon began to propagate and spread itself in all directions indifferently; after which the form of malady began to change, black spots or livid making their appearance in many cases on the arm or the thigh or elsewhere, now few and large, now minute and numerous. And as the gavocciolo had been and still was an infallible token of approaching death, such also were these spots on whomsoever they shewed themselves. Which maladies seemed to set entirely at naught both the art of the physician and the virtues of physic; indeed, whether it was that the disorder was of a nature to defy such treatment, or that the physicians were at fault . . . and, being in ignorance of its source, failed to apply the proper remedies; in either case, not merely were those that recovered few, but almost all died within three days of the appearance of the said symptoms, sooner or later, and in most cases without any fever or other attendant malady. ❑

The Decameron of Giovanni Boccaccio, trans. by J. M. Rigg (New York: Dutton, 1930), p. 5.

tions of Boccaccio, who recorded the varied reactions to the plague in the *Decameron* (1353), some sought a remedy in moderation and a temperate life; others gave themselves over entirely to their passions (sexual promiscuity among the stricken apparently ran high); and still others, "the most sound, perhaps, in judgment," chose flight and seclusion as the best medicine.

Among the most extreme social reactions were processions of flagellants. These were religious fanatics who beat their bodies in ritual penance until they bled,

A flagellant procession. Flagellants paraded from city to city, chanting songs and punishing their bodies in penance for sin. A typical flagellant parade lasted thirty-three days, one day for each year Christ lived. Note their bare backs and feet, hats with crosses, and rough penitential shirts. In their hands they carry candles and whips. [Koninlijke Bibliothek, Brussels.]

believing that such action would bring divine intervention. The Jews, who were hated by many because of centuries of Christian propaganda against them and the fact that they had become society's money lenders (a disreputable and resented profession) became scapegoats. Pogroms occurred in several cities, sometimes incited by the advent of flagellants. The terror created by the flagellants, whose dirty bodies may have actually served to transport the disease, became so socially disruptive and threatening even to established authority that the Church finally outlawed such processions.

SOCIAL AND ECONOMIC CONSEQUENCES. Among the social and economic consequences of the plague were a shrunken labor supply and the devaluation of the estates of the nobility. Villages vanished in the wake of the plague. As the number of farm laborers decreased, their wages increased, and those of skilled artisans soared. Many serfs now chose to commute their labor services by money payments, to abandon the farm altogether, and to pursue more interesting and rewarding jobs in skilled craft industries in the cities, an important new vocational option opened by the Black Death. Agricultural prices fell because of lowered demand, and the price of luxury and manufactured goods—the work of skilled artisans—rose. The noble landholders suffered the greatest decline in power from this new state of affairs. They were forced to pay more for finished products and for farm labor, and they received a smaller return on their agricultural produce. Everywhere their rents were in steady decline after the plague.

To recoup their losses, some landowners converted arable land to sheep pasture, substituting more profitable wool production for labor-intensive grain crops. Others abandoned the effort to farm their land and simply leased it to the highest bidder. Most ominously, legislation was sought to force peasants to stay on their farms and to freeze their wages at low levels, that is, to close off immediately the new economic opportunities opened for the peasantry by the demographic crisis. In France, the direct tax on the peasantry, the *taille*, was increased, and opposition to it was prominent among the grievances behind the *Jacquerie*, a great revolt of French peasants against the nobility in 1358. A Statute of Laborers was passed by the English Parliament in 1351 that limited wages to preplague levels and restricted the ability of peasants to leave the land of their traditional masters. Opposition to such legislation was also a prominent factor in the English Peasants' Revolt of 1381.

Although the plague hit urban populations especially hard, the cities and their skilled industries came, in time, to prosper from it. Cities had always been careful to protect their interests; as they grew, they passed legislation to regulate competition from rural areas and to control immigration. After the plague, their laws were progressively extended over the surrounding lands of nobles and feudal landlords, many of whom were peacefully integrated into urban life on terms very favorable to the cities.

The basic unit of urban industry was the master and his apprentices (usually one or two). Their numbers were purposely kept low and jealously guarded. As the craft of the skilled artisan was passed from master to apprentice only very slowly, the first wave of plague created a short supply of skilled labor almost overnight. But this short supply also raised the prices of available manufactured and luxury items to new heights. Ironically, the omnipresence of death whetted the appetite for the things that only skilled urban industries could produce. Expensive cloths and jewelry, furs from the north, and silks from the south were in great demand in the second half of the fourteenth century. Faced with life at its worst, people insisted on having the very best. The townspeople profited coming and going: as wealth poured into the cities and per capita income rose, the cost to urban dwellers of agricultural products from the countryside, which were now less in demand, actually declined.

The Church also profited from the plague as gifts and bequests multiplied. Although the Church, as a great landholder, also suffered losses, it had offsetting revenues from the vastly increased demand for religious services for the dead and the dying.

NEW CONFLICTS AND OPPORTUNITIES. By increasing the importance of skilled artisans, the plague contributed to new conflicts within the cities. The economic and political power of local artisans and trade guilds grew steadily in the late Middle Ages along with the demand for their goods and services. The merchant and patrician classes found it increasingly difficult to maintain their traditional dominance and grudgingly gave guild masters a voice in city government. As the guilds won political power, they encouraged restrictive legislation to protect local industries. These restrictions, in turn, brought confrontations between master artisans, who wanted to keep their numbers low and to expand their industries at a snail's pace, and the many journeymen, who were eager to rise to the rank of master. To the long-existing conflict between the guilds and the urban patriciate was now added a conflict within the guilds themselves.

Another indirect effect of the Great Plague was to assist monarchies in the development of centralized states. The plague caused the landed nobility to lose much of their economic power in the same period that the military superiority of paid professional armies over the traditional noble cavalry was being demonstrated by the Hundred Years' War. The plague also killed large numbers of clergy—perhaps one third of the German clergy fell victim to it as they heroically ministered to the sick and dying. This reduction in clerical ranks occurred in the same century in which the residence of the pope in Avignon (1309–1377) and the Great Schism (1378–1415; discussed later) were undermining the Church's popular support. After 1350, the two traditional "containers" of monarchy—the landed nobility and the Church—were on the defensive, and to no small degree as a consequence of the plague. Kings took full advantage of the new situation, as they drew on growing national sentiment to centralize their governments and economies.

Ecclesiastical Breakdown and Revival: The Late Medieval Church

During the reign of Pope Innocent III (1198–1216), papal power reached its height. Innocent elaborated the doctrine of papal plenitude of power and on that authority declared saints, disposed of benefices, and created a centralized papal monarchy with a clearly political mission.

What Innocent began, his successors perfected. The thirteenth-century papacy became a powerful political institution governed by its own law and courts, serviced by an efficient international bureaucracy, and preoccupied with secular goals.

Boniface VIII and Philip the Fair

Pope Boniface VIII (1294–1303) came to rule when England and France were maturing as nation-states. In England, a long tradition of consultation between the king and powerful members of English society evolved into formal "parliaments" during the reigns of Henry III (1216–1272) and Edward I (1272–1307), and these parliaments helped to create a unified kingdom. The reign of the French king Philip IV the Fair (1285–1314) saw France become an efficient, centralized monarchy. Boniface had the further misfortune of bringing to the papal throne memories of the way earlier popes had brought kings and emperors to their knees. He was to discover that the papal monarchy of the early thirteenth century was no match for the new political powers of the late thirteenth century.

France and England were on the brink of all-out war when Boniface became pope (1294). As both countries mobilized for war, they used the pretext of pre-

Pope Boniface VIII (1294–1303) who opposed the taxation of clergy by the kings of France and England and issued one of the strongest declarations of papal authority, the bull Unam Sanctam. *The statue is in the Museo Civico, Bologna, Italy. [Alinari/SCALA.]*

Marsilius of Padua Denies Coercive Power to the Clergy

According to Marsilius (CA. 1290–1342), a pamphleteer for the royal cause, the Bible gave the pope no right to pronounce and execute sentences on any person. The clergy held a strictly moral and spiritual rule, their judgments to be executed only in the afterlife, not in the present one. Here, on earth, they should be obedient to secular authority. Marsilius argued this point by appealing to the example of Jesus.

We now wish . . . to adduce the truths of the holy Scripture . . . which explicitly command or counsel that neither the Roman bishop called pope, nor any other bishop or priest, or deacon, has or ought to have any rulership or coercive judgment or jurisdiction over any priest or nonpriest, ruler, community, group, or individual of whatever condition. . . . Christ himself came into the world not to dominate men, nor to judge them [coercively] . . . not to wield temporal rule, but rather to be subject as regards the . . . present life; and moreover, he wanted to and did exclude himself, his apostles and disciples, and their successors, the bishops or priests, from all coercive authority or worldly rule, both by his example and by his word of counsel or command. . . . When he was brought before Pontius Pilate . . . and accused of having called himself king of the Jews, and [Pilate] asked him whether he had said this . . . [his] reply included these words . . . "My kingdom is not of this world," that is, I have not come to reign by temporal rule or dominion, in the way . . . worldly kings reign. . . . This, then, is the kingdom concerning which he came to teach and order, a kingdom which consists in the acts whereby the eternal kingdom is attained, that is, the acts of faith and the other theological virtues; not however, by coercing anyone thereto. ❑

Marsilius of Padua: The Defender of Peace: The Defensor Pacis, trans. by Alan Gewirth (New York: Harper, 1967), pp. 113–116.

---

paring for a crusade to tax the clergy heavily. Viewing English and French taxation of the clergy as an assault on traditional clerical rights, Boniface issued a bull, *Clericis Laicos*, which forbade lay taxation of the clergy without prior papal approval.

In England, Edward I retaliated by denying the clergy the right to be heard in the royal court, in effect removing from them the protection of the king. But it was Philip the Fair who struck back with a vengeance. In August 1296, he forbade the exportation of money from France to Rome, thereby denying the papacy revenues without which it could not operate. Boniface had no choice but to concede Philip the right to tax the French clergy "during an emergency."

In the year 1300, Boniface's fortunes appeared to revive. Tens of thousands of pilgrims flocked to Rome in that year for the Jubilee celebration. In a Jubilee year, all Catholics who visited Rome and there fulfilled certain conditions received a special indulgence, or remission of their sins. Heady with this display of popular religiosity, Boniface reinserted himself into international politics. Philip, seemingly spoiling for another fight with the pope, arrested Boniface's Parisian legate, Bernard Saisset, the bishop of Pamiers. Boniface demanded Saisset's unconditional release. A bull, *Ausculta Fili* ("Listen, My Son"), was sent to Philip in December 1301, pointedly informing him that "God has set popes over kings and kingdoms."

UNAM SANCTAM (1302). Philip unleashed a ruthless antipapal campaign. Boniface made a last-ditch stand against state control of national churches when on November 18, 1302, he issued the bull *Unam Sanctam*. This famous statement of papal power declared that temporal authority was "subject" to the spiritual power of the church.

After *Unam Sanctam*, the French moved against Boniface with force. An army of the king surprised the pope in mid-August 1303 at his retreat in Anagni. Boniface was badly beaten up and almost executed, before an aroused populace liberated him and returned him safely to Rome.

There was to be no papal retaliation by Boniface or his successors. Indeed, Pope Clement V (1305–1314), a former archbishop of Bordeaux, declared that *Unam Sanctam* should not be understood as in any way diminishing French royal authority. Clement established the papal court at Avignon, on the southeastern border of France, in 1309. There the papacy would remain until 1377.

After Boniface's humiliation, popes never again so seriously threatened kings and emperors, despite continuing papal excommunications and political intrigue. In the future, the relation between Church and State would tilt toward state control of religion within particular monarchies and the subordination of ecclesiastical to larger secular political purposes.

The Great Schism (1378–1417) and the Conciliar Movement to 1449

Pope Gregory XI (1370–1378) reestablished the papacy in Rome in January 1377, ending what had come to be known as the "Babylonian Captivity" of the church in Avignon, the reference being to the biblical bondage of the Israelites. The return to Rome proved to be short-lived, however. On Gregory's death on March 27, 1378, the cardinals, in Rome, elected an Italian archbishop as Pope Urban VI (1378–1389), who immediately proclaimed his intention to reform the Curia. This announcement came as an unexpected challenge to the cardinals, most of whom were French, and made them amenable to royal pressures to return the papacy to Avignon. The French king, Charles V, not wanting to surrender the benefits of a papacy located within the sphere of French influence, lent his support to a schism.

Five months after Urban's election, on September 20, 1378, thirteen cardinals, all but one of whom was French, formed their own conclave and elected a cousin of the French king as Pope Clement VII (1378–1397). They insisted, probably with some truth, that they had voted for Urban in fear of their lives, surrounded by a Roman mob that demanded the election of an Italian pope. Be that as it may, thereafter the papacy became a "two-headed thing" and a scandal to Christendom. Allegiance to the two papal courts divided along political lines: England and its allies (the Holy Roman Empire, Hungary, Bohemia, and Poland) acknowledged Urban VI, whereas France and its orbit (Naples, Scotland, Castile, and Aragon) supported Clement VII. Only the Roman line of popes, however, came to be recognized as official in subsequent Church history.

THE COUNCIL OF CONSTANCE (1414–1417). In 1409, a council was convened in Pisa that deposed both the Roman and the Avignon popes and elected in their stead its own new pope. But to the council's consternation, neither of these accepted its action, so after 1409, Christendom confronted the spectacle of three contending popes. This intolerable situation ended when the emperor Sigismund prevailed on the Pisan pope John XXIII to summon a "legal" council of the Church in Constance in 1414, a council also recognized by the reigning Roman pope Gregory XII. Gregory, however, soon resigned his office, raising grave doubts forevermore about whether the council was truly convened with Rome's blessing and hence valid. In a famous declaration entitled *Haec Sancta*, the council fathers asserted their supremacy and proceeded to conduct the business of the church.

They also executed the Bohemian reformer Jan Hus, on July 6, 1415. Hus was the rector of the Univer-

A German portrayal of the burning of Jan Hus for heresy and the dumping of his ashes into the Rhine to prevent their becoming relics. [Vincent Virga Archives.]

sity of Prague and he had been strongly influenced in his teaching by the English reformer John Wycliffe (D. 1384). Hus advocated communion for laity with both wine and bread (traditionally only the priest received both; the laity had received only bread, indicating the clergy's spiritual superiority over them); denied the dogma of transubstantiation (that wine and bread become the true body and blood of Christ by priestly consecration); and questioned the validity of sacraments performed by priests who led immoral lives.

In November 1417, the council successfully accomplished its main business when it elected a new pope,

Martin V (1417–1431), after the three contending popes had either resigned (Gregory XIII) or were deposed (Benedict XIII and John XXIII). The council made provisions for regular meetings of Church councils, scheduling a general council of the Church for purposes of reform within five, then seven, and thereafter every ten years. Constance has remained, however, an illegitimate Church council in official eyes: nor are the schismatic popes of Avignon and Pisa recognized as legitimate (for this reason another pope could take the name John XXIII in 1958).

THE COUNCIL OF BASEL (1431–1449). Conciliar government of the church both peaked and declined during the Council of Basel. This council curtailed papal powers of appointment and taxation and directly negotiated peace with the Hussites of Bohemia, conceding the latter's demands for communion with cup as well as bread, free preaching by their ordained clergy, and like punishment of clergy and laity for the same mortal sins. The council also recognized the right of the Bohemian church to govern its own internal affairs, much as the church in France and England had long since done.

During the pontificate of Pope Eugenius IV (1431–1447), the papacy regained much of its prestige and authority and successfully challenged the Council of Basel. The notion of conciliar superiority over popes died with the collapse of the Council of Basel in 1449. A decade later, the papal bull *Execrabilis* (1460) condemned appeals to councils as "erroneous and abominable" and "completely null and void."

But the conciliar movement was not a total failure. It planted deep within the conscience of all Western peoples the conviction that the leader of an institution must be responsive to its members and that the head exists to lead and serve, not to bring disaster on, the body.

Revival of Monarchy: Nation Building in the Fifteenth Century

After 1450, there was a progressive shift from divided feudal to unified national monarchies as "sovereign" rulers emerged. This is not to say that the dynastic and chivalric ideals of feudal monarchy did not continue. Territorial princes did not pass from the scene, and representative bodies persisted and in some areas even grew in influence. But in the late fifteenth and early sixteenth centuries, the old problem of the one and the many was decided clearly in favor of the interests of monarchy.

The feudal monarchy of the high Middle Ages was characterized by the division of the basic powers of government between the king and his semiautono-

mous vassals. The nobility and the towns acted with varying degrees of unity and success through such evolving representative assemblies as the English Parliament, the French Estates General, and the Spanish Cortes to thwart the centralization of royal power. Because of the Hundred Years' War and the schism in the Church, the nobility and the clergy were in decline in the late Middle Ages. The increasingly important towns began to ally with the king. Loyal, businesswise townspeople, not the nobility and the clergy, staffed the royal offices and became the king's lawyers, bookkeepers, military tacticians, and foreign diplomats. It was this new alliance between king and town that finally broke the bonds of feudal society and made possible the rise of sovereign states.

In a sovereign state, the power of taxation, war making, and law enforcement is no longer the local right of semiautonomous vassals but is concentrated in the monarch and is exercised by his chosen agents. Taxes, wars, and laws become national rather than merely regional matters. Only as monarchs were able to act independently of the nobility and the representative assemblies could they overcome the decentralization that had been the basic obstacle to nation building.

Monarchies also began to create standing national armies in the fifteenth century. As the noble cavalry receded and the infantry and the artillery became the backbone of armies, mercenary soldiers were recruited from Switzerland and Germany to form the major part of the "king's army."

The more expensive warfare of the fifteenth and sixteenth centuries increased the need to develop new national sources of royal income. The expansion of royal revenues was especially hampered by the stubborn belief among the highest classes that they were immune from government taxation. The nobility guarded their properties and traditional rights and despised taxation as an insult and a humiliation. Royal revenues accordingly grew at the expense of those least able to resist, and least able to pay. The king had several options. As a feudal lord he could collect rents from his royal domain. He could also levy national taxes on basic food and clothing, such as the *gabelle* or salt tax in France and the *alcabala* or 10 per cent sales tax on commercial transactions in Spain. The king could also levy direct taxes on the peasantry. This he did through agreeable representative assemblies of the privileged classes in which the peasantry did not sit. The French *taille* was such a tax. Sale of public offices and issuance of high-interest government bonds appeared in the fifteenth century as innovative fund-raising devices. But kings did not levy taxes on the powerful nobility. They turned to rich nobles, as they did to the great bankers of Italy and Germany, for loans, bargaining with the privileged classes, who in many instances remained as much the kings' creditors and competitors as their subjects.

France

There were two cornerstones of French nation building in the fifteenth century. The first was the collapse of the English holdings in France following the Hundred Years' War. The second was the defeat of Charles the Bold and the duchy of Burgundy. Perhaps Europe's strongest political power in the mid-fifteenth century, Burgundy aspired to dwarf both France and the Holy Roman Empire as the leader of a dominant middle kingdom. It might have succeeded in doing so had not the continental powers joined together in opposition. When Charles the Bold died in defeat in a battle at Nancy in 1477, the dream of Burgundian empire died with him.

The dissolution of Burgundy ended its constant intrigue against the French king and left Louis XI (1461–1483) free to secure the monarchy. The newly acquired Burgundian lands and his own Angevin inheritance permitted the king to end his reign with a kingdom almost twice the size of that with which he had started. Louis successfully harnessed the nobility, expanded the trade and industry, created a national postal system, and even established a lucrative silk industry at Lyons (later transferred to Tours).

A strong nation is a two-edged sword. It was because Louis' successors inherited such a secure and efficient government that France was able to pursue Italian conquests in the 1490s and to fight a long series of losing wars with the Habsburgs in the first half of the sixteenth century. By the mid-sixteenth century, France was again a defeated nation and almost as divided internally as during the Hundred Years' War.

Spain

Spain, too, became a strong country in the late fifteenth century. Both Castile and Aragon had been poorly ruled and divided kingdoms in the mid-fifteenth century. The marriage of Isabella of Castile (1474–1504) and Ferdinand of Aragon (1479–1516) changed that situation. The two future sovereigns married in 1469, despite strong protests from neighboring Portugal and France, both of which foresaw the formidable European power such a union would create. Castile was by far the richer and more populous of the two, having an estimated five million inhabitants to Aragon's population of under one million. Castile was also distinguished by its lucrative sheep-farming industry, which was run by a government-backed organization called the *Mesta*, another example of developing centralized economic planning. Although the two kingdoms were dynastically united by the marriage of Ferdinand and Isabella in 1469, they remained constitutionally separated, as each retained its respective government agencies—separate laws, armies, coinage, and taxation—and cultural traditions.

Ferdinand and Isabella could do together what neither was able to accomplish alone: subdue their realms, secure their borders, and venture abroad militarily. Townspeople allied themselves with the crown and progressively replaced the nobility within the royal administration. The crown also extended its authority over the wealthy chivalric orders, a further circumscription of the power of the nobility.

Spain had long been remarkable among European lands as a place where three religions—Islam, Judaism, and Christianity—coexisted with a certain degree of toleration. This toleration ended dramatically under Ferdinand and Isabella, who made Spain the prime example of state-controlled religion. Ferdinand and Isabella exercised almost total control over the Spanish church as they placed religion in the service of national unity. They appointed the higher clergy and the officers of the Inquisition. The Inquisition, run by Tomás de Torquemada (D. 1498), Isabella's confessor, was a key national agency established in 1479 to monitor the activity of converted Jews (*conversos*) and Muslims (*Moriscos*) in Spain. In 1492, the Jews were exiled and their properties were confiscated. In 1502, nonconverting Moors in Granada were driven into exile. Spanish spiritual life remained largely uniform and successfully controlled—a major reason for Spain's remaining a loyal Catholic country throughout the sixteenth century and providing a base of operation for the European Counter-Reformation.

Ferdinand and Isabella were rulers with wide horizons. They contracted anti-French marriage alliances that came to determine a large part of European history in the sixteenth century. In 1496, their eldest daughter, Joanna, later known as "the Mad," married Archduke Philip, the son of Emperor Maximilian I. The fruit of this union, Charles I of Spain, the first ruler over a united Spain, came by his inheritance and election as emperor Charles V in 1519 to rule over a European kingdom almost equal in size to that of Charlemagne. A second daughter, Catherine of Aragon, wed Arthur, the son of the English King Henry VII, and after Arthur's premature death, she married his brother, the future King Henry VIII. The failure of this latter marriage became the key factor in the emergence of the Anglican church and the English Reformation.

The new Spanish power was also revealed in Ferdinand and Isabella's promotion of overseas exploration. Their patronage of the Genoese adventurer Christopher Columbus (1451–1506), who discovered the islands of the Caribbean while sailing west in search of a shorter route to the spice markets of the Far East, led to the creation of the Spanish empire in Mexico and Peru, whose gold and silver mines helped to make Spain Europe's dominant power in the sixteenth century.

England

The last half of the fifteenth century was a period of especially difficult political trial for the English. Following the Hundred Years' War, a defeated England was subjected to internal warfare between two rival branches of the royal family, the House of York and the House of Lancaster. This conflict, known to us today as the War of the Roses (as York's symbol, according to legend, was a white rose, and Lancaster's a red rose), kept England in turmoil from 1455 to 1485.

The Lancastrian monarchy of Henry VI (1422–1461) was consistently challenged by the duke of York and his supporters in the prosperous southern towns. In 1461, Edward IV (1461–1483), son of the duke of York, successfully seized power and instituted a strong-arm rule that lasted over twenty years. Edward, assisted by loyal and able ministers, effectively bent Parliament to his will. His brother and successor was Richard III (1483–1485). During the reign of the Tudors, a tradition arose that painted Richard III as an unprincipled villain who murdered Edward's sons in the Tower of London to secure the throne. The best-known version of this characterization—unjust according to some—is found in Shakespeare's *Richard III*. Be that as it may, Richard's reign saw the growth of support for the exiled Lancastrian Henry Tudor. Henry returned to England to defeat Richard on Bosworth Field in August 1485.

Henry Tudor ruled as Henry VII (1485–1509), the first of the new Tudor dynasty that would dominate England throughout the sixteenth century. In order to bring the rival royal families together and to make the hereditary claim of his offspring to the throne uncontestable, Henry married Edward IV's daughter, Elizabeth of York. He succeeded in disciplining the English nobility through a special and much feared instrument of the royal will known as the *Court of Star Chamber*. Henry shrewdly construed legal precedents to the advantage of the crown, using English law to further his own ends. He managed to confiscate noble lands and fortunes with such success that he governed without dependence on Parliament for royal funds, always a cornerstone of strong monarchy. In these ways, Henry began to shape a monarchy that became one of early modern Europe's most exemplary governments during the reign of his granddaughter, Elizabeth I.

The Holy Roman Empire

Germany and Italy are the striking exceptions to the steady development of centralized nation-states in the last half of the fifteenth century. Unlike France, Spain, and England, the Holy Roman Empire saw the many thoroughly repulse the one. In Germany, territorial rulers and cities resisted every effort at national consolidation and unity. As in Carolingian times, rulers continued to partition their kingdoms, however small, among their sons, and by the late fifteenth century, Germany was hopelessly divided into some three hundred autonomous political entities.

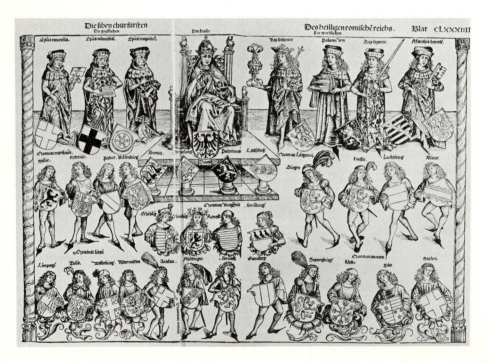

The Holy Roman Emperor is shown here with the seven electors. The three ecclesiastical electors are to his right and the four secular electors to his left. Also represented here are the territorial kingdoms or principalities (dukedoms, margraviates, landgraviates, and burgraviates) and the imperial cities. [Konrad Kolbl Reprint Verlag, Grunwald bei Munchen.]

The princes and the cities did work together to create the machinery of law and order, if not of union, within the divided empire. An agreement reached between the emperor Charles IV and the major German territorial rulers in 1356, known as the *Golden Bull*, established a seven-member electoral college consisting of the archbishops of Mainz, Trier, and Cologne; the duke of Saxony; the margrave of Brandenburg; the count Palatine; and the king of Bohemia. This group also functioned as an administrative body. They elected the emperor and, in cooperation with him, provided what transregional unity and administration existed. The figure of the emperor gave the empire a single ruler in law, if not in actual fact.

In the sixteenth and seventeenth centuries, German territorial princes became virtually sovereign rulers within their various domains. Such disunity aided religious dissent and conflict. It was in the cities and territories of still-feudal, fractionalized, backward Germany that the Protestant Reformation broke out in the sixteenth century.

The Renaissance in Italy (1375–1527)

In his famous study, *Civilization of the Renaissance in Italy* (1867), Jacob Burckhardt described the Renaissance as the prototype of the modern world. He believed that it was in fourteenth- and fifteenth-century Italy, through the revival of ancient learning, that new secular and scientific values first began to supplant traditional religious beliefs. This was the period in which people began to adopt a rational, objective, and statistical approach to reality and to rediscover the importance of the individual. The result, in Burckhardt's words, was a release of the "full, whole nature of man."

Other scholars have found Burckhardt's description too modernizing an interpretation of the Renaissance and have accused him of overlooking the continuity with the Middle Ages. His critics especially stress the strongly Christian character of Humanism and the fact that earlier "renaissances" also revived the ancient classics, professed interest in Latin language and Greek science, and appreciated the worth and creativity of individuals.

Most scholars nonetheless agree that the Renaissance was a time of transition from the medieval to the modern world. Medieval Europe, especially before the twelfth century, had been a fragmented feudal society with an agriculturally based economy, its thought and culture largely dominated by the Church. Renaissance Europe, especially after the fourteenth century, was characterized by growing national consciousness and political centralization, an urban economy based on organized commerce and capitalism, and ever greater lay and secular control of thought and culture.

It was especially in Italy between the late fourteenth and the early sixteenth centuries, from roughly 1375 to 1527, the year of the sack of Rome by imperial soldiers, that the distinctive features and achievements of the Renaissance, which also deeply influenced northern Europe, are most strikingly revealed.

The Italian City-State: Social Conflict and Despotism

Italy had always had a cultural advantage over the rest of Europe because its geography made it the natural gateway between East and West. Venice, Genoa, and Pisa traded uninterruptedly with the Near East throughout the Middle Ages and maintained vibrant urban societies. During the thirteenth and fourteenth centuries, trade-rich cities expanded to become powerful city-states, dominating the political and economic life of the surrounding countryside. By the fifteenth century, the great Italian cities had become the bankers of much of Europe.

The growth of Italian cities and urban culture was also assisted by the endemic warfare between the emperor and the pope. Either of these might have successfully challenged the cities. They chose instead to weaken one another and thus strengthened the merchant oligarchies of the cities. Unlike in northern Europe, where the cities tended to be dominated by kings and princes, Italian cities were left free to expand into states. They absorbed the surrounding countryside and assimilated the area nobility in a unique urban meld of old and new rich. There were five such major, competitive states in Italy: the duchy of Milan; the republics of Florence and Venice; the Papal States; and the kingdom of Naples (see Map 16.3).

Social strife and competition for political power were so intense within the cities that, for survival's sake, most had evolved into despotisms by the fifteenth century. Venice was the notable exception. It was ruled by a successful merchant oligarchy with power located in a patrician senate of three hundred members and a ruthless judicial body, the Council of Ten, that anticipated and suppressed rival groups. Elsewhere, the new social classes and divisions within society produced by rapid urban growth fueled chronic, near-anarchic conflict.

Florence was the most striking example. There were four distinguishable social groups within the city. The first was the old rich, or *grandi*, the nobles and merchants who had traditionally ruled the city. The second group was the emergent new-rich merchant class, capitalists and bankers known as the *popolo grasso*, or "fat people." They began to challenge the old rich for political power in the late thirteenth and early fourteenth centuries. Then there were the middle-burgher ranks of guild masters, shopkeepers, and professionals, those small businessmen who, in Florence as elsewhere, tended to take the side of the new rich against the conservative policies of the old rich. Finally, there was the omnipresent *popolo minuto*, the poor masses who lived from hand to mouth: in 1457, one third of the population of Florence, about thirty thousand people, were officially listed as paupers.

These social divisions produced conflict at every level of society. In 1378, a great revolt by the poor, known as the Ciompi Revolt, established a chaotic four-year reign of power by the lower Florentine classes. True stability did not return to Florence until the ascent to power in 1434 of Cosimo de' Medici (1389–1464).

The wealthiest Florentine and an astute statesman, Cosimo controlled the city internally from behind the scenes, skillfully manipulating the constitution and influencing elections. His grandson, Lorenzo the Magnificent (1449–1492), ruled Florence in almost totalitarian fashion during the last quarter of the fifteenth century.

A terra cotta bust of Lorenzo de' Medici by the sculptor Andrea del Verrocchio (CA. 1435–1488). [National Gallery of Art, Washington; Samuel H. Kress Collection.]

MAP 16-3   RENAISSANCE ITALY   *The city-states of Renaissance Italy were self-contained principalities whose internal strife was monitored by their despots and whose external aggression was long successfully controlled by treaty.*

Despotism was less subtle elsewhere. In order to prevent internal social conflict and foreign intrigue from paralyzing their cities, the dominant groups cooperated to install a hired strongman, known as a *podestá*, for the purpose of maintaining law and order. He held executive, military, and judicial authority, and his mandate was simple: to permit, by whatever means required, the normal flow of business. Because these despots could not depend on the divided populace, they operated through mercenary armies.

Political turbulence and warfare gave birth to diplomacy, by means of which the various city-states stayed abreast of foreign military developments and, if shrewd enough, gained power and advantage short of actually going to war. Most city-states established resident embassies in the fifteenth century. Their ambassadors not only represented them in ceremonies and as negotiators but also became their watchful eyes and ears at rival courts.

Whether within the comparatively tranquil republic of Venice, the strong-arm democracy of Florence, or the undisguised despotism of Milan, the wealthy Italian city proved a most congenial climate for an unprecedented flowering of thought and culture. Renaissance culture was promoted as vigorously by despots as by republicans and by secularized popes as enthusiastically as by the more spiritually minded.

Humanism

Some scholars describe Humanism as an unchristian philosophy that stressed the dignity of humankind and championed individualism and secular values. Others argue that the Humanists were true champions of authentic Catholic Christianity. Still others see Humanism as a form of scholarship consciously designed to promote a sense of civic responsibility and political liberty. One of the most authoritative modern commentators, Paul O. Kristeller, has accused all these views of dealing more with the secondary effects than with the essence of Humanism, which he believes, was no particular philosophy or value system but simply an educational program concentrated on rhetoric and sound scholarship for their own sake.

There is truth in each of these definitions. Humanism was the scholarly study of the Latin and Greek classics and the ancient Church Fathers both for their own sake and in the hope of a rebirth of ancient norms and values. Humanists were advocates of the *studia humanitatis*, a liberal arts program of study that embraced grammar, rhetoric, poetry, history, politics, and moral philosophy. The Florentine Leonardo Bruni (1374–1444) first gave the name *humanitas* ("humanity") to the learning that resulted from such scholarly pursuits. Bruni was a student of Manuel Chrysoloras, a Byzantine scholar who opened the world of Greek scholarship to a generation of young Italian Humanists when he taught at Florence between 1397 and 1403.

The first Humanists were orators and poets. They wrote original literature, in both the classical and the vernacular languages, inspired by the newly discovered works of the ancients, and they taught rhetoric within the universities. When Humanists were not employed as teachers of rhetoric, their talents were sought as secretaries, speech writers, and diplomats in princely and papal courts.

The study of classical and Christian antiquity existed before the Italian Renaissance. There were recoveries of ancient civilization during the Carolingian renaissance of the ninth century, within the cathedral school of Chartres in the twelfth century, during the great Aristotelian revival in Paris in the thirteenth century, and among the Augustinians in the early fourteenth century. However, these precedents only partially compare with the grand achievements of the Italian Renaissance of the late Middle Ages. The latter was more secular and lay-dominated, had broader interests, recovered more manuscripts, and possessed far superior technical skills than had been the case in the earlier "rebirths" of antiquity. Unlike their Scholastic rivals, Humanists were not content only to summarize and compare the views of recognized authorities on a question, but went directly to the original source itself and drew their own conclusions. Avidly searching out manuscript collections, Italian Humanists made the full sources of Greek and Latin antiquity available to scholars during the fourteenth and fifteenth centuries. Mastery of Latin and Greek was the surgeon's tool of the Humanist. There is a kernel of truth—but only a kernel—in the arrogant boast of the Humanists that the period between themselves and classical civilization was a "dark middle age."

PETRARCH, DANTE, AND BOCCACCIO. Francesco Petrarch (1304–1374) was the father of Humanism. He left the legal profession to pursue his love of letters and poetry. Although most of his life was spent in and around Avignon, he became caught up in Cola

Dante Aligheri as seen by his contemporary, Giotto. [The Granger Collection.]

Petrarch's Letter to Posterity

In old age, Petrarch wrote a highly personal letter to posterity in which he summarized the lessons he had learned during his lifetime. The letter also summarizes the original values of Renaissance Humanists: their suspicion of purely materialistic pleasure, the importance they attached to friendship, and their utter devotion to and love of antiquity.

I have always possessed extreme contempt for wealth; not that riches are not desirable in themselves, but because I hate the anxiety and care which are invariably associated with them . . . I have, on the contrary, led a happier existence with plain living and ordinary fare. . . .

The pleasure of dining with one's friends is so great that nothing has ever given me more delight than their unexpected arrival, nor have I ever willingly sat down to table without a companion. . . .

The greatest kings of this age have loved and courted me. . . . I have fled, however, from many . . . to whom I was greatly attached; and such was my innate longing for liberty that I studiously avoided those whose very name seemed incompatible with the freedom I loved.

I possess a well-balanced rather than a keen intellect—one prone to all kinds of good and wholesome study, but especially to moral philosophy and the art of poetry. The latter I neglected as time went on, and took delight in sacred literature. . . . Among the many subjects that interested me, I dwelt especially upon antiquity, for our own age has always repelled me, so that, had it not been for the love of those dear to me, I should have preferred to have been born in any other period than our own. In order to forget my own time, I have constantly striven to place myself in spirit in other ages, and consequently I delighted in history. . . .

If only I have lived well, it matters little to me how I have talked. Mere elegance of language can produce at best but an empty fame. ❑

Frederic A. Ogg (ed.), *A Source Book of Mediaeval History* (New York: American Book Company, 1908), pp. 470–473.

---

di Rienzo's popular revolt and two-year reign (1347–1349) in Rome as "tribune" of the Roman people. He also served the Visconti family in Milan in his later years. Petrarch celebrated ancient Rome in his *Letters to the Ancient Dead*, fancied personal letters to Cicero, Livy, Vergil, and Horace. He also wrote a Latin epic poem (*Africa*, a poetic historical tribute to the Roman general Scipio Africanus) and a set of biographies of famous Romans (*Lives of Illustrious Men*). He tirelessly collected ancient manuscripts; among his finds were some letters by Cicero. His critical textual studies, elitism, and contempt for the allegedly useless learning of the Scholastics were features that many later Humanists also shared. Petrarch's most famous contemporary work was a collection of highly introspective love sonnets to a certain Laura, a married woman whom he romantically admired from a safe distance. Medieval Christian values can be seen in his imagined dialogues with Saint Augustine and in tracts written to defend the personal immortality of the soul against the Aristotelians.

Petrarch was, however, far more secular in orientation than his famous near contemporary Dante Alighieri (1265–1321), whose *Vita Nuova* and *Divine Comedy* form, with Petrarch's sonnets, the cornerstones of Italian vernacular literature. Petrarch's student and friend Giovanni Boccaccio (1313–1375), author of the *Decameron*, one hundred bawdy tales told by three men and seven women in a country retreat from the plague that ravaged Florence in 1348, also pioneered Humanist studies. An avid collector of manuscripts, Boccaccio also assembled an encyclopedia of Greek and Roman mythology.

EDUCATIONAL REFORMS AND GOALS. Pietro Paolo Vergerio (1349–1420) left a classic summary of the Humanist concept of a liberal education:

We call those studies liberal which are worthy of a free man; those studies by which we attain and practice virtue and wisdom; that education which calls forth, trains, and develops those highest gifts of body and mind which ennoble men and which are rightly judged to rank next in dignity to virtue only, for to a vulgar temper, gain and pleasure are the one aim in existence, to a lofty nature, moral worth and fame.[1]

The ideal of a useful education and well-rounded people inspired far-reaching reforms in traditional education. Quintilian's *Education of the Orator*, the full text of which was discovered by Poggio Bracciolini (D. 1459) in 1416, became the basic classical guide for

[1] Cited by De Lamar Jensen, *Renaissance Europe: Age of Recovery and Reconciliation* (Lexington, Mass.: D. C. Heath, 1981), p. 111.

the Humanist revision of the traditional curriculum. The most influential Renaissance tract on education, Vergerio's *On the Morals that Befit a Free Man*, was written directly from classical models. Vittorino da Feltre (d. 1446) was a teacher who not only directed his students to a highly disciplined reading of Pliny, Ptolemy, Terence, Plautus, Livy, and Plutarch but also combined vigorous physical exercise and games with intellectual pursuits. Another educator, Guarino da Verona (d. 1460), rector of the new University of Ferrara and a student of the Greek scholar Manuel Chrysoloras, streamlined the study of classical languages and gave it systematic form. Baldassare Castiglione's famous *Book of the Courtier*, written for the cultured nobility at the court of Urbino, stressed the importance of integrating knowledge of language and history with athletic, military, and musical skills, as well as good manners and moral character.

THE FLORENTINE ACADEMY AND THE REVIVAL OF PLATONISM. Of all the important recoveries of the past made during the Italian Renaissance, none stands out more than the revival of Greek studies, especially the works of Plato, in fifteenth-century Florence. Many factors combined to bring this revival about. An important foundation was laid in 1397 when the city invited Manuel Chrysoloras to come from Constantinople and promote Greek learning. A half century later (1439), the ecumenical Council of Ferrara–Florence, having convened to negotiate the reunion of the Eastern and Western churches, opened the door for many Greek scholars and manuscripts to enter the West. After the fall of Constantinople to the Turks in 1453, Greek scholars fled to Florence for refuge. This was the background against which Platonic scholarship developed under the patronage of Cosimo de' Medici and the supervision of Marsilio Ficino (1433–1499) and Pico della Mirandola (1463–1494).

Although the thinkers of the Renaissance were interested in every variety of ancient wisdom, they seemed to be especially attracted to Platonism and those Church Fathers who had tried to synthesize Platonic philosophy and Christian teaching. In private residences, Ficino and other humanists met to discuss the works of Plato and the Neoplatonists: Plotinus, Proclus, Porphyry, and Dionysius the [Pseudo-]Areopagite. Historians have romanticized these meetings into the so-called "Florentine Academy." Ficino also edited and published the complete works of Plato.

The appeal of Platonism lay in its flattering view of human nature. Platonism distinguished between an eternal sphere of being and the perishable world in which humans actually lived. Human reason was believed to belong to the former, indeed, to have preex-

Pico della Mirandola States the Renaissance Image of Man

One of the most eloquent descriptions of the Renaissance image of mankind comes from the Italian Humanist Pico della Mirandola (1463–1494). In his famed Oration on the Dignity of Man *(CA. 1486) Pico described humans as free to become whatever they choose.*

The best of artisans [God] ordained that that creature (man) to whom He had been able to give nothing proper to himself should have joint possession of whatever had been peculiar to each of the different kinds of being. He therefore took man as a creature of indeterminate nature and, assigning him a place in the middle of the world, addressing him thus: "Neither a fixed abode nor a form that is thine alone nor any function peculiar to thyself have we given thee, Adam, to the end that according to thy longing and according to thy judgment thou mayest have and possess what abode, what form, and what functions thou thyself shalt desire. The nature of all other beings is limited and constrained within the bounds of laws prescribed by Us. Thou, constrained by no limits, in accordance with thine own free will, in whose hand We have placed thee, shall ordain for thyself the limits of thy nature. We have set thee at the world's center that thou mayest from thence more easily observe whatever is in the world. We have made thee neither of heaven nor of earth, neither mortal nor immortal, so that with freedom of choice and with honor, as though the maker and molder of thyself, thou mayest fashion thyself in whatever shape thou shalt prefer. Thou shalt have the power to degenerate into the lower forms of life, which are brutish. Thou shalt have the power, out of thy soul's judgment, to be reborn into the higher forms, which are divine." O supreme generosity of God the Father, O highest and most marvelous felicity of man! To him it is granted to have whatever he chooses, to be whatever he wills. ❑

Giovanni Pico della Mirandola, *Oration on the Dignity of Man*, in *The Renaissance Philosophy of Man*, ed. by E. Cassirer et al. (Chicago: Phoenix Books, 1961), pp. 224–225.

isted in this pristine world and to continue to commune with it, as their knowledge of mathematical and moral truth bore witness.

CRITICAL WORK OF THE HUMANISTS: LORENZO VALLA. Because they were guided by a scholarly ideal of philological accuracy and historical truthfulness, the Humanists could become critics of tradition even when that was not their intention. Dispassionate critical scholarship shook long-standing foundations, not the least of which were those of the medieval church.

The work of Lorenzo Valla (1406–1457), author of the standard Renaissance text on Latin philology, the *Elegance of the Latin Language* (1444), reveals the explosive character of the new learning. Although a good Catholic, Valla became a hero to later Protestants because of his defense of predestination against the advocates of free will and his exposé of the Donation of Constantine (see Chapter 13). The exposé of the Donation was not intended by Valla to have the devastating force that Protestants attributed to it. He only demonstrated in a careful, scholarly way what others had long suspected. Using the most rudimentary textual analysis and historical logic, Valla proved that the document contained such anachronistic terms as *fief* and made references that would have been meaningless in the fourth century. In the same dispassionate way, Valla also pointed out errors in the Latin Vulgate, then the authorized version of the Bible for the Roman Catholic church.

Such discoveries did not make Valla any less loyal to the church, nor did they prevent his faithful fulfillment of the office of Apostolic Secretary in Rome under Pope Nicholas V. Nonetheless, historical criticism of this type served those less loyal to the medieval church, and it was no accident that young Humanists formed the first identifiable group of Martin Luther's supporters (see Chapter 17).

Renaissance Art

In Renaissance Italy, as in Reformation Europe, the values and interests of the laity were no longer subordinated to those of the clergy. In education, culture, and religion, the laity assumed a leading role and established models for the clergy to imitate. This resulted in part from the Church's loss of its international power during the great crises of the late Middle Ages. But it was also encouraged by the rise of national sentiment, the creation of competent national bureaucracies staffed by laity rather than clerics, and the rapid growth of lay education during the fourteenth and fifteenth centuries. Medieval Christian values adjusted to a more this-worldly spirit. Men and women began again to appreciate and even glorify the secular world, secular learning, and purely human pursuits as ends in themselves.

This perspective on life is prominent in the painting and sculpture of the High Renaissance, the late fifteenth and early sixteenth centuries, when the art of the period reached its full maturity. In imitation of Greek and Roman art, painters and sculptors attempted to create harmonious, symmetrical, and properly proportioned figures and to portray the human form with a glorified realism. Whereas Byzantine and Gothic art had been religious and idealized in the extreme, Renaissance art, especially in the fifteenth century, became a realistic reproduction of nature and of man himself as a part of nature. Giotto (1266–1336), the father of Renaissance painting, signaled the new direction. An admirer of Saint Francis of Assisi, whose love of nature he shared, Giotto painted a more natural world than his Byzantine and Gothic predecessors. Though still filled with religious seriousness, his work was no longer quite so abstract and unnatural a depiction of the world.

Renaissance artists had the considerable advantage of new technical skills developed during the fifteenth century. In addition to the availability of oil paints, the techniques of using shading to enhance realism *(chiaroscuro)* and adjusting the size of figures so as to give the viewer a feeling of continuity with the painting (linear perspective) were perfected. Compared with their flat Byzantine and Gothic counterparts, Renaissance paintings seem filled with energy and life and stand out from the canvas in three dimensions.

Opposite: *The developing knowledge of human anatomy and physiology.*
A: *Medieval conception of the human body, from a manuscript of about* 1292, *depicting the venous system and what purport to be a few internal organs. Since post-mortems were forbidden, medieval renderings of the human body were based on a combination of speculation and animal dissection.* [The Bodleian Library, Oxford.]
B: *A chart showing the points of blood-letting, long an accepted medical practice. From the* Guidebook of the Barber Surgeons of York *(fifteenth century), now in the British Museum.* [Egerton MS. 2572, f. 50. Reproduced by permission of the British Library Board.]
C: *Leonardo da Vinci's drawings of the human fetus. Renaissance artists and scientists, in contrast to medieval artists, began to base their portrayal of the human body on the actual study of it.* [Bettmann Archive.]
D: *A woodcut illustration by John of Carcar from* De Humanis corporis fabrica (Structure of the Human body) (Basel, 1543), *by the great Flemish anatomist, Andreas Vesalius (1514-1564), the foundation work of modern knowledge of human anatomy.* [Bettmann Archive.]

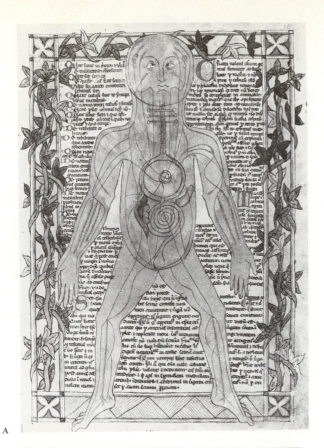

A

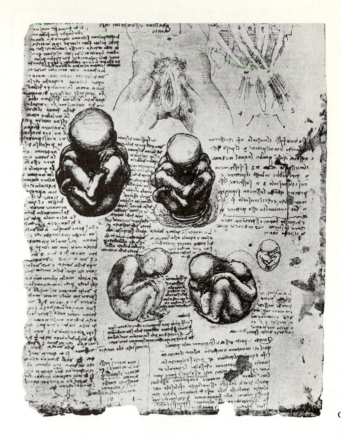

C

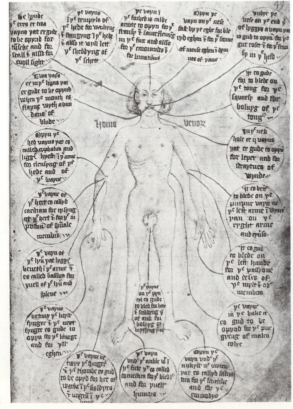

B

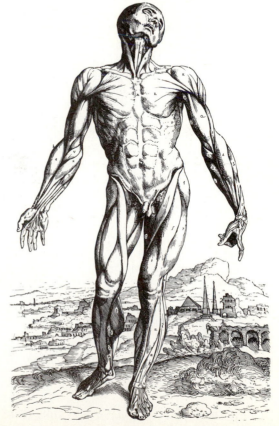

D

Madonna and Child, by Giotto. Giotto was the first artist to bring naturalism and realism to religious and spiritual subjects. [National Gallery of Art, Washington, D.C., Samuel H. Kress Collection.]

LEONARDO DA VINCI (1452–1519). More than any other person in the period, Leonardo exhibited the Renaissance ideal of the universal person, one who is not only a jack-of-all-trades but also a true master of many. One of the greatest painters of all time, Leonardo was also a military engineer for Ludovico il Moro in Milan, Cesare Borgia in Romagna, and the French king Francis I. Leonardo advocated scientific experimentation, dissected corpses to learn anatomy, and was an accomplished, self-taught botanist. His inventive mind foresaw such modern

Leonardo da Vinci's portrait of Ginevra de' Benci, an Italian noblewoman. The psychological acuity of Leonardo's portraits results in part from his technique. Leonardo was the first Italian to paint in oils, a medium that had been developed earlier in Northern Europe. Oils allow the artist to take more time and care and to produce colors that are more permanent and translucent. Leonardo was also the first to use light and shade effectively to bring a figure into the foreground of a painting. [National Gallery of Art, Washington, D.C., Alisa Mellon Bruce Fund.]

The School of Athens, fresco by Raphael in the Vatican in Rome, painted CA. 1510–1511. *The symmetry and organic unity of the painting, as well as its theme of antiquity, make it one of the most telling examples of Renaissance classicism.* [Bettmann Archive.]

machines as airplanes and submarines. Indeed, the variety of his interests was so great that it tended to shorten his attention span, so that he was constantly moving from one activity to another. His great skill lay in conveying inner moods through complex facial features, such as can be seen in the most famous of his paintings, the *Mona Lisa*.

RAPHAEL (1483–1520). Raphael, an unusually sensitive man whose artistic career was cut short by his premature death at thirty-seven, was apparently loved by contemporaries as much for his person as for his work. He is famous for his tender madonnas, the best known of which graces the monastery of San Sisto in Piacenza. Art historians praise his fresco *The School of Athens*, an involved portrayal of the great masters of Western philosophy, as one of the most perfect examples of Renaissance artistic theory and technique. It depicts Plato and Aristotle surrounded by the great philosophers and scientists of antiquity, who are portrayed with the features of Raphael's famous contemporaries, including Leonardo and Michelangelo.

MICHELANGELO (1475–1564). The melancholy genius Michelangelo also excelled in a variety of arts and crafts. His eighteen-foot godlike sculpture *David*, which long stood majestically in the great square of Florence, is a perfect example of the Renaissance artist's devotion to harmony, symmetry, and proportion, as well as his extreme glorification of the human form. Four different popes commissioned works by Michelangelo, the most famous of which are the frescoes for the Sistine Chapel, painted during the pontificate of Pope Julius II (1503–1513), who also set Michelangelo to work on the pope's own magnificent tomb. The Sistine frescoes originally covered 10,000 square feet and involved 343 figures, over half of which exceeded 10 feet in height. This labor of love and piety, painted while Michelangelo was lying on his back or stooping, took four years to complete and left Michel-

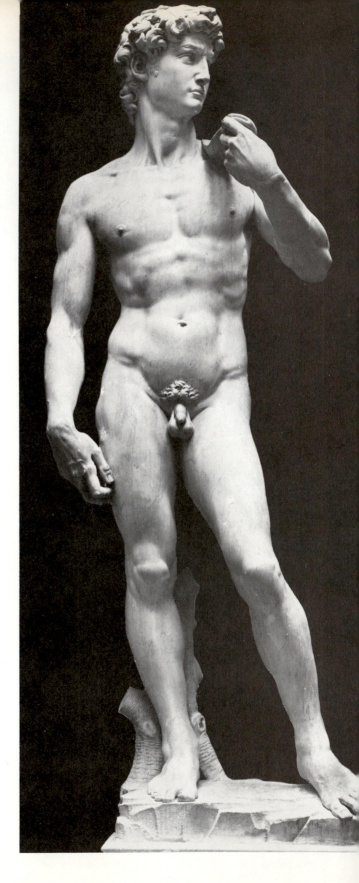

David, by Michelangelo. One of the most famous—and popular—of all the world's sculptures, it was carved in 1501–1504 and now stands in the Galleria dell' Accademia in Florence. [Alinari/SCALA.]

angelo partially crippled. A man who lived to be almost ninety, Michelangelo insisted on doing nearly everything himself and permitted his assistants only a few of the many chores involved.

His later works mark, artistically and philosophically, the passing of High Renaissance painting and the advent of a new, experimental style known as *mannerism*, which reached its peak in the late sixteenth and early seventeenth centuries. A reaction against the simplicity and symmetry of High Renaissance art, which also found expression in music and literature, mannerism made room for the strange and even the abnormal and gave freer reign to the subjectivity of the artist. It derived its name from the fact that it permitted the artist to express his own individual perceptions and feelings, to paint, compose, or write in a "mannered" or "affected" way. Tintoretto (D. 1594) and especially El Greco (D. 1614) became its supreme representatives.

Italy's Political Decline: The French Invasions (1494–1527)

The Treaty of Lodi

As a land of autonomous city-states, Italy's peace and safety from foreign invasion, especially from invasion by the Turks, had always depended on internal cooperation. Such cooperation had been maintained during the last half of the fifteenth century, thanks to a carefully constructed political alliance known as the Treaty of Lodi (1454–1455). The terms of the treaty brought Milan and Naples, long traditional enemies, into alliance with Florence. These three stood together for decades against Venice, which was frequently joined by the Papal States to create an internal balance of power that also made possible a unified front against Italy's external enemies.

The peace made possible by the Treaty of Lodi ended in 1494, when Naples, supported by Florence and the Borgia pope Alexander VI (1492–1503), prepared to attack Milan. At this point, the Milanese despot Ludovico il Moro made what proved to be a fatal response to these new political alignments: he appealed for aid to the French.

Charles VIII's March through Italy

The French king, Louis XI, had resisted the temptation to invade Italy, while nonetheless keeping French dynastic claims in Italy alive. His successor, Charles VIII (1483–1498), an eager youth in his twenties, responded to Ludovico's call with lightning speed. Within five months, he had crossed the Alps (August 1495) and raced as conqueror through Florence and the Papal States into Naples.

Charles' lightning march through Italy also struck terror in non-Italian hearts. Ferdinand of Aragon, whose native land and self-interests as king of Sicily now became vulnerable to a French–Italian axis, took the initiative to create a counteralliance: the League of Venice, formed in March 1495, with Venice, the Papal States, and the Emperor Maximilian I joining Ferdinand against the French. The stage was set for a conflict between France and Spain that would not end until 1559.

Ludovico il Moro meanwhile recognized that he had sown the wind; having desired a French invasion only so long as it weakened his enemies, he now saw Milan threatened by the whirlwind of events that he had himself created. In reaction, he joined the League of Venice, and this alliance was able to send Charles into retreat by May. Charles remained thereafter on the defensive until his death in April 1498.

Pope Alexander VI and the Borgia Family

The French returned to Italy under Charles' successor, Louis XII (1498–1515), this time assisted by a new Italian ally, the Borgia pope Alexander VI (1492–1503). Alexander, probably the most corrupt pope who ever sat on the papal throne, openly promoted the political careers of the children he had had before he became pope, Cesare and Lucrezia, as he placed the efforts of the powerful Borgia family to secure a political base in Romagna in tandem with papal policy there.

In Romagna, several principalities had fallen away from the church during the Avignon papacy, and Venice, the pope's ally within the League of Venice, continued to contest the Papal States for their loyalty. Seeing that a French alliance could give him the opportunity to reestablish control over the region, Alexander agreed to abandon the League of Venice, a withdrawal of support that made the league too weak to resist a French reconquest of Milan. In exchange, Cesare Borgia received the sister of the king of Navarre, Charlotte d' Albret, in marriage, a union that greatly enhanced Borgia military strength. Cesare also received land grants from Louis XII and the promise of French military aid in Romagna. His cunning and determination would make him the model for Machiavelli's The Prince.

All in all, it was a scandalous tradeoff, but one that made it possible for both the French king and the pope to realize their ambitions within Italy. Louis successfully invaded Milan in August 1499. In 1500, Louis and Ferdinand of Aragon divided Naples between them, while the pope and Cesare Borgia conquered the cities of Romagna without opposition.

Pope Julius II

Cardinal Giuliano della Rovere, a strong opponent of the Borgia family, became Pope Julius II (1503–1513). He suppressed the Borgias and placed their newly conquered lands in Romagna under papal jurisdiction. Julius came to be known as the "warrior pope" because he brought the Renaissance papacy to a peak of military prowess and diplomatic intrigue. Shocked as were other contemporaries by this thoroughly secular papacy, the Humanist Erasmus (CA. 1466–1536), who had witnessed in disbelief a bullfight in the papal palace during a visit to Rome, wrote a popular anonymous satire entitled Julius Excluded from Heaven. This humorous account purported to describe the pope's unsuccessful efforts to convince Saint Peter that he was worthy of admission to heaven.

Assisted by his powerful French allies, Pope Julius drove the Venetians out of Romagna in 1509, thereby ending Venetian claims in the region and fully securing the Papal States. Having realized this long-sought papal goal, Julius turned to the second major undertaking of his pontificate: ridding Italy of his former ally, the French invader. Julius, Ferdinand of Aragon, and Venice formed a second Holy League in October 1511, and within a short period, Emperor Maximilian I and the Swiss joined them. By 1512, the league had the French in full retreat, and Swiss armies soundly defeated them in 1513 at Novara.

The French invaded Italy still a third time under Louis' successor, Francis I (1515–1547). French armies massacred Swiss soldiers of the Holy League at Marignano in September 1515, revenging the earlier defeat at Novara. The victory won from the Medici pope, Leo X, the Concordat of Bologna in August 1516, an agreement that gave the French king control over the French clergy in exchange for French recognition of the pope's superiority over church councils and his right to collect taxes from the French clergy. This was an important compromise that helped keep France Catholic after the outbreak of the Protestant Reformation. But the new French entry into Italy also led to the first of four major wars with Spain in the first half of the sixteenth century: the Habsburg–Valois wars, none of which France won.

Niccolò Machiavelli

The period of foreign invasions made a shambles of Italy. The same period that saw Italy's cultural peak in the work of Leonardo, Raphael, and Michelangelo

Machiavelli Discusses the Most Important Trait for a Ruler

Machiavelli believed that the most important personality trait of a successful ruler was the ability to instill fear in his subjects.

Here the question arises; whether it is better to be loved than feared or feared than loved. The answer is that it would be desirable to be both but, since that is difficult, it is much safer to be feared than to be loved, if one must choose. For on men in general this observation may be made: they are ungrateful, fickle, and deceitful, eager to avoid dangers, and avid for gain, and while you are useful to them they are all with you, offering you their blood, their property, their lives, and their sons so long as danger is remote, as we noted above, but when it approaches they turn on you. Any prince, trusting only in their words and having no other preparations made, will fall to his ruin, for friendships that are bought at a price and not by greatness and nobility of soul are paid for indeed, but they are not owned and cannot be called upon in time of need. Men have less hesitation in offending a man who is loved than one who is feared, for love is held by a bond of obligation which, as men are wicked, is broken whenever personal advantage suggests it, but fear is accompanied by the dread of punishment which never relaxes. ❏

Niccolò Machiavelli, *The Prince* (1513), trans. and ed. by Thomas G. Bergin (New York: Appleton-Century-Crofts, 1947), p. 48.

---

also witnessed Italy's political tragedy. One who watched as French, Spanish, and Germany armies wreaked havoc on his country was Niccolò Machiavelli (1469–1527). The more he saw, the more convinced he became that Italian political unity and independence were ends that justified any means. A Humanist and a careful student of ancient Rome, Machiavelli admired the heroic acts of ancient Roman rulers, what Renaissance people called their *Virtù*. Romanticizing the old Roman citizenry, he lamented the absence of heroism among his compatriots. Such a perspective caused his interpretation of both ancient and contemporary history to be somewhat exaggerated. His Florentine contemporary, Guicciardini, a more sober historian less given to idealizing antiquity, wrote truer chronicles of Florentine and Italian history.

The juxtaposition of what Machiavelli believed the ancient Romans had been with the failure of contemporary Romans to realize such high ideals made him the famous cynic we know in the popular epithet *Machiavellian.* Only an unscrupulous strongman, he concluded, using duplicity and terror, could impose order on so divided and selfish a people.

It has been argued that Machiavelli wrote *The Prince* in 1513 as a cynical satire, not as a serious recommendation of unprincipled despotic rule. To take his advocacy of tyranny literally, it is argued, contradicts both his earlier works and his own strong family tradition of republican service. But Machiavelli seems to have been in earnest when he advised rulers to discover the advantages of fraud and brutality. He apparently hoped to see a strong ruler emerge from the restored powerful Medici family.

Whatever Machiavelli's hopes may have been, the Medicis were not destined to be Italy's deliverers. The second Medici pope, Clement VII (1523–1534), watched helplessly as Rome was sacked by the army of Emperor Charles V in 1527, also the year of Machiavelli's death.[2]

Suggested Readings

M. ASTON, *The Fifteenth Century: The Prospect of Europe* (1968). Crisp social history, with pictures.

H. BARON, *The Crisis of the Early Italian Renaissance*, Vols. 1 and 2 (1966). A major work, setting forth the civic dimension of Italian Humanism.

B. BERENSON, *Italian Painters of the Renaissance* (1901). Still incisive.

J. BURCKHARDT, *The Civilization of the Renaissance in Italy* (1867). The old classic that still has as many defenders as detractors.

W. K. FERGUSON, *The Renaissance* (1940). A brief, stimulating summary of the Renaissance in both Italy and northern Europe.

W. K. FERGUSON, *Europe in Transition* 1300–1520 (1962). A major survey that deals with the transition from medieval to Renaissance society.

F. GILBERT, *Machiavelli and Guicciardini* (1984). The two great Renaissance historians compared.

M. GILMORE, *The World of Humanism* 1453–1517 (1952). A comprehensive survey, especially strong in intellectual and cultural history.

R. S. GOTTFRIED, *The Black Death* (1983). Most up-to-date account.

[2] For the placement of the Renaissance in the West in world perspective, see the conclusion of Chapter 17.

J. R. Hale, *Renaissance Europe: The Individual and Society*, 1480–1520 (1971). A many-sided treatment of social history.

D. Hay, *Europe in the Fourteenth and Fifteenth Centuries* (1966). A many-sided treatment of political history.

J. Huizinga, *The Waning of the Middle Ages: A Study of the Forms of Life, Thought, and Art in France and the Netherlands in the Dawn of the Renaissance* (1924). A classic study of "mentality" at the end of the Middle Ages.

G. Huppert, *After the Black Death* (1986). A social historian's perspective on the transition from the Renaissance to modern times.

D. Jensen, *Renaissance Europe: Age of Recovery and Reconciliation* (1981).

R. J. Knecht, *Francis I* (1982). Up-to-date biography of the French king.

P. O. Kristeller, *Renaissance Thought: The Classic, Scholastic, and Humanist Strains* (1961). A master shows the many sides of Renaissance thought.

R. E. Lerner, *The Age of Adversity: The Fourteenth Century* (1968). A brief, comprehensive survey.

L. Martines, *Power and Imagination: City States in Renaissance Italy* (1980). Stimulating account of cultural and political history.

H. A. Miskimin, *The Economy of Early Renaissance Europe 1300–1460* (1969). Shows the interaction of social, political, and economic change.

E. Muir, *Civic Ritual in Renaissance Venice* (1981). A study of the use of pageantry for political purposes.

H. A. Oberman, *The Harvest of Medieval Theology* (1963). A demanding synthesis and revision.

E. Perroy, *The Hundred Years War*, trans. by W. B. Wells (1965). The most comprehensive one-volume account.

Y. Renovard, *The Avignon Papacy* 1305–1403, trans. by D. Bethell (1970). Standard narrative.

Q. Skinner, *The Foundations of Modern Political Thought I: The Renaissance* (1978). A broad survey, very comprehensive.

M. Spinka, *John Hus's Concept of the Church* (1966).

J. W. Thompson, *Economic and Social History of Europe in the Later Middle Ages* 1300–1530 (1958). A bread-and-butter account.

B. Tierney, *Foundations of the Conciliar Theory* (1955). An important study showing the origins of conciliar theory in canon law.

B. Tierney, *The Crisis of Church and State* 1050–1300 (1964). Part 4 provides the major documents in the clash between Boniface VIII and Philip the Fair.

W. Ullmann, *Origins of the Great Schism* (1948). A basic study by a controversial interpreter of medieval political thought.

C. T. Wood, *Philip the Fair and Boniface VIII* (1967). Excerpts from the scholarly debate over the significance of this confrontation.

H. B. Workman, *John Wyclif*, Vols. 1 and 2 (1926). Dated but still standard.

P. Ziegler, *The Black Death* (1969). A highly readable journalistic account.

Erasmus of Rotterdam in a 1526 engraving by Albrecht Durer. Erasmus influenced all of the reform movements of the sixteenth century. He was popularly said to have "laid the egg that Luther hatched." [National Gallery of Art, Washington, D.C.]

17 The Age of Reformation and Religious Wars

In the second decade of the sixteenth century, there began in Saxony in Germany a powerful religious movement that rapidly spread throughout northern Europe, deeply affecting society and politics as well as the spiritual lives of men and women. Attacking what they believed to be burdensome superstitions that robbed people of both their money and their peace of mind, Protestant reformers led a broad revolt against the medieval church. In a relatively short span of time, hundreds of thousands of people from all social classes set aside the beliefs of centuries and adopted a more simplified religious practice.

The Protestant Reformation challenged aspects of the Renaissance, especially its tendency to follow classical sources in glorifying human nature and its loyalty to traditional religion. Protestants were more impressed by the human potential for evil than by the inclination to do good and encouraged parents, teachers, and magistrates to be firm disciplinarians. On the other hand, Protestants also embraced many Renaissance values, especially in the sphere of educational reform and particularly with regard to training in ancient languages. Like the Italian Humanists, the Protestant reformers studied ancient languages and went directly to the original sources; only, for them, this meant the study of the Hebrew and Greek scriptures and the consequent challenge of traditional institutions founded on the authority of the Bible.

The road to the Reformation was long in preparation. As the Protestant ethic influenced an entire age, it was also itself born out of changes in European society beyond those within the purely religious and ecclesiastical spheres.

For Europe, the late fifteenth and the sixteenth centuries were a period of unprecedented territorial expansion and ideological experimentation. Permanent colonies were established within the Americas, and the exploitation of the New World's human and seem-

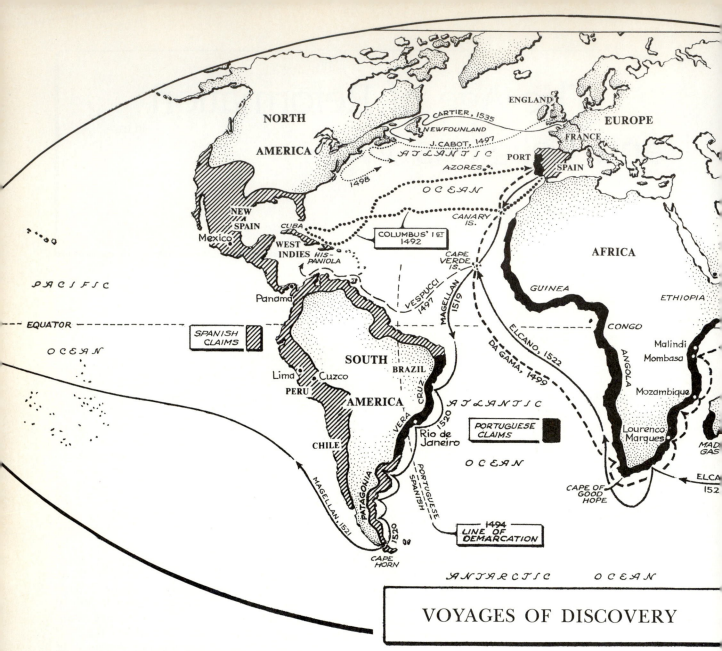

MAP 17-1 VOYAGES OF DISCOVERY *The map dramatizes the expansion of the area of European interest in the fifteenth and sixteenth centuries. Not until today's "space age" has a comparable widening of horizons been possible.*

ingly endless mineral resources was begun. The American gold and silver imported into Europe spurred scientific invention and a weapons industry and touched off an inflationary spiral that produced a revolution in prices by the end of the sixteenth century. The new bullion also helped to create international traffic in African slaves, who were used in ever-increasing numbers to work the mines and the plantations of the New World as replacements for the native Indians. This period further saw social engineering and political planning on a large scale as newly centralized governments developed long-range economic policies, a practice that came to be known as *mercantilism.*

The late fifteenth and the sixteenth centuries also marked the first wide-scale use of the printing press, an invention greatly assisted by the development of a process of cheap paper manufacture and publishers eager to exploit a fascinating new technology. Printing with movable type was invented by Johann Gutenberg (d. 1468) in the mid-fifteenth century in the German city of Mainz. Residential colleges and universities had greatly expanded in northern Europe during the

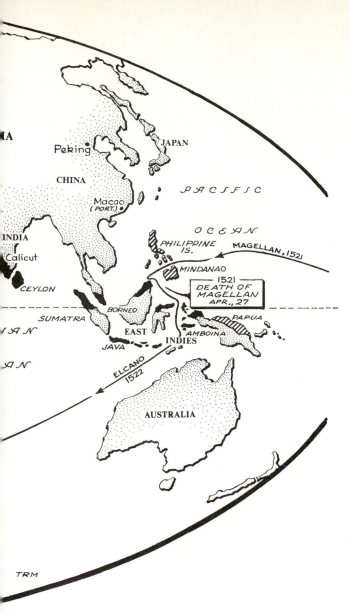

transference of commercial supremacy from the Mediterranean and the Baltic to the Atlantic seaboard. Mercenary motives, reinforced by traditional missionary ideals, inspired Prince Henry the Navigator (1394–1460) to sponsor the Portuguese exploration of the African coast. His main object was the gold trade, which for centuries had been an Arab monopoly. By the last decades of the fifteenth century, gold from Guinea entered Europe by way of Portuguese ships calling at the port cities of Lisbon and Antwerp, rather than by Arab land routes. Antwerp became the financial center of Europe, a commercial crossroads where the enterprise and derring-do of the Portuguese and the Spanish met the capital funds of the German banking houses of Fugger and Welser.

The rush for gold quickly expanded into a rush for the spice markets of India. In the fifteenth century, the diet of most Europeans was a dull combination of bread and gruel, cabbage, turnips, peas, lentils, and onions, together with what meat became available during seasonal periods of slaughter. Spices, especially pepper and cloves, were in great demand both to preserve food and to enhance its taste. Bartholomew Dias (d. 1500) opened the Portuguese empire in the East when he rounded the Cape of Good Hope at the

Model of a Portuguese caravel, a light, fast ship used extensively in trade and exploration. [National Maritime Museum, London.]

fourteenth and fifteenth centuries, creating a literate public in the cities eager to possess and read books. The new technology also made propaganda possible on a massive scale, as pamphlets could now be rapidly and inexpensively produced.

On the Eve of the Reformation

Voyages of Discovery

On the eve of the Reformation, the geographical as well as the intellectual horizons of Western people were broadening. The fifteenth century saw the beginning of Western Europe's global expansion and the tip of Africa in 1487. A decade later, in 1498, Vasco da Gama (d. 1524) reached the coast of India. When he returned to Portugal, he brought with him a cargo worth sixty times the cost of the voyage. In subsequent years, the Portuguese established themselves firmly on the Malabar Coast with colonies in Goa and Calicut and successfully challenged the Arabs and the Venetians for control of the European spice trade.

While the Portuguese concentrated on the Indian Ocean, the Spanish set sail across the Atlantic. They did so in the hope of establishing a shorter route to the rich spice markets of the East Indies. Rather than beating the Portuguese at their own game, however, Christopher Columbus (1451–1506) discovered the Americas instead. When he reached Cuba, he actually thought he was in Japan and the South American coast beyond he believed to be the mainland of China.

Amerigo Vespucci (1451–1512) and Ferdinand Magellan (1480–1521) demonstrated that these new lands were not the outermost territory of the Far East, as Columbus died believing, but an entirely new continent that opened on the still greater Pacific Ocean. Magellan died in the Philippines.

The discovery of gold and silver in vast quantities more than compensated for the disappointment of failing to find a shorter route to the Indies. Still greater mines opened in the 1520s and the 1530s when Hernando Cortes (1485–1547) conquered the Aztecs of Mexico and Francisco Pizarro (ca. 1470–1541) conquered the Incas of Peru, enslaving the native Indian populations and forcing them to work the new mines. As the forced labor and the new European diseases killed American natives in large numbers, another item of trade was created: African slaves. In the sixteenth century, they were transported in great numbers to replace less hearty native populations in the mines and on the sugar cane plantations of the New World.

The influx of spices and precious metals into Europe was not an unmixed blessing. It contributed to a steady rise in prices during the sixteenth century that created an inflation rate estimated at 2 per cent a year. The new supply of bullion from the Americas joined with enlarged European production to increase greatly the amount of coinage in circulation, and this increase in turn fed inflation. Fortunately, the increase in prices was by and large spread over a long period of time and was not sudden. Prices doubled in Spain by midcentury, quadrupled by 1600. In Luther's Wittenberg, the cost of basic food and clothing increased almost 100 per cent between 1519 and 1540. Generally, wages and rents remained well behind the rise in prices.

The new wealth enabled governments and private

Columbus Reports His Discovery of the Entrance to Paradise

During his third voyage, Columbus reached the mouth of the Orinoco River in Venezuela. He believed he was in the East Indies, where, according to tradition, Adam and Eve had first trod the earth. Columbus believed that he had now come upon the very entrance into paradise. In October 1498, he wrote of this discovery to his patrons, Ferdinand and Isabella, monarchs of Spain.

I have already described my ideas concerning this hemisphere and its form [he believed it to be pear-shaped]. I have no doubt that if I could pass below the equinoctial line, after reaching the highest point . . . I should find a much milder temperature and a variation in the stars and in the water. Not that I suppose that elevated point to be navigable, nor even that there is water there; indeed, I believe it is impossible to ascend to it, because I am convinced that it is the spot of the earthly paradise, whither none can go but by God's permission . . . .

I do not suppose that the earthly paradise is in the form of a rugged mountain, as the descriptions of it have made it appear, but that it is on the summit of the spot, which I have described as being in the form of the stalk of a pear. The approach to it . . . must be by constant and gradual ascent, but I believe that . . . no one could ever reach the top. I think also that the water I have described may proceed from it, though it be far off, and that stopping at the place which I have just left, it forms this lake. There are great indications of this being the terrestrial paradise, for its site coincides with the opinion of the holy and wise theologians whom I have mentioned. Moreover, the other evidences agree . . . for I have never read or heard of fresh water coming in so large a quantity in close conjunction with the water of the sea. The idea is also corroborated by the blandness of the temperature. If the water of which I speak does not proceed from the earthly paradise, it seems to be a still greater wonder, for I do not believe that there is any river in the world so large or so deep. ❑

Donald Weinstein (ed.), *The Renaissance and the Reformation* 1300–1600 (New York: Free Press, 1965), pp. 138–139.

Erasmus Describes the "Philosophy of Christ"

Although Erasmus called his ideal of how people should live the "philosophy of Christ," he found it taught by classical authors as well. In this selection, he commented on its main features, with obvious polemic against the philosophy of the Scholastics.

This kind of philosophy [the philosophy of Christ] is located more truly in the disposition of the mind than in syllogisms. Here life means more than debate, inspiration is preferable to erudition, transformation [of life] a more important matter than intellectual comprehension. Only a very few can be learned, but all can be Christian, all can be devout, and—I shall boldly add—all can be theologians. Indeed, this philosophy easily penetrates into the minds of all; it is an action in special accord with human nature. What else is the philosophy of Christ, which he himself calls a rebirth, than the restoration of human nature . . . ? Although no one has taught this more perfectly . . . than Christ, nevertheless one may find in the books of the pagans very much which does agree with it. There was never so coarse a school of philosophy that taught that money rendered a man happy. Nor has there ever been one so shameless that fixed the chief good in vulgar honors and pleasures. The Stoics understood that no one was wise unless he was good. . . . According to Plato, Socrates teaches . . . that a wrong must not be repaid with a wrong, and also that since the soul is immortal, those should not be lamented who depart this life for a happier one with the assurance of having led an upright life. . . . And Aristotle has written in the *Politics* that nothing can be a delight to us . . . except virtue alone. . . . If there are things that belong particularly to Christianity in these ancient writers, let us follow them. ❑

John C. Olin (ed. and trans.), *Christian Humanism and the Reformation: Desiderius Erasmus.* (New York: Harper, 1965), pp. 100–101.

---

entrepreneurs to sponsor basic research and expansion in the printing, shipping, mining, textile, and weapons industries—the growth industries of the Age of Reformation. There is also evidence of mercantilism or large-scale government planning in such ventures as the French silk industry and the Hapsburg–Fugger development of mines in Austria and Hungary.

In the thirteenth and fourteenth centuries, capitalist institutions and practices had already begun to develop in the rich Italian cities. Those who owned the means of production, either privately or corporately, were clearly distinguished from the workers who operated them. Wherever possible, monopolies were created in basic goods. High interest was charged on loans—actual, if not legal, usury. And the "capitalist" virtues of thrift, industry, and orderly planning were everywhere in evidence—all intended to permit the free and efficient accumulation of wealth.

The late fifteenth and sixteenth centuries saw the maturation of such capitalism together with its peculiar social problems. The new wealth and industrial expansion raised the expectations of the poor and the ambitious and heightened the reactionary tendencies within the established and wealthy classes. This effect, in turn, greatly aggravated the traditional social divisions between the clergy and the laity, the higher and the lower clergy, the urban patriciate and the guilds, masters and journeymen, and the landed nobility and the agrarian peasantry.

The Northern Renaissance

The scholarly works of northern Humanists created a climate favorable to religious and educational reforms on the eve of the Reformation. Northern Humanism was initially stimulated by the importation of Italian learning through such varied intermediaries as students who had studied in Italy, merchants, and the Brothers of the Common Life (an influential lay religious movement that began in the Netherlands). The northern Humanists tended to come from more diverse social backgrounds and to be more devoted to religious reforms than their Italian counterparts. They were also more willing to write for lay audiences.

The most famous of the northern Humanists was Desiderius Erasmus (1466–1536), the reputed "prince of the Humanists." Erasmus gained fame as both an educational and a religious reformer. He aspired to unite the classical ideals of humanity and civic virtue with the Christian ideals of love and piety. He believed that disciplined study of the classics and the Bible, if begun early enough, was the best way to reform both individuals and society. He summarized his own beliefs with the phrase *philosophia Christi*, a simple, ethical piety in imitation of Christ. He set this ideal in starkest contrast to what he believed to be the dogmatic, ceremonial, and factious religious practice of the later Middle Ages.

To promote his own religious beliefs, Erasmus edited the works of the Church Fathers and made a Greek edition of the New Testament (1516), which became the basis for his new, more accurate Latin translation (1519), later used by Martin Luther.

These various enterprises did not please Church authorities. At one point in the mid-sixteenth century, all of Erasmus' works were placed on the *Index of Forbidden Books*. Erasmus also received Luther's unqualified condemnation for his views on the freedom of human will. Still, Erasmus' didactic and scholarly works became basic tools of reform in the hands of both Protestant and Catholic reformers.

The best known of early English Humanists was Sir Thomas More (1478–1535), a close friend of Erasmus. It was while visiting More that Erasmus wrote his most famous work, *The Praise of Folly* (1511), an amusing and profound exposé of human self-deception that was quickly translated from the original Latin into many vernacular languages. More's *Utopia* (1516), a criticism of contemporary society, still rivals the plays of Shakespeare as the most-read sixteenth-century English work. *Utopia* depicts an imaginary society based on reason and tolerance that has overcome social and political injustice by holding all property and goods in common and by requiring all to earn their bread by the sweat of their own brow.

Although More remained staunchly Catholic, Humanism in England, as in Germany, played an important role in preparing the way for the English Reformation. A circle of English Humanists, under the direction of Henry VIII's minister Thomas Cromwell, translated and disseminated late medieval criticisms of the papacy and many of Erasmus' satirical writings.

Whereas in Germany, England, and France Humanism prepared the way for Protestant reforms, in Spain it entered the service of the Catholic church. Here the key figure was Francisco Jiménez de Cisneros (1437–1517), a confessor to Queen Isabella, and after 1508 Grand Inquisitor—a position from which he was able to enforce the strictest religious orthodoxy. Jiménez was a conduit for Humanist scholarship and learning. He founded the University of Alcalá near Madrid in 1509, printed a Greek edition of the New Testament, and translated many religious tracts that aided clerical reform and control of lay religious life. His greatest achievement, taking fifteen years to complete, was the *Complutensian Polyglot Bible*, a six-volume work that placed the Hebrew, Greek, and Latin versions of the Bible in parallel columns. Such scholarly projects and internal church reforms joined with the repressive measures of Ferdinand and Isabella to keep Spain strictly Catholic throughout the Age of Reformation.

Religious Life

The Protestant Reformation could not have occurred without the monumental crises of the medieval church during the "exile" in Avignon, the Great Schism, the conciliar period, and the Renaissance papacy. The late Middle Ages were marked by independent lay and clerical efforts to reform local religious practice and by widespread experimentation with new religious forms.

On the eve of the Reformation, Rome's international network of church offices, which had unified Europe religiously during the Middle Ages, began to fall apart in many areas, hurried along by a growing sense of regional identity—incipient nationalism—and local secular administrative competence. The long-entrenched benefice system of the medieval church, which had permitted important ecclesiastical posts to be sold to the highest bidders and had left parishes without active, resident pastors, did not result in a vibrant local religious life. The substitutes hired by nonresident holders of benefices, who lived elsewhere (mostly in Rome) and milked the revenues of their offices, performed their chores mechanically and had neither firsthand knowledge of nor much sympathy with local needs and problems. Rare was the late medieval German town that did not have complaints about the maladministration, concubinage, and/or fiscalism of their clergy, especially the higher clergy (i.e., bishops, abbots, and prelates).

Communities loudly protested the financial abuses of the medieval church long before Luther published his famous summary of economic grievances in the *Address to the Christian Nobility of the German Nation* (1520). The sale of indulgences, a practice greatly expanded on the eve of the Reformation had also been repeatedly attacked before Luther.

City governments attempted to improve local religious life on the eve of the Reformation by endowing preacherships. These beneficed positions provided for well-trained and dedicated pastors and regular preaching and pastoral care, which went beyond the routine performance of the Mass and traditional religious functions. In many instances, these preacherships became platforms for Protestant preachers.

Magistrates also restricted the growth of ecclesiastical properties and clerical privileges. During the Middle Ages, special clerical rights in both property and person had come to be recognized by canon and civil law. Because they were holy places, churches and monasteries had been exempted from the taxes and laws that affected others. They were treated as special places of "sacral peace" and asylum. It was considered inappropriate for holy persons (clergy) to be burdened with such "dirty jobs" as military service, compulsory labor, standing watch at city gates, and other obligations of citizenship. Nor was it thought right that the laity, of whatever rank, should sit in judgment on those who were their shepherds and intermediaries with God. The clergy, accordingly, came to enjoy an immunity of place (which exempted ecclesiastical properties from taxes and recognized their right of asylum) and an immunity of person (which exempted the clergy from the jurisdiction of civil courts).

On the eve of the Reformation, measures were passed to restrict these privileges and to end their abuses—efforts to regulate ecclesiastical acquisition of new property, to circumvent the right of asylum in churches and monasteries (a practice that posed a threat to the normal administration of justice), and to bring the clergy under the local tax code.

The Reformation

Martin Luther and the German Reformation to 1525

Unlike France and England, late medieval Germany lacked the political unity to enforce "national" religious reforms during the late Middle Ages. There were no lasting Statutes of Provisors (1351) and *praemunire* (1353, 1365), as in England, nor a Pragmatic Sanction of Bourges (1385), as in France, limiting papal jurisdiction and taxation on a national scale. What happened on a unified national level in England and France occurred only locally and piecemeal within German territories and towns. As popular resentment of clerical immunities and ecclesiastical abuses, especially regarding the selling of indulgences, spread among German cities and towns, an unorganized "national" opposition to Rome formed. German Humanists had long given voice to such criticism, and by 1517, it was pervasive enough to provide a solid foundation for Martin Luther's reform.

Luther (1483–1546) was the son of a successful Thüringian miner. He was educated in Mansfeld, Magdeburg, where the Brothers of the Common Life were his teachers, and in Eisenach. Between 1501 and 1505, he attended the University of Erfurt. After receiving his master of arts degree in 1505, Luther registered with the Law Faculty in accordance with his parents' wishes. But he never began the study of law. To the shock and disappointment of his family, he instead entered the Order of the Hermits of Saint Augustine in Erfurt on July 17, 1505. This decision had apparently been building for some time and was resolved during a lightning storm in which a terrified Luther, crying out to Saint Anne for assistance (Saint Anne was the pa-

Martin Luther Discovers Justification by Faith Alone

Many years after the fact, Martin Luther described his discovery that God's righteousness was not an active, punishing righteousness but a passive, transforming righteousness, which made those who believed in him righteous as God himself is righteous.

Though I lived as a monk without reproach, I felt that I was a sinner before God with an extremely disturbed conscience. I could not believe that he was placated by my satisfaction. I did not love, yes, I hated the righteous God who punishes sinners, and secretly, if not blasphemously, certainly murmuring greatly, I was angry with God, and said, "As if, indeed, it is not enough, that miserable sinners, eternally lost through original sin, are crushed by every kind of calamity by the law of the decalogue, without having God add pain to pain by the gospel and also by the gospel threatening us with his righteousness and wrath!" Thus I raged with a fierce and troubled conscience. Nevertheless, I beat importunately upon Paul at that place, most ardently desiring to know what St. Paul wanted.

At last, by the mercy of God, meditating day and night, I gave heed to the context of the words, namely, "In it the righteousness of God is revealed, as it is written, 'He who through faith is righteous shall live'" [Romans 1:17]. There I began to understand that the right-eousness of God is that by which the righteous lives by a gift of God, namely by faith. And this is the meaning: the righteousness of God is revealed by the gospel, namely, the passive righteousness with which merciful God justifies us by faith, as it is written, "He who through faith is righteous shall live." Here I felt that I was altogether born again and had entered paradise itself through open gates. There a totally other face of the entire Scripture showed itself to me. Thereupon I ran through the Scriptures from memory. I also found in other terms an analogy, as, the work of God, that is, what God does in us, the power of God, with which he makes us strong, the wisdom of God, with which he makes us wise, the strength of God, the salvation of God, the glory of God.

And I extolled my sweetest word with a love as great as the hatred with which I had before hated the word "righteousness of God." Thus that place in Paul was for me truly the gate to paradise. ❑

Preface to the Complete Edition of Luther's Latin Writings (1545), in *Luther's Works*, Vol. 34, ed. by Lewis W. Spitz (Philadelphia: Muhlenberg Press, 1960), pp. 336–337.

tron saint of travelers in distress), promised to enter a monastery if he escaped death.

Ordained in 1507, Luther pursued a traditional course of study, becoming in 1509 a *baccalaureus biblicus* and *sententiarius*, that is, one thoroughly trained in the Bible and the *Sentences* of Peter Lombard. In 1510, he journeyed to Rome on the business of his order, finding there justification for the many criticisms of the Church he had heard in Germany. In 1511, he was transferred to the Augustinian monastery in Wittenberg, where he earned his doctorate in theology in 1512, thereafter becoming a leader within the monastery, the new university, and the spiritual life of the city.

THE ATTACK ON INDULGENCES. Reformation theology grew out of a problem common to many of the clergy and the laity at this time: the failure of traditional medieval religion to provide either full personal or intellectual satisfaction. Luther was especially plagued by the disproportion between his own sense of sinfulness and the perfect righteousness that medieval theology taught that God required for salvation. Traditional Church teaching and the sacrament of penance proved to be of no consolation. Luther wrote that he came to despise the phrase "righteousness of God," for it seemed to demand of him a perfection he knew neither he nor any other human being could ever achieve. His insight into the meaning of "justification by faith alone" was a gradual process that extended over several years, between 1513 and 1518. The righteousness God demands, he concluded, was not one that came from many religious works and ceremonies but was present in full measure in those who simply believed and trusted in the work of Jesus Christ, who alone was the perfect righteousness satisfying to God. To believe in Christ was to stand before God clothed in Christ's sure righteousness.

This new theology made indulgences unacceptable. An indulgence was a remission of the temporal penalty imposed by the priest on penitents as a "work of satisfaction" for their committed mortal sins. According to medieval theology, after the priest had absolved penitents of guilt for their sins, they still remained under an eternal penalty, a punishment God justly imposed on them for their sins. After absolution, however, this eternal penalty had been transformed into a temporal penalty, a manageable "work of satisfaction" that the penitent could perform here and now (for example, through prayers, fasting, almsgiving, retreats, and pilgrimages). Penitents who defaulted on such prescribed works of satisfaction could expect to suffer for them in purgatory.

At this point, indulgences came into play as an aid to a laity made genuinely anxious by the belief in a future suffering in purgatory for neglected penances or unrepented sins. In 1343, Pope Clement VI (1342–1352) had proclaimed the existence of a "treasury of merit," an infinite reservoir of good works in the Church's possession that could be dispensed at the pope's discretion. It was on the basis of this declared treasury that the Church sold "letters of indulgence," which covered the works of satisfaction owed by penitents. In 1476, Pope Sixtus IV (1471–1484) extended indulgences also to purgatory. Originally, indulgences had been given only for the true self-sacrifice of going on a crusade to the Holy Land. By Luther's time, they

Luther and the Wittenberg reformers with Elector John Frederick of Saxony (1532–1547), painted about 1543 by Lucas Cranach the Younger (1515–1586). Luther is on the far left, Philip Melanchthon in the front row on the far right. [Toledo Museum of Art, Toledo, Ohio; gift of Edward Drummond Libbey.]

MAP 17-2   THE EMPIRE OF CHARLES V   *Dynastic marriages and simple chance concentrated into Charles's hands rule over the lands shown here, plus Spain's overseas possessions. Crowns and titles rained in on him; election in 1519 as emperor gave him new burdens and responsibilities.*

were regularly dispensed for small cash payments (very modest sums that were regarded as a good work of almsgiving) and were presented to the laity as remitting not only their own future punishments, but also those of their dead relatives presumed to be suffering in purgatory.

In 1517, a Jubilee indulgence, proclaimed during the pontificate of Pope Julius II (1503–1513) to raise funds for the rebuilding of Saint Peter's in Rome, was revived and preached on the borders of Saxony in the territories of Archbishop Albrecht of Mainz. Albrecht was much in need of revenues because of the large debts he had incurred in order to hold, contrary to church law, three ecclesiastical appointments. The selling of the indulgence was a joint venture by Albrecht, the Augsburg banking house of Fugger, and Pope Leo X (1513–1521), half the proceeds going to the pope and half to Albrecht and his creditors. The famous indulgence preacher John Tetzel (d. 1519) was enlisted to preach the indulgence in Albrecht's territories because he was a seasoned professional who knew how to stir ordinary people to action. As he exhorted on one occasion:

Don't you hear the voices of your dead parents and other relatives crying out, "Have mercy on us, for we suffer great punishment and pain. From this you could release us with a few alms. . . . We have created you, fed you, cared for you, and left you our temporal goods. Why do you treat us so cruelly and leave us to suffer in the flames, when it takes only a little to save us?"[1]

When on October 31, 1517, Luther posted his ninety-five theses against indulgences, according to tradition, on the door of Castle Church in Wittenberg, he protested especially against the impression created by Tetzel that indulgences actually remitted sins and released the dead from punishment in purgatory—claims he believed went far beyond the traditional practice and seemed to make salvation something that could be bought and sold.

ELECTION OF CHARLES V AND THE DIET OF WORMS.   The ninety-five theses were embraced by

[1] *Die Reformation in Augenzeugen Berichten*, ed. by Helmar Junghans (Düsseldorf: Karl Rauch Verlag, 1967), p. 44.

Humanists and other proponents of reform. They made Luther famous overnight and prompted official proceedings against him. As sanctions were being prepared against Luther, Emperor Maximilian I died (January 12, 1519), and this event, fortunate for the Reformation, turned all attention from heresy in Saxony to the contest for a new emperor.

The pope backed the French king, Francis I. However, Charles I of Spain, a youth of nineteen, succeeded his grandfather and became Emperor Charles V. Charles was assisted by both a long tradition of Habsburg imperial rule and a massive Fugger campaign chest, which secured the votes of the seven electors.

In the same month in which Charles was elected emperor, Luther entered a debate in Leipzig (June 27, 1519) with the Ingolstadt professor John Eck. During this contest, Luther challenged the infallibility of the pope and the inerrancy of Church councils, appealing, for the first time, to the sovereign authority of Scripture alone. All his bridges to the old Church were burned when he further defended certain teachings of Jan Hus that had been condemned by the Council of

A Catholic caricature of Martin Luther as a seven-headed demon. This picture served as the title page of a pamphlet by one of Luther's strongest Catholic critics, Johannes Cochlaeus.

A Protestant caricature of the pope as a monster with the characteristics of several beasts. Note the flag with the pope's "keys" to heaven and hell.

Constance. In 1520, Luther signaled his new direction with three famous pamphlets: the *Address to the Christian Nobility of the German Nation*, which urged the German princes to force reforms on the Roman church, especially to curtail its political and economic power in Germany; the *Babylonian Captivity of the Church*, which attacked the traditional seven sacraments, arguing that only two were proper, and which exalted the authority of Scripture, Church councils, and secular princes over that of the pope; and the eloquent *Freedom of a Christian*, which summarized the new teaching of salvation by faith alone. On June 15, 1520, the papal bull *Exsurge Domine* condemned Luther for heresy and gave him sixty days to retract. The final bull of excommunication, *Decet Pontificem Romanum*, was issued on January 3, 1521.

In April 1521, Luther presented his views before a diet of the empire in Worms, over which the newly elected Emperor Charles V presided. Ordered to recant, Luther declared that to do so would be to act against Scripture, reason, and his own conscience. On May 26, 1521, he was placed under the imperial ban and thereafter became an "outlaw" to secular as well as to religious authority. For his own protection, friends hid him in Wartburg Castle, where he spent almost a year in seclusion, from April 1521 to March 1522. During his stay, he translated the New Testament into German, using Erasmus' new Greek text, and he attempted by correspondence to oversee the first stages of the Reformation in Wittenberg.

The Reformation was greatly assisted in these early years by the emperor's war with France and the advance of the Ottoman Turks into eastern Europe. Against both adversaries Charles V, who also remained a Spanish king with dynastic responsibilities outside the empire, needed German troops, and to that end, he promoted friendly relations with the German princes. Between 1521 and 1559, Spain (the Habsburg dynasty) and France (the Valois dynasty) fought four major wars over disputed territories in Italy and along their borders. In 1526, the Turks overran Hungary at the Battle of Mohacs, while in western Europe the French-led League of Cognac formed against Charles for the second Habsburg–Valois war. Thus preoccupied, the emperor agreed through his representatives at the German Diet of Speyer in 1526 that each German territory was free to enforce the Edict of Worms (1521) against Luther "so as to be able to answer in good conscience to God and the emperor." That concession, in effect, gave the German princes territorial sovereignty in religious matters and the Reformation time to put down deep roots. Later (in 1555), such local princely control over religion would be enshrined in imperial law by the Peace of Augsburg.

THE PEASANTS' REVOLT. In its first decade, the Protestant movement suffered more from internal division than from imperial interference. By 1525, Luther had become as much an object of protest within Germany as was the pope. Original allies, sympathizers, and fellow travelers declared their independence from him.

Like the German Humanists, the German peasantry also had at first believed Luther to be an ally. The peasantry had been organized since the late fifteenth century against efforts by territorial princes to override their traditional laws and customs and to subject them to new regulations and taxes. Peasant leaders, several of whom were convinced Lutherans, saw in Luther's teaching about Christian freedom and his criticism of monastic landowners a point of view close to their own, and they openly solicited Luther's support of their political and economic rights, including their revolutionary request for release from serfdom. Luther and his followers sympathized with the peasants; indeed, for several years, Lutheran pamphleteers made *Karsthans*, the burly, honest peasant with his flail or hoe, a symbol of the simple life that God desired all people to live. The Lutherans, however, were not social revolutionaries, and when the peasants revolted against their masters in 1524–1525, Luther not surprisingly condemned them in the strongest possible terms as "unchristian" and urged the princes to crush their revolt without mercy. Tens of thousands of peasants (estimates run between 70,000 and 100,000) had died by the time the revolt was put down.

For Luther, the freedom of the Christian was an inner release from guilt and anxiety, not a right to restructure society by violent revolution. Had Luther supported the Peasants' Revolt, he would not only have contradicted his own teaching and belief but also ended any chance of the survival of his reform beyond the 1520s.

Zwingli and the Swiss Reformation

Switzerland was a loose confederacy of thirteen autonomous cantons or states and allied areas (see Map 17.3). Some cantons (e.g., Zurich, Bern, Basel, and Schaffhausen) became Protestant, some (especially around the Lucerne heartland) remained Catholic, and a few other cantons and regions managed to effect a compromise. Among the preconditions of the Swiss Reformation were the growth of national sentiment occasioned by opposition to foreign mercenary service (providing mercenaries for Europe's warring nations was a major source of Switzerland's livelihood) and a desire for Church reform that had persisted in Switzerland since the councils of Constance (1414–1417) and Basel (1431–1449).

THE REFORMATION IN ZURICH. Ulrich Zwingli (1484–1531), the leader of the Swiss Reformation, had been humanistically educated in Bern, Vienna, and Basel. He was strongly influenced by Erasmus, whom he credited with having set him on the path to reform. An eloquent critic of mercenary service, Zwingli believed such service threatened both the political sovereignty and the moral well-being of the Swiss confederacy. By 1518, Zwingli was also widely known for opposition to the sale of indulgences and religious superstition.

In 1519, Zwingli gained the position of people's priest in Zurich, the base from which he engineered the Swiss Reformation. In March 1522, he was part of a group who defied the Lenten fast—an act of protest analogous to burning one's national flag today. Zwingli's reform guideline was very simple and very effective: whatever lacked literal support in Scripture was to be neither believed nor practiced. A disputation held on January 29, 1523, concluded with the city government's sanction of Zwingli's Scripture test. Thereafter Zurich became, to all intents and purposes, a Protestant city and the center of the Swiss Reforma-

MAP 17-3   THE SWISS CONFEDERATION *While nominally still a part of the Holy Roman Empire, Switzerland grew from a loose defensive union of the central "forest cantons" in the thirteenth century to a fiercely independent association of regions with different languages, histories, and finally, religions.*

tion. A harsh discipline was imposed by the new Protestant regime, making Zurich one of the first examples of a puritanical Protestant city.

THE MARBURG COLLOQUY. Landgrave Philip of Hesse (1504–1567) sought to unite Swiss and German Protestants in a mutual defense pact, a potentially significant political alliance. His efforts were spoiled, however, by theological disagreements between Luther and Zwingli over the nature of Christ's presence in the Eucharist. Zwingli maintained a symbolic interpretation of Christ's words, "This is my body"; Christ, he argued, was only spiritually, not bodily, present in the bread and wine of the Eucharist. Luther, to the contrary, insisted that Christ's human nature could share the properties of his divine nature; hence, where Christ was spiritually present, he could also be bodily present, for his was a special nature.

Philip of Hesse brought the two Protestant leaders together in his castle in Marburg in early October 1529, but they were unable to work out their differences on this issue. Luther left thinking Zwingli a dangerous fanatic. Although cooperation between the two sides did not cease, the disagreement splintered the Protestant movement theologically and politically.

Anabaptists and Radical Protestants

The moderate pace and seemingly small ethical results of the Lutheran and Zwinglian reformations discontented many people, among them some of the original coworkers of Luther and Zwingli. Many desired a more rapid and thorough implementation of primitive Christianity and accused the major reformers of going only halfway. The most important of these radical groups were the Anabaptists, the sixteenth-century ancestors of the modern Mennonites and Amish. The Anabaptists were especially distinguished by their rejection of infant baptism and their insistence on only adult baptism (*anabaptism* derives from the Greek word meaning "to rebaptize"), believing that baptism as a consenting adult conformed to Scripture and was more respectful of human freedom.

Anabaptists physically separated from society to form a more perfect community in imitation of what they believed to be the example of the first Christians. Because of the close connection between religious and civic life in this period, such separatism was viewed by the political authorities as a threat to basic social bonds.

At first, Anabaptism drew its adherents from all social classes. But as Lutherans and Zwinglians joined with Catholics in opposition to the Anabaptists, a more rural, agrarian class came to make up the great majority. In 1529, rebaptism became a capital offense throughout the Holy Roman Empire. It has been estimated that between 1525 and 1618 at least one thousand and perhaps as many as five thousand men and women were executed for rebaptising themselves as adults.

Political Consolidation of the Lutheran Reformation

THE DIET OF AUGSBURG. Charles V returned to the empire in 1530 to direct the Diet of Augsburg, a meeting of Protestant and Catholic representatives assembled for the purpose of ending the religious divisions. With its terms dictated by the Catholic emperor, the diet adjourned with a blunt order to all Lutherans to revert to Catholicism. The Reformation was by this time too firmly established for that to occur, and in February 1531, the Lutherans responded with the formation of their own defensive alliance, the Schmalkaldic League, which achieved a stalemate with the emperor, who was again distracted by renewed war with France and the Turks.

THE EXPANSION OF THE REFORMATION. In the 1530s, German Lutherans formed regional consistories, judicial bodies composed of theologians and lawyers, which oversaw and administered the new Protestant churches. These consistories replaced the old Catholic episcopates. Under the leadership of Philip Melanchthon, Luther's most admired colleague, educational reforms were enacted that provided for compulsory primary education, schools for girls, a Humanist revision of the traditional curriculum, and catechetical instruction of the laity in the new religion. These accomplishments earned Melanchthon the title "praeceptor of Germany."

The Reformation also dug in elsewhere. Introduced into Denmark by Christian II (ruled 1513–1523), Danish Lutheranism throve under Frederick I (1523–1533), who joined the Schmalkaldic League. Under Christian III (1536–1559) Lutheranism became the state religion. In Sweden, Gustavus Vasa (1523–1560), supported by a Swedish nobility greedy for Church lands, confiscated Church property and subjected the clergy to royal authority at the Diet of Vesteras (1527).

In politically splintered Poland, Lutherans, Anabaptists, Calvinists, and even Antitrinitarians found room to practice their beliefs, as Poland, primarily because of the absence of a central political authority, became a model of religious pluralism and toleration in the second half of the sixteenth century.

REACTION AGAINST PROTESTANTS: THE INTERIM. Charles V made abortive efforts in 1540–1541 to enforce a compromise agreement between Protestants and Catholics. As these and other conciliar efforts failed, he turned to a military solution. In 1547, imperial armies crushed the Protestant Schmalkaldic League.

The emperor established puppet rulers in Saxony and Hesse and issued as imperial law the *Augsburg Interim*, a new order that Protestants everywhere

MAP 17-4   THE RELIGIOUS SITUATION ABOUT 1560   *By 1560 Luther, Zwingli, and Loyola were dead, Calvin near the end of his life, the English break from Rome fully accomplished, and the last session of the Council of Trent about to assemble. Here is the religious geography of Western Europe at this time.*

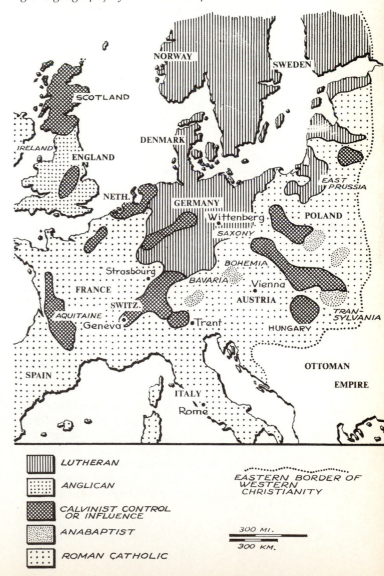

LUTHERAN

ANGLICAN

CALVINIST CONTROL OR INFLUENCE

ANABAPTIST

ROMAN CATHOLIC

EASTERN BORDER OF WESTERN CHRISTIANITY

300 MI.

300 KM.

must readopt old Catholic beliefs and practices. But the Reformation was too entrenched by 1547 to be ended even by brute force. Confronted by fierce Protestant resistance and weary from three decades of war, the emperor was forced to relent.

The Peace of Augsburg in September 1555 made the division of Christendom permanent. This agreement recognized in law what had already been well established in practice: *cuius regio, eius religio*, meaning that the ruler of a land would determine the religion of the land. Lutherans were permitted to retain all Church lands forcibly seized before 1552. Those discontented with the religion of their region were permitted to migrate to another.

Calvinism and Anabaptism were not recognized as legal forms of Christian belief and practice by the Peace of Augsburg. Anabaptists had long adjusted to such exclusion by forming their own separatist communities. Calvinists, however, were not separatists and could not choose this route; they remained determined not only to secure the right to worship publicly as they pleased but also to shape society according to their own religious convictions. While Anabaptists retreated and Lutherans enjoyed the security of an established religion, Calvinists organized to lead national revolutions throughout northern Europe in the second half of the sixteenth and the first half of the seventeenth century.

John Calvin and the Genevan Reformation

Calvinism was the religious ideology that inspired or accompanied massive political resistance in France, the Netherlands, and Scotland. It established itself within the Palatinate during the reign of Elector Frederick III (1559–1576). Believing strongly in both divine predestination and the individual's responsibility to reorder society according to God's plan, Calvinists became zealous reformers determined to transform and order society according to their religious beliefs. In a famous study, *The Protestant Ethic and the Spirit of Capitalism* (1904), the German sociologist Max Weber argued that this peculiar combination of religious confidence and self-disciplined activism produced an ethic that stimulated and reinforced emergent capitalism, bringing Calvinism and later Puritanism into close association with the development of modern capitalist societies.

POLITICAL REVOLT AND RELIGIOUS REFORM IN GENEVA. Whereas in Saxony religious reform paved the way for a political revolution against the emperor, in Geneva a political revolution against the local prince-bishop laid the foundation for the religious change. Genevans successfully revolted against the House of Savoy and their resident prince-bishop in the

The French reformer and theologian, John Calvin (1509–1564). [Musée Historique de la Réformation et Bibliothèque Calvinienne, Geneva. H. Pattusch.]

late 1520s. In late 1533, Bern dispatched Protestant reformers to Geneva. In the summer of 1535, after much internal turmoil, the Protestants triumphed, and the traditional Mass and other religious practices were removed. On May 21, 1536, the city voted officially to adopt the Reformation: "to live according to the Gospel and the Word of God . . . without . . . any more masses, statues, idols, or other papal abuses."

John Calvin (1509–1564), a reform-minded Humanist and lawyer, arrived in Geneva after these events, in July 1536. Guillaume Farel (1489–1565), the local Protestant reformer, successfully pleaded with him to stay and assist the Reformation.

Before a year had passed, Calvin had drawn up articles for the governance of the new church, as well as a catechism to guide and discipline the people, both of which were presented for approval to the city councils in early 1537. Because of the strong measures proposed to govern Geneva's moral life, the reformers were suspected by many of desiring to create a "new papacy." Both within and outside Geneva, Calvin and Farel were perceived as going too far too fast. In February 1538, the reformers were exiled from the city.

Calvin went to Strasbourg, a model Protestant city, where he became pastor to the French exiles there. During his two-year stay in Strasbourg, Calvin wrote biblical commentaries and a second edition of his masterful *Institutes of the Christian Religion*, which many consider the definitive theological statement of the Protestant faith. Calvin also married and participated in the ecumenical discussions urged on Protestants and Catholics by Charles V. Most important, he learned from the Strasbourg reformer Martin Bucer how to implement the Protestant Reformation successfully.

CALVIN'S GENEVA. In 1540, Geneva elected officials who were favorable to Calvin and invited him to return. This he did in September 1540, never to leave the city again. Within months of his arrival, new ecclesiastical ordinances were implemented that provided for cooperation between the magistrates and the clergy in matters of internal discipline. Following the Strasbourg model, the Genevan church was organized into four offices: (1) pastors, of whom there were five; (2) teachers or doctors to instruct the populace in and to defend true doctrine; (3) elders, a group of twelve laymen chosen by and from the Genevan councils and empowered to "oversee the life of everybody"; and (4) deacons to dispense church goods and services to the poor and the sick.

Calvin and his followers were motivated above all by a desire to transform society morally. Faith, Calvin taught, did not sit idly in the mind but conformed one's every action to God's law. The "elect" should live in a manifestly god-pleasing way, if they were truly God's elect. The majesty of God demanded nothing less. In the attempt to realize this goal, Calvin spared no effort. The consistory became his instrument of power. This body was composed of the elders and the pastors and was presided over by one of the four syndics. It enforced the strictest moral discipline, meting out punishments for a broad range of moral and religious transgressions—from missing church services (a fine of three sous) to fornication (six days on bread and water and a fine of sixty sous)—and, as time passed, increasingly for criticism of Calvin.

After 1555, the city's syndics were all devout Calvinists, and Geneva became home to thousands of exiled Protestants who had been driven out of France, England, and Scotland. Refugees (more than five thousand), most of them utterly loyal to Calvin, came to make up over one third of the population of Geneva. From this time until his death in 1564, Calvin's position in the city was greatly strengthened and the syndics were very cooperative.

Catholic Reform and the Counter-Reformation

SOURCES OF CATHOLIC REFORM. The Protestant Reformation did not take the medieval church completely by surprise. There were much internal criticism and many efforts at internal reform before there was a Counter-Reformation in reaction to Protestant successes. Before the Reformation, ambitious proposals had been set forth to bring about the long-demanded reform of the church in head and members. Catholic reformers were found within a variety of self-motivated lay and clerical movements. Two important organizations that brought reform-minded clergy and laity together were the Modern Devotion and the Oratory of Divine Love. The former, also known as the Brothers of the Common Life, was an organized group of laity and clergy who fostered the religious life outside formal ecclesiastical offices and apart from formal religious vows. The Oratory of Divine Love, founded in Rome in 1517, was an exclusive informal organization of earnest laity and clergy who were both learned and deeply committed to traditional religious devotion. Like Erasmus, whose religious writings the members admired, they taught that inner piety and good Christian living, not theological arguments and disputations, were the surest way to reform the church.

IGNATIUS OF LOYOLA AND THE JESUITS. Of the various reform groups, none was more instrumental in the success of the Counter-Reformation than the Society of Jesus, the new order of Jesuits, organized by Ignatius of Loyola in the 1530s and officially recognized by the Catholic church in 1540. The society grew within the space of a century from its original ten members to more than fifteen thousand scattered throughout the world, with thriving missions in India, Japan, and the Americas.

The founder of the Jesuits, Ignatius of Loyola (1491–1556), had been a dashing courtier and caballero in his youth. He began his spiritual pilgrimage in 1521 after he had been seriously wounded in the legs during a battle with the French. During a lengthy and painful convalescence, he passed the time by reading Christian classics. So impressed was he with the heroic self-sacrifice of the church's saints and their methods of overcoming mental anguish and pain that he underwent a profound religious conversion; henceforth he, too, would serve the Church as a soldier of Christ.

After recuperating, Ignatius applied the lessons he had learned during his convalescence to a program of religious and moral self-discipline that came to be embodied in the *Spiritual Exercises*. This psychologically perceptive devotional guide contained mental and emotional exercises designed to teach one absolute spiritual self-mastery over one's feelings. It taught that a person could shape his or her own behavior, even create a new religious self, through disciplined study and regular practice.

Whereas in Jesuit eyes Protestants had distinguished themselves by disobedience to Church authority and religious innovation, the exercises of Ignatius were intended to teach good Catholics to deny themselves and submit without question to higher Church authority and spiritual direction. Perfect discipline and self-control were the essential conditions of such obedience. To these was added the enthusiasm of tradi-

Ignatius of Loyola's "Rules for Thinking with the Church"

As leaders of the Counter-Reformation, the Jesuits attempted to live by and instill in others the strictest obedience to church authority. The following are some of the eighteen rules included by Ignatius in his Spiritual Exercises to give both Jesuits and lay Catholics positive direction. These rules also indicate the Catholic reformers' refusal to compromise with Protestantism.

In order to have the proper attitude of mind in the Church Militant we should observe the following rules:

1. Putting aside all private judgment, we should keep our minds prepared and ready to obey promptly and in all things the true spouse of Christ our Lord, our Holy Mother, the hierarchical Church.

2. To praise sacramental confession and the reception of the Most Holy Sacrament once a year, and much better once a month, and better still every week. . . .

3. To praise the frequent hearing of Mass. . . .

4. To praise highly the religious life, virginity, and continence; and also matrimony, but not as highly. . . .

5. To praise the vows of religion, obedience, poverty, chastity, and other works of perfection and supererogation. . . .

6. To praise the relics of the saints . . . [and] the stations, pilgrimages, indulgences, jubilees, Crusade indulgences, and the lighting of candles in the churches.

7. To praise the precepts concerning fasts and abstinences . . . and acts of penance. . . .

8. To praise the adornments and buildings of churches as well as sacred images. . . .

9. To praise all the precepts of the church. . . .

10. To approve and praise the directions and recommendations of our superiors as well as their personal behavior. . . .

11. To praise both positive and scholastic theology. . . .

12. We must be on our guard against making comparisons between the living and those who have already gone to their reward, for it is no small error to say, for example: "This man knows more than St. Augustine," "He is another Saint Francis, or even greater." . . .

13. If we wish to be sure that we are right in all things; we should always be ready to accept this principle: I will believe that the white that I see is black, if the hierarchical Church so defines it. For I believe that between . . . Christ our Lord and . . . His Church, there is but one spirit, which governs and directs us for the salvation of our souls. ❑

The Spiritual Exercises of St. Ignatius, trans. by Anthony Mottola (Garden City, N.Y.: Doubleday, 1964), pp. 139–141.

---

tional spirituality and mysticism—a potent combination that helped counter the Reformation and win many Protestants back to the Catholic fold, especially in Austria and Bavaria and along the Rhine.

THE COUNCIL OF TRENT (1545–1563). The broad success of the Reformation and the insistence of the Emperor Charles V forced Pope Paul III (1534–1549) to call a general council of the Church to define religious doctrine.

The long-delayed council met in 1545 in the city of Trent in northern Italy. There were three sessions, spread over eighteen years, from 1545 to 1563, with long interruptions due to war, plague, and imperial and papal politics. The council's most important reforms concerned internal Church discipline. Steps were taken to curtail the selling of Church offices and other religious goods. Many bishops who resided in Rome rather than within their dioceses were forced to move to their appointed seats of authority. The Council of Trent strengthened the authority of local bishops so that they could effectively discipline popular religious practice. The Council of Trent also sought to give the parish priest a brighter image by requiring him to be neatly dressed, better educated, strictly celibate, and active among his parishioners. To this end, the council also called for the construction of a seminary in every diocese.

The English Reformation to 1553

THE KING'S AFFAIR. Although Lollardy and Humanism may be said to have prepared the soil for the seeds of Protestant reform in England, it was King Henry VIII's unhappy marriage that furnished the plough that truly broke the soil. Henry had married Catherine of Aragon (d. 1536), daughter of Ferdinand and Isabella of Spain, and the aunt of Emperor Charles V. By 1527, the union had produced no male heir to the throne and only one surviving child, a daughter, Mary Tudor. Henry was justifiably concerned about the political consequences of leaving only

Progress of Protestant Reformation on the Continent

1513–1517	Fifth Lateran Council fails to bring about reform in the Catholic church
1517	Luther posts ninety-five theses against indulgences
1519	Charles I of Spain elected Holy Roman Emperor (as Charles V)
1519	Luther challenges infallibility of pope and inerrancy of Church councils at Leipzig Debate
1521	Papal bull excommunicates Luther for heresy
1521	Diet of Worms condemns Luther
1521–1522	Luther translates the New Testament into German
1524–1525	The Peasants' Revolt in Germany
1527	The *Schleitheim Confession* of the Anabaptists
1529	The Marburg Colloquy between Luther and Zwingli
1530	The Diet of Augsburg fails to settle religious differences
1531	Formation of Protestant Schmalkaldic League
1534–1535	Anabaptists assume political power in city of Münster
1536	Calvin arrives in Geneva
1540	Jesuits, founded by Ignatius of Loyola, recognized as order by pope
1546	Luther dies
1547	Armies of Charles V crush Schmalkaldic League
1548	Augsburg *Interim* outlaws Protestant practices
1555	Peace of Augsburg recognizes rights of Lutherans to worship as they please
1545–1563	Council of Trent institutes reforms and responds to the Reformation

By 1527, Henry, thoroughly enamored of Anne Boleyn, one of Catherine's ladies in waiting, decided to put Catherine aside and marry Anne. This he could not do in Catholic England without papal annulment of the marriage to Catherine. And therein lay a problem. The year 1527 was also the year when soldiers of the Holy Roman Empire mutinied and sacked Rome, and the reigning pope, Clement VII, was at the time a prisoner of Charles V, Catherine's nephew. Even if this had not been the case, it would have been virtually impossible for the pope to grant an annulment of the marriage. Not only had it survived for eighteen years but it had been made possible in the first place by a special papal dispensation required because Queen Catherine had previously been the wife of Henry's brother, Arthur.

After Cardinal Wolsey, Lord Chancellor of England since 1515, failed to secure the annulment, Thomas Cranmer (1489–1556) and Thomas Cromwell (1485–1540), both of whom harbored Lutheran sympathies, became the king's closest advisers. Finding the way to a papal annulment closed, Henry's new advisers struck a different course: Why not simply declare the king supreme in English spiritual affairs as he was in English temporal affairs? Then the king himself could settle the king's affair.

THE REFORMATION PARLIAMENT. In 1529, Parliament convened for what would be a seven-year session that earned it the title of "Reformation Parliament." During this period, it passed a flood of legislation that harassed and finally placed royal reins on the clergy. In January 1531, the clergy in Convocation (a legislative assembly representing the English clergy) publicly recognized Henry as head of the church in England "as far as the law of Christ allows." In 1533, Parliament passed the Submission of the Clergy, effectively placing canon law under royal control and thereby the clergy under royal jurisdiction.

In January 1533, Henry wed the pregnant Anne Boleyn, with Thomas Cranmer officiating. In 1534, Parliament ended all payments by the English clergy and laity to Rome and gave Henry sole jurisdiction over high ecclesiastical appointments. The Act of Succession in the same year made Anne Boleyn's children legitimate heirs to the throne, and the Act of Supremacy declared Henry "the only supreme head in earth of the church of England."

THE PROTESTANT REFORMATION UNDER EDWARD VI. Henry's political and domestic boldness was not carried over to the religious front, although the pope did cease to be the head of the English church and English Bibles were placed in English churches. Despite his political break with Rome, the king remained decidedly conservative in his religious

a female heir. People in this period believed it unnatural for women to rule over men: at best, a woman ruler meant a contested reign; at worst, turmoil and revolution. Henry even came to believe that his union with Catherine, who had numerous miscarriages and stillbirths, had been cursed by God, because prior to their marriage, Catherine had been the wife of his late brother, Arthur.

Hampton Court Palace, home to English royalty after it was taken over by Henry VIII from Cardinal Wolsey early in the sixteenth century. [British Tourist Authority, New York.]

beliefs, and Catholic doctrine remained prominent in a country seething with Protestant sentiment. Henry absolutely forbade the English clergy to marry and threatened any clergy who were twice caught in concubinage with execution. The Six Articles of 1539 reaffirmed transubstantiation, denied the Eucharistic cup

Thomas More Stands By His Conscience

More, loyal Catholic to the end, repudiated the Act of Supremacy as unlawful; he believed that it contradicted both the laws of England and the king's own coronation oath. More important, he believed that the act transgressed centuries of European tradition, by which he felt bound by conscience to stand, even if it meant certain death. In the following excerpt, More defended himself in a final interrogation, as reported by his prosecutors.

"Seeing that . . . ye are determined to condemn me [More said] . . . I will now in discharge of my conscience speak my mind plainly and freely. . . . Forasmuch as this indictment is grounded upon an Act of Parliament directly repugnant to the laws of God and his holy Church, the supreme government of which . . . may no temporal prince presume by any law to take upon him . . . it is . . . insufficient to charge any Christian man [who refuses to recognize this Act]."

For proof thereof, he [More] declared that this realm, being but one member and small part of the Church, might not make a particular law disagreeable with the general law of Christ's universal Catholic Church, no more than the city of London, being but one poor member in respect of the whole realm, might make a law against an Act of Parliament to bind the whole realm. So further showed he that it was contrary both to the laws and statutes of our own land . . . and also contrary to the sacred oath which the King's Highness himself and every Christian prince always with

great solemnity received at their coronations. . . .

Then . . . the Lord Chancellor . . . answered that seeing that all the bishops, universities, and best learned men of the realm had to this Act agreed, it was much marvel that he [More] alone against them all would so stiffly stick thereat. . . .

To this Sir Thomas replied . . . : "Neither as yet have I chanced upon any ancient writer or doctor that so advanceth, as your Statute doth, the supremacy of any secular and temporal prince . . . and therefore am I not bounde, my Lord, to conform my conscience to the Council of one realm against the general Council of [the whole of] Christendom. For of the foresaid holy bishops I have, for every bishop of yours, above one hundred. And for one Council or Parliament of yours (God knoweth what manner of one), I have all the Councils made these thousand years. And for this one Kingdom [of England], I have all other Christian realms." ❑

The Reformation in England: To the Accession of Elizabeth I, ed. by A. G. Dickens and Dorothy Carr (New York: St. Martin's Press, 1968), pp. 71–72.

1529	Reformation Parliament convenes
1532	Parliament passes the Submission of the Clergy, an act placing canon law and the English clergy under royal jurisdiction
1533	Henry VIII weds Anne Boleyn; Convocation proclaims marriage to Catherine of Aragon invalid
1534	Act of Succession makes Anne Boleyn's children legitimate heirs to the English throne
1534	Act of Supremacy declares Henry VIII "the only supreme head of the church of England"
1535	Thomas More executed for opposition to Acts of Succession and Supremacy
1535	Publication of Coverdale Bible
1539	Henry VIII imposes the Six Articles, condemning Protestantism and reasserting traditional doctrine
1547	Edward VI succeeds to the throne under protectorships of Somerset and Northumberland
1549	First Act of Uniformity imposes *Book of Common Prayer* on English churches
1553–1558	Mary Tudor restores Catholic doctrine
1558–1603	Elizabeth I fashions an Anglican religious settlement

to the laity, declared celibate vows inviolable, provided for private masses, and ordered the continuation of auricular confession.

Edward VI (1547–1553), Henry's son by his third wife Jane Seymour, gained the throne when he was only ten years old. Anne Boleyn had been executed in 1536 for adultery and her daughter Elizabeth declared illegitimate and thus ineligible to succeed to the English throne.

Under Edward, England fully enacted the Protestant Reformation. Henry's Six Articles and laws against heresy were repealed, and clerical marriage and communion with cup were sanctioned. In 1549, the Act of Uniformity imposed Thomas Cranmer's *Book of Common Prayer* on all English churches. Images and altars were removed from the churches in 1550. The Second Act of Uniformity, passed in 1552, imposed a revised edition of the *Book of Common Prayer* on all English churches. A forty-two-article confession of faith, also written by Thomas Cranmer, was adopted, setting forth a moderate Protestant doctrine.

All these changes were short-lived, however. In 1553, Catherine of Aragon's daughter, Mary Tudor, succeeded Edward (who had died in his teens) to the English throne and proceeded to restore Catholic doctrine and practice with a singlemindedness that rivaled that of her father. It was not until the reign of Anne Boleyn's daughter, Elizabeth (1558–1603), that a lasting religious settlement was worked out in England (to be discussed later).

The Wars of Religion

The late sixteenth century and the first half of the seventeenth century are described as an "age of religious wars" because of the bloody opposition of Protestants and Catholics across the length and breadth of Europe. In France, the Netherlands, England, and Scotland in the second half of the sixteenth century, Calvinists fought Catholic rulers for the right to form their own communities and to practice their chosen religion openly. In the first half of the seventeenth century, international armies of varying religious persuasions marched against one another in central and northern Europe during the Thirty Years' War. And by the middle of the seventeenth century, English Puritans had successfully revolted against the Stuart monarchy and the Anglican church. In the second half of the sixteenth century, the political conflict, which had previously been confined to central Europe and a struggle for Lutheran rights and freedoms, shifted to western Europe—to France, the Netherlands, England, and Scotland—and became a struggle for Calvinist recognition.

Genevan Calvinism and Tridentine Catholicism were two equally dogmatic, aggressive, and irreconcilable church systems. Calvinism adopted a presbyterian organization that magnified regional and local religious authority: boards of presbyters, or elders, representing the many individual congregations of Calvinists, directly shaped the policy of the Church at large. By contrast, the Counter-Reformation sponsored a centralized episcopal church system, hierarchically arranged from pope to parish priest, which stressed absolute obedience to the person at the top. The high clergy—the pope and his bishops—not the synods of local churches, ruled supreme. Calvinism proved attractive to proponents of political decentralization in contest with totalitarian rulers, whereas Catholicism remained congenial to the proponents of absolute monarchy determined to maintain "one king, one church, one law" throughout the land.

The French Wars of Religion (1562–1598)

Henry II died accidently during a tournament in 1559. His sickly fifteen-year-old son, Francis II, came to the throne under the regency of the queen mother, Catherine de Médicis. With the monarchy so weakened, three powerful families saw their chance to control France and began to compete for the young king's ear. They were the Bourbons, whose power lay in the south and west; the Montmorency-Châtillons, who controlled the center of France; and the Guises, who were dominant in eastern France. The Guises were far the strongest, and the name of Guise was interchangeable with militant, reactionary Catholicism. The Bourbon and Montmorency-Châtillon families, in contrast, developed strong Huguenot (as the French Protestants were called) sympathies, largely for political reasons. The Bourbon Louis I, prince of Condé (d. 1569), and

Catherine de Medicis (1519–1589). Following the death of her husband, King Henry II of France, in 1559. Catherine exercized much power during the reigns of her three sons, Francis II (1559–1560), Charles IX (1560–1574), and Henry III (1574–1589). [Bettmann Archive.]

the Montmorency-Châtillon Admiral Gaspard de Coligny (1519–1572) became the political leaders of the French Protestant resistance.

Often for quite different reasons, ambitious aristocrats and discontented townspeople joined Calvinist churches in opposition to the Guise-dominated French monarchy. In 1561, over two thousand Huguenot congregations existed throughout France, although Huguenots were a majority of the population in only two regions: Dauphiné and Languedoc. Although they made up only about one fifteenth of the population, Huguenots were in important geographic areas and were heavily represented among the more powerful segments of French society. Over two fifths of the French aristocracy became Huguenots. Many apparently hoped to establish within France a principle of territorial sovereignty akin to that secured within the Holy Roman Empire by the Peace of Augsburg (1555). In this way, Calvinism indirectly served the forces of political decentralization.

CATHERINE DE MÉDICIS AND THE GUISES. Following Francis II's death in 1560, Catherine de Médicis continued as regent for her minor son, Charles IX (1560–1574). Fearing the power and guile of the Guises, Catherine, whose first concern was always to preserve the monarchy, sought allies among the Protestants. In 1562, she granted Protestants freedom to worship publicly outside towns—although only privately within them—and to hold synods or church assemblies. In March, this royal toleration came to an abrupt end when the duke of Guise surprised a Protestant congregation at Vassy in Champagne and proceeded to massacre several score—an event that marked the beginning of the French wars of religion (March 1562).

Perpetually caught between fanatical Huguenot and Guise extremes, Queen Catherine always sought to balance the one side against the other. Like the Guises, she wanted a Catholic France; she did not, however, desire a Guise-dominated monarchy.

On August 22, 1572, four days after the Huguenot Henry of Navarre had married King Charles IX's sister, Marguerite of Valois—a sign of growing Protestant power—Coligny was struck down, although not killed, by an assassin's bullet. Catherine had apparently been a party to this Guise plot to eliminate Coligny. After its failure, she feared both the king's reaction to her complicity and the Huguenot response under a recovered Coligny. Summoning all her motherly charm and fury, Catherine convinced Charles that a Huguenot coup was afoot, inspired by Coligny, and that only the swift execution of Protestant leaders could save the crown from a Protestant attack on Paris. On the eve of Saint Bartholomew's Day, August 24, 1572, Coligny and three thousand fellow Hugue-

The massacre of Huguenots in Paris on Saint Batholomew's Day, August 24, 1572, as remembered by François Dubois, a Huguenot eyewitness. [The Granger Collection.]

nots were butchered in Paris. Within three days, an estimated twenty thousand Huguenots were executed in coordinated attacks throughout France. The event changed the nature of the struggle between Protestants and Catholics both within and beyond the borders of France. It was thereafter no longer an internal contest between Guise and Bourbon factions for French political influence, nor was it simply a Huguenot campaign to win basic religious freedoms. Henceforth, in Protestant eyes, it became an international struggle to the death for sheer survival against an adversary whose cruelty now justified any means of resistance.

THE RISE TO POWER OF HENRY OF NAVARRE. Henry III (1574–1589), who was Henry II's third son and the last to wear the French crown, found the monarchy wedged between a radical Catholic League, formed in 1576 by Henry of Guise, and vengeful Huguenots. Like the queen mother, Henry III sought to steer a middle course, and in this effort he received support from a growing body of neutral Catholics and Huguenots, who put the political survival of France above its religious unity. Such *politiques*, as they were called, were prepared to compromise religious creeds as might be required to save the nation.

In the mid-1580s the Catholic League, supported by the Spanish, became completely dominant in Paris. In what came to be known as the Day of the Barricades, Henry III attempted to rout the league with a surprise attack in 1588. The effort failed badly and the king had to flee Paris. Forced by his weakened position into guerrilla tactics, Henry successfully plotted the assassination of both the duke and the cardinal of Guise. The Catholic League reacted with a fury that matched the earlier Huguenot response to the Massacre of Saint Bartholomew's Day. The king now had only one course of action: He struck an alliance with his Protestant cousin, Henry of Navarre, in April 1589.

As the two Henrys prepared to attack the Guise stronghold of Paris, however, a fanatical Dominican friar stabbed Henry III to death. Thereupon the Bourbon Huguenot Henry of Navarre succeeded the childless Valois king to the French throne as Henry IV (1589–1610).

Henry IV came to the throne as a *politique*, weary of religious strife and prepared to place political peace above absolute religious unity. He believed that a royal policy of tolerant Catholicism would be the best way to achieve such peace. On July 25, 1593, he publicly abjured the Protestant faith and embraced the tra-

Philip II of Spain (1556–1598) at age 24, by Titian. Philip was the dominant ruler of the second half of the sixteenth century. However, he was finally denied victory over the two areas in which he most sought to impose his will, the Netherlands and England. [Museo del Prado, Madrid.]

ditional and majority religion of his country. "Paris is worth a Mass," he is reported to have said.

On April 13, 1598, a formal religious settlement was proclaimed in Henry IV's famous Edict of Nantes. This religious truce—and it was never more than that—granted the Huguenots, who by this time numbered well over one million, freedom of public worship, the right of assembly, admission to public offices and universities, and permission to maintain fortified towns. Most of the new freedoms, however, were to be exercised within their own towns and territories. As significant as it was, the edict only transformed a long hot war between irreconcilable enemies into a long cold war. To its critics, it had only created a state within a state.

Imperial Spain and the Reign of Philip II (1556–1598)

Until the English defeated his mighty Armada in 1588, no one person stood larger in the second half of the sixteenth century than Philip II of Spain. During the first half of Philip's reign, attention focused on the Mediterranean and Turkish expansion. In May 1571, a Holy League of Spain, Venice, and the pope defeated the Turks in the largest naval battle of the sixteenth century. A fleet under the command of Philip's half brother, Don John of Austria, engaged the Ottoman navy under Ali Pasha off Lepanto in the Gulf of Corinth on October 7, 1571. Before the engagement ended, thirty thousand Turks had died and over one third of the Turkish fleet was sunk or captured.

THE REVOLT IN THE NETHERLANDS. The spectacular Spanish military success in southern Europe was not repeated in northern Europe when Philip attempted to impose his will within the Netherlands and on England and France. The resistance of the Netherlands especially proved the undoing of Spanish dreams of world empire.

The Netherlands were the richest area not only of Philip's Habsburg kingdom, but of Europe as well. The merchant towns of the Netherlands were also, however, Europe's most independent; many, like magnificent Antwerp, were also Calvinist strongholds. A stubborn opposition to the Spanish overlords formed under William of Nassau, the Prince of Orange (1533–1584). Like other successful rulers in this period, William of Orange was a *politique* who placed the Netherlands' political autonomy and well-being above religious creeds. He personally passed through successive Catholic, Lutheran, and Calvinist stages.

The year 1564 saw the first fusion of political and religious opposition to Spanish rule, the result of Philip II's unwise insistence that the decrees of the Council of Trent be enforced throughout the Netherlands. A national covenant was drawn up called the *Compromise*, a solemn pledge to resist the decrees of Trent and the Inquisition.

Philip dispatched the duke of Alba to suppress the revolt. His army of ten thousand men journeyed northward from Milan in 1567 in a show of combined Spanish and papal might. A special tribunal, known to the Spanish as the Council of Troubles and among the Netherlanders as the Council of Blood, reigned over

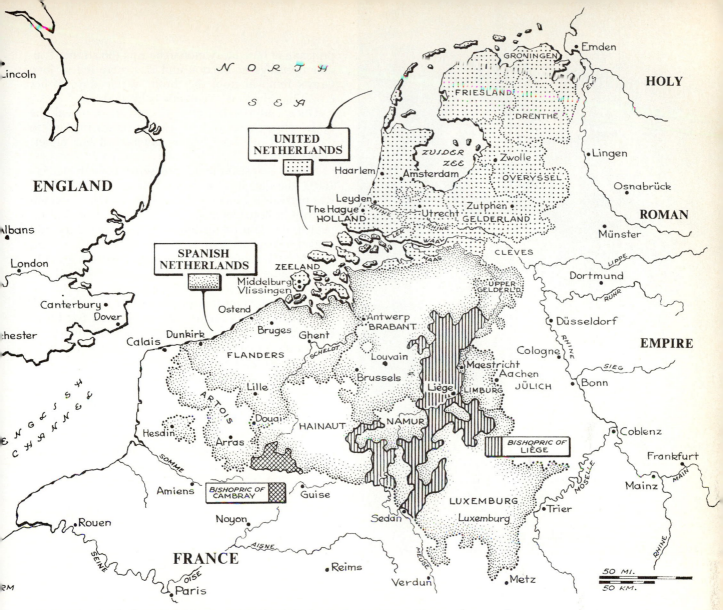

MAP 17-5 THE NETHERLANDS DURING THE REFORMATION *The northern and southern provinces of the Netherlands. The former, the United Provinces, were mostly Protestant in the second half of the sixteenth century, while the southern, the Spanish Netherlands, made peace with Spain and remained largely Catholic.*

the land. Several thousand suspected heretics were publicly executed before Alba's reign of terror ended.

William of Orange had been an exile in Germany during these turbulent years. He now emerged as the leader of a broad movement for the Netherlands' independence from Spain.

After a decade of persecution and warfare, the ten largely Catholic southern provinces (what is roughly modern Belgium) came together in 1576 with the seven largely Protestant northern provinces (what is roughly the modern Netherlands) in unified opposition to Spain. This union, known as the Pacification of Ghent,

was accomplished on November 8, 1576. It declared internal regional sovereignty in matters of religion. It was a Netherlands version of the territorial settlement of religious differences brought about in the Holy Roman Empire in 1555 by the Peace of Augsburg.

In January 1579, the southern provinces formed the Union of Arras and made peace with Spain. The northern provinces responded with the formation of the Union of Utrecht. Spanish preoccupation with France and England in the 1580s permitted the northern provinces to drive out all Spanish soldiers by 1593. In 1596, France and England formally recognized the indepen-

Elizabeth I of England painted in 1592 by Marcus Gheeraerts. Note that she is standing on a map of her kingdom. Elizabeth is considered by many to be the most successful ruler of the sixteenth century. [National Portrait Galley, London.]

principle of hereditary monarchy was too strong. Popular uprisings in London and elsewhere led to Jane Grey's removal from the throne within days of her crowning. She was eventually beheaded.

Once enthroned, Mary proceeded to repeal the Protestant statutes of Edward and return England to the strict Catholic religious practice of her father, Henry VIII.

Mary's half sister and successor, Elizabeth I (1558–1603), the daughter of Henry VIII and Anne Boleyn, was perhaps the most astute politician of the sixteenth century in both domestic and foreign policy. She repealed the anti-Protestant legislation of Mary and guided a religious settlement through Parliament that prevented England from being torn asunder by religious differences in the sixteenth century, as the Continent was.

Catholic extremists hoped to replace Elizabeth with the Catholic Mary Stuart, Queen of Scots. But Elizabeth acted swiftly against Catholic assassination plots and rarely let emotion override her political instincts.

Elizabeth dealt cautiously with the Puritans, who were Protestants working within the national church to "purify" it of every vestige of "popery" and to make its Protestant doctrine more precise. The Puritans had two special grievances: (1) the retention of Catholic ceremony and vestments within the Church of England, and (2) the continuation of the episcopal system of church governance.

Sixteenth-century Puritans were not separatists, however. They worked through Parliament to create an alternative national church of semiautonomous congregations governed by representative presbyteries (hence, Presbyterians), following the model of Calvin and Geneva. The more extreme Puritans wanted every congregation to be autonomous, a law unto itself, with neither higher episcopal nor presbyterian control. They came to be known as *Congregationalists*. Elizabeth refused to tolerate this group, whose views on independence seemed to her to be patently subversive.

DETERIORATION OF RELATIONS WITH SPAIN. A series of events led inexorably to war between England and Spain, despite the sincerest desires on the part of both Philip II and Elizabeth to avoid a direct confrontation. Following Don John's demonstration of Spain's seapower at the famous naval battle of Lepanto in 1571. England signed a mutual defense pact with France. Also in the 1570s, Elizabeth's famous seamen, John Hawkins (1532–1595) and Sir Francis Drake (1545?–1596), began to prey regularly on Spanish shipping in the Americas. Drake's circumnavigation of the glove between 1577 and 1580 was one in a series of dramatic demonstrations of English ascendancy on the high seas. In 1585, Elizabeth signed a treaty that committed English soldiers to the Nether-

dence of these provinces. Peace was not, however, concluded with Spain until 1609, when the Twelve Years' Truce gave the northern provinces their virtual independence. Full recognition came finally in the Peace of Westphalia in 1648.

England and Spain (1553–1603)

MARY I AND ELIZABETH I. Before Edward VI died in 1553, he had agreed to make the Protestant Lady Jane Grey—the teen-aged daughter of a powerful Protestant nobleman and, more important, the granddaughter on her mother's side of Henry VIII's *younger* sister Mary—his successor in place of the Catholic Mary Tudor (1553–1558). But popular support for the lands. These events made a tinderbox of English–Spanish relations. The spark that finally touched it off was Elizabeth's reluctant execution of Mary, Queen of Scots (1542–1587) on February 18, 1587, for complicity in a plot to assassinate Elizabeth. Philip II ordered his Armada to make ready.

On May 30, 1588, a mighty fleet of 130 ships bearing twenty-five thousand sailors and soldiers under the command of the duke of Medina-Sidonia set sail for England. But the day belonged completely to the English. The invasion barges that were to transport Spanish soldiers from the galleons onto English shores were prevented from leaving Calais and Dunkirk. The swifter English and Netherlands ships, assisted by an "English wind," dispersed the waiting Spanish fleet, over one third of which never returned to Spain.

The news of the Armada's defeat gave heart to Protestant resistance everywhere. Although Spain continued to win impressive victories in the 1590s, it never fully recovered from this defeat. Spanish soldiers faced unified and inspired French, English, and Dutch armies. By the time of Philip's death on September 13, 1598, his forces had been successfully rebuffed on all fronts.

The Thirty Years' War (1618–1648)

In the second half of the sixteenth century, Germany was an almost ungovernable land of 360 autonomous political entities. The Peace of Augsburg (1555) had given each a significant degree of sovereignty within its own borders. Each levied its own tolls and tariffs and coined its own money, practices that made land travel and trade between the various regions difficult, where not impossible. In addition, many of these little "states" were filled with great power pretensions. Political decentralization and fragmentation

MAP 17-6   RELIGIOUS DIVISIONS ABOUT 1600   *By 1600 few could seriously expect Christians to return to a uniform religious allegiance. In Spain and southern Italy Catholicism remained relatively unchallenged, but note the existence of large religious minorities, both Catholic and Protestant, elsewhere.*

NORTH SEA

DENMARK

BALTIC SEA

HOLSTEIN

MECKLEN-BURG

Hamburg
Bremen

UNITED PROVINCES
Amsterdam

BRANDEN-BURG
Berlin

MARCHE OF MAGDEB'G

POLAND

Königsbe

PRUSS

SPANISH NETHERLANDS

BISH. OF LIEGE

Cologne

Leipzig
SAXONY

SILESIA

LUXEM-BURG

Trier

PALATINATE

Mainz
Heidelberg

Prague
BOHEMIA

MORAVIA

FRANCE

Paris

LORRAINE

UPPER PALATINATE

WÜRTT-EMBERG

BAVARIA
Augsburg
Munich

Vienna
AUSTRIA

HUNGARY

HAPSBURG

OTTOMAN

FRANCH-COMTE

Basel
Zürich

SWISS CONFEDERATION

Geneva

ARCHB. OF SALZBURG

STYRIA

CARINTHIA

CARNIOLA

EMPIRE

BOUNDARY OF THE HOLY ROMAN EMPIRE

CATHOLIC GOVERNMENT

LUTHERAN GOVERNMENT

CALVINIST GOVERNMENT

TYROL

B. OF TRENT

VENICE

Milan

Genoa

PAPAL

STATES

150 MI.

150 KM.

MEDITERRANEAN SEA

TUSCANY

ITALY

MAP 17-7   THE HOLY ROMAN EMPIRE ABOUT 1618   *On the eve of the Thirty Years' War the Empire was politically and religiously fragmented, as revealed by the somewhat simplified map. Lutherans dominated the north and Catholics the south, while Calvinists controlled the United Provinces and the Palatinate and were important in Switzerland and Brandenburg.*

characterized Germany as the seventeenth century opened; it was not a unified nation like Spain, England, or even strife-filled France.

Religious conflict accentuated the international and internal political divisions (see Map 17.7). During this period, the population within the Holy Roman Empire was about equally divided between Catholics and Protestants, the latter having perhaps a slight numerical edge by 1600. The terms of the Peace of Augsburg (1555) had attempted to freeze the territorial holdings of the Lutherans and the Catholics. In the intervening years, however, the Lutherans had gained political control in some Catholic areas, as had the Catholics in a few previously Lutheran areas. There was religious strife in the empire not only between Protestants and Catholics but also between liberal and conservative Lutherans and between Lutherans and the growing numbers of Calvinists.

As elsewhere in Europe, Calvinism was the political and religious leaven within the Holy Roman Empire. Unrecognized as a legal religion by the Peace of Augsburg, Calvinism established a strong foothold within the empire when Frederick III (1559–1576), a devout convert to Calvinism, made it the official religion of his land on becoming Elector Palatine (ruler within the Palatinate) in 1559. By 1609, Palatine Calvinists headed a Protestant defensive alliance supported by Spain's sixteenth-century enemies: England, France, and the Netherlands.

If the Calvinists were active within the Holy Roman Empire, so also were their Catholic counterparts, the Jesuits. Staunchly Catholic Bavaria, supported by Spain, became militarily and ideologically for the Counter-Reformation what the Palatinate was for Protestantism. From there, the Jesuits launched successful missions throughout the empire. In 1609, Maximilian, duke of Bavaria, organized a Catholic League to counter a new Protestant alliance that had been formed in the same year under the leadership of the Calvinist Elector Palatine, Frederick IV (1583–1610). When the league fielded a great army under the command of Count Johann von Tilly, the stage was set, both internally and internationally, for the worst of the religious wars, the Thirty Years' War.

During its course, the war drew in every major western European nation—at least diplomatically and financially if not in terms of direct military involvement. It was the worst European catastrophe since the Black Death of the fourteenth century.

The Treaty of Westphalia in 1648 brought all hostilities within the Holy Roman Empire to an end. It firmly reasserted the major feature of the religious settlement of the Peace of Augsburg (1555), as the ruler of each land was again permitted to determine the religion of his land. The treaty also gave the Calvinists their long-sought legal recognition. The independence of the Swiss Confederacy and the United Provinces of Holland, long recognized in fact, was now proclaimed in law.

By confirming the territorial sovereignty of Germany's many political entities, the Treaty of Westphalia perpetuated German division and political weakness into the modern period. Only two German states attained any international significance during the seventeenth century: Austria and Brandenburg–Prussia. The petty regionalism within the empire also reflected on a small scale the drift of larger European politics. In the seventeenth century, distinctive nation-states, each with its own political, cultural, and religious identity, reached maturity and firmly established the competitive nationalism of the modern world.

Change and Conflict in Early Modern Society

Family Life

LATE MARRIAGES. Between 1500 and 1800, men and women married at later ages than they had done in previous centuries. Men tended to be in their mid- to late twenties rather than in their late teens and early twenties, and women in their early to mid-twenties rather than in their teens. In sixteenth-century Nuremberg, the legal minimum age for marriage without parental permission was set at twenty-five for men and twenty-three for women. The canonical or Church-sanctioned age for marriage remained fourteen for men and twelve for women, and marriage could still occur at such young ages if the parents agreed. As it had done throughout the high and later Middle Ages, the Church also recognized as valid the free, *private* exchange of vows between a man and a woman at these minimal ages. However, after the Reformation, which condemned such clandestine unions, the Church increasingly required both parental agreement and public vows in church for a fully licit marriage, a procedure it had, in fact, always preferred.

The late marriage pattern, generally observable in western Europe and England, resulted primarily from the difficulty a couple had supporting themselves as an independent family unit. Such support had become difficult because of the large population increase that occurred in the fifteenth and early sixteenth centuries, when western Europe was recovering from the great plague. Larger families meant more heirs and a greater division of resources. In Germanic and Scandinavian countries, the custom of a fair sharing of inheritance among all male children worked both to delay marriages, as more got less, and to encourage independent family units, as children did not have to remain in the family home indefinitely and live off the charity of the eldest brother after the death of their parents, as more often happened in England where primogeniture (right of the first-born son to inherit all property) remained strong. Still, it took the average couple a longer time to prepare themselves materially for marriage. Many never married. An estimated 20 per cent of all women remained spinsters in the sixteenth century. Combined with the estimated 15 per cent who were unmarried widows, this made up to a sizable unmarried female population.

Marriage tended to be "arranged" in the sense that the male heads of the two families met and discussed the terms of the marriage before they informed the prospective bride and bridegroom. However, it was rare for the two people involved not to know each other in advance or not to have a prior relationship. Parents did not force total strangers to live together, and children always had a legal right to protest and resist an unwanted marriage. A forced marriage was, by definition, invalid, and no one believed an unwanted marriage would last. The best marriage was one desired by both parties and supported by their families.

Later marriages meant marriages of shorter duration because couples who married in their thirties would not spend as much time together as couples who married in their twenties. Such marriages also contributed to more frequent remarriage because women bearing children for the first time at advanced ages had higher mortality rates than younger mothers. Later marriages also worked to slow overall population growth, although not by directly preventing older women from having as many children as younger women. Women who married later in life still had children in rapid succession, but with increased risk to health and life and hence with greater maternal mortality. As growing Church condemnation confirms, delayed marriage increased fornication. It also raised the number of illegitimate children, as is testified by the rapid growth of orphanages and foundling homes between 1600 and 1800.

FAMILY SIZE. The early modern family was conjugal or nuclear; that is, it consisted of a father and a mother and two to four children who managed to live into adulthood. The average husband and wife had six to eight children, a birth about every two years. Of these, however, an estimated one third died by age five, and one half were gone by age twenty. Rare was the family, at any social level, that did not learn first-

A sixteenth-century German family. This was a fairly comfortable household, as witnessed by the many toys and the maidservant. Note that the mother is nursing her youngest child herself. [Bildarchiv Preussicher Kulturbesitz.]

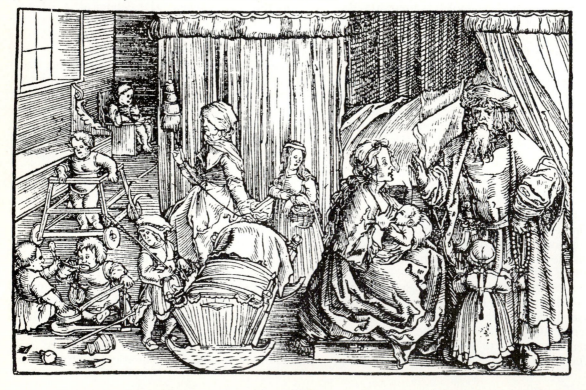

*Children's Games, by Pieter Brueghel, painted in 1560. Seventy-eight different games
are depicted. [Kunsthistorisches Museum, Vienna.]*

hand about infant mortality and child death. The Protestant reformer Martin Luther was typical. He married late in life (at forty-two, here atypical) and fathered six children, two of whom he lost, an infant daughter at eight months and another, more painfully, at thirteen years.

BIRTH CONTROL. Artificial birth control had existed since antiquity. (The ancient Egyptians used acidic alligator dung, and the use of sponges was equally old.) The Church's frequent condemnation of *coitus interruptus* (male withdrawal before ejaculation) in the thirteenth and fourteenth centuries suggests that a "contraceptive mentality"—that is, a conscious and regular effort at birth control—may have developed in the later Middle Ages. Birth control was not, however, very effective, and for both historical and moral reasons the Church firmly opposed it. During the eleventh century the Church suppressed an extreme ascetic sect, the Cathars, that had practiced birth control, when not abstaining from sex altogether,

on the grounds that to propagate the human species was to encase immortal souls in evil matter. But the Church also turned against contraception on moral grounds. According to its most authoritative theologian, Saint Thomas Aquinas, a moral act must always aid and abet, never frustrate, the natural end of a creaturely process. In the eyes of Aquinas and his church, the natural end of sex could be only the production of children and their subsequent rearing to the glory of God within the bounds of holy matrimony and the community of the Church.

Despite the Church's official opposition on contraception, it is likely that more general Christian moral teaching actually reinforced a contraceptive mentality within the early modern family by encouraging men to be more sensitive husbands and fathers. As men identified emotionally with wives who suffered painful, debilitating, unwanted, life-threatening, serial pregnancies (the chances of dying in childbirth were about one in ten) and with hungry children in overcrowded families, Christian love may also have persuaded a father that *coitus interruptus* was a moral course of action.

WET NURSING. The church allied with the physicians of early modern Europe on another intimate family matter: the condemnation of upper-class women who put their newborn children out to wet nurses for as long as eighteen months. Wet nurses were women who had recently had a baby or were suckling a child of their own, and who, for a fee, agreed also to suckle another child. The practice appears to have greatly increased the risk of infant mortality, as an infant received a strange and shared milk supply from a woman who was usually not as healthy as its own mother and who often lived under less sanitary conditions.

But nursing a child was a chore some upper-class women, and especially their husbands, found distasteful. Among women, vanity and convenience appear to have been motives for turning to wet nurses. For husbands, even more was at stake in the practice. Because the Church forbade sexual intercourse while a woman was lactating, and sexual intercourse was believed to spoil a lactating woman's milk, (pregnancy, of course, eventually ended her milk supply), a nursing wife often became a reluctant lover. In addition, nursing had a contraceptive effect (about 75 per cent effective). There is good evidence that some women prolonged nursing their children precisely in order to delay a new pregnancy—and loving husbands understood and cooperated in this form of family planning. For other husbands, however, especially wealthy burghers and noblemen who desired an abundance of male heirs, nursing seemed to rob them of sex and offspring and to jeopardize the patrimony. Hence, their strong support of wet nursing.

LOVING FAMILIES? The early modern family had features that seem cold and unloving. Not only did parents give infants to wet nurses, but later, when the children were between the ages of eight and thirteen, parents sent them out of their houses altogether into apprenticeships or to employment in the homes and businesses of relatives, friends, or even strangers. The affective ties between spouses seem to have been as tenuous as those between parents and children. Widowers and widows sometimes remarried within a few months of their spouse's death, and marriages with extreme disparity in age—especially between older men and younger women—also suggest low affection.

Love and affection, however, are as relative to time and culture as other values. A kindness in one historical period can be a cruelty in another. "What greater love," an early modern parent would surely have asked a modern critic, "can parents have for their children than to equip them to make their way vocationally in the world?" An apprenticed child was a child

with a future. Because of primitive living conditions, contemporaries could also appreciate the purely utilitarian and humane side of marriage and wink at quick remarriages. On the other hand, marriages with extreme disparity in age were no more the norm in early modern Europe than was the practice of wet nursing, and they received just as much criticism and ridicule.

Witchcraft and Witch-Hunts

Between 1400 and 1700, courts sentenced an estimated 70,000–100,000 people to death for harmful magic (*malificium*) and diabolical witchcraft. In addition to supposedly inflicting harm on their neighbors, these witches were said to attend mass meetings known as *sabbats*, to which they were believed to fly. They were also accused of indulging in sexual orgies with the Devil, who appeared at such gatherings in animal form, most often as a he-goat. Still other charges against them were cannibalism (they were alleged to be especially fond of small Christian children) and a variety of ritual acts and practices designed to insult every Christian belief and value.

Where did such beliefs come from? Their roots were in both popular and elite cultures, especially clerical culture.

In village societies, so-called cunning folk played a positive role in helping people cope with calamity. People turned to them for help when such natural disasters as plague and famine struck or when such physical disabilities as lameness or inability to conceive offspring befell either them or their animals. The cunning folk provided consolation and gave people hope that such natural calamities might be averted or reversed by magical means.

Possession of magical powers, for good or ill, made one an important person within village society. Not surprisingly, claims to such powers seem most often to have been made by the people most in need of security and influence, namely, the old and the impoverished, especially single or widowed women. But witch beliefs in village society may also have been a way of defying urban Christian society's attempts to impose its laws and institutions on the countryside. From this perspective, village Satanism became a fanciful substitute for an impossible social revolt, a way of spurning the values of one's new masters. It is also possible, although unlikely, that witch beliefs in rural society had a foundation in local fertility cults, whose semipagan practices, designed to ensure good harvests, acquired the features of diabolical witchcraft under Church persecution.

Popular belief in magic was the essential foundation on the great witch hunts of the sixteenth and seventeenth centuries. Had ordinary people not believed that certain gifted individuals could aid or harm others

A Confession of Witchcraft

A confession of witchcraft is here exacted from a burgomaster during a witch panic in seventeenth-century Bamberg in central Germany. The account, an official transcript, accurately describes the process by which an innocent victim was brought, step by step, to confession—from the confrontation with his accusers to the application of increasingly painful tortures. By at last concurring in the accusation (albeit reluctantly and only after torture), the victims were believed by their executioners to be saving the victims' souls as they lost their bodies. Having the victims' own confession may also have helped allay the executioners' consciences.

On Wednesday, June 28, 1628, was examined without torture Johannes Junius, Burgomaster at Bamberg, on the charge of witchcraft: how and in what fashion he had fallen into that vice. Is fifty-five years old, and was born at Niederwaysich in the Wetterau. Says he is wholly innocent, knows nothing of the crime, has never in his life renounced God; says that he is wronged before God and the world, would like to hear of a single human being who has seen him at such gatherings [as the witch sabbats].

Confrontation of Dr. Georg Adam Haan. Tells him to his face that he will stake his life on it, that he saw him, Junius, a year and a half ago at a witch-gathering in the electoral council-room, where they ate and drank. Accused denies the same wholly.

Confronted with Hopffens Elsse. Tells him likewise that he was on Haupts-moor at a witch-dance; but first the holy wafer was desecrated. Junius denies. Hereupon he was told that his accomplices had confessed against him and he was given time for thought.

On Friday, June 30, 1628, the aforesaid Junius was again without torture exhorted to confess, but again confessed nothing, whereupon, . . . since he would confess nothing, he was put to the torture, and first the

Thumb-screws were applied [both hands bound together, so that the blood ran out at the nails and everywhere]. Says he has never denied God his Saviour nor suffered himself to be otherwise baptized [i.e., initiated into devilish rites]. Will again stake his life on it; feels no pain in the thumb-screws.

Leg-screws. Will confess absolutely nothing; knows nothing about it. He has never renounced God; will never do such a thing; has never been guilty of this vice; feels likewise no pain. Is stripped and examined; on his right side is found a bluish mark, like a clover leaf, is thrice pricked therein, but feels no pain and no blood flows out.

Strappado [the binding of the prisoner's hands behind the back, and pulling them up by a rope attached to a pulley, resulting in the slow dislocation of the shoulders]. Says he never renounced God; God will not forsake him; if he were such a wretch he would not let himself be so tortured; God must show some token of his innocence. He knows nothing about witchcraft. . . .

On July 5, the above named Junius is without torture, but with urgent persuasions, exhorted to confess, and at last he . . . confesses. ❑

Translations and Reprints from the Original Sources of European History, Vol. 3 (Philadelphia: University of Pennsylvania, 1912), pp. 23–24.

by magical means, and had they not been willing to make accusations, the hunts could never have occurred. But the contribution of learned society was equally great. The Christian clergy also practiced a kind of magic, that of the holy sacraments, and the exorcism of demons had been one of their traditional functions within society. Fear of demons and the Devil, which the clergy actively encouraged, allowed them to assert their moral authority over people and to enforce religious discipline and conformity.

In the late thirteenth century, the Church declared that only its priests possessed legitimate magical power. Inasmuch as such power was not human, theologians reasoned, it had to come either from God or from the Devil. If it came from God, then it was obediently confined to and exercised only on behalf of the Church. Those who practiced magic outside the Church evidently derived their power from the Devil.

From such reasoning grew accusations of "pacts" between non-Christian magicians and Satan. This made the witch hunts a life-and-death struggle against Christian society's worst heretics and foes, those who had directly sworn allegiance to the Devil himself.

The Church based its intolerance of magic outside its walls on sincere belief in and fear of the Devil. But attacking witches was also a way for established Christian society to extend its power and influence into new areas. To accuse, try, and execute witches was also a declaration of moral and political authority over a village or territory. As the "cunning folk" were local spiritual authorities, revered and feared by people, their removal became a major step in the establishment of a Christian beachhead in village society.

About 80 per cent of the victims of witch hunts were women, the vast majority between forty-five and sixty years of age and widowed. This fact has suggested to some that misogyny fueled the witch-hunts. Based in male hatred and sexual fear of women, and occurring at a time when women threatened to break out from under male control, witch hunts, it is argued, were simply woman hunts. Older women may, however, have been vulnerable for more basic social reasons. As a largely nonproductive and dependent social group, ever in need of public assistance, older and widowed women became natural targets for the peculiar "social engineering" of the witch-hunts.

It may, however, be the case that gender played a purely circumstantial role. Because of their economic straits, more women than men laid claim to the supernatural powers that made them influential in village society. For this reason, they found themselves on the front lines in disproportionate numbers when the Church declared war against all who practiced magic without its blessing. Also, the involvement of many of these women in midwifery associated them with the deaths of beloved wives and infants and thus made them targets of local resentment and accusations. Both the Church and their neighbors were prepared to think and say the worst about these women. It was a deadly combination.

Why did the witch hunts come to an end in the seventeenth century? Many factors played a role. The emergence of a new, more scientific worldview made it difficult to believe in the powers of witches. When, in the seventeenth century, mind and matter came to be viewed as two independent realities, words and thoughts lost the ability to affect things. A witch's curse was merely words. With advances in medicine and the beginning of insurance companies people learned to rely on themselves when faced with natural calamity and physical affliction and no longer searched for supernatural causes and solutions.

Witch hunts also tended to get out of hand. Accused witches sometimes alleged that important townspeople had attended sabbats; even the judges could be so accused. At this point, the trials ceased to serve the purposes of those who were conducting them. They not only became dysfunctional but threatened anarchy.

Finally, the Reformation may have contributed to an attitude of mind that put the Devil in a more manageable perspective. Protestants ridiculed the sacramental magic of the old church as superstition and directed their faith to a sovereign God absolutely supreme over time and eternity. Even the Devil served God's purposes and acted only with His permission. Ultimately, God was the only significant spiritual force in the universe. This belief made the Devil a less fearsome creature. "One little word can slay him," Luther wrote of the Devil in the great hymn of the Reformation, and he often joked outrageously about witches.

Writers and Philosophers

The end of the sixteenth century saw much weariness with religious strife and incipient unbelief as many could no longer embrace either old Catholic or new Protestant absolutes. Intellectually as well as politically, the seventeenth century would be a period of transition, one already well prepared for by the thinkers of the Renaissance, who had reacted strongly against medieval intellectual traditions.

The writers and philosophers of the late sixteenth and seventeenth centuries were aware that they lived in a period of transition. Some embraced the emerging new science wholeheartedly (Hobbes and Locke), some tried to straddle the two ages (Cervantes and Shakespeare), and still others ignored or opposed the new developments that seemed mortally to threaten traditional values (Pascal).

MIGUEL DE CERVANTES SAAVEDRA. Spanish literature of the sixteenth and seventeenth centuries was influenced by the peculiar religious and political history of Spain in this period. Spain was dominated by the Catholic church and by the aggressive piety of the Spanish rulers Charles I—who became the Holy Roman Emperor as Charles V (1516–1556)—and his son, Philip II (1556–1598). The intertwining of Catholic piety and Spanish political power underlay literary preoccupation with medieval chivalric virtues—in particular, reflected in questions of honor and loyalty.

Generally acknowledged to be the greatest Spanish writer of all time, Cervantes (1547–1616), was preoccupied in his work with the strengths and weaknesses of religious idealism. Cervantes was the son of a nomadic physician. Having received only a smattering of formal education, he educated himself by insatiable reading in vernacular literature and immersion in the "school of life." As a young man, he worked in Rome for a Spanish cardinal. In 1570, he became a soldier and was decorated for gallantry in the Battle of Lepanto (1571). He conceived and began to write his most famous work, *Don Quixote*, in 1603, while languishing in prison after conviction for theft.

The first part of *Don Quixote* appeared in 1605, and a second part followed in 1615. If, as many argue, the intent of this work was to satirize the chivalric romances so popular in Spain, Cervantes failed to conceal his deep affection for the character he had created as an object of ridicule, Don Quixote. Don Quixote, a none-too-stable middle-aged man, is driven mad by reading too many chivalric romances. He comes to believe that he is an aspirant to knighthood and must prove his worthiness. To this end, he acquires a rusty suit of armor, mounts an aged horse, and chooses for his inspiration a quite unworthy peasant girl whom he fancies to be a noble lady to whom he can, with honor, dedicate his life.

Don Quixote's foil in the story—Sancho Panza, a clever, wordly-wise peasant who serves as Don Quixote's squire—watches with bemused skepticism, but also with genuine sympathy, as his lord does battle with a windmill (which he mistakes for a dragon) and repeatedly makes a fool of himself as he gallops across the countryside. The story ends tragically with Don Quixote's humiliating defeat by a well-meaning friend, who, disguised as a knight, bests Don Quixote in combat and forces him to renounce his quest for knighthood. The humiliated Don Quixote does not, however, come to his senses as a result. He returns sadly to his village to die a shamed and broken-hearted old man.

Throughout *Don Quixote*, Cervantes juxtaposed the down-to-earth realism of Sancho Panza with the old-fashioned religious idealism of Don Quixote. The reader perceives that Cervantes really admired the one as much as the other and meant to portray both as attitudes necessary for a happy life. Cervantes wanted his readers to remember that if they are to be truly happy, men and women need dreams, even impossible ones, just as much as they need a sense of reality.

WILLIAM SHAKESPEARE. There is much less factual knowledge about William Shakespeare (1564–1616), the greatest playwright in the English language, than one would expect of such an important figure. He apparently worked as a schoolteacher for a time and in this capacity acquired his broad knowledge of Renaissance learning and literature. There is none of the Puritan distress over worldliness in his work. He took the new commercialism and the bawdy pleasures of the Elizabethan Age in stride and with amusement. In matters of politics, as in those of religion, he was very much a man of his time and not inclined to offend his queen.

That Shakespeare was interested in politics is apparent from his history plays and the references to contemporary political events that fill all his plays. He seems to have viewed government simply, however, through the character of the individual ruler, whether Richard III or Elizabeth Tudor, not in terms of ideal systems or social goals. By modern standards, he was a political conservative, accepting the social rankings and the power structure of his day and demonstrating unquestioned patriotism.

Shakespeare knew the theater as one who participated in every phase of its life—as a playwright, an actor, and a part owner of a theater. He was a member and principal dramatist of a famous company of actors known as the King's Men.

Shakespeare's work was an original synthesis of the

The English dramatist and poet, William Shakespeare. This engraving by Martin Droeshout appears on the title page of the collected edition of his plays published in 1623 and is probably as close as we shall come to knowing what he looked like.

best past and current achievements. He mastered the psychology of human motivation and passion and had a unique talent for psychological penetration.

Shakespeare wrote histories, comedies, and tragedies. The tragedies are considered his unique achievement. Four of these were written within a three-year period: *Hamlet* (1603), *Othello* (1604), *King Lear* (1605), and *Macbeth* (1606). The most original of the tragedies, *Romeo and Juliet* (1597), transformed an old popular story into a moving drama of "star-cross'd lovers." Both Romeo and Juliet, denied a marriage by their factious families, die tragic deaths. Romeo, finding Juliet and thinking her dead after she has taken a sleeping potion, poisons himself. Juliet, awakening to find Romeo dead, stabs herself to death with his dagger.

Throughout his lifetime and ever since, Shakespeare has been immensely popular with both the playgoer and the play reader. As Ben Jonson, a contemporary classical dramatist who created his own school of poets, put it in a tribute affixed to the First Folio edition of Shakespeare's plays (1623): "He was not of an age, but for all time."

Pascal Meditates on Human Beings as Thinking Creatures

Pascal was both a religious and a scientific writer. Unlike other scientific thinkers of the seventeenth century, he was not overly optimistic about the ability of science to improve the human condition. Pascal believed that science and philosophy would instead help human beings to understand their situation better. In these passages from his Pensées (Thoughts), *he discussed the uniqueness of human beings as the creatures who alone in all the universe are capable of thinking.*

339

I can well conceive a man without hands, feet, head (for it is only experience which teaches us that the head is more necessary than feet). But I cannot conceive man without thought; he would be a stone or a brute.

344

Reason commands us far more imperiously than a master; for in disobeying the one we are unfortunate, and in disobeying the other we are fools.

346

Thought constitutes the greatness of man.

347

Man is but a reed, the most feeble thing in nature; but he is a thinking reed. The entire universe need not arm itself to crush him. A vapour, a drop of water suffices to kill him. But, if the universe were to crush him, man would still be more noble than that which killed him, because he knows that he dies and the advantage which the univese has over him: the universe knows nothing of this.

All our dignity consists, then, in thought. By it we must elevate ourselves, and not by space and time which we cannot fill. Let us endeavour, then, to think well: this is the principle of morality.

348

A thinking reed—It is not from space that I must seek my dignity, but from the government of my thought. I shall have no more if I possess worlds. By space the universe encompasses and swallows me up like an atom; by thought I comprehend the world. ❏

Blaise Pascal, *Pensées and The Provincial Letters* (New York: Modern Library, 1941), pp. 115–116.

BLAISE PASCAL. Pascal (1623–1662) was a French mathematician and a physical scientist widely acclaimed by his contemporaries. Torn between the continuing dogmatism and the new skepticism of the seventeenth century, he aspired to write a work that would refute both the Jesuits, whose casuistry (i.e., confessional tactics designed to minimize and even excuse sinful acts) he considered a distortion of Christian teaching, and the skeptics, who either denied religion altogether (atheists) or accepted it only as it conformed to reason (deists). Pascal never realized such a definitive work and his views on these matters exist only in piecemeal form. He wrote against the Jesuits in his *Provincial Letters* (1656–1657), and he left behind a provocative collection of reflections on humankind and religion that was published posthumously under the title *Pensées*.

Pascal was early influenced by the Jansenists, seventeenth-century Catholic opponents of the Jesuits. The Jansenists shared with the Calvinists St. Augustine's belief in the total sinfulness of human beings, their eternal predestination by God, and their complete dependence on faith and grace for knowledge of God and salvation.

Pascal believed that reason and science, although attesting to human dignity, remained of no avail in matters of religion. Here only the reasons of the heart and a "leap of faith" could prevail. Pascal saw two essential truths in the Christian religion: that a loving God, worthy of human attainment, exists, and that human beings, because they are corrupted in nature, are utterly unworthy of God. Pascal believed that the atheists and deists of the age had spurned the lesson of reason. For him, rational analysis of the human condition attested to humankind's utter mortality and corruption and exposed the weakness of reason itself in resolving the problems of human nature and destiny. Reason should rather drive those who truly heed it to faith and dependence on divine grace.

Pascal made a famous wager with the skeptics. It is a better bet, he argued, to believe that God exists and to stake everything on his promised mercy than not to do so, because if God does exist, everything will be gained by the believer, whereas the loss incurred by having believed in God should he prove not to exist is by comparison very slight.

Pascal was convinced that belief in God measurably improved earthly life psychologically and disciplined it morally, regardless of whether or not God proved in the end to exist. He thought that great danger lay in the surrender of traditional religious values. Pascal urged his contemporaries to seek self-understanding by "learned ignorance" and to discover humankind's greatness by recognizing its misery. Thereby he hoped to counter what he believed to be the false optimism of the new rationalism and science.

BARUCH SPINOZA. The most controversial thinker of the seventeenth century was Baruch Spinoza (1632–1677), the son of a Jewish merchant of Amsterdam. Spinoza's philosophy caused his excommunication by his own synagogue in 1656. In 1670, he published his *Treatise on Religious and Political Philosophy*, a work that criticized the dogmatism of Dutch Calvinists and championed freedom of thought. During his lifetime, both Jews and Protestants attacked him as an atheist.

Spinoza's most influential writing, the *Ethics*, appeared after his death in 1677. Religious leaders universally condemned it for its apparent espousal of pantheism. God and nature were so closely identified by Spinoza that little room seemed left either for divine revelation in Scripture or for the personal immortality of the soul, denials equally repugnant to Jews and to Christians. The *Ethics* is a very complicated work, written in the spirit of the new science as a geometrical system of definitions, axioms, and propositions.

The most controversial part of the *Ethics* deals with the nature of substance and of God. According to Spinoza, there is only one substance, which is self-caused, free, and infinite, and God is that substance. From this definition, it follows that everything that exists is in God and cannot even be conceived of apart from him. Such a doctrine is not literally pantheistic, because God is still seen to be more than the created world that he, as primal substance, embraces. Nonetheless, in Spinoza's view, statements about the natural world are also statements about divine nature. Mind and matter are seen to be extensions of the infinite substance of God; what transpires in the world of humankind and nature is a necessary outpouring of the divine.

Such teaching clearly ran the danger of portraying the world as eternal and human actions as unfree and inevitable, the expression of a divine fatalism. Such points of view had been considered heresies by Jews and Christians because the views deny the creation of the world by God in time and destroy any voluntary basis for personal reward and punishment.

THOMAS HOBBES. Thomas Hobbes (1588–1679) was the most original political philosopher of the seventeenth century. Although he never broke with the Church of England, he came to share basic Calvinist beliefs, especially the low view of human nature and the ideal of a commonwealth based on a covenant, both of which find eloquent expression in Hobbes' political philosophy.

Hobbes was an urbane and much-traveled man and one of the most enthusiastic supporters of the new scientific movement. During the 1630s, he visited Paris, where he came to know Descartes, and after the outbreak of the Puritan Revolution (see Chapter 19) in 1640, he lived as an exile in Paris until 1651. Hobbes also spent time with Galileo in Italy and took a special interest in the works of William Harvey (1578–1657). (See Chapter 23.) Harvey was a physiologist famed for the discovery of how blood circulated through the body; his scientific writings influenced Hobbes' own tracts on bodily motions.

Hobbes was driven to the vocation of political philosophy by the English Civil War. (See Chapter 19.) In 1651, his *Leviathan* appeared. Its subject was the political consequences of human passions, and its originality lay in (1) its making natural law, rather than common law (i.e., custom or precedent), the basis of all positive law, and (2) its defense of a representative theory of absolute authority against the theory of the divine right of kings. Hobbes maintained that statute law found its justification only as an expression of the law of nature and that political authority came to rulers by way of the consent of the people.

Hobbes viewed humankind and society in a thoroughly materialistic and mechanical way. Human beings are defined as a collection of material particles in motion. All their psychological processes begin with and are derived from bare sensation, and all their motivations are egoistical, intended to increase pleasure and minimize pain.

Despite this seemingly low estimate of human beings, Hobbes believed much could be accomplished by the reasoned use of science. All was contingent, however, on the correct use of that greatest of all human powers, one compounded of the powers of most people: the commonwealth, in which people are united by their consent in one all-powerful person.

The key to Hobbes' political philosophy is a brilliant myth of the original state of humankind. According to this myth, human beings in the natural state are generally inclined to a "perpetual and restless desire of power after power that ceases only in death."[2] As all people desire and in the state of nature have a natural right to everything, their equality breeds enmity, competition, and diffidence, and the desire for glory begets perpetual quarreling—"a war of every man against every man."[3]

Whereas earlier and later philosophers saw the

[2]*Leviathan Parts I and II*, ed. by H. W. Schneider (Indianapolis: Bobbs-Merrill, 1958), p. 86.

[3]Ibid., p. 106.

The famous title-page illustration for Hobbes's Leviathan. *The ruler is pictured as absolute lord of his lands, but note that he incorporates the mass of individuals whose self-interests are best served by their willing consent to accept and cooperate with him.*

original human state as a paradise from which humankind had fallen, Hobbes saw it as a corruption from which only society had delivered people. Contrary to the views of Aristotle and of Christian thinkers like Thomas Aquinas, in the view of Hobbes human beings are not by nature sociable, political animals; they are self-centered beasts, laws unto themselves, utterly without a master unless one is imposed by force.

According to Hobbes, people escape the impossible state of nature only by entering a social contract that creates a commonwealth tightly ruled by law and order. The social contract obliges every person, for the sake of peace and self-defense, to agree to set aside personal rights to all things and to be content with as much liberty against others as he or she would allow others against himself or herself.

Because words and promises are insufficient to guarantee this state, the social contract also establishes the coercive force necessary to compel compliance with the covenant. Hobbes believed that the dangers of anarchy were far greater than those of tyranny, and he conceived of the ruler as absolute and unlimited in power, once established in office. There is no room in Hobbes's political philosophy for political protest in the name of individual conscience, nor for resistance to legitimate authority by private individuals—features of the *Leviathan* criticized by his contemporary Catholics and Puritans alike.

John Locke

Locke (1632–1704) has proved to be the most influential political thinker[4] of the seventeenth century. His political philosophy came to be embodied in the Glori-

[4] Locke's scientific writings are discussed in Chapter 23.

ous Revolution of 1688–1689. Although he was not as original as Hobbes, his political writings were a major source of the later Enlightenment criticism of absolutism, and they gave inspiration to both the American and the French revolutions.

Locke read deeply in the works of Francis Bacon, René Descartes, and Isaac Newton and was a close friend of the English physicist and chemist Robert Boyle (1627–1691). Some argue that he was the first philosopher to be successful in synthesizing the rationalism of Descartes and the experimental science of Bacon, Newton, and Boyle.

Locke's two most famous works are the *Essay Concerning Human Understanding* (1690) (discussed in Chapter 23) and the *Two Treatises of Government* (1690). Locke wrote *Two Treatises of Government* against the argument that rulers were absolute in their power. Rulers, Locke argued, remain bound to the law of nature, which is the voice of reason, teaching that "all mankind [are] equal and independent, [and] no one ought to harm another in his life, health, liberty, or possessions,"[5] inasmuch as all human beings are the images and property of God. According to Locke, people enter into social contracts, empowering legislatures and monarchs to "umpire" their disputes, precisely in order to preserve their natural rights, and not to give rulers an absolute power over them.

Whenever that end [namely, the preservation of life, liberty, and property for which power is given to rulers by a commonwealth] is manifestly neglected or opposed, the trust must necessarily be forfeited and the power devolved into the hands of those that gave it, who may place it anew where they think best for their safety and security.[6]

From Locke's point of view, absolute monarchy was "inconsistent" with civil society and could be "no form of civil government at all."

Locke's main differences with Hobbes stemmed from the latter's views on the state of nature. Locke believed that the natural human state was one of perfect freedom and equality. Here the natural rights of life, liberty, and property were enjoyed, in unregulated fashion, by all. The only thing lacking in the state of nature was a single authority to give judgment when disputes inevitably arose because of the natural freedom and equality possessed by all. Contrary to the view of Hobbes, human beings in their natural state were not creatures of monomaniacal passion but were possessed of extreme goodwill and rationality. They did not surrender their natural rights unconditionally when they entered the social contract; rather, they established a means whereby these rights could be better preserved. The state of warfare that Hobbes believed characterized the state of nature emerged for Locke only when rulers failed in their responsibility to preserve the freedoms of the state of nature and attempted to enslave people by absolute rule, that is, to remove them from their "natural" condition. Only then were the peace, goodwill, mutual assistance, and preservation in which human beings naturally live and socially ought to live undermined, and a state of war was created.

The Renaissance and Reformation in World Perspective

During the Renaissance, Western Europe recovered its classical cultural heritage, from which it had been separated for almost eight centuries. No other world civilization had known such disjunction from its cultural past. It was due to the work of Byzantine and Islamic scholars that ancient Greek science and scholarship were rediscovered in the West. In this period, Western Europe also recovered from national wars to establish permanent centralized states and regional governments. Even the great population losses of the fourteenth century were recovered by 1500. By the late fifteenth and sixteenth centuries, Europeans were in a position to venture far afield to the shores of Africa, southern and eastern Asia, and the new world of the Americas directly confronting for the first time the different civilizations of the world from Japan to Brazil.

But Western history between 1500 and 1650 was especially shaped by an unprecedented schism in Christianity, as Lutherans and other Protestant groups broke with Rome. The religious divisions contributed to both national and international warfare, which by the seventeenth century devastated the empire on a scale unseen since the Black Death.

The other world civilizations moved more slowly, maintained greater social and political unity, and remained unquestionably more tolerant of religious belief than the West. Under Mongol rule (1279–1368), China tolerated all indigenous religions as well as Islam and Eastern Christianity. No crises on the scale of those that rocked the West struck China, although plagues in 1586–1589 and 1639–1644 killed 20–30 per cent of the inhabitants in populous regions. China moved steadily from Mongol to Ming (1368–1644) to Ching (1644–1911) rule without major social and political upheaval. By Western comparison, its society was socially static, and its rulers maintained unified, even despotic, control. Whereas the West also had highly centralized and authoritarian governments between 1350 and 1650, unlike China, it also managed more

[5] *The Second Treatise of Government*, ed. by T. P. Peardon (Indianapolis: Bobbs-Merrill, 1952), Ch. 2, sects. 4-6, pp. 4-6.

[6] Ibid. Ch. 13, sect. 149, p. 84.

successfully to balance the interests of the one with those of the many. In the West, parliaments and estates general, representing the nobility, and lesser representative political bodies gained a permanent right to express their views forcefully to higher authority.

Although parallels may be drawn between the court culture of the Forbidden Palace in Peking and that of King Louis XIV in seventeenth-century France, Chinese government and religious philosophy (Confucianism) remained more unified and patriarchal than their counterparts in the West. There was never the degree of political dissent and readiness to fragment Chinese society in the name of religion that characterized Western society even in the West's own "age of absolutism." On the other hand, the Chinese readily tolerated other religions, as their warm embrace of Jesuit missionaries attests. There is no similar Western demonstration of tolerance for Asian religious philosophy.

Voyages of exploration also set forth from Ming China, especially between 1405 and 1433, reaching India, the Arabian gulf, and East Africa. These voyages did not, however, prove to be commercially profitable as those of the West would be, nor did they spark any notable commercial development in China. It is an open question whether this was because the Chinese were less greedy, curious, or belligerent than the Portuguese and Spanish.

Like the West in the later Middle Ages, Japan experienced its own political and social breakdown after 1467, when the Bakufu government began to collapse. Japan's old manorial society progressively fell apart, and a new military class of vassalized foot soldiers, armed with spears and muskets, replaced the mounted samurai as the new military force. In 1590, Hideyoshi (1536–1598) disarmed the peasantry and froze the social classes, thereby laying the foundation for a new social and political order in Japan. On this achievement, Tokugawa rule (1600–1850) managed to stabilize and centralize the government by 1650. Much as Western kings had to "domesticate" their powerful noblemen to succeed, Japanese emperors learned to integrate the many regional daimyo lords into imperial government. Like Louis XIV, Tokugawa emperors required these lords to live for long periods of time at court, where their wives and children also remained. As in most Western countries, the emperors of Japan thus avoided both fragmented and absolutist government.

Like the Chinese, the Japanese were also admirers of the Jesuits, who arrived in Japan with the Portuguese in 1543. The admiration was mutual, leading to 300,000 Christian converts by 1600. As in China, the Jesuits treated native religion as a handmaiden and prelude to superior Christian teaching. But the tolerance of Christianity did not last as long in Japan as in China. Christianity was banned in the late sixteenth century as part of Hideyoshi's internal unification program. With the ascent of more tolerant Confucianism over Buddhism among the Japanese ruling classes, Christianity and Western culture would again be welcomed in the nineteenth century.

During the age of Reformation in the West, absolutist Islamic military regimes formed in the Ottoman empire, among the Safavids in Iran, and among the Mughals in India. In all three cultures, religion became tightly integrated into government, so that they never knew the divisiveness and political challenge periodically prompted in the West by Christianity. In opposition to the expansive Ottomans, Shah Abbas I (1588–1629) allied with the Europeans and welcomed Dutch and English traders. Embracing Shi'ite religion and the Persian language (the rest of the Islamic world was mostly Sunni and spoke Arabic or different regional languages), Iran progressively isolated itself. Unlike the West, the Timurid empire of the Indian Mughals, particularly under Akbar the Great (1556–1605), and extending into the late seventeenth century, encouraged religious toleration even to the point of holding discussions among different faiths at the royal court. As in China and Japan, India too was prepared to live with and learn from the West.

Suggested Readings

R. H. BAINTON, *Erasmus of Christendom* (1960). Charming presentation.

C. BOXER, *Four Centuries of Portuguese Expansion 1415–1825* (1961). A comprehensive survey by a leading authority.

F. BRAUDEL, *The Mediterranean and the Mediterranean World in the Age of Philip the Second*, Vols. 1 and 2 (1976). The widely acclaimed work of a French master historian.

O. CHADWICK, *The Reformation* (1964). Among the best short histories and especially strong on theological and ecclesiastical issues.

N. COHN, *The Pursuit of the Millennium* (1957). Traces millennial speculation and activity from the Old Testament to the sixteenth century.

A. G. DICKENS, *The Counter Reformation* (1969). A brief narrative with pictures.

A. G. DICKENS, *The English Reformation* (1974). The best one-volume account.

G. DONALDSON, *The Scottish Reformation* (1960). A dependable, comprehensive narrative.

R. DUNN, *The Age of Religious Wars* 1559–1689 (1979). An excellent brief survey of every major conflict.

M. DURAN, *Cervantes* (1974). Detailed biography.

J. H. ELLIOTT, *Europe Divided* 1559–1598 (1968). A direct, lucid narrative account.

G. R. ELTON, *England Under the Tudors* (1955). A masterly account.

G. R. Elton, *Reformation Europe* 1517–1559 (1966). Among the best short treatments and especially strong on political issues.

E. Erikson, *Young Man Luther: A Study in Psychoanalysis and History* (1962). A controversial study that has opened a new field of historiography.

H. O. Evennett, *The Spirit of the Counter Reformation* (1968). An essay on the continuity of Catholic reform and its independence from the Protestant Reformation.

J. H. Franklin (ed. and trans.), *Constitutionalism and Resistance in the Sixteenth Century: Three Treatises by Hotman, Beza, and Mornay* (1969). Three defenders of the right of people to resist tyranny.

R. Fülop-Miller, *The Jesuits: A History of the Society of Jesus*, trans. by F. S. Flint and D. F. Tait (1963). A critical survey, given to psychological analysis.

P. Geyl, *The Revolt of the Netherlands*, 1555–1609 (1958). The authoritative survey.

H. Grimm, *The Reformation Era: 1500–1650* (1973). Very good on later Lutheran developments.

J. L. Irwin (ed.), *Womanhood in Radical Protestantism, 1525–1675* (1979). A rich collection of sources.

H. Jedin, *A History of the Council of Trent*, Vols. 1 and 2 (1957–1961). Comprehensive, detailed, and authoritative.

D. Jensen, *Reformation Europe, Age of Reform and Revolution* (1981). An excellent, up-to-date survey.

T. F. Jessop, *Thomas Hobbes* (1960). A brief biographical sketch.

W. K. Jordan, *Edward VI: The Young King* (1968). The basic biography.

R. Kieckhefer, *European Witch Trials: Their Foundations in Popular and Learned Culture* 1300–1500 (1976). One of the very best treatments of the subject.

R. M. Kingdon, *Transition and Revolution: Problems and Issues of European Renaissance and Reformation History* (1974). Covers politics, printing, theology, and witchcraft.

A. Kors and E. Peters (eds.), *European Witchcraft, 1100–1700* (1972).

C. Larner, *Enemies of God: The Witchhunt in Scotland* (1981). One of the most detailed and authoritative accounts of witchhunting.

P. Laslett, *Locke's Two Treatises of Government*, 2nd ed. (1970). Definitive texts with very important introductions.

A. MacFarlane, *The Family Life of Ralph Josselin: A Seventeenth Century Clergyman* (1970). Exemplary family history.

J. R. Major, *Representative Institutions in Renaissance France* (1960). An essay in French constitutional history.

G. Mattingly, *The Armada* (1959). A masterpiece and novel-like in style.

J. McNeill, *The History and Character of Calvinism* (1954). The most comprehensive account and very readable.

J. E. Neale, *The Age of Catherine de Medici* (1962). A short, concise summary.

J. Neale, *Queen Elizabeth I* (1934). A superb biography.

D. Nugent, *Ecumenism in the Age of Reformation: The Colloquy of Poissy* (1974). A study of the last ecumenical council of the sixteenth century.

S. Ozment, *The Reformation in the Cities* (1975). An essay on why people thought they wanted to be Protestants.

S. Ozment, *The Age of Reform 1250–1550: An Intellectual and Religious History of Late Medieval and Reformation Europe* (1980).

S. Ozment, *When Fathers Ruled: Family Life in Reformation Europe* (1983).

J. H. Parry, *The Age of Reconnaissance* (1964). A comprehensive account of explorations from 1450 to 1650.

T. K. Rabb (ed.), *The Thirty Years' War* (1972). Excerpts from the scholarly debate over the war's significance.

E. F. Rice, Jr., *The Foundations of Early Modern Europe 1460–1559* (1970). A broad, succinct narrative.

J. H. M. Salmon (ed.), *The French Wars of Religion: How Important Were the Religious Factors?* (1967). Scholarly debate over the relation between politics and religion.

J. J. Scarisbrick, *Henry VIII* (1968). The best account of Henry's reign.

A. Soman (ed.), *The Massacre of St. Bartholomew's Day: Reappraisals and Documents* (1974). The results of an international symposium on the anniversary of the massacre.

L. Spitz, *The Religious Renaissance of the German Humanists* (1963). Comprehensive and entertaining.

J. Stayer, *Anabaptists and the Sword* (1972). One of the most lucid and sympathetic accounts.

G. Strauss (ed. and trans.), *Manifestations of Discontent in Germany on the Eve of the Reformation* (1971). A rich collection of sources for both rural and urban scenes.

R. H. Tawney, *Religion and the Rise of Capitalism* (1947). Advances beyond Weber's arguments relating Protestantism and capitalist economic behavior.

K. Thomas, *Religion and the Decline of Magic* (1971). Something of a classic on the subject.

E. Troeltsch, *The Social Teaching of the Christian Churches*, Vols. 1 and 2, trans. by Olive Wyon (1960).

M. Weber, *The Protestant Ethic and the Spirit of Capitalism*, trans. by Talcott Parsons (1958). First appeared in 1904–1905 and has continued to stimulate debate over the relationship between religion and society.

C. V. Wedgwood, *The Thirty Years' War* (1939). The authoritative account.

C. V. Wedgwood, *William the Silent* (1944). An excellent political biography.

F. Wendel, *Calvin: The Origins and Development of His Religious Thought*, trans. by Philip Mairet (1963). The best treatment of Calvin's theology.

G. H. Williams, *The Radical Reformation* (1962). A broad survey of the varieties of dissent within Protestantism.

Portfolio IV: Christianity

The teaching of Jesus gave birth to Christianity. His simple message of faith in God and love of neighbor attracted many people whose religious needs were not adequately met by the philosophies and religions of the ancient world. In the writings of St. Paul and the teachings of the early Church, Jesus became the Christ, the son of God, the long-awaited Messiah of Jewish prophecy. According to John's gospel, Jesus was also the *Logos*, the eternal principle of all being, after which the thinkers of antiquity had quested. Christianity thus offered people something more than philosophy, Law, and ritual.

Christianity proclaimed the very Incarnation of God in man, the visible presence of eternity in time. According to early Christian teaching, the power of God's Incarnation in Jesus lived on in the preaching and sacraments of the church under the guidance of the Holy Spirit. Christian thinkers here borrowed from the popular Oriental cults of the Roman world, which had also offered their followers a sacramental participation in deity and spiritual redemption from sin. But Christianity went beyond them all when it declared the source of all being to be no longer transcendant and proclaimed the Messiah to have arrived. The Christain message was that, in Jesus, eternity had made itself accessible to every person here and now and forevermore.

The first Christians were drawn from among the rich and poor alike. People flocked to the new religion for both materialistic and deeply religious reasons. For some believers, Christianity promised a better material life. But its appeal also lay in its unique ability to impart to people a sense of spiritual self-worth regardless of their place or prospects in society. The gospel of Jesus appealed to the hopelessly poor and powerless as readily as to the socially rising and well-to-do.

In the late second century, the Romans began persecuting Christians both as "heretics" (because of their rejection of the traditional Roman gods) and as social revolutionaries. At the same time, dissenting Christians, particularly sects claiming a direct spiritual knowledge of God apart from Scripture, brought new internal divisions to the young church by advocating Christian heresies of their own. Such challenges had to be met, and by the fourth century effective weapons against both state terrorism and Christian heresy were in place: an ordained official clergy, a hierarchical church organization, orthodox creeds, and a biblical canon, the New Testament. Christianity not only gained legal status within the Roman Empire, but, by the fourth century, was the favored religion of the emperor as well.

The fortunes of Christianity after the fall of Rome (A.D. 476) is one of history's great success stories. Aided by the enterprise of its popes and the example of its monks, the church cultivated an appealing lay piety centered on the Lord's Prayer, the Apostles' Creed, veneration of the Virgin, and the sacrament of the Eucharist. Clergy became both royal teachers and bureaucrats within the kingdom of the Franks. Despite a growing schism between the Eastern (Byzantine) and Western churches, and a final split in 1054, by 1000 the Church held real economic and political power. In the eleventh century, reform-minded prelates ended secular interference in its spiritual affairs; the traditional lay practice of investing clergy in their offices was condemned under penalty of excommunication. For several centuries thereafter the church would remain a formidable international force, successfully challenging kings and emperors and inspiring crusades against the non-Christian world.

By the fifteenth century, the new states of Europe had stripped the Church of much of this political power. It would henceforth be progressively confined to its present role of spiritual and moral authority. Christianity's greatest struggles ever since have been not with kings and emperors over political power, but with materialistic philosophies and worldly ideologies over spiritual and moral hegemony within an increasingly pluralistic and secular world. Since the sixteenth century, a succession of Humanists, Skeptics, Deists, Rationalists, Marxists, Freudians, Darwinians, and Atheists have attempted to explain away some of traditional Christianity's most basic teachings.

In addition, the church has endured major internal upheaval. After the Protestant Reformation (1517–1555) made the Bible widely available to the laity, the possibilities for internal criticism of Christianity multiplied geometrically. Beginning with the split between

Lutherans and Zwinglians in the 1520s, Protestant Christians have fragmented themselves into hundreds of sects, each claiming the true interpretation of Scripture. The Roman Catholic Church, by contrast, has maintained its unity through these perilous times. However, present-day discontent with papal authority threatens the modern Catholic Church almost as seriously as the Protestant Reformation once did.

But Christianity is nothing if not resilient. It continues to possess the simple, almost magically appealing, gospel of Jesus. It finds itself within a world whose religious needs and passions still remain deep and basic.

IV-1 Nativity. *A depiction of Jesus's birth by Giotto. In the foreground are Elizabeth and her son, John, born about the same time, who would later baptise Jesus. The birth is witnessed by choirs of angels and two shepherds with their flocks. A cow and a donkey seem to be equally involved in the event. In the foreground Joseph, Mary's husband, contemplates the marvelous occurrence. [Scala Art Resource.]*

IV-2 Crucifixion. *For Christians, the crucifixion of Jesus was God's redemption of mankind. Here is one of the most graphic representations of that event by Matthias Grünewald. Jesus's body is shown afflicted with lesions. John the Baptist stands to the right, pointing to the lamb of God, who takes away the sins of the world. Notice how the artist has distorted the figures to convey the drama and emotion of the event. This is a panel from the altarpiece in Isenheim, 1515. [Giraudon/Art Resource.]*

IV-3   Crusades. *Christians briefly recaptured the Holy Land in the late eleventh and early twelfth centuries. Here the crusaders are shown besieging Antioch in 1097 en route to Jerusalem, which fell to them in 1099. The buildings within the city, however, appear to be those of a European rather than a Middle Eastern city.* [Scala/Art Resource.]

IV-4   Images of Heaven & Hell. *According to Christian teaching, man and woman were created near perfect by their Maker and lived in harmony with both God and nature. In Heaven they would return again to such harmony. After humankind's fall, however, those unredeemed by God's grace would suffer eternally in Hell. Here are imaginative portrayals of Paradise and Hell by the Dutch painter, Hieronymus Bosch (CA. 1450–1516). These are the two side panels from Bosch's triptych known as the "Garden of Delights."* [Giraudon/Art Resource.]

IV-5 Popes and the Papacy. *Raphael's portrait of the great military pope Julius II (1503–1512) at Mass. Julius secured the Papal States by successfully driving the Venetians out of Romagna in 1509 and, with the help of powerful allies, the French out of Italy in 1512. His notorious worldliness and militarism led Erasmus to make him the object of a famous satire, in which Pope Julius, clad in his papal robes, is refused entrance into heaven by St. Peter, who failed to recognize him as a Christian. [Scala/Art Resource.]*

IV-6 Popes and the Papacy. *The efforts of Pope Boniface VIII (1294–1303) to stem the rising tide of secular political power, particularly in England and France, failed. A few years after his reign, in 1309, the papacy moved to Avignon, on the southeast border of France, and was never again the powerful political force it had been in the twelfth and thirteenth centuries. [Scala/Art Resource.]*

IV-7 Gothic Cathedrals. *The interior of the Gothic Cathedral at Reims is a space designed to impress upon the worshipper the smallness of man and the soaring majesty of God. [Scala/Art Resource.]*

IV-8 Baroque Church. *Baroque art and architecture is a grandiose, three-dimensional display of life and energy, and very congenial to post-Reformation Catholicism as it set forth to reclaim the lands and people lost to the Protestant Reformation. The style is the very reverse of the new Protestant churches, which were, by comparison, remarkably subdued. This is the Baroque Altar of the chapel of St. Ignatius in Rome. [Scala/Art Resource.]*

IV-9 Early Christian Art. *The catacombs were underground tunnels where Christians buried their dead. This is a drawing on the wall of the catacomb of Priscilla in Rome. [Scala/Art Resource.]*

IV-10 Church in Roman Empire. *(Early Byzantine Empire to 600 A.D.) The power of popes in the Western Church was based on Matthew 16:19, where Jesus describes Peter, or Peter's faith, as the "rock" on which his church is to be built. This passage set Peter above the other apostles, and, by extension, Rome and its bishops above the other episcopal sees of Christendom. Here is a fourth century mosaic from the apse of S. Costanza, Rome, portraying Jesus giving of the keys to heaven to Peter. [Scala/Art Resource.]*

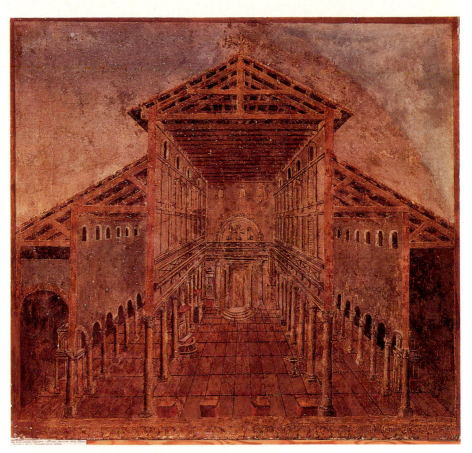

IV-11 Church in Roman Empire. *(Early Byzantine Empire to 600 A.D.) The old basilica of St. Peter was built during the reign of Constantine the Great (306–337). The financing of the rebuilding of this church by the selling of indulgences occasioned Martin Luther's famous protest and the eventual division of Christendom by the Protestant Reformation. [Scala/Art Resource.]*

IV-12 Church in Modern Europe. *Protestant churches generally were designed so that nothing might distract the eye and the mind from the preaching of God's word. Here for the Calvinists at worship in Lyon the preacher is absolutely at center stage. There are no decorations, paintings, statuary, or elaborate stained glass. In Zwinglian churches the walls were even whitewashed and no music or singing was permitted. Such simplicity contrasts starkly with the Baroque style of contemporary Catholic churches. [Bibliotheque Publique et Universitaire de Geneva.]*

IV-13 Church in Early Medieval Europe. *St. Jerome, seated in center, hands out copies of his Latin translation of the Bible (the Vulgate) for distribution by monks to the world. The Vulgate became Christendom's authoritative Bible until new translations from the Greek and Hebrew were adopted by Protestant Christians in the sixteenth century. This is a tenth century miniature. [Bibliotheque Nationale, Paris.]*

IV-14 Church in Early Medieval Europe. *The coronation of Charlemagne by Pope Leo III on Christmas Day 800, was an event that came to be regarded as the creation of the Holy Roman Empire, a revival of the old Roman Empire in the West. The church also gained a new importance and prestige by it. [Scala/Art Resource.]*

Index

Alcuin of York, 349–350
Alemanni, Rome and, 169
Aleppo, 404
Aleutian Islands, 913
Alexander I of Russia, 691, 694, 695, 697, 698, 704, 705, 711
Alexander II, Pope, 363
Alexander II of Russia, 743–744, 801
Alexander III. *See* Alexander the Great of Macedon
Alexander III, Pope, 383
Alexander III of Russia, 744, 745, 801
Alexander VI, Pope, 452, 453
Alexander the Great of Macedon, 11, 67, 114–117, 124, 184, 196, 198, 199, 204
Alexander Severus, 169
Alexandria, 119, 120
Alexandria Eschate, 116
Alexis, son of Peter the Great, 558
Alexis I, Emperor, 363
Alexis I of Russia, 555
Alfonsín, Raúl, 1051
Algeciras, 928
Algeria, 319, 633, 867, 869, 991, 1037, 1039
    France and, 712, 867, 921, 923
Algiers, Regency of, 633
Alhambra, 397
Ali, 319, 321, 323, 324, 325
Ali Pasha, 478
All Men Are Brothers, 511
Allahabad, 202
Allende, Salvador, 1048–1050
Allied Control Commission, 1001
Allies (Western)
    World War I and, 933, 935, 936, 939
    World War II and, 991, 993, 995, 998
Almagest (Ptolemy), 650
Almohads, 398, 399–400
Almoravids, 398–399, 416
Alps, 387, 453
    Hannibal and, 136
Alsace, 739
Alsace-Lorraine, 740, 924, 939, 942
Altaic, 247
Altar of Peace (*Ara Pacis*), 157
Alwa, 292, 634
Ambrose, 176
Amenhotep IV (Akhnaton), 14, 15
America
    discovery of, 460
    slave trade to, 638–640
    see also Latin America; North America; United States
American Federation of Labor (AFL), 771, 969
American Revolution, 493, 599, 605–610
Amida, 281, 516
Amiens, Treaty of, 687, 690
Amish, 468
Amitabha Buddha, 237, 308
Ammianus Marcellinus, 175
Amon, 13, 192
Amon-Re, 13, 15
Amorites, 7, 16
Amoy, 876
Amphipolis, 112
Amsterdam Congress of the Second International, 800
Amur River, 507, 878
An Lu-shan, 235
    rebellion, 236, 240
An Yang, 29
Anabaptism, 468–469, 470, 481
Anabasis (Arrian), 115
Anacreon of Teos, 87
Anagni, 438
Analects (Confucius), 40, 41
Anastasius I, Emperor, 343
Anatolia, 23, 196, 298, 319, 615, 626, 856

Timurids in, 405
Turks in, 402–403
see also Turkey
Anaxagoras of Clazomenae, 63
Anaximander, 62
Anaximenes, 62
Ancien régime, 561, 699
Ancient Learning School, in Japan, 528
Andes Mountains, 707
Andromeda (Euripides), 111
Andropov, Yuri, 1027
Angevin Empire, 382
Angilbert, 349
Anglican church, 441, 475, 480, 481, 535, 537, 538, 539, 812
Anglo-Japanese Alliance of 1902, 902–903, 908
Anglo-Saxons, 337, 382
Angola, 637, 638, 1018, 1037, 1048
Anhwei Army, 880
Anjou, 382
Ankara, 16
Anna, Empress of Russia, 580, 666
Anne, Saint, 463–464
Anne of England, 540, 546
Anschluss, 982
Anthony of Egypt, 342
Anti-Comintern Pact, 911, 981
Antigonid dynasty, 117
Antigonus I, 117
Antioch, 364
Antiochus I, 200
Antiochus III, 137
Antiochus the Great, 204, 205
Anti-Semitism. *See* Jews and Judaism
Antisthenes, 65
Antitrinitarians, 469
Antoninus Pius, 159
Antonius, 146, 148
Antrustiones, 354
Antwerp, 459, 478
Apamia, peace of, 137
Apartheid, 642, 1038–1039
Apedemak, 192
Apennines, 127, 128, 134
Aphrodite, 86
Apollo, 86–87, 157
Apostolic Succession, 167
Apoxyomenos (Lysippus), 112
Appeasement, policy of, 980, 981, 982
Appian, 143
Apulia, 134, 136
Aquinas, Thomas, Saint, 244, 389, 485, 492, 813
Aquitaine, 351, 383
Arabia, 21, 314, 315, 319, 321, 397, 400, 413, 1042
    Ottomans and, 615
    Wahhabis and, 854, 865
Arabian Desert, 6
Arabian Gulf, 1039
Arabian Sea, 193, 620
Arabic, 315, 323, 330
Arabs, 298, 314–315, 321, 323
    Charlemagne and, 347
    China and, 235
    early Middle Ages and, 339–341
    Franks and, 345
    Israeli conflict and, 939, 1040–1042
    Mediterranean and, 335
    oil and, 1042
Arachosia, 199, 204, 205, 206, 207
Arafat, Yassir, 1042
Aragon, 441
Aral Sea, 626, 627
Aramaic, 197, 205, 297, 299
Arausio, battle of, 144
Arcesilaus, 118
Arch, Roman, 163

Archimedes of Syracuse, 121
Ardashir, 298, 299
Ardennes, Forest of, 993
Areopagus, 90, 91, 102
Ares, 86
Arētē, 80
Argentina, 831–834, 1047, 1051
    Falkland Islands War, 1022
    hides and tallow from, 829
    Paraguayan War, 839–840
Argos, 87, 90, 102, 108
Arianism, 176–177, 339, 343
Aristagoras, 93
Aristarchus of Samos, 121
Aristobulus, 119
Aristocracy, of eighteenth-century Europe, 578–580
Aristocratic resurgence, 580
Aristophanes, 111
Aristotle, 6, 37, 64, 67, 68, 80, 108, 121, 370, 371, 492
Arius of Alexandria, 176–177
Arjun, Guru, 624
Arkwright, Richard, 575
Armada, 478, 481
Armenia, 193, 206, 298, 341, 858
    Islamic rule, 319
    Rome and, 161
    Seljuk Turks and, 402
    Timurids and, 405
Arminius, 152
Arms policy, United States and Soviet Union and, 1016, 1027, 1028
Arno River, 128
Arnold, Matthew, 811
Arouet, François Marie. *See* Voltaire
Arpinum, 144, 146
Arras, Union of, 479
Arrian, 115
Ars Amatoria (Ovid), 156
Arsacids, 206, 297
Art of War, The (Sun-tzu), 40
Arta, 193
Artaxerxes II, 107
Artaxerxes III, 196
Artemisium, Battle of, 94
Artemis, 86
Arthashastra, 200
Arthur (son of Henry VII of England and brother of Henry VIII), 441, 473
Articles of Confederation, 751, 754
Artillery, invention of heavy, 429
Artisan guilds, 581–582
Artisans, in eighteenth century, 582–583
Artisans Dwelling Act of 1875, 746
Artois, Count of, 680
Aryans
    Germany and, 23, 820, 821, 960
    India and, 18, 19, 21, 22–28, 38, 46, 47
    Iran and, 193
Asante, 419, 640, 864, 870
Asha, 193
Ashikaga *bakufu*, 278–279, 280, 282, 284, 285, 512, 513, 514, 524
Ashikaga Takauji, 279
Ashoka, 200–201, 202, 622
Asia Minor, 8, 14, 16, 61, 67, 76, 77, 78, 91, 93, 101, 116, 120, 137, 174
Asiento, 601, 602
Aspelta, King, 191
Asquith, Henry, 796
Assam, 302, 409
Assassins, 397, 400, 403, 404
Assembly, of Rome, 132
Assignats, 680
Association of God Worshippers, 878
Assos, 67
Assyria, 16, 196

Loyola, 469
Lu, Empress, 218
Lu Hsun, 886
Luanda, 637
Luba, 636
Luca, 147
Lucania, 134
Lucerne, 467
Lucian, 162
Lucretius, 154–155
Ludendorff, Erich, 933, 939, 954
Ludovico il Moro, 450, 452, 453
Lueger, Karl, 954
Luftwaffe, 986
Lumumba, Patrice, 1037
Lunda, 636
Lunéville, Treaty of, 687
Lusitania, 936
Luther, Martin, 448, 460, 461, 462, 463–467, 468, 485
Lutheranism, 470, 475, 481, 483
Luthuli, Albert, 1038
Luxembourg, 1002
    World War I and, 932
    World War II and, 986
Lwo, 297
Lyceum, 67, 118
Lydia, 93, 196
Lyell, Charles, 808, 810
Lyons, 441, 580
Lysander, 107
Lysippus, 112
Lytton, Earl of, 979
Lytton Report, 979

Ma Yin-ch'u, 1052–1053
Maasai, 297
Mabiki, 523
Macao, 508, 514
MacArthur, Douglas, 1058, 1060, 1064
Macartney mission, 508–509
Macaulay, Thomas Babington, 850
Macbeth (Shakespeare), 489
McCarthy, Joseph, 1006
MacDonald, John A., 779
MacDonald, Ramsay, 949
Macedon, 67
    Antigonid dynasty, 117
    Greeks and, 112–114
        Alexander the Great, 114–117
        Philip of Macedon, 112–114
    Hannibal and, 136
    Rome and, 137–138
Macedonia, 102, 138, 615, 930
Macedonian dynasty, 341
Macedonian Wars, 137–138, 139
Macemba, 870
Mach, Ernst, 814
Machiavelli, Niccoló, 453–454
Machu Picchu, 593
McKinley, William, 772, 775, 776
MacMahon, Marshal, 740
Macmillan, Harold, 1021
Madagascar, 296, 412, 413
Madeira, 638
Madero, Francisco, 837–838
Madison, James, 754
Madman's Diary, A (Lu Hsun), 886
Madonna and Child (Giotto), 450
Madrasa, 394–395, 403
Maecenas, 155
Magadha, 51, 183, 199, 301
Magdeburg, 463, 553
Magellan, Ferdinand, 458–459, 460
Magenta, battle at, 735
Maghili, Muhammad, al-, 633
Magi, 195, 206
Magic

preliterate human beings and, 4
    witch hunts and, 486–488
Maginot Line, 980, 984, 986
Magna Carta, 365, 368, 383, 384, 387
Magna Graecia, 81
Magnesia, Battle of, 137
Magyars, 353, 360, 550–551, 602, 665, 742, 743, 942
Mahabharata, 26, 202–203
Mahamud I, 618
Mahavira, 51–52, 199
Mahayana Buddhism, 273–274, 308, 309, 310
Mahdist uprising, 865–866
Mahmud of Ghazna, 401, 402, 409
Mahmud II, 857
Mai Dunama Dibbalemi, 419
Maimonides (Musa ibn Maymun), 398, 400
Main River, 738
Mainz, 443, 458
Maitreya, 237, 253
Malabar Coast, 460
Malacca, 514, 629
Malagasy, 296
Malawi, 863
Malay peninsula, 630
Malaya, 990
Malaysia, 413, 629
Malenkov, Georgy, 1025, 1026
Mali, 417–419, 634, 635
Malificium, 486
Malik, Abd al-, 326
Mallus, 349
Malta, 134, 1018
Malthus, Thomas, 808, 1052
Malvinas. *See* Falkland Islands
Mamluks, 292, 326, 400–401, 404, 615, 633
Ma'mun, al-, 326, 329
Manchester, 787
Manchu dynasty, 39, 248, 502, 504–505, 507, 508, 509, 558, 876–883
Manchukuo, 890
Manchuria, 249, 505, 904, 913, 924, 1053
    China and, 216
    Chinese Communist Party and, 892–893
    Japan and, 904, 908, 911, 990
    Manchus and, 504
    Russia and, 507, 885
    Soviet Union and, 995, 997
    T'ang dynasty and, 235
Manda, 413, 414
Mandarins, 502
Mandate system, World War I and, 942
Mande, 416, 418, 634
Mandela, Nelson, 1038
Mandinke, 418
Mani, 290, 300
Manichaeism
    in China, 236
    in Iran, 300
Manila, 500
Mannerism, 452
Manorialism, 335, 341, 350–351, 375–377
Mansa Musa, 418, 419, 634
Mansfield, 463
Mansi, 355
Mantinea, Battle of, 108
Manu, 305
Manura, 630
Man'yōshū, 271–272
Mao Tse-tung, 39, 887, 891, 892, 916, 1054–1055
Maqurra, 292
Marathas, 624, 848
Marathon, Battle of, 93
Marburg Colloquy, 468
March Enabling Act, 958
March Revolution, in Russia, 936–938, 940

Marcus Aurelius, 159, 160, 161, 164, 169
Mardonius, 95
Marduk, 55
Marengo, battle at, 687
Marguerite of Valois, 476
Maria Theresa, daughter of Charles VI, 551–552
Maria Theresa of Austria, 602, 665
Maria-Kannon, 516
Marie Antoinette of France, 676, 681, 684
Marie Louise, Austrian Archduchess, 693–694
Marie Thérèse, wife of Louis XIV, 544
Marignano, Battle of, 453
Maritime Customs Service, 882
Maritime Province, 878
Marius, Gaius, 144–145
Mark, Apostle, 340, 553
    Gospel of, 166
Marne, 939
    Battle of the, 933
Marrakesh, 398
Marriage
    between 1500 and 1800, 483–484
    early Industrial Revolution and, 718–720
    in eighteenth-century Europe, 563–564
Mars the Avenger, 156
Marshall, George C., 893, 1000
Marshall Plan, 1000–1001, 1002, 1006, 1018–1019, 1022, 1023
Marsilius of Padua, 429, 438
Marston Moor, Battle of, 537
Martin V, Pope, 440
Martin of Tours, Saint, 342, 349
Martinique, 588, 604
Marx, Karl, and Marxism, 720–722, 726, 798, 800, 801, 822, 887, 916, 1047–1051, 1052, 1053
Mary I of England, (Mary Tudor), 472, 475, 480
Mary, daughter of James II of England, 539
Mary Stuart, Queen of Scots, 480, 481, 535
Masaryk, Jan, 1001
Masaryk, Thomas, 1001
Massacre of Saint Bartholomew's Day, 476–477
Master K'ung, 40
Masurian Lakes, Battle of, 933
Matara, 290
Mathematical Principles of Natural Philosophy, The (Principia Mathematica) (Newton), 654
Mathura, 206
Mathura school, 304
Matsudaira Sadanobu, 522
Matsukata, 905
Matthew, 342, 344
    Gospel of, 168
Mauget, Marie, 796
Mauritania, 416
Mauritius, 631
Maurya, Chandragupta, 199–200, 202
Mauryans, 183, 199–202
Max of Baden, Prince, 939
Maximilian I, Emperor, 441, 453, 466
Maximilian of Austria, 739, 835–836
Maximilian, Duke of Bavaria, 483
Maximum Prices, Edict of, 172
May Fourth Movement, 886–887, 916
May Laws of 1873, 812
Mayas, 590–591
Maymun, Musa ibn. *See* Maimonides
Mayor of the palace, 344
Mazarin, Cardinal, 540
Mazdak, 301
Mazorca, 832
Mazowiecki, Tadeusz, 1032
Mazzini, Giuseppe, 734
Mbanza Kongo, 637

Mbundu people, 637
Meat Packing Act of 1906, 776
Mecca, 314, 315, 317, 318, 322, 323, 402
  Muhammad Ali in, 634
  Ottomans and, 615
Medea (Euripides), 105, 106
Medes, 193, 196, 197
Media, 18, 193
Medici family, 454
  Clement VII (Pope), 454
  Cosimo de', 444, 447
  Leo X, Pope, 453
  Lorenzo de' (the Magnificent), 444
Medina, 315, 318, 319, 322, 323, 402, 615
Medina-Sidonia, Duke of, 481
Mediterranean Sea, 6, 11, 14, 56, 75, 81, 134,
    137, 145, 335, 337, 341, 366, 668
Megalopolis, 131
Megara, 102
Megasthenes, 202
Mehmed the Conqueror, 615
Meiji state. *See under* Japan
Mein Kampf (Hitler), 954, 978
Melanchthon, Philip, 464, 469
Melos, 924
Melukka, 21
Melun Act of 1851, 787
Memphis, 11, 13, 190
Menander, 111, 205, 206
Mencius, 42
Mendel, Gregor, 808
Mendès-France, 1024
Menes, 11
Mennonites, 468
Mensheviks, 802, 937
Mercantilism, 458, 461, 588
Merchant class
  Black Death and, 436
  in high Middle Ages, 366–368, 378
Merchant guilds, 379
  in China, 242
Meroe, 189, 292
Meroitic Empire, 189–192
Merovich, 344
Merovingians, 344, 345, 346, 349, 351, 354
Mersen, Treaty of, 352
Meso-America, 5, 589–593
Mesopotamia, 6–11, 16, 21, 56, 57, 206, 339,
    341, 626
  Alexander the Great and, 116
  Neolithic societies in, 5
  Ottomans and, 615, 617
  Persia and, 168
  Rome and, 161
  Seleucid dynasty in, 117
  Timurids in, 405
Messana, 134
Messenia, 87–88
Messiah, Jesus and, 165
Mesta, 441
Metamorphoses (Ovid), 156
Metro, 786
Metternich, Klemens von, 704–705, 724
Mexico, 588, 827, 831, 834–839, 1052
  Aztecs of, 460, 590, 591–592
  Díaz, 836–837
  foreign relations
    Austria, 835–836
    United States, 835, 838
  independence, 834–835
  mining in, 829
  Partido Revolucionario Institucional (PRI),
      1052
  revolutionary politics in, 837–838
  Spanish empire in, 441
  Toltecs of, 591
  war and warfare
    Austria, 739

France, 835–836
  United States, 760, 835
  see also New Spain
Mexico City, 500
Mfecane era, 862–864
Miao Wars, 499
Michelangelo, 451–452
Middle Ages, 174
  early, 335–357
    Christianity in, 341–344, 345, 349–350,
        351, 352, 354
    feudalism, 341, 351, 353, 354–356
    Franks in, 336–339, 344–353
    Germanic invasions, 336–338
    Islam and, 339–341
  high, 359–390
    Christianity in, 354, 360–366, 379–380,
        390
    empire revival in, 360
    society in, 368–370, 372–382
    trade and growth of towns in, 366–370,
        378–379
    universities in, 370–372
  late, 439–443
    Black Death, 433–437
    Christianity in, 429, 436, 437–440, 462–
        463
    Hundred Years' War, 429, 430–433
  see also under Japan
Middle class
  in eighteenth century, 582
  in late nineteenth century, 784, 785, 787–
      788, *see also under* Cities
  women of, 792–794
Middle Comedy, 111
Middle East
  industrialization and, 574
  post-war history of, 1039–1042
  see also specific countries
Middle Kingdom, of Egypt, 13
Midway Island, Battle of, 913, 991
Milan, 173, 336, 443, 445, 446, 450, 452, 453,
    580
  Edict of, 342
Milan Decree of 1807, 691
Miletus, 93
Milinda, 206
Militia Ordinance, 537
Mill, John Stuart, 794
Millerand, Alexander, 799
Miltiades, 93, 101
Minamoto, 269, 285, 512, 517
Minaret tower, 331
Minas Gerais, 842
Ming dynasty, 493, 494, 497, 498–504, 505–
    507, 509–511, 514, 530
Ming History, 505
Minoans, 76
Minos, 76
Minseito, 910, 1059
Mirandola, Pico della, 447
Missi dominici, 349, 351, 389
Missile crisis, in Cuba, 1048
Mississippi River, 588, 756, 757
Missouri Compromise, 761
Missouri River, 756
Missouri, U.S.S., 995
Mita, 595
Mitannians, 16
Mithra, 165
Mithradates I, 206
Mithraism, 342
Mitsubishi combine, 899, 908
Mitsui, House of, 521
Mitterand, François, 1025
Mizuno Tadakuni, 522
Model T, 967
Modena, 736

Modern Devotion. *See* Brothers of the Com-
    mon Life
Modern Man in Search of a Soul (Jung), 819
Mogadishu, 413, 414
Mohacs, Battle of, 467
Mohammed. *See* Muhammad
Mohenjo-Daro, 18, 20, 21
Mohists, of China, 40
Moksha, 50–51
Moldavia, 733
Moldboard plow, 350
Molotov, Vyacheslav, 999
Moltke, Helmuth von, 932, 933
Moluccas, 413, 629
Mombasa, 413, 631
Mona Lisa (Leonardo da Vinci), 451
Monasticism, 342–343, 345, 374
  Cluny, 360–362
Money fiefs, 354–355
Mongolia, 248, 249, 253, 336, 625, 882
Mongols, 328, 387, 388, 403–405
  Assassins and, 400
  as Yuan dynasty in China, *see under* China
  in Iran, 400
  in Japan, 278, 389–390
  in Korea, 278
Monkey, 225
Monks. *See* Monasticism
Monnet, Jean, 1019
Monomatapa, 630
Monophytism, 292, 338–339, 343
Monotheism, 38, 56
  see also Christianity; Islam; Judaism
Monroe Doctrine, 705, 940, 945
Montagu, Mary Wortley, Lady, 547
Montcalm, Joseph, 604
Monte Cassino, 342
Montenegro, 925, 930
Montesquieu, Charles Secondat, Baron de,
    661–662, 663, 670, 752
Montevideo, 840
Montezuma, 592
Montgomery, Alabama, 1007
Montgomery, Bernard, 991
Montmartre, 787
Montmorency-Châtillons, 476
Moors, 322, 327, 339, 341, 370, 397–400, 441,
    630
Moravia, 550, 570, 724, 942
More, Thomas, Sir, 462, 474
Morelos y Pavón, José María, 834, 709
Morgan, J. P., 770, 775
Moriscos, 441
Morocco, 294, 319, 400, 633, 991, 1038, 1039
  Almohads in, 399–400
  Almoravids in, 398–399
  Germany and, 928, 929–930
  independence, 1024
  Sa'dids in, 633
Moravia, 1838 revolution, 723
Mosaddeq, Muhammad, 1043
Moscow, 251, 387, 388, 405, 695, 987
  Olympic Games in, 1016, 1027
Moses, 57, 59, 316
Moslem. *See* Muslim
Mosques, 331
Mossi, 416, 419
Most-favored-nation clause, in Treaty of Nan-
    king, 876
Mosul, 16
Motoori Norinaga, 528, 529
Mo-tzu, 40
Mountain (Jacobins), 682, 683
Mozambique, 631, 863, 1037
Mozarabs, 399
Mpinda, 637
Mu'awiya, 319, 321–322, 324
Mughals, 494, 848

Noah, 316
Nobiles, 132
Nobility
    Black Death and, 436, 437
    Middle Ages and, 372–374, 378–379
Nobunaga, 515, 517, 519
Nok culture, 188–189, 294, 421
Nomarchs, 13
Nomes, 13
Nonconformist denominations, in Great Britain, 812
Norman Conquest, of England, 382, 383
Normandy, 353, 382
    D-Day at, 993
    Hundred Years' War and, 431, 432
Normans, 352–353, 383
North, Lord, 606, 608, 609, 610
North Africa. *See* Africa
North America, 588
    American Revolution, 493, 599, 605–610
    Great Britain in, 588
    King William's War, 544
    Seven Years' War, 603–604
    see also America; Canada; United States
North Atlantic Treaty Organization (NATO), 1002, 1011, 1018, 1019, 1024
North Briton, 609
North German Confederation, 738, 739
North Korea, 1052, 1063–1064
North Vietnam, 1065–1066, 1067
Northern Ireland, Great Britain and, 1022
Northern Rhodesia. *See* Zambia
Northern Society, 711
Northern Sung, 240, 241, 242, 243, 246, 247, 249
Northern Wei, 220, 229–230
Northmen. *See* Normans
Norway, 796, 1002
    democracy in, 797
    World War II and, 986
Notre-Dame, Cathedral of, 370, 683
Novara, Battle of, 453
Nova Scotia, 588, 777
Novgorod, 251
Novum Organum (Bacon), 653
Novus homo, 144
Nubia, 185, 188, 400, 635
Nuclear Test Ban Treaty, 1016, 1024
Numantia, 138
Numidia, 144
Nun Shōgun, 277, 278
Nuns, in Middle Ages, 374, 380
Nuremberg Laws, 960
Nuremberg trials, 989
Nyamwezi, 864
Nystad, Peace of, 557

Oberman, Heiko, 429
Ocean River, 116
O'Connell, Daniel, 714
Octavian, 148, 151–152
    see also Augustus
October Manifesto, 802
Oda Nobunaga, 512, 513
Oder-Neisse river line, 1024
Odes (Horace), 155
Odoacer, 337
Odyssey (Homer), 77, 78–80, 138
Ogata Kōrin, 524
O'Higgins, Bernardo, 707
Ohio River, 588, 756, 757
Oikos, 105
Oil
    Arab states and, 1042
    Mexico and, 1052
Ōishi Karanosuke, 521
Old Babylonian dynasty, 7

Old Believers, 556–557
Old Comedy, 111
Old Kingdom, of ancient Egypt, 12–13
Old regime, European society under, 561
Old Stone Age, in Japan, 261
Old Testament, 56, 57, 60, 168
Oligarchs, in Japan, 902, 905
Olmec civilization, 589–590
Olympia, 82, 86
Olympic Games, in Moscow, 1016, 1027
Olympus, Mount, 86
Oman, 324, 1039
Omanis, 630–631
On, 55
On Christian Doctrine (Saint Augustine), 371
On Divine and Secular Learning (Cassiodorus), 371
On the Morals that Befit a Free Man (Vergerio), 447
On the Motion of Mars (Kepler), 652
On the Revolutions of the Heavenly Spheres (Copernicus), 646–651, 652
One Day in the Life of Ivan Denisovich (Solzhenitsyn), 1026
Oni, 421
Ono no Komachi, 285
Open-door policy, 885, 924
Operation Barbarossa, 987
Opium War, 876–878
Opportunism, in France, 799–800
Optimates, 143
Orange, Prince William of, 544
Orange Free State, 864
Orange River, 185, 641, 863, 864
Oration on the Dignity of Man (Mirandola), 447
Oratory of Divine Love, 471
Order of the Hermits of Saint Augustine, 463, 464
Ordinance of 1787, 754
Oregon, 760
Organic Articles of 1802, 688–689
Organization for Economic Cooperation and Development (OECD), 1019
Organization for European Economic Cooperation (OEEC), 1018–1019
Origin of the Species, The (Darwin), 808
Orinoco River, 460
Orlando, Vittorio Emanuele, 939
Orléans, Hundred Years' War and, 432–433
Orthodox Christianity, 344
Orthopraxy, 395–396
Osaka, 263, 519, 520, 524, 525, 527
Osaka Cotton Spinning Mill, 900
Osiris, 165
Osman, 615
Osmanlis. *See* Ottoman Empire
Ostpolitik, 1023
Ostrogoths, 173, 337–338, 339
Othello (Shakespeare), 489
Othman, 615
Otto I of Germany, 352, 360, 362
Otto IV of Germany, 384, 386–387
Otto of Brunswick, 386
Ottoman Empire, 341, 494, 615–619, 627
    Acheh and, 630
    Balkans and, 928–929
    Christianity in, 618
    eastern Europe and, 467
    Egypt and, 401, 631
    end of, 942
    Hungary and, 550, 551
    North Africa and, 631, 633–634
    Parliament, 848
    Russia and, 667–668
    Seljuks and, 403
    Tanzimat reforms, 857, 858
    war and warfare

Balkans, 930
Crimean War, 733–734
Funj, 635
Italy, 930
Janissaries, 617, 854, 857
Russia, 856, 857
Russo-Turkish War, 924–925
Safavid Shi'ites, 620
Spain, 478
West and, 855–856, 857–858
Young Turks, 929
    see also Turkey
Ottoman guilds, 854
Ottonians, 352, 360
Ovid, 155–156
Oxford University, 370, 371, 745
Oxus River, 207, 233, 319, 320, 401, 620, 622, 624, 627
Oyo, 419

Pacific Ocean, 247, 460
Paedagogus, 141
Paekche, 264–265
Paganism, 175
Pahlavas, 207
Pahlavi rule, in Iran, 299, 300, 1042–1043
Paine, Thomas, 607
Pakistan, 18, 853, 854, 1044–1046, 1053
Palaestra, 86
Palatinate, 443, 470, 483, 544
Palatine Hill, 156–157
Paleolithic Age, 3–4
    in India, 18
    in Italy, 127
Palermo, 736
Palestine, 13, 14, 16, 56, 57, 315, 342, 366, 404, 1039
    Antiochus and, 137
    Balfour Declaration, 939
    Great Britain and, 942
    as homeland for Jews, 1039–1040
    Israel and, 1041–1042
    Saladins and, 400
Palestine Liberation Organization, 1041, 1042
Paley, William, 810
Palmer, Robert, 665
Pamir Mountains, 233
Pan Ku, 222
Panaetius, 138, 140
Panama, United States and, 830
Panama Canal, United States and, 830
Pangaeus, Mount, 112
Pani, 24
Panini, 202
Pankhurst, Emmeline, Christabel and Sylvia, 795–796
Pan-Slavic movement, 925, 930, 932
Pantheon, 163
Panther, 929, 930
Papacy. *See* popes and papacy *under* Christianity
Papal primacy doctrine, 343
Papal States, 346, 360, 443, 452, 453, 736
Papen, Franz von, 957
Paraguay, 831
    independence of, 707
    Paraguayan War, 839–840, 842
Parens scientiarum, 370
Pareto, Vilfredo, 820
Paris, 242, 353, 378, 383, 580, 676, 677, 681
    Commune, 681, 682, 740, 786, 798, 799
    French Revolution and, 675, 676–678, 681, 684, 685–686
    nineteenth-century redesign, 786–787
    Parlement of, 674, 675
    socialism and, 798
    summit conference at, 1014–1015